MCTS: Microsoft Windows 7 Configuration Study Guide

MCTS: Microsoft Windows 7 Configuring (70-680) Objectives

OBJECTIVE	CHAPTER
Installing, Upgrading, and Migrating to Windows 7	
Perform a clean installation.	1
Upgrade to Windows 7 from previous versions of Windows.	1
Migrate user profiles.	1
Deploying Windows 7	
Capture a system image.	2
Prepare a system image for deployment.	2
Deploy a system image.	2
Configure a VHD.	7
Configuring Hardware and Applications	
Configure devices.	5
Configure application compatibility.	5
Configure application restrictions.	6
Configure Internet Explorer.	5
Configuring Network Connectivity	
Configure IPv4 network settings.	7
Configure IPv6 network settings.	7
Configure networking settings.	7
Configure Windows Firewall.	7
Configure remote management.	7
Configuring Access to Resources	
Configure shared resources.	6, 7
Configure file and folder access.	6
Configure user account control (UAC).	6
Configure authentication and authorization.	6
Configure BranchCache.	7

Sybex®
An Imprint of
WILEY

OBJECTIVE	CHAPTER
Configuring Mobile Computing	
Configure BitLocker and BitLocker To Go.	6
Configure DirectAccess.	7
Configure mobility options.	4
Configure remote connections.	4
Monitoring and Maintaining Systems that Run Windows 7	
Configure updates to Windows 7.	1
Manage disks.	3
Monitor systems.	8
Configure performance settings.	4, 8
Configuring Backup and Recovery Options	
Configure backup.	9
Configure system recovery options.	9
Configure file recovery options.	9

Exam specifications and content are subject to change at any time without prior notice and at Microsoft's sole discretion. Please visit the Microsoft Learning website (`www.microsoft.com/learning/mcp`) for the most current information on exam content.

Sybex®
An Imprint of
WILEY

MCTS

Microsoft® Windows® 7 Configuration

Study Guide

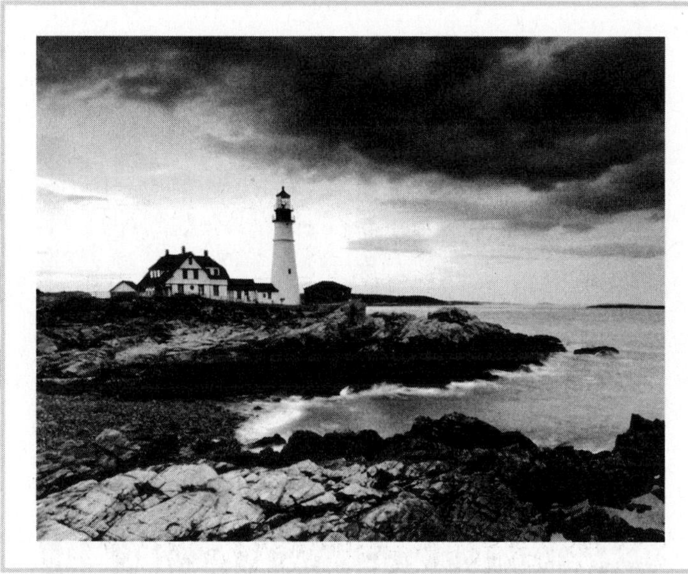

MCTS

Microsoft® Windows® 7 Configuration

Study Guide

William Panek

Wiley Publishing, Inc.

Acquisitions Editor: Jeff Kellum
Development Editor: Sara Barry
Technical Editors: Randy Muller and Rodney Fournier
Production Editor: Christine O'Connor
Copy Editor: Judy Flynn
Editorial Manager: Pete Gaughan
Production Manager: Tim Tate
Vice President and Executive Group Publisher: Richard Swadley
Vice President and Publisher: Neil Edde
Media Project Manager 1: Laura Moss-Hollister
Media Associate Producer: Shawn Patrick
Media Quality Assurance: Doug Kuhn
Book Designer: Judy Fung and Bill Gibson
Proofreader: Kristy Eldredge, Word One New York
Indexer: Robert Swanson
Project Coordinator, Cover: Lynsey Stanford
Cover Designer: Ryan Sneed

Published simultaneously in Canada

ISBN: 978-0-470-56875-0

For general information on our other products and services or to obtain technical support, please contact our Customer Care Department within the U.S. at (877) 762-2974, outside the U.S. at (317) 572-3993 or fax (317) 572-4002.

Wiley also publishes its books in a variety of electronic formats. Some content that appears in print may not be available in electronic books.

Library of Congress Cataloging-in-Publication Data

Panek, William, 1970–
MCTS : Microsoft Windows 7 configuration study guide (70-680) / William Panek. —1st ed.
p. cm.
Includes bibliographical references and index.
ISBN 978-0-470-56875-0 (paper/cd-rom : alk. paper)
1. Electronic data processing personnel—Certification. 2. Microsoft software—Examinations—Study guides. 3. Microsoft Windows (Computer file) I. Title.
QA76.3.P354 2010
005.4'46—dc22

2010003133

10 9 8 7 6 5 4 3

Dear Reader,

Thank you for choosing *MCTS: Microsoft Windows 7 Configuration Study Guide.* This book is part of a family of premium-quality Sybex books, all of which are written by outstanding authors who combine practical experience with a gift for teaching.

Sybex was founded in 1976. More than 30 years later, we're still committed to producing consistently exceptional books. With each of our titles, we're working hard to set a new standard for the industry. From the paper we print on, to the authors we work with, our goal is to bring you the best books available.

I hope you see all that reflected in these pages. I'd be very interested to hear your comments and get your feedback on how we're doing. Feel free to let me know what you think about this or any other Sybex book by sending me an email at `nedde@wiley.com`. If you think you've found a technical error in this book, please visit `http://sybex.custhelp.com`. Customer feedback is critical to our efforts at Sybex.

Best regards,

Neil Edde
Vice President and Publisher
Sybex, an Imprint of Wiley

This book is dedicated to my wife, Crystal, and my two girls, Alexandria and Paige.

Acknowledgments

I would like to thank my wife, Crystal, and my two daughters, Alexandria and Paige, for all of their love and support during the time I was writing all my books. They make it all worthwhile.

I want to thank my family and especially my brothers, Rick, Gary, and Rob. They have always been there for me.

I have to thank Tylor Wentworth. He is a great business partner, a confidant, a terrific family man, and most importantly, my friend. I always end up laughing every time we get together, and that's important in this world.

I would like to thank Jeremy Hodgson, my training partner, who spends more time with me on the road than anyone else. His sense of humor keeps me smiling even when I am homesick.

Finally, I want to thank everyone from Sybex who backed me up on this book, especially Sara Barry, who helped me make this the best book possible, and Randy Muller, who was my technical editor. I would also like to thank Christine O'Connor, who did a great job keeping everything organized, and Jeff Kellum, who was the lead for the entire book. He is always there for me and he is great to write for. Thanks to you all and everyone else behind the scenes on this book.

About the Author

William Panek (MCP®, MCP+I®, MCSA®, MCSA® W/SECURITY & MESSAGING, MCSE—NT (3.51 & 4.0)®, MCSE—2000 & 2003®, MCSE W/SECURITY & MESSAGING, MCDBA®, MCT®, MCTS®, MCITP®, CCNA®, CHFI®)

After many successful years in the computer industry and a degree in computer programming, William Panek decided that he could better use his talents and his personality as an instructor. He started teaching for such schools as Boston University, Clark University, and Vtec, to name just a few.

In 1998 William Panek started Stellacon Corporation. Stellacon has become one of New England's most respected training companies. Stellacon is also a two-time winner of the Best Computer School award in Portsmouth, New Hampshire.

William brings years of real-world expertise to the classroom and strives to ensure that each and every student has an understanding of the course material.

William currently lives in New Hampshire with his wife and two girls. In his spare time he likes to golf, ski, and snowmobile. William is also a commercially rated helicopter pilot.

Contents at a Glance

Contents

Table of Exercises

Introduction

Microsoft's certification program contains three primary series: Technology, Professional, and Architect. The Technology Series of certifications is intended to allow candidates to target specific technologies and is the basis for obtaining the Professional Series and Architect Series of certifications. The Technology Series consists of one to three exams, each of which focuses on a specific technology, and does not include job-role skills. By contrast, each of the certifications in the Professional Series focuses on a job role and not necessarily on a single technology but rather a comprehensive set of skills for performing the job role being tested. The certifications in the Architect Series offered by Microsoft are premier certifications that consist of passing a review board of previously certified architects. To apply for the Architect Series of certifications, you must have a minimum of 10 years of industry experience.

When obtaining a Technology Series certification, you are recognized as a Microsoft Certified Technology Specialist (MCTS) on the specific technology or technologies on which you have been tested. The Professional Series certifications include Microsoft Certified IT Professional (MCITP) and Microsoft Certified Professional Developer (MCPD). Passing the review board for an Architect Series certification will allow you to become a Microsoft Certified Architect (MCA).

This book has been developed to give you the critical skills and knowledge you need to prepare for the Microsoft Windows 7, Configuring exam (Exam 70-680).

The Microsoft Certified Professional Program

Since the inception of its certification program, Microsoft has certified more than 2 million people. As the computer network industry continues to increase in both size and complexity, this number is sure to grow—and the need for *proven* ability will also increase. Certifications can help companies verify the skills of prospective employees and contractors.

Microsoft has developed its Microsoft Certified Professional (MCP) program to give you credentials that verify your ability to work with Microsoft products effectively and professionally. Several levels of certification are available based on specific suites of exams. With the release of Windows Vista, Microsoft created a new generation of certification programs:

Microsoft Certified Technology Specialist (MCTS) The MCTS can be considered the entry-level certification for the new generation of Microsoft certifications. The MCTS certification program targets specific technologies instead of specific job roles. You must take and pass one to three exams.

Microsoft Certified IT Professional (MCITP) The MCITP certification is a Professional Series certification that tests network and system administrators on job roles rather than only on a specific technology. The MCITP certification program generally consists of one to three exams in addition to obtaining an MCTS-level certification.

Microsoft Certified Professional Developer (MCPD) The MCPD certification is a Professional Series certification for application developers. Similar to the MCITP, the MCPD is focused on a job role rather than on a single technology. The MCPD certification program generally consists of one to three exams in addition to obtaining an MCTS-level certification.

Microsoft Certified Architect (MCA) The MCA is Microsoft's premier certification series. Obtaining the MCA requires a minimum of 10 years of experience and passing a review board consisting of peer architects.

How Do You Become Certified on Windows 7?

Attaining Microsoft certification has always been a challenge. In the past, students have been able to acquire detailed exam information—even most of the exam questions—from online "brain dumps" and third-party "cram" books or software products. For the new generation of exams, this is simply not the case.

Microsoft has taken strong steps to protect the security and integrity of its new certification tracks. Now prospective candidates should complete a course of study that develops detailed knowledge about a wide range of topics. It supplies them with the true skills needed, derived from working with the technology being tested.

The new generations of Microsoft certification programs are heavily weighted toward hands-on skills and experience. It is recommended that candidates have troubleshooting skills acquired through hands-on experience and working knowledge.

Fortunately, if you are willing to dedicate the time and effort to learn Windows 7, you can prepare yourself well for the exam by using the proper tools. By working through this book, you can successfully meet the exam requirements to pass the Windows 7 Configuration exam.

This book is part of a complete series of Microsoft certification Study Guides published by Sybex Inc. that together cover the new MCTS, MCITP, MCPD exams as well as the core operating system requirements you need to know for the MCSA and MCSE exam requirements. Visit the Sybex website at `www.sybex.com` for complete program and product details.

MCTS Exam Requirements

Candidates for MCTS certification on Windows 7 must pass at least one Windows 7 exam. Other MCTS certifications may require up to three exams. For a more detailed description of the Microsoft certification programs, including a list of all the exams, visit the Microsoft Learning website at `www.microsoft.com/learning/mcp`.

The Microsoft Windows 7 Client Configuration Exam

The Windows 7 Client Configuration exam covers concepts and skills related to installing, configuring, and managing Windows 7 computers. It emphasizes the following elements of Windows 7 support and administration:

- Installing, upgrading, and migrating to Windows 7
- Deploying Windows 7

- Configuring hardware and applications
- Configuring network connectivity
- Configuring access to resources
- Configuring mobile computing
- Monitoring and maintaining systems that run Windows 7
- Configuring backup and recovery options

This exam is quite specific regarding Windows 7 requirements and operational settings, and it can be particular about how administrative tasks are performed within the operating system. It also focuses on fundamental concepts of Windows 7 operations.

In addition to being a core requirement for achieving the MCTS: Windows 7 Configuration certification, the 70-680 exam can be used as an elective toward the MCSE or MCSA certifications on the Windows Server 2003 track. Careful study of this book, along with hands-on experience, will help you prepare for this exam.

Microsoft provides exam objectives to give you a general overview of possible areas of coverage on its exams. Keep in mind, however, that exam objectives are subject to change at any time without prior notice and at Microsoft's sole discretion. Please visit the Microsoft Learning website (`www.microsoft.com/learning/mcp`) for the most current listing of exam objectives.

Types of Exam Questions

In an effort to both refine the testing process and protect the quality of its certifications, Microsoft has focused its newer certification exams on real experience and hands-on proficiency. There is a greater emphasis on your past working environments and responsibilities and less emphasis on how well you can memorize. In fact, Microsoft says that certification candidates should have hands-on experience before attempting to pass any certification exams.

Microsoft will accomplish its goal of protecting the exams' integrity by regularly adding and removing exam questions, limiting the number of questions that any individual sees in a beta exam, limiting the number of questions delivered to an individual by using adaptive testing, and adding new exam elements.

Exam questions may be in a variety of formats: Depending on which exam you take, you'll see multiple-choice questions as well as select-and-place and prioritize-a-list questions. Simulations and case study–based formats are included as well. Let's take a look at the types of exam questions and examine the adaptive testing technique so you'll be prepared for all of the possibilities.

Multiple-Choice Questions

Multiple-choice questions come in two main forms. One is a straightforward question followed by several possible answers, of which one or more is correct. The other type of multiple-choice question is more complex and based on a specific scenario. The scenario may focus on several areas or objectives.

Select-and-Place Questions

Select-and-place exam questions involve graphical elements that you must manipulate to successfully answer the question. A typical diagram will show computers and other components next to boxes that contain the text "Place here." The labels for the boxes represent various computer roles on a network, such as a print server and a file server. Based on information given for each computer, you are asked to select each label and place it in the correct box. You need to place *all* of the labels correctly. No credit is given for the question if you correctly label only some of the boxes.

In another select-and-place problem you might be asked to put a series of steps in order by dragging items from boxes on the left to boxes on the right and placing them in the correct order. One other type requires that you drag an item from the left and place it under an item in a column on the right.

For more information on the various exam question types, go to `www.microsoft.com/learning/`.

Simulations

Simulations are the kinds of questions that most closely represent actual situations and test the skills you use while working with Microsoft software interfaces. These exam questions include a mock interface on which you are asked to perform certain actions according to a given scenario.

Because of the number of possible errors that can be made on simulations, be sure to consider the following recommendations from Microsoft:

- Do not change any simulation settings that don't pertain to the solution directly.
- When related information has not been provided, assume that the default settings are used.
- Make sure that your entries are spelled correctly.
- Close all the simulation application windows after completing the set of tasks in the simulation.

The best way to prepare for simulation questions is to spend time working with the graphical interface of the product on which you will be tested.

Case Study–Based Questions

Case study–based questions first appeared in the MCSD program. These questions present a scenario with a range of requirements. Based on the information provided, you answer a series of multiple-choice and select-and-place questions. The interface for case study–based questions has a number of tabs, each of which contains information about the scenario. At present, this type of question appears only in most of the Design exams.

Microsoft will regularly add and remove questions from the exams. This is called *item seeding*. It is part of the effort to make it more difficult for individuals to merely memorize exam questions that were passed along by previous test-takers.

Tips for Taking the Windows 7 Client Configuration Exam

Here are some general tips for achieving success on your certification exam:

- Arrive early at the exam center so that you can relax and review your study materials. During this final review, you can look over tables and lists of exam-related information.
- Read the questions carefully. Don't be tempted to jump to an early conclusion. Make sure you know *exactly* what the question is asking.
- Answer all questions. If you are unsure about a question, mark it for review and come back to it at a later time.
- On simulations, do not change settings that are not directly related to the question. Also, assume default settings if the question does not specify or imply which settings are used.
- For questions you're not sure about, use a process of elimination to get rid of the obviously incorrect answers first. This improves your odds of selecting the correct answer when you need to make an educated guess.

Exam Registration

You may take the Microsoft exams at any of more than 1,000 Authorized Prometric Testing Centers (APTCs) around the world. For the location of a testing center near you, call Prometric at 800-755-EXAM (755-3926). Outside the United States and Canada, contact your local Prometric registration center.

Find out the number of the exam you want to take, and then register with the Prometric registration center nearest to you. At this point, you will be asked for advance payment for the exam. The exams are $125 each and you must take them within one year of payment. You can schedule exams up to six weeks in advance or as late as one working day prior to the date of the exam. You can cancel or reschedule your exam if you contact the center at least two working days prior to the exam. Same-day registration is available in some locations, subject to space availability. Where same-day registration is available, you must register a minimum of two hours before test time.

You may also register for your exams online at `www.prometric.com`. At the time this book was written, VUE no longer offers Microsoft exams. If you have taken Microsoft exams with VUE, continue to watch VUE's website (`www.vue.com`) to see if it starts offering Microsoft exams again.

When you schedule the exam, you will be provided with instructions regarding appointment and cancellation procedures, ID requirements, and information about the testing center location. In addition, you will receive a registration and payment confirmation letter from Prometric.

Microsoft requires certification candidates to accept the terms of a nondisclosure agreement before taking certification exams.

Is This Book for You?

If you want to acquire a solid foundation in Windows 7 and your goal is to prepare for the exam by learning how to use and manage the new operating system, this book is for you. You'll find clear explanations of the fundamental concepts you need to grasp and plenty of help to achieve the high level of professional competency you need to succeed in your chosen field.

If you want to become certified as an MCTS, this book is definitely for you. However, if you just want to attempt to pass the exam without really understanding Windows 7, this Study Guide is *not* for you. It is written for people who want to acquire hands-on skills and in-depth knowledge of Windows 7.

What's in the Book?

What makes a Sybex Study Guide the book of choice for hundreds of thousands of MCPs? We took into account not only what you need to know to pass the exam, but what you need to know to take what you've learned and apply it in the real world. Each book contains the following:

Objective-by-objective coverage of the topics you need to know Each chapter includes a list of the objectives it covers.

The topics covered in this Study Guide map directly to Microsoft's official exam objectives. Each exam objective is covered completely.

Assessment test Directly following this introduction is an assessment test that you should take. It is designed to help you determine how much you already know about Windows 7. Each question is tied to a topic discussed in the book. Using the results of the assessment test, you can figure out the areas where you need to focus your study. Of course, we do recommend you read the entire book.

Exam Essentials To highlight what you learn, you'll find a list of exam essentials at the end of each chapter. The Exam Essentials section briefly highlights the topics that need your particular attention as you prepare for the exam.

Glossary Throughout each chapter, you will be introduced to important terms and concepts that you will need to know for the exam. These terms appear in italics within the chapters, and at the end of the book, a detailed glossary gives the definitions for these terms as well as other general terms you should know.

Review questions, complete with detailed explanations Each chapter is followed by a set of review questions that test what you learned. The questions are written with the exam in mind, meaning they are designed to have the same look and feel as what you'll see on the exam. Question types are just like the exam, including multiple choice, exhibits, and select-and-place.

Hands-on exercises In each chapter, you'll find exercises designed to give you the important hands-on experience that is critical for your exam preparation. The exercises support the topics of the chapter, and they walk you through the steps necessary to perform a particular function.

Real World Scenarios Because reading a book isn't enough for you to learn how to apply these topics in your everyday duties, we have provided Real World Scenarios in special sidebars. These explain when and why a particular solution would make sense, in a working environment you'd actually encounter.

Interactive CD Every Sybex Study Guide comes with a CD complete with additional questions, flashcards for use with an interactive device, and the book in electronic format. Details are in the following section.

What's on the CD?

With this new member of our best-selling Study Guide series, we are including quite an array of training resources. The CD offers bonus exams and flashcards to help you study for the exam. We have also included the complete contents of the Study Guide in electronic form. The CD's resources are described here:

The Sybex E-book for Windows 7 Many people like the convenience of being able to carry their whole Study Guide on a CD. They also like being able to search the text via computer to find specific information quickly and easily. For these reasons, the entire contents of this Study Guide are supplied on the CD, in PDF. We've also included Adobe Acrobat Reader, which provides the interface for the PDF contents as well as the search capabilities.

The Sybex Test Engine This is a collection of multiple-choice questions that will help you prepare for your exam. There are four sets of questions:

- Two bonus exams designed to simulate the actual live exam.
- All the questions from the Study Guide, presented in a test engine for your review. You can review questions by chapter or by objective, or you can take a random test.
- The assessment test.

Here is a sample screen from the Sybex test engine:

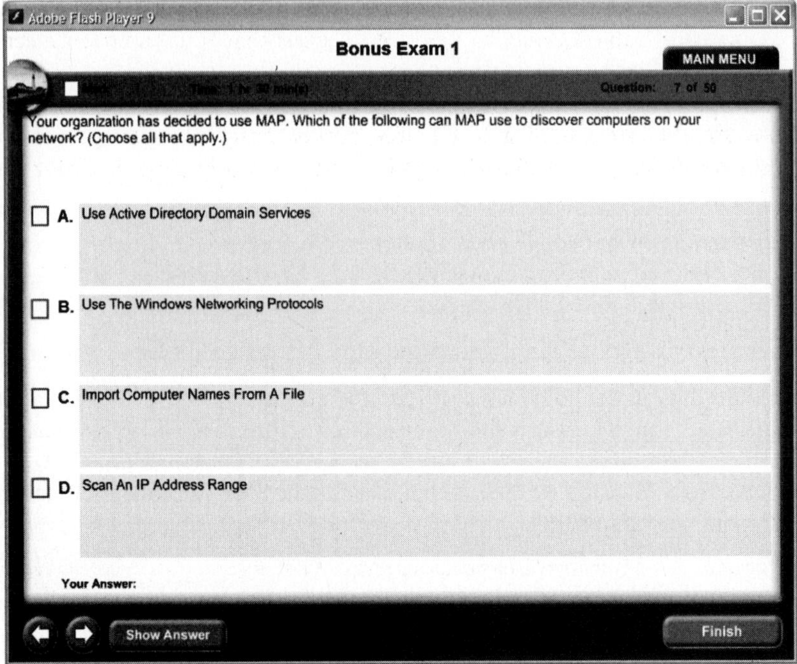

Sybex Flashcards for PCs and Handheld Devices The "flashcard" style of question offers an effective way to quickly and efficiently test your understanding of the fundamental concepts covered in the exam. The Sybex Flashcards set consists of 100 questions presented in a special engine developed specifically for this Study Guide series. Here's what the Sybex Flashcards interface looks like:

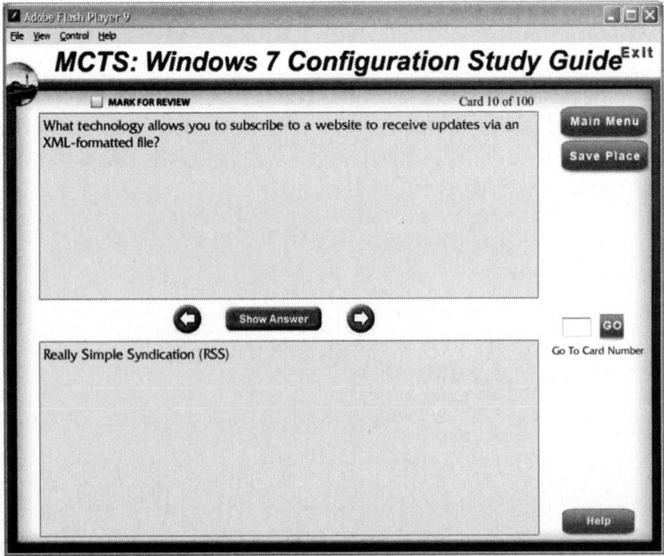

Hardware and Software Requirements

You should verify that your computer meets the minimum requirements for installing Windows 7 as listed in Table 1.3 in Chapter 1. We suggest that your computer meets or exceeds the recommended requirements for a more enjoyable experience.

The exercises in this book assume that your computer is configured in a specific manner. Your computer should have at least a 20 GB drive that is configured with the minimum space requirements and partitions. Other exercises in this book assume that your computer is configured as follows:

- 20 GB C: partition with the NTFS file system
- Optional D: partition with the FAT32 file system
- 15 GB or more of free space

Of course, you can allocate more space to your partitions if it is available.

The second exercise in the book assumes that you are performing a clean installation and not an upgrade. Your partitions should be created and formatted as previously specified.

Contacts and Resources

To find out more about Microsoft Learning materials and programs, to register with Prometric, or to obtain other useful certification information and additional study resources, check the following resources:

Microsoft Learning Home Page

`www.microsoft.com/learning`

This website provides information about the MCP program and exams. You can also order the latest Microsoft Roadmap to Education and Certification.

Microsoft TechNet Technical Information Network

`www.microsoft.com/technet`

800-344-2121

Use this website or phone number to contact support professionals and system administrators. Outside the United States and Canada, contact your local Microsoft subsidiary for information.

Prometric

`www.prometric.com`

800-755-3936

Contact Prometric to register to take an MCP exam at any of more than 800 Prometric Testing Centers around the world.

MCP Magazine Online

www.mcpmag.com

Microsoft Certified Professional Magazine is a well-respected publication that focuses on Windows certification. This site hosts chats and discussion forums and tracks news related to the MCSE program. Some of the services cost a fee, but they are well worth it.

Stellacon Training Center

www.stellacon.com

877-778-6107

Stellacon Training offers IT certification exam preparation materials for Microsoft exams, along with classes on all Microsoft certifications. William Panek, the author, is a trainer with Stellacon Training Center.

Assessment Test

1. What filename extension is applied by default to custom consoles that are created for the MMC?

   A. `.mmc`

   B. `.msc`

   C. `.con`

   D. `.mcn`

2. You want to create roaming profiles for users in the sales department. They frequently log on at computers in a central area. The profiles should be configured as mandatory and roaming profiles. Which users are able to manage mandatory profiles on Windows 7 computers?

   A. The user who uses the profile

   B. Server operators

   C. Power users

   D. Administrators

3. You want to monitor the CPU, memory, and disk usage on your computer to ensure that there are no bottlenecks. Which MMC snap-in would you load to access System Monitor?

   A. System Monitor

   B. Reliability Monitor

   C. ActiveX Control

   D. Performance Logs and Alerts

4. If you wanted to require that a user enter an Administrator password to perform administrative tasks, what type of user account should you create for the user?

   A. Administrator User account

   B. Standard User account

   C. Power User account

   D. Authenticated User account

5. You have installed a clean installation of Windows 7 on your computer. You want to create an image of the new installation to use as a basis for remote installs. What Windows 7 utility should you use to accomplish this?

   A. WDS

   B. Windows SIM

   C. ImageX

   D. Sysprep

6. Which of the following statements is true regarding the built-in Administrator account in Windows 7? (Choose all that apply.)
   - **A.** The built-in Administrator account does not exist in Windows 7.
   - **B.** The built-in Administrator account is disabled by default in Windows 7.
   - **C.** The built-in Administrator account has no permissions in Windows 7.
   - **D.** The built-in Administrator account is not a member of the Administrators group in Windows 7.

7. You have a user with limited vision. Which accessibility utility is used to read aloud screen text, such as the text in dialog boxes, menus, and buttons?
   - **A.** Read-Aloud
   - **B.** Orator
   - **C.** Dialog Manager
   - **D.** Narrator

8. You have just purchased a new computer that has Windows 7 preinstalled. You want to migrate existing users from a previous computer that was running Windows XP Professional. Which two files would you use to manage this process through the User State Migration Tool?
   - **A.** `usmt.exe`
   - **B.** `ScanState.exe`
   - **C.** `LoadState.exe`
   - **D.** `Windows7Migrate.exe`

9. You have scheduled a specific program that is required by the accounting department to run as a scheduled task every day. When you log on as an administrator, you can run the task, but when the scheduled task is supposed to run, it does not run properly. You have already verified that the Task Scheduler task is running. What else should you check?
   - **A.** Verify that the task has been configured to run in unattended mode.
   - **B.** Make sure the user who is scheduled to run the task has the appropriate permissions.
   - **C.** Make sure the time is properly synchronized on the computer.
   - **D.** Verify that the Process Manager task is running.

10. You are the network administrator for your company. Recently, one of your users in the accounting department has reported that they were unsure whether a banking website was legitimate or not. You want to configure a utility that will verify whether a website is known to be fraudulent. Which utility should you configure?
    - **A.** Pop-up Blocker
    - **B.** RSS Reader
    - **C.** Phishing Filter
    - **D.** Add-on Manager

11. You have a user, Jan, who suspects that her Windows 7 computer has been infected with spyware. You remove the spyware from her computer and want to prevent spyware from infecting it in the future. Which of the following Windows 7 utilities should you configure?

    A. Windows Defender

    B. Phishing Filter

    C. Pop-up Blocker

    D. Windows OneCare

12. You are configuring power settings on your laptop. You configure the laptop to enter sleep mode after a specified period of inactivity. Which of the following will occur when the computer enters Sleep mode?

    A. The computer will be shut down gracefully.

    B. Data will be saved to the hard disk.

    C. The monitor and hard disk will be turned off, but the computer will remain in a fully active state.

    D. The user session will not be available when you resume activity on the computer.

13. You are using Internet Explorer to access several RSS feeds that you subscribe to. One of the feeds stores only the 10 most recent updates. You want to ensure that the last 100 updates are stored. What should you do?

    A. Configure the RSS feed to automatically download attached files.

    B. Modify the schedule so that the RSS feed is updated more than once a day.

    C. Turn on feed reading view in IE.

    D. Modify the archive setting so that the last 100 items are stored.

14. What is the CIDR equivalent for 255.255.255.224?

    A. /24

    B. /25

    C. /26

    D. /27

15. You are configuring a new Windows 7 computer for a new employee. You configure the new user with a standard user account. Which of the following functions will the new employee be allowed to perform? (Choose all that apply.)

    A. Install a printer.

    B. Install network drivers.

    C. Configure WPA keys.

    D. Modify the Desktop settings.

16. You are the network administrator for Stellacon. Your network consists of 200 Windows 7 computers, and you want to assign static IP addresses rather than use a DHCP server. You want to configure the computers to reside on the 192.168.10.0 network. What subnet mask should you use with this network address?

    A. 255.0.0.0

    B. 255.255.0.0

    C. 255.255.255.0

    D. 255.255.255.255

17. You are using a laptop running Windows 7 Home Premium. You want to synchronize files between your laptop and a network folder. Which of the following actions must you perform first in order to enable synchronization to occur between your laptop and the network folder?

    A. Upgrade your laptop to Windows 7 Ultimate.

    B. Enable one-way synchronization between the laptop and the network folder.

    C. Enable two-way synchronization between the laptop and the network folder.

    D. Configure the files on your laptop as read-only.

18. You have a DNS server that contains corrupt information. You fix the problem with the DNS server, but one of your users is complaining that they are still unable to access Internet resources. You verify that everything works on another computer on the same subnet. Which command can you use to fix the problem?

    A. `IPCONFIG /flush`

    B. `IPCONFIG /flushdns`

    C. `PING /flush`

    D. `GROPE /flushdns`

19. Which of the following information can be configured on a VPN client so that it can access a VPN server? (Choose two answers.)

    A. IP address

    B. MAC address

    C. Domain name

    D. Connection address

20. Which of the following statements are true regarding the creation of a group in Windows 7? (Choose two.)

    A. Only members of the Administrators group can create users on a Windows 7 computer.

    B. Group names can be up to 64 characters.

    C. Group names can contain spaces.

    D. Group names can be the same as usernames but not the same as other group names on the computer.

21. You need to expand the disk space on your Windows 7 computer. You are considering using spanned volumes. Which of the following statements is/are true concerning spanned volumes? (Choose all that apply.)

    A. Spanned volumes can contain space from 2 to 32 physical drives.

    B. Spanned volumes can contain space from 2 to 24 physical drives.

    C. Spanned volumes can be formatted as FAT32 or NTFS partitions.

    D. Spanned volumes can be formatted only as NTFS partitions.

22. Which of the following versions of Windows 7 support the Windows Aero interface? (Choose all that apply.)

    A. Windows 7 Home Basic

    B. Windows 7 Home Premium

    C. Windows 7 Business

    D. Windows 7 Ultimate

23. Your home computer network is protected by a firewall. You have configured your Windows 7 home computer to use Windows Mail. After you configure your email accounts, you discover that you are unable to send email messages from Windows Mail. Your email provider uses POP3 and SMTP. What port should you open on the firewall?

    A. 25

    B. 110

    C. 443

    D. 995

24. You need Windows 7 to be the primary operating system on a dual-boot machine. Which file do you configure for this?

    A. `boot.ini`

    B. **`bcdedit`**

    C. `bcboot.ini`

    D. `bcdboot`

25. Which of the following versions of Windows 7 can be upgraded to Windows 7 Ultimate Edition? (Choose all that apply.)

    A. Windows 7 Home Starter

    B. Windows 7 Professional

    C. Windows 7 Home Premium

    D. Windows 7 Business

26. You are configuring a Windows 7 computer that is going to be used by your children. You are configuring access restrictions using the Parental Controls feature of Windows 7. Which of the following can be configured by setting Parental Controls? (Choose all that apply.)

   A. When your children can access the computer

   B. What websites your children can view

   C. What programs your children can access

   D. What other computers on your home network your children can access

27. How do you access the Advanced Boot Menu in Windows 7 during the boot process?

   A. Press the spacebar.

   B. Press F6.

   C. Press F8.

   D. Press F10.

28. You have two remote sites with Windows 7 machines. You need to share data across the slow sites. What feature can help with this?

   A. Link Detection

   B. BranchCache

   C. DirectAccess

   D. DirectCache

29. Which utility is used to upgrade a FAT32 partition to NTFS?

   A. UPFS

   B. UPGRADE

   C. Disk Manager

   D. CONVERT

30. You want to be able to track which users are accessing the `C:\PAYROLL` folder and whether the access requests are successful. Which of the following audit policy options allows you to track events related to file and print object access?

   A. File And Object Access

   B. Audit Object Access

   C. Audit File And Print Access

   D. Audit All File And Print Events

Answers to Assessment Test

1. B. When you create a custom console for the MMC, the `.msc` filename extension is automatically applied. See Chapter 3 for more information.

2. D. Only members of the Administrators group can manage mandatory profiles. See Chapter 6 for more information.

3. C. Select ActiveX Control in the Add/Remove Snap-in dialog box. Then, from the Insert ActiveX Control dialog box, select System Monitor Control to access the System Monitor utility. You can also access the System Monitor view by opening Performance Monitor. See Chapter 8 for more information.

4. B. You would create a standard user account for the user. Standard users must provide the credentials of an administrator account when prompted by User Account Control (UAC) in order to perform administrative tasks. See Chapter 6 for more information.

5. C. You can use the ImageX utility to create an image of a Windows 7 installation. After the image has been created, you can prepare the image with a utility such as the System Preparation Tool (Sysprep). The image can then be used for remote installations of Windows 7. See Chapter 2 for more information.

6. B. The built-in Administrator account is disabled by default in Windows 7. However, it can be enabled through Local Users and Groups or by modifying the Accounts: Administrator Account Status GPO setting. See Chapter 6 for more information.

7. D. The Narrator utility uses a sound output device to read onscreen text. See Chapter 4 for more information.

8. B, C. Windows 7 ships with a utility called the User State Migration Tool (USMT) that is used by administrators to migrate users from one computer to another via a command-line utility. The USMT consists of two executable files: `ScanState.exe` and `LoadState.exe`. See Chapter 1 for more information.

9. B. If you are using Task Scheduler and your jobs are not running properly, make sure the Task Scheduler service is running and is configured to start automatically. You should also ensure that the user who is configured to run the scheduled task has sufficient permissions to run it. See Chapter 8 for more information.

10. C. Internet Explorer 8 ships with Phishing Filter, which can help verify whether a website is known to be fraudulent or not. Phishing Filter helps to prevent malicious websites from masquerading as legitimate sites in order to obtain your personal or financial information. See Chapter 5 for more information.

11. A. Windows Defender is an antispyware program included with Windows 7. It offers real-time protection from spyware and other unwanted software. You can also configure Windows Defender to scan for spyware on a regular basis. See Chapter 6 for more information.

12. B. Sleep mode is a combination of Standby mode and Hibernation mode. When Sleep mode is configured, the user's session is quickly accessible on wakeup, but the data is saved to the hard disk. Sleep mode is the preferred power-saving mode in Windows 7. See Chapter 4 for more information.

13. D. Internet Explorer 8 provides the ability to read and subscribe to RSS feeds. You can configure several options for RSS feeds, such as how often the feed is checked for updates, whether attachments are automatically downloaded, and how many updates are stored for the feed. See Chapter 5 for more information.

14. D. A subnet mask of 255.255.255.224 equals a CIDR of /27. CIDR is the number of on bits See Chapter 7 for more information.

15. A, C, D. Standard users are allowed to perform a variety of tasks, such as install printers, configure wireless keys, and modify their Desktop settings. See Chapter 6 for more information.

16. C. You should use the subnet mask 255.255.255.0 on your network in this scenario. The IP network address 192.168.10.0 is a Class C address. Class C addresses, by default, use the subnet mask 255.255.255.0. The network portion of the address is 192.168.10, and the host portion of the address can be 1 to 254. See Chapter 7 for more information.

17. A. To enable synchronization of files between your laptop and a network folder, you must first upgrade your laptop to a version of Windows 7 that supports synchronization with network folders, such as Windows 7 Ultimate. Windows Sync Center also supports synchronization of files between computers and mobile devices. See Chapter 4 for more information.

18. B. The `IPCONFIG /flushdns` command is used to purge the DNS Resolver cache. The `IPCONFIG` command displays a computer's IP configuration. See Chapter 7 for more information.

19. A, C. When you configure a VPN connection, you must specify the IP address or host domain name of the computer to which you'll connect. See Chapter 4 for more information.

20. A, C. Only administrators can create new groups on a Windows 7 computer. Group names can contain up to 256 characters and can contain spaces. Group names must be unique to the computer, different from all the other usernames and group names that have been specified on that computer. See Chapter 6 for more information.

21. A, C. You can create a spanned volume from free space that exists on a minimum of 2 to a maximum of 32 physical drives. When the spanned volume is initially created in Windows 7, it can be formatted with FAT32 or NTFS. If you extend a volume that already contains data, however, the partition must be NTFS. See Chapter 3 for more information.

22. B, C, D. The new Windows Aero interface is not available on Windows 7 Home Basic. It is available on Windows 7 Home Premium, Windows 7 Business, and Windows 7 Ultimate. See Chapter 4 for more information.

23. A. Port 25 should be opened on the firewall. SMTP is used for outbound mail and uses port 25. POP3, which is used for receiving inbound mail, uses port 110. See Chapter 7 for more information.

24. B. You should configure the `bcdedit` utility to configure your boot order. See Chapter 1 for more information.

25. B, D. You can upgrade Windows 7 Professional, and Windows 7 Business to Windows 7 Ultimate Edition. See Chapter 1 for more information.

26. A, B, C. Using Parental Controls, you can configure what websites your children can access, when they can use the computer, what games they can play, and what programs they can run, and you can view reports regarding their activity. See Chapter 5 for more information.

27. C. During the boot process, you are prompted to press F8 to access the Advanced Boot Menu. See Chapter 9 for more information.

28. B. BranchCache allows multiple sites with slower links to share data quickly and efficiently. See Chapter 7 for more information.

29. D. The CONVERT utility is used to convert an FAT32 partition to NTFS. See Chapter 3 for more information.

30. B. Though all four options seem plausible, only the Audit Object Access option actually exists. Audit Object Access is used to enable auditing of access to files, folders, and printers. Once you enable auditing of object access, you must enable file auditing through NTFS security or enable print auditing through printer security. See Chapter 6 for more information.

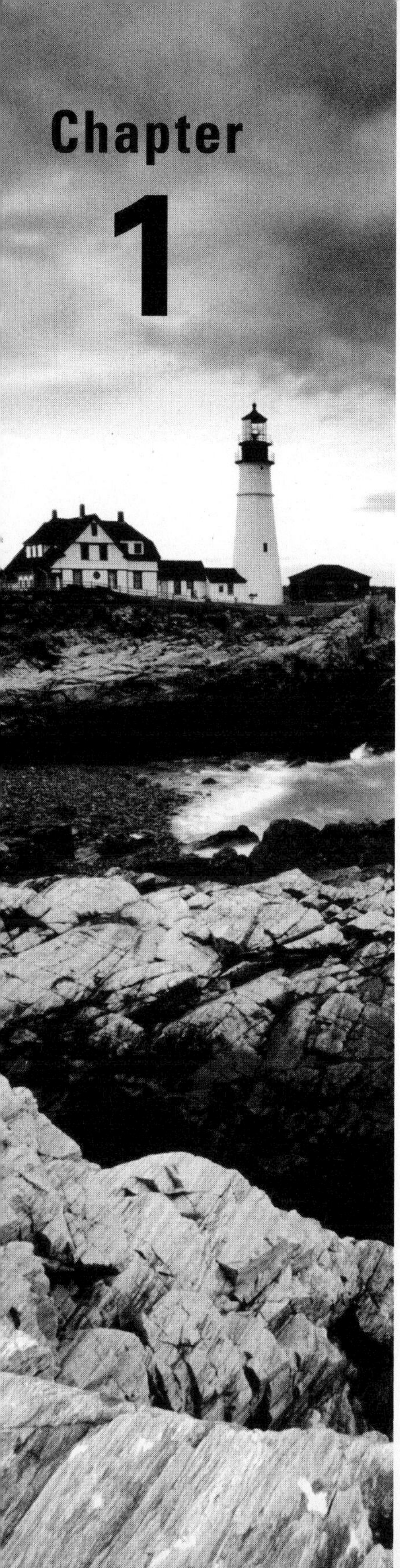

Installing Windows 7

MICROSOFT EXAM OBJECTIVES COVERED IN THIS CHAPTER:

✓ **Perform a clean installation.**

- This objective may include but is not limited to: identifying hardware requirements; setting up as the sole operating system; setting up as dual boot; installation methods; boot from the source of installation; preparing the installation source: USB, CD, network share, WDS

✓ **Upgrade to Windows 7 from previous versions of Windows.**

- This objective may include but is not limited to: upgrading from Windows Vista; migrating from Windows XP; upgrading from one edition of Windows 7 to another edition of Windows 7

✓ **Migrate user profiles.**

- This objective may include but is not limited to: migrating from one machine to another; migrating from previous versions of Windows; side-by-side vs. wipe and load

✓ **Configure updates to Windows 7.**

- This objective may include but is not limited to: configuring update settings; determining source of updates; configuring Windows Update policies; reviewing update history; checking for new updates; rolling back updates

In this chapter I will show you how to install Windows 7 because, before you can master any Microsoft product, you must first know how to properly install the product.

Preparing for the installation of Windows 7 involves making sure your hardware meets the minimum requirements and that your hardware is supported by the operating system.

Once you've completed all the planning, you are ready to install Windows 7. This is a straightforward process that is highly automated and user friendly.

Another consideration when installing Windows 7 is whether you are going to upgrade from a previous version of Windows or install a clean copy on your computer. An upgrade attempts to preserve existing settings; a clean install puts a fresh copy of the operating system on your computer. Installation preparation also involves making choices about your system's configuration, such as selecting a disk-partitioning scheme.

To complete the Windows 7 installation, you will need to activate the product through Windows Activation. This process is used to reduce software piracy. After Windows 7 is installed, you can keep the operating system up-to-date with post-installation updates.

When you install Windows 7, you should also consider whether the computer will be used for dual-boot or multi-boot purposes. Dual-booting or multi-booting allows you to have your computer boot with operating systems other than Windows 7.

Introducing Windows 7

Unless you have been living on another planet, you know that Windows 7 is not Microsoft's first client operating system. Before I start explaining Windows 7, you should know about some of the features of Windows XP and Windows Vista and how they affect Windows 7.

I understand that many IT professionals did not make the move from Windows XP to Windows Vista and that is why we give a brief overview of some of the features of both.

Overview of Windows XP

Microsoft introduced Windows XP in 2001. Microsoft Windows XP was a replacement to the Millennium operating system. Windows XP was a stable environment that catered to both the home user and work environment user.

Windows XP was the first operating system to introduce the dual column Start menu, shown in Figure 1.1. The Windows XP operating system also redesigned how the Control Panel was structured.

FIGURE 1.1 Windows XP Start menu

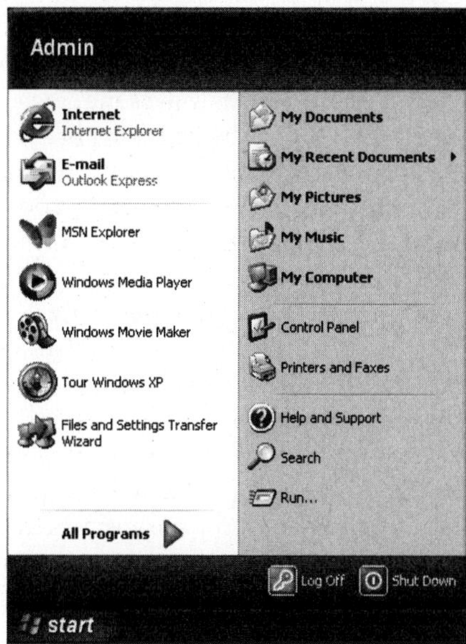

Windows XP was also the first operating system to use the new core called the kernel. Previous versions of Microsoft used a 9*x* version of the core systems, but this new kernel was more stable and ran more efficiently.

Windows XP also introduced Remote Assistance (which is still in use in Windows 7). This allows an administrator to accept an invitation from a user and then connect to that user's machine to help the user technically from a remote location.

Windows XP made it easier to keep your machine up-to-date with the ability to schedule Windows updates with the Microsoft website, also included with Windows 7. This allows users to guarantee that their machines are always running with the latest security patches and also with the latest versions of the XP system files.

Another feature that was introduced into the XP operating system and is still used in Windows 7 is driver signing. If a manufacturer of a device did not adhere to Microsoft's standards and the devices were not digitally signed, you have the ability to stop the installation of the drivers.

As Microsoft developed Windows Vista, it incorporated some new features. These features are available for Windows XP only if you install Service Pack 3, but they are included with Windows 7.

Windows XP Service Pack 3

With the release of Windows XP Service Pack 3, the operating system obtained some new benefits over the basic XP system. First off, Service Pack 3 includes all previous service pack fixes and patches. It also includes all required security fixes. The following features are some of the enhancements included in Service Pack 3.

Network Access Protection (NAP) Network Access Protection (NAP) is a compliancy checking platform that is included with Windows 2008 Server, Windows Vista, Windows 7, and Windows XP with SP3. NAP allows you to create compliancy policies that check computers before allowing them access to the network.

Windows Product Activation Users have the ability to install the complete integrated operating system with SP3 without the need of a product key. The operating system will ask the user to provide a product key at a later time.

Microsoft Cryptographic Module The `rsaenh.dll` file has been redesigned with the SHA2 hashing algorithms (SHA256, SHA382, and SHA512) in X.509 certificate validation already included.

Now that we have looked at some of the features of XP and how these features affect Windows 7, let's take a look at Windows Vista and some of the features that are still included with Windows 7.

Overview of Windows Vista

Windows Vista was the next generation of Microsoft's client operating system to be released after Windows XP. Since the majority of the IT market did not switch to Windows Vista, it is important to understand some basics about it. Windows 7 has many of the same features and attributes.

There were many new features and changes from Windows XP to Windows Vista. Let's take a look at some of them.

New Improved Desktop Windows Vista introduced a new improved desktop called Windows Aero. Windows Aero offers Vista Home Premium, Vista Business, Vista Ultimate, and Vista Enterprise users a more stable desktop. Computers running Windows Aero will require a compatible graphics adapter. Windows 7 also includes the Windows Aero Desktop.

Windows Sidebar Windows Vista introduced a new vertical bar that is displayed on the side of the desktop called the Windows Sidebar. The Windows Sidebar has mini applications called gadgets running within it. Windows 7 has removed the Windows Sidebar, but you can still add gadgets to the Windows 7 Desktop.

Gadgets are mini applications that allow you to easily perform and see useful functions such as a clock, a slide show, an Internet feed, a calendar, weather reports, a stocks feed, a currency exchange, and so forth. Many downloadable gadgets are available from Microsoft's website. Gadgets will be explained in detail in Chapter 4, "Managing the Windows 7 Environment."

Parental Controls Parental controls allow the computer administrator (or parent) to configure how other family members will be able to use the computer system. You can set which sites specific users can visit and what times a specific user can use the computer system. Parental controls have been improved and are still included on Windows 7.

Improved Windows Firewall Firewalls are hardware devices or software applications that either restrict or allow users and data from an internal or external source. Microsoft Vista has included an improved version of Microsoft's software-based firewall, as shown in Figure 1.2.

FIGURE 1.2 Windows Vista Firewall

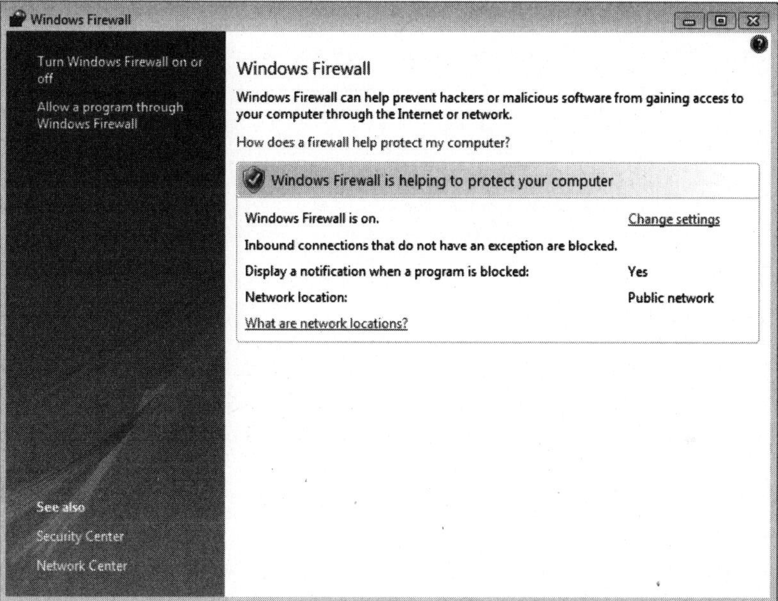

This improved version helps protect your computer system by restricting operating system resources if they operate in an unusual way. For example, let's say you have an application that uses a particular port to function properly. If that application tries to use a different port, the system stops the application, thus protecting other computer systems from possible problems. Windows 7 also includes Windows Firewall.

Windows Vista User Account Control Introduced in Windows Vista and Windows Server 2008, the User Account Control (UAC) is a new security feature that allows a standard user to perform many functions without needing to use a non-administrative account.

Windows Search Windows Search, also included with Windows 7, allows you to search files or applications quickly and easily from anywhere in Windows Vista. One of the nice features of Windows Search is that when you start typing in your search term, all files, folders, and applications that have names starting with the first letters you type start to appear. For example, if you type **No,** everything with names starting with *no*, including Notepad, appear.

Live Icons If you have a compatible video adapter and choose to run Windows Aero (also included with Windows 7), you have the ability to use live icons. When you mouse over a live icon, you can see what is in the application or folder it represents.

Windows Vista is easy to install but you must verify that the machine that you are loading Vista onto can handle the installation. Table 1.1 lists the requirements for a Windows Vista–capable PC as well as the requirements for Windows Vista Premium.

TABLE 1.1 Hardware requirements (non-network Installation)

Component	Windows Vista–capable PC	Windows Vista Premium PC
Processor	800 MHz 32-bit (x86) or 64-bit (x64) processor; Intel Core/Pentium/Celeron, AMD, Via, or compatible	1 GHz 32-bit (x86) or 64-bit (x64) processor; Intel Core/Pentium/Celeron, AMD, Via, or compatible
Memory	512 MB	1 GB
Disk space	20 GB hard drive with 15 GB of free disk space	40 GB hard drive with 15 GB free disk space
Graphics	DirectX 9 video card capable of SVGA at 800×600 resolution (WDDM driver support recommended)	DirectX 9 video card that supports a WDDM driver, Pixel Shader 2.0 in hardware, and 32 bits per pixel; graphics card memory dependent on desired resolution

Processors with Windows Vista

Windows Vista supports computers with one or two physical processors. Windows Vista Starter, Windows Vista Home Basic, and Windows Vista Home Premium support one physical processor. Windows Vista Business, Windows Vista Enterprise, and Windows Vista Ultimate support two physical processors. There is no limit to the number of processor cores these editions support, so you will be able to use quad-core processor architectures with Windows Vista.

Now that we have taken a look at Windows XP and Windows Vista, it's time to take a look at some of the features of Windows 7. Microsoft Vista did not take off the way Microsoft had anticipated. Vista got a bad reputation from the get-go due to the higher-end machine requirements. To allow Vista to run properly, you needed a dual core processor and a beefed-up machine.

Many smaller IT departments do not even have dual-core processors in their servers, and they were not about to rebuy all of their client machines. Also, Vista took much more hard disk space compared to its predecessor, XP. So many organizations held off installing Vista.

Microsoft heard the masses and started building a new operating system. What it came up with is now called Windows 7. Microsoft Windows 7 is the newest version of Microsoft's client operating system software. Windows 7 combines the best of Windows XP and Windows Vista.

Microsoft currently has six different versions of the Windows 7 operating system:

- Windows 7 Starter
- Windows 7 Home Basic
- Windows 7 Home Premium
- Windows 7 Professional
- Windows 7 Enterprise
- Windows 7 Ultimate

The Windows 7 hardware requirements are discussed in greater detail in Chapter 2, "Automating the Windows 7 Installation."

New Features in Windows 7

Windows 7 has improved in many of the weak areas plaguing Windows Vista. Windows 7 has a much faster boot time and shutdown compared to Windows Vista. It is also easier to install and configure.

The Windows 7 operating system functions are also faster than its previous counterparts. Opening, moving, extracting, compressing, and installing files and folders are also more efficient than they were in previous versions of Microsoft's client operating systems.

Let's take a look at some of the improvements and features of Windows 7. This is just an overview of some of the benefits to using Windows 7.

Windows 7 Taskbar In the previous versions of Windows, you had a Quick Launch bar on the left-hand side, and on the right-hand side you could see which programs were loaded and running. The Quick Launch bar is now gone and has been replaced by the Windows 7 Taskbar and Jump List, as shown in Figure 1.3.

FIGURE 1.3 Windows 7 Taskbar

The Windows Taskbar allows a user to quickly access the programs they use the most. One advantage to having the applications on the Windows 7 Taskbar is fewer icons on the Desktop, thus allowing for a more manageable Desktop environment.

Jump Lists Jump Lists are a new feature to the Windows lineup, and they allow you to quickly access files that you have been working on. For example, if you have the Word icon in the Taskbar, you can right-click it to see all the files that you have been working with recently. In the case of Internet Explorer, you could view all the websites that you have visited recently.

Another advantage to using Jump Lists is that you can preset certain applications, like Windows Media Player.

New Preview Pane Windows XP and Windows Vista have a preview pane, but Windows 7 has improved on the preview pane by allowing you to now view text files, music files, picture files, HTML files, and videos. Another new advantage is if you have installed Microsoft Office and Adobe Acrobat Reader, you now have the ability to also view Office files and PDF files.

Windows Touch This is one of the cooler features included with Windows 7. Windows Touch allows you to control the operating system and its applications by using a touchscreen.

For example, you can open a picture and then move it around, make it larger or smaller, or place it anywhere on the Desktop, all with the touch of your fingers on the screen.

Touchscreens are placed on laptops, tabletops, GPS devices, phones, and now on the Windows 7 operating system.

Windows XP Mode Microsoft realizes that many organizations are running Windows XP and older applications on these Windows XP systems. Windows XP Mode allows an organization that chooses to upgrade to Windows 7 to still have the ability to run older Windows XP applications on the Windows 7 operating system.

In Windows XP Mode, Windows 7 uses virtualized technology to run a virtual XP operating system to allow the use of the older applications.

Simpler Home Networking Windows 7 networking has been made easier with the improvement of HomeGroups. Using HomeGroups is an easy way to set up a network with Windows 7. Windows 7 searches for your home network, and if one is found, it connects after you enter the HomeGroup password.

If a home network is not found, a networking wizard automatically creates a password for the HomeGroup. This password allows you to connect all of your other computers to the same network, and it can be changed anytime after the installation of Windows 7.

Device Stage Device Stage is new to the Windows operating systems family. It allows you to connect a compatible device to your PC and have a picture of the device appear. Using Device Stage, you can easily share files between devices and computers.

Before Windows 7 Device Stage, when you connected a device to the PC, you might see multiple devices. For example, when you add a multifunction printer (printer, scanner, and copier), it might be added as three separate devices. Device Stage helps resolve this issue.

Another feature of the Device Stage is that the device vendors can customize the icons for the Device Stage, so that the same multi-function printer can have the ability to order ink from the Device Stage.

View Available Networks (VAN) If you have used a laptop, you have used this feature. When you use a wireless network adapter and you right-click the icon in the system tray, you can choose the wireless network to which you want to connect. Connecting to a wireless network is done through the wireless network adapter. Now that same functionality is built into the Windows 7 operating system.

Windows Internet Explorer 8 Windows 7 includes the newest version of Internet Explorer (IE8). IE8, shown in Figure 1.4, allows a user to work faster and more efficiently on the Internet due to new search features, address bars, and favorites.

FIGURE 1.4 IE8

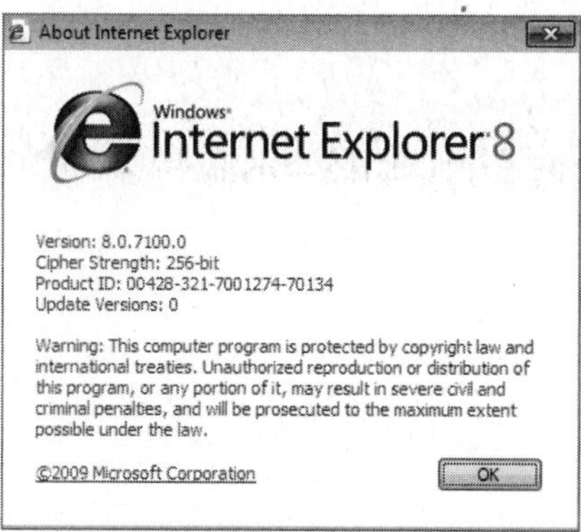

The following list includes some of the new features of IE8:

Instant Search This feature allows you to quickly access search requests without typing in the entire search criteria. As you start typing in the search request, you start seeing suggestions for your search.

The advantage to Instant Search is that it will also use your browsing history to narrow down the suggestions. If one of the suggestions is what you are looking for, you can choose it without finishing the query.

Accelerators This new feature allows you to accelerate actions on Internet services and applications. For example, if you were looking for a street address and you clicked the blue accelerator icon, a map would appear right there on the screen.

Microsoft accelerators can be used for email, searching, and so forth. Websites such as eBay and Facebook also offer accelerators for their services.

Web Slices Web Slices are instances on a website that you can access without the need of accessing the site itself. For example, you can get stock quotes, sports scores, or auction items without visiting the respective sites. With Web Slices, as the information that you are watching changes, the updates will show immediately.

Real World Scenario

Choosing an Appropriate Operating System

As an IT consultant, I have clients who want to stay on the leading edge of technology but don't have the money to replace all of their equipment. This is where I have to convince the client that it is better to slowly migrate their equipment.

Try presenting a timeline to your customers or organization that shows the migration to Windows 7. Your clients will be happy, and you will have the time needed to migrate your organization.

I understand that you are reading this book so that you can install Windows 7 in your organization, but since not all of your machines will be able to run Windows 7, it is important to know the minimum requirements for Windows XP and Vista.

Windows 7 Architecture

Windows 7 is built on the Windows Vista core, but Windows 7 has limited the files that load at startup to help with the core performance of the operating system. Microsoft has also removed many of the fluff items that Windows Vista used, allowing for better performance.

When Microsoft first released Windows 7 as a beta, there was a 64-bit version but no 32-bit version. This did not go over well with the Internet bloggers. I even saw a petition online to have a 32-bit version released.

The funny thing is that I also saw a petition asking Microsoft to *not* release a 32-bit version. The logic behind this petition was that the release of a 32-bit version would force users and manufacturers to upgrade everything to 64-bit. Regardless, Microsoft has released Windows 7 as both 32-bit and 64-bit version.

Microsoft could not release just a 64-bit version of Windows 7. This would alienate many users with 32-bit computer systems, and it would cost Microsoft a large share of the client-side software market (it's already had to deal with the PC/Mac commercials). So you have a choice of either using Windows 7 32-bit or 64-bit.

32-bit versus 64-bit

The terms *32-bit* and *64-bit* are referring to the CPU, or processor. The number represents how the data is processed. It is processed either as 2^{32} or 2^{64}. The larger the number is, the larger the amount of data that can be processed at any one time.

To get an idea of how 32-bit and 64-bit processors operate, think of a large highway with 32 lanes. Vehicles can travel on those 32 lanes only, so when traffic gets backed up, the result is delays. Now think of how many more vehicles can travel on a 64-lane highway.

The problem here is that a 32-lane highway can't handle the number of vehicles a 64-lane highway could. You need to have the infrastructure to allow for that volume of vehicles. The same is true for computers. Your computer has to be configured to allow you to run a 64-bit processor.

So what does all of this mean to the common user or administrator? It's all about Random Access Memory, or RAM. A 32-bit operating system can handle up to 4 GB of RAM, and a 64-bit processor can handle up to 16 exabytes of RAM. The problem is that Windows and most motherboards can't handle this much RAM.

None of this is new. Although 64-bit processors are just starting to get accepted with Windows, other operating systems, such as Apple, have been using 64-bit processors for many years.

So should you switch all of your users to 64-bit? The answer is no. Most users do not need to have large amounts of RAM, and many manufactures do not have 64-bit-compliant components.

For example, I am writing this book on a 64-bit computer, but if I open Internet Explorer and go to any website that uses Adobe Flash Player, it will not work. Currently, Adobe does not have a 64-bit Flash Player.

Computer processors are typically rated by speed. The speed of the processor, or central processing unit (CPU), is rated by the number of clock cycles that can be performed in 1 second. This measurement is typically expressed in gigahertz (GHz). One GHz is one billion cycles per second. Keep in mind that processor architecture must also be taken into account when considering processor speed. A processor with a more efficient pipeline will be faster than a processor with a less efficient pipeline at the same CPU speed.

Now that you have seen the new features of Windows 7, let's look at how to prepare the machine to install Windows 7.

Preparing to Install Windows 7

Installing Windows 7 is very simple because of the installation wizard. The installation wizard will walk you through the entire installation of the operating system.

The harder part of installing Windows 7 is preparing and planning for the installation. One thing I often say to IT professionals is, "An hour of planning will save you days of work." Planning a Windows 7 rollout is one of the hardest and most important tasks that you will perform when installing Windows 7.

There are many decisions that should be made before you insert the actual Windows 7 media into the machine. The first decision is which version of Windows 7 you want to install. Let's take a look at the different versions of Windows 7.

Different Versions of Windows 7

Microsoft has six different versions of the Windows 7 operating system. This allows an administrator to custom fit a user's hardware and job function to the appropriate version of Windows 7. The six different versions of Windows 7 are:

- Windows 7 Starter
- Windows 7 Home Basic
- Windows 7 Home Premium
- Windows 7 Professional
- Windows 7 Enterprise
- Windows 7 Ultimate

Many times Microsoft releases multiple editions of the operating system contained within the same Windows 7 media disk. You can choose to unlock the one you want based on the product key you have. Let's take a closer look at the different versions of Windows 7.

Windows 7 Starter

The Windows 7 Starter edition was designed for small notebook PCs, and it is now available worldwide. This is a change from the previous versions of the Windows Starter editions. Previously, the Starter editions were available only to certain locations. Windows 7 Starter edition has some features that work well on small notebook PCs:

- A safe, reliable, and supported operating system
- HomeGroup, which allows a user to easily share media, documents, and printers across multiple PCs in homes or offices without the need of a domain

- Improved Windows Taskbar and Jump Lists
- Broad application and device compatibility with unlimited concurrent applications

At the time this book was written, the three concurrent applications restriction was removed. Concurrent applications restriction meant that you could only run a certain amount of applications at any one time. This was a limitation in Vista Starter Edition. If you plan on using the Windows 7 Starter edition, please check Microsoft's website for any possible changes to this restriction.

There are many limitations to using the Windows 7 Starter edition. Windows 7 Starter edition does not include the following:

- Aero Glass. You are allowed to use only the Windows Basic or other opaque themes. Also, you do not get to use the Live Taskbar Previews or Aero Peek.
- Personalization features for changing Desktop backgrounds, window colors, and sound schemes.
- The ability to easily switch between users. You must log off to change users.
- Multi-monitor support.
- DVD playback or Windows Media Center for watching recorded TV or other media.
- Remote media streaming for streaming your videos, music, and recorded TV from your home computer.
- Domain support for business customers.
- XP Mode for those who want the ability to run older Windows XP programs on Windows 7.

Windows 7 Home Basic

The Windows 7 Home Basic edition is going to be issued only to limited areas throughout the world. The Home Basic edition, at the time this was written, is not going to be available to U.S. customers. Only emerging markets will be able to purchase the Home Basic edition so that they can have an inexpensive version of Windows 7. The Home Basic edition has some of the following features:

- Broad application and device compatibility with unlimited concurrent applications
- A safe, reliable, and supported operating system
- HomeGroup, which allows a user to easily share media, documents, and printers across multiple PCs in homes or offices without the need of a domain
- Improved Taskbar and Jump Lists
- Live thumbnail previews and an enhanced visual experience

- Advanced networking support (ad hoc wireless networks and Internet connection sharing)
- Windows Mobility Center

Windows 7 Home Premium

Windows 7 Home Premium is the main operating system for the home users. Home Premium offers many features, including these:

- Broad application and device compatibility with unlimited concurrent applications
- A safe, reliable, and supported operating system
- HomeGroup, which allows a user to easily share media, documents, and printers across multiple PCs in homes or offices without the need of a domain
- Improved Taskbar and Jump Lists
- Live thumbnail previews and an enhanced visual experience
- Advanced networking support (ad hoc wireless networks and Internet connection sharing)
- Mobility Center
- Windows Aero transparent glass design and advanced Windows navigation
- Easy networking and sharing across all your PCs and devices
- Improved media format support and enhancements to Windows Media Center and media streaming, including Play To
- Multitouch
- Improved handwriting recognition

Windows 7 Professional

Windows 7 Professional was designed with the small business owner in mind. Microsoft has designed Windows 7 Professional so that you can get more done and safeguard your data. Professional offers the following features:

- Broad application and device compatibility with unlimited concurrent applications
- A safe, reliable, and supported operating system
- HomeGroup, which allows a user to easily share media documents and printers across multiple PCs in homes or offices without the need of a domain
- Improved Taskbar and Jump Lists
- Live thumbnail previews and an enhanced visual experience
- Advanced networking support (ad hoc wireless networks and Internet connection sharing)
- Mobility Center

- Action Center, which makes it easier to resolve many IT issues yourself
- Aero transparent glass design and advanced Windows navigation
- Easy networking and sharing across all your PCs and devices
- Improved media format support and enhancements to Windows Media Center and media streaming, including Play To
- Multitouch
- Improved handwriting recognition
- Domain Join, which enables simple and secure server networking
- Encrypting File System, which protects data with advanced network backup
- Location Aware Printing, which helps find the right printer when moving between the office and home
- Windows XP Mode to enable customers to run many Windows XP productivity applications

Windows 7 Enterprise and Ultimate

Windows 7 Enterprise and Ultimate are the two versions designed for mid-size and large organizations. These two operating systems have the most features and security options out of all Windows 7 versions. Here are some of the features:

- Broad application and device compatibility with unlimited concurrent applications
- A safe, reliable, and supported operating system
- HomeGroup, which allows a user to easily share media, documents, and printers across multiple PCs in homes or offices without the need of a domain
- Improved Taskbar and Jump Lists
- Live thumbnail previews and an enhanced visual experience
- Advanced networking support (ad hoc wireless networks and Internet connection sharing)
- Mobility Center
- Aero transparent glass design and advanced Windows navigation
- Easy networking and sharing across all your PCs and devices
- Improved media format support and enhancements to Windows Media Center and media streaming, including Play To
- Multitouch
- Improved handwriting recognition
- Domain Join, which enables simple and secure server networking
- Encrypting File System, which protects data with advanced network backup

- Location Aware Printing, which helps find the right printer when you are moving between the office and home
- Windows XP Mode, which enables customers to run many Windows XP productivity applications
- BitLocker, which protects data on removable devices
- DirectAccess, which links users to corporate resources from the road without a virtual private network (VPN)
- BranchCache, which makes it faster to open files and web pages from a branch office
- AppLocker, which restricts unauthorized software and also enables greater security

Windows 7 Ultimate also includes the multilanguage pack; Windows 7 Enterprise does not.

Table 1.2 shows a comparison of all the Windows 7 versions and what they include. This table, based on Microsoft's websites, is only a partial representation of the features and applications that are included on all the different versions.

TABLE 1.2 Windows 7 edition comparison

	Starter Edition	Home Basic Edition	Home Premium Edition	Professional Edition	Enterprise and Ultimate Edition
Processor (32-bit or 64-bit)	Both	Both	Both	Both	Both
Multiprocessor support	No	No	Yes	Yes	Yes
32-bit maximum RAM	4 GB	4 GB	4 GB	4 GB	4 GB
64-bit maximum RAM	8 GB	8 GB	16 GB	192 GB	192 GB
Windows HomeGroup	Yes	Yes	Yes	Yes	Yes
Jump Lists	Yes	Yes	Yes	Yes	Yes
Internet Explorer 8	Yes	Yes	Yes	Yes	Yes
Media Player 12	Yes	Yes	Yes	Yes	Yes
System Image	Yes	Yes	Yes	Yes	Yes
Device Stage	Yes	Yes	Yes	Yes	Yes
Sync Center	Yes	Yes	Yes	Yes	Yes

	Starter Edition	Home Basic Edition	Home Premium Edition	Professional Edition	Enterprise and Ultimate Edition
Windows Backup	Yes	Yes	Yes	Yes	Yes
Remote Desktop	Yes	Yes	Yes	Yes	Yes
ReadyDrive	Yes	Yes	Yes	Yes	Yes
ReadyBoost	Yes	Yes	Yes	Yes	Yes
Windows Firewall	Yes	Yes	Yes	Yes	Yes
Windows Defender	Yes	Yes	Yes	Yes	Yes
Taskbar Previews	No	Yes	Yes	Yes	Yes
Mobility Center	No	Yes	Yes	Yes	Yes
Easy User Switching	No	Yes	Yes	Yes	Yes
Windows Aero Glass	No	No	Yes	Yes	Yes
Multi-touch	No	No	Yes	Yes	Yes
DVD playback	No	No	Yes	Yes	Yes
Windows Media Center	No	No	Yes	Yes	Yes
XP Mode	No	No	No	Yes	Yes
Encrypting File System (EFS)	No	No	No	Yes	Yes
BitLocker	No	No	No	No	Yes
AppLocker	No	No	No	No	Yes
BranchCache	No	No	No	No	Yes
DirectAccess	No	No	No	No	Yes

Hardware Requirements

Before you can insert the Windows 7 DVD and install the operating system, you must make sure the machine's hardware can handle the Windows 7 operating system.

To install Windows 7 successfully, your system must meet or exceed certain hardware requirements. Table 1.3 lists the requirements for a Windows 7–capable PC.

TABLE 1.3 Hardware requirements

Component	Requirements
CPU (processor)	1 GHz 32-bit or 64-bit processor
Memory (RAM)	1 GB of system memory
Hard disk	16 GB of available disk space
Video adapter	Support for DirectX 9 graphics with 128 MB memory (to enable the Aero theme)
Optional drive	DVD-R/W drive
Network device	Compatible network interface card

The hardware requirements listed in Table 1.3 were those specified at the time this book was written. Always check Microsoft's website for the most current information.

The Windows 7–capable PC must meet or exceed the basic requirements to deliver the core functionality of the Windows 7 operating system. These requirements are based on the assumption that you are installing only the operating system without any premium functionality. For example, you may be able to get by with the minimum requirements if you are installing the operating system just to learn the basics of the software. Remember, the better the hardware, the better the performance.

The requirements for the graphics card depend on the resolution at which you want to run. The required amount of memory is as follows:

- 64 MB is required for a single monitor at a resolution of 1,310,720 pixels or less, which is equivalent to a 1280×1024 resolution.
- 128 MB is required for a single monitor at a resolution of 2,304,000 pixels or less, which is equivalent to a 1920×1200 resolution.
- 256 MB is required for a single monitor at a resolution larger than 2,304,000 pixels.

In addition, the graphics memory bandwidth must be at least 1,600 MB per second, as assessed by the Windows 7 Upgrade Advisor.

Real World Scenario

Deciding on Minimum Hardware Requirements

The company you work for has decided that everyone will have their own laptop running Windows 7. You need to decide on the new computers' specifications for processor, memory, and disk space.

The first step is to determine which applications will be used. Typically, most users will work with an email program, a word processor, a spreadsheet, presentation software, and maybe a drawing or graphics program. Additionally, an antivirus application will probably be used. Under these demands, a 1 GHz Celeron processor and 1,000 MB of RAM will make for a very slow-running machine. So for this usage, you can assume that the minimum baseline configuration would be higher than a 1 GHz processor with at least 2 GB of RAM.

Based on your choice of baseline configuration, you should then fit a test computer with the applications that will be used on it and test the configuration in a lab environment simulating normal use. This will give you an idea of whether the RAM and processor calculations you have made for your environment are going to provide a suitable response.

Today's disk drives have become capable of much larger capacity while dropping drastically in price. So for disk space, the rule of thumb is to buy whatever is the current standard. At the time this book was written, 500 GB drives were commonplace, which is sufficient for most users. If users plan to store substantial graphics or video files, you may need to consider buying larger-than-standard drives.

Also consider what the business requirements will be over the next 12 to 18 months. If you will be implementing applications that are memory- or processor-intensive, you may want to spec out the computers with hardware sufficient to support upcoming needs to avoid costly upgrades in the near future.

Measurement Used for Disk Space and Memory

Hard disks are commonly rated by capacity. The following measurements are used for disk space and memory capacity:

- 1 MB (megabyte) = 1,024 KB (kilobytes)
- 1 GB (gigabyte) = 1,024 MB
- 1 TB (terabyte) = 1,024 GB
- 1 PB (petabyte) = 1,024 TB
- 1 EB (exabyte) = 1,024 PB

If you are not sure if your machine meets the minimum requirements, Microsoft includes some tools that can help you determine if the machine is Windows 7–compatible.

The Hardware Compatibility List (HCL)

Along with meeting the minimum requirements, your hardware should appear on the *Hardware Compatibility List (HCL)*. The HCL is an extensive list of computers and peripheral hardware that have been tested with the Windows 7 operating system.

The Windows 7 operating system requires control of the hardware for stability, efficiency, and security. The hardware and supported drivers on the HCL have been put through rigorous tests to ensure their compatibility with Windows 7. Microsoft guarantees that the items on the list meet the requirements for Windows 7 and do not have any incompatibilities that could affect the stability of the operating system.

If you call Microsoft for support, the first thing a Microsoft support engineer will ask about is your configuration. If you have any hardware that is not on the HCL, you may not be able to get support from Microsoft.

To determine if your computer and peripherals are on the HCL, check the most up-to-date list at `https://winqual.microsoft.com/HCL/Default.aspx`.

BIOS Compatibility

Before you install Windows 7, you should verify that your computer has the most current Basic Input/Output System (BIOS). This is especially important if your current BIOS does not include support for Advanced Configuration and Power Interface (ACPI) functionality. ACPI functionality is required for Windows 7 to function properly. Check the computer's vendor for the latest BIOS version information.

Driver Requirements

To successfully install Windows 7, you must have the critical device drivers for your computer, such as the hard drive device driver. The Windows 7 media comes with an extensive list of drivers. If your computer's device drivers are not on the Windows 7 installation media, you should check the device manufacturer's website. If you can't find the device driver on the manufacturer's website and no other compatible driver exists, you are out of luck. Windows 7 will not recognize devices that don't have Windows 7 drivers.

New Install or Upgrade

Once you've determined that your hardware meets the minimum requirements, you need to decide whether you want to do an upgrade or a clean install.

An upgrade allows you to retain your existing operating system's applications, settings, and files. If you currently have a computer with Windows Vista, you are eligible to use an upgrade copy of Windows 7.

The bad news is that you must always perform a clean install with Windows XP or earlier versions of Windows. You can, however, use the Windows Easy Transfer utility to migrate files and settings from Windows XP to Windows 7 on the same computer. The steps to do this will be shown later in this chapter.

Another possibility is to upgrade your Windows XP machine to Windows Vista and then upgrade the new Vista operating system to Windows 7.

You can perform an upgrade to Windows 7 if the following conditions are true:

- You are running Windows Vista.
- You want to keep your existing applications and preferences.
- You want to preserve any local users and groups you've created.

You must perform a clean install of Windows 7 if any of the following conditions are true:

- There is no operating system currently installed.
- You have an operating system installed that does not support an in-place upgrade to Windows 7 (such as DOS, Windows 9*x*, Windows NT, Windows Me, Windows 2000 Professional, or Windows XP).
- You want to start from scratch, without keeping any existing preferences.
- You want to be able to dual-boot between Windows 7 and your previous operating system.

Table 1.4 shows each Vista operating system that can be upgraded and the edition of Windows 7 to which it should be updated.

TABLE 1.4 Windows Vista Upgrade Options

Windows Vista Edition	Windows 7 Edition
Home Premium edition	Home Premium edition
Business edition	Professional edition
Ultimate edition	Ultimate edition

Upgrade Considerations

Almost all Windows Vista applications should run with the Windows 7 operating system. However, the following are a few possible exceptions to this statement:

- Applications that use file-system filters, such as antivirus software, may not be compatible.
- Custom power-management tools may not be supported.

Before upgrading to Windows 7, be sure to stop any antivirus scanners, network services, or other client software. These software packages may see the Windows 7 install as a virus and cause installation issues.

If you are performing a clean install to the same partition as an existing version of Windows, the contents of the existing Users (or Documents And Settings), Program Files, and Windows directories will be placed in a directory named `Windows.old`, and the old operating system will no longer be available.

Hardware Compatibility Issues

You need to ensure that you have Windows 7 device drivers for your hardware. If you have a video driver without a Windows 7–compatible driver, the Windows 7 upgrade will install the Standard VGA driver, which will display the video with an 800×600 resolution. Once you get the Windows 7 driver for your video, you can install it and adjust video properties accordingly.

Application Compatibility Issues

Not all applications that were written for earlier versions of Windows will work with Windows 7. After the upgrade, if you have application problems, you can address the problems as follows:

- If the application is compatible with Windows 7, reinstall the application after the upgrade is complete.
- If the application uses dynamic-link libraries (DLLs), and there are migration DLLs for the application, apply the migration DLLs.
- Use the Microsoft Application Compatibility Toolkit (ACT) to determine the compatibility of your current applications with Windows 7. ACT will determine which applications are installed, identify any applications that may be affected by Windows updates, and identify any potential compatibility problems with User Account Control and Internet Explorer. Reports can be exported for detailed analysis.
- If applications were written for earlier versions of Windows but are incompatible with Windows 7, use the Windows 7 Program Compatibility Wizard. From Control Panel, click the Programs icon and then click the Run Programs From Previous Versions link to start the Program Compatibility Wizard. If the application is not compatible with Windows 7, upgrade your application to a Windows 7–compliant version.

Windows 7 Upgrade Advisor

To assist you in the upgrade process, the Windows 7 Setup program can check the compatibility of your system, devices, and installed applications and then provide the results to you. You can then analyze these results to determine whether your hardware or software applications will port properly from previous Windows versions to Windows 7.

You can download the Windows 7 *Upgrade Advisor* from Microsoft's website at `www.microsoft.com/downloads`. The Windows 7 Upgrade Advisor is compatible with Windows 7, Windows Vista, and Windows XP with Service Pack 2 or higher.

When you are running the Upgrade Advisor on a machine running Windows XP, if you do not have the .NET Framework 2.0, you will be asked to download and install it. After the .NET Framework is installed, you can restart the Upgrade Advisor installation.

After your computer is scanned, the Upgrade Advisor will determine whether any incompatibilities exist between your computer and Windows 7. It will also tell you which edition of Windows 7 seems to be best for your computer. However, you are by no means limited to upgrading to the recommended edition. The Upgrade Advisor compatibility reports are broken up into three categories:

System Requirements The System Requirements report will alert you to any shortcomings your system might have when running certain editions of Windows 7. For example, my lab computer should have no problems accessing all the features of Windows 7 Enterprise but it won't be able to access all of the features of Windows 7 Home Premium or Windows 7 Ultimate because it doesn't have a TV tuner card.

Devices The Devices report will alert you to any potential Windows 7 driver issues. Each device in your system will be listed in this section as either a device to be reviewed or a device that should automatically work after Windows 7 is installed. You will need a driver for the network card after Windows 7 is installed.

Programs The Programs report will alert you to any potential application compatibility issues.

You can also save or print a task list that tells you the most compatible Windows 7 edition, your current system configuration, and the steps you need to take before and after installing Windows 7.

In Exercise 1.1, I will walk you through the Windows 7 Upgrade Advisor. The Upgrade Advisor will need to be downloaded from Microsoft's website.

EXERCISE 1.1

Using the Windows 7 Upgrade Advisor

1. Go to `www.microsoft.com/downloads` and download the Windows 7 Upgrade Advisor.
2. After the download is complete, run the `.msi` installation.
3. The Windows 7 Upgrade Advisor Wizard will start. Click the Next button.

EXERCISE 1.1 *(continued)*

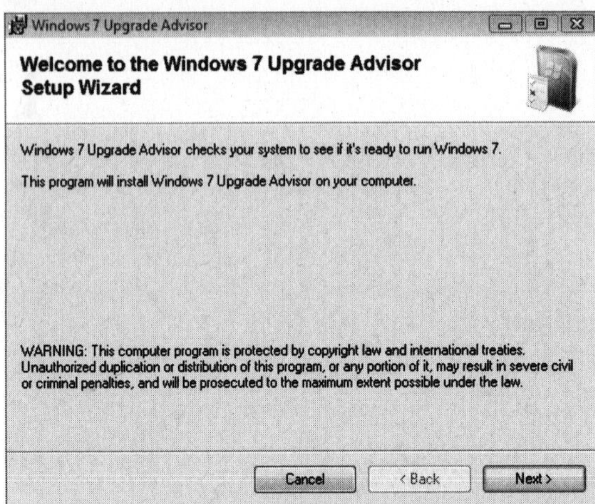

4. At the License screen, click the I Accept The License Terms check box and click Next.
5. At the Select Installation Folder screen, accept the defaults or choose a directory location where you would like this program installed. Click Install.

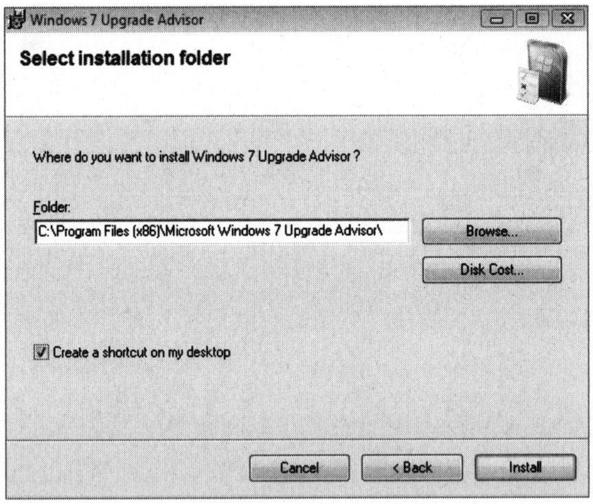

6. At the Installation Complete screen, click the Close button.

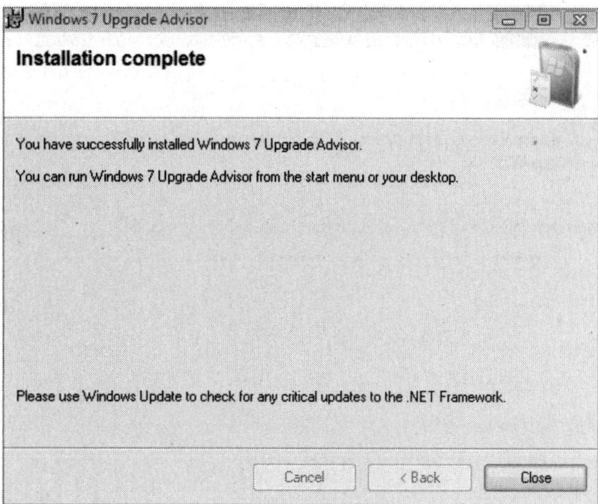

7. On the Desktop, double-click the Windows 7 Upgrade Advisor icon.
8. When the Windows 7 Upgrade Advisor starts, click the Start Check button to start the scan of the machine.

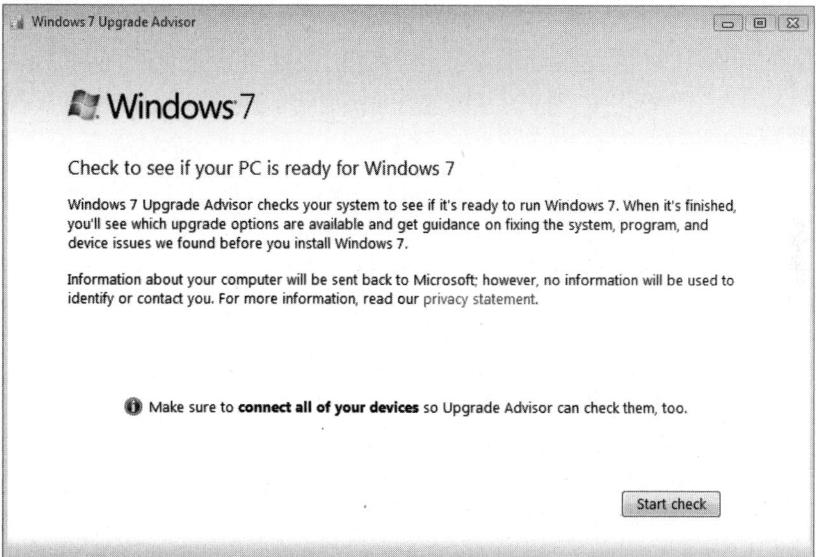

9. Once the system scan is complete, the Upgrade Advisor will give you the results. You can print or save them. Close the Upgrade Advisor.

An Upgrade Checklist

Once you have made the decision to upgrade, you should develop a plan of attack. The following upgrade checklist (valid for upgrading from Windows Vista) will help you plan and implement a successful upgrade strategy.

- Verify that your computer meets the minimum hardware requirements for Windows 7.
- Be sure your hardware is on the HCL.
- Make sure you have the Windows 7 drivers for the hardware. You can verify this with the hardware manufacturer.
- To audit the current configuration and status of your computer, run the Windows 7 Upgrade Advisor tool from the Microsoft website, which also includes documentation on using the utility. It will generate a report of any known hardware or software compatibility issues based on your configuration. You should resolve any reported issues before you upgrade to Windows 7.
- Make sure your BIOS is current. Windows 7 requires that your computer have the most current BIOS. If it does not, it may not be able to use advanced power-management features or device-configuration features. In addition, your computer may cease to function during or after the upgrade. Use caution when performing BIOS updates because installing the incorrect BIOS can cause your computer to fail to boot.
- Take an inventory of your current configuration. This inventory should include documentation of your current network configuration, the applications that are installed, the hardware items and their configuration, the services that are running, and any profile and policy settings.
- Back up your data and configuration files. Before you make any major changes to your computer's configuration, you should back up your data and configuration files and then verify that you can successfully restore your backup. Chances are if you have a valid backup, you won't have any problems. Chances are if you don't have a valid backup, you will have problems.
- Delete any unnecessary files or applications, and clean up any program groups or program items you don't use. Theoretically, you want to delete all the junk on your computer before you upgrade. Think of this as the spring-cleaning step.
- Verify that there are no existing problems with your drive prior to the upgrade. Perform a disk scan, a current virus scan, and defragmentation. These, too, are spring-cleaning chores. This step just prepares your drive for the upgrade.
- Perform the upgrade. In this step, you upgrade from the Windows Vista operating system to Windows 7.
- Verify your configuration. After Windows 7 has been installed, use the inventory to compare and test each element that was inventoried prior to the upgrade to verify that the upgrade was successful.

Handling an Upgrade Failure

Before you upgrade, you should have a contingency plan in place. Your plan should assume the worst-case scenario. For example, what happens if you upgrade and the computer doesn't work anymore? It is possible that, after checking your upgrade list and verifying that everything should work, your attempt at the actual upgrade may not work. If this happens, you may want to return your computer to the original, working configuration.

Indeed, I have made these plans, created my backups (two, just in case), verified them, and then had a failed upgrade anyway—only to discover that I had no clue where to find the original operating system CD. A day later, with the missing CD located, I was able to get up and running again. My problem was an older BIOS, and the manufacturer of my computer did not have an updated BIOS.

Disk Space Partitioning

Disk partitioning is the act of taking the physical hard drive and creating logical partitions. A logical drive is how space is allocated to the drive's primary and logical partitions. For example, if you have a 500 GB hard drive, you might partition it into three logical drives: a C: drive, which might be 200 GB; a D: drive, which might be 150 GB; and an E: drive, which might be 150 GB.

The following are some of the major considerations for disk partitioning:

- The amount of space required
- The location of the system and boot partition
- Any special disk configurations you will use
- The utility you will use to set up the partitions

Partition Size One important consideration in your disk-partitioning scheme is determining the partition size. You need to consider the amount of space taken up by your operating system, the applications that will be installed, and the amount of stored data. It is also important to consider the amount of space required in the future.

Microsoft recommends that you allocate at least 16 GB of disk space for Windows 7. This allows room for the operating system files and for future growth in terms of upgrades and installation files that are placed with the operating system files.

The System and Boot Partitions When you install Windows 7, files will be stored in two locations: the system partition and the boot partition. The system partition and the boot partition can be the same partition.

The system partition contains the files needed to boot the Windows 7 operating system. The system partition contains the Master Boot Record (MBR) and boot sector of the active drive partition. It is often the first physical hard drive in the computer and normally contains the necessary files to boot the computer. The files stored on the system partition do not take any significant disk space. The active partition is the system partition that is used to start your computer. The C: drive is usually the active partition.

The boot partition contains the files that are the Windows 7 operating system files. By default, the Windows operating system files are located in a folder named Windows.

Special Disk Configurations Windows 7 supports several disk configurations. Options include simple, spanned, and striped volumes. These configuration options are covered in detail in Chapter 3, "Managing Disks."

Disk Partition Configuration Utilities If you are partitioning your disk prior to installation, you can use several utilities, such as the DOS or Windows FDISK program, or a third-party utility such as Norton's Partition Magic. You can also configure the disks during the installation of the Windows 7 operating system.

You might want to create only the first partition where Windows 7 will be installed. You can then use the Disk Management utility in Windows 7 to create any other partitions you need. The Windows 7 Disk Management utility is covered in Chapter 3.

Language and Locale

Language and locale settings determine the language the computer will use. Windows 7 supports many languages for the operating system interface and utilities.

Locale settings are for configuring the format for items such as numbers, currencies, times, and dates. For example, English for the United States specifies a short date as mm/dd/yyyy (month/day/year), while English for South Africa specifies a short date as yyyy/mm/dd (year/month/day).

Installing Windows 7

You can install Windows 7 either from the bootable DVD or through a network installation using files that have been copied to a network share point. You can also launch the `setup.exe` file from within the Windows 7 operating system to upgrade your operating system.

The Windows 7 DVD is bootable. To start the installation, you simply restart your computer and boot to the DVD. The installation process will begin automatically. You will walk through the steps of installing Windows 7 from the DVD in Exercise 1.2.

If you are installing Windows 7 from the network, you need a distribution server and a computer with a network connection. A distribution server is a server that has the Windows 7 distribution files copied to a shared folder. The following steps are used to install Windows 7 over the network:

1. Boot the target computer.
2. Attach to the distribution server and access the share that has the files copied to it.

3. Launch `setup.exe`.
4. Complete the Windows 7 installation using either the clean install method or the upgrade method. These methods are discussed in detail in the following sections.

Performing a Clean Install of Windows 7

On any installation of Windows 7, there are three stages to the installation.

Collecting Information During the collection phase of the installation, Windows 7 gathers the information necessary to complete the installation. This is where Windows 7 gathers your local time, location, keyboard, license agreement, installation type, and installation disk partition.

Installing Windows This section of the installation is where your Windows 7 files are copied to the hard disk and the installation is completed. This phase takes the longest as the files are installed.

Set Up Windows In this phase, you set up a username, computer name, password, product key, and security settings and review the date and time. After this is finished, your installation will be complete.

As explained earlier, you can run the installation from the optical media or over a network. The only difference in the installation procedure is your starting point: from your optical drive or from a network share. The steps in the following exercise assume you are using the Windows 7 DVD to install Windows 7.

Setting Up Your Computer for Hands-On Exercises

Before beginning Exercise 1.2, verify that your computer meets the requirements for installing Windows 7 as listed in Table 1.3. For Exercise 1.2, it is assumed you are not currently running a previous version of Windows that will be upgraded.

The exercises in this book are based on your computer being configured in a specific manner. Your computer should have at least a 20 GB drive that is configured with the minimum space requirements and partitions.

When you boot to the Windows 7 installation media, the Setup program will automatically start the Windows 7 installation. In Exercise 1.2, you will perform a clean install of Windows 7. This exercise assumes that you have access to Windows 7 Ultimate; other editions may vary slightly. You can also download an evaluation version of Windows 7 from Microsoft's website.

EXERCISE 1.2

Performing a Clean Install of Windows 7

1. Insert the Windows 7 DVD into the machine and start the computer.
2. If you are asked to Hit Any Key to start the DVD, press Enter.
3. The first screen will ask you to enter your language, local time, and keyboard. After filling in these fields, click Next.

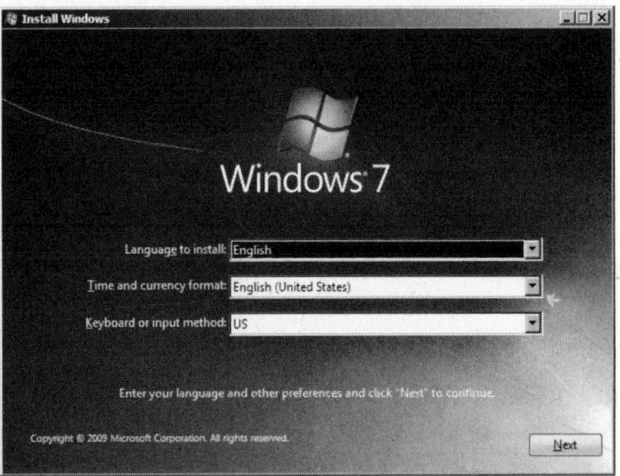

4. At the next screen, click the Install Now button.

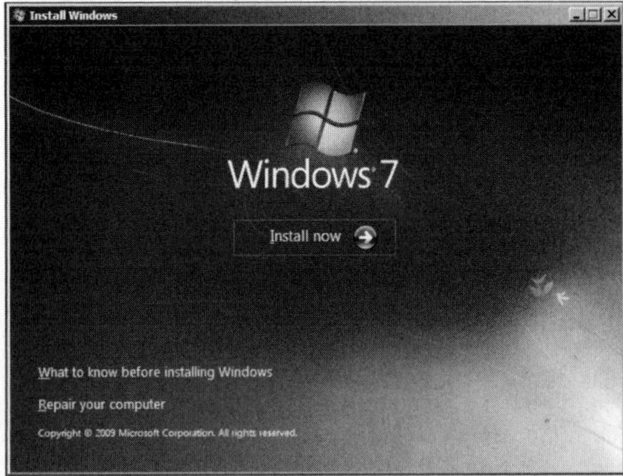

5. A message appears to tell you that the setup is starting. The licensing screen will be first. Read the license agreement and then check the I Accept The License Terms check box. Click Next.

6. When asked which type of installation you want, click Custom (Advanced).

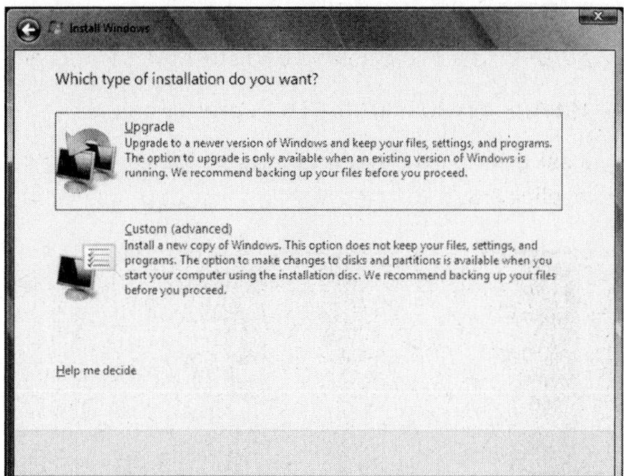

7. The next screen asks you to identify the disk to which you would like to install Windows 7. Choose an unformatted free space or a partition (partition will be erased) with at least 20 GB available. You can also click the Drive Options (Advanced) link to create your own partition. After you choose your partition, click Next.

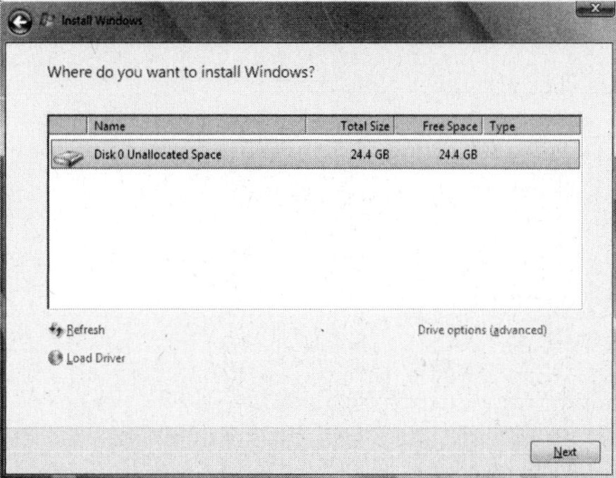

8. When your partition is set, the installation will start. You will see the progress of the installation during the entire process. When the installation is complete, the machine will reboot.

9. After the installation is complete, the Username And Computer Name screen will appear. Type in your username and computer name and click Next.

EXERCISE 1.2 *(continued)*

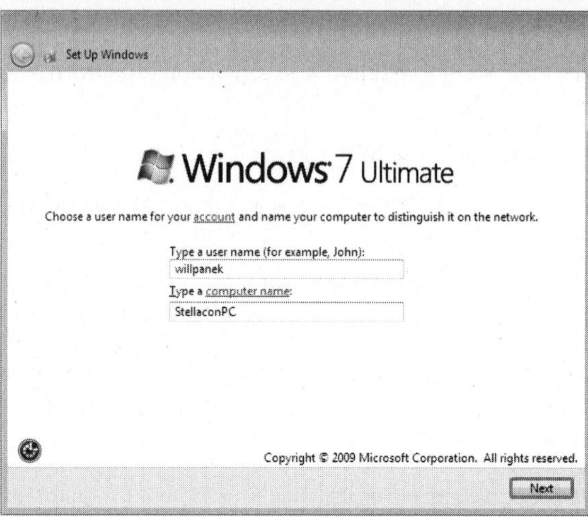

10. Set your password on the next screen. Enter your password twice and enter your hint. Click Next.

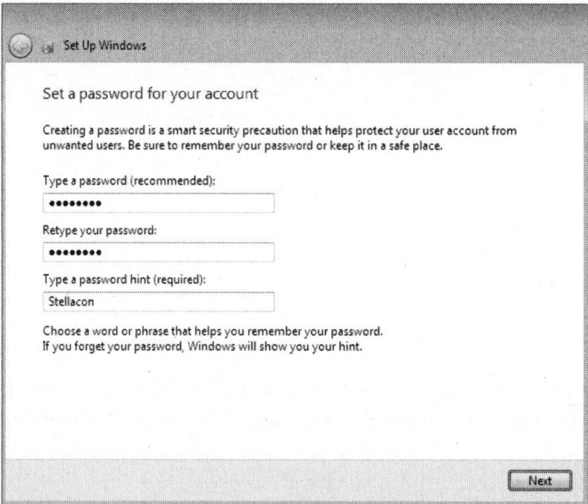

11. The next screen asks you to enter your 25-digit product key. Enter your product key and make sure the check box—to automatically register your machine when you're online—is checked. Click Next.

12. Settings related to Windows Update and security will appear next. You can use the recommended settings, install important updates for Windows only, or have the

computer ask you later. If you select the option to use the recommended settings, the following settings will be configured:

- Windows Update will be enabled and updates will automatically install.
- Windows Defender will be installed and any collected information will be sent to Microsoft.
- Errors will automatically be sent to Microsoft.
- The latest drivers for your hardware will automatically be downloaded from Windows Update.

13. You will now be able to verify your time and date settings. Configure your time, time zone, and date. Click Next.
14. The next step is to set your computer's current location. You have the ability to choose from a home, work, or public location. Choose the location where your computer is located.

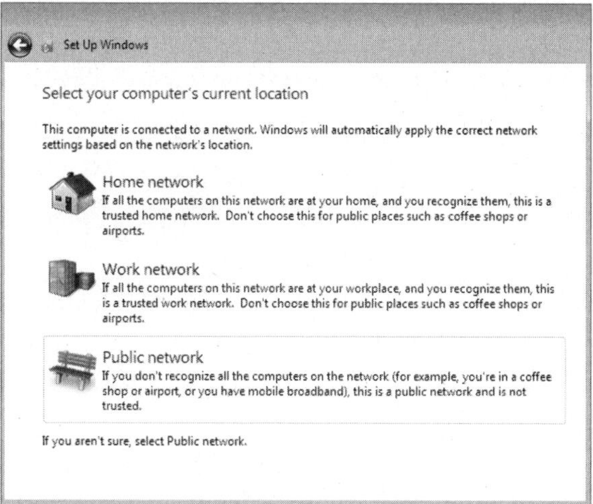

15. Windows will finalize your setup and the installation will be complete.

Performing an Upgrade to Windows 7

This section describes how to perform an upgrade to Windows 7 from Windows Vista. Similar to a clean install, you can run the installation from the installation DVD or over a network. The only difference in the installation procedure is your starting point: from your optical drive or from a network share. For the steps in the following sections, it is assumed that you are using the Windows 7 DVD to install the Windows 7 operating system.

The three main steps in the Windows 7 upgrade process are very similar to the process for a clean install. The three steps of upgrading to Windows 7 are:

1. Collecting information
2. Installing Windows
3. Setting up Windows

In Exercise 1.3, you will go through the process of installing Windows 7 by upgrading Windows Vista.

EXERCISE 1.3

Upgrading Windows Vista to Windows

1. Insert the Windows 7 DVD.
2. If Autorun does not start, navigate to the DVD drive and click `setup.exe`. Once the setup starts (via either `setup.exe` or Autorun), click Install Windows 7.
3. You are prompted to update your current operating system. If you choose not to update, the installation might fail. You can also choose to send information to Microsoft during this process.
4. The Microsoft Windows 7 license terms appear. The installation will not allow you to click Next until you have accepted the license terms.
5. You are prompted to select the type of installation you want to perform. Choose the Upgrade link.
6. You will see a compatibility report that will alert you of any applications or drivers that are not supported in Windows 7. Click Next.

   The following steps will take place in the Installing Windows section of the upgrade.

7. During the Installing Windows phase, all the files required by the Setup program will be copied to the hard drive. The computer automatically reboots during the installation process. This process takes several minutes and proceeds automatically without user intervention. The following steps appear on the screen along with a completion percentage for each:

   - Copying Windows files
   - Gathering files, settings, and programs
   - Expanding Windows files
   - Installing features and updates
   - Transferring files, settings, and programs

   Once your computer finishes copying files and reboots, you will be in the Setup Windows phase of the installation. The following steps are involved with completing an upgrade.

8. You'll be asked for your Windows product key. Type in your 25-digit product key and click Next.
9. Settings related to Windows Update and security appear. You can use the recommended settings, install important updates for Windows only, or have the computer ask you later.
10. On the next screen, set up your local time and date and choose whether you want daylight savings time. Click Next.
11. The installation completes.

Troubleshooting Installation Problems

The Windows 7 installation process is designed to be as simple as possible. The chances for installation errors are greatly minimized through the use of wizards and the step-by-step process. However, it is possible that errors may occur.

Identifying Common Installation Problems

As most of you are aware, installations seldom go off without a hitch. You might encounter some of the following installation errors:

Media Errors Media errors are caused by defective or damaged DVDs. To check the disc, put it into another computer and see if you can read it. Also check your disc for scratches or dirt—it may just need to be cleaned.

Insufficient Disk Space Windows 7 needs at least 16 GB of free space for the installation program to run properly. If the Setup program cannot verify that this space exists, the program will not let you continue.

Not Enough Memory Make sure your computer has the minimum amount of memory required by Windows 7 (1 GB). Having insufficient memory may cause the installation to fail or blue-screen errors to occur after installation.

Not Enough Processing Power Make sure your computer has the minimum processing power required by Windows 7 (1 GHz). Having insufficient processing power may cause the installation to fail or blue-screen errors to occur after installation.

Hardware That Is Not on the HCL If your hardware is not listed on the HCL, Windows 7 may not recognize the hardware or the device may not work properly.

Hardware with No Driver Support Windows 7 will not recognize hardware without driver support.

Hardware That Is Not Configured Properly If your hardware is Plug and Play compatible, Windows 7 should configure it automatically. If your hardware is not Plug and Play compatible, you will need to manually configure the hardware per the manufacturer's instructions.

Incorrect Product Key Without a valid product key, the installation will not go past the Product Key screen. Make sure you have not typed in an incorrect key (check your Windows 7 installation folder or your computer case for this key).

Failure to Access TCP/IP Network Resources If you install Windows 7 with typical settings, the computer is configured as a DHCP client. If there is no DHCP server to provide IP configuration information, the client will still generate an auto-configured IP address but be unable to access network resources through TCP/IP if the other network clients are using DHCP addresses.

Installing Nonsupported Hard Drives If your computer is using a hard disk that does not have a driver included on the Windows 7 media, you will receive an error message stating that the hard drive cannot be found. You should verify that the hard drive is properly connected and functional. You will need to obtain a disk driver for Windows 7 from the manufacturer and then specify the driver location by selecting the Load Driver option during partition selection.

Troubleshooting with Installation Log Files

When you install Windows 7, the Setup program creates several log files. You can view these logs to check for any problems during the installation process. Two log files are particularly useful for troubleshooting:

- The action log includes all of the actions that were performed during the setup process and a description of each action. These actions are listed in chronological order. The action log is stored as `\Windows\setupact.log`.
- The error log includes any errors that occurred during the installation. For each error, there is a description and an indication of the severity of the error. This error log is stored as `\Windows\setuperr.log`.

In Exercise 1.4, you will view the Windows 7 Setup logs to determine whether there were any problems with your Windows 7 installation.

EXERCISE 1.4

Troubleshooting Failed Installations with Setup Logs

1. Select Start ➢ Computer.
2. Double-click Local Disk (C:).
3. Double-click Windows.
4. In the Windows folder, double-click the `setupact.log` file to view your action log in Notepad. When you are finished viewing this file, close Notepad.
5. Double-click the `setuperr.log` file to view your error file in Notepad. If no errors occurred during installation, this file will be empty. When you are finished viewing this file, close Notepad.
6. Close the directory window.

Migrating Files and Settings

Rather than perform an in-place upgrade, you can choose to migrate your files and settings from an existing installation. In this case, you can use the User State Migration Tool (USMT) or the Windows Easy Transfer utility.

User State Migration Tool

You can download a utility called the *User State Migration Tool (USMT)* that is used by administrators to migrate large numbers of users over automated deployments. The USMT for Windows 7 is now part of the Windows Automated Installation Kit (Windows AIK). The USMT is similar to Windows Easy Transfer with the following differences:

- The USMT is more configurable and can use XML files to specify which files and settings are transferred.
- The USMT is scriptable and uses command-line utilities to save and restore user files and settings.

The USMT consists of two executable files: `ScanState.exe` and `LoadState.exe`. In addition, there are three premade migration rule information files: `Migapp.xml`, `Migsys.xml`, and `Miguser.xml`. Finally, you can create a `Config.xml` file that specifies what should and should not be migrated. The purpose of these files is as follows:

- `ScanState.exe` collects user data and settings information based on the configuration of the `Migapp.xml`, `Migsys.xml`, and `Miguser.xml` files and stores it as an image file.
- `LoadState.exe` then deposits the information that is collected to a computer running a fresh copy of Windows 7.

The following information is migrated:

- From each user:
  - Documents
  - Video
  - Music
  - Pictures
  - Desktop files
  - Start menu
  - Quick Launch toolbar
  - Internet Explorer Favorites
- From the All Users profile:
  - Shared Documents
  - Shared Video
  - Shared Music

- Shared Desktop files
- Shared Pictures
- Shared Start menu
- Shared Internet Explorer Favorites
- Files with certain filename extensions, including .doc, .dot, .rtf, .txt, .wps, .wri, .xls, .csv, .wks, .ppt, .pps, .pot, .pst, and more
- Access control lists (ACLs)

USMT will not migrate hardware settings, drivers, passwords, application binaries, synchronization files, DLL files, or other executables.

Using the USMT

The USMT is downloadable software from Microsoft's website. In its simplest form, you use the USMT in the following manner:

1. Run ScanState.exe on the source computer. ScanState.exe will copy the user state data to an intermediate store. The intermediate store (for example, a CD-RW) must be large enough to accommodate the data that will be transferred. Scanstate.exe would commonly be executed as a shortcut sent to users that they would deploy in the evening or through a scheduled script.
2. Install a fresh copy of Windows 7 on the target computer.
3. Run LoadState.exe on the target computer. LoadState.exe will access the intermediate store to restore the user settings.

When you use the USMT, you can create a script that can be run manually or can be used as an automated process at a scheduled time. Table 1.5 defines the options for the Scanstate.exe and Loadstate.exe commands.

TABLE 1.5 Options for Scanstate.exe and Loadstate.exe

Option	Description
/config	Specifies the Config.xml file that should be used
/encrypt	Encrypts the store (Scanstate.exe only)
/decrypt	Decrypts the store (Loadstate.exe only)
/nocompress	Disables data compression
/genconfig	Generates a Config.xml file but does not create a store
/targetxp	Optimizes ScanState for use with Windows XP

Option	Description
`/all`	Migrates all users
`/ue`	User exclude: excludes the specified user
`/ui`	User include: includes the specified user
`/uel`	Excludes user based on last login time
`/v verboselevel`	Used to identify what verbosity level will be associated with the log file on a scale of 0–13, with 0 being the least verbose

Windows Easy Transfer

Windows 7 ships with a utility called *Windows Easy Transfer* that is used to transfer files and settings from one computer to another. You can transfer some or all of the following files and settings from a computer running Windows XP with Service Pack 2 or Windows Vista:

- User accounts
- Folders and files
- Program settings
- Internet settings
- Favorites
- Email messages, contacts, and settings

You can transfer the migrated files and settings using the following methods:

- Easy Transfer Cable, which is a USB cable that connects to the source and destination computers
- CD or DVD
- Removable media, such as a USB flash drive or a removable hard drive
- Network share
- Direct network connection

You can password-protect the migrated files and settings if you use CDs, DVDs, removable media, or a network share.

Upgrading from Windows XP to Windows 7

Since the upgrade option from Windows XP to Windows 7 is not available, you can use Windows Easy Transfer to integrate settings from Windows XP to Windows 7 on the same computer.

The first step in this migration process is to copy your files to removable media such as an external hard drive or thumb drive or to a network share. After the installation of the Windows 7 operating system, you can then migrate these files onto the Windows 7 system.

Exercise 1.5 shows how to accomplish the goal of migrating Windows XP to Windows 7.

EXERCISE 1.5

Migrating Windows XP to Windows 7

First, copy files using Windows Easy Transfer.

1. Insert the Windows 7 DVD while running Windows XP. If the Windows 7 installation window opens automatically, close it.
2. Open Windows Explorer by right-clicking the Start menu, and then clicking Explore.
3. Browse to the DVD drive on your computer and click `migsetup.exe` in the Support\Migwiz directory.
4. When the Windows Easy Transfer window opens, click Next.
5. Select an external hard disk or USB flash drive.
6. Click This Is My Old Computer. Windows Easy Transfer scans the computer.
7. Click Next. You can also determine which files should be migrated by selecting only the user profiles you want to transfer or by clicking Customize.
8. Enter a password to protect your Easy Transfer file, or leave the box blank, and then click Save.
9. Browse to the external location on the network or to the removable media where you want to save your Easy Transfer file, and then click Save.
10. Click Next. Windows Easy Transfer displays the file name and location of the Easy Transfer file you just created.

Then, use the Windows 7 DVD to install the operating system.

1. Start Windows 7 Setup by browsing to the root folder of the DVD in Windows Explorer and then double clicking `setup.exe`.
2. Click Go Online To Get The Latest Updates (Recommended) to retrieve any important updates for Windows 7. This step is optional. If you choose not to check for updates during Setup, click Do Not Get The Latest Updates.
3. Read and accept the Microsoft Software License Terms. Click I Accept The License Terms (required to use Windows), and then click Next. If you click I Decline (cancel installation), Windows 7 Setup will exit.

4. Click Custom to perform an upgrade to your existing Windows installation.
5. Select the partition where you would like to install Windows. To move your existing Windows installation into a `Windows.old` folder and replace the operating system with Windows 7, select the partition where your current Windows installation is located.
6. Click Next and then click OK.
7. Windows 7 Setup will proceed without further interaction.

Finally, migrate files to the destination computer.

1. If you saved your files and settings in an Easy Transfer file on a removable media such as a UFD rather than on a network share, insert the removable media into the computer.
2. Click Start, click All Programs, click Accessories, click System Tools, and then click Windows Easy Transfer.
3. The Windows Easy Transfer window opens; click Next.
4. Click an external hard disk or USB flash drive.
5. Click This Is My New Computer.
6. Click Yes, Open The File.
7. Browse to the location where the Easy Transfer file was saved. Click the filename, and then click Open.
8. Click Transfer to transfer all files and settings. You can also determine which files should be migrated by selecting only the user profiles you want to transfer or by clicking Customize.
9. Click Close after Windows Easy Transfer has completed moving your files.

After the migration process is complete, you should regain the disk space used by the Windows XP system by deleting the `Windows.old` directory, using the Disk Cleanup tool. The following steps show you how to use the Disk Cleanup tool.

1. Open Disk Cleanup. Click Start, click All Programs, click Accessories, click System Tools, and then click Disk Cleanup.
2. Click Clean Up System Files.
3. Previous installations of Windows are scanned. After they are scanned, select Previous Windows Installation(s) and any other categories of files you want to delete.
4. Click OK and then click Delete Files.

Upgrading to Windows 7

Another important decision that should be considered is whether to upgrade your Windows XP clients to Windows Vista first and then upgrade the machine to Windows 7.

As you have seen, you can migrate your users' data, but let's say you have software installed and you can't locate the CD/DVD for that software package. It may be beneficial to a user or organization to upgrade the Windows XP machine to Windows Vista. After that installation is complete, upgrade the Vista machine to Windows 7.

This is just another option that is available to you when migrating your users to the Windows 7 operating system.

Supporting Multiple-Boot Options

You may want to install Windows 7 but still be able to run other operating systems. *Dual-booting* or multibooting allows your computer to boot multiple operating systems. Your computer will be automatically configured for dual-booting if there was a supported operating system on your computer prior to the Windows 7 installation, you didn't upgrade from that operating system, and you installed Windows 7 into a different partition.

One reason for dual-booting is to test various systems. If you have a limited number of computers in your test lab and you want to be able to test multiple configurations, you should dual-boot. For example, you might configure one computer to multiboot with Windows XP Professional, Windows Vista, and Windows 7.

Here are some keys to successful dual-boot configurations:

- Make sure you have plenty of disk space.
- Windows 7 must be installed on a separate partition in order to dual-boot with other operating systems.
- Install older operating systems before installing newer operating systems. If you want to support dual-booting with Windows XP and Windows 7, Windows XP must be installed first. If you install Windows 7 first, you cannot install Windows XP without ruining your Windows 7 configuration. This requirement also applies to Windows 9*x*, Windows 2000, and Windows Vista.
- Never, ever upgrade to Windows 7 dynamic disks. Dynamic disks are seen only by Windows 2000, Windows XP Professional, Windows Server 2003, Windows Vista, and Windows 7 and are not recognized by any other operating system, including Windows NT and Windows XP Home Edition.
- Only Windows NT 4.0 (with Service Pack 4), Windows 2000, Windows XP, Windows Vista, Windows 7, Windows Server 2003, and Windows Server 2008 can recognize

NTFS file systems. Other Windows operating systems use FAT16 or FAT32 and cannot recognize NTFS. All Windows-based operating systems can recognize FAT partitions.

- If you will dual-boot with Windows 9*x*, you must turn off disk compression or Windows 7 will not be able to read the drive properly.
- Do not install Windows 7 on a compressed volume unless the volume was compressed using NTFS compression.
- Files that are encrypted with Windows 7 will not be available to Windows NT 4.

If you are planning on dual-booting with Windows NT 4, you should upgrade to NT 4 Service Pack 4 (or higher), which provides NTFS version 5 support.

Once you have installed each operating system, you can choose the operating system that you will boot to during the boot process. You will see a boot selection screen that asks you to choose which operating system you want to boot.

The Boot Configuration Data (BCD) store contains boot information parameters that were previously found in `boot.ini` in older versions of Windows. To edit the boot options in the BCD store, use the bcdedit utility, which can be launched only from a command prompt. To open a command prompt window, you can do the following:

1. Launch `\Windows\system32\cmd.exe`.
2. Open the Run command by pressing the [Windows] key + R and then entering **`cmd`**.
3. Type **`cmd.exe`** in the Search Programs And Files box and press Enter.

After the command prompt window is open, type **`bcdedit`** to launch the **`bcdedit`** utility. You can also type **`bcdedit/?`** to see all the different `bcdedit` commands. A few `bcdedit` commands may be needed when dual-booting a machine. Table 1.6 shows a few of the `bcdedit` commands that may be needed when dual-booting.

TABLE 1.6 `Bcdedit` commands

Command	Explanation
`/default`	Allows you to specify which operating system will start when the time-out expires.
`/displayorder`	Shows the display order that the boot manager uses when showing the display order to the user.
`/timeout`	Specifies the amount of time used before the system boots into the default operating system.

Using Windows Activation

Windows Activation is Microsoft's way of reducing software piracy. Unless you have a corporate license for Windows 7, you will need to perform postinstallation activation. This can be done online or through a telephone call. Windows 7 will attempt automatic activation three days after you log on to it for the first time. There is a grace period when you will be able to use the operating system without activation. After the grace period expires, you will not be able to create new files or save changes to existing files until Windows 7 is activated. When the grace period runs out, the Windows Activation Wizard will automatically start (see Figure 1.5); it will walk you through the activation process.

FIGURE 1.5 The Windows Activation Wizard screen

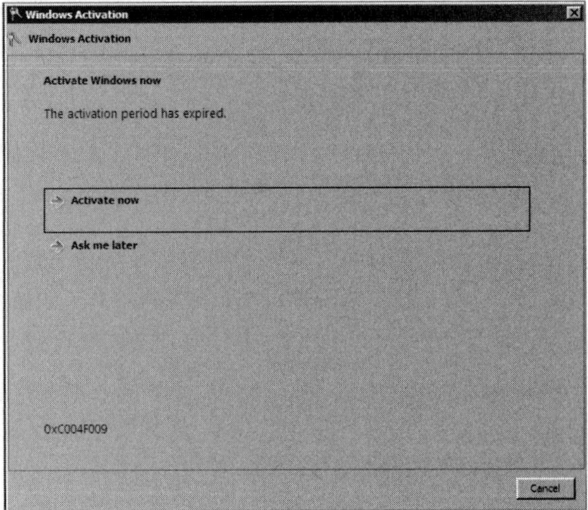

Using Windows Update

Windows Update, shown in Figure 1.6, is a utility that connects to Microsoft's website and checks to ensure that you have the most up-to-date versions of Microsoft products.

FIGURE 1.6 Windows Update

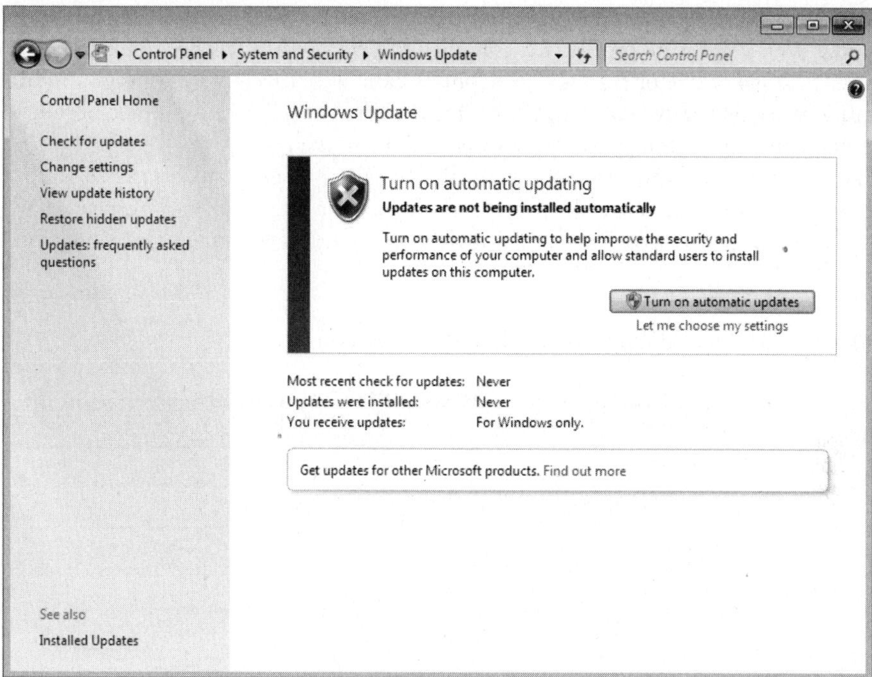

Some of the common update categories associated with Windows Update are as follows:

- Critical updates
- Service packs
- Drivers

Follow these steps to configure Windows Update:

1. Select Start ➢ Control Panel.
   - From Windows Icons View, select Windows Update.
   - From Windows Category View, select System And Security, Windows Update.
2. Configure the options you want to use for Windows Update, and click OK.

   The options you can access from Windows Update include the following:

- Check For Updates
- Change Settings
- View Update History

- Restore Hidden Updates
- Updates: Frequently Asked Questions
- Installed Updates

Check for Updates

When you click Check For Updates, Windows Update will retrieve a list of available updates from the Internet. You can then click View Available Updates to see what updates are available. Updates are marked as Important, Recommended, or Optional. Figure 1.7 shows a sample list of updates.

FIGURE 1.7 Checking for updates

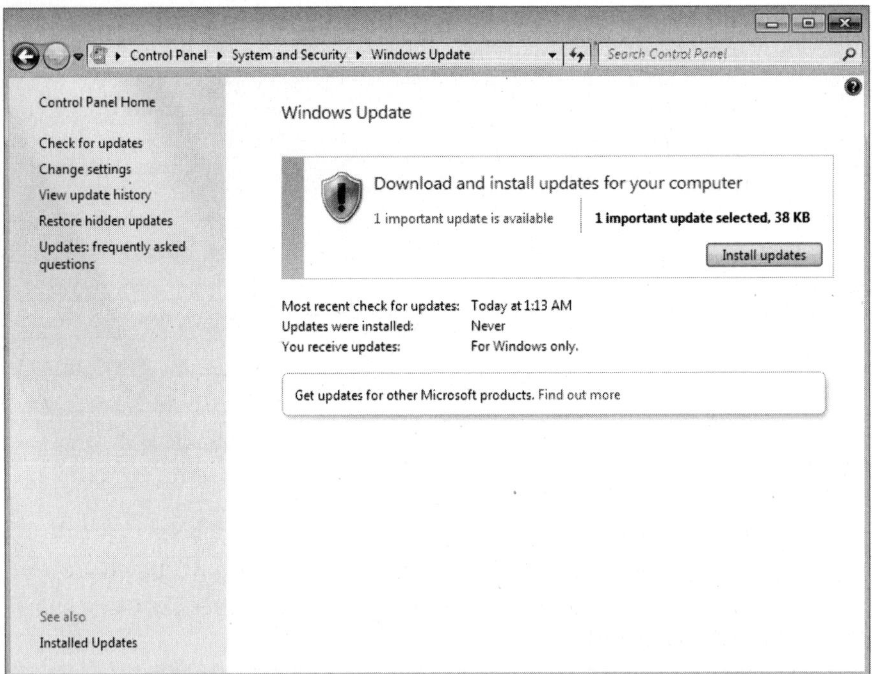

Change Settings

Clicking Change Settings allows you to customize how Windows can install updates. You can configure the following options:

- "Install updates automatically (recommended)"
- "Download updates but let me choose whether to install them"

- "Check for updates but let me choose whether to download and install them"
- "Never check for updates (not recommended)"

Figure 1.8 shows the settings that can be configured for Windows Update.

FIGURE 1.8 Windows Update Change settings

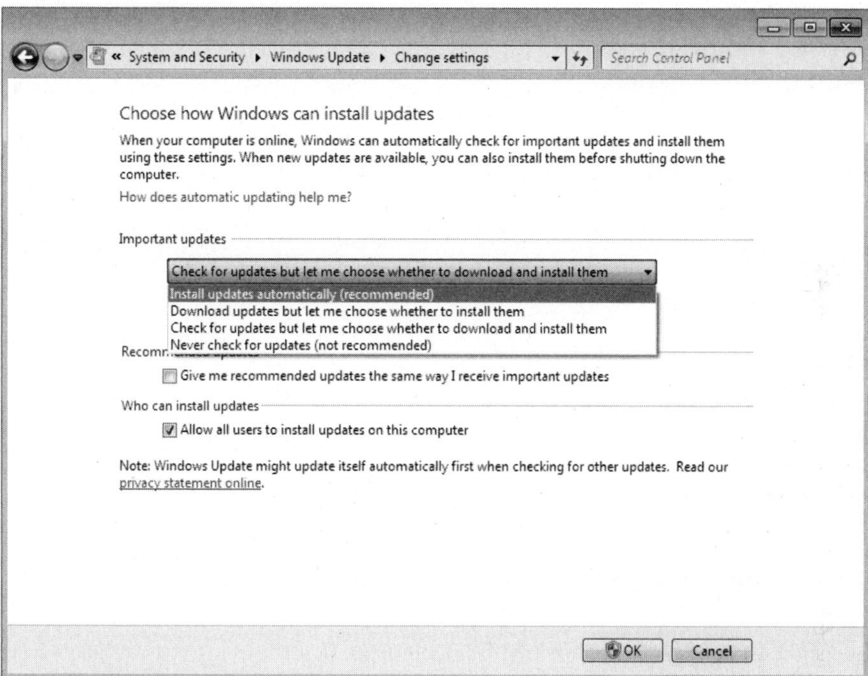

View Update History

View Update History, as shown in Figure 1.9, is used to view a list of all of the installations that have been performed on the computer. You can see the following information for each installation:

- Update Name
- Status (Successful, Unsuccessful, or Canceled)
- Importance (Important, Recommended, or Optional)
- Date Installed

FIGURE 1.9 Windows Update, View Update History

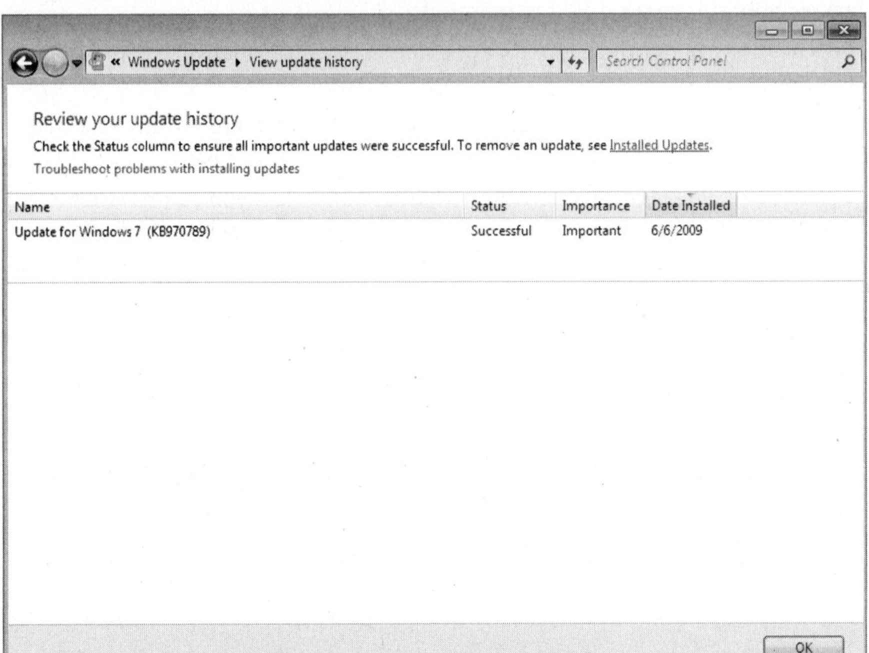

Restore Hidden Updates

With Restore Hidden Updates you can list any updates that you have hidden from the list of available updates. An administrator might hide updates that they do not want users to install.

Sometimes it is important for an administrator to test and verify updates before the users can install them. This area allows you to see hidden updates so that they can be tested before deployment.

Installed Updates

Installed Updates allows you to see the updates that are installed and to uninstall or change them if necessary. The Installed Updates feature is a part of the Programs And Features applet in the Control Panel, which allows you to uninstall, change, and repair programs.

Installing Windows Service Packs

Service packs are updates to the Windows 7 operating system that include bug fixes and product enhancements. Some of the options that might be included in service packs are security fixes or updated versions of software, such as Internet Explorer.

Prior to installing a service pack, you should perform the following steps:

1. Back up your computer.
2. Check your computer to ensure that it is not running any malware or other unwanted software.
3. Check with your computer manufacturer to see whether there are any special instructions for your computer prior to installing the service pack.

You can download service packs from `www.microsoft.com`, you can receive service packs via Windows Update, or you can pay for a copy of the service pack to be mailed to you on disc. Before you install a service pack, you should read the release note that is provided for each service pack on Microsoft's website.

Summary

In this chapter I started with a discussion of how Windows XP introduced many new features to the normal user. I also discussed how Windows XP was the first operating system to use the new core called the kernel.

Windows Vista introduced many new features, such as a new improved Desktop, Windows Sidebar, parental controls, improved Windows Firewall, Windows Vista User Account Control (UAC), Windows Search, and live icons.

Microsoft then took the best of both worlds (XP and Vista) and created Windows 7. Windows 7 has introduced many new features, such as the Windows 7 Taskbar, Jump Lists, a new preview pane, Windows Touch, Windows XP Mode, simpler home networking, Device Stage, View Available Networks (VAN), and the new Windows Internet Explorer 8 (IE8).

We also took at look at the difference between 64-bit and 32-bit operating systems and showed some of the advantages that 64-bit entails, like greater RAM and processor speed.

Then you learned about installing Windows 7. Installation is an easy process, but you must first make sure the machine is compatible with the Windows 7 operating system.

There are two main ways to install Windows 7: upgrade or clean install. You can upgrade a Windows Vista machine to Windows. You can migrate the user's data and information from a Windows XP machine, but there is no upgrade option.

After the Windows 7 installation is complete, you'll want to make sure all updates and service packs are installed. You can use Microsoft Windows Update to complete that task.

Exam Essentials

Understand the Windows 7 hardware requirements. The minimum hardware requirements to run Windows 7 properly are a CPU (processor) of at least 1 GHz (32-bit or 64-bit processor), at least 1 GB of memory (RAM), hard disk with 16 GB of available disk space, video adapter, support for DirectX 9 graphics with 128 MB memory (to enable the Aero theme), DVD-R/W drive, and a compatible network interface card.

Understand the Hardware Compatibility List. The Hardware Compatibility List (HCL) is an extensive list of computers and peripheral hardware that have been tested with the Windows 7 operating system. The hardware and supported drivers on the HCL have been put through rigorous tests to ensure their compatibility with Windows 7. Microsoft guarantees that the items on the list meet the requirements for Windows 7 and do not have any incompatibilities that could affect the stability of the operating system.

Understand how to complete a clean install. If your machine meets the minimum hardware requirements, you can install Windows 7. There are a few different ways to install Windows 7 onto a computer. You can install Windows 7 using the installation disk, over a network, or from an image (see Chapter 2, "Automating the Windows 7 Installation").

Understand how to complete an upgrade. You can upgrade a Windows Vista machine to Windows 7. To complete an upgrade on a Windows Vista machine, insert the Windows 7 DVD into the Vista machine or connect to the Windows 7 files over the network and complete an upgrade on the computer.

You can't upgrade a Windows XP machine to Windows 7. If the machine is running Windows XP, you have to use a migration tool to migrate all the user data from Windows XP to a Windows 7 machine.

Understand how to migrate a user to Windows 7. If you can't perform an upgrade on the computer, you can choose to migrate your files and settings from an existing installation. In this case, you can use the Windows Easy Transfer utility or the User State Migration Tool (USMT).

Review Questions

1. You are the network administrator for a mid-size organization that wants to start looking at migrating their computer systems to Windows 7. They have asked you to explain the new features of Windows 7 to all the department heads. Which of the following are new features to Windows 7? (Choose all that apply.)

   A. Windows 7 Taskbar

   B. Jump List

   C. Windows XP Mode

   D. Windows Touch

2. You are the network administrator for a small company that has just switched its machines from Windows XP to Windows Vista and Windows 7. One of the users who has Windows Vista asks you why there is a vertical sidebar on the screen. What feature of Windows Vista is this?

   A. Parental controls

   B. Jump List

   C. Windows Sidebar

   D. Windows Firewall

3. Your company has asked you to implement Network Access Protection (NAP) on the network. You already have Windows Server 2008 installed on your servers but your organization wants to know which client operating systems will support NAP. What operating systems support NAP? Choose all that apply.

   A. Windows XP with SP2

   B. Windows XP with SP3

   C. Windows Vista

   D. Windows 7

4. You are the IT manager for a medium-size organization. Your organization is looking at upgrading its Windows XP machines to Windows 7. The managers have heard of a new feature that allows you to connect a device to the machine and then the Windows 7 operating system shows a graphical picture of the device for use. Which Windows 7 feature are they referring to?

   A. Device Manager

   B. Device Stage

   C. Staging Manager

   D. ADD/Remove Hardware

5. You are the IT manager for your organization. The organization is looking at upgrading all of its machines from Windows XP to Windows 7. Many of the managers are concerned that their Windows XP applications won't be compatible with Windows 7. Which Windows 7 feature can you use to assure the managers that all of their Windows XP applications will continue to work?

   A. Windows XP Compatibility Checker

   B. Windows XP Application Center

   C. Windows XP Mode

   D. Windows XP Application Upgrade tool

6. Your organization has approached you to give a presentation on the new Internet Explorer 8. During the presentation, one of the managers asks you to let them know what some of its new features are. Which of the following can you tell them about? (Choose all that apply.)

   A. Instant Search

   B. Root Hints

   C. Accelerators

   D. Web Slices

7. You are the IT administrator for a large computer training company that uses laptops for all its employees. Currently the users have to connect to the wireless network through the wireless network adapter. Windows 7 now includes this built in as which feature?

   A. Available Network Finder (ANF)

   B. View Networks (VN)

   C. Network Availability Viewer (NAV)

   D. View Available Networks (VAN)

8. You are the network administrator for a mid-size company. One of the managers has come into your office and asked you about setting up a network in his house. He wants to use Windows 7. What feature allows him to set up a home network using Windows 7?

   A. Home Networking

   B. HomeGroups

   C. Quick Connect

   D. Networking Groups

9. Which new Windows 7 feature allows you to quickly access files that you have been working on?

   A. Quick Connect

   B. Jump Lists

   C. File Finder

   D. Quick File Access

10. You are the IT Manager for a pharmaceutical company. The company wants to create a medication dispenser that can be used on the floors of hospital units. The dispensers have to work through touchscreen technology. Which Windows 7 feature has built-in touchscreen technology?

A. Windows Touch Screen

B. Windows Pure Touch

C. Windows Touch

D. Windows Pure Screen

11. You are the network administrator for a large organization that has decided to convert all of its Windows XP machines to Windows 7. How can it put Windows 7 on all the Windows XP machines without losing the users' information?

A. Upgrade all the Windows XP machines to Windows 7.

B. Format all the XP machines and do a clean install of Windows 7.

C. Use a migration tool to migrate all the users' data and then load a clean copy of Windows 7.

D. Do nothing. The Windows XP machines can't be upgraded without losing all the user's data.

12. You are the network administrator for a mid-size organization. You have a machine with Windows Vista and you need to load Windows 7. You want to make the machine dual-boot. You install Windows 7 on a new partition on the machine. You want the machine to start in Windows Vista by default. How do you accomplish this?

A. Change the `Boot.ini` file so that Windows Vista is the default.

B. Edit `Bcdedit.exe` with the `/default` parameter to set Windows Vista as the default.

C. Delete the Windows 7 `Boot.ini` file so the machine reverts to Vista by default.

D. Edit the `Bcdedit.exe` with the `/order` parameter to set Windows Vista as the default.

13. Alexandria, your network manager, has been asked by the organization to verify that all machines in the company that are running Windows Vista can upgrade to Windows 7. How can Alexandria perform this task?

A. She can check the Windows Vista machines against the Hardware Compatibility List.

B. She can install Windows 7 on all the machines to see if they operate properly.

C. She can call the manufacture of all the machines and ask to see if each machine is compatible.

D. She can ask each user to email her the specifications of their machines and then go online to the machine manufacturer to find out if they will run Windows 7 properly.

14. You have just completed the install on one of your new Windows 7 machines. After the install is complete, what's the next step in making sure the machine is ready to be used?

    A. Set up the machine to dual-boot.

    B. Check Microsoft's website for all updates and patches.

    C. Configure the `sethc.exe` file.

    D. Load Microsoft Office.

15. You are the network administrator for an organization that wants to convert all of its Windows XP machines to Windows 7. Your organization wants to keep as much user data as possible. You decide to use Windows Easy Transfer. Which of the following can be migrated to the new machines using Windows Easy Transfer? (Choose all that apply.)

    A. User accounts

    B. Folders and files

    C. Program settings

    D. Internet settings

    E. Favorites

    F. Email messages, contacts, and settings

16. Which of the following options can be configured in Windows Update? (Choose all that apply.)

    A. Check For Updates

    B. Change Settings

    C. View Update History

    D. Restore Hidden Updates

17. You are the network administrator for a small organization that needs to consolidate equipment. You want to make sure all machines are multibootable between Windows 7, Windows Vista, and Windows XP. In what order do you load the operating system to accomplish this task?

    A. Windows 7, Windows Vista, Windows XP

    B. Windows 7, Windows XP, Windows Vista

    C. Windows XP, Windows Vista, Windows 7

    D. Windows Vista, Windows 7, Windows XP

18. You are installing Windows 7 on a new machine. The machine has encountered installation errors. Which files can you view to see the errors or issues? (Choose two.)

    A. `setupact.log`

    B. `setuplog.log`

    C. `setupdc.log`

    D. `setuperr.log`

19. You are a network administrator that has decided to implement Windows 7. You have to be able to use the Encrypting File System (EFS). Which Windows 7 versions can you install? (Choose all that apply.)

    A. Home Edition

    B. Home Premium Edition

    C. Professional Edition

    D. Enterprise Edition

20. You have a machine that is currently running Windows Vista Ultimate edition. You would like to upgrade this machine to Windows 7. Which Windows 7 editions can you upgrade this machine to? Choose all that apply.

    A. Home Premium Edition

    B. Professional Edition

    C. Enterprise Edition

    D. Ultimate Edition

Answers to Review Questions

1. A, B, C, D. Windows 7 has included many new features, including the Windows 7 Taskbar, Jump Lists, a new preview pane, Windows Touch, Windows XP Mode, simpler home networking, Device Stage, View Available Networks (VAN), and the new Windows Internet Explorer 8 (IE8).

2. C. Windows Vista introduced a new vertical bar that is displayed on the side of the Desktop, and this is called the Windows Sidebar. The Windows Sidebar has mini applications running within the bar called gadgets. Windows 7 has removed the sidebar, but you can still continue to use gadgets.

3. B, C, D. Network Access Protection (NAP) is a compliancy checking platform that is included with Windows 2008 Server, Windows Vista, Windows 7, and Windows XP with SP3. NAP allows you to create compliancy policies that check computers before allowing them access to the network.

4. B. Device Stage is new to the Windows 7 operating system family. Device Stage allows you to connect a compatible device to your PC and a picture of the device will appear. This allows you to easily share files between devices and computers.

5. C. With Windows XP Mode, an organization that chooses to upgrade to Windows 7 will still have the ability to run older Windows XP applications on the Windows 7 operating system.

6. A, C, D. Some of the new features of IE8 are Instant Search, accelerators, and Web Slices. Instant Search allows you to quickly access search requests without typing in the entire search criteria. Accelerators allow you to accelerate actions on Internet services and applications. Web Slices are instances on a website that you want to access without accessing the site.

7. D. The feature the question is referring to is View Available Networks (VAN). Before Windows 7, when you used a wireless network adapter, you would choose the wireless network that you want to connect to by using the wireless network adapter properties. In Windows 7, this is built into the operating system.

8. B. HomeGroups provide an easy way to set up a network using Windows 7. Windows 7 will search for your home network, and if one is found, it will connect after the HomeGroup password is entered. If a home network is not found, a networking wizard will automatically create a password for the HomeGroup so other computers can join.

9. B. Jump Lists are a new feature in Windows 7 that allows you to quickly access files that you have been working on. Another advantage to using Jump Lists is that certain applications, like Windows Media Player, can be preset, and in the case of Internet Explorer, you could view all the recent websites that you have visited.

10. C. Windows Touch allows you to control the operating system and its applications by using a touchscreen. Touchscreens can be placed on laptops, tabletops, GPS devices, phones, and now on the Windows 7 operating system.

11. C. You can't upgrade Windows XP to Windows 7, so you must use a migration tool to migrate all the users' data and then install a clean copy of Windows 7.

12. B. Windows 7 and Windows Vista no longer use a `boot.ini` file to control the boot order. Using the `Bcdedit /default` command will allow you to configure Vista as the default operating system.

13. A. To find out if a machine is compatible with Windows 7, just check the machine with the Hardware Compatibility List. The hardware listed on the HCL has been tested to verify compatibility.

14. B. After you install the Windows 7 operating system, the next step would be to load all updates and patches. You can download these patches for free from Microsoft's website by using Windows Update.

15. A, B, C, D, E, F. The Windows Easy Transfer can migrate everything listed in the options.

16. A, B, C, D. Windows Update also includes Updates: Frequently Asked Questions and Installed Updates as two other configurable options.

17. C. To make the machine multibootable, you must make sure the oldest operating systems is always be loaded first. So, for example, if you want to dual-boot Windows 7 and Windows Vista, Windows Vista must be loaded first.

18. A, D. The action log includes all of the actions that were performed during the setup process and a description of each action. The action log is stored as `\Windows\setupact.log`. The error log includes any errors that occurred during the installation. The error log is stored as `\Windows\setuperr.log`.

19. C, D. To use the Encrypting File System (EFS), you must install Windows 7 Professional, Windows 7 Enterprise, or Windows 7 Ultimate.

20. D. If you are upgrading a version of Windows Vista Ultimate, you must upgrade the machine to Windows 7 Ultimate.

Automating the Windows 7 Installation

MICROSOFT EXAM OBJECTIVES COVERED IN THIS CHAPTER:

✓ **Capture a system image.**

- This objective may include but is not limited to: preparing system for capture; creating a WIM file; automated capture; manual capture

✓ **Prepare a system image for deployment.**

- This objective may include but is not limited to: inserting an application into a system image; inserting a driver into a system image; inserting an update into a system image; configuring tasks to run after deployment

✓ **Deploy a system image.**

- This objective may include but is not limited to: automated deployment methods; manually deploying a customized image

It's important to understand how to automate a Windows 7 deployment for the Windows 7 (70-680) exam, but it's also a tool that you will use in a corporate environment. Many companies use third-party tools to create and deploy Windows 7 machines, but there are other ways.

Installing Windows 7 is quick and easy, but as an IT manager or IT professional, you may have to install hundreds of copies of Windows 7. It is not a good practice to install them one at a time.

You can automate the installation of Windows 7 in several ways: by using an unattended installation, by using Windows Deployment Services (WDS) to remotely deploy unattended installations (which requires a Windows Server 2008 machine), or by using the System Preparation Tool for disk imaging. To help customize these options for automating remote installations, you can also use answer files. Answer files are used with automated installations to provide answers to the questions that are normally asked during the installation process. After you've installed Windows 7, you can also automate the installation of applications by using Windows Installer packages.

This chapter begins with an overview of the automated deployment options available with Windows 7. Then I describe how to access the deployment tools available for Windows 7. Next is a detailed discussion of the following topics: the use of unattended installation, WDS, how the System Preparation Tool (along with ImageX) is used to create disk images for automated installation, and how to use Windows System Image Manager (SIM) to create unattended answer files.

Choosing Automated Deployment Options

If you need to install Windows 7 on multiple computers, you could manually install the operating system on each computer, as described in Chapter 1, "Windows 7 Installation." However, automating the deployment process will make your job easier, more efficient, and more cost effective if you have a large number of client computers to install.

Windows 7 comes with several utilities that can be used for deploying and automating the Windows 7 installation. With access to multiple utilities with different functionality, administrators have increased flexibility in determining how to best deploy Windows 7 within a large corporate environment.

The following sections contain overviews of the automated deployment options, which will help you choose which solution is best for your requirements and environment.

Each utility will then be covered in more detail throughout this chapter. The options for automated deployment of Windows 7 are as follows:

- Microsoft Deployment Toolkit (MDT) 2010
- Unattended installation, or unattended setup, which uses `Setup.exe`
- Windows Automated Installation Kit (WAIK)
- WDS, which requires Windows Server 2008 for deployment
- System Preparation Tool (`Sysprep.exe`), which is used to create and deploy disk imaging or cloning

Later in the chapter, you will see a table that summarizes the features and requirements of each installation deployment option.

Another option that you have to deploy Windows 7 is through Systems Management Server (SMS). Since SMS is its own application, it is beyond the scope of this book. You can learn more about SMS on the Microsoft website at `http://www.microsoft.com`.

An Overview of the Microsoft Deployment Toolkit (MDT) 2010

At the time this book was written, Microsoft had released a new beta program called the *Microsoft Deployment Toolkit (MDT) 2010*. It is used to automate desktop and server deployment. The MDT allows an administrator to have some of the following benefits:

- Administrative tools that allow for the deployment of desktops and servers through the use of a common console (see Figure 2.1)

FIGURE 2.1 MDT console

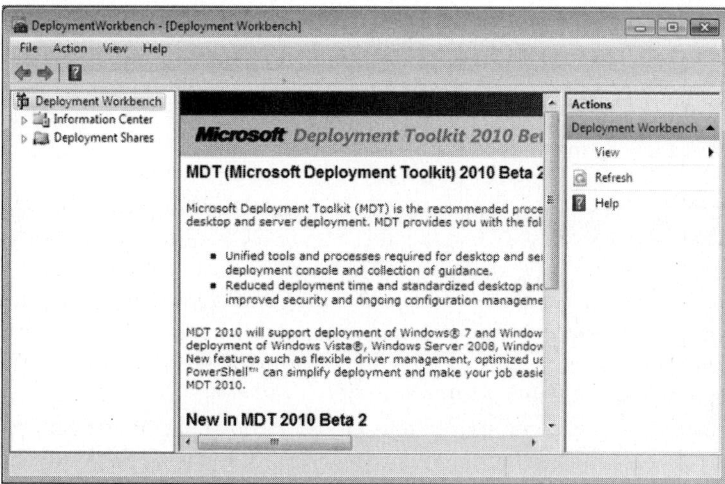

- Quicker deployments and the capabilities of having standardized desktop and server images and security
- Zero touch deployments of Windows 7, Windows Server 2008, Windows Vista, Windows Server 2003, and Windows XP

To install the MDT 2010 package onto your computer (regardless of the operating system being deployed), you must first meet the minimum requirements of MDT. These requirements need to be installed only on the computer where MDT 2010 is being installed:

- Microsoft Management Console (MMC) 3.0
- Microsoft .NET Framework 2.0 or higher
- Windows PowerShell command-line interface, version 1.0 or 2.0 Community Technology Preview (CTP) 3 (or higher)
- Windows Automated Installation Kit (Windows AIK) for Windows 7

You can install MDT 2010 without installing WAIK first, but you will not be able to use the package fully until WAIK is installed.

For Zero Touch deployments, MDT 2010 requires certain components.

- If you're deploying Windows 7 or Windows Server 2008, Microsoft System Center Configuration Manager 2007 Service Pack 2 (SP2) is required.
- If you want to deploy previous versions of Windows using MDT 2010, System Center Configuration Manager 2007 Service Pack 1 (SP1) can be used but you cannot use Deployment Workbench in this configuration to maintain an MDT database. If you are using an MDT database with System Center Configuration Manager, you should use System Center Configuration Manager 2007 SP2.

In Exercise 2.1, you will download and install MDT 2010. You can install MDT 2010 on the Windows 7 operating system machine that you installed in Chapter 1. If you decide to install the MDT onto a server or production machine, I recommend that you perform a full backup before completing Exercise 2.1. Installing MDT 2010 will replace any previous version of MDT that the machine may currently being using.

EXERCISE 2.1

Downloading and Installing MDT 2010

To download and install MDT 2010, follow these steps:

1. Download the MDT 2010 utility from Microsoft's website.

2. Double-click on the `MicrosoftDeploymentToolkit_x86.exe` to start the installation. If you downloaded the 64-bit version, click on that version.
3. At the Welcome screen, click Next.
4. At the License screen, click the I Accept The Terms In The License Agreement radio button and click Next.
5. At the Custom Setup screen, click the down arrow next to Microsoft Deployment Toolkit and choose Entire Feature Will Be Installed On Local Hard Drive. Click Next.

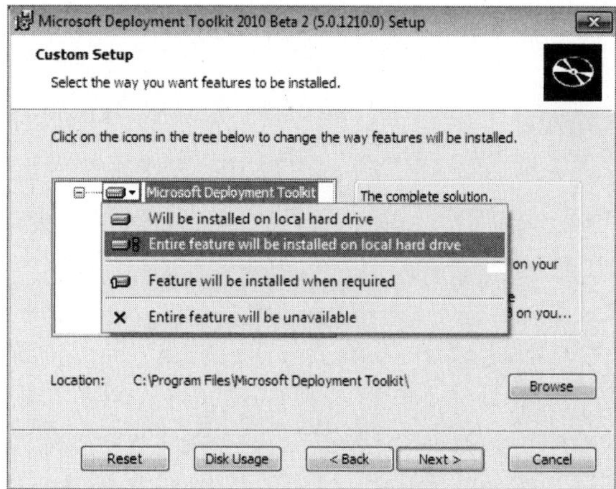

6. At the Ready To Install screen, click the Install button.
7. When the installation completes, click the Finish button.

Now that you have installed MDT 2010, you are going to configure the package. In Exercise 2.2, you will configure MDT 2010 and set up a distribution share and database.

EXERCISE 2.2

Configuring MDT 2010

To configure MDT 2010, follow these steps:

1. Create a shared folder on your network called Distribution and give the Everyone group full control for this exercise.

EXERCISE 2.2 *(continued)*

2. Open the MDT workbench by choosing Start ➤ All Programs ➤ Microsoft Development Toolkit ➤ Deployment Workbench.
3. If the User Account Control box appears, click Yes.
4. In the left-hand pane, click Deployment Shares and then right-click on the deployment shares and choose New Deployment Share.

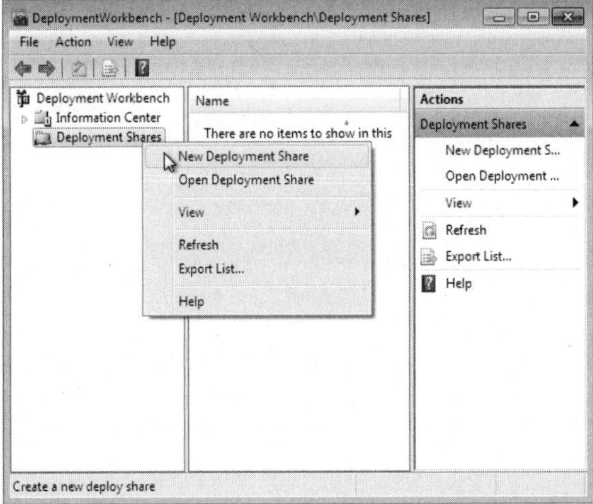

5. The New Deployment Share Wizard begins. At the first screen, you will choose the directory where the deployments will be stored. Click the Browse button and choose the Distribution share that you created in step 1. Then click Next.
6. At the Share Name screen, accept the default, Distribution. Click Next.
7. At the Deployment Share Description screen, accept the default description name and click Next.
8. At the Allow Image Capture screen, make sure the check box labeled Ask If An Image Should Be Captured is checked. Images can be captured after they are deployed to a domain. Checking this box gives you the option to either capture or not capture the image after deployment. Click Next.

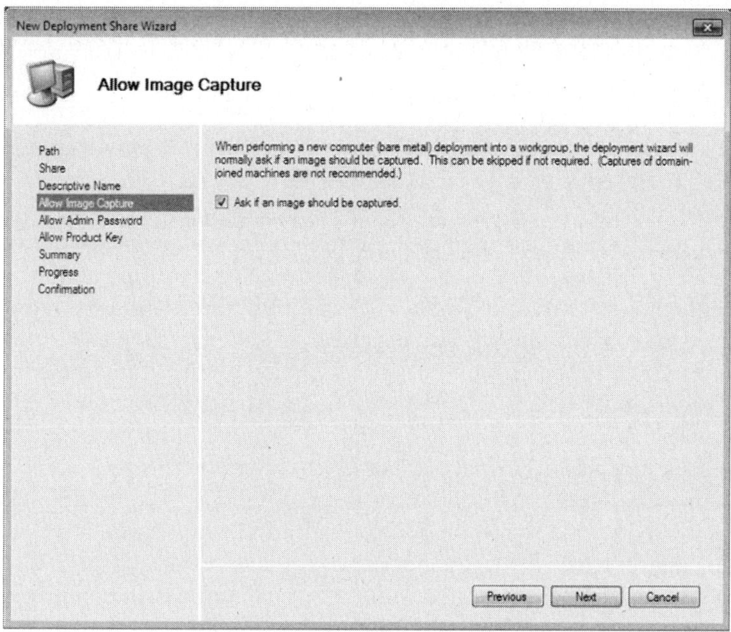

9. At the Allow Admin Password screen, check the box that allows the user to set the admin password for the local machine. If this box is checked, the user can set the local admin password. If the box is not checked, you can preset the password before deployment.
10. At the Allow Product Key screen, check the Ask Users To Enter A Product Key At Time Of Installation box. You can also preset the product key and then the user would not be required to supply the product key. Many organizations have site licenses and the user would not be required to enter a product key. Click Next.
11. At the Summary screen, verify all of your settings and click Next.
12. After the installation is complete, a confirmation screen will appear. Click Finish. Close the MDT workbench.

Now that you have seen how to install the MDT 2010 utility, let's take a look at some other ways to automatically install Windows 7.

An Overview of Unattended Installation

Unattended installation is a practical method of automatic deployment when you have a large number of clients to install and the computers require different hardware and software configurations. Unattended installations utilize an answer file called `Autounattend.xml` to provide configuration information during the unattended installation process.

Think about the Windows 7 installation from the previous chapter. You are asked for your locale, type of installation, and so on. The answer file allows these questions to be answered without user intervention.

With an unattended installation, you can use a distribution share to install Windows 7 on the target computers. You can also use a Windows 7 DVD with an answer file located on the root of the DVD, on a floppy disk, or on a universal flash device (UFD), such as an external USB flash drive.

Unattended installations allow you to create customized installations that are specific to your environment. Custom installations can support custom hardware and software installations. Since the answer file for Windows 7 is in XML format, all custom configuration information can be contained within the `Autounattend.xml` file. This is different from past versions of Windows where creating automated installation routines for custom installations required multiple files to be used. In addition to providing standard Windows 7 configuration information, you can use the answer file to provide installation instructions for applications, additional language support, service packs, and device drivers.

If you use a distribution share, it should contain the Windows 7 operating system image and the answer file to respond to installation configuration queries. The target computer must be able to connect to the distribution share over the network. After the distribution share and target computers are connected, you can initiate the installation process. Figure 2.2 illustrates the unattended installation process.

FIGURE 2.2 Unattended installation with distribution share and a target computer

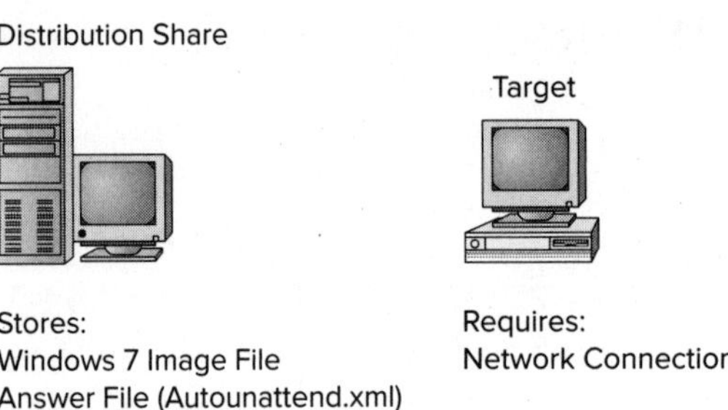

Advantages of Unattended Installation

In a mid-size or large organization, it just makes sense to use automated setups. As stated earlier, it is impossible to install hundreds of Windows 7 machines one at a time. But there are many advantages to using unattended installations as a method for automating Windows 7:

- Unattended installation saves time and money because users do not have to interactively respond to each installation query.
- It can be configured to provide automated query response while still selectively allowing users to provide specified input during installations.
- It can be used to install clean copies of Windows 7 or upgrade an existing operating system (providing it is on the list of permitted operating systems) to Windows 7.

- It can be expanded to include installation instructions for applications, additional language support, service packs, and device drivers.
- The physical media for Windows 7 does not need to be distributed to all computers on which it will be installed.

Disadvantages of Unattended Installation

A client operating system is one of the most important items that you will install onto a machine. As an IT manager and consultant, I have always felt better installing a client operating system when I am physically doing it. This way, if there are any glitches, I can see and deal with them immediately.

As stated earlier, a manual installation is not practical for mass installations. But one of the biggest disadvantages to performing an unattended installation is that an administrator does not physically walk through the installation of Windows 7. If something happens during the install, you may never know it, but the end user may experience small issues throughout the entire lifetime of the machine.

Some of the other disadvantages of using unattended installations as a method for automating Windows 7 installations are listed here:

- They require more initial setup than a standard installation of Windows 7.
- Someone must have access to each client computer and must initiate the unattended installation process on the client side.

An Overview of Windows Deployment Services

Windows Deployment Services (WDS) is an updated version of Remote Installation Services (RIS). WDS is a suite of components that allows you to remotely install Windows 7 on client computers.

A WDS server installs Windows 7 on the client computers, as illustrated in Figure 2.3. The WDS server must be configured with the Preboot Execution Environment (PXE) boot files, the images to be deployed to the client computers, and the answer file. WDS client computers must be PXE capable. PXE is a technology that is used to boot to the network when no operating system or network configuration has been installed and configured on a client computer.

FIGURE 2.3 Windows Deployment Services (WDS) uses a WDS server and WDS clients.

WDS Server

WDS Client

Stores:
PXE Boot Files and Boot Images
Windows 7 Boot Images
Answer File(s)

Requires:
PXE-Compatible Boot

The WDS clients access the network with the help of a Dynamic Host Configuration Protocol (DHCP) server. This allows the WDS client to remotely install the operating system from the WDS server. The network environment must be configured with a DHCP server, a Domain Name System (DNS) server, and Active Directory to connect to the WDS server. No other client software is required to connect to the WDS server. Remote installation is a good choice for automatic deployment when you need to deploy to large numbers of computers and the client computers are PXE compliant.

Advantages of WDS

The advantages of using WDS as a method for automating Windows 7 installations are as follows:

- Windows 7 installations can be standardized across a group or organization.
- The physical media for Windows 7 does not need to be distributed to all computers that will be installed.
- End-user installation deployment can be controlled through the Group Policy utility. For example, you can configure what choices a user can access or are automatically specified through the end-user Setup Wizard.

Disadvantages of WDS

The disadvantages of using WDS as a method for automating Windows 7 installations include the following:

- WDS can be used only if your network is running Windows Server 2003 or Windows Server 2008 with Active Directory installed.
- The clients that use WDS must be PXE capable.

An Overview of the System Preparation Tool and Disk Imaging

The *System Preparation Tool* (`Sysprep.exe`) is used to prepare a computer for disk imaging, and the disk image can then be captured using ImageX—a new imaging management tool included with Windows 7—or third-party imaging software.

Disk imaging is the process of taking a snapshot of a computer and then using that snapshot to create new computers, thus allowing for automated deployments. The reference, or source, computer has Windows 7 installed and is configured with the settings and applications that should be installed on the target computers. The image (snapshot) is then created and can be transferred to other computers, thus installing the operating system, settings, and applications that were defined on the reference computer.

Advantage of Imaging

Using the System Preparation Tool and disk imaging is a good choice (and the most commonly used in the real world) for automatic deployment when you have a large number of computers with similar configuration requirements or machines that need to be rebuilt frequently.

For example, Stellacon Training Center, a Microsoft education center that I work for, reinstalls the same software every week for new classes. Imaging is a fast and easy way to simplify the deployment process.

Using Imaging Software

As I have stated before, I am a consultant and trainer, but I was an IT manager for many years. In the real world, imaging software is the most common way to install or reinstall corporate computers.

Most organizations use images to create new machines quickly and easily, but they also use them to reimage end users' machines that crash.

In most companies, end users will have space on a server (home folders) to allow them to store data. We give our end users space on the server because this way, we need to back up only the servers at night and not the end users' machines. If your end users place all of their important documents on the server, it gets backed up.

Now, if we are also using images in our company and an end user's machine crashes, we just reload the image and they are backed up and running in minutes. Since their documents are being saved on the server, they do not lose any of their information.

Many organizations use third-party imaging software instead of using `Sysprep.exe` and ImageX. This is another good way of imaging your Windows 7 machines. Just make sure your third-party software supports the Windows 7 operating system.

To perform an unattended install, the System Preparation Tool prepares the reference computer by stripping away any computer-specific data, such as the security identifier (SID), which is used to uniquely identify each computer on the network; any event logs; and any other unique system information. The System Preparation Tool also detects any Plug and Play devices that are installed and can adjust dynamically for any computers that have different hardware installed.

When the client computer starts an installation using a disk image, you can customize what is displayed on the Windows Welcome screen and the options that are displayed through the setup process. You can also fully automate when and how the Windows Welcome screen is displayed during the installation process by using the `/oobe` option with the System Preparation Tool and an answer file named `Oobe.xml`.

Sysprep is a utility that is good only for setting up a new machine. You do not use Sysprep to image a computer for upgrading a current machine. There are a few switches that you can use in conjunction with Sysprep to configure the Sysprep utility for your specific needs. Table 2.1 shows you some of the Sysprep switches and what they will do for you when used.

TABLE 2.1 Sysprep switches

Switch	Explanation
`/pnp`	Forces a mini-setup wizard to start at reboot so that all Plug and Play devices can be recognized.
`/generalize`	This allows Sysprep to remove all system-specific data from the Sysprep image. If you're running the GUI version of Sysprep, this is a check box option.
`/oobe`	Initiates the Windows Welcome screen at the next reboot.
`/audit`	Initiates Sysprep in Audit mode.
`/nosidgen`	Sysprep does not generate a new SID on the computer restart. Forces a mini-setup on restart.
`/reboot`	Stops and restarts the computer system.
`/quiet`	Runs without any confirmation dialog messages being displayed.
`/mini`	Tells Sysprep to run the mini-setup on the next reboot.

The Windows System Preparation Tool is a free utility that comes on all Windows operating systems. By default, the Sysprep utility can be found on Windows Server 2008 and Windows 7 operating systems in the `\Windows\system32\sysprep` directory.

Real World Scenario

The Problems with Deployment Software

For many years, when you had to create many machines that each had a Microsoft operating system on it, you would have to use files to help deploy the multiple systems.

Then, multiple third-party companies came out with software that allowed you to take a picture of the Microsoft operating system and you could deploy that picture to other machines. One advantage of this is that all the software that is installed on the system could also be part of that picture. This was a great way to copy all the software on a machine over to another machine.

There was one major problem for years—SID numbers. All computers get assigned a unique number that represents them on a domain network and that number is called a *security identifier (SID)* number. The problem for a long time was that when you copied a machine to another machine, the SID number was also copied.

Microsoft released Sysprep many years ago and that helped solve this problem. Sysprep would allow you to remove the SID number so that a third-party software package could image it to another machine. Many third-party image software products now also remove the SID numbers, but Sysprep was one of the first utilities to help solve this problem.

When you decide to use Sysprep to set up your images, there are a few rules that you must follow for Sysprep to work properly:

- You can use images to restart the Windows activation clock. The Windows activation clock starts to decrease as soon as Windows starts for the first time. You can restart the Windows activation clock only three times using Sysprep.
- The computer on which you're running Sysprep has to be a member of a workgroup. The machine can't be part of a domain. If the computer is a member of the domain, when you run Sysprep, the computer will automatically be removed from the domain.
- When installing the image, the system will prompt you for a product key. During the install you can use an answer file, which in turn will have all the information needed for the install and you will not be prompted for any information.
- A third-party utility or ImageX is required to deploy the image that is created from Sysprep.
- If you are using Sysprep to capture an NTFS partition, any files or folders that are encrypted will become corrupt and unreadable.

One new advantage to Sysprep and Windows 7 is that you can use Sysprep to prepare a new machine for duplication. You can use Sysprep to image a Windows 7 machine. The following steps are necessary to image a new machine:

1. Install the Windows 7 operating system.
2. Install all components on the OS.
3. Run Sysprep `/generalize` to create the image.

When you image a computer using the Windows Sysprep utility, a Windows image (`.wim`) file is created. Most third-party imaging software products can work with the Windows image file.

Advantages of the System Preparation Tool

The following are advantages of using the System Preparation Tool as a method for automating Windows 7 installations:

- For large numbers of computers with similar hardware, it greatly reduces deployment time by copying the operating system, applications, and Desktop settings from a reference computer to an image, which can then be deployed to multiple computers.
- Using disk imaging facilitates the standardization of Desktops, administrative policies, and restrictions throughout an organization.
- Reference images can be copied across a network connection or through DVDs that are physically distributed to client computers.

Disadvantages of the System Preparation Tool

There are some disadvantages of using the System Preparation Tool as a method for automating Windows 7 installations:

- ImageX, third-party imaging software, or hardware disk-duplicator devices must be used for an image-based setup.
- The version of the System Preparation Tool that shipped with Windows 7 must be used. An older version of Sysprep cannot be used on a Windows 7 image.
- The System Preparation Tool will not detect any hardware that is not Plug and Play compliant.

Overview of the Windows Automated Installation Kit (Windows AIK)

Another way to install Windows 7 is to use the *Windows Automated Installation Kit (Windows AIK)*. The Windows AIK is a set of utilities and documentation that allows an administrator to configure and deploy Windows operating systems. An administrator can use the Windows AIK to do the following:

- Capture Windows images with ImageX
- Configure and edit images by using the Deployment Image Servicing and Management (DISM) utility
- Create Windows PE images
- Migrate user data and profiles using the User State Migration Tool (USMT)
- Centrally manage volume activations by using the Volume Activation Management Tool (VAMT)

The Windows AIK can be installed and configured on the following operating systems:

- Windows 7
- Windows Server 2008
- Windows Server 2003 with SP2
- Windows Vista with SP1

The Windows AIK is a good solution for organizations that need to customize the Windows deployment environments. The Windows AIK allows an administrator to have the flexibility needed for mass deployments of Windows operating systems. Since every organization's needs are different, the Windows AIK allows you to use all or just part of the deployment tools available. It allows you to manage deployments by using some additional tools.

Microsoft Deployment Toolkit The tools included with this part of the Windows AIK will allow an administrator to easily deploy and configure Windows operating systems and images.

Application Compatibility Toolkit When new Windows operating systems are installed, applications that ran on the previous version of Windows may not work properly. The Application Compatibility Toolkit allows an administrator to help solve these issues before they occur.

Microsoft Assessment and Planning (MAP) Toolkit The MAP toolkit is a utility that will locate computers on a network and then perform a thorough inventory of them. This inventory can then be used to determine which machines can have Windows 7 installed. The MAP utility will be explained and installed later in this chapter in the Microsoft Assessment and Planning section.

Summary of Windows 7 Deployment Options

Table 2.2 summarizes the installation options for Windows 7 and notes the required client hardware, server requirements, and whether the option supports a clean install or upgrade.

TABLE 2.2 Summary of Windows 7 installation options

	MDT 2010	Windows AIK	Unattended Installation	WDS	System Preparation Tool
Required Client Hardware	PC that meets Windows 7 requirements, access to the network	PC that meets Windows 7 requirements	PC that meets Windows 7 requirements, access to the network	PC that meets the Windows 7 requirements and is PXE compliant	Reference computer with Windows 7 installed and configured; PC that meets the Windows 7 requirements; ImageX, third-party disk imaging software, or hardware disk-duplicator device

TABLE 2.2 Summary of Windows 7 installation options *(continued)*

	MDT 2010	Windows AIK	Unattended Installation	WDS	System Preparation Tool
Required Server Hardware and Services	Network installation, distribution server.	None. Windows AIK can be installed on any compatible machine.	None with DVD; if using network installation, distribution server with preconfigured client images.	Windows Server 2003 w/ SP1 or Windows Server 2008 to act as a WDS server with image files, Active Directory, DNS server, and DHCP server.	None.
Clean Install or Upgrade Only	Clean install	Clean install	Clean install or upgrade	Clean install	Clean install

Table 2.3 summarizes the installation tools and files that are used with unattended, automated installations of Windows 7, the associated installation method, and a description of each tool.

TABLE 2.3 Summary of Windows 7 unattended deployment utilities

Tool or File	Automated Installation Option	Description
`Setup.exe`	Unattended installation	Program used to initiate the installation process
`Autounattend.xml`	Unattended installation	Answer file used to customize installation queries
`Windows System Image Manager`	Unattended installation	Program used to create answer files to be used for unattended installations

Tool or File	Automated Installation Option	Description
ImageX.exe	Sysprep	Command-line utility that works in conjunction with Sysprep to create and manage Windows 7 image files for deployment
Sysprep.exe	Sysprep	System Preparation Tool, which prepares a source reference computer that will be used in conjunction with a distribution share or with disk duplication through ImageX, third-party software, or hardware disk-duplication devices

The Windows 7 installation utilities and resources relating to automated deployment are found in a variety of locations. Table 2.4 provides a quick reference for each utility or resource and its location.

TABLE 2.4 Location of Windows 7 deployment utilities and resources

Utility	Location
`Sysprep.exe`	Included with Windows 7; installed to `%WINDIR%\system32\sysprep`
ImageX	Installed with the WAIK; installed to `C:\Program Files\Windows AIK\Tools\x86\imagex.exe`
Windows System Image Manager	Installed with WAIK; installed to `C:\ProgramFiles\Windows AIK\Tools\Image Manager\ImgMgr.exe`

Now that you have seen some of the ways you can install Windows 7, let's take a more detailed look at each one.

Deploying Unattended Installations

You can deploy Windows 7 installations or upgrades through a Windows 7 distribution DVD or through a distribution server that contains Windows 7 images and associated files, such as `Unattend.xml` for unattended installations. Using a DVD can be advantageous if the computer on which you want to install Windows 7 is not connected to the network or is connected via a low-bandwidth network. It is also typically faster to install a Windows 7 image from DVD than to use a network connection.

Unattended installations rely on options configured in an answer file that is deployed with the Windows 7 image. Answer files are XML files that contain the settings that are typically supplied by the installer during attended installations of Windows 7. Answer files can also contain instructions for how programs and applications should be run.

The Windows Setup program is run to install or upgrade to Windows 7 from computers that are running compatible versions of Windows, as discussed in Chapter 1. In fact, Windows Setup is the basis for the other types of installation procedures I'll be discussing in this chapter, including unattended installations, WDS, and image-based installations.

The Windows Setup program (`Setup.exe`) replaces `Winnt32.exe` and `Winnt.exe`, which are the setup programs used in versions of Windows prior to Windows Vista. Although it's a graphical tool, Windows Setup can be run from the command line. For example, you can use the following command to initiate an unattended installation of Windows 7:

```
setup.exe /unattend:answerfile
```

The Windows Setup program has several command-line options that can be applied. Table 2.5 describes the `Setup.exe` command-line options.

TABLE 2.5 `Setup.exe` command-line options and descriptions

Setup.exe Option	Description
`/1394debug:` *`channel`* `[baudrate:`*`baudrate`*`]`	Enables kernel debugging over a FireWire (IEEE 1394) port for troubleshooting purposes. The [baudrate] optional parameter specifies the baud rate for data transfer during the debugging process.
`/debug:`*`port`* `[`*`baudrate`*`:` *`baudrate`*`]`	Enables kernel debugging over the specified port for troubleshooting purposes. The [`baudrate`] optional parameter specifies the baud rate for data transfer during the debugging process.
`/dudisable`	Used to prevent a dynamic update from running during the installation process.
`/emsport:{com1|com2|usebiossettings|off}[/emsbaudrate:`*`baudrate`*`]`	Configures EMS to be enabled or disabled. The [baudrate] optional parameter specifies the baud rate for data transfer during the debugging process.
`/m:`*`folder_name`*	Used with Setup to specify that replacement files should be copied from the specified location. If the files are not present, Setup will use the default location.
`/noreboot`	Normally, when the downlevel phase of `Setup.exe` is complete, the computer restarts. This option specifies that the computer should not restart so that you can execute another command prior to the restart.

Setup.exe Option	Description
/tempdrive:*drive letter*	Specifies the location that will be used to store the temporary files for Windows 7 and the installation partition for Windows 7.
/autounattend: [*answerfile*]	Specifies that you will be using an unattended installation for Windows 7. The answerfile variable points to the custom answer file you will use for installation.

Next we'll look at the System Preparation Tool (Sysprep); using it is one of many ways to install Windows 7 automatically.

Using the System Preparation Tool to Prepare an Installation for Imaging

You can use disk images to install Windows 7 on computers that have similar hardware configurations. Also, if a computer is having technical difficulties, you can use a disk image to quickly restore it to a baseline configuration.

To create a disk image, you install Windows 7 on the source computer with the configuration that you want to copy and use the System Preparation Tool to prepare the installation for imaging. The source computer's configuration should also include any applications that should be installed on target computers.

Once you have prepared the installation for imaging, you can use imaging software such as ImageX to create an image of the installation.

The System Preparation Tool (Sysprep.exe) is included with Windows 7, in the %WINDIR%\system32\sysprep directory. When you run this utility on the source computer, it strips out from the master copy information that must be unique for each computer, such as the SID. Table 2.6 defines the command options that you can use to customize the Sysprep.exe operation.

TABLE 2.6 System preparation command-line options

Switch	Description
/audit	Configures the computer to restart into audit mode, which allows you to add drivers and applications to Windows or test the installation prior to deployment
/generalize	Removes any unique system information from the image, including the SID and log information
/oobe	Specifies that the Windows Welcome screen should be displayed when the computer reboots

TABLE 2.6 System preparation command-line options *(continued)*

Switch	Description
`/quiet`	Runs the installation with no user interaction
`/quit`	Specifies that the System Preparation Tool should quit after the specified operations have been completed
`/reboot`	Restarts the target computer after the System Preparation Tool completes
`/shutdown`	Specifies that the computer should shut down after the specified operations have been completed
`/unattend`	Indicates the name and location of the answer file to use

In the following sections, you will learn how to create a disk image and how to copy and install from it.

Preparing a Windows 7 Installation

To run the System Preparation Tool and prepare an installation for imaging, take the following steps:

1. Install Windows 7 on a source computer. The computer should have a similar hardware configuration as the destination computer(s). The source computer should not be a member of a domain. (See Chapter 1 for instructions on installing Windows 7.)
2. Log on to the source computer as an administrator and, if desired, install and configure any applications, files (such as newer versions of Plug and Play drivers), or custom settings (for example, a custom Desktop) that will be applied to the target computer(s).
3. Verify that your image meets the specified configuration criteria and that all applications are properly installed and working.
4. Select Start ➢ Computer, and navigate to `C:\%WINDIR%\System32\sysprep`. Double-click the Sysprep application icon.
5. The Windows System Preparation Tool dialog box appears. Select the appropriate options for your configuration.
6. If configured to do so, Windows 7 will be rebooted into setup mode, and you will be prompted to enter the appropriate setup information.
7. You will now be able to use imaging software to create an image of the computer to deploy to other computers.

In Exercise 2.3, you will use the System Preparation Tool to prepare the computer for disk imaging. The Sysprep utility must be run on a machine with a clean version of Windows 7. If you upgraded a Windows Vista machine to Windows 7, you will not be able to run the Sysprep utility.

EXERCISE 2.3

Using the System Preparation Tool

1. Log on to the source computer as Administrator and, if desired, install and configure any applications that should also be installed on the target computer.
2. Select Start ➢ Computer, and navigate to `C:\%WINDIR%\System32\sysprep`. Double-click the Sysprep application icon.
3. In the System Preparation Tool dialog box, select Enter System Out-Of-Box Experience (OOBE) in the system cleanup action.
4. Under the shutdown options, depending on the options selected, the System Preparation Tool will quit, the computer will shut down, or the computer will be rebooted into setup mode, where you will need to configure the setup options. Choose the Reboot option. Click OK.
5. Configure the Sysprep utility and name the image `image.wim`.

After creating the Sysprep image, you need to use some type of third-party software to install it. Windows includes a utility called ImageX for just that purpose.

Using ImageX to Create a Disk Image

After you've run the System Preparation Tool on the source computer, you can create an image from the installation, and you can then install the image on target computers.

To create an image, you can use ImageX, which is a command-line utility that can be used to create and manage Windows image (`.wim`) files.

Creating a Disk Image

To run the ImageX utility to create a disk image of a Windows 7 installation, follow these steps:

1. Reboot the computer into the Windows Preinstallation Environment (PE).
2. At the resulting command prompt, access the ImageX utility by typing **D:\Tools\ImageX** and entering the appropriate options. For example, to create an image named Windows 7, you could enter the following command:

   ```
   D:\ImageX.exe /capture C: C:\Images\image.wim "Windows 7" /verify
   ```

3. You can copy the new image to a network share or to the local computer for hardware disk duplication. To copy the image to a network share, you can use the `net use` *`dir network share`* command along with the `copy` *`file dir`* command to copy the file.

In Exercise 2.4, you will use the ImageX utility to create a disk image of a Windows 7 installation.

EXERCISE 2.4

Using the ImageX Utility to Create a Disk Image

1. Boot the computer into the Windows Preinstallation Environment (Windows PE).
2. Type the following command in Windows PE, assuming that your DVD\CD drive is configured as the D: drive:

   ```
   D:\ImageX.exe /capture C: C:\Images\image.wim "Windows 7" /verify
   ```

3. Copy the new image to a network share at `\\Server\Images` by using the following commands:

   ```
   net use z: \\Server\Images
   copy  C:\Images\image.wim z:
   ```

After you create the disk image, the next step is to install the disk image. In the next section, you'll learn to install the disk image to a new machine.

Installing from a Disk Image

After you've run the System Preparation Tool and ImageX on the source computer, you can copy the image and then install it on the target computer.

After the image is copied, you should boot the destination computer into the Windows Preinstallation Environment (Windows PE). If the computer has been used previously, it may be necessary to reformat the hard drive, which you can do using the `diskpart` command in Windows PE. If the image is stored over the network, you should then copy the image to the destination computer by using the `net use [dir] [network share]` and `copy [file] [dir]` commands. Then, you should use the `/apply` option of the ImageX utility to apply the image to the local computer. If an answer file has not been deployed along with the image, you may have to apply such information as regional settings, the product key, the computer name, and the password to the new computer after the destination computer is rebooted.

In Exercise 2.5, you will use the stripped image that was created in Exercise 2.4 to simulate the process of continuing an installation from a disk image.

EXERCISE 2.5

Installing Windows 7 from a Disk Image

1. Boot the target computer into the Windows PE environment.
2. Copy the image created in Exercise 2.4 to the local computer by using the following commands:

   ```
   net use z: \\Server\Images
   copy  Z:\Images\image.wim C:
   ```

3. Apply the image to the target computer using the following ImageX command:

   ```
   D:\ImageX.exe /apply C:\Images\image.wim C:
   ```

When you install Windows 7, the installation wizard asks you questions such as your username and computer name. There is a way to answer these questions without actually being in front of the computer. As you'll see in the next section, you can do this by using an answer file.

Using Windows System Image Manager to Create Answer Files

Answer files are automated installation scripts used to answer the questions that appear during a normal Windows 7 installation. You can use answer files with Windows 7 unattended installations, disk image installations, or WDS installations. Setting up answer files allows you to easily deploy Windows 7 to computers that may not be configured in the same manner, with little or no user intervention. Because answer files are associated with image files, you can validate the settings within an answer file against the image file.

You can create answer files by using the Windows System Image Manager (SIM) utility. There are several advantages to using Windows SIM to create answer files:

- You can easily create and edit answer files through a graphical interface, which reduces syntax errors.
- It simplifies the addition of user-specific or computer-specific configuration information.
- You can validate existing answer files against newly created images.
- You can include additional application and device drivers in the answer file.

In the following sections, you will learn about options that can be configured through Windows SIM, how to create answer files with Windows SIM, how to format an answer file, and how to manually edit answer files.

Configuring Components Through Windows System Image Manager (SIM)

You can use Windows SIM to configure a wide variety of installation options. The following list defines what components can be configured through Windows SIM and gives a short description of each component:

auditSystem Adds additional device drivers, specifies firewall settings, and applies a name to the system when the image is booted into audit mode. Audit mode is initiated by using the `sysprep /audit` command.

auditUser Executes `RunSynchronous` or `RunAsynchronous` commands when the image is booted into audit mode. Audit mode is initiated by using the `sysprep /audit` command.

generalize Removes system-specific information from an image so that the image can be used as a reference image. The settings specified in the generalize component will only be applied if the `sysprep /generalize` command is used.

offlineServicing Specifies the language packs and packages to apply to an image prior to the image being extracted to the hard disk.

oobeSystem Specifies the settings to apply to the computer the first time the computer is booted into the Windows Welcome screen, which is also known as the Out-Of-Box Experience (OOBE). To boot to the Welcome screen, the `sysprep /oobe` command should be used.

specialize Configures the specific settings for the target computer, such as network settings and domain information. This configuration pass is used in conjunction with the generalize configuration pass.

Windows PE Sets the Windows PE–specific configuration settings, as well as several Windows Setup settings, such as partitioning and formatting the hard disk, selecting an image, and applying a product key.

Creating Answer Files with Windows System Image Manager

To create an answer file with the Windows System Image Manager, the first thing you must do is install the Windows Automated Installation Kit (WAIK). In Exercise 2.6, you will download and install the WAIK, which is a free download from Microsoft's website.

EXERCISE 2.6

Downloading and Installing the WAIK

1. Download the `WAIK.iso` file from Microsoft's website.
2. You must transfer the `.iso` file to a DVD.
3. Insert the DVD into your Windows 7 machine.
4. When Autoplay starts, click Run `StartCD.exe`. If Autorun does not start, open Windows Explorer and click `StartCD.exe` under the DVD drive.
5. At the User Account Control screen, click the Yes button.
6. The Welcome To Windows Automated Installation Kit screen appears. Click the Windows AIK Setup link.

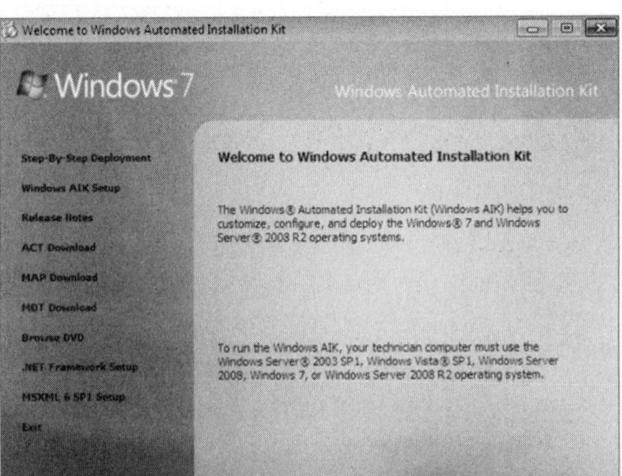

7. The Welcome screen to the wizard appears. Click Next.
8. At the License Terms screen, click the I Agree radio button and click Next.
9. At the Select Installation Folder screen, choose where you want to install the WAIK files. You can also choose who has the rights to use the WAIK. In this example, the Everyone radio button is selected. Click Next.

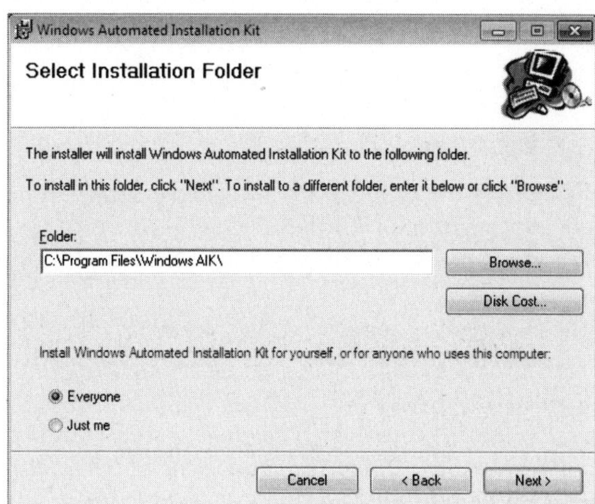

10. At the Confirmation screen, verify your settings and click Next.
11. At the Installation Complete screen, verify that there are no errors and click Close.
12. Close the WAIK installation screen.

After you have installed the WAIK, you can run the Windows SIM utility to create a new answer file or edit existing answer files. Exercise 2.7 describes how to create a new answer file using Windows SIM.

EXERCISE 2.7

Using the Windows SIM Utility

1. Select Start > All Programs > Microsoft Windows AIK, and click Windows System Image Manager.
2. Windows System Image Manager displays an empty screen with five panes: a pane for selecting distribution shares, a pane for selecting Windows image files, the answer file pane, a properties pane, and a pane for displaying validation messages.

EXERCISE 2.7 *(continued)*

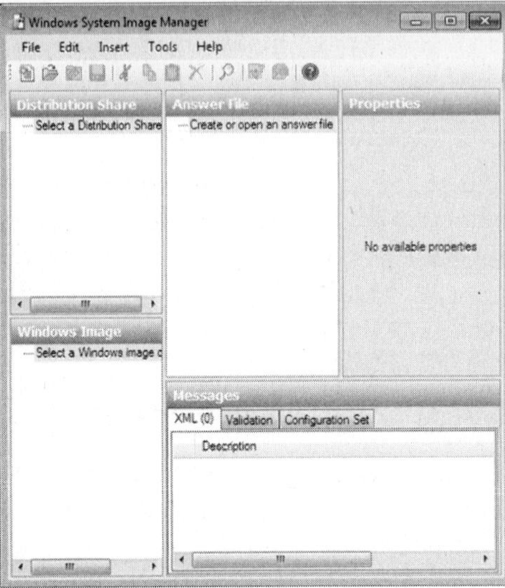

3. Select the Windows 7 image file for which a new answer file should be created by clicking the File ➤ Select Windows Image or catalog file option or by right-clicking the Windows Image pane in Windows SIM and clicking Select Windows Image, and then choosing the image you created in Exercise 2.4.

4. Select File ➤ New Answer File or right-click the Answer File pane and select New Answer File from the context menu to generate the structure of the new answer file.

5. Right-click each component as desired to modify the configuration pass options that are specific to the new environment. You can drill down within a component to provide specific customizations, or you can modify parent-level components.

6. When you have finished customizing the answer file for the desired environment, choose File ➤ Save Answer File to save the answer file.

You can use an answer file to provide automated answers for a DVD-based installation. Simply create a new answer file named `Unattend.xml` and copy it to the root of the DVD. Insert the Windows 7 DVD and set the BIOS to boot from the DVD drive. As the installation begins, Windows Setup will implicitly search for answer files in a number of locations, including the root of removable media drives.

Using Windows Deployment Services (WDS)

Another way that many IT departments deploy operating systems has been through the use of Remote Installation Services (RIS). RIS was a utility that allowed an administrator to deploy an operating system remotely. On the client machine that was receiving the operating system, you would use a set of disks (RIS client disks) that would automatically initiate a network card, connect to the RIS server, and download the operating system.

For Windows 7 and Windows Server 2008, a new version of RIS has been developed, and it's called Windows Deployment Services (WDS). WDS (see Figure 2.4) allows an IT administrator to install a Windows operating system without using a CD or DVD installation disk. Using WDS allows you to deploy the operating system through a network installation. WDS can deploy Windows XP, Windows Server 2003, Windows Vista, Windows 7, and Microsoft Windows Server 2008.

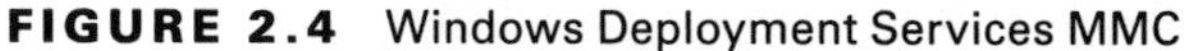

FIGURE 2.4 Windows Deployment Services MMC

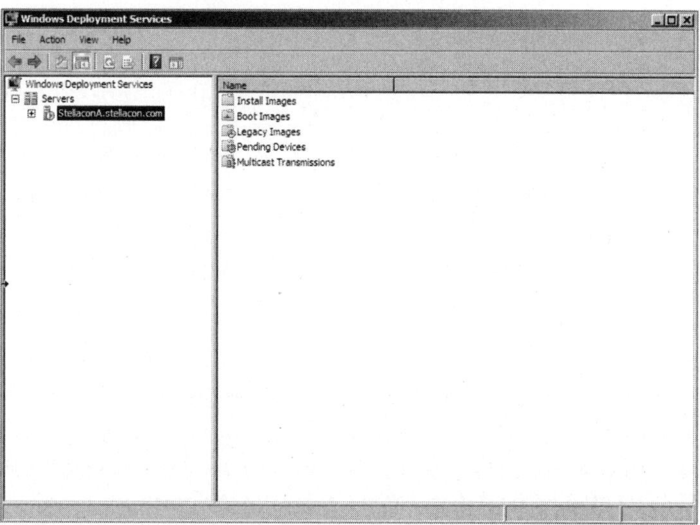

The following are some of the advantages of using WDS for automated installation:

- You can remotely install Windows 7.
- The procedure simplifies management of the server image by allowing you to access Windows 7 distribution files from a distribution server.
- You can quickly recover the operating system in the event of a computer failure.

Here are the basic steps of the WDS process from a PXE-enabled WDS client:

1. The WDS client initiates a special boot process through the PXE network adapter (and the computer's BIOS configured for a network boot). On a PXE client, the client presses F12 to start the PXE boot process and to indicate that they want to perform a WDS installation.
2. A list of available Windows Preinstallation Environment (PE) boot images is displayed. The client should select the appropriate Windows PE boot image from the boot menu.
3. The Windows Welcome screen is displayed. The client should click the Next button.
4. The WDS client is prompted to enter credentials for accessing and installing images from the WDS server.
5. A list of available operating system images is displayed. The client should select the appropriate image file to install.
6. The WDS client is prompted to enter the product key for the selected image.
7. The Partition And Configure The Disk screen is displayed. This screen provides the ability to install a mass storage device driver, if needed, by pressing F6.
8. The image copy process is initiated, and the selected image is copied to the WDS client computer.

The following sections describe how to set up the WDS server and the WDS clients and how to install Windows 7 through WDS.

Preparing the WDS Server

With the WDS server, you can manage and distribute Windows 7 operating system images to WDS client computers. The WDS server contains any files necessary for PXE booting, Windows PE boot images, and the Windows 7 images to be deployed.

The following steps for preparing the WDS server are discussed in the upcoming sections:

1. Make sure the server meets the requirements for running WDS.
2. Install WDS.
3. Configure and start WDS.
4. Configure the WDS server to respond to client computers (if this was not configured when WDS was installed).

For WDS to work, the server on which you will install WDS must meet the requirements for WDS and be able to access the required network services.

WDS Server Requirements

The WDS server must meet these requirements:

- The computer must be a domain controller or a member of an Active Directory domain.
- At least one partition on the server must be formatted as NTFS.
- WDS must be installed on the server.
- The operating system must be Windows Server 2003 or Windows Server 2008.
- A network adapter must be installed.

Network Services

The following network services must be running on the WDS server or be accessible to the WDS server from another network server:

- TCP/IP installed and configured.
- A DHCP server, which is used to assign DHCP addresses to WDS clients. (Ensure that your DHCP scope has enough addresses to accommodate all the WDS clients that will need IP addresses.)
- A DNS server, which is used to locate the Active Directory controller.
- Active Directory, which is used to locate WDS servers and WDS clients as well as authorize WDS clients and manage WDS configuration settings and client installation options.

Installing the WDS Server Components

You can configure WDS on a Windows Server 2003 or Windows Server 2008 computer by using the Windows Deployment Services Configuration Wizard or by using the WDSUTIL command-line utility. Table 2.7 describes the WDSUTIL command-line options.

TABLE 2.7 WDSUTIL command-line options

WDSUTIL Option	Description
`/initialize-server`	Initializes the configuration of the WDS server
`/uninitialized -server`	Undoes any changes made during the initialization of the WDS server
`/add`	Adds images and devices to the WDS server

TABLE 2.7 WDSUTIL command-line options *(continued)*

WDSUTIL Option	Description
/convert-ripimage	Converts Remote Installation Preparation (RIPrep) images to WIM images
/remove	Removes images from the server
/set	Sets information in images, image groups, WDS servers, and WDS devices
/get	Gets information from images, image groups, WDS servers, and WDS devices
/new	Creates new capture images or discover images
/copy- image	Copies images from the image store
/export-image	Exports to WIM files images contained within the image store
/start	Starts WDS services
/stop	Stops WDS services
/disable	Disables WDS services
/enable	Enables WDS services
/approve-autoadddevices	Approves Auto-Add devices
/reject-autoadddevices	Rejects Auto-Add devices
/delete-autoadddevices	Deletes records from the Auto-Add database
/update	Uses a known good resource to update a server resource

The first step in setting up WDS to deploy operating systems to the clients is to install the WDS role. You do this by using Server Manager. You must make sure that DNS, DHCP, and Active Directory are installed before doing this exercise. Exercise 2.8 will take you through the install of WDS.

DNS and DHCP are discussed in detail in *MCTS: Windows Server 2008 Network Infrastructure Configuration Study Guide* by William Panek, Tylor Wentworth, and James Chellis (Sybex, 2008).

EXERCISE 2.8

Installing WDS on Windows Server 2008

1. Start Server Manager by choosing Start ➤ Administrative Tools ➤ Server Manager.
2. On the left side, click Roles.
3. In the right window pane, click the Add Roles link.
4. At the Add Roles Wizard, click Next at the Before You Begin screen.
5. Click the Windows Deployment Services check box. Click Next.
6. At the Overview Screen, click Next.
7. On the Select Role Services screen, make sure both check boxes (Deployment Server and Transport Server) are checked and click Next.
8. At the Confirmation screen, verify the installation selections and click Install.
9. At the Installation Results screen, click close.
10. Close the Server Manager MMC.

Configuring the WDS Server to Respond to Client Requests

Now that you have installed the Windows Deployment Services role, you need to configure the server. In Exercise 2.9, you will configure the WDS server.

EXERCISE 2.9

Configuring the WDS Server

Follow these steps to configure the WDS server:

1. Start the WDS MMC by choosing Start ➤ Administrative Tools ➤ Windows Deployment Services.
2. In the left window pane, expand the Servers link. Click the name of your server and then right-click. Choose Configure Server.
3. The Welcome Page appears, explaining that you need DHCP, DNS, Active Directory, and an NTFS partition. If you meet these minimum requirements, click Next.
4. The Remote Installation Folder Location screen appears; accept the defaults by clicking Next.
5. A System Volume Warning dialog box appears; click Yes.
6. The DHCP Option 60 screen will be next. Check both boxes and click Next.

EXERCISE 2.9 ***(continued)***

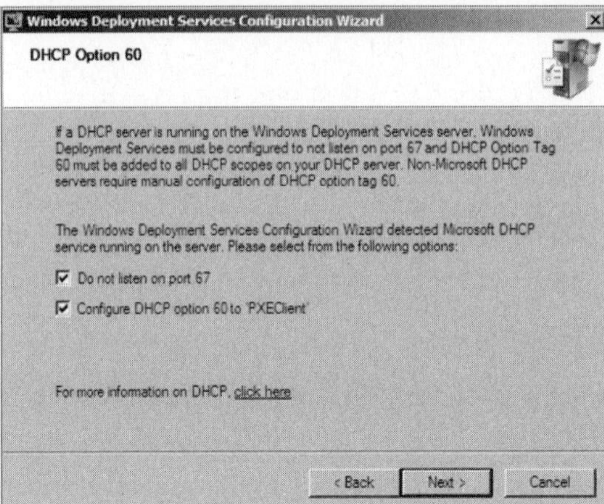

7. On the PXE Server Initial Settings screen, choose how PXE will respond to clients. Choose the Respond To All (Known And Unknown) Client Computers radio button. Click Finish.

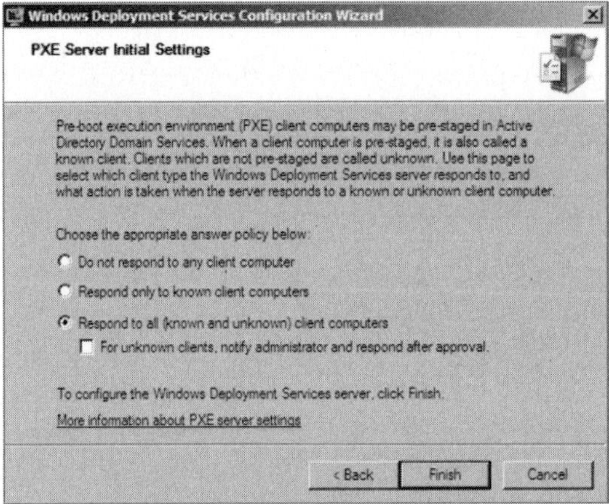

8. At the Configuration Complete screen, make sure the check box Add Image To The Windows Deployment Server Now is unchecked. Click Finish.

One of the advantages of using the Windows deployment server is that WDS can work with Windows image (`.wim`) files. As stated in the previous section, Windows image files can be created through the use of the Windows Sysprep utility.

One component that you need to pay attention to when using the Windows deployment server is Preboot Execution Environment (PXE) network devices. PXE boot devices are network interface cards (NICs) that can talk to a network without the need for an operating system. PXE boot NIC adapters are network adapters that have a set of preboot commands within the boot firmware.

This is important when using WDS because PXE Boot adapters connect to a WDS server and requests the data needed to load the operating system remotely. Remember, most of these machines that you are using WDS for do not have an operating system on the computer. You need NIC adapters that can connect to a network without the need for an operating system for WDS to work properly.

For the same reason, you must set up DHCP to accept PXE machines. Those machines need a valid TCP/IP address so that they can connect to the WDS server.

Preparing the WDS Client

The WDS client is the computer on which Windows 7 will be installed. WDS clients rely on a technology called PXE, which allows the client computer to remotely boot and connect to a WDS server.

To act as a WDS client, the computer must meet all the hardware requirements for Windows 7 (see Chapter 1) and have a PXE-capable network adapter installed, and a WDS server must be present on the network. Additionally, the user account used to install the image must be a member of the Domain Users group in Active Directory.

After the WDS server has been installed and configured, you can install Windows 7 on a WDS client that uses a PXE-compliant network card.

To install Windows 7 on the WDS client, follow these steps:

1. Start the computer. When prompted, press F12 for a network service boot. The Windows PE appears.
2. The Windows Welcome screen appears. Click the Next button to start the installation process.
3. Enter the username and password of an account that has permissions to access and install images from the WDS server.
4. A list of available operating system images stored on the WDS server appears. Select the image to install, and click Next.
5. Enter the product key for the selected Windows 7 image, and click Next.
6. The Partition And Configure The Disk screen appears. Select the desired disk partitioning options, or click OK to use the default options.
7. Click Next to initiate the image copying process. The Windows Setup process will begin after the image is copied to the WDS client computer.

Microsoft Assessment and Planning (MAP) Toolkit

This chapter is all about installing Windows 7 on multiple computers. One utility that you can use to help design your network is the *Microsoft Assessment and Planning (MAP) toolkit*. MAP is a utility that will locate computers on a network and then perform a thorough inventory of them. To obtain this inventory, MAP uses multiple utilities, such as Windows Management Instrumentation (WMI), the Remote Registry Service, and the Simple Network Management Protocol (SNMP).

Having this information will allow an administrator to determine if the machines on their network will be able to load Microsoft Windows Vista, Windows 7, Windows Server 2008, Microsoft Office 2007, and Microsoft Application Virtualization. One advantage of using MAP when determining the needs for Windows 7 is that MAP will also advise you of any hardware upgrades needed for a machine or of device driver availability.

Anyone who has been in the industry for a while can see the potential of using MAP. A utility that goes out and discovers your network hardware and then advises you of the resources you need for the operating system to operate properly is a tool that should be in every administrator's arsenal.

You have multiple ways to locate the computers on your network. The following are your discovery options and how they try to discover the computers:

Use Active Directory Domain Services Select this checkbox to find computer objects in Active Directory.

Use The Windows Networking Protocols Select this check box to find computers in workgroups and Windows NT 4.0 domains.

Import Computer Names From A File Select this check box to import computer names from a file.

Scan An IP Address Range Select this check box to find computers within a specified IP address range.

Manually Enter Computer Names And Credentials Select this check box to enter computer names individually.

As a network administrator, one thing that is always difficult to determine is how many servers are needed for your Windows 7 end users and where to place them on your network. One feature included with MAP is the ability to obtain performance metric data from the computers. MAP will also generate a report that recommends which machines can be used for Windows 7.

MAP generates your report in both Microsoft Excel and Microsoft Word. These reports can provide information to you in both summary and full detail modes. MAP can generate reports for you for some of the following scenarios:

- Currently installed client operating systems and their requirements for migrating to Windows 7
- Currently installed Windows Server systems and their requirements for migrating to Windows Server 2008
- Currently installed Microsoft Office software and their requirements for migrating to Microsoft Office 2007

- Server performance by using the Performance Metrics Wizard
- Hyper-V or Virtual Server 2005 server consolidation and placement
- Assessment of machines (Clients, Servers) for installation of Microsoft Application Virtualization (formally known as SoftGrid)

Next we'll look at system requirements and how to install MAP.

MAP System Requirements

Your system must meet these requirements to use MAP:

Supported Operating Systems Windows Server 2008; Windows Server 2003; Windows 7, Windows Vista with Service Pack 1; Windows XP Professional Edition.

CPU Architecture One advantage to the Microsoft Assessment and Planning Solution Accelerator is that it can be installed on both the 32-bit and 64-bit versions of any of the operating systems listed above.

Hardware Requirements Your system must meet the following hardware requirements:

1.6-GHz-or-faster processor minimum or dual-core for Windows 7

1.5 GB of RAM minimum / 2.0 GB for Windows 7 or Windows Vista

Minimum 1 GB of available hard-disk space

Network card that supports 10/100 Mbps

Additional Requirements Microsoft SQL Server 2005 Express Edition, Microsoft Word (2003 with SP2 or 2007), and Microsoft Excel (2003 with SP2 or 2007).

Microsoft Assessment and Planning toolkit is free to use but it must be downloaded from Microsoft's website or installed from the Windows AIK installation disk. Exercise 2.10 will walk you through the steps to install the Microsoft Assessment and Planning toolkit from the Windows AIK installation utility.

EXERCISE 2.10

Installing the Microsoft Assessment and Planning Toolkit

1. Insert the Windows AIK DVD on your machine.
2. When Autoplay starts, click Run `StartCD.exe`. If Autorun does not start, open Windows Explorer and click `StartCD.exe` under the DVD drive.
3. At the User Account Control screen, click the Yes button.
4. The Welcome To Windows Automated Installation Kit screen appears. Click the MAP Download link. This will take you to the Microsoft website where you can download MAP.

EXERCISE 2.10 *(continued)*

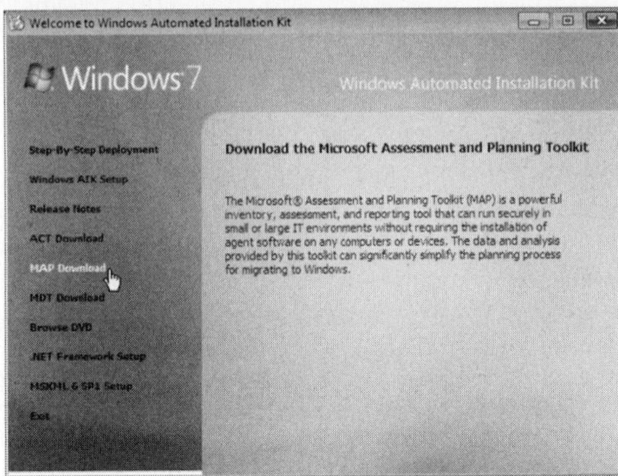

5. Scroll down to the bottom of the page and click the download button for the `Microsoft_Assessment_and_Planning_Solution_Setup.x64.exe` or `x86.exe`.
6. Click the Save Button. Save the file to your hard drive.
7. After the file is downloaded to your hard drive, click the Run button.
8. The Microsoft Assessment and Planning Solution Accelerator Setup Wizard appears. Make sure the check box to automatically check for device compatibility is checked and click Next.

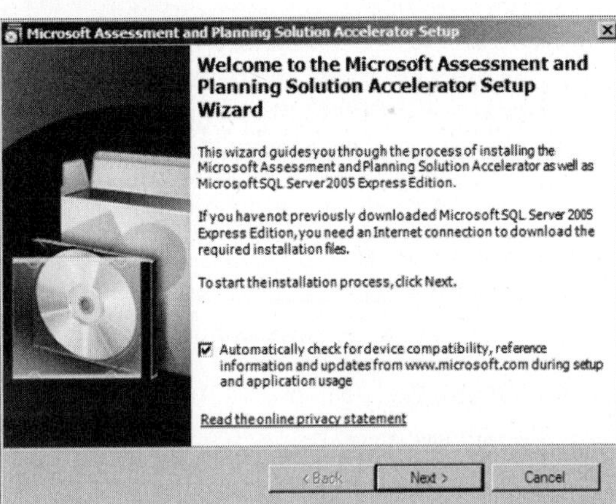

9. The License Agreement screen appears next. Click the I Accept The Terms Of The License Agreement radio button and click Next.
10. At the Installation Folder screen, just accept the default location by clicking Next.
11. A screen appears asking about SQL Server 2005 Express. If you have a previous version of SQL Server 2005 Express on your machine, click the Install From Previous Downloaded Installation Files radio button. If you do not have a previous copy of SQL, make sure the Download And Install radio button is checked. Click Next.

12. The SQL Server 2005 Express License Agreement screen appears next. Click the I Accept The Terms Of The License Agreement radio button and click Next.
13. At the Ready to Install screen, click the Install button.
14. The Installing The Microsoft Assessment And Planning Solution Accelerator status screen will appear and show you the status of the install.
15. After the installation is complete, the Installation Successful screen will appear.

Now that you have installed the Microsoft Assessment and Planning toolkit, it's time to configure and test your server. In Exercise 2.11, you will create your database for testing.

EXERCISE 2.11

Configuring MAP

1. Start the Microsoft Assessment and Planning toolkit by choosing Start ➤ All Programs ➤ Microsoft Planning And Assessment Solution Accelerator ➤ Microsoft Planning And Assessment Solution.
2. The first thing you need to do is select your database. You are going to create your database at this time. To accomplish this, click Select A Database in either the center or right window pane.

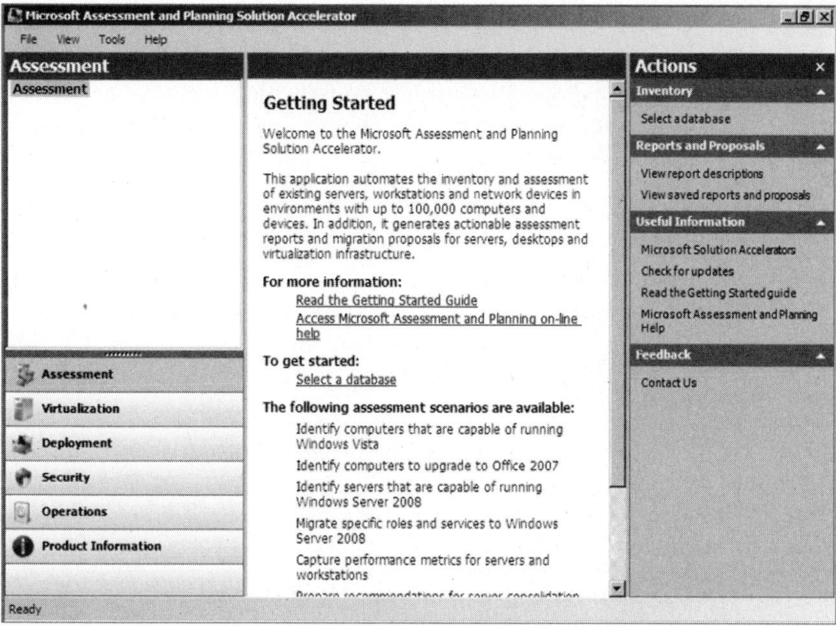

3. The Create Or Select A Database screen appears. Make sure the Create An Inventory Database radio button is clicked. In the Name Field, type **Windows 7** and click the OK button.

After your database is created, you have the ability to run the different options to test the machines and servers. This is where you decide which scenarios you would like to test for your network.

As a consultant and system administrator for many years, I find it very useful to have a utility like MAP to help not only detect the network and its operating systems but also recommend enhancements.

Summary

In this chapter, we discussed automated installation of Windows 7. Installing Windows 7 through an automated process is an effective way to install the Windows 7 operating system onto multiple computers.

There are multiple methods for automated installation: unattended installations, Windows Deployment Services (WDS), Windows Automated Installation Kit (WAIK), third-party applications, unattended installations, and using the System Preparation Tool along with ImageX.

Windows Deployment Services (WDS) is an updated version of Remote Installation Services (RIS). WDS is a suite of components that allows you to remotely install Windows 7 on client computers.

The Windows AIK is a set of utilities and documentation that allows an administrator to configure and deploy Windows operating systems.

You can use unattended answer files to automatically respond to the queries that are generated during the normal installation process.

You can also prepare an installation for imaging by using the System Preparation Tool (`Sysprep.exe`) and creating a disk image by using the ImageX utility or a third-party utility.

Microsoft Deployment Toolkit (MDT) 2010 is a way of automating desktop and server deployment. With the MDT, an administrator can deploy desktops and servers through the use of a common console, which allows for quicker deployments, having standardized desktop and server images and security, and Zero Touch deployments of Windows 7, Windows Server 2008, Windows Vista, Windows Server 2003, and Windows XP.

Exam Essentials

Know the difference between unattended installation methods. Understand the various options available for unattended installations of Windows 7 and when it is appropriate to use each installation method.

Understand how to use unattended installations for Windows 7 deployment. Know when it is appropriate to use unattended installations for Windows 7 deployment.

Understand the features and uses of WDS. Know when it is appropriate to use WDS to manage unattended installations. Be able to list the requirements for setting up WDS servers and WDS clients. Be able to complete an unattended installation using WDS.

Be able to use disk images for unattended installations. Know how to perform unattended installations of Windows 7 using the System Preparation Tool and disk images.

Know how to use Windows System Image Manager to create and edit answer files. Understand how to access and use Windows System Image Manager to create answer files. Be able to edit the answer files and know the basic options that can be configured for them.

Understand the Microsoft Deployment Toolkit (MDT) 2010. Know that the MDT is a way of automating desktop and server deployment. Understand that the MDT allows an administrator to deploy desktops and servers through the use of a common console.

Review Questions

1. You are the network administrator of a large corporation. Your company has decided to use WDS to install 100 client computers. You have set up the WDS server and now want to test a single WDS client to make sure the installation will go smoothly. Which of the following services are required to use WDS? (Choose all that apply.)

   A. DNS

   B. WINS

   C. DHCP

   D. Active Directory

2. You are the network administrator for a large organization. You are in charge of developing a plan to install 200 Windows 7 computers in your company's data center. You decide to use WDS. You are using a Windows Server 2008 domain and have verified that your network meets the requirements for using WDS services. What command-line utility should you use to configure the WDS server?

   A. ImageX

   B. WDSUTIL

   C. `Setup.exe`

   D. The WDS icon in Control Panel

3. Your company has a variety of client computers that are running Windows XP Professional. You want to upgrade these machines to Windows 7 using WDS. What requirement must be met on a client computer to upgrade to Windows 7 from a WDS server?

   A. The computer must use a PXE-based boot ROM.

   B. The computer must contain an NTFS partition.

   C. The computer must use identical hardware configurations as the reference image.

   D. There is no option to upgrade with WDS.

4. Will is the network manager for a large company. He has been tasked with creating a deployment plan to automate installations for 100 computers that need to have Windows 7 installed. Will wants to use WDS for the installations. To fully automate the installations, he needs to create an answer file. Will does not want to create the answer files with a text editor. What other program can he use to create unattended answer files via a GUI interface?

   A. ImageX

   B. Answer Manager

   C. Windows System Image Manager

   D. System Preparation Tool

5. Bob is using WDS to install 100 clients that are identically configured. The first 65 computers are installed with no problems. When he tries to install the other 35, the machines all receive a 169.254.*x*.*x* number along with an error. Which of the following would cause this failure?

   A. The WDS server has been authorized to serve only 65 clients.

   B. The WINS server is no longer available.

   C. The DHCP server does not have enough IP addresses to allocate to the WDS clients.

   D. The network bandwidth has become saturated.

6. You run a training department that needs the same software installed from scratch on the training computers each week. You decide to use ImageX to deploy disk images. Which Windows 7 utility can you use in conjunction with ImageX to create these disk images?

   A. UAF

   B. Answer Manager

   C. Setup Manager

   D. System Preparation Tool

7. You are trying to decide whether you want to use WDS as a method of installing Windows 7 within your company. Which of the following options is *not* an advantage to using a WDS automated installation?

   A. The Windows 7 security is retained when you restart the computer.

   B. Windows 7 installation media does not need to be deployed to each computer.

   C. Unique information is stripped out of the installation image so that it can be copied to other computers.

   D. You can quickly recover the operating system in the event of a system failure.

8. You are the network manager of the XYZ Corporation. You are in charge of developing an automated deployment strategy for rolling out new Windows 7 computers. You want to install a WDS server and are evaluating whether an existing server can be used as a WDS server for Windows 7 deployment. Which of the following is *not* a requirement for configuring the WDS server?

   A. The remote installation folder must be NTFS version 3.0 or later.

   B. The remote installation folder must reside on the system partition.

   C. RIS must be installed on the server.

   D. The existing server must run Windows Server 2003 with Service Pack 1 installed.

9. You are using WDS to install 20 Windows 7 computers. When the clients attempt to use WDS, they are not able to complete the unattended installation. You suspect that the WDS server has not been configured to respond to client requests. Which one of the following utilities would you use to configure the WDS server to respond to client requests?

   A. Active Directory Users and Computers

   B. Active Directory Users and Groups

   C. WDS MMC snap-in

   D. WDSMAN

10. You want to install a group of 25 computers using disk images created in conjunction with the System Preparation Tool. Your plan is to create an image from a reference computer and then copy the image to all the machines. You do not want to create a SID on the destination computer when you use the image. Which `Sysprep.exe` command-line option should you use to set this up?

    A. `/specialize`

    B. `/generalize`

    C. `/oobe`

    D. `/quiet`

11. You are planning on deploying 100 new Windows 7 computers throughout your company. Each new computer is similarly configured. You want to create a reference image that will then be applied to the remaining images. Which of the following utilities should you use?

    A. WDSUTIL

    B. `Setup.exe`

    C. Windows SIM

    D. ImageX

12. You are a network technician for your company, and you need to deploy Windows 7 to multiple computers. You want to automate the installation of Windows 7 so that no user interaction is required during the installation process. Which of the following utilities could you use?

    A. Windows SIM

    B. ImageX

    C. System Preparation Tool

    D. WDSUTIL

13. You want to initiate a new installation of Windows 7 from the command line. You plan to accomplish this by using the `Setup.exe` command-line setup utility. You want to use an answer file with this command. Which command-line option should you use?

    A. `/unattend`

    B. `/apply`

    C. `/noreboot`

    D. `/generialize`

14. You have manually created an answer file that you want to use to deploy an image that you have previously created. Before deploying the image, you want to ensure that your answer file will work with the image. Which of the following tools could you use to validate the answer file?

    A. System Preparation Tool

    B. Windows SIM

    C. ImageX

    D. WDSUTIL

15. You have created a Windows 7 image that you will copy to a DVD and deploy to several new computers. You want to use an answer file to automate the setup process. Where should the answer file be located so that you can use it during installation?

    A. On a network share

    B. On a WDS server

    C. On a separate DVD

    D. At the root of the DVD

16. You are planning on deploying a new Windows 7 image to 100 client computers that are similarly configured. You are using the Windows SIM tool to create an answer file that will be used to automate the installation process. You want each computer to contain two partitions, one for the system partition and one that will function as a data partition. You need to modify the answer file to support this configuration. Which component of the answer file will you need to modify?

    A. oobeSystem

    B. auditSystem

    C. Windows PE

    D. specialize

17. Your company has recently hired a new employee. You need to deploy Windows 7 on the new employee's computer. You have previously created a Windows 7 image using the ImageX utility and have successfully deployed it to other computers. You want to use ImageX to deploy the image to the new employee's computer. Which ImageX option will you need to use?

    A. `/apply`

    B. `/capture`

    C. `/mount`

    D. `/verify`

18. You are using WDS to deploy Windows 7 images across your organization, and you are using the WDSUTIL command-line utility to perform this task. You want to copy a previously created image from the image store using this utility. Which option of WDSUTIL should you use?

    A. `/move`

    B. `/copy-image`

    C. `/get`

    D. `/enable`

19. You are using the Windows SIM tool to create an answer file to be used when deploying new Windows 7 images. You are editing the configuration passes too so that the desired settings are entered during the installation process. You are currently editing the specialize component of the answer file. Which of the following information should you include in this component of the answer file?

    A. Hard disk partitioning information

    B. Product key information

    C. Windows Welcome screen settings

    D. Domain and network settings

20. You have recently installed Windows 7 onto a reference computer that will be used to create an image that can then be deployed to sales employees' computers. You have installed and configured several proprietary sales applications on the computer. You have previously used the System Preparation Tool to remove any system-specific information from the computer, and you plan to use ImageX to create the image from this reference computer. Which option of the ImageX utility can you use to accomplish your goal?

    A. `/apply`

    B. `/capture`

    C. `/mount`

    D. `/verify`

Answers to Review Questions

1. A,C,D. DNS, DHCP, and Active Directory must be properly configured and running for WDS services to work. The WDS server must also be installed and configured.

2. B. WDSUTIL is a command-line utility that can be used to configure the WDS server. Several other configuration options need to be specified on the WDS server and you can set them using WDSUTIL.

3. D. If you are using WDS, it is not possible to upgrade from Windows XP Professional; you can only install a fresh copy of Windows 7. Unattended installations can be used to support automated upgrades.

4. C. Windows System Image Manager (SIM) is used to create unattended answer files in Windows 7. It uses a GUI-based interface to set up and configure the most common options that are used within an answer file.

5. C. To access the WDS server, the WDS clients must be able to access the DHCP server. Each WDS client will use an IP address from the DHCP server's scope, so you should ensure that the DHCP server has enough addresses to accommodate all of the WDS clients.

6. D. Once you have a reference computer installed, you can use the System Preparation Tool to prepare the computer to be used with disk imaging. ImageX is a utility that can be used to create a disk image after it is prepared using the System Preparation Tool. The image can then be transferred to the destination computer(s).

7. C. Unique information is stripped out of the installation image when you use the System Preparation Tool to create a disk image—for example, the unique SID that is applied to every computer. Unique information is then generated when the target computer is installed.

8. B. When you configure your WDS server, the remote installation folder should not reside on the system partition.

9. C. You enable WDS servers to respond to client requests through the Windows Deployment Services (WDS) Microsoft Management Console (MMC) snap-in. In the PXE Properties dialog box, enable the option Respond To Client Computers.

10. B. The `/generalize` options prevents system-specific information from being included in the image. The `Sysprep.exe` command can be used with a variety of options. You can see a complete list by typing `sysprep /?` at a command-line prompt.

11. D. ImageX is a command-line utility that can be used to create and manage Windows 7 image (`.wim`) files. You can configure a reference installation as desired and then use ImageX to create an image of the installation that can then be deployed to the remaining computers.

12. A. SIM is a graphical utility that can be used to create an answer file. Answer files can be used to automate the installation routine so that no user interaction is required.

13. A. The `/unattend` option can be used with the `Setup.exe` command to initiate an unattended installation of Windows 7. You should also specify the location of the answer file to use when using the `Setup.exe` utility.

14. B. You can use the SIM tool to validate an answer file, even if the answer file was manually created in a text editor.

15. D. During a DVD-based setup, an answer file can be used to automate the installation process. The Windows Setup program implicitly searches for an answer file in several locations, including the root of the DVD.

16. C. You would configure formatting and partitioning information in the Windows PE component of the answer file. The options specified in this configuration pass will occur before the image will be copied to the local computer.

17. A. To deploy the Windows 7 image using ImageX, you will need to use the `/apply` option. This option applies the selected image to a specified drive volume.

18. B. You should use the `/copy` option of the WDSUTIL utility to copy an image from the image store.

19. D. The specialize component of the answer file will contain information specific to the target computer, such as domain information and network settings.

20. B. To create a Windows 7 image from a reference computer using the ImageX utility, you should use the `/capture` option. This option captures the image into a new WIM file.

Managing Disks

MICROSOFT EXAM OBJECTIVES COVERED IN THIS CHAPTER:

✓ **Manage disks.**

- This objective may include but is not limited to: managing disk volumes; managing system fragmentation; RAID; removable device policies

As you've probably noticed, there are not many objectives that are required for the Microsoft Windows 7 (70-680) exam in this chapter, but this is a very important topic. Not only is managing disks important for the exam, but properly configuring your hard disks is a task that every IT professional should know how to accomplish, because an improperly configured hard disk can cause many issues for an IT team.

When you install Windows 7, you designate the initial configuration for your disks. Through Windows 7's utilities and features, you can change that configuration and perform disk-management tasks.

For file system configuration, it is recommended that you use NTFS, although you could also format the disk drive as FAT32. You can also update a FAT32 partition to NTFS. This chapter covers the features of each file system and how to use the Convert utility to upgrade to NTFS.

Another factor in disk management is choosing the configuration for your physical drives. Windows 7 supports basic, dynamic, and GPT disks. When you install Windows 7 or upgrade from Windows 7 using basic disks, the drives are configured as basic disks. Dynamic disks are supported by Windows 7, Windows Vista, Windows XP Professional, Windows 2000 (all versions), Windows Server 2003, and Windows Server 2008 and allow you to create simple volumes, spanned volumes, and striped volumes.

Once you decide how your disks should be configured, you implement the disk configurations through the Disk Management utility. This utility helps you view and manage your physical disks and volumes. In this chapter, you will learn how to manage both types of storage and how to upgrade from basic storage to dynamic storage. The other disk-management features covered in this chapter are data compression, data encryption, disk defragmentation, disk cleanup, and disk error checking.

Configuring File Systems

Each partition (each logical drive that is created on your hard drive) you create under Windows 7 must have a file system associated with it.

When selecting a file system, you can select FAT32 or NTFS. You typically select file systems based on the features you want to use and whether you will need to access the file system using other operating systems. If you have a FAT32 partition and want to update it to NTFS, you can use the Convert utility. The features of each filesystem and the procedure for converting file systems are covered in the following sections.

File System Selection

Your file system is used to store and retrieve the files stored on your hard drive. One of the most fundamental choices associated with file management is the choice of your file system's configuration. It is recommended that you use NTFS with Windows 7 because doing so will allow you to take advantage of features such as local security, file compression, and file encryption. You should choose FAT32 if you want to dual-boot your computer with a version of Windows that does not support NTFS, because these file systems are backward compatible with other operating systems.

Table 3.1 summarizes the capabilities of each file system, and they are described in more detail in the following sections.

TABLE 3.1 File system capabilities

Feature	FAT32	NTFS
Supporting operating systems	Windows 95 OSR2, Windows 98, Windows ME, Windows 2000, Windows XP, Windows Server 2003, Windows Server 2008, Windows Vista, and Windows 7	Windows NT, Windows 2000, Windows XP, Windows Server 2003, Windows Vista, and Windows 7
Long filename support	Yes	Yes
Efficient use of disk space	Yes	Yes
Compression support	No	Yes
Encryption support	No	Yes
Support for local security	No	Yes
Support for network security	Yes	Yes
Maximum volume size	32 GB	16 TB with 4 KB clusters or 256 TB with 64 KB clusters

Windows 7 also supports Compact Disk File System (CDFS). However, CDFS cannot be managed. It is used only to mount and read CDs. Let's start looking at the supported file systems.

FAT32

FAT32 is an updated version of File Allocation Table (FAT). The FAT32 version was first shipped with Windows 95 OSR2 (Operating System Release 2) and can be used by Windows 7.

One of the main advantages of FAT32 is its support for smaller cluster sizes, which results in more efficient space allocation than was possible with FAT16. Files stored on a FAT32 partition can use 20 to 30 percent less disk space than files stored on a FAT16 partition. FAT32 supports drive sizes from 512 MB up to 2 TB, although if you create and format a FAT32 partition through Windows 7, the FAT32 partition can only be up to 32 GB. Because of the smaller cluster sizes, FAT32 can also load programs up to 50 percent faster than programs loaded from FAT16 partitions.

The main disadvantages of FAT32 compared to NTFS are that it does not provide as much support for larger hard drives and it does not provide very robust security options. It also offers no native support for disk compression. Now that you understand FAT32, let's take a look at NTFS.

NTFS

NTFS, which was first used with the NT operating system, offers the highest level of service and features for Windows 7 computers. NTFS partitions can be up to 16 TB with 4 KB clusters or 256 TB with 64 KB clusters.

NTFS offers comprehensive folder- and file-level security. This allows you to set an additional level of security for users who access the files and folders locally or through the network. For example, two users who share the same Windows 7 computer can be assigned different NTFS permissions so that one user has access to a folder but the other user is denied access to that folder.

NTFS also offers disk-management features—such as compression and encryption services—and data recovery features. The disk-management features are covered later in this chapter. The data-recovery features are covered in Chapter 8, "Monitoring and Maintaining Windows 7."

You should also be aware that there are several different versions of NTFS. Every version of Windows 2000 uses NTFS 3.0. Windows 7, Windows Vista, Windows XP, and Windows Server 2003 use NTFS 3.1. NTFS versions 3.0 and 3.1 use similar disk formats, so Windows 2000 computers can access NTFS 3.1 volumes and Windows 7 computers can access NTFS 3.0 volumes. NTFS 3.1 includes the following features:

- When files are read or written to a disk, they can be automatically encrypted and decrypted.
- Reparse points are used with mount points to redirect data as it is written or read from a folder to another volume or physical disk.
- There is support for sparse files, which is used by programs that create large files but allocate disk space only as needed.
- Remote storage allows you to extend your disk space by making removable media (for example, external tapes) more accessible.
- You can use recovery logging on NTFS metadata, which is used for data recovery when a power failure or system problem occurs.

Now that you have seen the differences between FAT32 and NTFS, let's discuss how to change a FAT32 drive to a NTFS drive.

File System Conversion

In Windows 7, you can convert FAT32 partitions to NTFS. File system conversion is the process of converting one file system to another without the loss of data. If you format a drive as another file system, as opposed to converting it, all the data on that drive will be lost.

To convert a partition, you use the Convert command-line utility. The syntax for the Convert command is as follows:

```
Convert [drive:] /fs:ntfs
```

For example, if you wanted to convert your D: drive to NTFS, you would type the following from a command prompt:

```
Convert D: /fs:ntfs
```

When the conversion process begins, it will attempt to lock the partition. If the partition cannot be locked—perhaps because it contains the Windows 7 operating system files or the system's page file—the conversion will not take place until the computer is restarted.

In Exercise 3.1, you will convert your D: drive from FAT32 to NTFS. For this exercise, it is assumed that you have a D: drive that is formatted with the FAT32 file system.

Using the Convert Command

You can use the /v switch with the Convert command. This switch specifies that you want to use verbose mode, and all messages will be displayed during the conversion process. You can also use the /NoSecurity switch, which specifies that all converted files and folders will have no security applied by default so they can be accessed by anyone.

EXERCISE 3.1

Converting a FAT32 Partition to NTFS

1. Copy some folders to the D: drive.
2. Select Start, then type `cmd` into the Search box to open a command prompt.
3. In the Command Prompt dialog box, type Convert **D: /fs:ntfs** and press Enter.
4. After the conversion process is complete, close the Command Prompt dialog box.
5. Verify that the folders you copied in step 1 still exist on the partition.

Stopping a Conversion

If you choose to convert a partition from FAT32 to NTFS, and the conversion has not yet taken place, you can cancel the conversion by editing the Registry with the REGEDIT or REGEDT32 commands. The key that needs to be edited is:

`HKEY_LOCAL_MACHINE\System\CurrentControlSet\Control\SessionManager.`

The BootExecute value needs to be changed from autoconv `\DosDevices\x: /FS:NTFS` to `autocheck autochk*`.

After you decide which file system you want to use, you need to decide what disk storage type you want to configure. Let's take a look at some of the disk storage options you have.

Configuring Disk Storage

Windows 7 supports three types of disk storage: basic, dynamic, and GUID partition table (GPT). Basic storage is backward compatible with other operating systems and can be configured to support up to four partitions. Dynamic storage is supported by Windows 2000, Windows XP, Windows Server 2003, Windows Server 2008, Windows Vista, and Windows 7 and allows storage to be configured as volumes. GPT storage allows you to configure volume sizes larger than 2 TB and up to 128 primary partitions. The following sections describe the basic storage, dynamic storage, and GPT storage configurations.

Basic Storage

Basic storage consists of primary and extended partitions and logical drives. The first partition that is created on a hard drive is called a primary partition and is usually represented as the C: drive. Primary partitions use all of the space that is allocated to the partition, and a single drive letter is used to represent the partition. Each physical drive can have up to four partitions and only four partitions. You can set up four primary partitions, or you can have three primary partitions and one extended partition. With an extended partition, you can allocate the space however you like, and each suballocation of space (called a logical drive) is represented by a different drive letter. For example, a 500 MB extended partition could have a 250MB D: partition and a 250MB E: partition.

At the highest level of disk organization, you have a physical hard drive. You cannot use space on the physical drive until you have logically partitioned the physical drive. A partition is a logical definition of hard drive space.

One of the advantages of using multiple partitions on a single physical hard drive is that each partition can have a different file system. For example, the C: drive might be FAT32 and the D: drive might be NTFS. Multiple partitions also make it easier to manage security requirements.

Basic storage is the default, and this is the type that many users continue to use. But what if you want some additional functionality from your storage type? Let's take a look at some of the more advanced disk storage options.

Dynamic Storage

Dynamic storage is a Windows 7 feature that consists of a dynamic disk divided into dynamic volumes. Dynamic volumes cannot contain partitions or logical drives.

Dynamic storage supports three dynamic volume types: simple volumes, spanned volumes, and striped volumes. Dynamic storage also supports Redundant Array of Independent Disks (RAID).

To set up dynamic storage, you create or upgrade a basic disk to a dynamic disk. When converting a basic disk to dynamic, you do not lose any of your data. After the disk is converted, you can then create dynamic volumes within the dynamic disk.

You create dynamic storage with the Windows 7 Disk Management utility, which is discussed after the descriptions of the dynamic volume types. Let's take a closer look at the different types of dynamic volumes.

Simple Volumes

A *simple volume* contains space from a single dynamic drive. The space from the single drive can be contiguous or noncontiguous. Simple volumes are used when you have enough disk space on a single drive to hold your entire volume. Figure 3.1 illustrates two simple volumes on a physical disk.

FIGURE 3.1 Two simple volumes

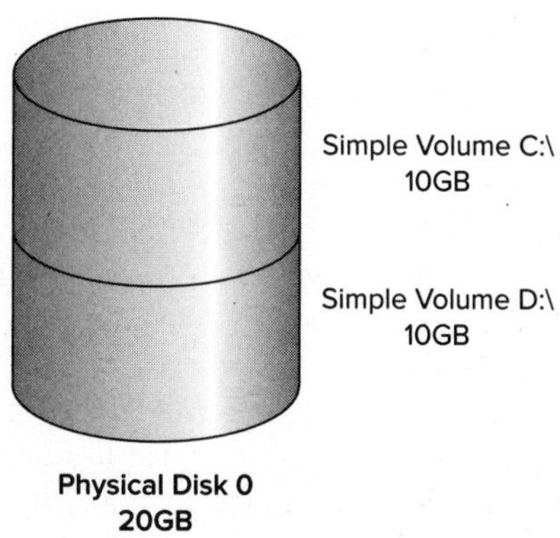

Spanned Volumes

A *spanned volume* consists of disk space on two or more dynamic drives; up to 32 dynamic drives can be used in a spanned volume configuration. Spanned volume sets are used to dynamically increase the size of a dynamic volume. When you create spanned volumes, the data is written sequentially, filling space on one physical drive before writing to space on the next physical drive in the spanned volume set. Typically, administrators use spanned volumes when they are running out of disk space on a volume and want to dynamically extend the volume with space from another hard drive.

You do not need to allocate the same amount of space to the volume set on each physical drive. This means you could combine a 500MB partition on one physical drive with two 750MB partitions on other dynamic drives, as shown in Figure 3.2.

FIGURE 3.2 A spanned volume set

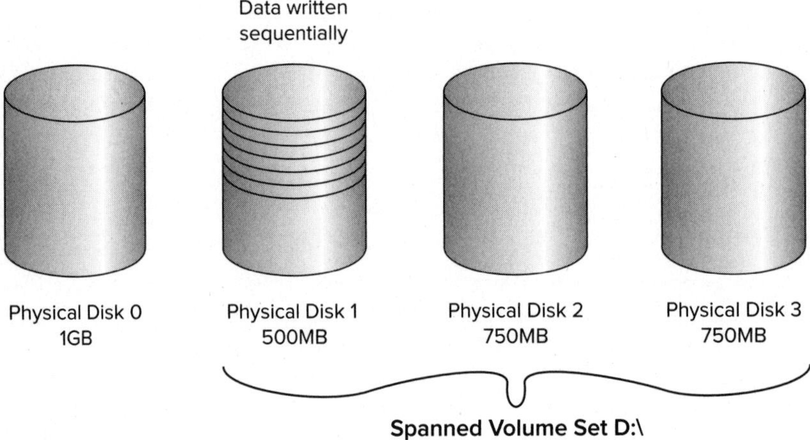

Because data is written sequentially, you do not see any performance enhancements with spanned volumes as you do with striped volumes (discussed next). The main disadvantage of spanned volumes is that if any drive in the spanned volume set fails, you lose access to all of the data in the spanned set.

Striped Volumes

A *striped volume* stores data in equal stripes between two or more (up to 32) dynamic drives, as illustrated in Figure 3.3. Since the data is written sequentially in the stripes, you can take advantage of multiple I/O performance and increase the speed at which data reads and writes take place. Typically, administrators use striped volumes when they want to combine the space of several physical drives into a single logical volume and increase disk performance.

FIGURE 3.3 A striped volume set

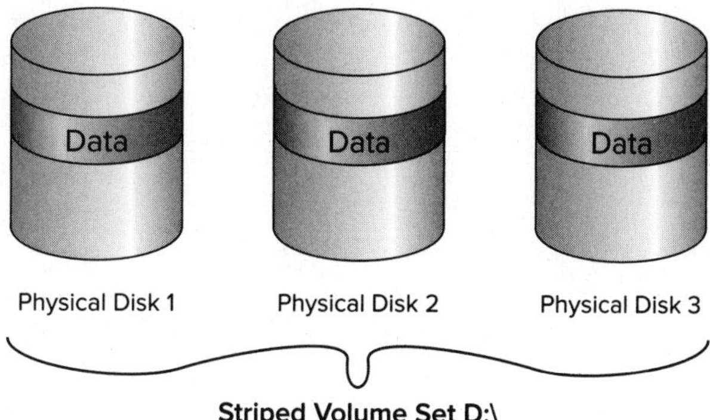

The main disadvantage of striped volumes is that if any drive in the striped volume set fails, you lose access to all of the data in the striped set.

In the last few years a new storage type has emerged in the Microsoft computer world, and as with most new technologies, it also has some advantages over the previous technologies. Let's take a look at the newest advantage to storage types.

GUID Partition Table (GPT)

The *GUID Partition Table (GPT)* is available for Windows 7 and was first introduced as part of the Extensible Firmware Interface (EFI) initiative from Intel. Basic and dynamic disks use the Master Boot Record (MBR) partitioning scheme that all operating systems have been using for years. Basic and Dynamic disks use Cylinder-Head-Sector (CHS) addressing with the MBR scheme.

The GPT disk partitioning system uses the GUID Partition Table to configure the disk area. GPT uses a newer addressing scheme called Logical Block Addressing (LBA). Another advantage is that the GPT header and partition table is written to both the front and the back end of the disk, which in turn provides for better redundancy.

The GPT disk partitioning system gives you many benefits over using the MBR system:

- Allows a volume size larger than 2 TB
- Allow up to 128 primary partitions
- Used for both 32-bit or 64-bit Windows 7 editions
- Includes Cyclical Redundancy Check (CRC) for greater reliability

This is one disadvantage to using the GPT drives. You can convert a GPT drive only if the disk is empty and unpartitioned. I will show you the steps to creating a GPT disk later in this chapter.

To convert any disk or format any volume or partition, you can use the Disk Management utility. Let's take a look at how to manage your disks using the Disk Management Utility.

Using the Disk Management Utility

The Disk Management utility is a Microsoft Management Console (MMC) snap-in that gives administrators a graphical tool for managing disks and volumes within Windows 7. In this section, you will learn how to access the Disk Management utility and use it to manage basic tasks, basic storage, and dynamic storage. You will also learn about troubleshooting disks through disk status codes.

But before we dive into the Disk Management utility, let's take a look at the Microsoft Management Console (MMC). It is important to understand the MMC since Disk Management (like many other tools) is actually a MMC snap-in.

Using the Microsoft Management Console

The *Microsoft Management Console (MMC)* is the console framework for application management. The MMC provides a common environment for snap-ins. Snap-ins are administrative tools developed by Microsoft or third-party vendors. Some of the MMC snap-ins that you may use are Computer Management, Active Directory Users and Computers, Active Directory Sites and Services, Active Directory Domains and Trusts, and DNS Management.

Knowing how to use and configure the MMC snap-ins will allow you to customize your work environment. For example, if you are in charge of Active Directory Users and Computers and DNS, you can add both of these snap-ins into the same window. This would then allow you to open just one application to configure all your tasks. The MMC offers many other benefits:

- The MMC is highly customizable—you add only the snap-ins you need.
- Snap-ins use a standard, intuitive interface, so they are easier to use than previous versions of administrative utilities.
- You can save MMC consoles and share them with other administrators.
- You can configure permissions so that the MMC runs in authoring mode, which an administrator can manage, or in user mode, which limits what users can access.
- You can use most snap-ins for remote computer management.

As shown in Figure 3.4, by default the MMC console contains three panes: a console tree on the left, a details pane in the middle, and an optional Actions pane on the right. The console tree lists the hierarchical structure of all snap-ins that have been loaded into the console. The details pane contains a list of properties or other items that are part of the snap-in that is highlighted in the console tree. The Actions pane provides a list of actions that the user can access depending on the item selected in the details pane.

FIGURE 3.4 The MMC console tree, details pane, and Actions pane

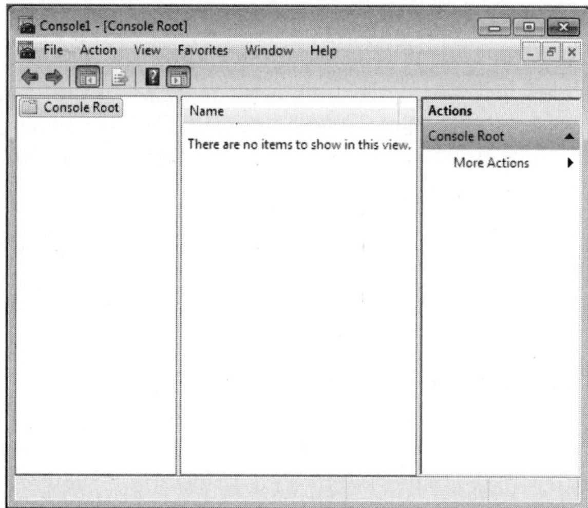

On a Windows 7 computer, to open the MMC, click the Start button and type **MMC** in the Search dialog box. When you first open the MMC, it contains only the Console Root folder, as shown in Figure 3.4. The MMC does not have any default administrative functionality. It is simply a framework used to organize administrative tools through the addition of snap-in utilities.

The first thing that you should decide when using the MMC is the different administrative mode types. You need to decide which mode type is best suited to use for your organization.

Configuring MMC Modes

You can configure the MMC to run in author mode, for full access to the MMC functions, or in one of three user modes, which have more limited access to the MMC functions. To set a console mode, while in the MMC editor, select File ➢ Options to open the Options dialog box. In this dialog box, you can select from the console modes listed in Table 3.2.

TABLE 3.2 MMC console modes

Console Mode	Description
Author mode	Allows use of all the MMC functions.
User mode—full access	Gives users full access to window management commands, but they cannot add or remove snap-ins or change console properties.

TABLE 3.2 MMC console modes (*continued*)

Console Mode	Description
User mode—limited access, multiple window	Allows users to create new windows but not close any existing windows. Users can access only the areas of the console tree that were visible when the console was last saved.
User mode—limited access, single window	Allows users to access only the areas of the console tree that were visible when the console was last saved, and they cannot create new windows.

After you decide which administrative role you are going to run, it's time to start configuring your MMC snap-ins.

Adding Snap-Ins

The biggest advantage of using the MMC is to configure snap-ins the way your organization needs them. Adding snap-ins is a very simple and quick procedure. To add snap-ins to the MMC console and save it, complete Exercise 3.2.

EXERCISE 3.2

Adding a MMC Snap-In

1. To start the MMC editor, click Start, type **MMC** into the search box, and press Enter.
2. From the main console window, select File ➤ Add/Remove Snap-In to open the Add/Remove Snap-In dialog box.
3. Highlight the snap-in you want to add, and click the Add button.

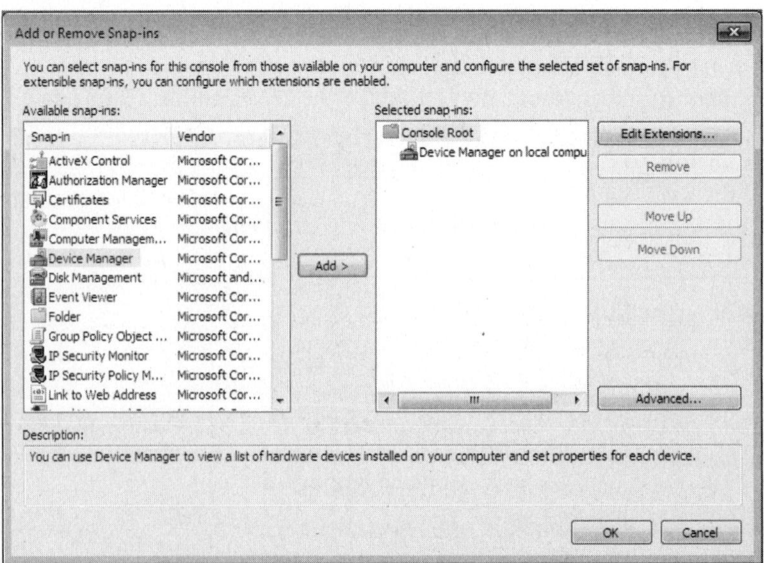

4. If prompted, specify whether the snap-in will be used to manage the local computer or a remote computer. Then click the Finish button.

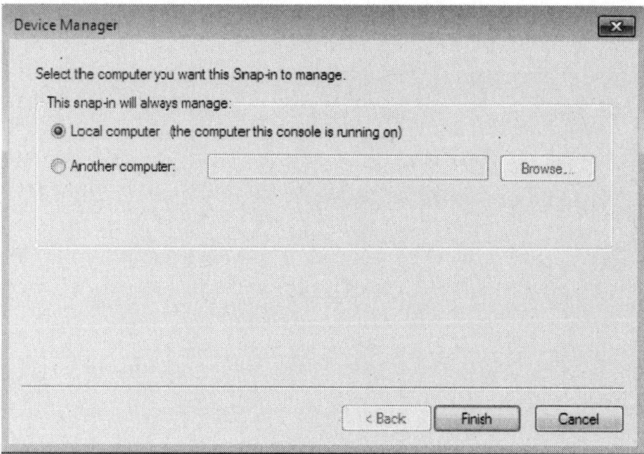

5. Repeat steps 2 and 3 to add each snap-in you want to include in your console.
6. When you have finished adding snap-ins, click OK.
7. Click OK to return to the main console screen.
8. After you have added snap-ins to create a console, you can save it by selecting File ➢ Save As and entering a name for your console.

You can save the console to a variety of locations, including a program group or the Desktop. By default, custom consoles have an `.msc` filename extension.

Many applications that are MMC snap-ins, including Disk Management, are already configured for you under the Administrative Tools section of Windows 7. Next let's take a look at the Disk Management utility.

Understanding the Disk Management Utility

The Disk Management utility, located under the Computer Management snap-in by default, is a one-stop shop for configuring your disk options.

First off, to have full permissions to use the Disk Management utility, you must be logged on with Administrative privileges. You can access the Disk Management utility a few different ways. You can right-click Computer from the Start menu and select Manage and, then in Computer Management, select Disk Management. You could also use Control Panel ➢ Administrative Tools ➢ Computer Management.

The Disk Management utility's opening window, shown in Figure 3.5, shows the following information:

- The volumes that are recognized by the computer
- The type of disk, either basic or dynamic

- The type of file system used by each partition
- The status of the partition and whether the partition contains the system or boot partition
- The capacity (amount of space) allocated to the partition
- The amount of free space remaining on the partition
- The amount of overhead associated with the partition

FIGURE 3.5 The Disk Management window

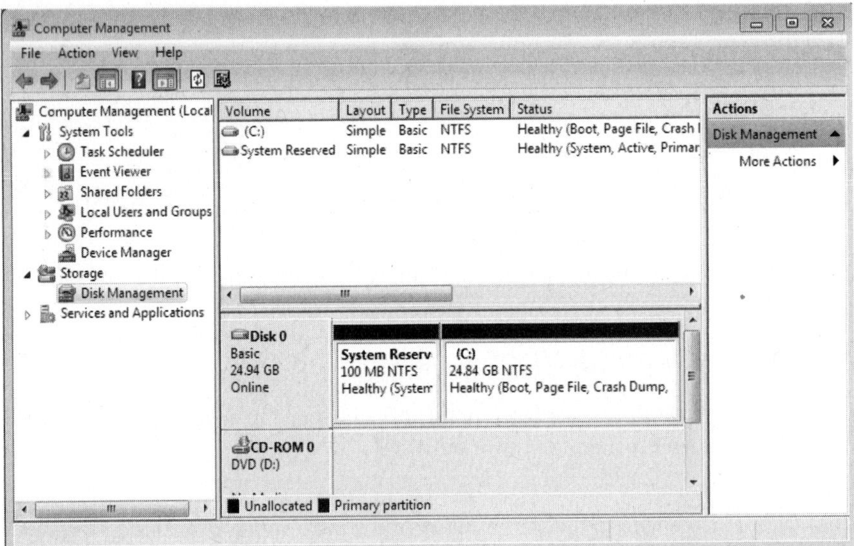

Windows 7 also includes a command-line utility called Diskpart, which can be used as a command-line alternative to the Disk Management utility. You can view all of the options associated with the Diskpart utility by typing **Diskpart** at a command prompt and then typing ? at the Diskpart prompt.

The Disk Management utility allows you to configure and manage your disks. Let's take a look at some of the tasks that you can perform in disk administration.

Managing Administrative Hard Disk Tasks

The Disk Management utility allows you to perform a variety of hard drive administrative tasks. These tasks are discussed in the sections that follow:

- View disk properties.
- View volume and local disk properties.
- Add a new disk.
- Create partitions and volumes.

- Upgrade a basic disk to a dynamic disk.
- Change a drive letter and path.
- Delete partitions and volumes.

Viewing Disk Properties

To view the properties of a disk, right-click the disk number in the lower panel of the Disk Management main window and choose Properties from the context menu. This brings up the disk's Properties dialog box. Click the Volumes tab to see the volumes associated with the disk, as shown in Figure 3.6, which contains the following disk properties:

- The disk number
- The type of disk (basic, dynamic, CD-ROM, removable, DVD, or unknown)
- The status of the disk (online or offline)
- The capacity of the disk
- The amount of unallocated space on the disk
- The logical volumes that have been defined on the physical drive

FIGURE 3.6 The Volumes tab of a disk's Properties dialog box

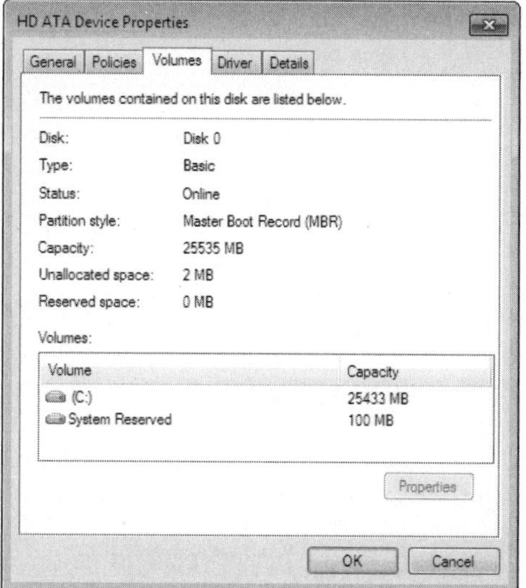

If you click the General tab of a disk's Properties dialog box, the hardware device type, the hardware vendor that produced the drive, the physical location of the drive, and the device status are displayed.

Viewing Volume and Local Disk Properties

On a dynamic disk, you manage volume properties. On a basic disk, you manage partition properties. Volumes and partitions perform the same function, and the options discussed in the following sections apply to both. (The examples here are based on a dynamic disk using a simple volume. If you are using basic storage, you will view the local disk properties rather than the volume properties.)

To see the properties of a volume, right-click the volume in the upper panel of the Disk Management main window and choose Properties. This brings up the volume's Properties dialog box. Volume properties are organized on seven tabs: General, Tools, Hardware, Sharing, Security, Quotas, and Previous Versions. The Security tab and Quotas tab appear only for NTFS volumes. All these tabs are covered in detail in the following sections.

General The information on the General tab of the volume's Properties dialog box, as seen in Figure 3.7, gives you a general idea of how the volume is configured. This dialog box shows the label, type, file system, used and free space, and capacity of the volume. The label is shown in an editable text box, and you can change it if desired. The space allocated to the volume is shown in a graphical representation as well as in text form.

FIGURE 3.7 General properties for a volume

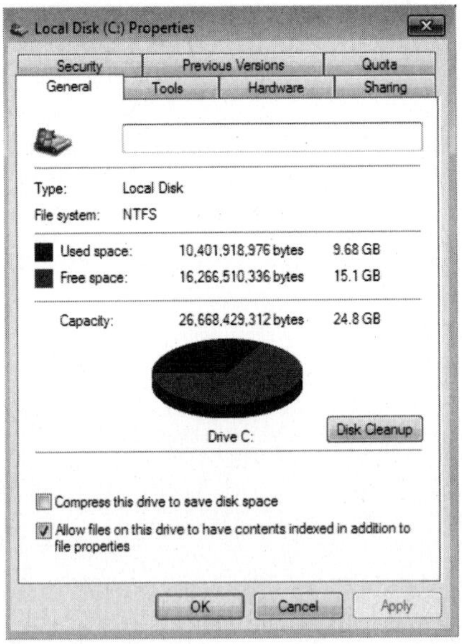

The label on a volume or local disk is for informational purposes only. For example, depending on its use, you might give a volume a label such as APPS or ACCTDB.

The Disk Cleanup button starts the Disk Cleanup utility, which you can use to delete unnecessary files and free disk space. This utility is discussed later in this chapter in the section "Using the Disk Cleanup Utility."

This tab also allows you to configure compression for the volume and to indicate whether the volume should be indexed.

Tools The Tools tab of the volume's Properties dialog box, shown in Figure 3.8, provides access to three tools.

FIGURE 3.8 The Tools tab of the volume's Properties dialog box

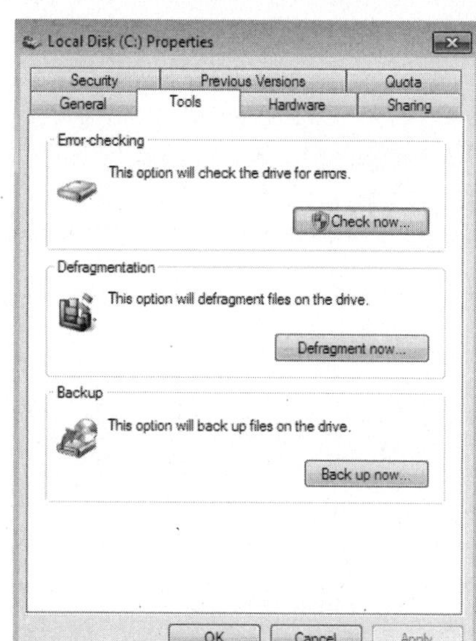

Click the Check Now button to run the Error-checking utility to check the volume for errors. You would do this if you were experiencing problems accessing the volume or if the volume had been open during a system restart that did not go through a proper shutdown sequence. This utility is covered in more detail in "Troubleshooting Disk Management" later in this chapter.

Click the Defragment Now button to run the Disk Defragmenter utility. This utility defragments files on the volume by storing the files contiguously on the hard drive. Defragmentation is discussed later in this chapter, in the section "Using the Disk Defragmenter Utility."

Click the Back Up Now button to open the Backup Status And Configuration dialog box, which allows you to configure backup procedures.

Hardware The Hardware tab of the volume's Properties dialog box, shown in Figure 3.9, lists the hardware associated with the disk drives that are recognized by the Windows 7 operating system. The bottom half of the dialog box shows the properties of the device that is highlighted in the top half of the dialog box.

FIGURE 3.9 The Hardware tab of the volume's Properties dialog box

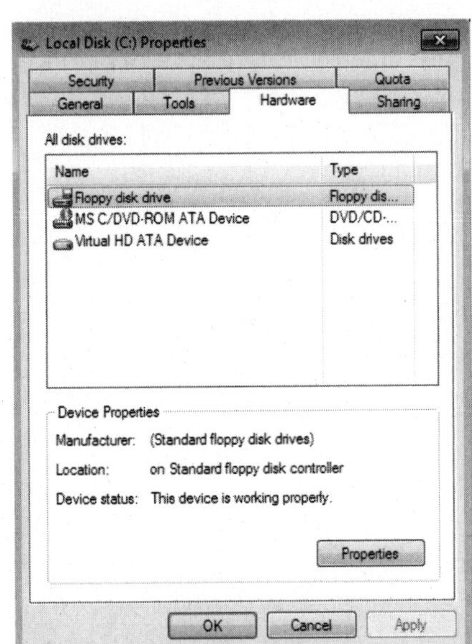

For more details about a hardware item, highlight it and click the Properties button in the lower-right corner of the dialog box. This brings up a Properties dialog box for the item. Your Device Status field should report that "this device is working properly." If that's not the case, you can click the Troubleshoot button to get a troubleshooting wizard that will help you discover the problem.

Sharing On the Sharing tab of the volume's Properties dialog box, shown in Figure 3.10, you can specify whether or not the volume is shared. Volumes are not shared by default. To share a volume, you can click the Advanced Sharing button, which will allow you to specify whether the volume is shared and, if so, what the name of the share should be. You will also be able to specify who will have access to the shared volume.

FIGURE 3.10 The Sharing tab of the volume's Properties dialog box

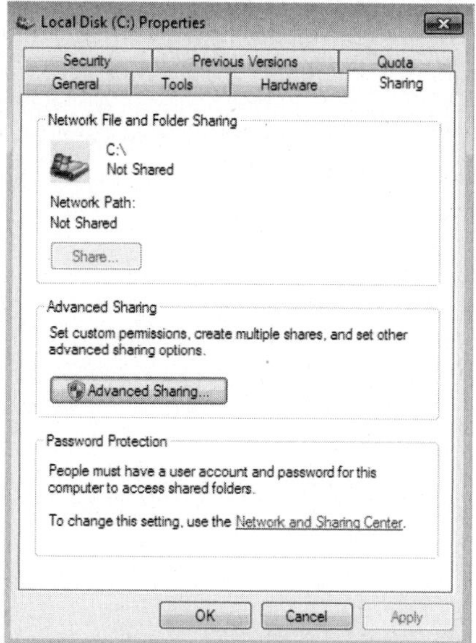

Security The Security tab of the volume's Properties dialog box, shown in Figure 3.11, appears only for NTFS volumes. The Security tab is used to set the NTFS permissions for the volume.

FIGURE 3.11 The Security tab of the volume's Properties dialog box

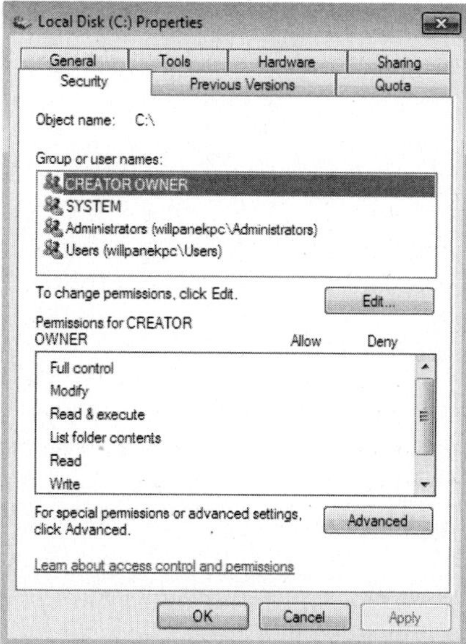

Previous Versions The Previous Versions tab displays shadow copies of the files that are created by System Restore, as shown in Figure 3.12. Shadow copies of files are backup copies created by Windows in the background to allow you to restore the system to a previous state. On the Previous Versions tab, you can select a copy of the volume and either view the contents of the shadow copy or copy the shadow copy to another location. If System Restore is not enabled, then shadow copies of a volume will not be created.

FIGURE 3.12 The Previous Versions tab of the volume's Properties dialog box

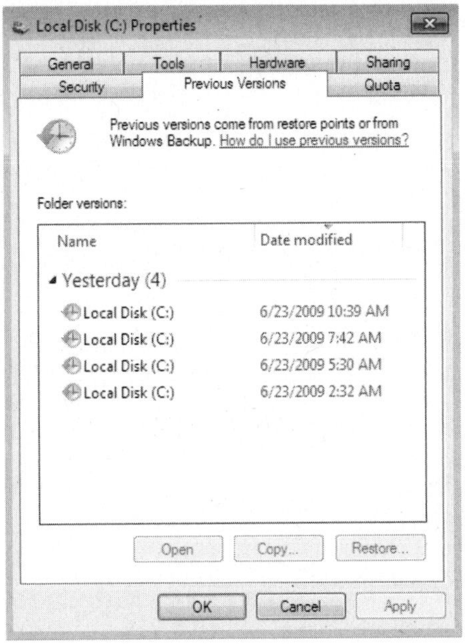

Quotas Quotas give you the advantage to limit the amount of hard disk space that a user can have on a volume or partition (see Figure 3.13). There are a few options that can be configured when enabling quotas. By default, quotas are disabled. To enable quotas, check the Enable Quota Management check box.

FIGURE 3.13 The Quota tab of the volume's Properties dialog box

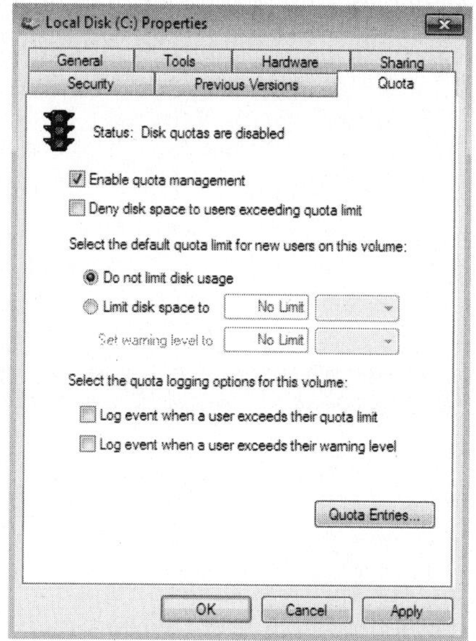

The Deny Disk Space To Users Exceeding Quota Limit check box is another option. When this box is enabled, any user who exceeds their quota limit will be denied disk storage. You can choose not to enable this option, which allows you to just monitor the quotas. You also have the ability to set the quota limit and warning size. You can also log all quota events as they happen.

Adding a New Disk

New hard disks can be added to a system to increase the amount of disk storage you have. This is a fairly common task that you will need to perform as your application programs and files grow larger.

How you add a disk depends on whether your computer supports hot swapping of drives. Hot swapping is the process of adding a new hard drive while the computer is turned on. Most desktop computers do not support this capability. Remember, your user account must be a member of the Administrators group to install a new drive. The following list specifies configuration options:

Computer doesn't support hot swapping If your computer does not support hot swapping, you must shut down the computer before you add a new disk. Then add the drive according to the manufacturer's directions. When you've finished, restart the computer. You should find the new drive listed in the Disk Management utility.

Computer supports hot swapping If your computer does support hot swapping, you don't need to turn off your computer first. Just add the drive according to the manufacturer's directions. Then open the Disk Management utility and select Action ➢ Rescan Disks. You should find the new drive listed in the Disk Management utility.

Creating Partitions and Volumes Once you add a new disk, the next step is to create a partition (on a basic disk) or a volume (on a dynamic disk). Partitions and volumes fill similar roles in the storage of data on disks, and the processes for creating them are the same.

Creating a Volume or a Partition

Creating a volume or partition is a fairly easy process. To create the new volume or partition, you right-click on the unformatted free space and start the wizard.

Exercise 3.3 walks you through the New Volume Wizard for creating a new volume.

EXERCISE 3.3

Creating a New Volume

1. In the Disk Management utility, right-click an area of free storage space and choose the type of volume to create. If only one drive is installed, you will be able to create only a simple volume. You can click New Simple Volume to create a new simple volume.
2. The Welcome To The New Simple Volume Wizard appears. Click the Next button to continue.
3. The Select Volume Size screen appears. Select the size of volume to create, and then click Next to continue.
4. Next you see the Assign Drive Letter Or Path screen. You can specify a drive letter, mount the volume as an empty folder, or choose not to assign a drive letter or drive path. If you choose to mount the volume as an empty folder, you can have an unlimited number of volumes, negating the drive-letter limitation. If you choose not to assign a drive letter or path, users will not be able to access the volume. Make your selections, and click Next to continue.

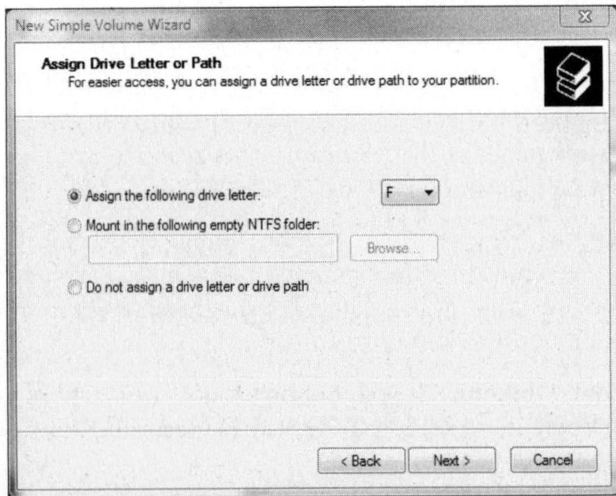

5. The Format Partition screen appears. This screen allows you to choose whether you will format the volume. If you choose to format the volume, you can format it as FAT32 or NTFS. You can also select the allocation block size, enter a volume label (for information only), specify a quick format, or choose to enable file and folder compression. After you've made your choices, click Next.

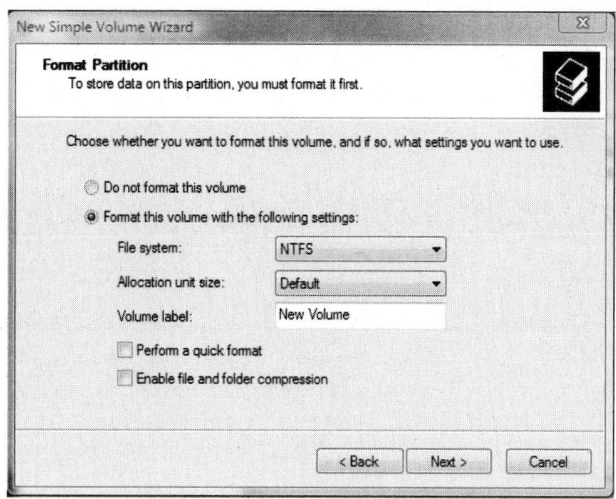

6. The Completing The New Volume Wizard screen appears next. Verify your selections. If you need to change any of them, click the Back button to reach the appropriate screen. When everything is correctly set, click the Finish button.

Now that you know how to create a new volume or partition, let's take a look at how to convert a basic disk to dynamic or GPT.

Upgrading a Basic Disk to a Dynamic or GPT Disk

When you install a fresh installation of Windows 7, your drives are configured as basic disks. To take advantage of the features offered by Windows 7 dynamic or GPT disks, you must upgrade your basic disks to either dynamic or GPT disks.

Upgrading basic disks to dynamic disks is a one-way process as far as preserving data is concerned and is a potentially dangerous operation. Before you perform this upgrade (or make any major change to your drives or volumes), create a new backup of the drive or volume and verify that you can successfully restore the backup.

Any basic partition can be converted to a dynamic disk but only unformatted free space can be converted to a GPT disk. Exercise 3.4 walks you through how to convert a drive to a GPT.

EXERCISE 3.4

Converting a Drive to a GPT Disk

1. If the volume or partition that you want to convert has data, first delete the partition or volume.
2. Open the Disk Management utility by clicking the Start button, right-clicking Computers, and choosing Manage.
3. Click Disk Management in the lower-left section.
4. Right-click the drive letter and choose Convert To GPT Disk.

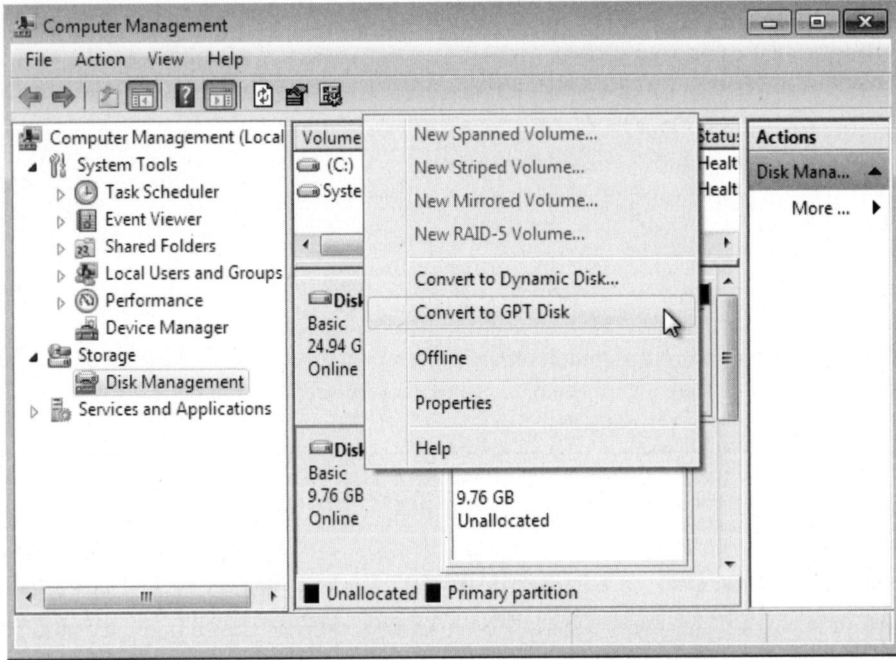

5. After the disk converts, you can right-click on the disk and see that the Convert To MBR Disk is now available.

There are a few other methods for converting a basic disk to a GPT disk. You can use the Diskpart utility and type in the Convert GPT command. You can also create a GPT disk when you first install a new hard drive. After you install the new hard drive, during the initialization phase, you can choose GPT disk.

Another type of conversion that you may need to perform is converting a basic disk to a dynamic disk. Complete exercise 3.5 to convert a basic disk to a dynamic disk.

EXERCISE 3.5

Converting a Basic Disk to a Dynamic Disk

1. In the Disk Management utility, right-click the disk you want to convert and select the Convert To Dynamic Disk option.
2. In the Convert To Dynamic Disk dialog box, check the disk that you want to convert and click OK.
3. In the Disks To Convert dialog box, click the Convert button.
4. A confirmation dialog box warns you that you will no longer be able to boot previous versions of Windows from this disk. Click the Yes button to continue to convert the disk.

As you are configuring the volumes or partitions on the hard drive, another thing that you may need to configure is the drive letter and paths.

Changing the Drive Letter and Path

There may be times when you need to change drive letters and paths when you add new equipment. Let's suppose you have a hard drive with two partitions: drive C: assigned as your first partition and drive D: assigned as your second partition. Your DVD is assigned the drive letter E:. You add a new hard drive and partition it as a new volume. By default, the new partition is assigned as drive F:. If you want your logical drives to be listed before the DVD drive, you can use the Disk Management utility's Change Drive Letter And Paths option to rearrange your drive letters.

When you need to reassign drive letters, right-click the volume for which you want to change the drive letter and choose Change Drive Letter And Paths. This brings up the dialog box shown in Figure 3.14. Click the Change button to access the Change Drive Letter Or Path dialog box (Figure 3.15). Use the drop-down list next to the Assign The Following Drive Letter option to select the drive letter you want to assign to the volume.

FIGURE 3.14 The dialog box for changing a drive letter or path

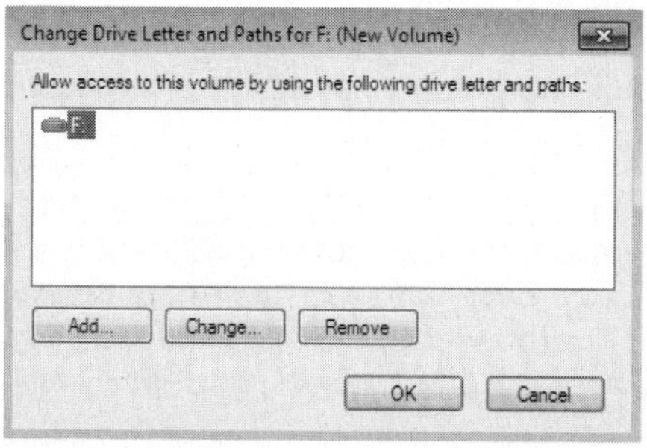

FIGURE 3.15 Editing the drive letter

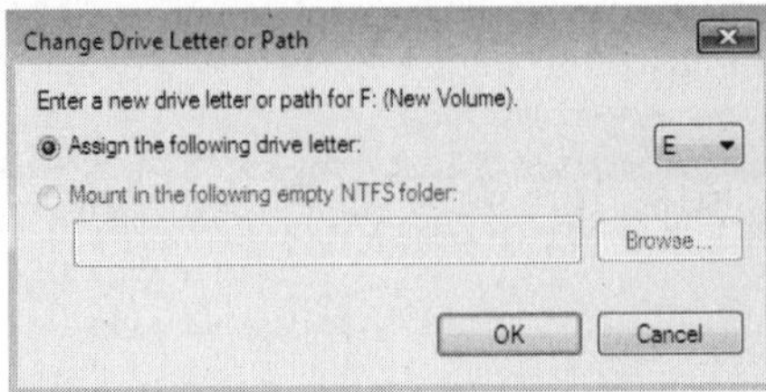

In Exercise 3.6, you will edit the drive letter of the partition you created.

EXERCISE 3.6

Editing a Drive Letter

1. Select Start ➢ Control Panel ➢ System and Maintenance ➢ Administrative Tools. Double-click Computer Management; then expand Storage and then Disk Management.
2. Right-click a drive that you have created and select Change Drive Letter And Paths.
3. In the Change Drive Letter And Paths dialog box, click the Change button.
4. In the Change Drive Letter Or Path dialog box, select a new drive letter and click OK.
5. In the dialog box that appears, click the Yes button to confirm that you want to change the drive letter.

Another task that you may need to perform is deleting a partition or volume that you have created. The next section looks at these tasks.

Deleting Partitions and Volumes

When configuring your hard disks, there may be a time that you want to reconfigure your drive by deleting the partitions or volumes on the hard drive. You may also want to delete a volume so that you can extend another volume. These are tasks that can be configured in Disk Management.

When deleting a volume or partition, you will see a warning that all the data on the partition or volume will be lost. You have to click Yes to confirm that you want to delete the volume or partition. This confirmation is important because once you delete a partition or volume, it's gone for good.

The system volume, the boot volume, or any volume that contains the active paging (swap) file can't be deleted through the Disk Management utility. If you are trying to remove these partitions because you want to delete Windows 7, you can use a third-party disk-management utility.

In the Exercise 3.7, you will delete a partition that you have created. Make sure that if you delete a partition or volume, it is an empty partition or volume or back up all the data before the deletion.

EXERCISE 3.7

Deleting a Partition

1. In the Disk Management utility, right-click the volume or partition that you want to remove and choose Delete Volume.
2. A warning box appears stating that once this volume is deleted, all data will be lost. Click Yes.
3. The volume will be removed and the area will be returned as unformatted free space.

You may be worried about your users removing devices from their Windows 7 machines. Microsoft has helped you in this situation. You can use removable device policies to help restrict your users from removing their hardware. Removable device policies can be created through the use of a group policy object (GPO) on the server. GPOs are policies that are set on a computer or user and allow you to manipulate the Windows 7 environment.

Group Policy Objects are discussed in greater detail in Chapter 6, "Managing Users, Groups, and Security.

Now that we have looked at some of the basic tasks of Disk Management, let's take a look at how to manage storage.

Managing Storage

The Disk Management utility offers support for managing storage. You can create, delete, and format partitions or volumes on your hard drives. You can also extend or shrink volumes on dynamic disks. Additionally, you can delete volume sets and striped sets. The first topic I am going to cover is dynamic storage and volumes.

Managing Dynamic Storage

As noted earlier in this chapter, a dynamic disk can contain simple, spanned, or striped volumes. Through the Disk Management utility, you can create volumes of each type. You can also create an extended volume, which is the process of adding disk space to a single simple volume. The following sections describe these disk-management tasks.

Creating Simple, Spanned, and Striped Volumes

As explained earlier, you use the New Volume Wizard to create a new volume. To start the New Volume Wizard, in the Disk Management utility right-click an area of free space where you want to create the volume. Then, you can choose the type of volume you want to create: simple, spanned, or striped.

When you choose to create a spanned volume, you are creating a new volume from scratch that includes space from two or more physical drives, up to a maximum of 32 drives.

When you choose to create a striped volume, you are creating a new volume that combines free space from 2 to 32 drives into a single logical partition. The free space on all drives must be equal in size. Data in the striped volume is written across all drives in 64 KB stripes. (Data in spanned and extended volumes is written sequentially.)

Striped volumes are RAID-0 because striped volumes do not offer any type of redundancy. Striped volumes offer you better performance and are normally used for temporary files or folders. The problem with a striped volume is if you lose one of the drives in the volume, the entire striped volume is lost.

Another option that you have with volumes is extending the volumes to create a larger storage area. In the next section we will look at extending volumes.

Creating Extended Volumes

When you create an extended volume, you are taking a single, simple volume (maybe one that is almost out of disk space) and adding more disk space to it, using free space that exists on the same physical hard drive. When the volume is extended, it is seen as a single drive letter. To extend a volume, the simple volume must be formatted as NTFS. You cannot extend a system or boot partition.

An extended volume assumes that you are using only one physical drive. A spanned volume assumes that you are using two or more physical drives. Exercise 3.8 shows you how to create an extended volume.

EXERCISE 3.8

Creating an Extended Volume

1. In the Disk Management utility, right-click the volume you want to extend and choose Extend Volume.
2. The Extend Volume Wizard starts. Click Next.
3. The Select Disks screen appears. You can specify the maximum size of the extended volume. The maximum size you can specify is determined by the amount of free space that exists in all of the dynamic drives on your computer. Click Next to continue.

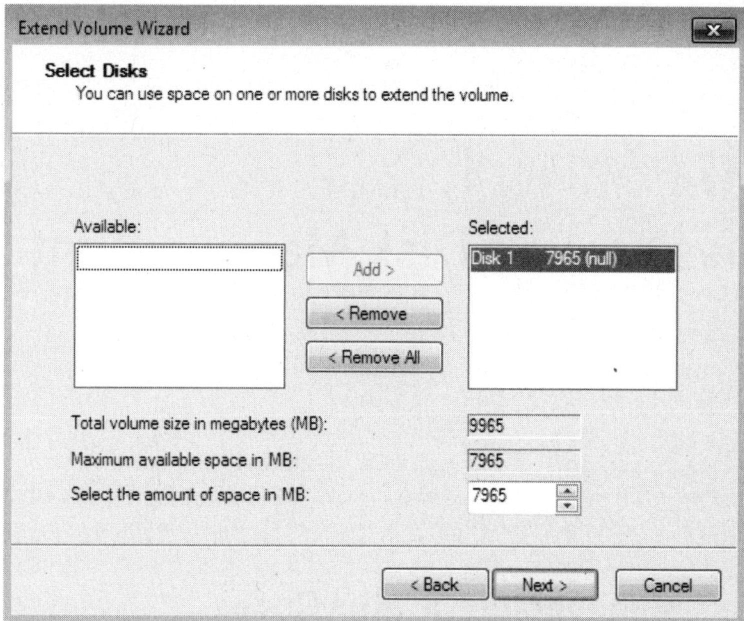

4. The Completing The Extend Volume Wizard screen appears. Click the Finish button.

Once a volume is extended, no portion of the volume can be deleted without losing data on the entire set. (However, you can shrink a volume without losing data by using the Shrink Volume option in Disk Management.)

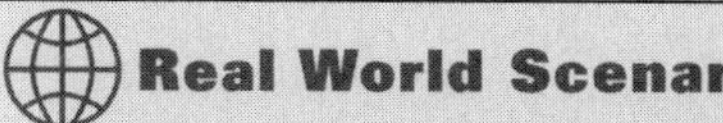

Real World Scenario

You're Running Out of Disk Space

Crystal, a user on your network, is running out of disk space. The situation needs to be corrected so she can be brought back up and running as quickly as possible. Crystal has a 250 GB drive (C:) that runs a very large customer database. She needs additional space added to the C: drive so the database will recognize the data because it must be stored on a single drive letter. Crystal's computer has a single IDE drive with nothing attached to the second IDE channel.

You have two basic options for managing space in these circumstances. One is to upgrade the disk to a larger disk, but this will necessitate reinstalling the OS and the applications and restoring the user's data. The other choice is to add a temporary second drive and extend the volume. This will at least allow Crystal to be up and running—but it should not be considered a permanent solution. If you do choose to extend the volume and then either drive within the volume set fails, the user will lose access to both drives. When Crystal's workload allows time for maintenance, you can replace the volume set with a single drive.

One issue you may run into with hard drives is that they go bad from time to time. If you have never heard a hard drive fail, it is a distinct clicking. Once you have experienced it, you will never forget it. When drives go bad, Disk Management can help determine which drive and what the issue may be. In the next section, we will look at hard disk errors.

Troubleshooting Disk Management

The Disk Management utility can be used to troubleshoot disk errors through a set of status codes; however, if a disk will not initialize, no status code will be displayed. Disks will not initialize if there is no valid disk signature.

The problem with disk errors is that you don't know when a disk fails or which disk failed. Disk Management can help you with this. When disks have problems or errors, status codes get assigned. Knowing what these codes mean will help you determine what the problem is and, more important, what steps need to be taken to fix the problem.

Using Disk Management Status Codes

The main window of the Disk Management utility displays the status of disks and volumes. The following list contains the possible status codes and a description of each code; these are very useful in troubleshooting disk problems.

Online Indicates that the disk is accessible and that it is functioning properly. This is the normal disk status.

Online (Errors) Used only with dynamic disks. Indicates that I/O errors have been detected on the dynamic disk. One possible fix for this error is to right-click the disk and select Reactivate Disk to attempt to return the disk to Online status. This fix will work only if the I/O errors were temporary. You should immediately back up your data if you see this error and suspect that the I/O errors are not temporary.

Healthy Specifies that the volume is accessible and functioning properly.

Healthy (At Risk) Used to indicate that a dynamic volume is currently accessible but I/O errors have been detected on the underlying dynamic disk. This option is usually associated with Online (Errors) for the underlying disk.

Offline or Missing Used only with dynamic disks. Indicates that the disk is not accessible. This can occur if the disk is corrupted or the hardware has failed. If the error is not caused by hardware failure or major corruption, you may be able to re-access the disk by using the Reactivate Disk option to return the disk to Online status. If the disk was originally offline and then the status changed to Missing, it indicates that the disk has become corrupted, has been powered down, or was disconnected.

Unreadable This can occur on basic or dynamic disks. Indicates that the disk is inaccessible and might have encountered hardware errors, corruption, or I/O errors or that the system disk configuration database is corrupted. This message may also appear when a disk is spinning up while the Disk Management utility is rescanning the disks on the computer.

Failed Can be seen with basic or dynamic volumes. Specifies that the volume can't be started. This can occur because the disk is damaged or the file system is corrupted. If this message occurs with a basic volume, you should check the underlying disk hardware. If the error occurs on a dynamic volume, verify that the underlying disks are online.

Unknown Used with basic and dynamic volumes. Occurs if the boot sector for the volume becomes corrupted—for example, from a virus. This error can also occur if no disk signature is created for the volume.

Incomplete Occurs when you move some, but not all, of the disks from a multidisk volume. If you do not complete the multivolume set, then the data will be inaccessible.

Foreign This error can occur if you move a dynamic disk from a computer running Windows 2000 (any version), Windows 2008, Windows XP Professional, Windows Vista, or Windows Server 2003 to a Windows 7 computer. This error is caused because configuration data is unique to computers where the dynamic disk was created. You can correct this error by right-clicking the disk and selecting the option Import Foreign Disks. Any existing volume information will then be visible and accessible.

In addition to errors, there are some other issues that can arise when installing or configuring disks. One issue that may occur is that a disk fails to initialize when installed.

Troubleshooting Disks That Fail to Initialize

When you add a new disk to your computer in Windows 7, the disk does not initially contain a disk signature, which is required for the disk to be recognized by Windows. Disk signatures are at the end of the sector marker on the Master Boot Record (MBR) of the drive.

When you install a new drive and run the Disk Management utility, a wizard starts and lists all new disks that have been detected. The disk signature is written through this process. If you cancel the wizard before the disk signature is written, you will see the disk status Not Initialized. To initialize a disk, you right-click the disk you want to initialize and select the Initialize Disk option.

So as you have know seen, Disk Management can be a very useful tool in your computer management arsenal. If you decide to format your partition or volume using NTFS, you then receive added benefits like compression, encryption, quotas, and security. In the next section, we will start taking a looking at some of these benefits.

Managing Data Compression

One of the advantages of using NTFS over FAT32 is the ability to compress data. I teach IT administrators data compression and I like to refer to a well-known infomercial as an example. Have you seen the commercial where people put all of the blankets into a large bag and then hook a vacuum to the bag and suck all the air out? This is a great example of how compression works. Data compression is the process of storing data in a form that takes less space than uncompressed data.

If you have ever “zipped” or “packed” a file, you have used a form of data compression. The compression algorithms support cluster sizes only up to 4 KB, so if you are using larger cluster sizes, NTFS compression support is not available. If you have the Modify permission on an NTFS volume, you can manage data compression through Windows Explorer or the Compact command-line utility.

Files as well as folders in the NTFS file system can be either compressed or uncompressed. Files and folders are managed independently, which means that a compressed folder can contain uncompressed files, and an uncompressed folder can contain compressed files.

Access to compressed files by applications is transparent. For example, if you access a compressed file through Microsoft Word, the file will be uncompressed automatically when it is opened and then automatically compressed again when it is closed.

Compression happens very quickly, but if, for example, you compress a 500 GB hard drive, there is no guarantee that there won’t be any lag time on your machine or server.

Data compression is available only on NTFS partitions. Because of this, if you copy or move a compressed folder or file to a FAT32 partition, Windows 7 automatically uncompresses the folder or file.

Certain system files (e.g. `Pagefile.sys`) can’t be compressed. You also have the ability to show compressed files and folders with an alternate color.

In Exercise 3.9, you will compress and uncompress folders and files.

EXERCISE 3.9

Compressing and Uncompressing Folders

1. Select Start > Run, and then type **Explorer** and click OK.
2. In Windows Explorer, find and select Computer, Local Disk (C:), and then a folder on the C: drive. The folder you select should contain files.
3. Right-click the folder and select Properties. In the General tab of the folder’s Properties dialog box, note the value listed for Size On Disk. Then click the Advanced button.
4. In the Advanced Attributes dialog box, check the Compress Contents To Save Disk Space option. Then click OK.

5. In the Confirm Attribute Changes dialog box, select the option Apply Changes To This Folder, Subfolders and Files. (If this confirmation dialog box does not appear, you can display it by clicking the Apply button in the Properties dialog box.) Click OK to confirm your changes.
6. On the General tab of the folder's Properties dialog box, note the value that now appears for Size On Disk. This size should have decreased because you compressed the folder.

To uncompress folders and files, repeat the steps in Exercise 3.9 and uncheck the Compress Contents To Save Disk Space option in the Advanced Attributes dialog box.

As I stated earlier, you can specify that compressed files be displayed in a different color from the uncompressed files. To do so, in Windows Explorer, select Organize ➤ Folder And Search Options ➤ View. Under Files And Folders, check the Show Encrypted Or Compressed NTFS Files In Color option.

In addition to compressing files and folders in Windows Explorer, you can compress the files and folders using the Compact command-line utility.

Using the Compact Command-Line Utility

The command-line options for managing file and folder compression are Compact and Expand. You can access these commands from a command prompt. The Compact command offers you more control over file and folder compression than Windows Explorer. For example, you can use the Compact command with a batch script or to compress only files that meet a specific criterion (for example, all the DOC files in a specific folder). Some of the options that can be used with the Compact command are shown in Table 3.3.

TABLE 3.3 Compact commands

Command	Description
/C	Compresses the specified file or folder
/U	Uncompresses the specified file or folder
/S:dir	Used to specify which folder should be compressed or uncompressed
/A	Displays any files that have been hidden or system file attributes
/I	Indicates that any errors should be ignored
/F	Forces a file to be compressed
/Q	Used with reporting, to report only critical information
/?	Displays help

Another way that you can save disk space is by zipping folders. In the following section we will discuss how to save space using zipped folders.

Using Compressed (Zipped) Folders

Windows 7 also supports compressed (zipped) folders. This feature is different from NTFS compressed folders. The advantage of using compressed (zipped) folders is that it is supported on FAT32 or NTFS volumes. In addition, you can use compressed (zipped) folders to share data with other programs that use zipped files. The downside to using compressed (zipped) folders is that it is slower than using NTFS compression.

Within Windows Explorer, you create a zipped folder (or file) by right-clicking on the folder and selecting Send To ➤ Compressed (Zipped) Folder. You create a zipped file by right-clicking on a file and selecting New ➤ Compressed (Zipped) Folder. When you create a compressed folder, it will be displayed as a folder with a zipper.

Compression is a nice advantage to using NTFS, but another advantage is data encryption. In the following section, I will discuss the benefits to using data encryption.

Managing Data Encryption with EFS

Data encryption is a way to increase data security. Encryption is the process of translating data into code that is not easily accessible to users other than the person who encrypted the data. Once data has been encrypted, you must have the correct key (SID number) to decrypt the data. Unencrypted data is known as plain text, and encrypted data is known as ciphertext.

The *Encrypting File System (EFS)* is the Windows 7 technology that is used to store encrypted files on NTFS partitions. Encrypted files add an extra layer of security to your file system. A user with the proper key can transparently access encrypted files. A user without the proper key is denied access. If the user who encrypted the files is unavailable, you can use the data recovery agent (DRA) to provide the proper key to decrypt folders or files. The following EFS features are among those included with Windows 7:

- Automatically color-codes encrypted files in green text so you can easily identify files that have been encrypted
- Support so that offline folders can also be encrypted
- A shell user interface (UI) that is used to support encrypted files for multiple users
- Control over who can read the encrypted files

In the following sections, you will learn how to encrypt and decrypt data, how to create and manage DRAs, how to recover encrypted files, how to share encrypted files, and how to use the Cipher utility.

Encrypting and Decrypting Folders and Files

To use EFS, a user specifies that a folder or file on an NTFS partition should be encrypted. The encryption is transparent to users. However, when other users try to access the file, they will not be able to unencrypt it—even if those users have Full Control NTFS permissions. Instead, they will receive an error message.

Windows 7 does not allow you to have a folder or file compressed and encrypted at the same time. A feature included with Windows Server 2003 and Windows Server 2008 is support for concurrent compression and encryption.

In Exercise 3.10, you will use EFS to encrypt a folder. Before encrypting any data, you will create a new user.

EXERCISE 3.10

Encrypting a Folder

1. To create a new user, select Start ➢ Control Panel ➢ System And Maintenance ➢ Administrative Tools. Under System Tools, expand Local Users And Groups and right-click the Users folder. Choose New User.

2. Create a new user named Paige and make her password P@ssw0rd. Deselect the User Must Change Password At Next Logon option for this user. Click Create.

EXERCISE 3.10 *(continued)*

3. Close Computer Management.
4. Select Start and type **Explorer** in the Search box.
5. In Windows Explorer, find and select a folder on the C: drive. The folder you select should contain files. Right-click the folder and select Properties.
6. On the General tab of the folder's Properties dialog box, click the Advanced button.
7. In the Advanced Attributes dialog box, check the Encrypt Contents To Secure Data option. Then click OK.
8. In the Confirm Attribute Changes dialog box (if this dialog box does not appear, click the Apply button in the Properties dialog box to display it), select Apply Changes To This Folder, Subfolders And Files. Then click OK.
9. Log off as Administrator and log on as Paige.
10. Open Windows Explorer and attempt to access one of the files in the folder you encrypted. You should receive an error message stating that the file is not accessible.
11. Log off as Paige and log on as Administrator.

To decrypt folders and files, repeat the steps in Exercise 3.10, but uncheck the Encrypt Contents To Secure Data option in the Advanced Attributes dialog box.

The problem here is that the user who encrypts the data is the only one who can open the files. But the owner of the data can share the encrypted files with other users. In the next section, we will look at how to share your encrypted data with other users.

Managing EFS File Sharing

In Windows 7, it is possible to share encrypted files with another person or between two computers. To share encrypted files, you must have a valid EFS certificate for the user who should have access to the file. By implementing EFS file sharing, you provide an additional level of recovery in the event that the person who encrypted the files is unavailable.

Complete Exercise 3.11 to implement EFS file sharing.

EXERCISE 3.11

Implementing EFS File Sharing

1. Encrypt the file if it is not already encrypted (see Exercise 3.10 for the steps involved).
2. Through Windows Explorer, access the encrypted file's properties. At the bottom of the dialog box, click the Advanced button.

3. The Advanced Attributes dialog box appears. In the Compress Or Encrypt Attributes section of the Advanced Attributes dialog box, click the Details button, which brings up the Encryption Details dialog box.
4. In the Encryption Details dialog box, click the Add button to add any additional users who should have access to the encrypted file (provided they have a valid certificate for EFS in Active Directory or that you have imported a valid certificate onto the local computer).
5. Close the Properties box for the folder.

Someone may have encrypted files or folders and then left the company. There are a few different ways to unencrypt the data, as you'll see in the next section.

Using the DRA to Recover Encrypted Data

If a user who encrypted folders or files is unavailable or no longer with the company and you need to decrypt the folders or files, you can use the data recovery agent (DRA) to access the encrypted files. DRAs are implemented differently depending on the version of your operating system and the configuration of your computer:

- For Windows 7 computers that are a part of a Windows 2008 Active Directory domain, the domain Administrator user account is automatically assigned the role of DRA.
- For Windows 7 computers that are installed as stand-alone computers or if the computer is a part of a workgroup, no default DRA is assigned.

You should use extreme caution when using EFS on a stand-alone Windows 7 computer. If the key used to encrypt the files is lost, there is no default recovery process, and all access to the files will be lost.

Creating a DRA on a Stand-Alone Windows 7 Computer

If Windows 7 is installed on a stand-alone computer or on a computer that is part of a workgroup, then no DRA is created by default. To manually create a DRA, you use the Cipher command-line utility as follows:

```
Cipher /R:filename
```

The `/R` switch is used to generate two files, one with a `.pfx` filename extension and one with a `.cer` extension. The PFX file is used for data recovery and the CER file includes a self-signed EFS recovery agent certificate.

The CER file (self-signed public key certificate) can then be imported into the local security policy and the PFX file (private key) can be stored in a secure location. Cipher is explained further in the next section.

Once you have created the public and private keys to be used with EFS, you can specify the DRA through Local Security Policy, using the steps in Exercise 3.12.

EXERCISE 3.12

Using the Local Security Policy

1. Through Local Security Policy, which can be accessed through Administrative Tools or the Local Computer Policy MMC snap-in, expand Public Key Policies and then Encrypting File System.

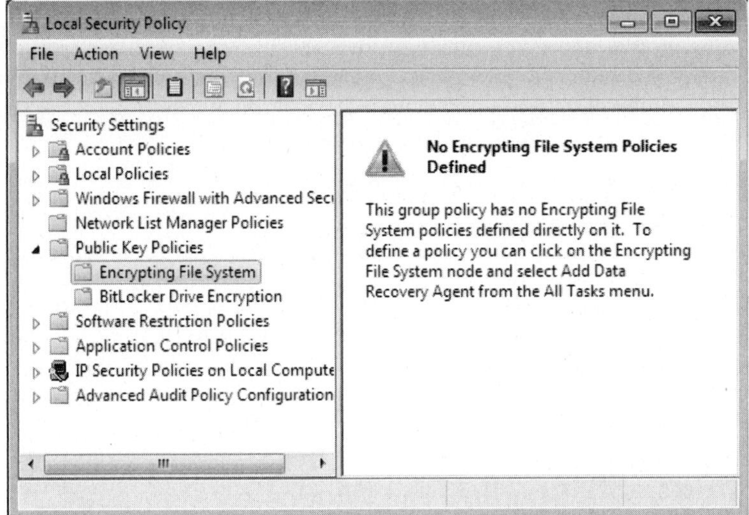

2. Right-click Encrypting File System and select Add Data Recovery Agent.
3. The Add Recovery Agent Wizard starts. Click the Next button to continue.
4. The Select Recovery Agents screen appears. Click the Browse Folders button to access the CER file you created with the Cipher `/R:`*filename* command. Select the certificate and click Next.

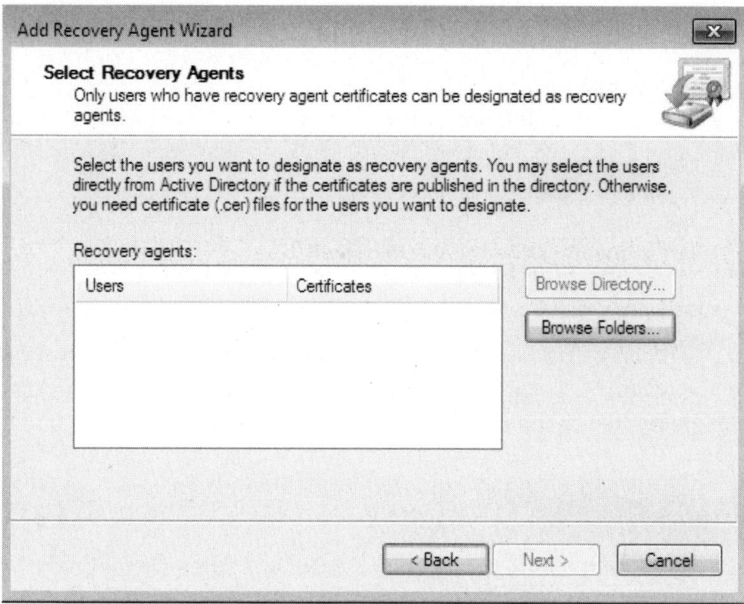

5. The Completing The Add Recovery Agent Wizard screen appears. Confirm that the settings are correct and click the Finish button.

You will see the data recovery agent listed in the Local Security Settings dialog box, under Encrypting File System. Let's continue our look at encryption with a discussion of recovering encrypted files in the next section.

Recovering Encrypted Files

If the DRA has the private key to the DRA certificate (that was created through `Cipher /R:`*`filename`*), the DRA can decrypt files in the same manner as the user who originally encrypted the file. Once the encrypted files are opened by a DRA, they are available as unencrypted files and can be stored as either encrypted or unencrypted files.

Using the Cipher Utility

Cipher is a command-line utility that can be used to encrypt files on NTFS volumes. The syntax for the Cipher command is as follows:

```
Cipher /[command parameter] [filename]
```

Table 3.4 lists common command parameters associated with the `Cipher` command.

TABLE 3.4 Cipher command parameters

Parameter	Description
/E	Specifies that files or folders should be encrypted. Any files that are subsequently added to the folder will be encrypted.
/D	Specifies that files or folders should be decrypted. Any files that are subsequently added to the folder will not be encrypted.
/S:dir	Specifies that subfolders of the target folder should also be encrypted or decrypted based on the option specified.
/I	Causes any errors that occur to be ignored. By default, the Cipher utility stops whenever an error occurs.
/H	By default, files with hidden or system attributes are omitted from display. This option specifies that hidden and system files should be displayed.
/K	Creates a new certificate file and certificate key.
/R	Used to generate a recovery agent key and certificate for use with EFS.
/X	Used to back up the EFS certificate and key into the specified file name.

Exercise 3.13 will show you how to use the Cipher utility to encrypt files. Make sure that you have encrypted a folder on the C: drive before completing these steps.

EXERCISE 3.13

Using the Cipher Utility

1. Select Start ➤ All Programs ➤ Accessories ➤ Command Prompt.
2. In the Command Prompt dialog box, type **C:** and press Enter to access the C: drive.
3. From the C:\> prompt, type **cipher**. You will see a list of folders and files and the state of encryption. The folder you encrypted should be indicated by an *E*.
4. Type **MD TEST** and press Enter to create a new folder named Test.
5. Type **cipher /e test** and press Enter. You will see a message verifying that the folder was encrypted.

In the next section we will look at how to protect your disks using Redundant Array of Independent Disks (RAID).

Understanding RAID

One concern for any computer department is the loss of data and hard drive failures. *Redundant Array of Independent Disks (RAID)* allows an administrator to recover data from a single hard disk failure.

The important factor to remember about Microsoft RAID is that you can recover from only a single disk failure. If multiple hard disks fail, RAID will no longer be an option.

There are two types of RAID: hardware based and software based. Hardware RAID, which is the best option, is built into the physical machine. Software RAID is used through the use of the Windows operating system.

The downside to hardware RAID is cost. A server or computer that has hardware RAID built in can cost thousands of dollars. Software RAID is free, but remember the old saying, "You get what you pay for."

In the next section we will look at the different models of RAID and how each model operates.

RAID Models

There are many different models of RAID but Microsoft Windows 7 uses three main models: RAID-0, RAID-1, and RAID-5. Let's take a look at each.

RAID-0 (Stripped Volume) RAID-0 has no data recoverability but it is used for better performance. With RAID-0 you can have a minimum of two hard disks, and these two disks work together as a single volume. Because the two disks work together, the disks both use their own read/write heads, giving you better performance.

The downside to RAID-0 is that if you lose either disk, you lose the entire stripped volume. RAID-0 is good for temp files or noncritical data since RAID-0 is not recoverable in the event of a hard disk failure.

RAID-1 (Mirroring) RAID-1, also known as mirroring, allows you to set up two volumes or disks that mirror each other. The advantage to mirroring is that if you lose one disk or volume, you can boot to the second disk or volume (the mirror) and recover your data. The downside to mirroring is that it is more expensive than other RAID options.

RAID-5 Volume A RAID-5 volume, which many years ago was known as a stripe set with parity, uses a minimum of 3 disks (maximum of 32 disks) that work together as one volume. The advantage to a RAID-5 volume is that the volume uses a parity bit, which allows you to recover your data in the event of a single hard disk failure.

When it comes to hardware RAID and software RAID, recoverability is night and day. Hardware RAID is much faster and easier when a hard disk fails. Many hardware RAID systems are hot-swappable, meaning that when a disk fails, you just slide it out, place a new disk in, and the RAID gets back to work.

This is not the case with software RAID. Recoverability for a single hard disk failure can take time, which in turn costs an organization money. Software RAID is set up through the Disk Management utility (explained earlier in this chapter) and is not available unless you have multiple hard disks installed in the Windows 7 machine.

In the next section we will look at how to keep your disk volumes and partitions running at peak performance.

Using Disk Maintenance Tools

As IT professionals, part of our job is to keep our systems running the best that they can. Most of us have seen machines running very quickly when they are new, but then they start to slow down over time, even when we do not install any new software.

Microsoft Windows 7 includes a few utilities that you can run to help keep your system running efficiently. In the next sections we will discuss three of these utilities: Disk Defragment, Disk Cleanup, and Check Disk.

Using the Disk Defragmenter Utility

Data is normally stored sequentially on the disk as space is available. Fragmentation naturally occurs as users create, delete, and modify files. The access of noncontiguous data is transparent to the user; however, when data is stored in this manner, the operating system must search through the disk to access all the pieces of a file. This slows down data access.

Disk defragmentation rearranges the existing files so they are stored contiguously, which optimizes access to them. In Windows 7, you use the Disk Defragmenter utility to defragment your disk.

To access the Disk Defragmenter, select Start ➢ Control Panel ➢ System And Maintenance ➢ Administrative Tools ➢ Computer Management. Expand Storage and select Disk Management, right-click the drive to defragment, select the Tools tab, and then click the Defragment Now button. The Disk Defragmenter window appears (Figure 3.16); you can schedule when the Disk Defragmenter should run or run the Disk Defragmenter tool immediately.

FIGURE 3.16 The Disk Defragmenter window

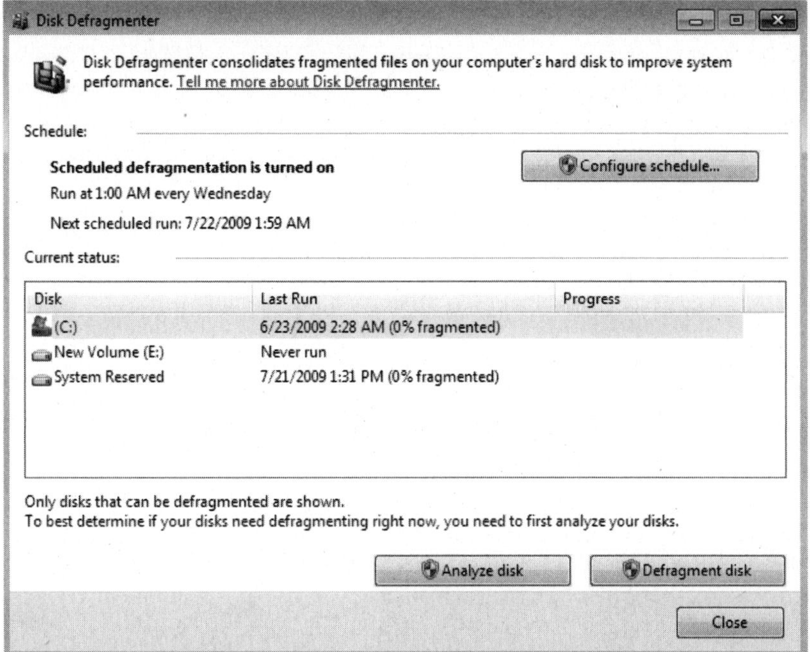

You can also defragment disks through the command-line utility Defrag. The disk needs to have at least 15 percent free space for Defrag to run properly. You can analyze the state of the disk by using `Defrag` *`VolumeName`* `/a`.

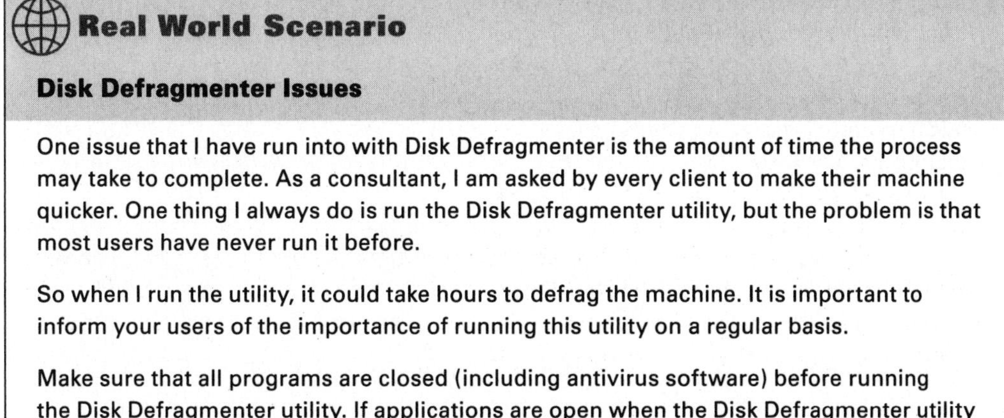

Real World Scenario

Disk Defragmenter Issues

One issue that I have run into with Disk Defragmenter is the amount of time the process may take to complete. As a consultant, I am asked by every client to make their machine quicker. One thing I always do is run the Disk Defragmenter utility, but the problem is that most users have never run it before.

So when I run the utility, it could take hours to defrag the machine. It is important to inform your users of the importance of running this utility on a regular basis.

Make sure that all programs are closed (including antivirus software) before running the Disk Defragmenter utility. If applications are open when the Disk Defragmenter utility runs, it could cause the Disk Defragmenter utility to stop working or run even slower than normal.

Complete Exercise 3.14 to defragment your Windows 7 machine.

EXERCISE 3.14

Defragmenting Windows 7

1. Start the Disk Defragmenter utility by opening Computer Management.
2. Right-click the C: drive and choose Properties.
3. Click the Tools tab.
4. Click the Defragment Now button.
5. Either schedule a defragment or click the Defragment Disk button to start the defragment immediately.

It is a good practice to run Disk Defragmenter at least once a week on a Windows 7 machine that is constantly being used. If the machine is not used that often, you can space out how often you defrag the machine.

In the next section we will look at another tool that is included with Windows 7—the Disk Cleanup utility.

Using the Disk Cleanup Utility

One concern that we as IT professionals face is how to conserve hard disk space for our users. Hard drives continue to get larger and larger, but so do applications. This is where the Disk Cleanup utility can help.

The Disk Cleanup utility identifies areas of disk space that can be deleted to free up hard disk space. Disk Cleanup works by identifying temporary files, Internet cache files, and unnecessary program files.

To access this utility, select Start ➤ Control Panel ➤ System And Maintenance ➤ Administrative Tools ➤ Computer Management. Right-click the drive letter and choose Properties and then Disk Cleanup. The Disk Cleanup utility then runs and calculates the amount of disk space you can free up.

Complete Exercise 3.15 to run the Disk Cleanup utility on the Windows 7 operating system.

EXERCISE 3.15

Running the Disk Cleanup Utility

1. Select Start ➤ Control Panel ➤ System And Maintenance ➤ Administrative Tools ➤ Computer Management.
2. Right-click the drive and choose Properties.

3. On the General tab, click the Disk Cleanup button.
4. The Disk Cleanup utility will start to calculate the system data.
5. After the analysis is complete, you will see the Disk Cleanup dialog box listing files that are suggested for deletion and showing how much space will be gained by deleting those files. Click OK.

6. When you are asked to confirm that you want to delete the files, click the Yes button. The Disk Cleanup utility deletes the files and automatically closes the Disk Cleanup dialog box.

Another issue that you may run into is bad sectors on your hard disk. Windows 7 also includes a utility to help you troubleshoot disk devices and volumes.

Using the Check Disk Utility

If you are having trouble with your disk devices or volumes, you can use the Windows 7 Check Disk utility. This utility detects bad sectors, attempts to fix errors in the file system, and scans for and attempts to recover bad sectors. To use Check Disk, you must be logged in as a member of the Administrators group.

File system errors can be caused by a corrupted file system or by hardware errors. If you have software errors, the Check Disk utility may help you find them. There is no way to fix hardware errors through software, however. If you have excessive hardware errors, you should replace your disk drive.

Complete Exercise 3.16 to run the Check Disk utility.

EXERCISE 3.16

Using the Check Disk Utility

1. Select Start ➤ Control Panel ➤ System And Maintenance ➤ Administrative Tools.
2. Double-click Computer Management, and then expand Storage and select Disk Management.
3. Right-click the C: drive and choose Properties.
4. Click the Tools tab, and then click the Check Now button.
5. In the Check Disk dialog box, you can choose one or both of the options to automatically fix file system errors and to scan for and attempt recovery of bad sectors. For this exercise, check both of the disk option check boxes. Then click the Start button.

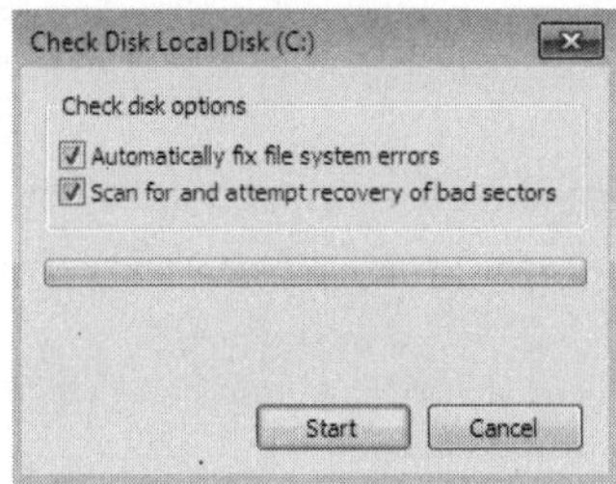

Another way to run the Check Disk utility is from the command line, using the command `Chkdsk`. `Chkdsk` is used to create and display a status report, which is based on the file system you are using.

Summary

There are a two different ways that you can format your hard disk in a Windows 7 operating system: FAT32 and NTFS. NTFS has many advantages over FAT32, including security, encryption, disk quotas, and compression, just to name a few.

Besides the way you format your hard disk, you can configure your hard disk as a basic disk, dynamic disk, or a GPT disk. You can use the Disk Management MMC snap-in to configure your hard disks and file system.

Another option within the Disk Management utility is RAID. RAID-1 and RAID-5 allow you to recover your data in the event of a single hard disk failure. RAID-0 allows you to achieve better performance but has no data recoverability in the event of a hard disk failure.

After the hard disks are installed and configured, there will be some maintenance issues that need to be tended to. There are utilities that allow you to achieve these maintenance issues, like the Disk Defragmenter and Check Disk utilities.

In the next chapter we will examine how to manage the user environment on the Windows 7 operating system.

Exam Essentials

Understand the different file format options. There are two ways to format a hard disk in Windows 7: FAT32 and NTFS. Understand that NTFS offers many benefits over FAT32, including security, encryption, compression, and disk quotas.

Understand the different hard disk storage types. Windows 7 supports three types of disk storage: basic, dynamic, and GUID partition table (GPT). Basic storage is backward compatible with other operating systems and can be configured to support up to four partitions. Dynamic storage is supported by Windows 2000, Windows XP, Windows Server 2003, Windows Vista, and Windows 7 and allows storage to be configured as volumes. GPT storage allows you to configure volume sizes larger than 2 TB and up to 128 primary partitions.

Know the disk management utilities. Microsoft Windows 7 includes a few utilities that you can run to help keep your system running efficiently. These utilities include the Disk Defragmenter, Disk Cleanup, and Check Disk.

Review Questions

1. Will has installed Windows 7 on his Windows XP computer. The machine is now a dual-boot computer. He has FAT32 for Windows XP and NTFS for Windows 7. In addition, he boots his computer to Windows XP Professional for testing an application's compatibility with both operating systems. Which of the following file systems will be seen by both operating systems?

   A. Only the FAT32 partition will be seen by both operating systems.

   B. Only the NTFS partition will be seen by both operating systems.

   C. Neither the FAT32 partition nor the NTFS partition will be seen by both operating systems.

   D. Both the FAT32 partition and the NTFS partition will be seen by both operating systems.

2. You are the network administrator for a large company that has decided to use EFS. You have two Windows 7 machines, named machine1 and machine2. Both of these Windows 7 machines are part of a Windows Server 2008 domain. From machine1 you can recover all EFS encrypted files for all users in the entire domain. You need to be able to do the same from machine2. How do you accomplish this task?

   A. From machine1, export the data recovery agent certificate and import that certificate onto machine2.

   B. On a domain controller, add machine1 as the master EFS machine.

   C. From machine1, export the data recovery agent certificate and import that certificate onto the EFS server.

   D. On a domain controller, add machine2 as the EFS recovery agent machine.

3. Alexandria is the payroll manager and stores critical files on her local drive for added security on her Windows 7 computer. She wants to ensure that she is using the disk configuration with the most fault tolerance and the highest level of consistent availability. Which of the following provisions should she use?

   A. Disk striping

   B. Spanned volumes

   C. Mirrored volumes

   D. Extended volume

4. Paige is considering upgrading her basic disk to a dynamic disk on her Windows 7 computer. She asks you for help in understanding the function of dynamic disks. Which of the following statements are true of dynamic disks in Windows 7? (Choose all that apply.)

   A. Dynamic disks can be recognized by older operating systems such as Windows NT 4 in addition to new operating systems such as Windows 7.

   B. Dynamic disks are supported only by Windows 2000 Server and Windows Server 2003.

   C. Dynamic disks support features such as simple partitions, extended partitions, spanned partitions, and striped partitions.

   D. Dynamic disks support features such as simple volumes, extended volumes, spanned volumes, mirrored volumes, and striped volumes.

5. Cindy is using Windows 7 on her laptop computer, and the C: partition is running out of space. You want to identify any areas of free space that can be reclaimed from temporary files. What utility should you use?

   A. Disk Cleanup

   B. Disk Manager

   C. Disk Administrator

   D. Disk Defragmenter

6. Rob is using Windows 7 to store video files. He doesn't access the files very often and wants to compress the files to utilize disk space. Which of the following options allows you to compress files in Windows 7?

   A. `Compression.exe`

   B. `Cipher.exe`

   C. `Packer.exe`

   D. Windows Explorer

7. Maggie wants the highest level of security possible for her data. She stores the data on an NTFS partition and has applied NTFS permissions. Now she wants to encrypt the files through EFS (Encrypting File System). Which command-line utility can she use to manage data encryption?

   A. Encrypt

   B. Cipher

   C. Crypto

   D. EDS

8. You have compressed a 4 MB file into 2 MB. You are copying the file to another computer that has a FAT32 partition. How can you ensure that the file will remain compressed?

   A. When you copy the file, use the XCOPY command with the `/Comp` switch.

   B. When you copy the file, use the Windows Explorer utility and specify the option Keep Existing Attributes.

   C. On the destination folder, make sure that you set the option Compress Contents To Save Disk Space in the folder's properties.

   D. You can't maintain disk compression on a non-NTFS partition.

9. Julie wants to allow her assistant, Tylor, access to several files that she has encrypted with EFS. How can she allow Tylor to access the files on her computer?

   A. Julie should export and email her encryption key to Tylor.

   B. Julie should configure NTFS permissions to provide Tylor with full access to the files.

   C. Julie should import Tylor's encryption key and add Tylor's certificate to each file to which Tylor should have access.

   D. Julie should configure share permissions to provide Tylor with full access to the files over the network.

10. Will is the manager of human resources in your company. He is concerned that members of the Administrators group, who have implied access to all NTFS resources, will be able to easily view the contents of the sensitive personnel files. What is the highest level of security that can be applied to the payroll files?

    A. Apply NTFS permissions to the files.

    B. Encrypt the files with EFS.

    C. Secure the files with the `Secure.exe` command.

    D. Encrypt the files with HSP.

11. Bruce frequently works with a large number of files. He is noticing that the larger the files get, the longer it takes to access them. He suspects that the problem is related to the files being spread over the disk. What utility can be used to store the files sequentially on the disk?

    A. Disk Defragmenter

    B. Disk Manager

    C. Disk Administrator

    D. Disk Cleanup

12. You are the network administrator for a small company. You have a laptop that you use to test an application that is deployed to several users who have access to only a Windows XP computer. To accommodate the testing of the application, you have a laptop that dual-boots between Windows 7 and Windows XP. You currently have Windows XP on the C: drive and Windows 7 on the D: drive. Both partitions are formatted with FAT32. You decide to convert the D: drive to NTFS so that you can apply additional security to some of the files. You use the Convert command-line utility to convert the D: drive. Before you reboot and convert the drive, you realize that you should not have converted the drive. How can you cancel the conversion process?

   A. Use `Convert D: /cancel`.

   B. Use `Convert D: /fs:FAT`.

   C. In Disk Administrator, select Tools ➢ Cancel Conversion for Drive C:.

   D. Edit the Registry setting for `HKEY_LOCAL_MACHINE\System\CurrentControlSet\Control\SessionManager to autocheck autochk *`.

13. Cathy is the payroll manager at your company. The day before the payroll is processed, Cathy is involved in a minor car accident and spends two days in the hospital. She has Windows 7 installed as a part of a workgroup and has encrypted the payroll files with EFS. All of the EFS settings for the computer are set to default values. How can these files be accessed in her absence?

   A. The Administrator user account can access the files by backing up the files, restoring the files on the computer where the recovery agent is located, and disabling the files' Encrypt The Contents To Secure Data option.

   B. The Administrator user account can access the files by using the `unencrypt` command-line utility.

   C. The Administrator user account can access the files by using the `encrypt -d` command.

   D. Unless a DRA has been configured, there will be no access to the files.

14. You have an extremely large database that needs to be stored on a single partition. Your boss asks you about the maximum capacity for an NTFS partition. Assuming you are using 4 KB clusters, what is the correct answer?

   A. 16 TB

   B. 64 GB

   C. 132 GB

   D. 32 GB

15. You have just added a new disk to your computer that supports hot swapping. Your computer now has three physical drives. What is the fastest way to allow Windows 7 to recognize the new disk?

   A. Restart the computer.

   B. In Disk Manager, select Action ➢ Rescan Disk.

   C. In Disk Management, select Action ➢ Rescan Disk.

   D. In System Tools, select Update Disks.

16. You have a 10 MB image file that you want to email to another user in the marketing department. Which of the following should you do in order to email the image?
    A. Encrypt the image with EFS.
    B. Configure compression on the directory in which the image file is stored.
    C. Right-click the image file and select Send To ➢ Compressed (Zipped) folder.
    D. Use the Compact command-line utility.

17. You are installing a new hard drive into your computer, which dual-boots between Windows 7 and Windows XP. You will be storing large and sensitive files on this drive. You will need to access these files from either operating system. You need to determine the file system to use when formatting the disk. Which of the following should you use?
    A. NTFS
    B. FAT32
    C. FAT16
    D. CDFS

18. You are administering a Windows 7 computer. You suspect that the disk in the computer may have some bad sectors. You want to determine if the disk does have any bad sectors and fix them if possible. Which utility could you use to accomplish this?
    A. DiskPart
    B. Check Disk
    C. Disk Cleanup
    D. Disk Defragmenter

19. You are the human resources administrator for your company. You have recently been assigned a Windows 7 laptop computer. You have added a new directory named HR to the computer. You want to ensure that all files that are stored within the HR directory are encrypted. You will use the Cipher utility to accomplish this. Which of the following options should you use with the Cipher utility?
    A. `/D`
    B. `/E`
    C. `/R`
    D. `/X`

20. You are a system administrator for your company. You are managing a Windows 7 computer. You issue the following command at a command prompt: **Compact /C**. Which of the following will occur as a result of issuing this command?
    A. All files located on the C: drive will be compressed.
    B. All files located on the C: drive will be uncompressed.
    C. All files within the specified directory will be compressed.
    D. All files within the specified directory will be uncompressed.

Answers to Review Questions

1. D. Both Windows 7 and Windows XP Professional support FAT32 and the NTFS file systems, so both file systems will be viewable on both operating systems.

2. A. In Windows 7, it is possible to share encrypted files with another person or between computers. To share encrypted files, you must have a valid EFS certificate for the user who should have access to the files.

3. C. Windows 7 supports mirrored volumes and mirrored volumes allow you to have fault tolerance in the event of a single hard disk failure.

4. D. Dynamic disks are supported by Windows 7 as well as by Windows XP, Windows Vista, Windows 2000, Windows Server 2003, and Windows Server 2008. Windows 7 supports mirrored volumes.

5. A. The Disk Cleanup utility is used to identify areas of space that may be reclaimed through the deletion of temporary files or Recycle Bin files.

6. D. In Windows 7, one way you can compress files is through Windows Explorer. Windows 7 has no programs called Compression or Packer. The Cipher program is used to encrypt or decrypt files. The command-line option for managing file and folder compression is Compact.

7. B. The Cipher utility is used to encrypt or decrypt files. Windows 7 doesn't have a program called Encrypt, Crypto, or EDS. If you want to manage file encryption through a GUI utility, you can use Windows Explorer.

8. D. Windows 7 data compression is supported only on NTFS partitions. If you move the file to a FAT32 partition, then it will be stored as uncompressed.

9. C. To allow Tylor to access her encrypted files, Julie should import Tylor's encryption key and then add that key to each file to which Tylor should have access. Adding share permissions or NTFS permissions will not allow another user to access an encrypted file unless that user's encryption key has been added to the file. Exporting and emailing Julie's key to Tylor will not allow Tylor to access the file.

10. B. You can increase the level of security on folders and files on an NTFS partition by using Encrypting File System (EFS). Only a user who is configured as a DRA with the correct private key or who has explicitly been provided permission can access this data.

11. A. The Disk Defragmenter utility is used to rearrange files so that they are stored contiguously on the disk. This optimizes access to those files. You can also defragment disks through the command-line utility Defrag.

12. D. The only way to cancel an NTFS conversion prior to reboot is to edit the Registry setting for `HKEY_LOCAL_MACHINE\System\CurrentControlSet\Control\SessionManager` to `autocheck autochk *`. Once the conversion has taken place, there is no way to reverse the conversion process.

13. D. By default, a Windows 7 computer that is installed as a stand-alone computer or a part of a workgroup has no DRA automatically configured. You will not be able to access her files.

14. A. You can have NTFS partitions that are up to 16 TB with 4 KB clusters or 256 TB with 64 KB clusters. NTFS supports the largest partitions of any of the file systems supported by Windows 7.

15. C. Select Action ➤ Rescan Disk in the Disk Management utility. The disk will then be listed through the Disk Management utility and can be configured as needed.

16. C. You can send the image in a compressed file in order to limit the size of the image while emailing it. Compressing an image in a zipped file can often drastically reduce the size of the image file and make it easier to email to other users. To send the image file to a compressed folder, you can right-click the file and select Send To ➤ Compressed (Zipped) Folder.

17. A. You should use NTFS when formatting the new disk. Only NTFS supports both file encryption and file compression. Both Windows XP and Windows 7 can access NTFS partitions, so file access should not be a problem.

18. B. To check a disk to determine if it has any bad sectors, you can use the Check Disk utility, which can be accessed from the command line by typing **Chkdsk**. The Check Disk utility can discover and attempt to fix bad sections on hard disks.

19. B. You should use the `/E` option with the Cipher utility. The `/E` option encrypts the specified directory and configures all files subsequently added to the directory to be encrypted.

20. C. By issuing the command `Compact /C`, you ensure that all files within the specified directory will be compressed. The Compact utility can be used to compress files and directories from a command line. The `/C` option compresses the selected files.

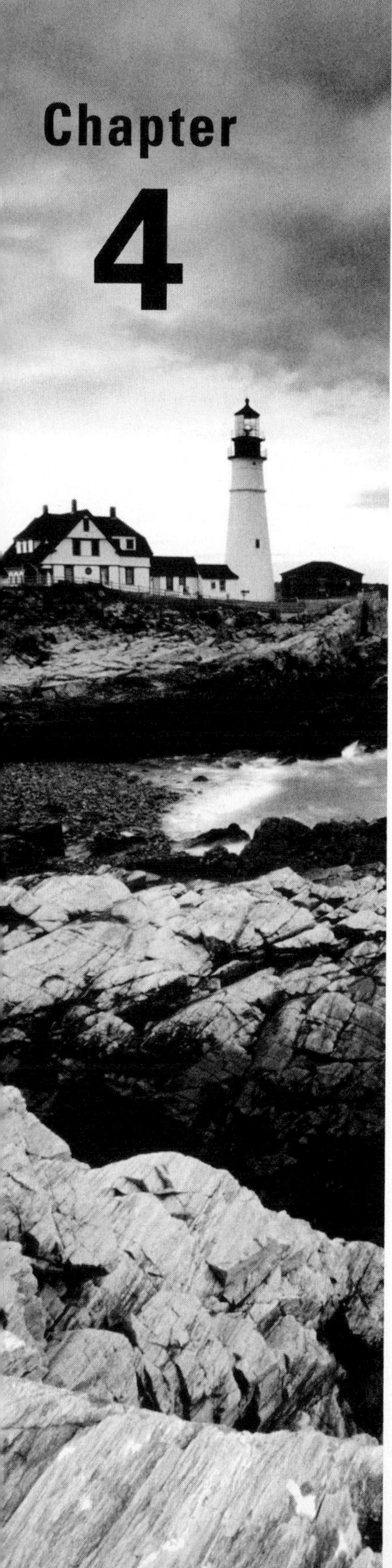

Managing the Windows 7 Environment

MICROSOFT EXAM OBJECTIVES COVERED IN THIS CHAPTER:

✓ **Configure performance settings.**

- This objective may include but is not limited to: configuring page files; configuring power plans; configuring desktop environments; configuring services and programs to resolve performance issues; configuring power

✓ **Configure mobility options.**

- This objective may include but is not limited to: creating and migrating power policy

✓ **Configure remote connections.**

- This objective may include but is not limited to: establishing VPN connections and authentication; enabling a VPN reconnect; dial-up connections; remote desktop

After you've installed Windows 7, you will need to configure the system. In this chapter, we will examine the process of configuring the Windows 7 environment, beginning with an overview of the main configuration utilities.

Control Panel is one of the most important configuration areas of Windows 7. It includes many icons that can help us optimize, maintain, and personalize the operating system. One of the most important icons in Control Panel is the System icon. The System icon not only has operating system information—it allows you to configure devices, remote settings, and system protection.

If you use Windows 7 on a laptop computer, it is important to properly configure your power and mobility options. Configuring these options on a laptop will allow you to get the most out of your laptop and Windows 7. There are many different mobility options that you can choose from to help customize the laptop to each individual user.

We will also examine how services operate and how to configure your services to start manually or automatically. We will examine how to configure services in the event of a service error.

Configuring the Windows 7 Operating System

After Windows 7 is installed, the next important step is configuration. If a Windows 7 machine is not configured properly, it will not run properly.

The following sections describe many of the configuration options for customizing Windows 7 for each individual user's needs. We will start with configuring the Windows 7 Desktop environment.

Configuring the Desktop Environment

Before we configure the Windows 7 Desktop, let's discuss what the Windows 7 Desktop actually is. The Windows 7 Desktop is the interface that appears when a user logs into the operating system. The Desktop includes the wallpaper, Start menu, gadgets, and icons (see Figure 4.1).

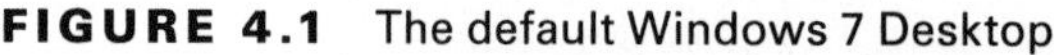

FIGURE 4.1 The default Windows 7 Desktop

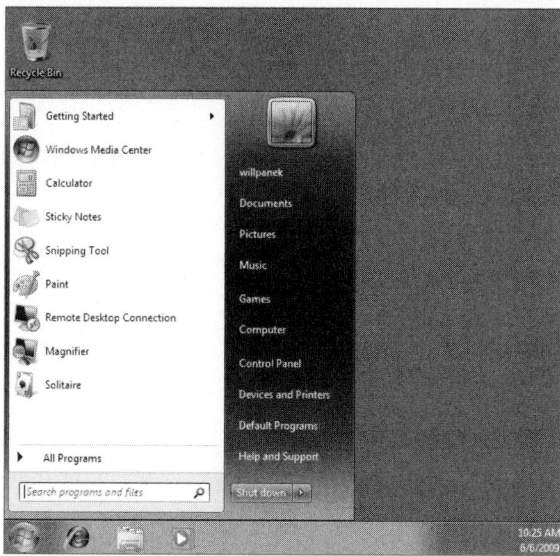

The Windows 7 Desktop default settings also include the default All Programs section, shown in Figure 4.2. One of the advantages of the Windows 7 Desktop is that you can configure the Desktop the way you like it.

FIGURE 4.2 The default All Programs section

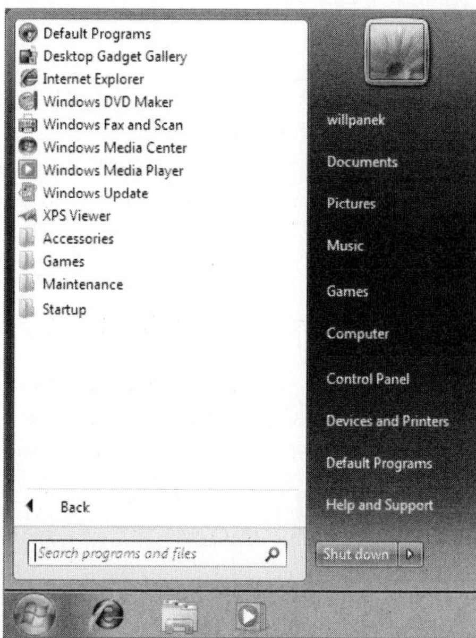

Microsoft includes premade Desktops called themes. You can set Windows 7 to use the Windows 7 Aero theme, the Windows 7 Standard theme, the Windows 7 Basic theme, the Windows Classic theme, or any customized theme you want.

The Windows 7 default Desktop appears after a user has logged on to a Windows 7 computer for the first time. Users can then configure their Desktops to suit their personal preferences and to work more efficiently.

When you install Windows 7 from a clean install, you will notice that the Desktop is clean except for the Recycle Bin. The following list shows the common default options that appear on the Start menu and the All Programs section.

Getting Started This is used to access preset tasks (see Figure 4.3). Some of these tasks are Discover Windows 7, Personalize Windows, Transfer Your Files, Add New Users, and Back Up Your Files.

FIGURE 4.3 Getting Started tasks

Calculator This shortcut starts the Calculator program.

Sticky Notes This application places a sticky note on your desktop, as shown in Figure 4.4. You can then type a message or reminder into the sticky note. It will remain on the Desktop until you remove it.

FIGURE 4.4 Sticky notes application

Snipping Tool This tool allows a user to capture an item on the Desktop (see Figure 4.5). The user clicks the Snipping Tool and drags the cursor around an area that will then be captured. The captured area can then be drawn on, highlighted, or saved as a file.

FIGURE 4.5 Snipping Tool

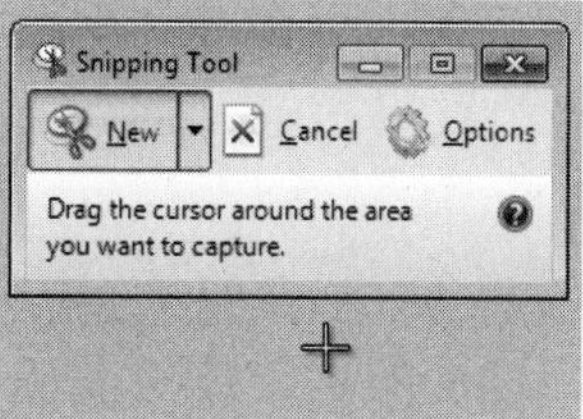

Paint This is a shortcut that starts the Paint program. The Paint program is an application that allows you to change or manipulate graphics files.

Remote Desktop Connection This program allows a user to connect remotely to another machine. To connect to another computer, the Remote Desktop Connection must be enabled on the receiving computer.

Magnifier The Magnifier utility is one of the Ease of Access utilities. The Ease of Access utilities are included with Windows 7 to allow users who may have difficulties seeing experience Windows 7 more easily. The Magnifier, Narrator, and On-Screen keyboard are among the Ease of Access utilities.

Solitaire This shortcut starts the Solitaire game. This game can also be accessed from the Games section of the Start menu.

Default Programs When you choose the Default Programs shortcut, there will be four different configuration items that can be accessed: Set Your Default Programs, Associate A File Type Or Protocol With A Program, Change AutoPlay Settings, and Set Program Access And Computer Defaults.

Default Gadget Gallery This shortcut opens the default gadget gallery. Gadgets are mini applications that can be placed on the Desktop. They are explained in greater detail later in this chapter.

Internet (Internet Explorer 8) This shortcut starts the built-in web browser. When used with an Internet connection, Internet Explorer 8 (IE8) provides an interface for accessing the Internet or a local intranet.

Windows DVD Maker This application is used to view and edit photo and video files to create your own personal DVDs.

Windows Fax and Scan This application is allows you to create and manage scans and faxes. Windows Fax and Scan allows users to send or receive faxes from their workstation.

Windows Media Center Windows Media Center allows you to watch TV on your computer or laptop. When you start the Media Center for the first time, a wizard will walk you through the TV setup. Windows Media Center also allows you to play DVD movies and music.

Windows Media Player The Windows Media Player allows you to play all your media files. It allows you to play videos, music, pictures, and recorded TV.

Windows Update This shortcut allows you to receive updates from either Microsoft's web server or a Windows Server Update Services (WSUS) machine. Windows Updates allows you to receive updates and security patches for the Windows 7 operating system.

XPS Viewer The XPS viewer is a new application that allows you to view Microsoft XML Paper Specification (`.xps`) files. The XPS viewer also allows you to print these files.

Accessories The Accessories section includes many Windows 7 tools (see Figure 4.6), such as the calculator, the command prompt, Windows PowerShell, the Ease of Access utility, Run, Paint, and Notepad.

FIGURE 4.6 The Accessories section of the Start menu

Games This section opens up the games that are included with Windows 7. Some of the games that are included are Chess Titans, FreeCell, Hearts, Internet Backgammon, Internet Checkers, Internet Spades, Mahjong Titans, Minesweeper, Purble Place, Solitaire, and Spider Solitaire.

Maintenance The Maintenance section includes important maintenance utilities like Backup and Restore, Create a System Repair Disk, Help and Support, and Windows Remote Assistance.

Startup The Startup section allows you to place application shortcuts within the Startup section. Once these shortcuts are placed in the Startup section, the applications will automatically start when the system user logs in.

User Documents This shortcut (shown as `willpanek` in Figure 4.2 earlier) opens the user's personnel folders.

Documents By default, this folder stores the documents that are created. Each user has a unique Documents folder, so even if a computer is shared, each user will have their own personal folder.

Pictures This application shows any pictures that are in the user's Pictures folder.

Music This shortcut will show any music that is in the My Music folder.

Computer This shortcut allows you to centrally manage your computer's files, hard drives, and devices with removable storage. It also allows you to manage system tasks and other places (such as other computers on the network) and to view details about your computer.

Control Panel Control Panel holds many utilities and tools that allow you to configure your computer. It is discussed in greater detail later in this chapter.

Devices and Printers This shortcut opens the Devices and Printers section. In the Devices and Printers section you can add or configure any of your hardware devices or printers.

Help and Support This shortcut is used to access the Windows 7 Help and Support resources. You can also access Windows 7 online help from the Help and Support utility.

Search Use this option to search for pictures, music, video, documents, files and folders, computers, or people.

Shut Down Button This button is used to shut down the computer. There is an arrow next to the button that you can use to switch users, log off, lock the machine, restart the machine, or cause the machine to sleep. Configuring the Shut Down button is discussed later in this chapter.

If you use any kind of remote management tools, you may want to rename the Computer icon with the computer's actual name. This allows you to easily identify which computer you're accessing.

When configuring the Desktop, you have the ability to switch between background and Desktop themes. To switch between these different themes, right-click an area of open space on the Desktop, select Personalize, and then click Theme. In the Theme Settings dialog box, you can select the theme you want to use.

The Desktop also includes the Recycle Bin. The Recycle Bin is a special folder that holds the files and folders that have been deleted, assuming that your hard drive has enough free space to hold the deleted files. If the hard drive is running out of disk space, the files that were deleted first will be copied over. You can retrieve and clear files (for permanent deletion) from the Recycle Bin.

You can configure the Desktop by customizing the taskbar and Start menu, adding shortcuts, and setting display properties. I'll describe these configurations in the following sections. Let's start with the Desktop themes that you can configure and choose from.

Configuring Windows Aero

Windows Aero is the user interface component of Windows 7. When the Windows Aero theme is configured, open windows are displayed with a transparent glass effect and subtle animations.

Windows Aero Minimum Requirements

Enabling Windows Aero on a computer that has less than 1 GB of random access memory (RAM) and less than 128 MB of video RAM could adversely affect the performance of the computer. Ensure that your computer meets the minimum requirements before enabling Windows Aero. Windows 7 minimum requirements are discussed in detail in Chapter 1, "Windows 7 Installation."

To enable Windows Aero, you must first ensure that the Windows 7 theme is selected. This can be accomplished through the Personalization Control Panel option. You can open this Control Panel option by right-clicking the Desktop and selecting Personalize. Then choose the Windows 7 theme by clicking the theme you want in the Aero Theme (7) section.

After the Windows 7 theme is chosen, you can configure the theme's background picture, color, sounds, and screen savers. To configure the theme's background picture, click the Background link on the bottom and then choose the picture you like. To configure the Windows Aero color scheme, just click on the Color link below and select the color you want from the Color Scheme list.

You would do the same for the sounds and screen savers. Just click the link below the themes box and select the sounds and screen saver you want to use with your theme.

The Personalization dialog box also includes several configurable options that control various aspects of your theme:

Desktop Background This lets you pick your Desktop background, which uses a picture or an HTML document as wallpaper.

Windows Color and Appearance This allows you to fine-tune the color and style of your windows.

Sounds This lets you choose the sounds that will be played based on the action taken. Each action can have its own sound.

Screen Saver This lets you select a screen saver that will start after the system has been idle for a specified amount of time. You can also specify a password that must be used to reaccess the system after it has been idle. When the idle time has been reached, the computer will be locked and the password of the user who is currently logged on must be entered to access the computer again. You can also adjust monitor power settings.

Windows 7 includes many different screen saver options that can be used and configured:

- None
- 3D Text
- Blank
- Bubbles
- Mystify
- Photos
- Ribbons

Change Desktop Icons This allows you to customize the desktop icons. You also have the ability to change shortcut icons.

Change Mouse Pointers This allows you to customize the appearance of the mouse pointers.

Change Your Account Picture This lets you change your account picture. Your account picture is the picture next to your account name when you log on.

Complete Exercise 4.1 to configure your theme and choose your additional options.

EXERCISE 4.1

Configuring Windows 7 Theme Options

1. Right-click on an open area of the Desktop and choose Personalize.
2. Scroll down to the Aero Themes (7) section and choose a theme.
3. Select Desktop Background, and then select the Picture Library option from the drop-down menu. Click the Clear All box. Then put a check mark in the picture that you want to use for your Desktop background. In the Picture Position box, choose Fill. Click Save Changes.
4. Click Screen Saver, select the 3D Text, and specify a wait of five minutes. Click OK.

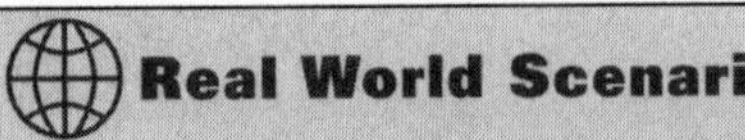

Configuring Personal Preferences

One thing that I noticed as an IT manager is that the most common configuration change made by users is to configure their Desktop. This lets them use the computer more efficiently, and the customization makes them more comfortable with it.

To help users work more efficiently with their computers, I would determine which applications or files are frequently and commonly used and verify that shortcuts or Start menu items were added for those elements. You can also remove shortcuts or Start menu items for elements that are seldom used or used not at all, helping to make the work area less cluttered and confusing.

Less-experienced users will feel more comfortable with their computer if they have a Desktop personalized to their preferences. This might include their choice of Desktop theme (for example, Windows 7 Aero or Windows Classic themes) and screen saver.

In Exercise 4.2, you will complete the steps needed to change your account picture.

EXERCISE 4.2

Changing the Account Picture

1. Right-click on your Desktop and choose Personalize.
2. Click the Change Your Account Picture link in the upper-left corner.
3. Choose a new picture for your account.
4. Click the Change Picture button.

You also have the ability to add more pictures to your choices by browsing the pictures on your computer system. Users can also download pictures that can be used for the account picture.

Windows 7 includes several utilities for managing various aspects of the operating system configuration. In the following sections, you will learn how to configure your operating system using Control Panel and the Registry Editor.

We will start with Control Panel and the different utilities included within the Control Panel.

Using Control Panel

Control Panel is a set of GUI utilities that allow you to configure Registry settings without the need to use a Registry editor. The Registry is a database used by the operating system to store configuration information.

Let's take a closer look at the utilities that are available through Control Panel. I have set Control Panel to Large Icons view but you can also set it to Small Icons view.

Action Center The Action Center has two configurable sections: Security and Maintenance. The Security section allows you to configure three different options:

- Spyware and unwanted software protection allows you to update Windows Defender.
- Virus protection allows you to install and configure virus protection.
- Windows Update allows you to update Windows 7.

You can use the Maintenance section to set up a backup. Backup and Windows Update will be explained later in this section.

Administrative Tools This icon has multiple administrative tools that can help you configure and monitor the Windows 7 operating system. These tools include:

- Computer Services
- Computer Management
- Data Sources (ODBC)
- Event Viewer
- iSCSI Initiator
- Local Security Policy
- Performance Monitor
- Print Management
- Services
- System Configuration
- Task Scheduler
- Windows Firewall with Advanced Security
- Windows Memory Diagnostics
- Windows PowerShell Modules

AutoPlay This icon lets you configure media disks and will autostart when inserted into the media player (see Figure 4.7). Each media type has different configuration settings, but the basic choices are as follows:

- Play Media Using The Windows Media Player
- Open The Folder To View Files Using Windows Explorer
- Take No Action
- Ask Me Every Time

FIGURE 4.7 AutoPlay options

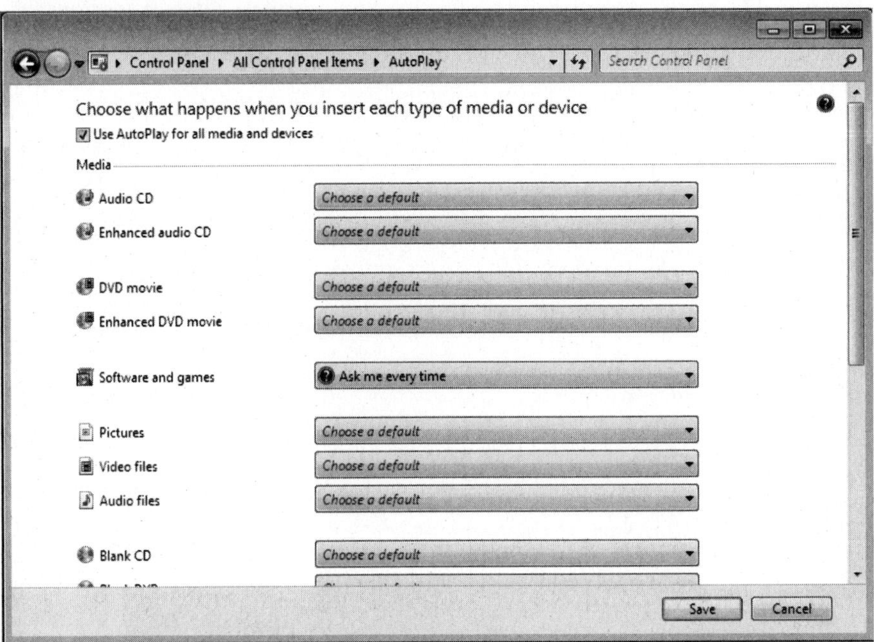

Backup and Restore The Backup And Restore icon allows you to install and configure your backup media. Users can make copies of all important data on their machine to avoid losing it in the event of a hardware failure or disaster. Backups will be discussed in greater detail in Chapter 9, "Configuring Backups and Recovery."

BitLocker Drive Encryption BitLocker Drive Encryption helps prevent unauthorized users from accessing files stored on the hard drives. The user is able to use the computer as they normally would, but unauthorized users cannot read or use any of their files. BitLocker Drive Encryption will be discussed in greater detail in Chapter 8, "Monitoring and Maintaining Windows 7."

Color Management The Color Management icon allows you to configure some of the video adapters settings, as shown in Figure 4.8. You can configure the Windows color system defaults, the ICC Rendering Intent to WCS Gamut Mapping settings, and display calibration, and you can change the system defaults.

FIGURE 4.8 Color Management

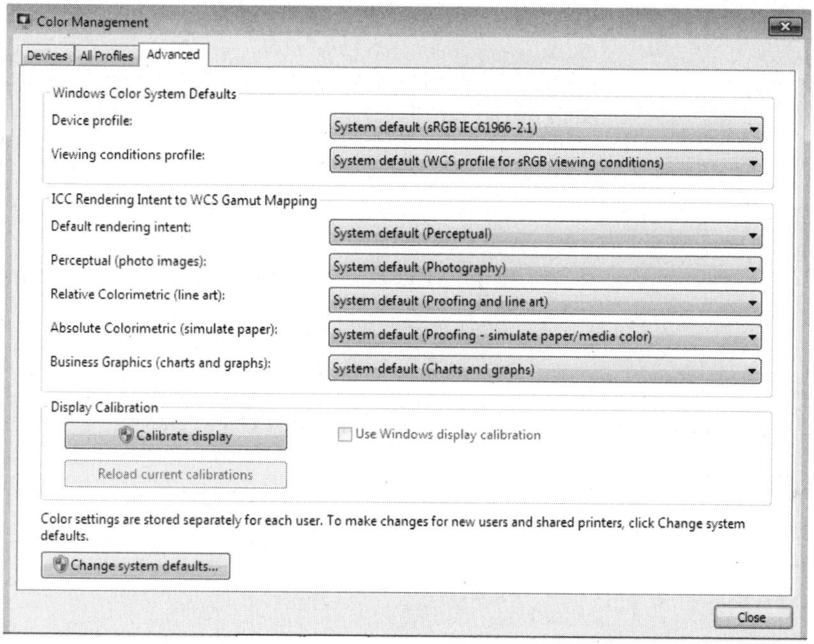

Credential Manager You use the Credential Manager to store credentials such as usernames and passwords. These usernames and passwords get stored in vaults so that you can easily log onto computers or websites.

There are three sections in the Credential Manager: Windows Credentials, Certificate-Based Credentials, and Generic Credentials. You can add credentials by clicking the link next to each of the three credential sections, shown in Figure 4.9.

FIGURE 4.9 Credentials Manager

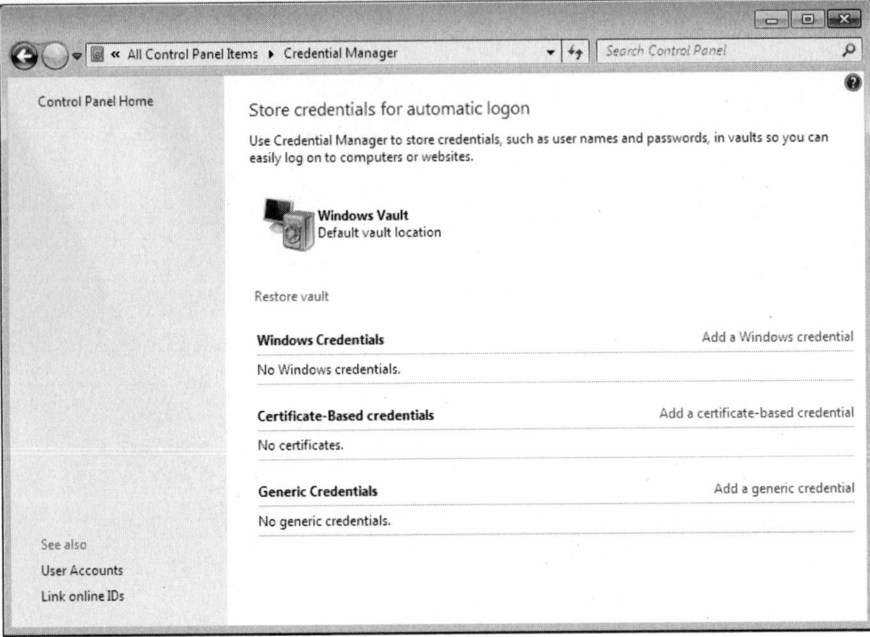

Date and Time The Date and Time icon allows you to configure your local date and time for the Windows 7 machine. You also have the ability to synchronize your clock with the Internet, as shown in Figure 4.10.

FIGURE 4.10 Time synchronization

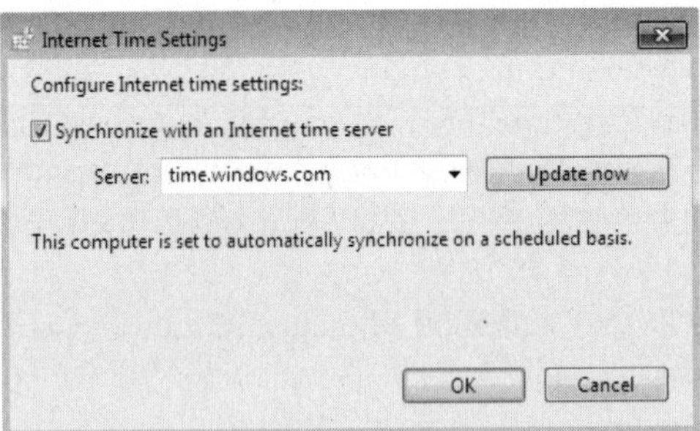

Default Programs The Default Programs icon allows you to choose the programs that Windows will use by default. For example, you can set Internet Explorer 8 to be the default web browser (see Figure 4.11).

FIGURE 4.11 Default Programs

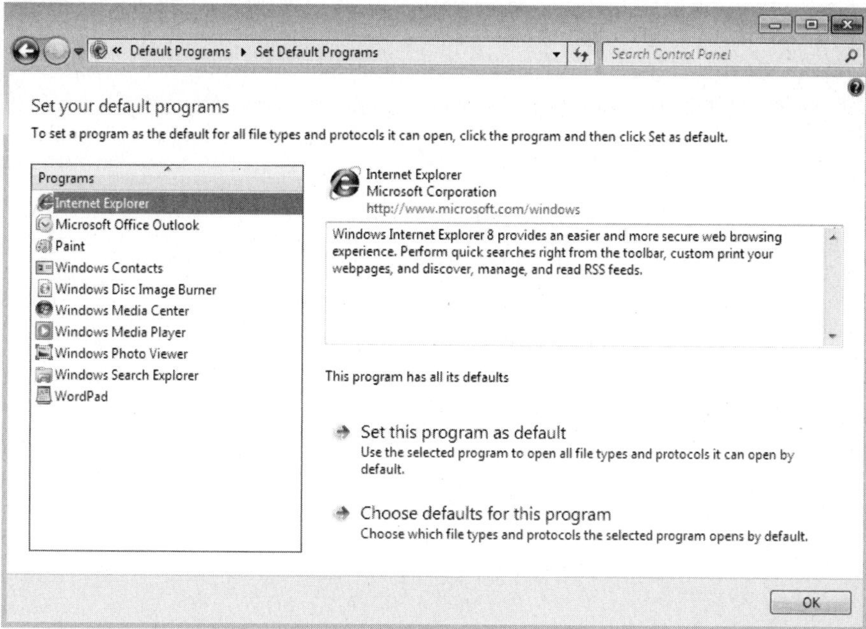

Desktop Gadgets With Desktop Gadgets icon, you can set up the different gadgets for your Windows 7 Desktop. Windows gadgets are programs that provide quick, visual representations of information, such as the weather, RSS feeds, your calendar, and the current time.

Windows gadgets are installed by default on Windows 7, but they have to be added to the Windows 7 Desktop.

Device Manager The Device Manager icon allows you to configure the different devices on your Windows 7 machine. You can configure such devices as disk drives, display adapters, DVD/CD-ROM drives, monitors, and network adapters. Device Manager is explained in greater detail in Chapter 5, "Configuring Hardware and Applications."

Devices and Printers You can use the Devices and Printers icon so you can add or configure the devices on your machine and your printers. Devices and Printers will be discussed further in Chapter 5.

Display The Display icon allows you to configure your display. You can change the size of the text and other items on your screen. You also have the ability to change the resolution, calibrate colors, change display settings, adjust ClearType text, and change custom text size.

Ease of Access Center The Ease of Access Center allows you to set up your accessibility options.

Folder Options The Folder Options icon allows you to configure how you view folders on the Windows 7 machine by default. You have the ability to set up how you browse and navigate folders, which files and folders you can view (see Figure 4.12), and how folders are searched.

FIGURE 4.12 Folder Options

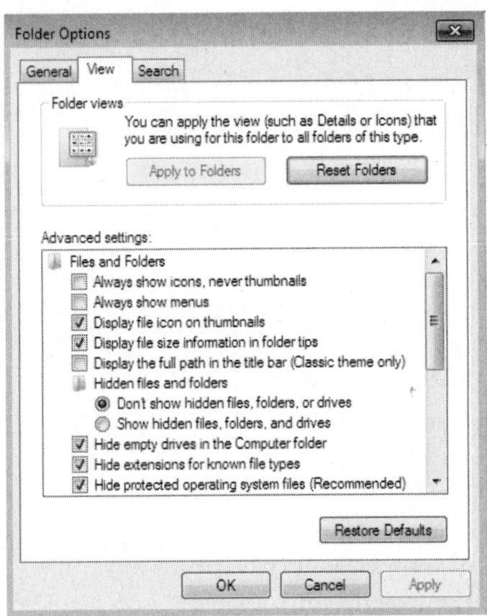

Fonts The Fonts icon is where you can install, preview, delete, show, hide, and configure the fonts that the applications on your Windows 7 operating system can use. The Fonts icon allows you to get fonts online, adjust ClearType text, find a character, and change font size.

Getting Started The Getting Started icon allows you to learn about and configure your Windows 7 operating system. In the Getting Started icon you can do the following:

- Go online to find out what's new in Windows 7
- Personalize Windows
- Transfer files and settings from another computer
- Use a HomeGroup to share with other computers in your home
- Choose when to be notified about changes to your computer
- Go online to get Windows Live Essentials

- Back up your files
- Add new users to your computer
- Change the size of the text on your screen

HomeGroup HomeGroups are small local networks that you can easily configure at home and work.

When you install HomeGroups on your first computer, a password is assigned so that you can connect other computers to this HomeGroup. The password can be changed from the HomeGroup icon. HomeGroups are discussed in greater detail in Chapter 7, "Configuring Network Connectivity."

Indexing Options Windows uses indexing to perform very fast searches of common files on your computer. The Indexing Option feature gives you the ability to configure which files and applications get indexed (see Figure 4.13).

FIGURE 4.13 Indexing advanced options

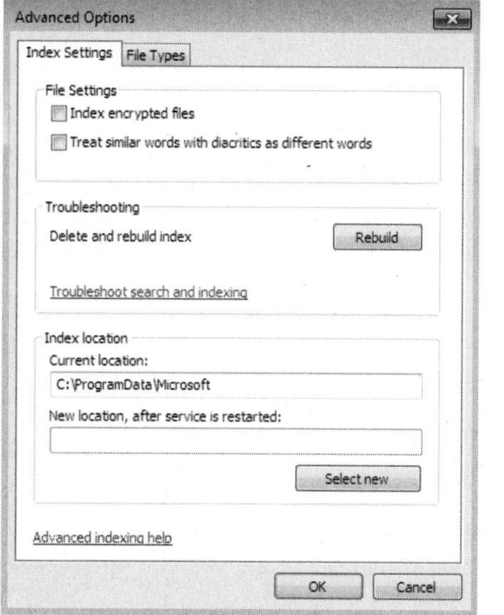

Internet Properties The Internet Properties icon allows you to configure how the Internet will operate (see Figure 4.14). From this icon you can configure your home page, browsing history, tabs, security, privacy, content, connections, and programs. Internet Explorer will be discussed in greater detail in Chapter 5.

FIGURE 4.14 Internet Properties

Keyboard Keyboard Properties allows you to configure how the keyboard will react when used. You can set the Character repeat speed (how fast the keyboard will repeat what you are typing) and the cursor speed. You can also configure the keyboard drivers from these properties.

Location and Other Sensors Sensors are either software or hardware devices that pick up information from the surrounding area for your computer. Windows 7 supports both hardware and software sensors.

Examples of hardware sensors are motion detectors and an example of a software sensor is your computer reacting to a network packet. The following is a list of the sensors that are supported in Windows 7:

- GPS
- Accelerometer
- Proximity
- Light
- RFID
- Compass
- Camera

- Microphone
- Temperature
- Moisture
- Motion detector
- Traffic
- Weather station

Mail When you set the Mail properties, you set up your client-side mail settings. In the Mail properties, you can set up different user profiles (mailboxes) and the local mail servers or Internet mail servers to which they connect.

Mouse Mouse Properties gives you the ability to configure how the mouse will operate (see Figure 4.15). You can configure the buttons, click speed, clicklock, pointer type, pointer options, center wheel, and hardware properties.

FIGURE 4.15 Mouse Properties

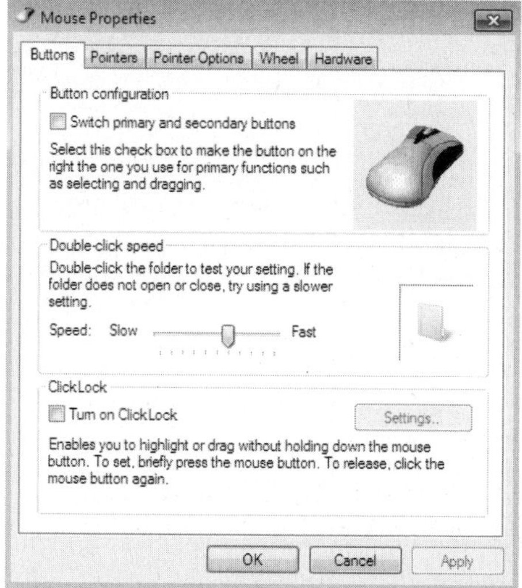

Network and Sharing Center The Network and Sharing properties configure your Windows 7 machine to connect to a local network or the Internet. You can configure TCP/IP, set up a new network, connect to a network, choose a HomeGroup, and configure the network adapter. Network and Sharing Center is discussed in greater detail in Chapter 7.

Notification Area Icon The Notification Area is the icon in the lower right-hand window of Windows 7 (next to the time) taskbar. The Notification Area icon in Control Panel allows you to configure which icons will appear on the Taskbar and which notifications will be shown.

Parental Controls Parental Controls lets you manage how children can use the Windows 7 computer. With Parental Controls, you can set the hours that they can use the computer, the programs that they can access, and the type of games they can play.

When children try to access applications or games that they are not allowed to use, a notification will let them know that these are restricted. The restricted child can click a link that will then ask for access to the application or game and then the parent can accept or decline the request.

Performance Information and Tools The Performance Information and Tools icon gives you the ability to run a Windows Experience Index measurement (see Figure 4.16). The Windows Experience Index measures the performance of the computer system.

FIGURE 4.16 Performance Information and Tools

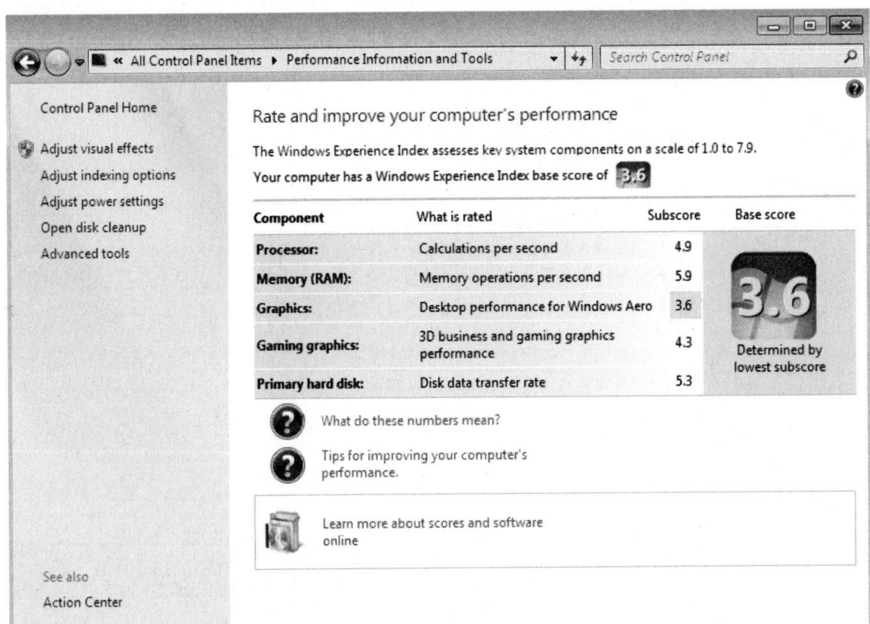

The results will be issued as a base score. The higher the base score, the better your machine is performing. Performance Information and Tools will also show you how you can improve the performance of the machine.

Personalization Personalization allows you to set up your Desktop environment.

Phone and Modem The Phone and Modem properties are used to set up your local dialing properties and modem options. You can set up your dialing location, modem properties, and telephony providers.

Power Options Power plans allow a user to maximize their Windows 7 machine's performance and/or conserve energy. You have the ability to enter your own power restrictions to customize your machine. Power options are important settings when you are dealing with laptops. Since many laptops use batteries, power options allow you to get the most time from their batteries. Power management will be discussed later in this chapter.

Programs and Features The Programs and Features icon was the Add/Remove Programs icon in Windows XP. Programs and Features allows you to uninstall, change, or repair programs and features, as shown in Figure 4.17.

FIGURE 4.17 Programs and Features

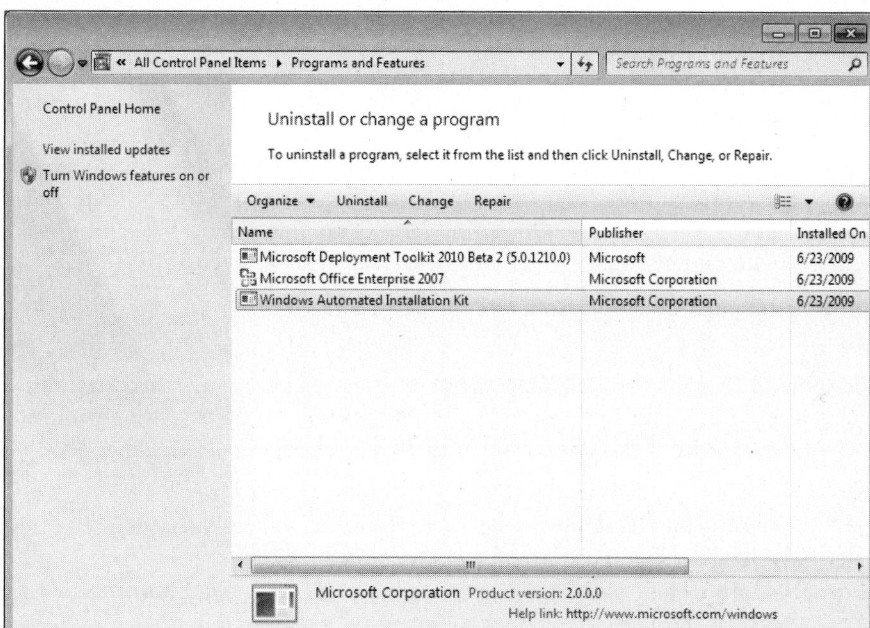

The Programs and Features icon also allows you to choose which Windows 7 features you want installed on the machine (see Figure 4.18). Some of the features that you can enable are Games, Indexing Services, Telnet client, Telnet server, etc.

FIGURE 4.18 Windows Features

Recovery The Recovery icon allows a user or administrator to recover the Windows 7 system to a previously captured restore point. System Restore is one of the first recovery options that appear when your Windows 7 system is experiencing problems. Recovery will be discussed in detail in Chapter 9, "Configuring Backups and Recovery."

Region and Language The Region and Language tool allows you to configure your local regional settings.

RemoteApp and Desktop Connections RemoteApp and Desktop Connections allows you to access programs and Desktops on your network. To connect to these resources (Remote Applications and Desktops), you must have the proper permission to access these resources.

With the RemoteApp and Desktop Connections, you can connect to either a remote computer or a virtual computer. To create a new connection, use the Set Up A New Connection Wizard included with the RemoteApp and Desktop Connections icon.

Sound The Sound tool allows you to configure your machine's audio. You can configure output (speakers and audio drivers) and your input devices (microphones).

Speech Recognition The Speech Recognition icon allows you to configure your speech properties. Speech Recognition allows you to speak into the computer and that speech will be displayed on the system. Many programs like Microsoft Office can type in the words as you speak them into the system. In the Speech Recognition icon, you can complete the following items:

- Start Speech Recognition
- Set up a microphone
- Take speech tutorials
- Train your computer to better understand you
- Open the Speech Reference Card

Sync Center The Sync Center allows you to configure synchronization between the Windows 7 machine and a network server. The Sync Center also allows you to see when synchronization had occurred, if the synchronization was successful, and if there were any errors.

System The System icon is one of the most important icons in Control Panel. The System icon allows you to view which operating system your machine is using, check system resources (processor, RAM), change the computer name/domain/workgroup, and activate Windows 7. From the System icon you can also configure the following settings:

- Device Manager
- Remote Settings
- System Protection
- Advanced Settings

Taskbar and Start Menu The Taskbar and Start Menu icon allows you to configure how the Taskbar, Start menu, and toolbars will operate.

Troubleshooting The Troubleshooting icon in Control Panel allows you to troubleshoot common Windows 7 problems (see Figure 4.19). You can troubleshoot:

- Program issues
- Hardware and Sound
- Network and Internet
- Appearance and Personalization
- System and Security issues

FIGURE 4.19 Troubleshooting options

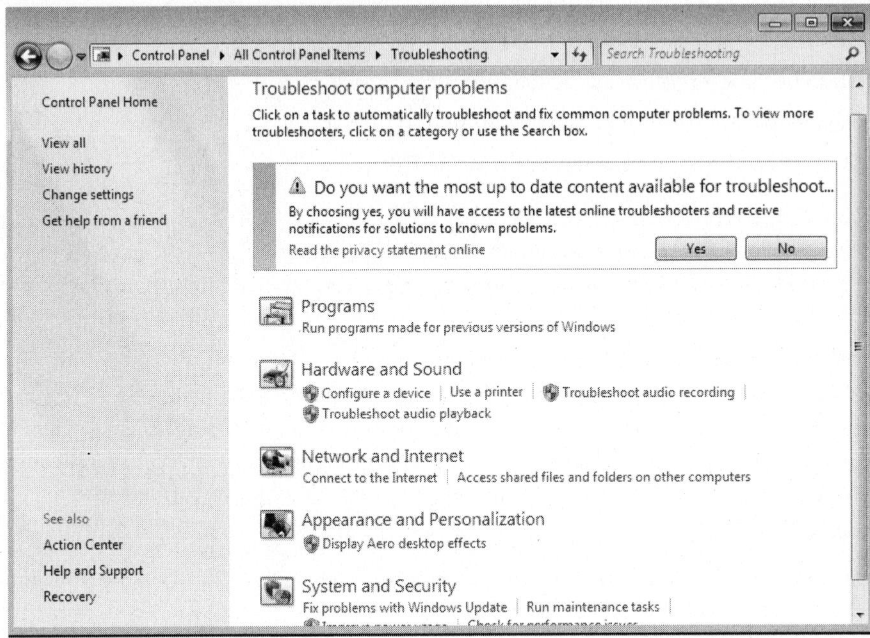

User Accounts The User Accounts icon allows you to create and modify user accounts. In the User Account icon, you can perform the following tasks:

- Change user passwords
- Remove passwords
- Change the account picture
- Change the account name
- Change the account type
- Manage Accounts
- Change User Account Control settings

Creating user accounts will be discussed in greater detail in Chapter 6, "Managing Users, Groups, and Security."

Windows CardSpace Windows CardSpace is a new way for you to interact with websites and online services. Windows CardSpace allows you to replace the username and passwords that you currently use with online services. Here are some of the things you can do with Windows CardSpace:

- Review the identity of the site
- Manage your information by using Information Cards
- Review card information before you send it to a site
- Receive requests for information from websites

Windows Defender Windows Defender is a built-in Windows 7 application that protects your system from spyware. It is included free with the operating system, and once you turn it on, it starts automatically protecting your system. Windows Defender can operate in two modes:

Real-time Protection In Real-time Protection mode, Windows Defender runs in the background and protects your system as you are working live on the Internet or a network.

Scanning Options When it's in Scanning Option mode, you can run a system scan at any time to check for spyware. This option does not require Windows Defender to always be running.

Windows Firewall Windows Firewall, shown in Figure 4.20, helps prevent unauthorized users or hackers from accessing your Windows 7 machine from the Internet or the local network. Windows Firewall is explained in detail in Chapter 8.

FIGURE 4.20 Windows Firewall

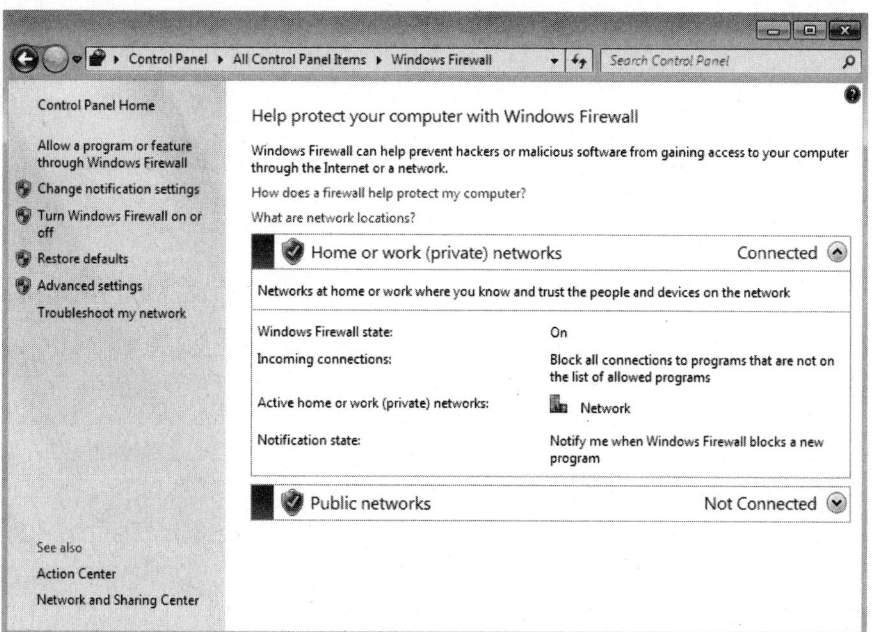

Windows Update The Windows Update icon allows you to configure the way the Windows 7 operating system will receive updates from Microsoft's website. The Windows Update icon is explained in greater detail in Chapter 1, "Windows 7 Installation."

In Exercise 4.3, you'll install the Telnet client on the Windows 7 operating system.

EXERCISE 4.3

Installing Features

1. Open the Programs And Features tool by clicking Start ➤ Control Panel ➤ Programs And Features.
2. Click the Turn Windows Features On Or Off link in the upper-left corner.
3. Scroll down the features list and check the Telnet client check box.
4. Click OK.

Real World Scenario

Using Telnet

As an IT manager, my job does not just consist of working on Windows machines. I also need to understand and work on routers.

When working with most routers, you can use the Telnet client to connect to most routers. Using the Telnet client, you can configure the router to operate the way your organization needs it to operate.

I mentioned Windows Firewall in the section "Using Control Panel." I do not recommend that you use Windows Firewall as your main line of defense against hackers. You need to purchase a good router/firewall to complete this task. Knowing how to configure this router using the Telnet client will help you accomplish your networking needs.

Its fine to use Windows Firewall on all the clients as an added line of defense, but do not make it your main line of defense.

Now that we have taken a look at all the icons in Control Panel, let's now take a look at the System icon in greater detail.

Understanding the System Icon

The System icon in Control Panel is a very useful set of utilities and tasks that can allow you to set Remote Access, System Devices, System Protection, and the computer name, just to name a few.

Let's take a look at the different utilities and tasks that can be configured in Control Panel.

Windows Edition The Windows Edition section shows you which edition of Windows the machine is currently using. The Windows Edition section also shows if service packs are installed.

System The System section shows information about the system hardware. The System sections shows the following information:

- Rating
- Processor
- Installed Memory (RAM)
- System Type
- Pen and Touch

Computer Name, Domain, and Workgroup Settings In the Computer Name, Domain, And Workgroup settings section, you can change the name of the computer system and also change the workgroup or domain (see Figure 4.21). Windows 7 works well with Windows Server 2008 R2, which is explained in greater detail in Chapter 7, "Configuring Network Connectivity."

FIGURE 4.21 Change the computer name, domain, or workgroup

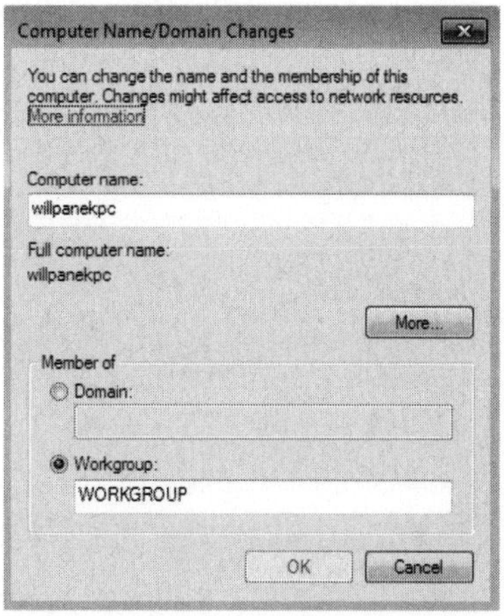

Windows Activation The Windows Activation section allows you to activate your Windows 7 operating system. The Windows Activation section also allows you to change your Product key before activating.

Remote Settings In the Remote Settings section, you can set the Remote Assistance and Remote Desktop settings for the Windows 7 system, as shown in Figure 4.22. Windows Remote Assistance allows an administrator to connect to a machine and control the mouse and keyboard while the user is on with the administrator. This option can be enabled or disabled.

FIGURE 4.22 Remote settings screen

Remote Desktop allows you to have your own session on the Windows 7 operating system. While you are logged on to the Windows 7 operating system through Remote Desktop, the user of the machine can't view the session. There are three Remote Desktop options from which you can choose:

Don't allow connections from this machine Choosing this option denies anyone the ability to connect to this machine through Remote Desktop.

Allow connections from computers running any version of Remote Desktop (less secure) This setting allows any computer running Remote Desktop to connect to this

Windows 7 machine. These machines do not need to use Network Level Authentication, and that's what makes this connection type less secure.

Allow connections only from computers running Remote Desktop with Network Level Authentication (more secure) Network Level Authentication is a new authentication method used for Remote Desktop (Windows Vista and higher). It allows Remote Desktop users to connect to the Windows 7 operating system securely.

You also have the ability in Remote Desktop to specify which users have access to the Windows 7 machine through the use of Remote Desktop.

System Protection The System Protection section is for configuring restore points and recoverability for the Windows 7 operating system (see Figure 4.23). You can also manage disk space and manage all of your restore points from the System Protection section.

FIGURE 4.23 System Protection screen

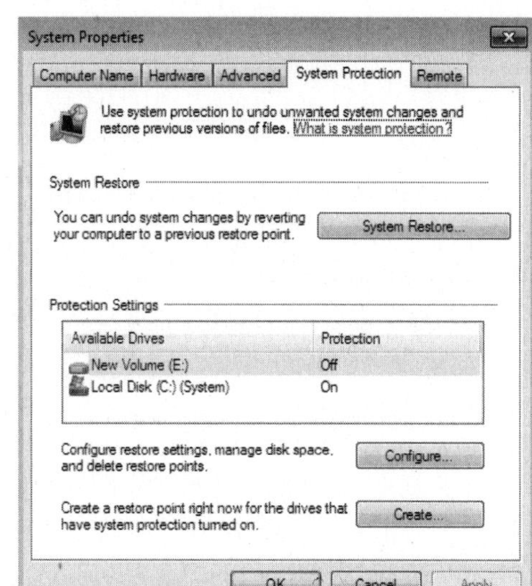

Advanced System Settings The Advanced System Settings section allows you to set up such items as visual effects, processor scheduling, memory usage, virtual memory, Desktop settings, system startup, and recoverability (see Figure 4.24).

FIGURE 4.24 Advanced System Settings

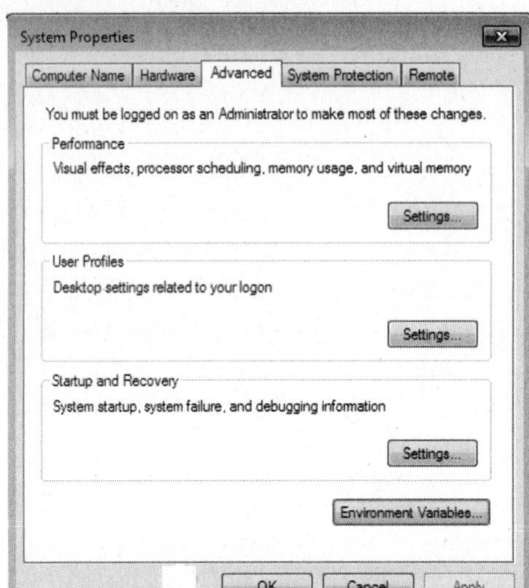

There are three main sections within the Advanced System Settings section:

Performance The Performance section allows you to configure the visual effects, the virtual memory, processor scheduling, and the Data Execution Prevention for the Windows 7 operating system.

The virtual memory is a section of the hard drive that is used by the system and RAM. Think of RAM as a pitcher of water. As the water fills up the pitcher, the pitcher becomes full. Once it's full, more water would cause it to overflow. The virtual memory is the overflow for RAM. When RAM fills up, the oldest data in RAM gets put into the virtual memory. This way the system does not need to look at an entire hard drive for that data. It finds it in the virtual memory.

The Data Execution Prevention section helps protect against damage from viruses and other security threats.

User Profiles The User Profiles section allows you to copy, delete, or move a user's Desktop profile to another location or user account. User's profiles were discussed in Chapter 6, "Managing Users, Groups, and Security."

Startup and Recovery The Startup and Recovery section (see Figure 4.25) allows you to configure which operating system will be booted by default (important for dual-booting machines) and what should happen when the system gets a startup error.

FIGURE 4.25 Startup and Recovery

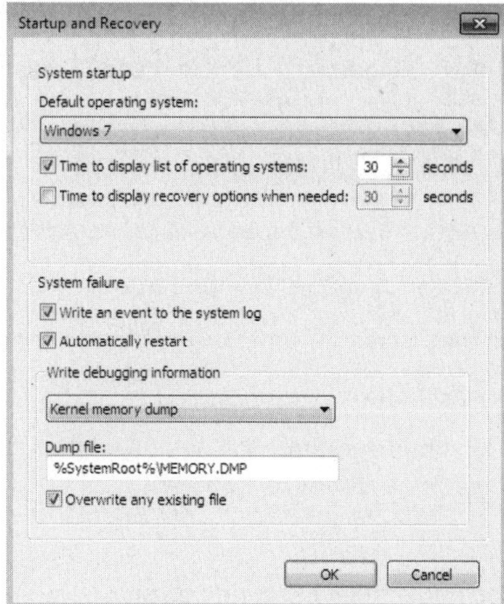

You can also configure the Device Manager from the System icon. The Device Manager is discussed in greater detail in Chapter 5, "Configuring Hardware and Applications."

Let's now take a look at how to configure some of the options using the System icon. Complete Exercise 4.4 to change the computer name.

EXERCISE 4.4

Changing the Computer Name

1. Open the System tool by clicking Start ➢ Control Panel ➢ System.
2. Under the Computer Name, Domain, And Workgroup settings section, click the Change Settings link.
3. Click the Change button in the To Rename This Computer section.
4. In the Computer Name field, rename your computer. Click OK.
5. A dialog box asking you to reboot the machine will appear. Click the OK button.
6. Click the Close button. Click the Restart Now button.

Now that you have renamed the computer, let's take a look at how to configure performance options. Complete Exercise 4.5 to manipulate your system's virtual memory.

EXERCISE 4.5

Changing the System's Virtual Memory

1. Open the System tool by clicking Start ➢ Control Panel ➢ System.
2. In the left-hand side, click the Advanced System Settings link.
3. Under the Performance section, click the Settings button.
4. When the Performance option screen appears, click the Advanced center tab.
5. In the Virtual Memory section, click the Change button.
6. Uncheck the check box that states Automatically Manage Paging File Size For All Drives.
7. Click the Custom Size radio button.
8. Set the Minimum and Maximum settings to one and a half times RAM. For example, if your RAM is 1,024 MB, set the settings to 1,536 MB.
9. Click the Set button.
10. Click OK. Click OK at the Performance Options screen.
11. Close the System Properties screen.

Microsoft Windows 7 handles the virtual memory requirements by default, but I recommend increasing the virtual memory on your machine if hard drive space is available. I use the rule of thumb of one and a half to two times the size of RAM. You want to make sure that the virtual memory is at least the same size as your RAM at a minimum.

Now let's take a look at how to set up some recoverability options for your operating system. Complete Exercise 4.6 to create a restore point.

EXERCISE 4.6

Creating a Restore Point

1. Open the System tool by clicking Start ➢ Control Panel ➢ System.
2. In the left side, click the System Protection link.
3. When the System Protection screen appears, click the Create button in the Create A Restore Point Right Now section.
4. A dialog box asks you to type in a description to help identify which restore point it is. Type in today's date and click the Create button.

5. Next, a dialog box stating that the restore was created successfully appears. Click the Close button.
6. Now click the System Restore button.
7. At the System Restore box, click Next.
8. At the "Restore your computer to the state it was in before the selected event" screen, you should see the restore point that you just created.
9. If the restore that you created is there, click Cancel. If the restore is not there, repeat steps 2 through 5.

Another way to configure options within the Windows 7 operating system is to configure the settings directly in the Registry. To do this, you use a Registry editor. In the next section we will discuss using the Registry editor.

Using the Registry Editor

You use the Registry Editor program to edit the Registry. This utility is designed for advanced configuration of the system. Usually, when you make changes to your configuration, you use other utilities, such as Control Panel, which was discussed in the previous section.

Only experienced administrators should use the Registry Editor. It is intended for making configuration changes that can be made only directly through the Registry. For example, you might edit the Registry to specify an alternate location for a print spool folder. Improper changes to the Registry can cause the computer to fail to boot. Use the Registry Editor with extreme caution.

Windows 7 uses the REGEDIT or REGEDT32 programs as the primary utility for Registry editing in Windows 7. These programs support full editing of the Registry. To use REGEDIT, select Start and type **REGEDIT** in the Search dialog box. To use REGEDT32, type **REGEDT32** into the Search dialog box.

The Registry is organized in a hierarchical tree format of keys and subkeys that represent logical areas of computer configuration. By default, when you open the Registry Editor, you see five Registry key listings, as shown in Figure 4.26 and described in Table 4.1.

FIGURE 4.26 The Registry Editor window

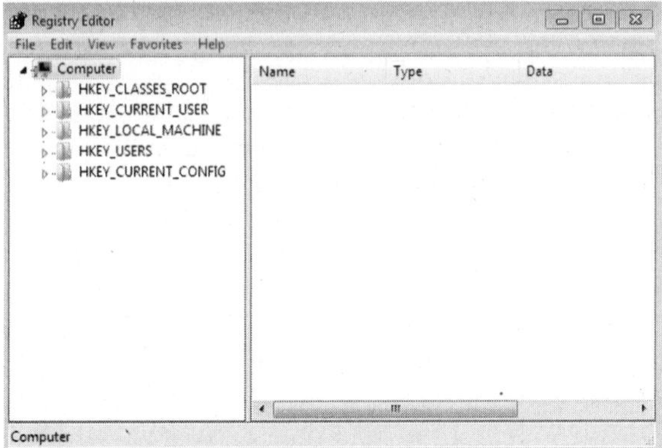

TABLE 4.1 Registry Keys

Registry Key	Description
HKEY_CURRENT_USER	Configuration information for the user who is currently logged on to the computer. This key is a subkey of the HKEY_USERS key.
HKEY_USERS	Configuration information for all users of the computer.
HKEY_LOCAL_MACHINE	Computer hardware configuration information. This computer configuration is used regardless of the user who is logged in.
HKEY_CLASSES_ROOT	Configuration information used by Windows Explorer to properly associate file types with applications.
HKEY_CURRENT_CONFIG	Configuration of the hardware profile that is used during system startup.

Real World Scenario

Using the Registry Editors

As an IT manager, I have used the Registry Editors many times in my career. One change that I like to make to my servers is the ShutDownWithoutLogon entry.

If you start your Registry Editor and do a search on ShutDownW (it's the only one, so you do not need to type it out completely), a value of zero will be shown. I change this value to a one. Now what does this do?

> When you log on to a server, by default at the logon screen, the Shutdown button is grayed out. It is set this way by default because you may not want just anyone shutting down the computer. So you want them to log in before shutting down.
>
> If my servers are locked in a secure computer room, I change the Shutdown button so that it is active. I do this so that if I need to use the Last Known Good option to recover the Registry, I can shut down at the logon screen.

Earlier in this chapter I showed you that Remote Desktop Connection is one of the configurable Windows 7 options. In the next section, we will look at configuring different ways to remotely connect using the Windows 7 operating system and how to allow others to remotely connect to you for assistance.

Configuring Remote Connections

End user support for most IT departments is a major concern and a time-consuming endeavor. Anything we can do to provide a more efficient solution to user issues is a major benefit. Basic telephone or chat support works in many cases, but what if you could see what the end user sees or even interface with their machine? By using Remote Assistance and Remote Desktop, you can. If you've been using them with XP and Vista, you're really going to be pleased with the improvements with Windows 7.

Remote Assistance in Windows Vista provided many enhancements over previous versions, including improvements in security, performance, and usability. Windows 7 goes even further by adding Easy Connect, which makes it even easier for novice users to request help from expert users. Group Policy support has been increased. There is command-line functionality (meaning we can add scripting), bandwidth optimization, logging, and even more.

Remote Desktop is a tool that allows you to take control of a remote computer's keyboard, video, and mouse. This tool does not require someone collaborating with you on the remote computer. Remote Desktop is used to access remote machines' applications and troubleshoot issues as well as provide end user needs where you want complete control of the remote machine. Let's start the discussion with Remote Assistance.

Remote Assistance

Remote Assistance provides a method for inviting help by instant message, email, a file, or now an Easy Connect option. To use Remote Assistance, the computer requesting help and the computer providing help must have Remote Assistance capabilities and both computers must have network connectivity (they have to be able to talk to each other).

Remote Assistance is designed to have an expert user provide assistance to a novice user. The "expert" and "novice" terms are used to describe the assistor (expert) and assistee (novice). When assisting a novice user, the expert can use text-based chat built into Remote Assistance. The expert can also take control of a novice user's desktop (with permission of course). Here are some common examples of when you would use Remote Assistance:

- Diagnosing problems that are difficult to explain or reproduce. Remote Assistance can allow an expert to remotely view the computer and the novice user can show the expert an error or problem.
- Guiding a novice user to perform a complex set of instructions. The expert can also take control of the computer and complete the tasks if necessary.

Easy Connect

The Easy Connect method for getting remote assistance is new for Windows 7. Easy Connect uses Peer Name Resolution Protocol (PNRP) to set up direct peer-to-peer transfer using a central machine on the Internet to establish the connection. PNRP uses IPv6 and Teredo tunneling to register a machine as globally unique. You're not using IPv6? You are with PNRP; Windows 7 (as well as Vista and Windows Server 2008) has IPv6 turned on natively as well as the currently used standard of IPv4. You will, however, be able to use only Easy Connect with Windows 7 and beyond. We'll discuss IPv6 in more detail in a later chapter, but to give you an idea, you can see the structure of the PNRP Teredo IPv6 packet in Figure 4.27.

FIGURE 4.27 Teredo and IPv6 PNRP structure

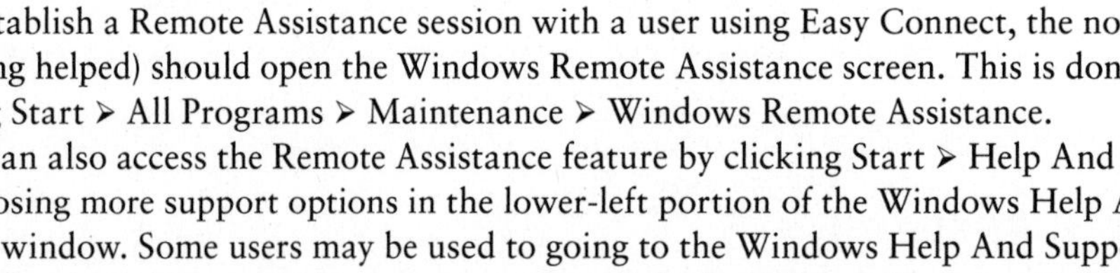

	Time	Source	Destination	Protocol	Info
88	15.301866	2001:0:4137:9e50:2810	2001:0:4137:9e50:1864	IPv6	IPv6 no next header
89	15.310901	2001:0:4137:9e50:2810	2002:d093:467d::d093:	ICMPv6	Echo request
90	15.321489	192.168.1.124	70.41.124.129	UDP	Source port: 59021 Des
91	15.321832	2001:0:4137:9e50:2810	2001:0:4137:9e50:205c	IPv6	IPv6 no next header
92	15.330986	65.55.129.172	192.168.1.124	UDP	Source port: pnrp-port

User Datagram Protocol, Src Port: 59021 (59021), Dst Port: teredo (3544)
Teredo IPv6 over UDP tunneling

To establish a Remote Assistance session with a user using Easy Connect, the novice (the user being helped) should open the Windows Remote Assistance screen. This is done by selecting Start ➢ All Programs ➢ Maintenance ➢ Windows Remote Assistance.

You can also access the Remote Assistance feature by clicking Start ➢ Help And Support and choosing more support options in the lower-left portion of the Windows Help And Support window. Some users may be used to going to the Windows Help And Support window from previous operating system versions. It looks different, but it's still there. You can also launch the Windows Remote Assistance screen by typing **msra** in the integrated search box from the Start menu (click the Start button).

Whichever way the novice or the expert launches the feature, the Windows Remote Assistance screen will become available. To start using Easy Connect, the novice user will select Invite Someone You Trust To Help You. The initial Remote Assistance window where the novice will initiate an invitation is shown in Figure 4.28.

FIGURE 4.28 Remote Assistance initial screen

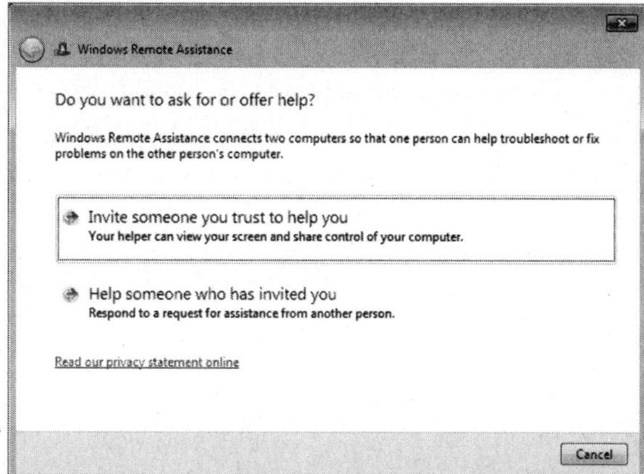

The Windows 7 machine is configured by default to allow Remote Assistance. If this has been disabled in the configuration, an error will be generated here and you must enable Remote Assistance. To enable a remote computer to allow Remote Desktop access, select Start ➢ Control Panel ➢ System And Security ➢ System. Click Remote Settings in the left pane. Select the Allow Remote Assistance Connections To This Computer check box and click OK. This will create an exception in Windows Firewall to allow Remote Assistance.

The Windows Remote Assistance screen (Figure 4.29) will ask, "How do you want to invite your trusted helper?" and will offer the user the option to use Easy Connect.

FIGURE 4.29 Remote Assistance invite screen

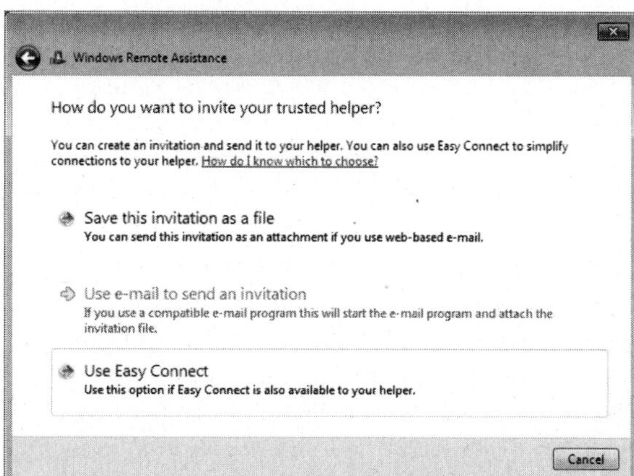

One nice feature of Easy Connect is that if the novice user has already established an Easy Connect session previously with an expert user, the screen after selecting Use Easy Connect will offer the novice the ability to connect to the same expert. The novice user can also choose to invite someone new and/or delete the old contact if necessary. The expert user will have the same option after choosing Use Easy Connect from the machine used for a previous Easy Connect session.

After the Use Easy Connect option is selected, Windows 7 will verify network connectivity briefly. This is the point at which the PNRP actions take place and the novice user's information is added to a cloud in the Internet space. The cloud is the group of machines holding little pieces of information, the identifiers of users needing connectivity, set up in a peer-to-peer sharing environment. PNRP uses this distributed infrastructure for its peer-to-peer name resolution. The novice user's contact information is entered into the PNRP cloud and an associated password is created and displayed to the novice user.

The novice user will now relay the password to the expert by text message, telephone, or any convenient conversation method. The novice will simply have to wait for the expert to initiate their part. The novice user will still have to accept the connection once the expert starts the remote assistance session.

The expert user needs to start a Remote Assistance session the same way the novice did, but the expert will choose Help Someone Who Has Invited You from the Windows Remote Assistance screen (Figure 4.30).

FIGURE 4.30 Remote Assistance

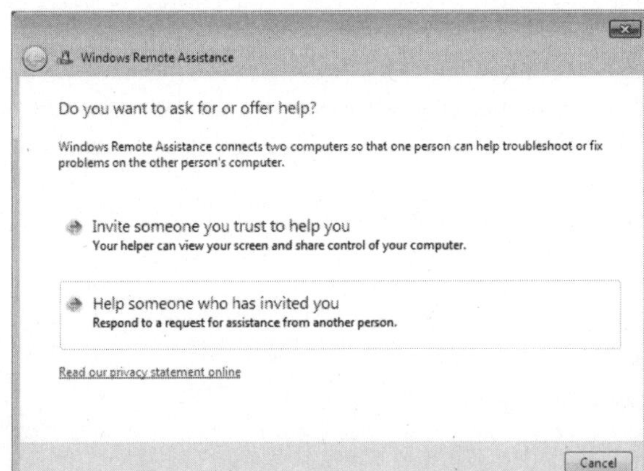

The expert user will be presented a dialog box to enter the password given by the novice user (Figure 4.31) who is initiating the Remote Assistance session.

FIGURE 4.31 Remote Assistance screen for entering a password

After a few moments of querying the PNRP cloud and finding the connection path back to the novice user, Remote Assistance presents the novice user a confirmation box verifying that the user wants to allow help from the expert.

The novice user will then have a control bar on their screen indicating that the Remote Assistance session is active. From this control bar, the novice can initiate a chat session with the expert and modify some general session settings (bandwidth, logging, contact information exchange, and sharing control).

The expert user will be shown the novice user's Desktop within a separate Remote Assistance window. The expert user will also have some general configuration-setting capabilities as well as an option to request control of the novice user's desktop. The novice user will, of course, be allowed to accept or reject the expert's request.

The expert and novice user can now have a interactive session in which the necessary assistance can be provided. This method of help really takes out the "can you tell me what you see on your screen" issues between two users. The Easy Connect feature takes one more problem out of the equation, getting a novice user to send an invitation to another user. The one caveat here is that both users must be using Windows 7 for Easy Connect to be an option.

Now what if the user is not available to send you the invitation? You can still connect to a user's computer using Remote Desktop, which I will discuss in the next section.

Remote Desktop

Remote Desktop is a tool in Windows 7 that allows you to take control of a remote computer's keyboard, video, and mouse. This tool does not require someone to be available to collaborate with you on the remote computer. While the remote computer is being accessed, it remains locked and any actions that are performed remotely will not be visible to the monitor that is attached to the remote computer.

New/Updated Features

Windows 7 Remote Desktop is, again, an enhanced version of the remote desktop functionality that has been with us for many of the previous versions of Windows, both client and server operating systems. Remote Desktop uses Remote Desktop Protocol (RDP) to provide the data between a host and a client machine. Windows 7 is using the latest version of RDP, RDP 7.0. Windows 7 Remote Desktop enhancements are as follows:

- RDP Core Performance Enhancements
- True Multi-Monitor Support
- Direct 2D and Direct 3D 10.1 Application Support
- Windows 7 Aero Support
- Bi-directional Audio Support
- Multimedia and Media Foundation Support

There are many uses for Remote Desktop, but the most common use is that of the administrator attempting to perform a task on an end user's machine (or server).

Another use is the end user connecting to a machine from their home or on the road. If you have noticed the enhancements of Remote Desktop (which are enhancements to the RDP protocol), you can see that one of the main goals of enhancing Remote Desktop is to make the user experience as comfortable and seamless as possible.

Real World Scenario

Using Remote Desktop Functionality

I have mentioned many times about using Remote Desktop for troubleshooting client computers. As an administrator, I like to just take control of an end user machine and fix it. Although this can be done in Remote Assistance, the end user is required to allow us to have access and then can watch what we do. In Remote Desktop, we just take control and close the interactive session at the remote machine (yes, the remote end user can block us or take over the session, but not if they want their problem solved).

But there are other uses as well. We provide a server with resources to our clients, and that server may need to be changed or updated on a regular basis (sometimes a couple of changes in a day). Remote Desktop allows us to maintain our server and database from wherever we are without impacting the clients or other administrators.

Remote Desktop Connection Options

When connecting to a Remote Desktop host machine, there are several options available to enhance the client user session. The options allow configuration for general settings, display options, local resource access, programs to be executed on startup, the user experience, and advanced options for security and Remote Desktop gateway access. The options are available by selecting the Options button in the lower-left area of the initial Remote Desktop connection screen. Figure 4.32 shows the options window both hidden and displayed.

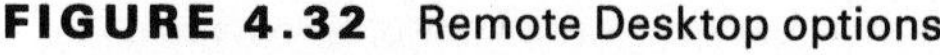

FIGURE 4.32 Remote Desktop options

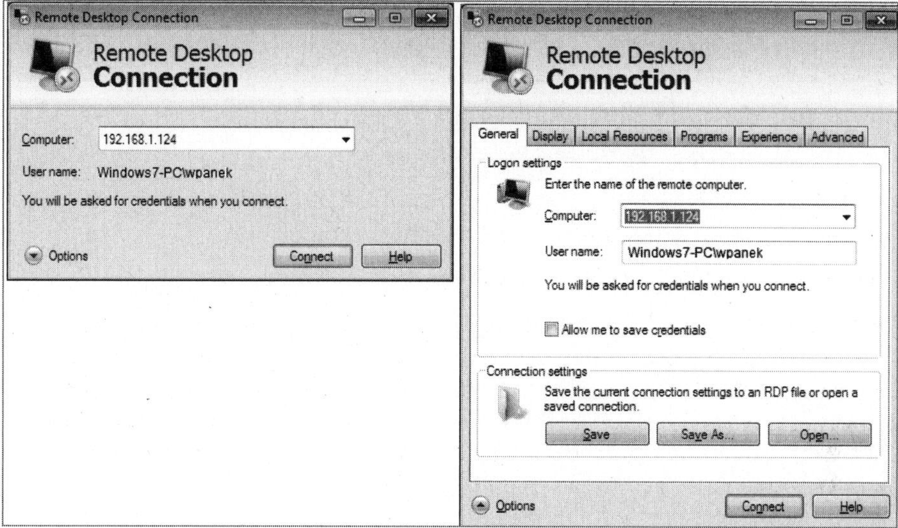

From the General tab, the host computer and username can be selected. User credentials can be saved from this tab as well. The connection settings can be saved to a file or an existing RDP file can be opened from the General tab.

From the Display tab (Figure 4.33), the size of the display screen can be chosen. This is also where the option to use multiple monitors will be selected. The color depth (color quality) is selected in the Display tab. The option to display the connection bar when using full screen display is available here as well.

FIGURE 4.33 Remote Desktop Display options

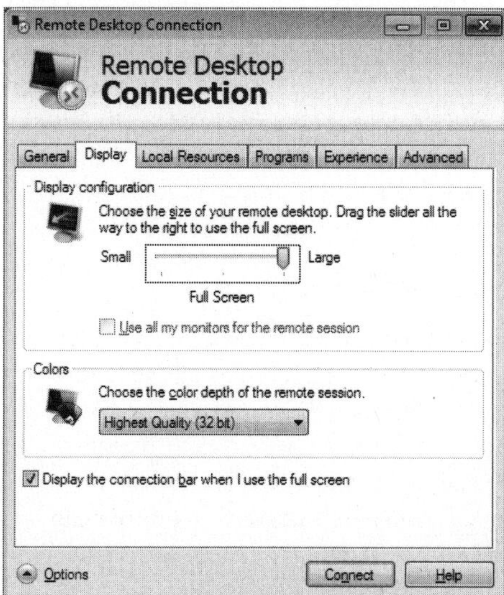

From the Local Resources tab (Figure 4.34), remote audio settings, keyboard settings, and local device and resource access can be configured.

FIGURE 4.34 Remote Desktop Local Resources options

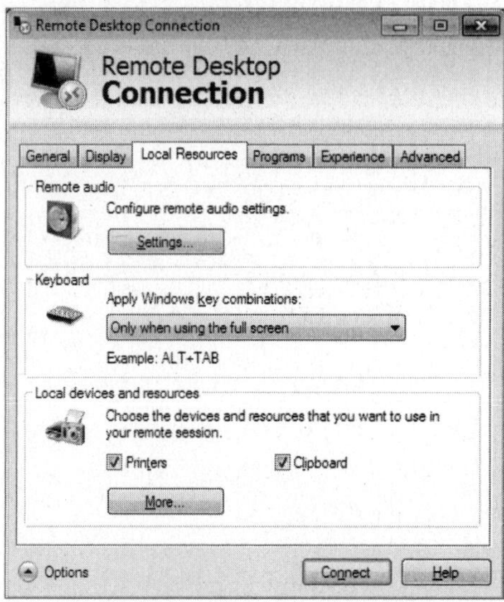

The Programs tab (Figure 4.35) for Remote Desktop options allows the selection of a program to run at connection startup. The program name and path are specified as well as a startup folder if necessary.

FIGURE 4.35 Remote Desktop Programs options

The end user experience is important to the overall success of using Remote Desktop in the user environment. Remember, Remote Desktop can be used to provide a user with the ability to connect to their machine and "remote in." The most seamless environment from the user to the remote location is desirable, but that will be dependent on the bandwidth available. The more bandwidth, the more high-end features can be made available to the end user.

This is also nice for the administrator who is working on an end user machine. The Experience tab (Figure 4.36) allows the configuration of the end user experience.

FIGURE 4.36 Remote Desktop Experience options

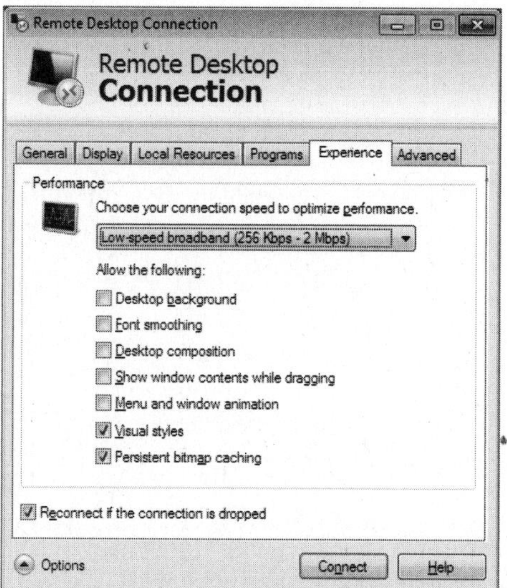

Controlling the behavior of the Remote Desktop connection with regard to security is configured on the Advanced tab of the Remote Desktop options dialog. The Advanced tab also supports the configuration of a Remote Desktop gateway to allow Remote Desktop connections to be established from any Internet location through SSL. The user must still be authorized and the Remote Desktop client must still be available.

In Exercise 4.7, you will enable the Windows 7 machine to allow Remote Desktop connections.

EXERCISE 4.7

Enabling Remote Desktop

1. Open the System tool by clicking Start ➢ Control Panel ➢ System.
2. In the left-hand side, click the Remote Settings link.

EXERCISE 4.7 *(continued)*

3. In the Remote Desktop section, click the radio button that allows connections from computers running any version of Remote Desktop (less secure).
4. Make sure the Allow Remote Assistance Connections To This Computer check box is checked.
5. Click OK.
6. Close the System Properties screen.

Another way a Windows 7 user can connect to a server is through the use of a virtual private network (VPN) connection. In the next section, we will look at how to configure a VPN connection on Windows 7.

Configuring a VPN Connection

A virtual private network (VPN) is a way to establish a connection between a client machine (VPN client) and server machine (VPN server). A VPN gives you the ability to connect (called tunneling) to a server through the use of the Internet or a dial-up connection (hopefully not dial-up). In a nutshell, a VPN allows you to connect to a private network from a public network.

VPN connections can be secured using different protocols. The following list shows you some of the different tunneling protocols that can be used when connecting a Windows 7 machine to a remote server.

Secure Socket Tunneling Protocol (SSTP) *Secure Socket Tunneling Protocol (SSTP)* is the newest of the tunneling protocols and it is available when tunneling with a Windows Server 2008 server. The way SSTP works is that SSTP allows encapsulated Point-to-Point Protocol (PPP) packets to be transmitted over an HTTP connection. Because of this, firewalls or Network Address Translation (NAT) devices allow SSTP VPN connections to be more easily established. SSTP is the best choice for securing a VPN connection.

Point-to-Point Tunneling Protocol (PPTP) *Point-to-Point Tunneling Protocol (PPTP)* is one of the predecessors to SSTP and it also allows point-to-point packets to have encryption for secure connections. PPTP uses TCP/IP for the encryption. PPTP encapsulates PPP frames in the IP protocol section and uses the TCP protocol section for the management side of the PPTP protocol.

Layer 2 Tunneling Protocol (L2TP) *Layer 2 Tunneling Protocol (L2TP)* is a tunneling protocol that has no encryption included in the protocol. L2TP uses the IP Security protocol (IPSec) to make L2TP secure. L2TP with IPSec is a much more secure tunneling option than PPTP.

To set up a VPN connection in Windows 7, you use the Network and Sharing Center. In Exercise 4.8, you will set up a new VPN connection.

EXERCISE 4.8

Setting Up a VPN Connection

1. Start the Network and Sharing Center by clicking Start ➢ Control Panel ➢ Network And Sharing Center.
2. Choose the Set Up A New Connection Or Network link.
3. Choose Connect To A Workplace. Click Next.

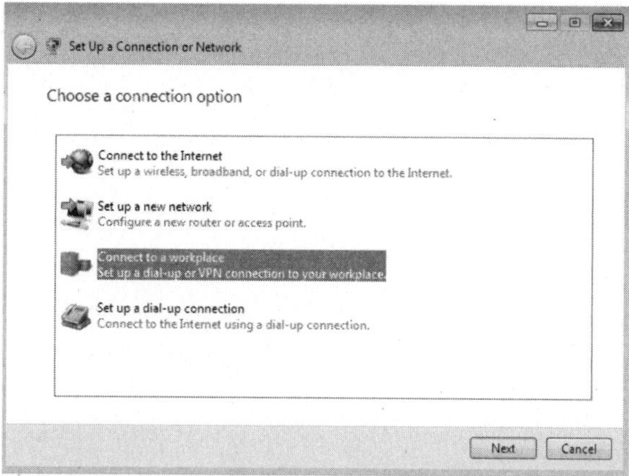

4. Choose the Use My Internet Connection (VPN) option.
5. The Connect To A Workplace screen appears. You need to type in the TCP/IP address of a Windows Server 2008 machine and name this VPN connection. In this window, you also have the ability to use a smart card, allow other people to use this connection, and to set up just the VPN but not connect at this time (the option I chose). After you type in a TCP/IP address and name the VPN connection, click Next.

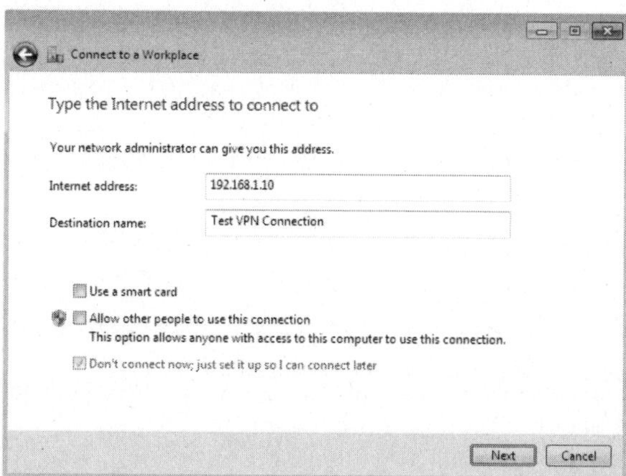

EXERCISE 4.8 *(continued)*

6. The next screen asks you for your logon credentials. Type in your username, password, and domain name. Click Create.

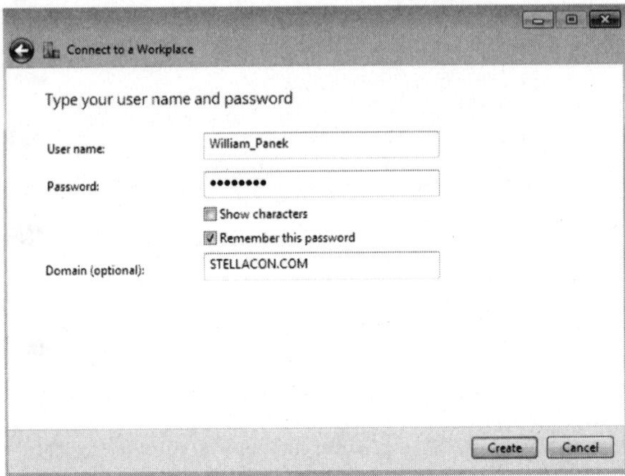

7. Now that the connection is created, I'll show you the steps needed to use it. In the Network and Sharing Center, click the Connect To A Network link.

8. A box appears showing your connections. To connect to the VPN connection, choose the corresponding link.

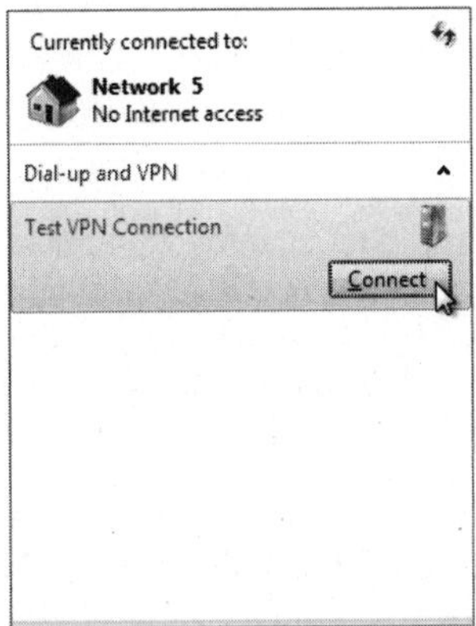

9. When the Connect Dialog box appears, make sure your username, password, and domain name are present and click the Connect button.

10. After the connection is established, close it and close the Network and Sharing Center.

In many organizations Windows 7 will be loaded onto a laptop computer. In the next section, we will look at how to configure Windows 7 mobile computing.

Configuring Mobile Computing

Windows 7 includes several features that are particularly useful for laptop computers. For example, through Power Options in Control Panel, you can select a power plan and enable power-management features. Enabling a power plan gives the user a chance to conserve battery life and get the most out of mobility.

To see many of the power options, you must be using Windows 7 on a laptop computer. If you are running Windows 7 on a desktop, you will see many but not all of the features covered in the following sections.

Recognizing the Improvements to Power Management

Windows 7 builds upon the power-management features that were introduced with Windows XP with some the following enhancements:

- Battery meter, which provides a notification icon in the system tray that details the computer's battery power
- Power plans, which are collections of hardware and software settings optimized for a specific function

- Sleep power state, which combines the speed of standby with the features of hibernate mode
- ReadyDrive, which provides faster booting and resume times when used in conjunction with ReadyDrive-capable hard drives

These power enhancements were present with Windows Vista but I listed them here because I understand that many users and administrators did not switch to Windows Vista.

After looking at some of the features of Windows 7 Power Management, let's take a look at managing the different power options.

Managing Power States

In Windows 7, the Advanced Configuration Power Interface (ACPI) specifies different levels of power states:

- Fully active PC
- Sleep
- Hibernation
- Complete shutdown of PC

The sleep power state is a new power state introduced with Windows 7 that combines the features of hibernate and standby. When a computer enters the sleep power state, data including window locations and running applications is saved to the hard disk, and that session is available within seconds when the computer wakes. The computer can thus be put into a power-saving state when not in use but allows quick access to the in-process user session, so the user can begin working more quickly than if the computer were shut down or put into hibernation.

Hibernation falls short of a complete shutdown of the computer. With hibernation, the computer saves your Desktop state as well as any open files. To use the computer again, you need to press the power button. The computer should start more quickly than from a complete shutdown because it does not have to go through the complete startup process. You will have to again log on to the computer. Similar to when the computer is put into sleep mode, all the documents that were open when the computer went into hibernation are still available. With hibernation you can easily resume work where you left off. You can configure your computer to hibernate through Power Options or by choosing Start, then clicking the arrow and selecting Hibernate from the drop-down menu. This option will appear only if hibernation has been enabled through Power Options.

Unless you want to completely shut down the computer, configuring the computer to enter Sleep mode is typically the best power-saving option. You may need to upgrade your computer's BIOS in order to use advanced power modes such as sleep

The Hibernation mode may not be available on your Windows 7 laptop machine by default. You must make sure your firmware can support Hibernation. If it does not appear by default and your system can support Hibernation, complete the following steps to enable the Hibernate function.

EXERCISE 4.9

Enabling the Hibernate Feature

1. Open an elevated command prompt (right-click on the command prompt and choose Run As Administrator).

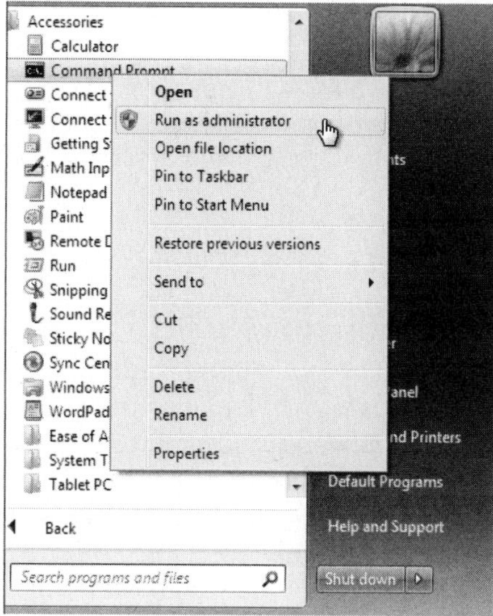

2. Click Yes at the dialog box.
3. At the prompt, type `powercfg -h` **on** and press Enter. Entering the same command and using the Off switch would disable Hibernation on the machine.
4. Close the command prompt.

Now let's take a look at the different types of power options that you can configure.

Managing Power Options

You configure power options through the Power Options Properties dialog box. To access this dialog box, access Control Panel ➢ Power Options. The Power Options dialog box provides the ability to manage power plans and to control power options, such as when the display is turned off, when the computer sleeps, and what the power button does.

Configuring Power Plans

Windows 7 includes three configurable power plans: Balanced, Power Saver, and High Performance. Power plans control the trade-off between quick access to an existing computer session and energy savings. In Windows 7, each power plan contains default options that can be customized to meet the needs of various scenarios.

The Balanced power plan, as its name suggests, provides a balance between power savings and performance. By default, this plan is configured to turn off the display after 20 minutes and to put the computer to sleep after 1 hour of idle time. These times can be modified as needed. Other power options that can be modified include Wireless Adapter settings and Multimedia settings. Wireless adapters can be configured for maximum power savings or maximum performance. By default, the Balanced power plan configures wireless adapters for maximum performance. The Multimedia settings can be configured so that the computer will not be put into Sleep mode when sharing media. For example, if the computer is acting as a Media Center device, then you can configure the computer to remain on by setting the Prevent Idling To Sleep option so that other computers can connect to it and stream media from it even when the computer is not being used for other purposes.

The Power Saver power plan is optimized for power savings. By default, the display is configured to be turned off after 20 minutes of inactivity, and the computer will be put into sleep mode after 1 hour of inactivity. Additionally, this power plan configures hard disks to be turned off after 20 minutes of inactivity.

The High Performance power plan is configured to provide the maximum performance for portable computers. By default, the computer will never enter Sleep mode, but the display will be turned off after 20 minutes. When this setting is configured, by default the Multimedia settings are configured with the Allow The Computer To Enter Away Mode option, which allows the computer to enter into a new power state called Away mode. Away mode configures the computer to look like it's off to users but remain accessible for media sharing. For example, the computer can record television shows when in Away mode.

You can modify the existing power plans to suit your needs by clicking Change Plan Settings or you can use the preconfigured power plans listed in Table 4.2.

TABLE 4.2 Windows 7 power plans

Power Plan	Turn Off Display	Put Computer to Sleep
Balanced	After 20 minutes	1 hour
Power Saver	After 20 minutes	1 hour
High Performance	After 20 minutes	Never

Other Desktop options you can use are the Shutdown button and switching users. Let's take a look at these features.

Configuring the Power Button

Unless you decide to run your computer 24 hours a day, you will eventually want to shut it down. By default on the Start menu, you have a Shut Down button (this is called the power button). When you click this button, your machine will power off. But the power button does not have to be set to the Shut Down option. You can configure this button to Switch User, Logoff, Lock, Restart, or Shut Down.

You may have a machine that is shared by multiple users and it may be better for you to have the Switch User button on the Start menu instead of the Shut Down button. Configuring the Switch User option would make it easier on your users.

In Exercise 4.10 you will complete the following steps to configure the power button to the Switch User option.

EXERCISE 4.10

Changing the Power Button

1. Right-click the Shut Down button and choose Properties.
2. The Taskbar and Start Menu Properties dialog box appears. Make sure you are working on the Start Menu tab.
3. From the Power Button Action drop-down menu, choose Switch User.
4. Click OK.
5. Click the Start menu and verify that the power button is now set to Switch User.

After you decide how the power button is going to be used, you may want to configure some of the advanced power options. In the next section we will look at the different power options.

Configuring Advanced Power Settings

Each power plan contains advanced settings that can be configured, such as when the hard disks will be turned off and whether a password is required on wakeup. To configure these advanced settings, you click Control Panel ➤ Power Options and select the power plan to use. You then click Change Advanced Power Settings to open the Advanced Settings tab of the Power Options dialog box, shown in Figure 4.37.

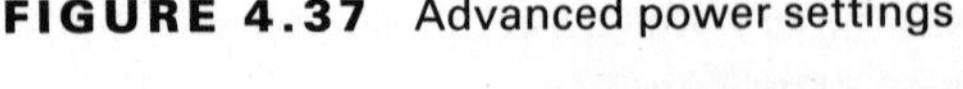

FIGURE 4.37 Advanced power settings

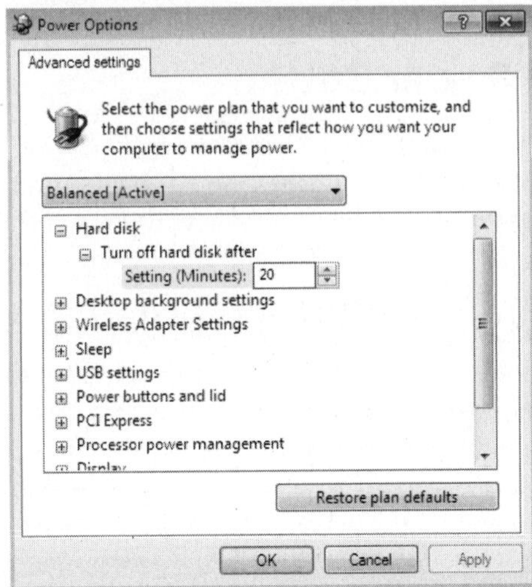

You can then modify the settings as desired or restore the plan defaults. For example, one option that you might want to change if you are using a mobile computer is the Power Buttons And Lid option, which configures what happens when you press the power button or close the lid of the mobile computer. When either of these actions occurs, the computer can be configured to do nothing, shut down, go into Sleep mode, or go into Hibernation mode.

Configuring Hibernation

Although Sleep is the preferred power-saving mode in Windows 7, Hibernation is still available for use. Hibernation for a computer means that anything stored in memory is also stored on your hard disk. This ensures that when your computer is shut down, you do not lose any of the information that is stored in memory. When you take your computer out of hibernation, it returns to its previous state.

To configure your computer to hibernate, access the Advanced Settings tab of the Power Options dialog box. The Hibernate option appears under the Sleep option.

Complete Exercise 4.11 to configure a power plan for your computer. If Hibernate is not present, complete the steps in Exercise 4.9 to enable hibernation.

EXERCISE 4.11

Configuring a Power Plan

1. Select Start ➢ Control Panel ➢ Power Options.
2. Select a power plan to modify from the Preferred Plans list and click Change Plan Settings.

3. Configure the power plan options for your computer based on your personal preferences. Click Change Advanced Power Settings to modify advanced power settings. When all changes have been made, click Save Changes.
4. Close Control Panel.

There is a useful tool when you're using a laptop on the battery that allows you to see how much time you have left until the battery dies. Let's take a look at the Battery Meter.

Managing Power Consumption Using the Battery Meter

Windows 7 includes a battery meter that you can use to monitor the battery power consumption on your computer. The battery meter also provides notification on what power plan is being used.

The battery meter appears in the notification area of the Windows Taskbar and indicates the status of the battery, including the percentage of battery charge. As the battery charge gets lower, the battery meter provides a visual indication of the amount of charge left. For example, when the battery charge reaches the low-battery level, a red circle with a white X is displayed.

The battery meter also provides a quick method for changing the power plan in use on the computer. By clicking the battery meter icon, you can select between the three preferred power plans available with Windows 7.

Using Windows ReadyBoost and Windows 7

With Windows Vista, Microsoft introduced several new technologies to help boost operating system performance. Windows ReadyBoost is a new technology that was introduced with Windows Vista and is also available in Windows 7.

Windows ReadyBoost allows for the use of multiple nonvolatile flash memory devices as an additional memory cache. When the physical memory devices become full on a computer with Windows ReadyBoost configured, data is written to the flash device instead of to the hard drive. This improves performance because data can be read more quickly from the flash drive than from the hard drive.

When a compatible device is installed on a Windows 7 computer, a ReadyBoost tab is displayed on the device's Properties dialog that can be used to configure Windows ReadyBoost.

To use a flash memory device with Windows ReadyBoost, the device must meet the following specifications:

- The device must have a storage capacity of at least 256 MB.
- The device must support USB 2.0.
- The device must support a throughput of 2.5 MB/sec for 4 K random reads and 1.75 MB/sec for 512 K random writes.

Using ReadyDrive and Windows 7

ReadyDrive is also a technology included with Windows 7 that you can use to speed up the boot process, resume from a hibernation state faster, and conserve battery power for mobile computers. ReadyDrive relies on new hybrid hard disks, which use flash memory technology in conjunction with mechanical hard disk technology.

When you use ReadyDrive, data is written to flash memory instead of to the mechanical hard disk. This saves battery power because the mechanical hard disk does not need to perform as many read/write actions. Additionally, read/write times with flash memory are quicker than with traditional hard disk media, so resuming from hibernation occurs faster.

Configuring the power options on a laptop can help save energy and extend battery life.

Another important item to look at when configuring Windows 7 is how you are managing your Windows services.

Managing Windows 7 Services

A service is a program, routine, or process that performs a specific function within the Windows 7 operating system. You can manage services through the Services window (Figure 4.38), which can be accessed in a variety of ways. If you go through the Computer Management utility, right-click Computer, select Manage, expand Services And Applications, and then expand Services. You can also go through Administrative Tools or set up Services as an MMC snap-in.

FIGURE 4.38 The Services window

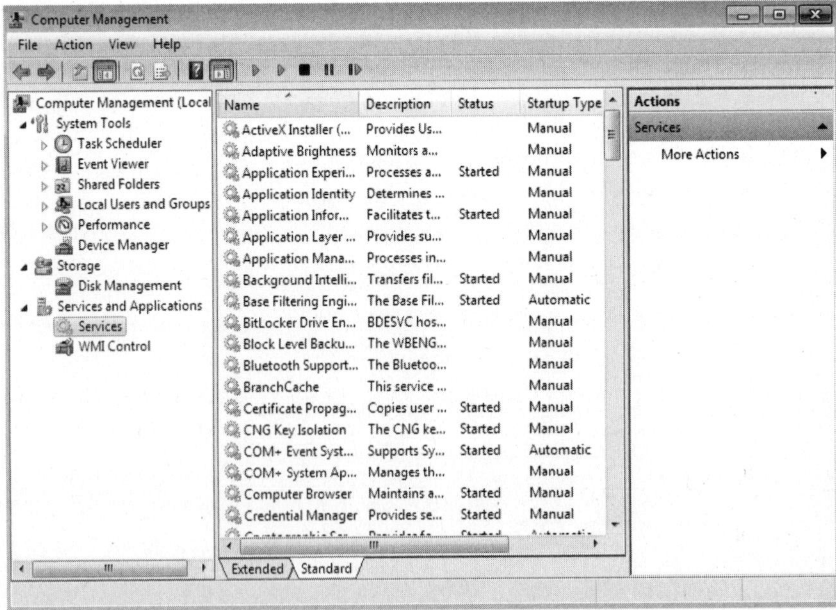

The Services window lists the name of each service, a short description, the status, the startup type, and the logon account that is used to start it. To configure the properties of a service, double-click it to open its Properties dialog box, shown in Figure 4.39. This dialog box contains four tabs of options for services: General, Log On, Recovery, and Dependencies.

FIGURE 4.39 The Properties dialog box for a service

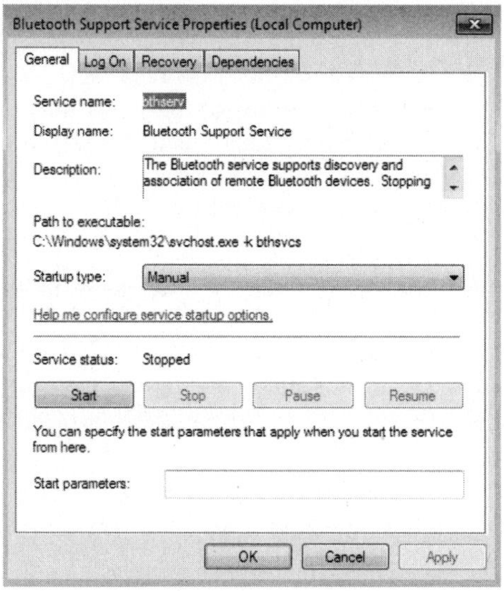

General Allows you to view and configure the following options:

- The service display name
- Display name
- A description of the service
- The path to the service executable
- The startup type, which can be automatic, manual, or disabled
- The current service status
- Start parameters that can be applied when the service is started

In addition, the buttons across the lower part of the dialog box allow you change the service status to start, stop, pause, or resume the service.

Log On The Log On tab allows you to configure the logon account that will be used to start the service. Choose the local system account or specify another logon account.

Recovery The Recovery tab allows you to designate what action will be taken if the service fails to load. For the first, second, and subsequent failures, you can select from the following actions:

- Take No Action
- Restart The Service
- Run A Program
- Restart The Computer

If you choose Run A Program, specify it along with any command-line parameters. If you choose Restart The Computer, you can configure a message that will be sent to users who are connected to the computer before it is restarted. You can also specify how long until a machine is restarted if an error occurs.

Dependencies The Dependencies tab lists any services that must be running in order for the specified service to start. If a service fails to start, you can use this information to examine the dependencies and then make sure each one is running. In the bottom panel, you can verify whether any other services depend on this service before you decide to stop it.

In Exercise 4.12 you will complete the steps needed to configure services in the Windows 7 operating system.

EXERCISE 4.12

Configuring Services

1. Start Computer Management by clicking Start and then right-clicking Computer. Choose Manage.
2. In the Computer Management MMC, expand the Services And Applications section.
3. Click the Services link.
4. Scroll down the list and double-click Remote Desktop Configuration.
5. Under the Startup Type, choose Automatic.
6. Under the Logon tab, click the This Account radio button.
7. Click the Browse button and choose the local administrator account. Click OK.

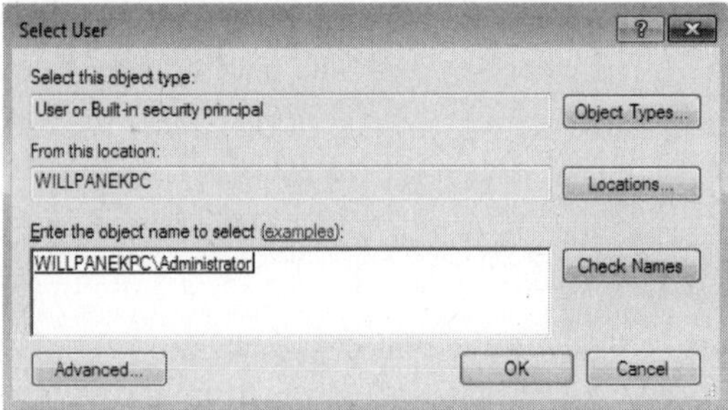

8. In the Password boxes, type and verify the Administrator password.
9. In the Recovery tab, make sure the following settings are configured.

   Action — Response

   First Failure — Restart The Service

   Second Failure — Restart The Service

   Subsequent Failures — Take No Action

   Reset Fail Count After — 1 Day

   Restart Service After — 10 Minutes
10. Click the OK button.
11. Close the Computer Management MMC.

Real World Scenario

Services

As an IT professional, I have had to troubleshoot many problems while doing my job. One of the very first things I always check when encountering an error with an application is the services for that application. Many times you need to just set the service from Manual to Automatic to solve the problem.

If the service is set to Automatic and it is still not starting properly, check the Dependencies tab. It will show you that all the other services that are required to start this service are configured and running properly.

Services are just another troubleshooting and configuring tool that is part of your arsenal of troubleshooting techniques. When services are working properly, your Windows 7 operating system works properly.

Summary

Besides actually installing Windows 7, configuring the operating system properly is one of the most important tasks that an IT team can perform.

Configuring the desktop environment allows an administrator to configure an environment that is comfortable for the end user, which in turn makes the user more productive.

Understanding the Start menu and Control Panel icons allows you to configure and operate the Windows 7 applications more efficiently. Knowing how to configure the System icon properly in Control Panel allows you to fine-tune the Windows 7 operating system and get the best performance possible out of it.

Besides using Control Panel to configure the Windows 7 operating system, you can edit the Registry directly using the REGEDIT utility.

Another important consideration when configuring Windows 7 is how the operating system will function on a laptop. By configuring the power options on a laptop, you can extend the life of your battery.

We also took a look at services that run on Windows 7 and how to configure and troubleshoot them when they don't run properly. In the next chapter, we will look at how to configure applications and hardware properly within Windows 7.

Exam Essentials

Be able to configure Desktop settings. Understand how to customize and configure the Windows 7 Desktop settings, including configuring Windows Aero, adding gadgets to the Desktop, creating shortcuts, and configuring the Taskbar and Start menu.

Be able to support mobile computers through power management features. Understand the new power features that are available in Windows 7 and be able to configure a laptop computer to use them.

Understand Remote Connections. Know how to configure and connect to machines through remote connections. You can use Remote Assistance, Remote Desktop, and a VPN.

Know how to configure services. Understand how to stop, start, monitor, pause, and configure services on the Windows 7 operating system. Know how to configure the different properties available through services.

Review Questions

1. You are the system administrator for your company. You are configuring the services on a Windows 7 computer. You want to ensure that if a service fails to load, it will attempt to restart. Which tab of the service's Properties dialog box should you use?

   A. General

   B. Log On

   C. Recovery

   D. Dependencies

2. The system administrator of your network wants to edit the Registry, including setting security on the Registry keys. What primary utility or utilities that support full editing of the Windows 7 Registry should the system administrator use? (Choose all that apply.)

   A. REGEDIT

   B. REDIT

   C. REGEDT32

   D. REGEDITOR

3. Kayla is dissatisfied with the configuration of her keyboard and mouse. She wants to reset the keyboard speed and the mouse pointer rate. Which utility should she use to configure the keyboard and mouse properties?

   A. Control Panel

   B. Computer Management

   C. Microsoft Management Console

   D. Registry Editor

4. Denise is using a laptop computer that uses ACPI. She wants to see what percentage of the battery power is still available. She also wants to know if Hibernation has been configured. Which of the following utilities should she use?

   A. Device Manager

   B. Computer Manager

   C. Battery meter

   D. MMC

5. You are administering a computer that is used by several customer support representatives for your company. The support representatives use a custom application to report support incidents. After the application is updated, it stops functioning properly and one of the programmers who wrote the application indicates that a Registry change needs to be made to the computer. You need to ensure that the change is applied for each user of the computer. Which Registry key should you modify?

   A. HKEY_CLASSES_ROOT

   B. HKEY_CURRENT_USER

   C. HKEY_LOCAL_MACHINE

   D. HKEY_USERS

6. You have a user, Rob, who uses a laptop computer running Windows 7. You have configured the laptop to enter Sleep mode after 30 minutes of inactivity. What will occur when the computer enters Sleep mode?

   A. The data will be saved to the hard disk, and the computer will shut down.

   B. The data will be erased from RAM, and the computer will shut down.

   C. The monitor will be turned off, but the hard disks will remain active.

   D. The data will be saved to the hard disk, and the computer will be put into a power-saving state.

7. You want to speed up the resume time on your computer after it is put into Hibernation mode. You have installed a hybrid hard disk drive into your Windows 7 computer. Which technology should you use to accomplish your goal?

   A. ReadyDrive

   B. ReadyBoost

   C. Superfetch

   D. SuperDrive

8. A new employee named Crystal has been supplied with a Windows 7 laptop computer. You have configured Crystal's computer with the Power Saver power plan, and you used the default options. Which of the following will occur after 20 minutes of inactivity on Crystal's computer?

   A. The display will be turned off, but the hard disk will remain active.

   B. The hard disk will be turned off, but the display will remain active.

   C. Both the hard disk and the display will be turned off.

   D. No components will be turned off.

9. You are the network administrator for a medium-sized company. You support all user Desktop issues. Gary is using the default Windows 7 Desktop on his laptop computer. Gary wants to change his Desktop settings. Which of the following options should Gary use to configure the Desktop in Windows 7?

   A. Right-click an empty space on the Desktop and choose Personalize from the context menu.

   B. Select Control Panel ➤ System.

   C. Right-click My Computer and choose Manage from the context menu.

   D. Right-click My Computer and choose Properties from the context menu.

10. You work on the help desk for a large company. One of your users calls you and reports that they just accidentally deleted their `C:\Documents\Timesheet.xls` file. What is the easiest way to recover this file?

    A. In Folder Options, click the Show Deleted Files option.

    B. In Folder Options, click the Undo Deleted Files option.

    C. Click the Recycle Bin icon on the Desktop and restore the deleted file.

    D. Restore the file from your most recent tape backup.

11. Dennis has a new display adapter and monitor. He wants to set display properties for his Desktop. Which of the following options are *not* set through the Personalization dialog box?

    A. Desktop background

    B. Screen saver

    C. Special visual effects for your Desktop

    D. Contrast and brightness of the monitor

12. You sit in a busy area of the office. Sometimes, you forget to log off or lock the computer when you leave your desk. How can you configure your computer so that it will become password-protected if it is idle for more than 10 minutes?

    A. Through the Logon/Logoff icon in Control Panel

    B. Through the Screen Saver option on the Personalization dialog box

    C. Through the Security icon in Control Panel

    D. Through the Security properties of Local Users and Groups

13. You are an administrator for your company's network. You want to configure the clock and stock ticker to be displayed on the Desktop of your users' computers. How can you accomplish this task?

    A. Through Control Panel ➤ Personalization

    B. Through Control Panel ➤ Desktop Gadgets

    C. Through Control Panel ➤ Windows Sidebar Properties

    D. Through Control Panel ➤ Ease of Access Center

14. You are configuring an image of Windows 7 that will be deployed to a new office location for your company. You are configuring the Desktop. You want to automatically hide the Taskbar when it's not being used. You also do not want the Taskbar to be moved by the users. How can you configure these options?

    A. By right-clicking an empty space of the Taskbar, selecting Properties, and clicking the Toolbars tab

    B. By right-clicking an empty space of the Taskbar, selecting Properties, and configuring the Taskbar tab

    C. By right-clicking an empty space of the Taskbar, selecting Properties, and clicking the Notification Area tab

    D. By right-clicking an empty space of the Taskbar, selecting Properties, and clicking the Start Menu tab

15. You are the network administrator for a manufacturing company. You are configuring several Windows 7 computers for a group of newly hired engineers. You want to optimize the new computers to use the Windows Aero theme. How can you accomplish this task?

    A. By right-clicking an empty space of the Desktop, selecting Personalize, and clicking Display Settings

    B. By right-clicking an empty space of the Desktop, selecting Personalize, and clicking Desktop Background

    C. By right-clicking an empty space of the Desktop, selecting Personalize, and clicking Screen Saver

    D. By right-clicking an empty space of the Desktop and selecting Personalize. Then choose your theme.

16. You are configuring a computer to be deployed to another network administrator. You want to allow the other administrator to quickly access the Administrative Tools options available with Windows 7. How can you accomplish this task?

    A. By right-clicking an empty space of the Taskbar, selecting Properties, and clicking Desktop on the Toolbars tab

    B. By right-clicking an empty space of the Taskbar, selecting Properties, and clicking Show Quick Launch on the Taskbar tab

    C. By right-clicking an empty space of the Taskbar, selecting Properties, and clicking the Customize button on the Start Menu tab

    D. By right-clicking an empty space of the Taskbar, selecting Properties, and clicking Customize on the Notification Area tab

17. You are the network administrator for a large company. One of your users calls and states that they are getting an error every time they start an application. You want to see what the user is doing and what the error is. How can you accomplish this?

    A. Remote Desktop

    B. Hyper-V

    C. Remote Assistance

    D. Virtual PC

18. You are a consultant for a large organization. Some employees contact you at 11:00 p.m. and state that one of the servers is down. No one is in the office to fix the problem. How can you connect to the server fix the problem?

    A. Remote Desktop

    B. Hyper-V

    C. Remote Assistance

    D. Virtual PC

19. You are the network administrator for a large organization that wants to set up a secure VPN between two of the company's locations using the Internet. Both sides of the VPN use Windows Server 2008. What is the best protocol to use to set up the VPN?

    A. PPTP

    B. L2TP

    C. SSTP

    D. PPP

20. You are the network administrator for a large organization. You have a user that needs you to connect and help them with a Windows 7 issue. You want to use Remote Assistance for the connection. Which of the following allows you to easily set up a Remote Assistance session?

    A. Easy Connect

    B. Quick Connect

    C. User Connect

    D. Fast Connect

Answers to Review Questions

1. C. You can configure what actions will occur if the service fails to start on the Recovery tab of the service's Properties dialog box. For example, you can configure the service to attempt to restart, or you can configure the computer to reboot.

2. A, C. In Windows 7, you can edit the Registry with REGEDIT or REGEDT32. You should always use extreme caution when editing the Registry because improper configurations can cause the computer to fail to boot.

3. A. You configure keyboard and mouse properties in Control Panel.

4. C. On a laptop computer, Denise can use the battery meter to view the amount of battery power available and to change the power plan configured for the computer.

5. C. You will need to make the Registry modification in the HKEY_LOCAL_MACHINE Registry key. This key provides configuration information that is accessible regardless of who is logged onto the computer.

6. D. When the computer enters Sleep mode, the data will be saved to the hard disk and the computer will be put into a power-saving state. Sleep mode combines the features of standby and Hibernation so that all data is saved to the hard disk, but the computer restores faster than if the computer were put into Hibernation mode.

7. A. You should use the Windows ReadyDrive technology to help speed the resume time of your computer after it has been put into Hibernation mode. ReadyDrive is a new technology that is used in conjunction with hybrid hard disk drives, which combine flash memory with standard hard disk technology. This allows data to be stored in flash memory, which enables the hard disk to remain spun down longer and also improves the time required for the computer to resume after being put into Hibernation mode.

8. C. When a Windows 7 computer is configured with the Power Saver power plan, the computer's display and hard disk will be turned off after 20 minutes of inactivity in order to conserve energy. The computer will be put into sleep mode after 1 hour of inactivity when using the Power Saver power plan.

9. A. The easiest way to configure the Desktop is by right-clicking an open area of the Desktop and choosing Personalize.

10. C. The easiest way to recover a deleted file is to restore it from the Recycle Bin. The Recycle Bin holds all of the files and folders that have been deleted as long as there is space on the disk. From this utility, you can retrieve or permanently delete files.

11. D. Through the Personalization dialog box, you can set your Desktop background, the screen saver to be used by your computer, and any special visual effects for your Desktop. Contrast and brightness of the monitor are typically set through the monitor's controls.

12. B. The Screen Saver option of the Personalization dialog box allows you to select a screen saver that will start after the computer has been idle for a specified amount of time. You can configure the screen saver options to require the user's password in order to resume the computer's normal function. When the password is invoked, the computer will be locked. To access the locked computer, you must enter the password of the user who is currently logged on or an administrator password.

13. B. You can configure notification area options, such as displaying the clock and stock ticker, through Control Panel ➤ Desktop Gadgets. Windows 7 has removed the Windows Vista Sidebar.

14. B. You can configure Taskbar options by right-clicking an empty space of the Taskbar, selecting Properties, and then configuring the Taskbar tab. This tab contains several options for configuring the Taskbar, such as Lock The Taskbar, Auto-Hide The Taskbar, and Use Small Icons.

15. D. You can configure user interface settings by clicking an empty space on the Desktop and selecting Personalize. The Themes for Windows 7 will appear. The Windows 7 Aero theme includes user interface elements, such as transparent windows and color schemes.

16. C. You can configure Start Menu options by clicking an empty space of the Taskbar, selecting Properties, and clicking the Customize button on the Start Menu tab, which opens the Customize Start Menu dialog box. This dialog box provides a list of configuration options that customize how items are displayed on the Start menu. The System Administrative Tools option configures how the Administrative Tools icon is displayed. You can configure the Administrative Tools icon to be displayed on the All Programs menu, to be displayed on both the All Programs menu and the Start Menu, or not to be displayed on either the Start Menu or the All Programs menu.

17. C. Remote Assistance is what you want to use to see the user's actions and the error. Remote Desktop does not allow a user to work with you during your connection. Hyper-V and Virtual PC have nothing to do with remote connections.

18. A. Remote Desktop allows you to connect to a machine and take over the session. Remote Assistance requires that a user invite you to the connection.

19. C. SSTP is the newest of the tunneling protocols and it is available when tunneling with a Windows 2008. The way SSTP works is that SSPT allows encapsulated Point-to-Point Protocol (PPP) packets to be transmitted over an HTTP connection.

20. A. The Easy Connect method for getting remote assistance is new for Windows 7. Easy Connect uses Peer Name Resolution Protocol (PNRP) to set up direct peer-to-peer transfer using a central machine on the Internet to establish the connection.

Configuring Hardware and Applications

MICROSOFT EXAM OBJECTIVES COVERED IN THIS CHAPTER:

✓ **Configure devices.**

- This objective may include but is not limited to: updating, disabling, and uninstalling drivers; signed drivers; conflicts between drivers; configuring driver settings; resolving problem device drivers

✓ **Configure application compatibility.**

- This objective may include but is not limited to: setting compatibility mode; implementing shims; compatibility issues with Internet Explorer

✓ **Configure Internet Explorer.**

- This objective may include but is not limited to: configuring compatibility view; configuring security settings; configuring providers; managing add-ons; controlling InPrivate mode; certificates for secure websites

Getting hardware up and running in today's operating systems is not usually a problem. With Plug and Play technology, the initial installation and configuration will typically go smoothly. However, the software controlling the hardware (drivers) will usually need to be updated over time and may need to be rolled back in case of an issue in a new package.

There will also be times when the drivers need to be installed manually for legacy hardware. You may also need to verify hardware configuration and make adjustments. The utility provided to perform these functions is Device Manager.

Device Manager displays all installed hardware. It also keeps information on storage, both removable and fixed, and communication devices like network interface cards and wireless and Bluetooth devices.

What you won't see for hardware in Device Manager are printers, unless of course they're USB. In that case, you will see the USB port and thus the printer will be identified, but you won't be able to configure the printer from Device Manager. You will use the Devices And Printers applet for configuring and troubleshooting printers. There is new functionality in Windows 7 that integrates some Device Manager functionality into Devices And Printers. The new functionality is known as Device Stage.

We will also take a look how to configure applications on Windows 7. One of the issues with applications is that they may not work properly on a newer operating system. We will look at the ways to allow older applications to work on Windows 7.

We will also take a look at Internet Explorer. Internet Explorer, also known as IE, has been the web browser for Microsoft operating systems since its introduction as Microsoft Internet Explorer Version 1 in 1995. As the Internet and the World Wide Web have increased exponentially in both content and features, Microsoft has continually enhanced and added new functionality to its world-class browser up to the current version being released with Windows 7. The current version is Windows Internet Explorer 8, or IE8.

With the increase in the functionality of browsers and in their ease of use, there has been an increase in the way websites are used to provide content for end users in the public space (Internet browsing) as well as for private corporate browsing. With the introduction of IE8, Microsoft has taken the usability end users want to new levels as well as providing a good deal of security enhancement. This gives the user the best and easiest browsing environment as well as providing a balance of security information about the sites and pages being viewed.

Configuring Hardware

Device Manager in Windows 7 works the same way it did in Windows Vista and XP. *Device Manager* is designed to display information about the hardware installed on your computer and as an interface to add and configure new hardware.

Hardware today follows a Plug and Play standard. So most of the time, simply connecting hardware will allow Device Manager (well, the OS processes controlling the device that is displayed to you) to automatically configure it. Devices that are not Plug and Play–compatible can be installed manually from Device Manager as well.

In Windows 7, a new functionality known as Device Stage has been added. It is a more enhanced graphic output giving better details and functionality to installed devices such as cameras.

You can use Device Manager to ensure that all devices are working properly and to troubleshoot misbehaving devices. For each device installed, you can view specific properties down to the resources being used, such as I/O port (input/output) and IRQ (interrupt request). Through Device Manager, you can take the following specific actions:

- View a list of all hardware installed on your computer
- Determine which device driver is installed for each device
- Manage and update device drivers
- Install new devices
- Disable, enable, and uninstall devices
- Use driver rollback to return to a previous version of a driver
- Troubleshoot device problems

New/Updated Features—Device Stage

Throughout the evolution of technologies and PCs, one of the greatest features is how we can use such a wide array of devices on PCs. Device Manager has allowed us see all the hardware connected and make configuration changes, but utilizing the features of the devices themselves has been left up to alternate programs outside the Windows interface. Windows 7 introduces a new specification for hardware vendors (knowing that most hardware comes with software for the user to interface with), allowing them to provide user access within Windows. The new feature and specification is known as Device Stage. Windows 7 Devices And Printers is the interface for displaying and accessing hardware supporting Device Stage. The Windows 7 Devices And Printers screen is shown in Figure 5.1.

FIGURE 5.1 Devices And Printers

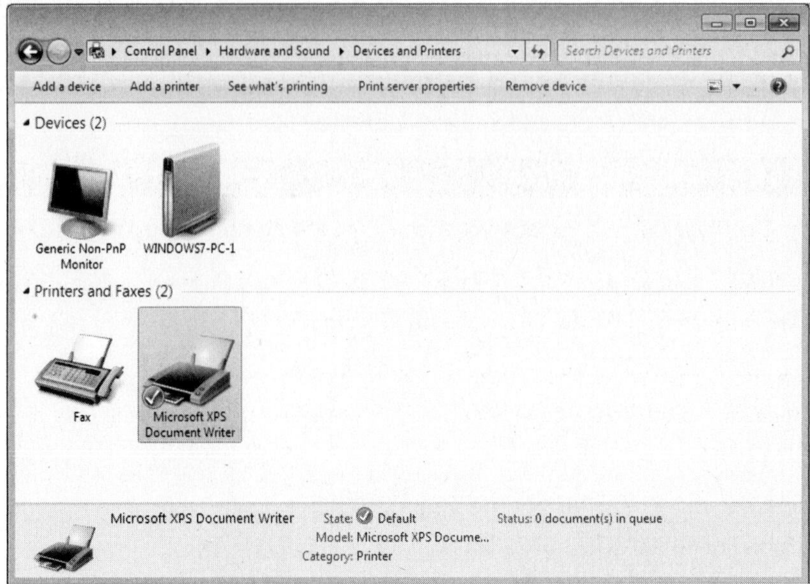

Take, for example, a digital camera. When you connect the camera to the PC, the PC recognizes the device (Plug and Play) and typically displays the camera as a mass storage device. Users wanting advanced features like downloading and editing the photos use another program. When you plug in a device that supports Device Stage technology, Device Stage displays a single window that gives you easy access to common device tasks, such as, in the case of a camera, importing pictures, launching the vendor-supplied editing programs, and simply browsing, all from one interface.

With Windows 7, you'll be able to access all of your connected and wireless devices from the single Devices And Printers screen, and the device will be displayed in the Windows 7 enhanced Taskbar (Figure 5.2). From here, you can work with your devices, browse files they might contain, and manage device settings.

FIGURE 5.2 Device options display from the Windows 7 Taskbar

Wireless and Bluetooth devices are also supported by Device Stage, making managing these resources much more effortless for the end user. As portable devices are disconnected and reconnected, the Device Stage–driven Devices And Printers screen will update in real time. Exercise 5.1 will guide you through opening and viewing devices recognized on your Windows 7 machine.

EXERCISE 5.1

Opening Devices and Printers to View Device Stage–Supported Devices

1. Choose Start ➢ Control Panel ➢ Hardware And Sound.
2. Choose Devices And Printers from the main window.
3. To see options specific to a device, right-click the device.

To make it easier for the end user, Devices And Printers is also available directly from the Start menu:

1. Choose Start ➢ Control Panel ➢ Devices And Printers.
2. To see options specific to a device, right-click the device.

Even simpler yet, you can click the Start button and type **device** into the integrated search box to launch Devices And Printers, the first applet in the search list.

Next we'll take a look at using Device Manager to configure devices.

Using Device Manager

Device Manager is the component in Windows 7 you'll use first to see which devices are connected to your machine. More appropriately (and importantly), you can see which devices Windows 7 has recognized. That is, if you install or connect new piece of hardware and Windows 7 doesn't recognize it at all, it won't be seen in Device Manager.

This would be an unusual occurrence given the sophistication of today's hardware vendors and the standards like Plug and play which are implemented. However, this is an important step in seeing just which devices are known to Windows 7. Keep in mind that we've been using Device Manager for many versions of Windows, so what I'm discussing is applicable to legacy versions as well. As seen in Figure 5.3, Device Manager has a fairly simple opening screen, but it has a lot of functionality behind it.

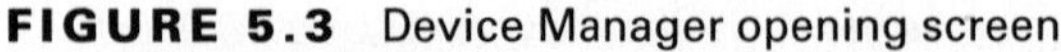

FIGURE 5.3 Device Manager opening screen

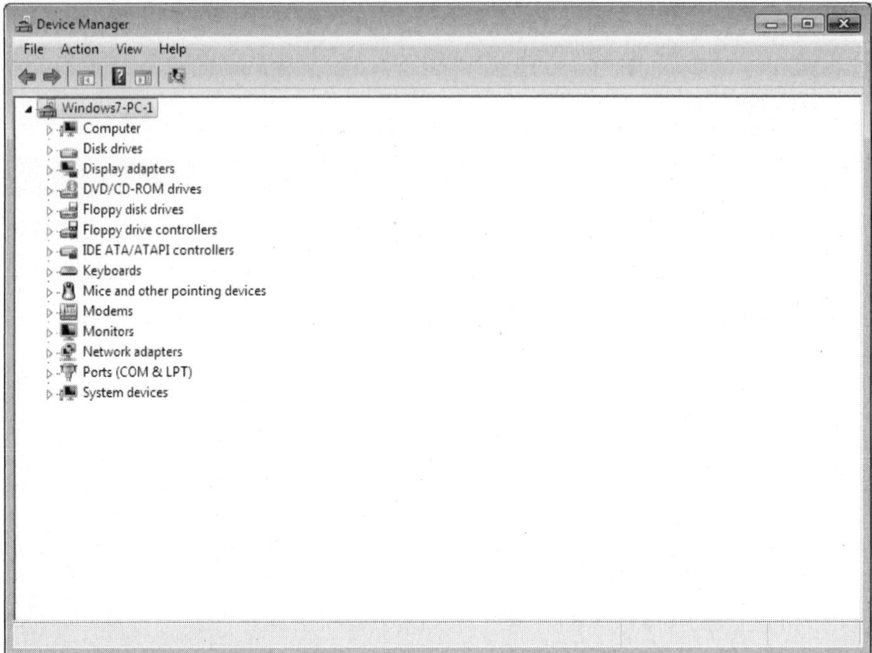

From the opening screen, you get a good first feeling for the hardware that's installed and recognized and for any major issues, such as a device that's recognized but has no drivers installed or is not working correctly. You'll see a warning symbol displayed over the misbehaving device. For example, suppose you have just installed a new network adapter but the device does not seem to be working. You can open Device Manager and open the Network Adapter option to start the troubleshooting process. Figure 5.4 shows an issue with a network adapter.

To continue troubleshooting the network adapter within Device Manager, you would right-click the misbehaving adapter and choose Properties to see its Properties dialog box (Figure 5.5). This is just a small part of the functionality within Device Manager.

There are many reasons to view the devices installed and configured on a machine. One reason is to verify the type and status of hardware. For example, if someone in your organization has given you documentation for a specific user machine with the machine's hardware specifications and you are concerned that the stated network adapter for the machine may not be the one actually installed, you can use Device Manager on the machine in question to see the network adapters Windows 7 recognizes in the machine.

FIGURE 5.4 Device Manager showing an issue with a network adapter

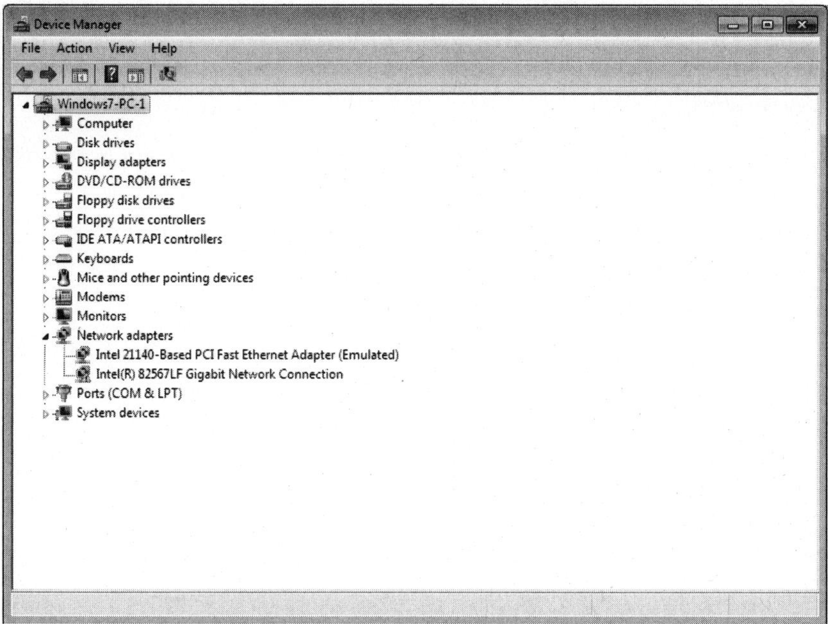

FIGURE 5.5 Device Manager network adapter properties

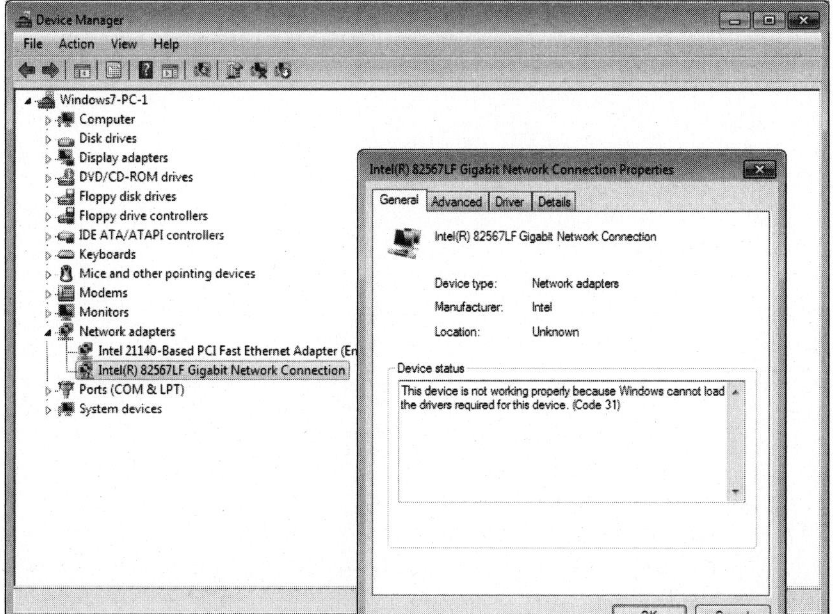

In Exercise 5.2, you will view devices using Device Manager.

EXERCISE 5.2

Using Device Manager

1. Choose Start ➤ Control Panel ➤ Hardware And Sound ➤ Device Manager (under Devices And Printers).
2. Click the triangle next to Network Adapters (or double-click Network Adapters) to expand Network Adapters.

The steps in Exercise 5.2 show one way to launch Device Manager, through Control Panel. This is a valid method that shows you where the application resides, but it is not how administrators usually do it.

You may want to try the following method because it puts Device Manager into a more functional MMC, allowing access to more administrative tools from one location:

1. Choose Start and then right-click Computer.
2. Select Manage.
3. In the Navigation pane of the MMC, select Device Manager.

I also sometimes type **Device Manager** into the Windows integrated search box and press Enter. Or I right-click Computer and choose Properties. All of these are means to the same end.

Device Properties Available within Device Manager

Once you have opened Device Manager and have access to the installed devices on your machine, you can view their Properties dialog boxes. From there, you can view and change configuration parameters if necessary. You will find that the tabs available in the Properties dialog boxes will vary from device to device because the parameters that are available will vary with different hardware. Most devices will have at a minimum a General tab, a Driver tab, and a Detail tab, as seen in Figure 5.6.

The Properties dialog box for most devices will include more specific tabs for the hardware configuration, such as for a network adapter, which also has an Advanced tab for more specific configuration parameters. Figure 5.7 shows a network adapter's Advanced tab selected with Connection Type selected and the Value drop-down box active to show possible choices.

FIGURE 5.6 A Device Manager Properties dialog box

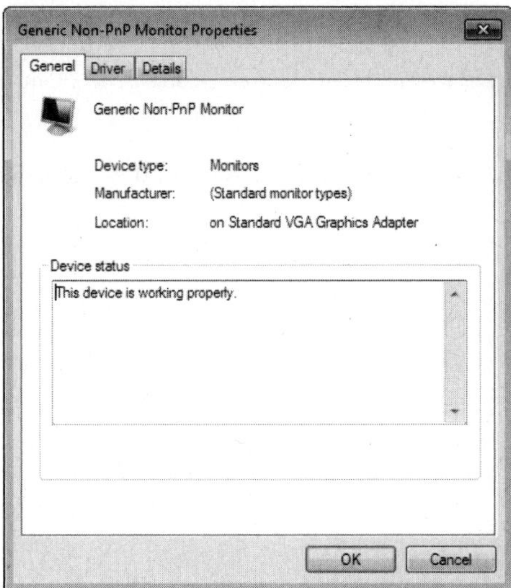

FIGURE 5.7 Advanced network interface properties

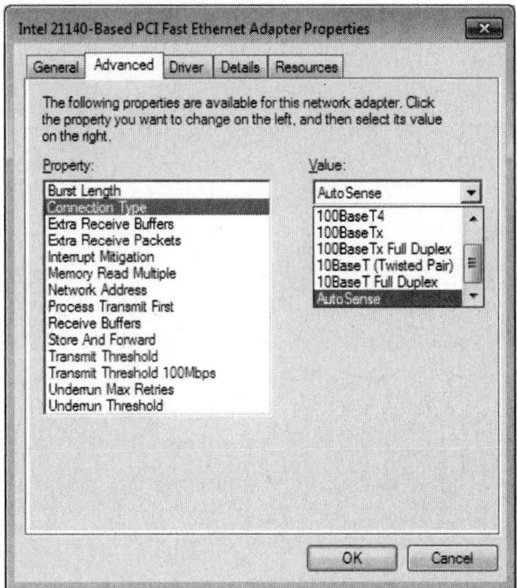

If you need to change the hardware configuration properties, Device Manager is the best way to access the parameters. Exercise 5.3 will show you how to view configurable properties for a network adapter through the Advanced tab.

EXERCISE 5.3

Configuring Network Adapter Advanced Properties

1. Choose Start ➢ Control Panel ➢ Hardware And Sound ➢ Device Manager (under Devices And Printers).
2. Click the triangle next to Network Adapters (or double-click Network Adapters) to expand it.
3. Right-click your network adapter and select Properties.
4. Choose the Advanced tab.
5. Select various properties and view the parameters.

In addition to setting up devices, you will need to install and configure device drivers, which I will cover in the next section.

Installing and Updating Device Drivers

Device drivers are the controlling code actually interfacing the hardware components with the operating system. The commands are specific to each piece of hardware, and there may be different commands, memory locations, or actions even within the same type of hardware. A network interface card (NIC) from one vender may actually have a different set of instructions than a NIC from a different manufacturer.

An operating system or software works best when it can issue a standard command and have the same functionality across the hardware regardless of vendor. This is where *drivers* come in; the driver takes a standard instruction from the operating system and issues the command to the hardware to perform the desired function.

Drivers need to be updated. For example, a command set for a driver may perform a function incorrectly. This can produce errors and would need to be fixed. The hardware vendor will update the driver to fix the problem. Or new or better functionality may be necessary or wanted, so the hardware vendor would need to change the driver code to add functionality or provide better performance, in turn leading to an update.

Real World Scenario

Driver Code Causing an Arbitrary Nonreproducible Error

While working on a consulting job for a company where I was installing a new program and hardware to provide bar code scanning, I was plagued by the bar code readers connected to PCs randomly failing.

The bar code readers seemed to install correctly, and they showed as functioning properly within Device Manager. However, periodically the hardware readers would fail to input data into the application I was using. I could reboot the affected machine and the bar code reader would work fine again (for a while). It's easy to blame the operating system because the reboot seemed to fix the problem, but the operating system wasn't to blame.

After several days of troubleshooting and working with the manufacturer, it was determined that the driver interfacing the operating system with the hardware was not releasing memory resources correctly, causing the driver to fail. We received an updated driver and applied the update to the machines, and the problem was resolved. Be careful not to blame the operating system prematurely, and be sure to investigate other areas for possible problems.

Typical first-time installation of drivers today happens automatically with the Plug and Play specification. After the hardware is installed, Windows 7 will recognize it and launch the driver installation program. Let's take, for example, the connection of a digital camera to the USB port of your computer.

Windows 7 will recognize that a device has been plugged in and will gather the information about the USB device. Windows 7 will then install the best driver it knows about (and if it doesn't know about the device, it will ask you how to proceed). Figure 5.8 shows the message indicating that the operating system found a driver and is installing it automatically.

FIGURE 5.8 Automatic driver installation

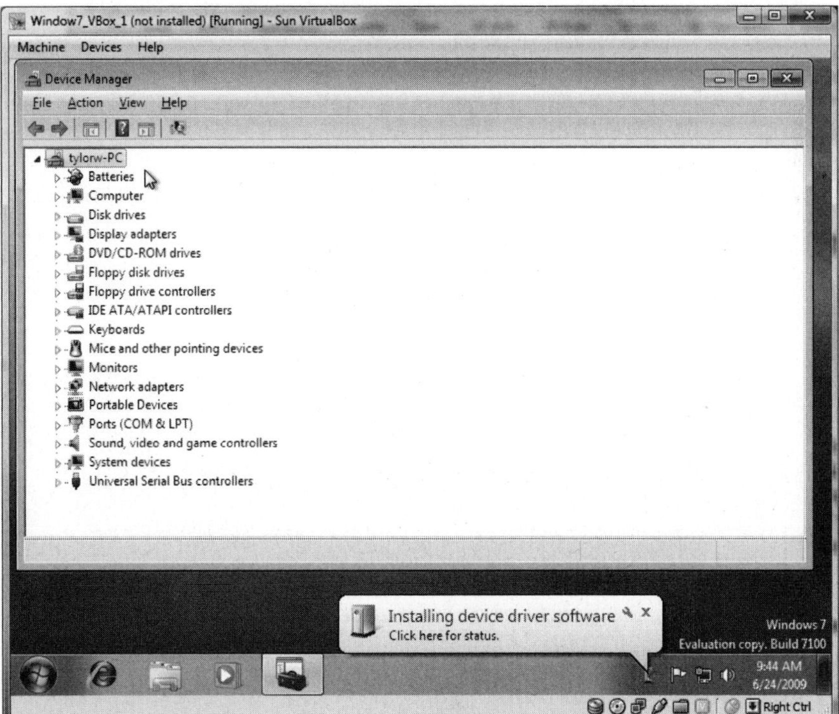

The installation completes and the device is now available in Device Manager. Figure 5.9 shows the digital camera as a hardware item you can now access as we did with the network adapter previously.

FIGURE 5.9 New device availability in Device Manager

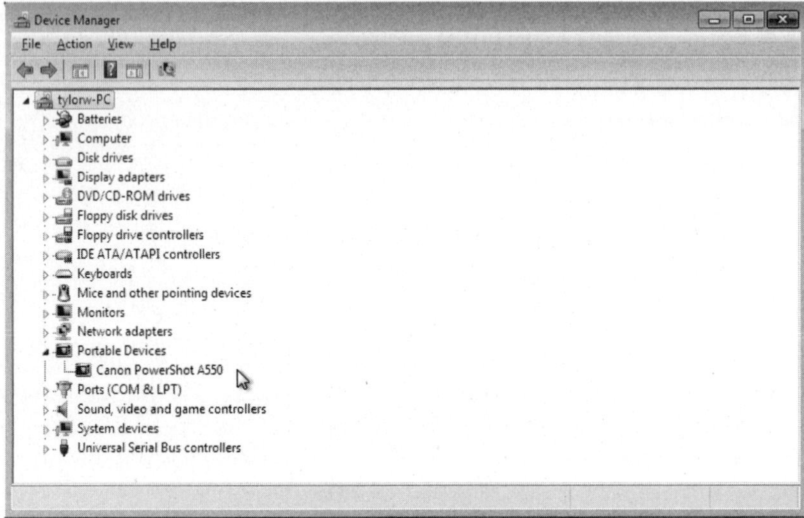

If you need to review the driver details for your newly installed device, the digital camera in this case, you can right-click the device in Device Manager and choose Properties. Figure 5.10 shows the right-click menu (also known as the context menu); note that the top choice in this menu is a quick launch to update the driver software, if that's what you're trying to do.

FIGURE 5.10 Right-click menu for a device in Device Manager

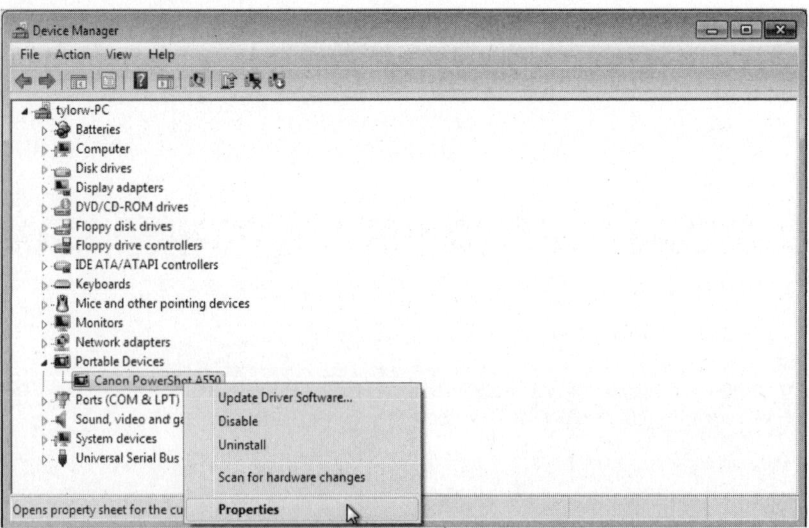

You may want to verify general information about the driver, like the provider or version. You can see that information in the driver tab of the Properties dialog box. You can also choose to view the driver details, which are the supporting files and associated paths. Figure 5.11 shows the Properties dialog box of the digital camera after the Driver tab has been selected and the Driver Details button clicked.

FIGURE 5.11 Driver details within Device Manager

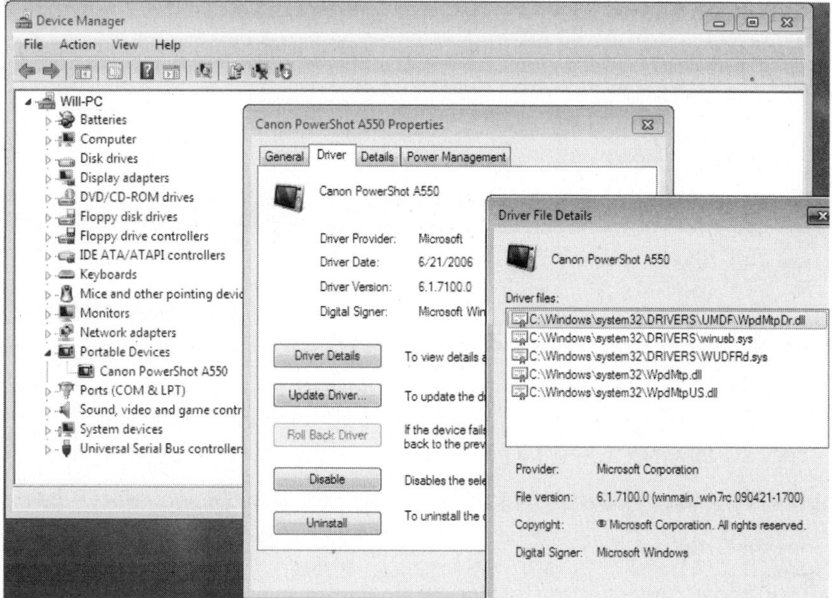

Sometimes when you're having issues with a hardware device, you will go online and read forums or search engine queries for ideas from other administrators. Someone might mention that they had a problem with a specific driver for the hardware you're researching. They might even mention the exact version of the driver and suggest a fix. Having the ability to view information on drivers and update them is helpful in a situation such as this. Exercise 5.4 walks you through looking at driver details.

EXERCISE 5.4

Viewing Driver Details

Follow these steps to view the details of a device driver:

1. Choose Start > Control Panel > Hardware And Sound > Device Manager (or type **device manager** in the integrated search window).
2. Click the triangle next to the category in which you want to view driver details to expand the item list; you can also double-click the category name. For example, double-click the category Portable Devices to see the portable devices connected to the machine.

EXERCISE 5.4 *(continued)*

3. Right-click the hardware item (e.g., Cannon PowerShot A550) and select Properties.
4. Choose the Driver tab.
5. View the driver version.
6. Click the Driver Details button to see the files associated with the hardware.

Another task may be updating the drivers. In exercise 5.5 we will look at updating a driver.

EXERCISE 5.5

Updating a Driver

1. Choose Start ➢ Control Panel ➢ Hardware And Sound ➢ Device Manager (or type **device manager** in the integrated search window).
2. Click the triangle next to category for which you want to update the driver to expand the item list; you can also double-click the category name (e.g., double-click Portable Devices as a category to see the portable devices connected to the machine).
3. Right-click the hardware item (e.g., Cannon PowerShot A550) and select Properties.
4. Choose the Driver tab.
5. Click the Update Driver button; a window launches asking how you want to search for the driver.

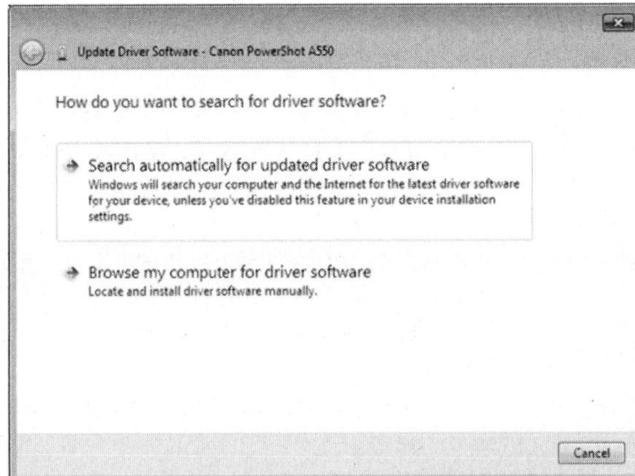

6. Choose Search Automatically For Updated Driver Software to have Windows 7 search for you, or you can choose Browse My Computer For Driver Software if you have the new drivers already.
7. Windows 7 searches for and update the drivers or reports back that you have the most current version.

Not only will you update drivers because of a failure or hardware issue—you will install new drivers for new or updated functionality. But there will be times when a hardware driver gets updated and the update breaks a piece of functioning hardware or doesn't solve a problem. You will want to go back to the previous version, or "roll back" the driver. In Exercise 5.6, you will learn how to do a driver rollback.

EXERCISE 5.6

Rolling Back a Driver

1. Choose Start ➢ Control Panel ➢ Hardware And Sound ➢ Device Manager (or type **device manager** in the integrated search window).
2. Click the triangle next to the category for which you want to roll back the driver to expand the item list; you can also double-click the category name (e.g., double-click Portable Devices as a category to see the portable devices connected to the machine).
3. Right-click the hardware item (e.g., Cannon PowerShot A550 as an item) and select Properties.
4. Choose the Driver tab.
5. Click the Roll Back Driver button. Note that if the Roll Back Driver button is grayed out, there isn't a previous version of the driver available.
6. The previous driver will be installed and the hardware will return to its previous state of functionality.

The Driver tab for a piece of installed hardware in Device Manager also provides functionality for disabling and uninstalling a driver. Why would you want to disable a driver? There are several possibilities, but troubleshooting is one of the most common reasons.

Disabling the driver effectively disables the hardware; it will no longer function as designed. Uninstalling the device driver also has a similar effect, but if the hardware is still installed, you can uninstall and perform a scan to ensure that the hardware is still recognized and induce a reinstallation.

I have often disabled a device from Device Manager to eliminate one part of an issue I am having with a system. If I'm confident that the problem is with the hardware, I will uninstall the driver and let the operating system reinstall it as part of the troubleshooting procedure. This works much of the time and is a good place to start. In Exercise 5.7, you will disable and enable a device driver.

EXERCISE 5.7

Disabling and Enabling a Device in Device Manager

1. Choose Start ➢ Control Panel ➢ Hardware And Sound ➢ Device Manager (or type **device manager** in the integrated search window).
2. Click the triangle next to the appropriate category to expand the item list; you can also double-click the category name (e.g., double-click Portable Devices to see the portable devices connected to the machine).
3. Right-click the hardware item (e.g.. Cannon PowerShot A550) and select Properties. Note that you can select Disable directly from the context menu if desired.
4. Choose the Driver tab.
5. Click the Disable button. (This is a toggle button; it will be labeled Disable if the device is enabled and Enable if the device is disabled.)
6. The device driver and hence the device will be disabled and will no longer function. There will be a down arrow on the item in Device Manager and the General tab will show the device disabled. Close the properties dialog box for that device.
7. Right-click the hardware item (e.g., Cannon PowerShot A550) and select Properties.
8. Choose the Driver tab.
9. Click the Enable button. (This is a toggle button; it will say Enable if the device is disabled, or Disable if the device is enabled.)
10. The device driver will become enabled and the hardware will work as designed (barring any other issues). Close Device Manager.

It may be beneficial at times to uninstall and reinstall a device driver. Many times when you uninstall and reinstall a device driver, the default configuration parameters will be reset to their original specifications.

Any changes you have made will need to be reconfigured, but if the device driver worked previously and has stopped for some unknown reason (if you knew the reason, you'd simply fix it, eh?), uninstalling and reinstalling is worth a try. You may also consider using a different device driver than Windows 7 is set up to use via Plug and Play.

Uninstalling the device driver and manually installing a different version may be a solution as well. It should be noted here that uninstalling a device driver does not delete the driver files from the machine; uninstalling the device drivers removes the operating system configuration for the hardware.

You may want or need to find the files and delete them manually in some cases. Remember, you can find the files (and thus the filenames) from Driver Details found within the Driver tab of the Properties dialog box of the hardware from Device Manager.

If you have determined that the device driver for your misbehaving hardware is potentially causing the problem you are having, you can decide to uninstall and reinstall (automatically) the drivers. In Exercise 5.8, you will uninstall and then reinstall a device driver.

EXERCISE 5.8

Uninstalling and Reinstalling a Device Driver

1. Choose Start ➤ Control Panel ➤ Hardware And Sound ➤ Device Manager (or type **device manager** in the integrated search window).
2. Click the triangle next to category for the device you want to uninstall to expand the item list; you can also double-click the category name (e.g., double-click Portable Devices to see the portable devices connected to the machine).
3. Right-click the hardware item (e.g., Cannon PowerShot A550) and select Properties. Note that you can select Uninstall directly from the context menu.
4. Choose the Driver tab.
5. Click the Uninstall button.
6. Click OK in the Confirm Device Uninstall dialog box. A progress box appears as the device driver is uninstalled. Once the driver is uninstalled, Device Manager will no longer show it.
7. From Device Manager, choose the Action menu item and select Scan For Hardware Changes; alternatively. you can right-click the machine name in Device Manager and select Scan For Hardware Changes from the context menu.

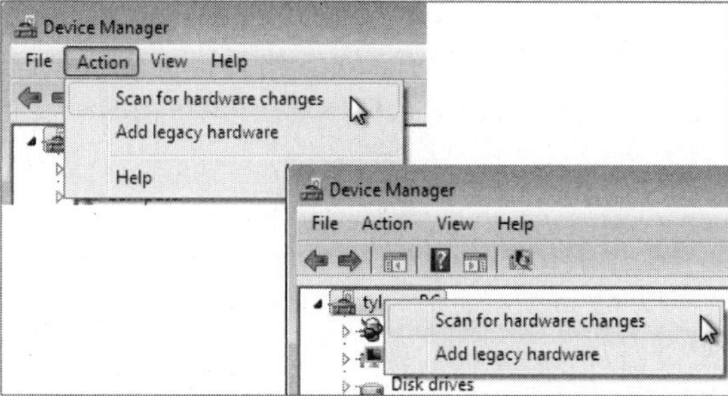

8. Windows 7 will initiate the process of discovering the Plug and Play device and will reinstall the device driver configuration into the operating system. The hardware will be available again within Device Manager.

A lot of hardware manufacturers would like you to install the driver files and some software for their device before the operating system has a chance to discover it. This may be just so the software program controlling some of the hardware functionality will be installed first so its configuration file can accurately reference the installed drivers, or it could be to add the driver files to the driver configuration directories of the operating system before the operating system discovers the device.

This is usually done by inserting and running a setup program from a provided CD or DVD. I will say the hardware vendors know what's best. As an Admin, it's sometimes hard not to just install the hardware and go from there, but following the vendor's recommendations will most often produce a better result.

Real World Scenario

Follow the Hardware Vendor's Recommendation

Like many other admins, I sometimes think I know the right way to proceed in installing a piece of hardware. Seriously, how hard can it be? I once installed a new wireless USB adapter into a machine I was using by just plugging it in despite the great big red sticker that said, "Run the setup on the CD FIRST!?!"

Sure enough, Windows found the adapter and proceeded to install the drivers. The hardware showed up in Device Manager but would not work. Now, being the good troubleshooter I am, I decided to run the Setup program on the CD. It turns out the driver files on the CD were a different version (actually older) than the installed files and Windows would not replace the installed drivers.

Even after I manually uninstalled them? Yes, I had to go back and find five different files in numerous locations and delete each one. Finding the files to delete was not a simple operation; a lot of online research went into solving this problem, and several hours of my time was wasted.

Simply following the hardware vendor instructions would have been much easier. I did the same installation on another machine following the vendor recommendations, and everything worked perfectly.

But then again, that's how we all learn these valuable lessons in life.

There are also situations we run into requiring a manual installation of hardware. This may be for legacy hardware you are using, for drivers not supplied in the operating system distribution files, or drivers which may perform different functions from the default drivers available. You can also do this within Windows 7, from Device Manager through the Add Hardware Wizard.

In the manual installation process, you can have Windows 7 go out to the internet to find a current driver, or you can specify a location of your choosing locally. From Device Manager you launch the Add Hardware Wizard by choosing Add Legacy Hardware from either the Action menu or the context menu of the machine as shown in Figure 5.12.

FIGURE 5.12 Add Hardware Wizard initial window

The next step is to tell Windows 7 where to look for the driver. This is the next page of the Add Hardware Wizard, as Figure 5.13 shows.

FIGURE 5.13 Driver file location choices

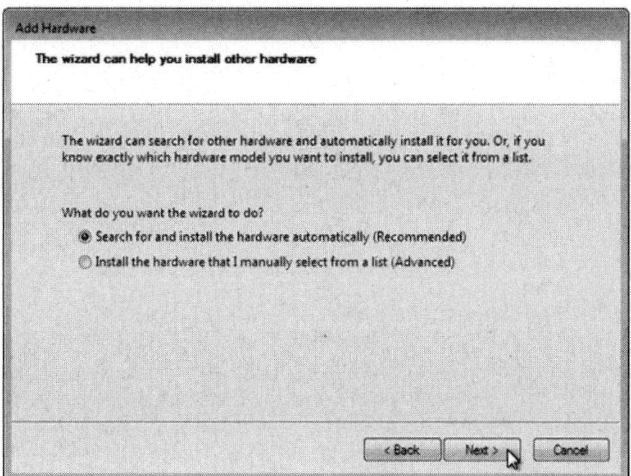

To choose a piece of hardware from a list of supplied drivers or, more importantly, to choose a specific path, select the option Install The Hardware That I Manually Select For A List (Advanced) and choose Next. This allows you select a device or choose Show All Devices (Figure 5.14); the Show All Devices choice and Next will give you the ability to choose a location.

FIGURE 5.14 Add Hardware Device Wizard select hardware window

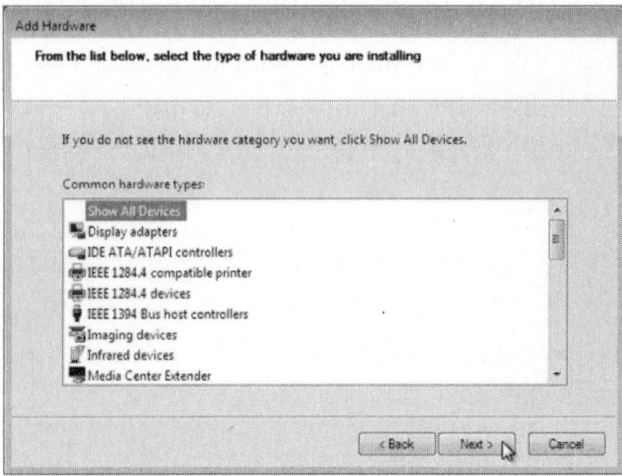

If you have a disk or have the appropriate drivers stored in an accessible location, click the Have Disk button (as seen in Figure 5.15) and browse to the driver files you need to install. If all goes as planned, the hardware device drivers will be installed and Device Manager will display the newly installed hardware.

FIGURE 5.15 Add Hardware Device Wizard, Have Disk

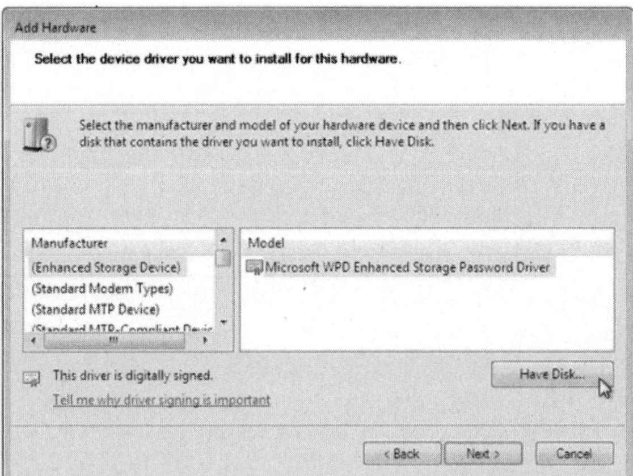

Driver Signing

In this world of hackers and viruses, one issue that needs to be addressed is the possibility that drivers that are downloaded have viruses or worms.

To help combat this problem, drivers that are created from reputable companies (like Dell, Compaq, etc.) assign a digital file certificate to the driver to show its validity.

One way to verify that all the drivers on your machine are verified is to run the Sigverif.exe from the Search Programs and Files box on the Start menu. When you run the Sigverif.exe program, the program will verify that all drivers on the machine are verified.

Exercise 5.9 walks you through the steps of verifying the drivers on your machine.

EXERCISE 5.9

Verifying Signed Drivers

1. Run the `Sigverif.exe` program by clicking Start and typing **Sigverif.exe** in the Search Programs And Files box and then pressing Enter.
2. The File Signature Verification box appears. Click Start.

3. You will notice that the system scan begins. When the system is finished verifying the drivers, a message will appear. Click OK.

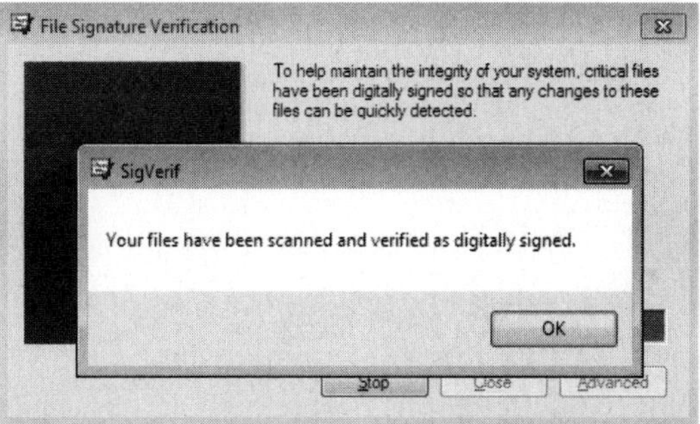

4. If there are any programs with unsigned drivers, they will be displayed at this time. Click Close to close the `Sigverif.exe` program.

Knowing how to properly install and configure drivers is an important part of an IT professional's job. Another task that we must perform is managing input/output devices.

Managing I/O Devices

The devices you use to get information into and out of your Windows 7 machine are your I/O (input/output) devices. I/O devices include your keyboard, mouse, scanner, and printer. Your devices may be connected to your computer by standard cabling or by USB, or they may use a wireless technology such as IrDA (infrared) or RF (radio frequency).

Configuring Removable Storage Devices

Removable storage devices have been part of our computing world since the beginning. CDs, DVDs, and floppy disks are examples of removable storage. Today, we're using other types of removable storage as well, including flash-based electronics like USB sticks, memory cards, USB or FireWire external rotating hard drives, cameras, phones, and so on. These devices (or media) are learned dynamically as the devices are connected.

We'll be concentrating in this section on dynamically connected devices utilizing the USB/Firewire connectivity and memory cards. These devices present challenges to the administrative team, as end users utilizing the technology may not follow guidelines for protecting their data from loss, or for keeping it secure.

Windows 7 includes improvements to the Safely Remove Hardware (eject) menu. For example, it's now possible to eject just one memory card at the same time (from a single hub) and keep the ports available for future use. Removable media is now listed under its label through Devices And Printers (Figure 5.16) rather than just its drive letter as it was in previous versions of Windows. This is also part of the new Device Stage functionality of Windows 7; hardware vendors can include configuration information about portable devices and give users more resources from one location.

FIGURE 5.16 Devices And Printers with USB stick installed

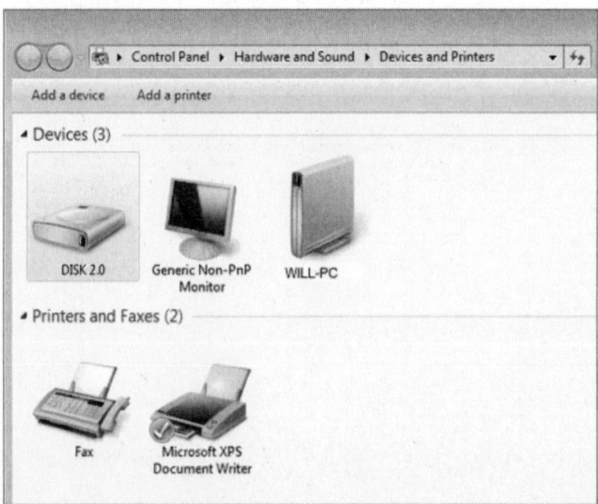

There are considerations in terms of data access performance with the portable devices as well. To make data access and saves faster, it's possible to have the operating system cache the data and write it to the portable device later (when there's free processor time). However, this allows the possibility of a user just removing the portable device before the write is actually made, which would result in a loss of data.

Windows 7 defaults to writing the data immediately, minimizing the chance of data loss and the cost of performance. The configuration for optimizing the portable device for quick removal or better performance is found in the Policies tab of the Properties dialog box for the hardware in Device Manager.

In Exercise 5.10, we will walk through the steps to configure input/output devices through the use of Device Manager.

EXERCISE 5.10

Configuring Input/Output Devices

1. Choose Start ➤ Control Panel ➤ Hardware And Sound ➤ Device Manager (under Devices And Printers) or type **device manager** into the integrated search window of Windows 7.
2. Click the triangle next to Disk Drives (or double-click Disk Drives) to expand the item.
3. Right-click the USB Disk hardware item and select Properties.

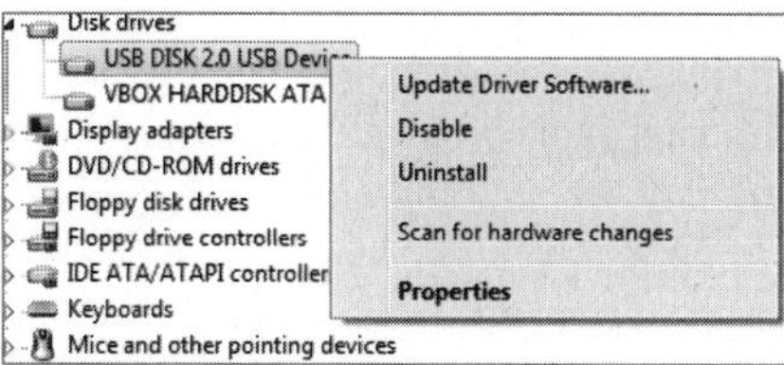

4. Choose the Policies tab.
5. Select the Better Performance radio button and then click OK.

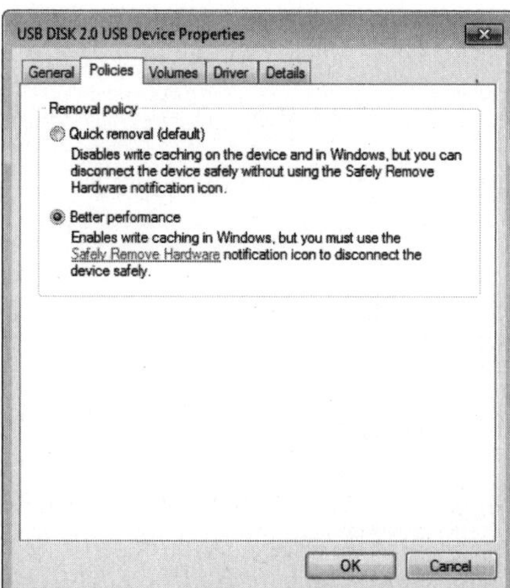

In Exercise 5.10, you changed the USB portable storage device to write cache policy for better performance; this means writes to the portable device may be saved and written at a later time (when the processor has clock cycles available). To ensure no loss of data, it is fairly important to eject the device through Windows 7 before physically removing it.

Choosing the icon in the Taskbar to eject the device initiates a stop for the hardware, forcing any cached writes in memory to be written to the device. You can also stop the portable hardware device from the Devices And Printers window by choosing Eject from the context menu of the device.

The device will close, meaning the writes have been made, and you will be presented with a window saying it's safe to remove the hardware.

Another important piece of hardware that needs to be configured is the printer. In the next section, I will discuss managing printers.

Managing Printers

Printers have been an issue for IT teams around the world and will continue to be as far as I can tell. Every new update/release/version of an operating system has new software intelligence to make the installation and maintenance easier, but printer technology continues to grow and hardware vendors continue to make changes.

The driver base for all the different printers out there is huge, and even for the same printer, there are numerous variations. Printers themselves have lots of options that can be made available, and this all has to be controlled by the operating system, through the drivers.

Basic Definitions in the Printer World

I should point out here that I have already referred (in the first section) to printers and devices; I have been talking about the physical piece of hardware and its functions. In the IT world, we need to distinguish between the functionality of the hardware and of the software (both the driver software and the controlling software).

To this end, a lot of us know the physical device that has paper in it as the print device, not "the printer." The printer is the software application on the local machine controlling the print device. The printer driver is the software shim between the operating system and the locally installed software (the printer).

You will find in most organizations that there is not a print device attached to every computer. They are usually shared between users. This is cost effective on many levels, but it tends to cause issues. Most of us, end users and the IT team, need to print something once in a while, and so we send our documents or web pages to the print device to be printed.

The print device may be connected to someone's machine and shared for others to use, or it may be a stand-alone device. You may have a server on your network that has one or more print devices attached, and everyone sends their documents to a central location. Each user machine will have a printer installed and the appropriate drivers to allow Windows 7 to send the document to the print device through the printer with the appropriate instructions.

Of course, the print device can't physically print a document at the speed at which the printer can send the data to it. This is where a software component called the spool (spooler, print spool, etc.) comes in. There need to be software components that can buffer the print job until the print device can complete it. In fact, there may be more than one user sending documents to be printed to the same print device at the same time (I'm sure this happens), and yes, the spool handles this as well.

Real World Scenario

What, No Spool?

I was working on a networking problem for a local veterinary clinic. The employees were complaining about issues they were having with their PCs being extremely slow sometimes but faster other times, and they were sure the network hardware was the cause. We discussed things that had changed recently—they had upgraded a piece of their software package to allow more functionality, which included having a couple of centralized printers for the docs and techs to use. It seemed as though every time someone printed, the network bogged down to the point of uselessness.

Casual discussions ensued. The network bog-down affected only the machine (or machines) actively sending a print job. Looking into the problem a little further showed that the vendor installation defaulted to printing directly to the print device, no spooling. Each machine had to wait for the print job to complete before releasing any local resources (yes, that's right, not even background printing), and the other machines on the network ended up waiting as well. Allowing the machines to spool their print jobs solved the problem of slow networking (clearly not a networking issue in the end).

Installing Printers

Installing printers to a machine is done in two distinct ways—one where the print device is physically connected to the machine, one where it is not (it's connected over the network). There have to be software drivers in either case, and they can be on a CD/DVD, on a network share, or even in the Windows distribution files. Printers in Windows 7 will be located in the Devices And Printers window and will allow the Device Stage configuration to accommodate a full range of functionality from this one location.

To add a printer to a machine locally, you will usually run the Setup program on the CD/DVD (following the manufacturer's instructions). The manufacturer's Setup program in a wizard format will ask the appropriate questions. You can set up the printer through Windows 7 as well using the Add Printer functionality of Devices And Printers. To add a printer using the Windows 7 functionality, choose Start ➢ Devices And Printers, and then choose Add A Printer, as shown in Figure 5.17. USB printers will be automatically detected and their drivers will be installed (or at least looked for automatically).

FIGURE 5.17 Adding a printer from Devices And Printers

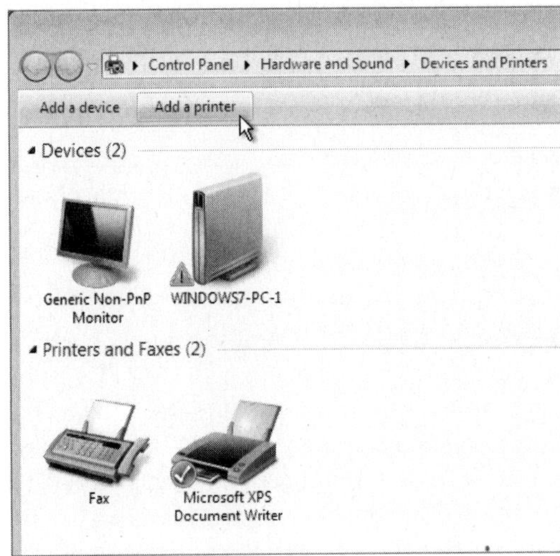

Choosing the Add Printer menu choice launches the Add Printer Wizard (starting at the screen shown in Figure 5.18) and will bring up the screen where you make the choice of installing the printer and print device locally or installing the printer locally to access a print device remotely.

FIGURE 5.18 Add Printer Wizard local or remote choice

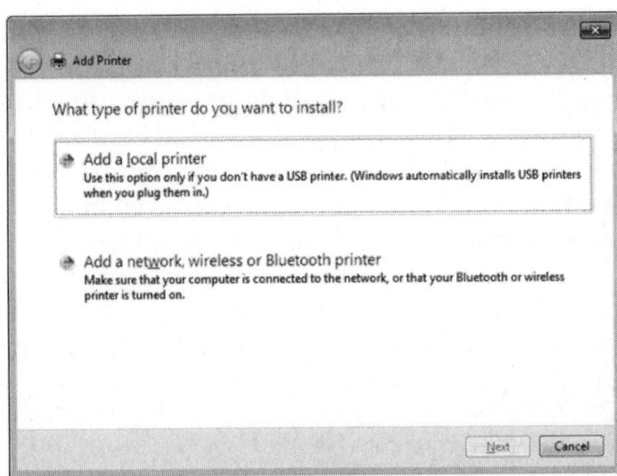

From the opening screen you can follow the following example to install the printer for a physically connected print device to a machine. We're going on the premise that the setup program on the CD/DVD (if one existed) was not run and we're installing the printer from the wizard associated with Windows.

EXERCISE 5.11

Installing a Printer

1. Choose Start ➤ Devices And Printers.
2. Choose Add Printers.
3. Select the Add A Local Printer option.
4. In the Add Printer window, choose the Use An Existing Port radio button and use the drop-down window to select LPT1: (Printer Port). Then click Next.

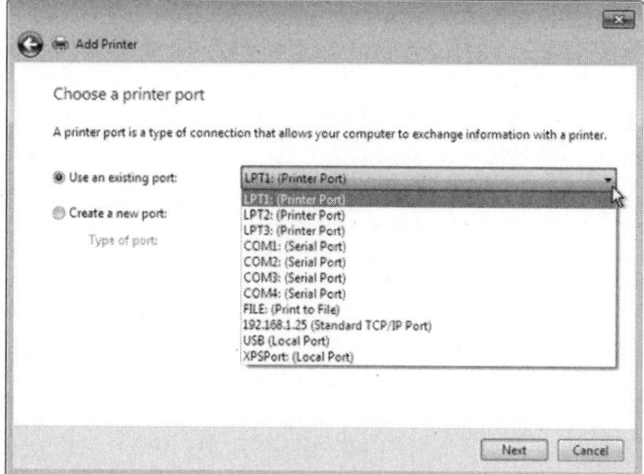

5. Select the manufacturer of your print device and the printer model you want to install. If you don't find your model in the list, it wasn't included in the distribution files; you can click the Windows Update button to get more choices from Microsoft. If you still don't have your model available and you have the original disk, you can choose Have Disk and browse to the driver files. OK, if you had the disk, wouldn't you have just run the setup? Ah, you didn't have the disk, you went on to the internet and downloaded the drivers . . . use the Have Disk option to browse to the folder with the `.inf` file for the printer drivers.

EXERCISE 5.11 *(continued)*

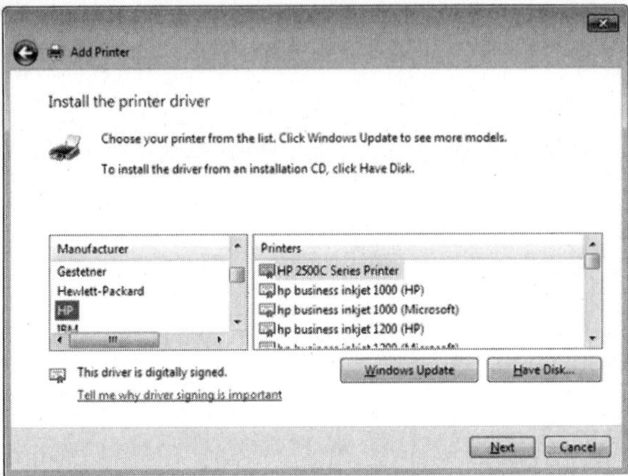

6. If there was a driver previously installed, you will be given the option to use the existing driver or replace it.

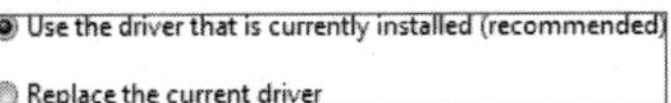

7. After choosing the appropriate device driver or using the existing driver and clicking Next, you will choose the name of the printer. An intuitive name is always a good choice here. Enter the name and click Next.

8. You can make the print device available on the network by sharing it. The next page of the Add Printer Wizard gives you the opportunity to do so. For most of the options within the wizard, you can change the values or function from the Properties dialog box (if, for example, you change your mind later). After making your choice, click Next.

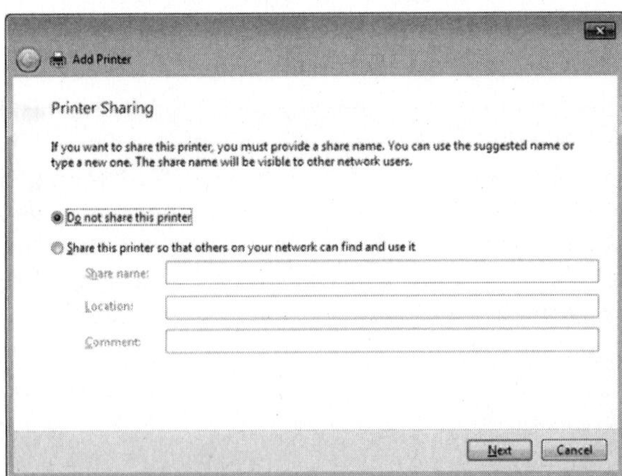

9. On the final page of the Add Printer Wizard, select the Set As The Default Printer check box (to make this the default printer for any application on the machine) and click Print A Test Page. Once the test page prints, click Finish. The printer for the locally connected print device is installed on the local machine.

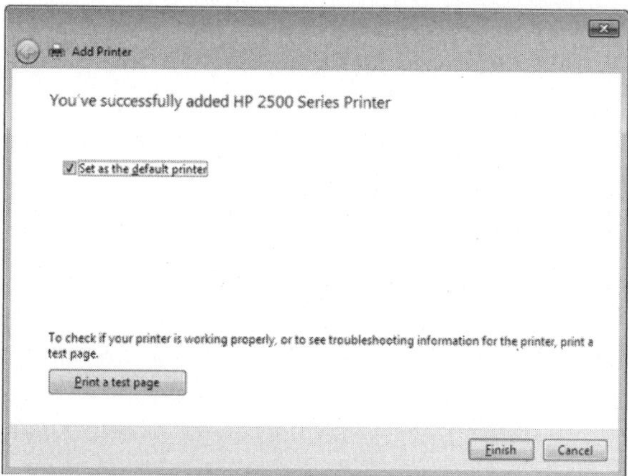

Do not remove the printer you installed in Exercise 5.11. You will use it in a later exercise.

Once you have completed the Add Printer Wizard or let the hardware vendor's setup program install your printer, you can open the Devices And Printers window and see it. Using the context menu, you will have access to the Properties dialog box as well as some of the standard printing functions we've had in Windows past. As hardware vendors start implementing functionality for Windows 7, you will have access to a full array of software components from the Devices And Printers window, at least for the vendors who are going to participate in the Device Stage specification.

What about installing a printer on a machine that needs to access a print device connected to another machine? That's fine; that is the functionality we want. You will launch the Add Printer Wizard and go through the process of installing the printer but point to a share or stand-alone network printer.

Knowing that not all machines on any company's network are going to have print devices physically attached, there is functionality to allow sharing of networked devices and to install printers (software) on client machines. In Exercise 5.12, we will look at how to connect to a network printer.

EXERCISE 5.12

Installing a Shared Network Print Device

1. Choose Start ➤ Devices And Printers.
2. Choose the Add Printers menu item.
3. Select Add A Network, Wireless Or Bluetooth Printer.
4. The Add Printers Wizard will search the locally available network for print devices that are available.
5. Select the networked print device from the Select A Printer section. If the device is not listed, you can choose The Printer That I Want Is Not Listed and enter the parameters for the networked print device.
6. The print device will be detected, the driver will be discovered and installed, and you will be able to use the printer. It will be available at this time in Devices And Printers.

Once the printer is installed for either a print device physically connected to the local machine or a network-connected printer, you can view the configuration parameters and modify them if necessary from the Properties dialog box. Access the property pages from Devices And Printers. Right-click the printer (Figure 5.19) and select Properties for the hardware properties and Printer Properties for the software components.

FIGURE 5.19 Printer context menu from Devices And Printers

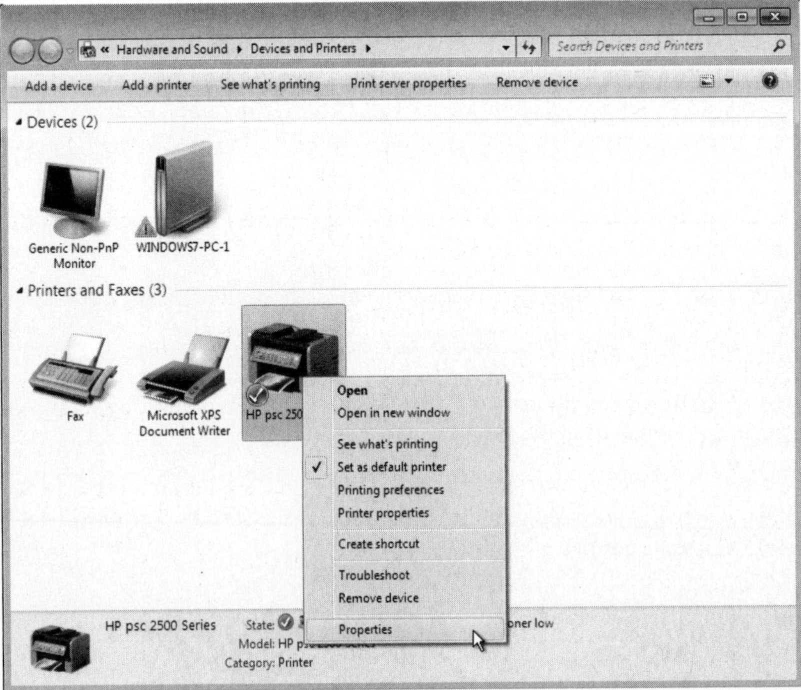

The Properties dialog boxes for printers follow a standard that Microsoft has in place, but the content is really up to the manufacturer. Some vendors will supply more information than others. Most printers will provide a basic set of pages (tabs):

General Tab The printer name, location, and comment are displayed here. The model is typically shown as well as the features of the specific print device and available paper. The printer preferences page is available by clicking the Preferences button, and you can print a test page by clicking the Print Test Page button.

Sharing Tab The Sharing tab allows you to share a printer if it wasn't shared during its installation or to stop sharing it if it was previously shared. You can also add drivers for other flavors of operating systems so the locally installed and shared printer can supply drivers for other machines attempting to connect and use it.

Ports Tab Available ports and print devices connected to them can be viewed on the Ports tab. You can add a port, delete a port, and configure ports from the tab as well. Bidirectional support for print devices supporting this functionality (sending codes back from the print device to the printer for control). Printer pooling is also available here. Printer pooling gives the IT staff the ability to configure multiple print devices (using identical drivers) to appear as one printer to connected users. The print jobs will be printed on one of the devices in the pool (first available print device prints the job). If a print device fails, the others will keep working, making life better for the users (always a goal).

Security Tab Group or user access permissions are controlled in the Security tab. Advanced permissions can be controlled here as well.

Advanced Tab The Advanced tab provides various configuration parameters to control the printer and print device functions. When the printer is available by time is a configuration parameter on the advanced tab. Installed drivers for the print device is a button option as well as adding a new driver (by launching an Add Printer Driver Wizard). Spool options include whether to spool or not, and whether to start printing immediately upon job submission, or start printing after the last page is spooled. The Advanced tab includes the following buttons:

Printing Defaults Button Launches the printer properties for the vendor as they apply to the documents.

Print Processor Button Lets you choose whether to use the vendor-supplied print processor or the built-in Windows print processor. You can also choose the default data type to be sent to the print device.

Separator Page Button Allows a specific page to be inserted between print jobs, making the separation of different documents easier.

Device Settings Specific parameters for each print device are set up on the Device Settings tab. Items like Form To Tray Assignment, Font Substitution, and other installable options for the print device are configurable here.

Once the configuration is complete and the printer and print device are working in harmony, life is good. You can see the status of the document currently being printed as well as documents waiting to be printed. This is what we call the queue. The queue used to be viewed by choosing the queue option in the context menu for the printer. Windows 7 calls it See What's Printing (Figure 5.20).

FIGURE 5.20 See What's Printing

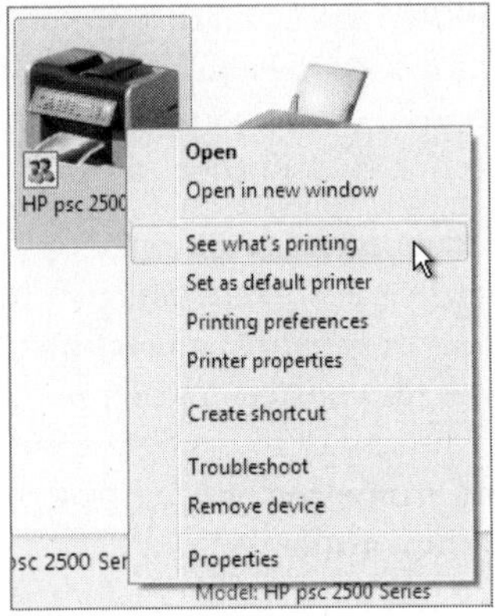

Selecting See What's Printing opens the window that shows you what's going on with your printer (as far as document/job control). Figure 5.21 shows the queue available in Windows 7.

FIGURE 5.21 See What's Printing display window

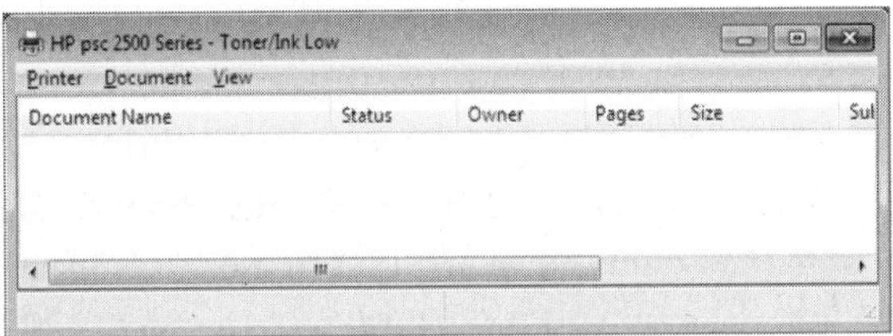

To take a look at the better functionality of Device Stage, you can select the context window from Devices And Printers. To get a graphical view of Device Stage, double-click the printer in Devices And Printers to get a consolidated view and the popular (as decided by the vendor) menu choices. Figure 5.22 shows a printer and its options as seen when you double-click it in Devices And Printers.

FIGURE 5.22 Printer window from Devices And Printers

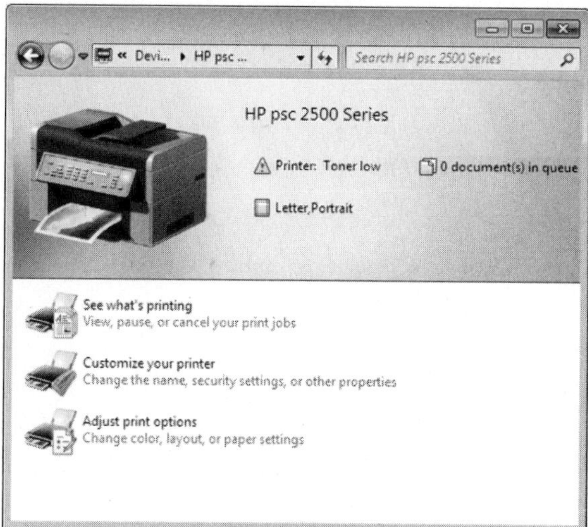

You've installed printers in previous exercises for both a locally connected and a network-connected printer. In Exercise 5.13, let's take a look at sending a print job to the locally connected printer that you set up in a previous exercise and view the document properties.

EXERCISE 5.13

Managing Documents in the Local Queue

1. Choose Start ➢ Devices And Printers.
2. Double-click the printer previously installed as the locally connected printer. If you haven't installed the printer yet, you can return to and complete Exercise 5.11.
3. To pause printing, open the printer window; double-click the See What's Printing area in the body of the window or single-click the Printer item in the top of the window.
4. Choose Printer ➢ Pause Printing from the menu.
5. View the status bar of the printer to verify that the printer is paused; there will also be a check mark next to Pause Printing in the menu.

Now, let's send a test document to the paused locally connected printer:

1. From the Printer window, select Printer ➢ Properties.
2. On the General tab of the Properties window, click the Print Test Page button.

EXERCISE 5.13 *(continued)*

3. An information box will appear stating a test page has been sent to the printer; click the Close button.
4. Click the OK button in the printer Properties window.
5. The Printer window will display the print job in the queue.

You can view document properties from a job in the print queue.

1. In the Printer window, single-click the document you want to view (the print job you want to view).
2. Choose Document ➢ Properties to view the document properties; you can also right-click the print job and select Properties from the context menu. The General tab will show you the document properties, the other tabs are vendor supplied to control additional printer functionality for the document.
3. Choose OK or Cancel to close the Properties window. OK will save any changes made and close the window, Cancel will close the window without saving any changes. If you have made any configuration changes, the Apply button will become available; selecting Apply saves any changes made but does not close the window.

Now, delete a document from the queue.

1. In the Printer windows, single click the job you want to cancel (the document you want to delete).
2. Choose Document ➢ Cancel From The Printer Window Menu Structure to delete the document. You can also right-click the document and select Cancel to delete the print job. Either method will prompt a confirmation message box asking Are You Sure You Want To Cancel The Document? Choose Yes.
3. The document will no longer be in the queue in the Printer window.
4. Choose Printer ➢ Close to close the Printer window.

There may also be times you will want to delete a printer, either one that's locally connected or a network printer, from your Windows 7 machine. This will be done from the Devices And Printers window. Removing a printer will remove the software configuration but not necessarily the files (drivers and software) from the local machine.

There will be times in any administrator's life where a previously installed printer will need to be removed. This may be due to a replacement of an older print device or to moving a user to a new print device. In either case, the old one is no longer needed. In exercise 5.14 we will remove a printer.

EXERCISE 5.14

Removing a Printer from Devices and Printers

To remove a printer, follow these steps:

1. Choose Start ➤ Devices And Printers.
2. Right-click the printer you want to remove and select Remove Device from the context menu, or you can choose Remove Device from the menu of Devices And Printers to unpair the printer from the machine.
3. Click Yes in the dialog box with the question Are You Sure You Want To Remove This Device?
4. You are presented with a status box during the removal process, and then the device is no longer available in Devices And Printers.

Now that you've seen how to configure hardware, let's take a look at how to manage applications on a Windows 7 machine.

Managing Applications

As IT professionals, many of us think of managing applications as installing the application on the computer. But there are other details that may need to be configured to allow applications to run better, faster, and more efficiently.

Configuring Applications

As operating systems evolve, one issue that you can run into is that your applications may not work properly on the newer operating system. Microsoft has developed a few different ways to help you combat this issue.

Windows 7 XP Mode

One technology that has started to sweep the computer industry is called virtualization. Virtualization is the ability to run one operating system on top of another. For example, Microsoft Hyper-V is a virtualization feature on Windows Server 2008 R2 that allows you to run multiple versions of operating systems simultaneously on one computer.

Microsoft has a virtualization environment that can operate on its client software called *Windows Virtual PC*. Windows Virtual PC allows you to create and manage virtual machines without the need for a server operating system. The advantage here is that you can run operating systems in a client environment like Windows XP, Windows Vista, or Windows 7. You must have Windows 7 Professional, Enterprise, or Ultimate to download and run Windows XP Mode. All other versions must use Windows Virtual PC. All other Windows 7 versions can just download Windows Virtual PC.

Windows Virtual PC gives you the ability to set up virtualization on a client operating system. This is very beneficial for anyone in the industry who has to do testing or configuration. Windows Virtual PC is not really meant to run a network like Hyper-V, but it does give an administrator the ability to test software and patches before installing them live on a network or running applications in an operating system other than the installed one. Also, it is very beneficial to research problems in a controlled environment and not on a live server where you can end up doing more harm than good.

Finally, Windows Virtual PC gives you a training advantage. Think about having the ability to train users on a real product like Windows Server 2008 or Windows 7 without needing to purchase additional equipment. Windows Virtual PC allows you to train users on products and software while using only one machine.

Real World Scenario

Using Windows Virtual PC

As an instructor and consultant, I can't say enough about how valuable Microsoft Virtual PC can be as a tool. I have used it on many occasions to either test a piece of software before installation or find an answer to a problem in a controlled environment.

Currently, at the time this book is being written, I use Microsoft Windows Vista on my laptop. On that same laptop I have a version of Windows Virtual PC with both Windows Server 2008 and Windows 7 Ultimate operating system virtual machines.

While I am on a client site or while I am in the classroom, having a way to test and research problems using multiple operating systems on one client computer system is invaluable.

To run Windows Virtual PC, you need a minimum of a 400 MHz Pentium-compatible processor (1.0 GHz or faster recommended) and at least 35 MB of free disk space. You can load Windows Virtual PC on Windows 7, Windows Vista with SP1 (Enterprise, Business, Ultimate), and Windows XP with SP3.

Professional and Ultimate can use the Windows XP Mode. All other versions complete the following steps to download and configure Windows Virtual PC on a Windows 7 machine.

EXERCISE 5.15

Downloading and Configuring Windows Virtual PC

1. Download Microsoft Virtual PC (currently version 2007) at `www.microsoft.com/downloads/details.aspx?FamilyId=28C97D22-6EB8-4A09-A7F7-F6C7A1F000B5&displaylang=en`.

2. After the download completes, install the application to your system.
3. Once the product is installed, open the Windows Virtual PC application by choosing Start ➢ All Programs ➢ Windows Virtual PC.
4. When you start Windows Virtual PC, the New Virtual Machine Wizard will automatically appear. Click Next.
5. At the Options screen, click the Create A Virtual Machine radio button.
6. At the virtual machine Name and Location screen, type **VirtualWin7** and then click Next.
7. At the Operating System screen, choose Other in the pull-down box (if you are going to install Windows 7 32-bit). Click Next.
8. At the Memory screen, choose the Adjust The RAM radio button and set it to 1024 (512 minimum if needed). Click Next.
9. At the Virtual Hard Disk screen, click the New Virtual Hard Disk radio button and click Next.
10. At the Virtual Hard Disk Name And Location screen, accept the default location and click Next. You can change the name or location if needed.
11. At the Completing The New Virtual Machine screen, verify the settings and click Finish.
12. The Windows Virtual PC console will now show the VirtualWin7 virtual machine. Click the virtual machine and choose Settings under the Actions menu.
13. The Settings for VirtualWin7 will appear. Here is where you can change or verify your settings for this virtual machine. Click on CD/DVD drive and verify that you are using the local DVD drive. Click OK.
14. Put the Windows 7 32-bit DVD in the physical drive. At the Windows Virtual PC console screen, click VirtualWin7 and click Start.
15. Install Windows 7 onto the virtual machine. If for any reason the DVD does not get recognized, click the CD menu item and choose the Use Physical CD option. Click Enter and finish the install.
16. After Windows 7 is installed, close the VirtualWin7 virtual machine and save the changes.

If you are using Windows 7 Enterprise, Ultimate, or Professional, Microsoft has an XP virtual machine insert that allows you to run Windows XP applications on Windows 7. This is known as *Windows 7 XP Mode*. If you have applications that ran properly on Windows XP but aren't running well on Windows 7, running the applications in XP Mode solves this issue.

Understanding Shims

When new operating systems get released, older applications may not run and you may not be able to get a newer version. For example, a vendor that sold you an application has gone out of business, but the application is still needed in your organization.

If you install the application on Windows 7, there may be issues. This is where shims apply. The *shim* (known as Shim Infrastructure) is a coding fix that allows the application to function properly.

The Shim Infrastructure (`http://technet.microsoft.com/en-us/library/dd837644(WS.10).aspx`) consists of application programming interface (API) hooking. What this means is that the Shim Infrastructure uses linking to redirect API calls from the Windows operating system to the alternative code called the shim.

To have shims created, you must first contact Microsoft. Microsoft must create the shim; Microsoft does not offer any custom tools to allow for private creation. Microsoft does include shims with Windows 7 and new shims will be available through Windows Update as they are created.

Windows 7 Compatibility Mode

Another way to try to run an older application in Windows 7 is by setting the compatibility mode. Let's say that an application worked fine in Windows XP but it is not working correctly in Windows 7. You can set that application to run in compatibility mode for a previous operating system (see Figure 5.23).

FIGURE 5.23 Application compatibility mode

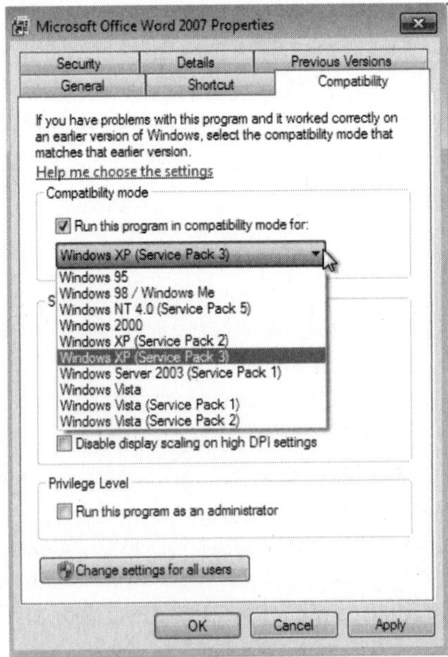

There are some other features that you can enable when setting the compatibility options:

- Run In 256 Color
- Run In 640 × 480 Screen Resolution
- Disable Visual Themes
- Disable Desktop Composition
- Disable Display Scaling On High DPI Settings
- Run This Program As An Administrator

File Extension Association

One task that may need to be performed is associating a file to a particular application. For example, you may want all files with the filename extension .asx to be played through Windows Media Player. You have the ability to set these file extension associations in Default Programs in Control Panel. Within Default Programs, there is an Associate A File Type Or Protocol With A Program link, as shown in Figure 5.24.

FIGURE 5.24 Filename extension association

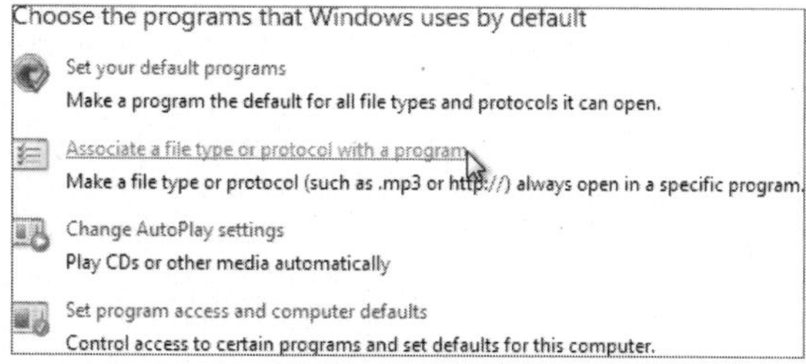

Another application that is used in Windows 7 that we need to discuss is Internet Explorer 8. In the next section we will look at configuring and managing Internet Explorer 8.

Overview of Internet Explorer 8

Windows Internet Explorer 8, or IE8, is the latest web browser developed and released by Microsoft Corporation in the popular Internet Explorer series. IE8 was release in March 2009 and available for Windows XP and Windows Server 2003 with at least SP2 in both the 32-bit and 64-bit operating systems.

IE8 is available for Windows Vista and Windows Server 2008 in both the 32-bit and 64-bit versions and is the browser shipped with Windows 7 (both 32-bit and 64-bit). Windows Internet Explorer 8 is the successor to Windows Internet Explorer 7, released in 2006.

With the explosion of Internet use—even for the inexperienced end user browsing the Internet for personal reasons as well as for those who use it for work-related tasks—enhancing the user interface (UI) while providing better levels of security (which include privacy) has been the focus in the development of IE8.

Windows Internet Explorer 8 is loaded with new user features to provide end users with a better and simpler way to get the information they desire from their browsing experience.

Using New User Features of IE8

The new features added to Windows Internet Explorer 8 are designed to give end users an easy way to browse the Internet for the information they're looking for while providing a secure environment for networks by recognizing potentially bad sites (those attempting to sneak viruses or Trojan horses into the network), phishing sites (those that attempt to steal private information about the user), or invasive sites that users may go to either on purpose or inadvertently.

I will cover the security and safety features of IE8 later in this chapter. But first, we will take a look at additions related to the user experience. Microsoft has added Accelerators to give users a faster way to access online services, Web Slices to let users see if parts of a website have changed automatically, and Compatibility View to ensure that older web pages display appropriately in IE8.

Defining IE8 Accelerators

Windows Internet Explorer 8 includes a new feature that allows you to gain access to Internet services with a click. By highlighting a word within a web page and clicking the Accelerator icon, you have access to a range of various services by default and can add more Accelerators if you desire. In Figure 5.25, you can see the word *cryptographic* highlighted and the Accelerator icon selected. Clicking the Accelerator icon will bring up a list of currently available services.

FIGURE 5.25 The Accelerator icon

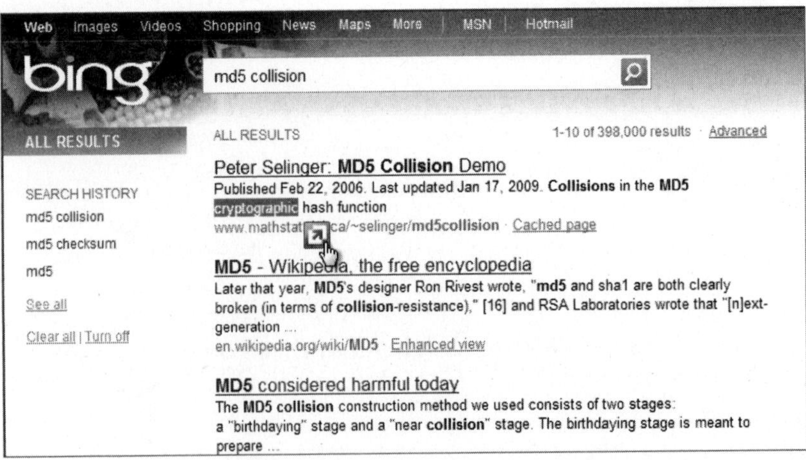

The default set of Accelerator services are shown in Figure 5.26 and are available to launch a web page to provide information about the selected text. In this example, I'm going to search Bing for the term *cryptographic* by choosing Search With Bing.

FIGURE 5.26 The Search With Bing Accelerator

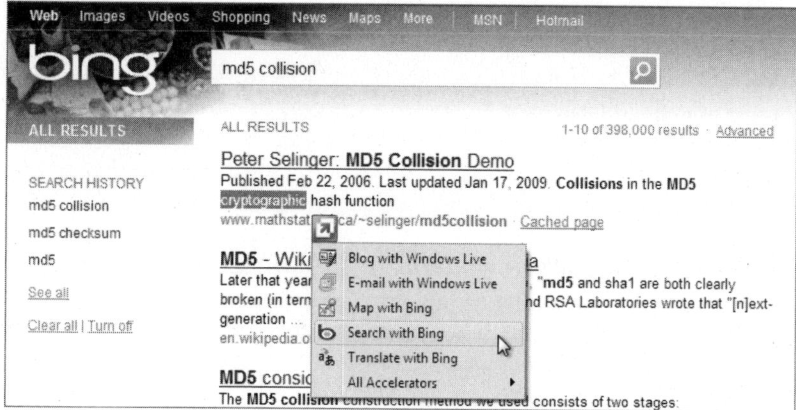

Figure 5.26 shows the set of Accelerator services installed by default in IE8, but there are several more currently available and more to be available as time goes on. You add more Accelerators from the same menu by choosing All Accelerators and Find More Accelerators (Figure 5.27).

FIGURE 5.27 Adding more Accelerators

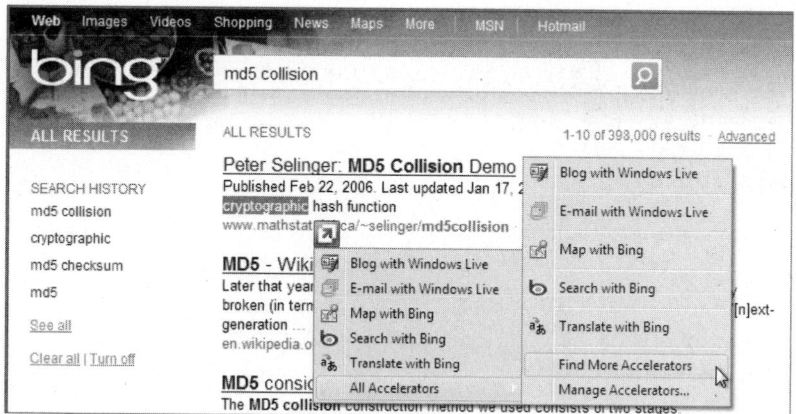

Adding Accelerators to IE8 will certainly provide a more feature-rich and efficient browsing experience. Most of the time while browsing, a second browser or new tab is opened to do further research about the page you're currently viewing. Lots of times this is just for a quick look at a new piece of information or to look something up. If you're used to going to a certain page to find the "extra" information, this would be a great candidate to add to your Accelerators.

In Exercise 5.16, you'll add an Accelerator to IE8 from a currently open web page.

EXERCISE 5.16

Adding an Accelerator to IE8

1. Open Windows Internet Explorer 8 and open a web page.
2. Select a word or phrase and choose the Accelerator icon.
3. Choose All Accelerators and then Find More Accelerators.
4. Review the available Accelerators and select the Define With Bing Accelerator:

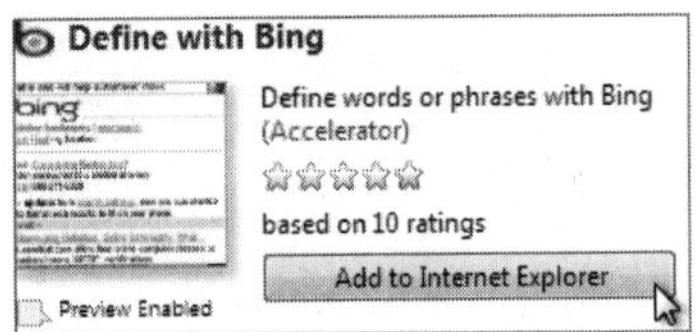

5. A confirmation box appears asking if you're sure you want to add this Accelerator and if you want to make it the default for this Accelerator category. Select the check box to make it the default and choose Add.
6. You can verify the installation of the Define With Bing Accelerator by returning to the web page (or going to any web page), highlighting a word or phrase, and choosing the Accelerator icon. The Define With Bing option will now be available.

You can also add Accelerators directly from the IE8 menus, which is also where you can manage any of the Accelerators you have installed (and that includes deleting them).

Managing IE8 Accelerators

To manage the installed Accelerators or add new Accelerators directly from the IE8 program interface, perform the following steps:

1. Open Windows Internet Explorer 8.
2. Choose the Tools then Manage Add-ons menu choice
3. From the Manage Add-ons window, select Accelerators from the Add-on Types section
4. Select the Accelerator in the right pane that you would like to manage or Select the Find More Accelerators menu choice in the bottom left of the Manage Add-Ons window to add more Accelerators to IE8.

Using Accelerators in IE8

Let's take a look at some of the different capabilities of the Accelerators in Windows Internet Explorer 8. In the previous section, we installed the Define With Bing Accelerator. We discussed the addition of the Define With Bing Accelerator as being a quick launch of Bing with a define search functionality implemented in a new tab of IE8.

This is true; however, the Accelerator provides an even more useful function by giving you a "preview" of the search without opening a new tab. If you select a word in a web page you are viewing and would like a definition of the word, you can open the Accelerators menu by clicking the icon and simply pausing the mouse pointer over the Define With Bing option. IE8 will use Bing and display a quick definition in the current window, as shown in Figure 5.28, with *cryptographic* highlighted and the mouse pointer paused over Define With Bing.

FIGURE 5.28 A quick definition from an Accelerator

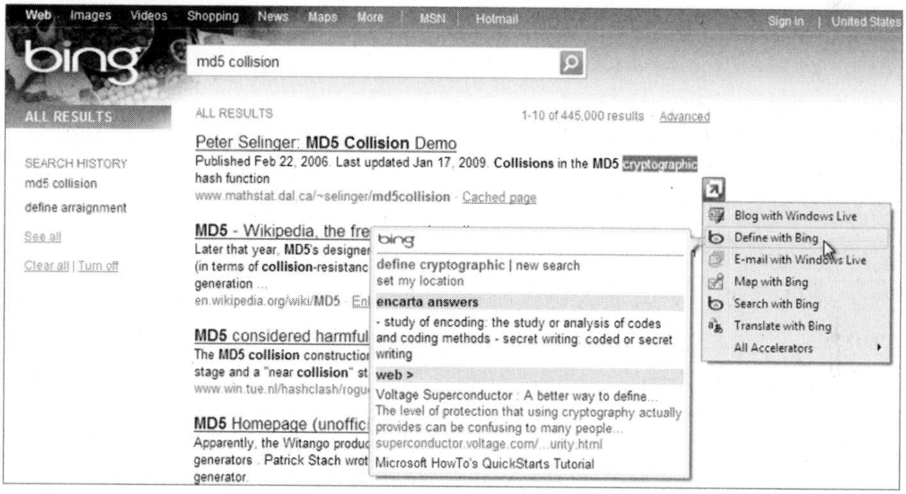

If you think this is cool, hold on; it gets even better. The default Map With Bing Accelerator works like Define With Bing. It will open a new tab in IE8 with a highlighted location address entered and searched with Bing. The Map With Bing Accelerator also has the preview capability and will show you an insert in your current page if you hover the pointer over the address. If you check out Figure 5.29, you can see that I searched on the latitude and longitude of a lighthouse in Maine.

FIGURE 5.29 Quick map from an Accelerator

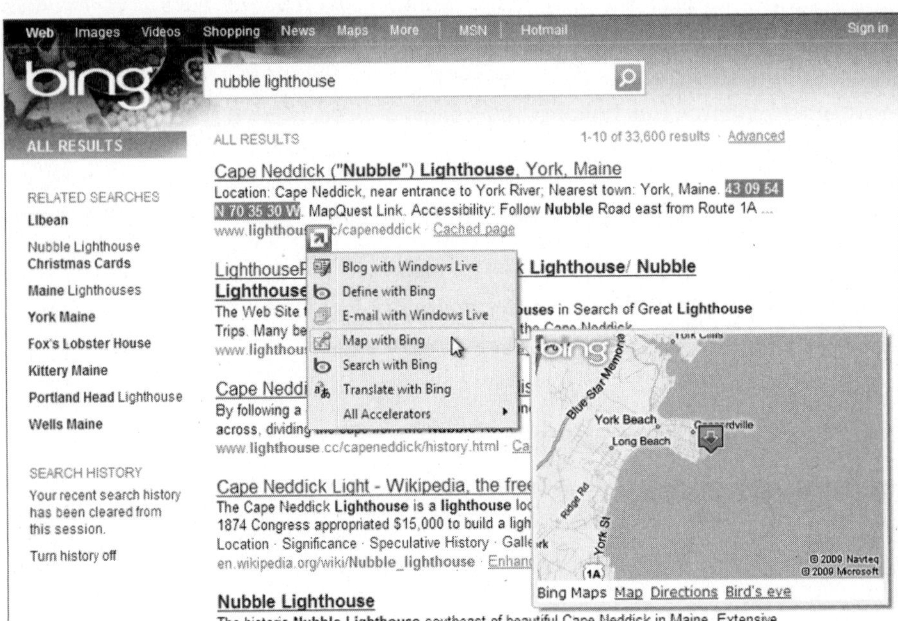

The list of Accelerators providing internet services is extensive at this time, with Accelerators available for most of your favorite providers. I've used examples from Bing here, but if you prefer other search engines and mapping providers, they already have Accelerators available.

Facebook, eBay, Hotmail, Google, LinkedIn, Trip Advisor, Currency Converter, Wal-Mart, TechNet, MSDN, UPS Tracking, and USPS Tracking are just a short list of Accelerators available. As you get used to using the Accelerators, the functionality they provide will make the browsing experience so much faster you'll wonder what you did without it. There are other more new services available in IE8, like Web Slices.

Defining IE8 Web Slices

Web Slices in Windows Internet Explorer 8 allows IE8 to check for updates to web page content you may frequently want to have. How many times in the course of the day do you check your local weather or stock quotes or even watch an auction item on eBay? Most of the time you either keep a tab open and refresh it periodically or even re-surf to the website with the content you would like to review.

With Web Slices, you can add the piece of the web page with the content you're looking for to the new favorites bar and IE8 will check it for you and give you a visual clue when the content changes. You can control how often IE8 checks for changes as well as have IE8 play a sound when Web Slice content is found on a page and even when an update to content is discovered.

Web Slice content is being added to provider pages continually and its functionality will grow over time. Even as Windows 7 and IE8 are being released, the available content makes this new feature a welcome addition and Web Slices are already at the top of my list of favorite functions. If there is Web Slice content available on a web page, the green Web Slice icon will become active on the Favorites toolbar as well as becoming visible as you move your mouse pointer over the available Web Slice content in the page itself. Figure 5.30 shows the Web Slice icon on the IE8 new Favorites toolbar.

FIGURE 5.30 Web Slice icon on the Favorites toolbar

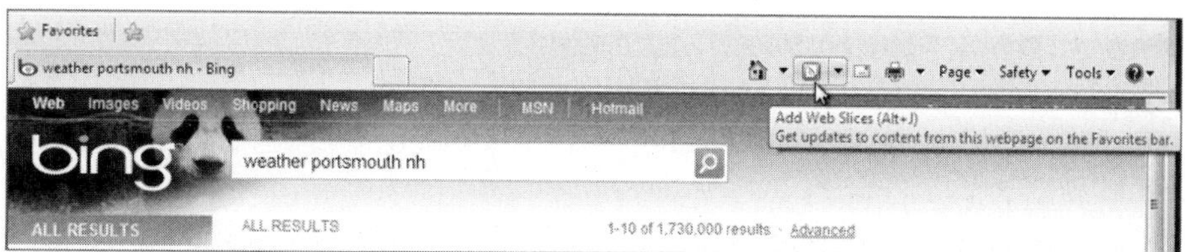

Figure 5.31 shows the result of a Bing query for a weather forecast for Portsmouth, New Hampshire, and the option icon available to add the forecast content as a Web Slice to the IE8 Favorites toolbar. Clicking the down arrow associated with the Favorites toolbar Web Slice icon will display all of the Web Slices available on the current web page. In the case of eBay, for example, all the items matching your search will be individual Web Slices you can pick from, allowing you to watch just one (or more if you add more than one Web Slice) item.

FIGURE 5.31 Web Slice icon within a web page

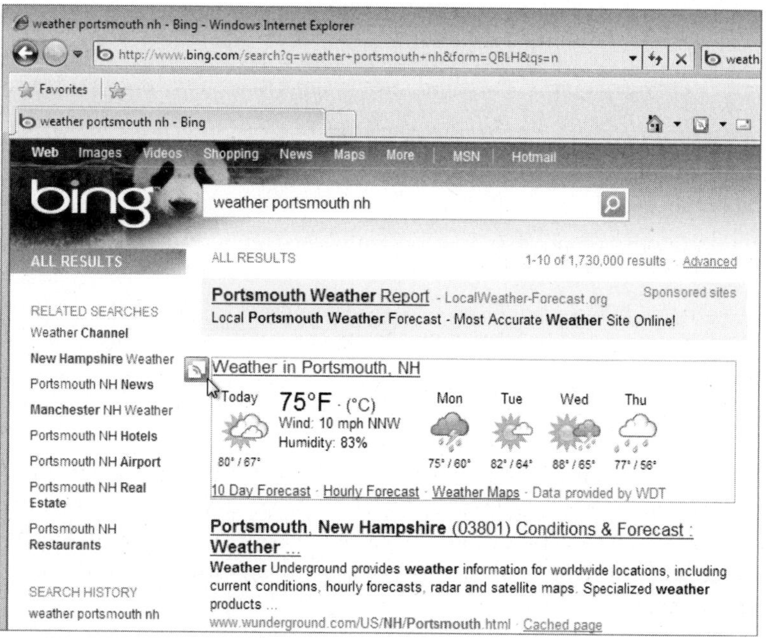

When the user chooses a Web Slice icon from the web page content, they'll see a confirmation box for adding the Web Slice to the Favorites bar. Once accepted, the Web Slice is available to be viewed at any time, even if you browse away from the originating page.

Once the Web Slice has been added to IE8, the browser will periodically check the source of the content for changes. If there have been changes to the content, the text of the Web Slice on the Favorites bar will change to bold and the background color of the Favorites bar behind the Web Slice will flash a color indicating that an update has been detected. Adding a Web Slice to your browser is a simple task you will find extremely convenient.

Adding a Stock Quote Web Slice to IE8

You may like to monitor a company's stock prices throughout the course of the day. Complete Exercise 5.17 to add Microsoft's stock quote (Web Slice) to your IE8 interface.

EXERCISE 5.17

Adding a Stock Quote Web Slice to IE8

1. Open Windows Internet Explorer 8 and browse to `www.Bing.com`.
2. Enter **msft** into the search box in Bing and click the Search button.
3. Choose the drop-down arrow from the Web Slice icon on the IE8 Favorites toolbar and select Microsoft Corp. Web Slice.
4. Select the Add To Favorites Bar button in the Internet Explorer confirmation window.
5. Verify that the Web Slice is available in the IE8 Favorites toolbar.
6. Click the down arrow of the Bing Microsoft Corp. Web Slice and you will be presented with the current information from the Web Slice of the original page, with updated information if it's available.

You could have also added the Web Slice by clicking the Web Slice icon associated with the content on the page. Once the Web Slice is added, you can change certain parameters associated with it, such as how often the content is checked for updates or whether a sound is associated with Web Slices.

After adding Web Slices to Windows Internet Explorer 8, you may want to tweak the properties to allow a more frequent update check. The default update interval for a Web Slice is dependent on the website content developer. The eBay interval shows up as 3,600+ seconds for an item, expiring a long time from when the Web Slice is added. The weather Web Slice from Bing defaults to 360 seconds.

You can change the properties for the Web Slice timing by adjusting the values from the Properties dialog box of the Web Slice. Right-clicking (alternate mouse click) the Web Slice from the new IE8 Favorites bar and selecting Properties opens the Properties dialog box. Exercise 5.18 will show you how to manage a Web Slice.

EXERCISE 5.18

Managing IE8 Web Slices

1. Perform the tasks associated with Adding A Stock Quote Web Slice located earlier in this section if you have not done so already.
2. Right-click (alternate mouse click) the Bing Microsoft Corp. Web Slice in the favorites bar and select properties.
3. Choose the Use Custom Schedule Radio button.
4. Choose the down arrow from the Frequency: drop down list box and choose a new interval.
5. Choose the OK button to close the Properties box and save your changes.

You can also set other properties for the Web Slices from the properties pages as well by choosing the Settings button from the Update Schedule section; sound options and display options for the Web Slices can be set from this Feed and Web Slice Settings page.

If you have to enter credentials for a Web Slice, you can add or modify the information from the Web Slice properties pages by selecting the Settings button from the Web Slice Properties page main section next to the User name and password item. The Web Slice display text can be changed in the Web Slice Properties page and the Uniform Resource Locator (URL) for the Web Slice is available on the properties page too.

Once you're done with a Web Slice, you remove it from the favorites bar by right-clicking it and selecting Delete from the context menu; you will be asked to confirm the deletion. The alternate-click context menu also provides shortcuts to Web Slice properties such as choosing to bold a new entry and modifying the text or icons shown on the Favorites bar.

You will find using Web Slices a fast and convenient way to keep up-to-date with content you review periodically throughout the day or to keep track of web content that may need to be addressed as it changes. As Windows Internet Explorer continues to advance, content providers can make use of the new features. However, there may be older pages that don't display correctly. Windows Internet Explorer 8 adds Compatibility View, allowing IE8 to present older content correctly.

Using IE8 Compatibility View

Windows Internet Explorer 8 is included in Windows 7 as a new release of Microsoft's web browser, and some websites may not be updated to use the new features of IE8 or display their content correctly. Problems may exist displaying misaligned images or text. By using Compatibility View, IE8 will display a web page the way it would have been displayed in Internet Explorer 7 (which should correct any display issues). To display a page in Compatibility View, click the Compatibility View button in the IE8 address bar.

Once you have chosen Compatibility View for a website, you will not need to make the choice again. IE8 will display the site in Compatibility View the next time you browse to it. If the website gets updated in the future or you decide you would prefer to see it in the native IE8 standard mode, you can simply click the Compatibility View button again to return to the standard view. The Compatibility View option can also be selected from the IE8 tools menu Compatibility View menu option.

There is also a Compatibility View Settings option you can use to manage the sites currently set to be viewed in Compatibility View mode by adding or deleting sites by name. Many companies have extensive websites, and it may take time to update to IE8 features. The Compatibility View Settings page has the default setting for all intranet sites to be displayed in Compatibility View. You also have to the choice to display all websites in Compatibility View.

Compatibility View will help in the transition to the new Windows Internet Explorer 8, allowing users to view pages in a consistent manner. The new features—Accelerators, Web Slices, and Compatibility View—are all a definite plus in the overall browsing experience. Windows Internet Explorer 8 also includes a wide range of security enhancements and updated safety features.

Using New Security and Safety Features of IE8

The new security and safety features of Windows Internet Explorer 8 are designed to help protect end users from malicious attacks or attempts to get personal information from the user without their knowledge. Users expect things to be as they appear which is not always the case. Because we all use the internet and our corporate intranets to provide information every day, online crime has risen dramatically.

The new type of criminal we face are known as cybercriminals, and they are using extremely deceptive and sophisticated methods for getting information from end users. One method is the use of malware to steal private information through software pretending to be an expected website. This malware could be a program running on your PC which reads everything you type (including login information from a web browser) and reports the info back to a cybercriminal. Phishing is another technique used by cybercriminals to gain personal information from users. Phishing can be perpetrated by the cybercriminal pretending to be a legitimate website such as the user's banking site or credit card site and getting the end user to enter information into a fraudulent page.

New features of IE8 helping to identify malware and phishing schemes will make it easier for end users to quickly identify potential issues and allow the administrators to spend less time "fixing" the network and user-compromised data. Domain Highlighting, Cross Site Scripting Filter, Click-Jacking prevention, Smart Screen filters, a -InPrivite Browsing, and InPrivate Filtering are new additions to Windows Internet Explorer 8.

Using Domain Highlighting

Domain Highlighting is one of the new features in Windows Internet Explorer 8 that gives the user more feedback about the website they are visiting. When a user surfs to a website, they normally type in a Uniform Resource Locater (URL) in the form of, for example, `www.bing.com`. This is displayed in the address bar of the browser, and the user can see it during the entire browsing session. This may or may not be apparent to the user as it is in nondescript text and nothing jumps out at them. In IE8, the displayed URL is shown to the user with the domain highlighted, for example, `www.bing.com`. As the user continues to surf to other pages within Bing, the domain portion, `bing.com`, remains clear (the other text softens to gray) so if the user is redirected to another site, there is a visual clue jumping out at the user.

Real World Scenario

Getting Users to Help Themselves with Security

One of the biggest issues I face when working with users is getting them to think outside of their box while they're using a browser. The main problem is that users really do expect the world to be a kind place where no one is going to try to trick them. How many times have we told users, both those well versed in technology and those who are not quite so strong, that they should not click links in an e-mail, that instead they should go where the e-mail says the link will take them instead of where they think they're going. How many times do we tell users to make sure they get the lock icon if they're surfing to a secure site and/or to look at the protocol being used (`https:` vs `http:`). Educating the user and getting them to "do what you say" are two completely different things.

I have set up phishing websites and had corporate users go to my site (unbeknownst to them it was a fake) and enter company credentials to gain access. The phishing site did not use the correct name for the company, and, in some cases, where the connection was meant to be secure, we did not use `https:`, but the users still entered their credentials.

I have contemplated numerous times just what I could do to help the user see that there is a problem and provide some feedback. Although not a perfect solution (some users just won't look), the Domain Highlighting feature of IE8 seems to be working. The fact that the link changes as the user surfs and that the domain name appears in bold at least has a few users looking and asking, "is this the right place?" We do have other features in IE8 where we, as administrators, are controlling the users, but Domain Highlighting seems to be scratching the surface with users and they're at least pondering the domain changes. Whether the change is good or bad (some sites will in fact send you to another domain), at least they're looking!

If you take a look at Figure 5.32, you can see the same search string issued in both Windows IE7 and IE8. Notice how much better `bing.com` stands out in the Windows Internet Explorer 8 address bar.

FIGURE 5.32 Domain Highlighting in IE8

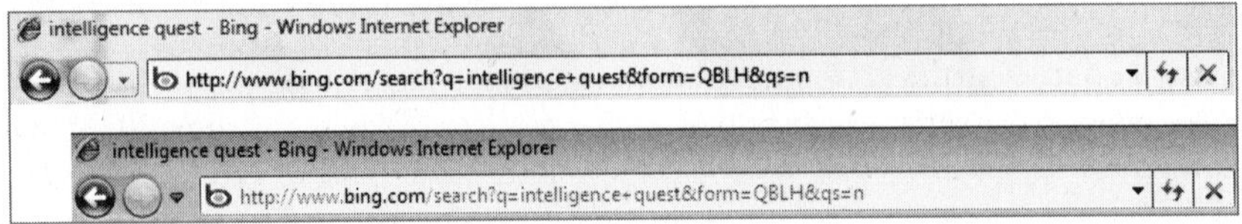

Domain Highlighting and user education are a good starting place for security and safety, but are there features that can be added to proactively help the user? Yes, one of the more common phishing/malware activities is Cross Site Scripting (XSS), where the user inadvertently runs a script in a website link exploiting a flaw in the website, or Clickjacking, where a user clicks a link that says one thing on the page but sends the user somewhere else. IE8 has proactive software to help identify these types of phishing/malware attacks before they can happen.

Defending Against Cross-Site Scripting and Click-Jacking

Cross-site scripting (XSS) attacks attempt to exploit vulnerabilities that exist in the websites you use. XSS attacks are set up by inserting an address to a malicious website in a link a user might click on in an email. The data in the link directs the browser to a legitimate website that has been compromised to contain malicious code that can capture keystrokes, letting the cybercriminal capture a user's login credentials (user name and password).

As a leading compromise today, Windows Internet Explorer 8 includes a Cross Site Scripting filter that attempts to detect these types of attacks and disable the harmful scripts. If users surf to a website that has been compromised, the problem can be detected and IE8 can modify the request, avoiding the potential risk.

A message will appear at the top of IE8 page indicating to the user that "Internet Explorer has modified this page to help prevent cross-site scripting." Figure 5.33 shows the message displayed when a malformed query is issued to a search engine. The user can click the message to get further information about the compromise.

FIGURE 5.33 Cross-site scripting filter message

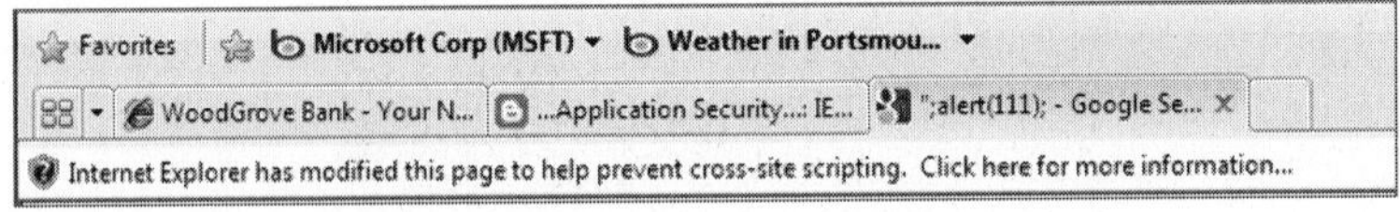

As with all of technology and cybercrime, it's a cat-and-mouse game between the administrators and users, and the cybercriminals. Every time the good guys find a way to block or mitigate an attack, the bad guys (good or bad I guess depends on your point of view) find a different way to perpetrate an exploit. Click-jacking is a growing threat to our online community. A savvy cybercriminal can create a website where a real page is placed in a frame in the attacker's page.

Clicking on an item in the attacker's page allows the attacker to manipulate your input and have you view an advertisement at best or change your browser parameters at worst. Windows Internet Explorer 8 includes code that will allow developers to prevent their websites from getting inserted into a frame in the IE8 interface, helping to mitigate the click-jacking problem.

The cross-site scripting filter and click-jack prevention code offer protection against malicious code in a website. There is also a set of tools included in Windows Internet Explorer 8 that help prevent the user from visiting a website that has been reported as unsafe or downloading content that has been reported as unsafe. This protection is known as Smart Screen filtering.

Working with SmartScreen Filters

Microsoft maintains a database of unsafe websites that is checked while a user is browsing through websites. If an unsafe website is chosen, IE8 will block the user's request and present a page displaying the fact that the page has been identified as unsafe and changing the background color of the address bar to reflect the same.

The user can continue to the web page if they are confident of the safety of the website by choosing More Options and continuing to the website. This functionality is part of the IE8 suite of technologies helping to protect the users from the deceptive practices of cybercriminals. The SmartScreen filters also have the ability to block malware or phishing from within initially safe sites by including specific pages identified as unsafe in the Microsoft unsafe website database.

Another new feature added to SmartScreen filters is the ability to protect the user from unsafe downloads. If a user attempts to download a file and the file has been reported as unsafe (and accepted into the Microsoft database as unsafe), an Unsafe Download security warning dialog box is generated and the user is prevented from downloading the file. As with the unsafe website filters, the user can still choose to continue the download if they are confident the file they are requesting is safe, as shown in Figure 5.34.

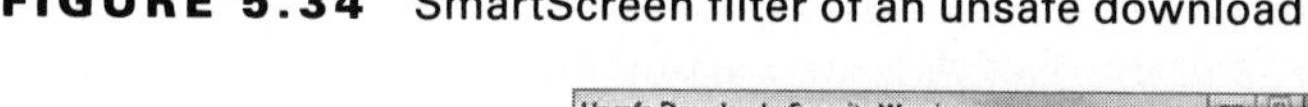

FIGURE 5.34 SmartScreen filter of an unsafe download

Administrators do have the option of configuring Group Policy for Windows Internet Explorer 8 to disable the ability of the users to download unsafe files if this is desired. You do have the ability to manage Smart Screen Filtering functionality from the Safety menu of IE8. Figure 5.35 shows the option to select Turn Off Smart Screen Filter. . . . From the Smart Screen filter menu choice you do have the ability to check whether the current site has been reported as unsafe (let's say you turned off Smart Screen Filtering but would like to check a specific site).

FIGURE 5.35 Smart Screen Filter options menu

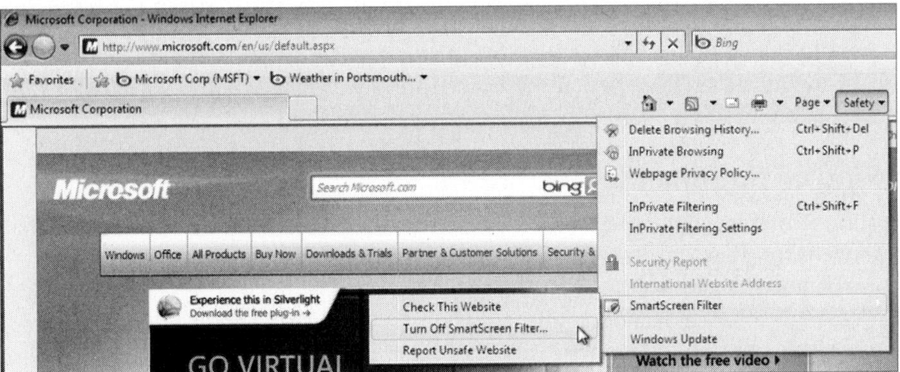

The Smart Screen Filter menu option also gives you the ability to report a website as unsafe. Once submitted, Microsoft will review the site and add it to their database if they determine it meets the criteria they have put in place for an unsafe website. Microsoft has also added two new features to protect a user's personal information. The new features are InPrivate Browsing and InPrivate Filtering.

Using InPrivate Browsing and InPrivate Filtering

InPrivate browsing provides some level of privacy to users using Windows Internet Explorer 8. The privacy maintained with InPrivate browsing relates to current browsing where an InPrivate session has been enabled. The InPrivate session prevents the browsing history from being recorded nor will temporary internet files be retained. Cookies, usernames, passwords, and form data will not remain in IE8 following the closing of the InPrivate session nor will there be any footprints or data pertaining to the InPrivate browsing session.

This is a good method of protecting user data if you are not surfing from your own machine or are surfing from a public location (always a bad place to leave personal information). InPrivate browsing can also be used if you don't want anyone to be able to see data from your internet browsing session.

There are several ways to launch an InPrivate IE8 browsing session. One way is to open a new tab and select the Open An InPrivate Browsing Window option from the Browse With InPrivate section. This will open a new tab and the tab will be an InPrivate session. You can also choose to open Windows Internet Explorer 8 and start an InPrivate session directly by choosing the Safety menu item and selecting the InPrivate Browsing menu choice.

You can also open a new IE8 browser and press Control+Shift+P. Figure 5.36 shows an InPrivate session launched with Control+Shift+P and going to `login.live.com`. This will ensure any of my login and browsing information will not be saved to this computer.

FIGURE 5.36 InPrivate Browsing session

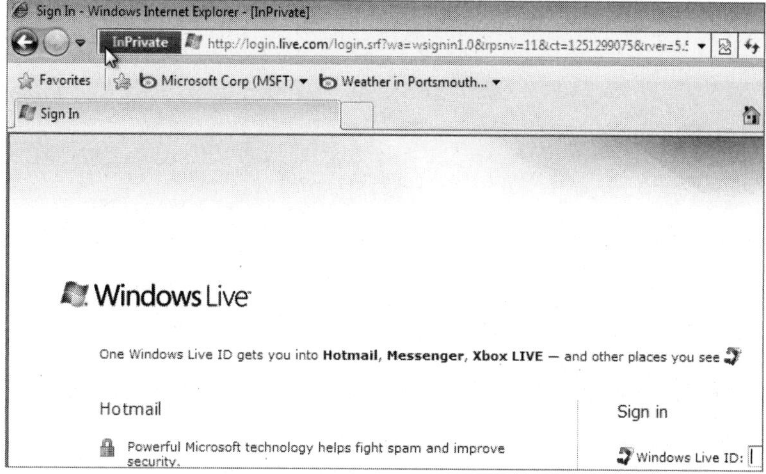

InPrivate Browsing keeps information from being saved to the local machine while the session is active, but don't get lulled into a false sense of security; malware, phishing, and other methods that send data out of the local machine are still valid and can provide personal information to a cybercriminal.

InPrivate Filtering takes a slightly different approach in providing security and safety to the user who is surfing using Windows Internet Explorer 8. Many of today's websites gather content from different sources as they present a web page to you. Some of these sources are websites outside the main location, and they provide third-party companies with tracking information about where you surf and what you look at.

This information can then be used to provide statistics as well as send advertisements back to you. InPrivate Filtering provides an added layer of control for the user to decide what information third-party websites will have access to while the user is browsing, limiting the ability of third-party websites to track their browsing usage.

InPrivate Filtering is not enabled by default and must be enabled per browsing session. It is enabled from the Safety menu in IE8. You can alternatively use Control+Shift+F to enable InPrivate Filtering.

Once you choose InPrivate Filtering, you will be given the option to have IE8 automatically block some third-party content or choose to let the user select which third-party providers will receive the user's browsing information (Figure 5.37). You can always go back and change the options later or turn off InPrivate Filtering if you desire.

FIGURE 5.37 InPrivate Filtering options

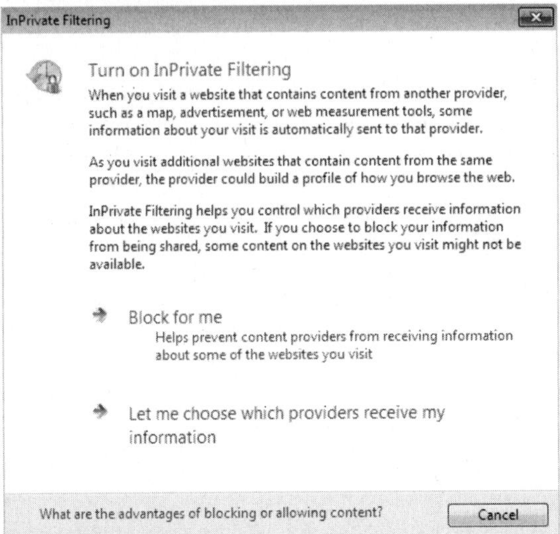

After InPrivate Filtering is enabled, you can see which pages have been blocked as third-party queries from the InPrivate Filtering Settings dialog box. The InPrivate Filtering Settings dialog is an alternate location for enabling InPrivate Filtering (as shown in Figure 5.38) or disabling it. You open InPrivate Filtering Settings from the Safety menu item of Windows Internet Explorer 8.

FIGURE 5.38 InPrivate Filtering settings

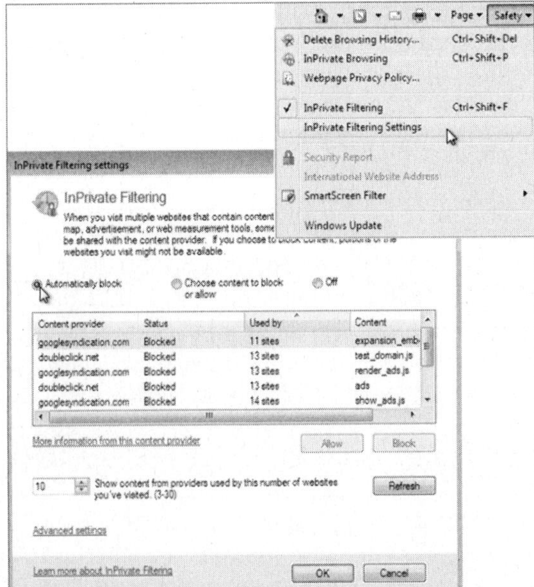

Along with the new security and safety features of Windows Internet Explorer 8, there are several enhancements to existing features. Some of the enhanced items include Data Execution Prevention, Automatic Crash Recovery, and Enhanced Delete Browsing History.

One of the many advantages of IE8 is that you can configure the web content filter. IE8 also allows you to set up and configure the Allow and Block lists. The Allow and Block lists are lists that you can subscribe to that will automatically filter out certain websites.

Installing Add-Ons to IE8

Windows Internet Explorer 8 provides the ability to install add-ons to extend the functionality of the browser. Add-ons can improve the user's experience by providing a simpler approach to resources, enhancing security, or simply providing enjoyment (a joke of the day add-on, for example). Add-ons can be created by Microsoft, but many times you will find third-party add-ons to be equally useful.

To enable, disable, or install add-ons, you will select the Tools menu item and choose Manage Add-Ons. The Manage Add-Ons window will open. The Manage Add-Ons window is a consolidation of tools where you will be able to manage add-on toolbars and functionality in the Add-On Types section and by selecting Toolbars And Extensions.

After selecting the Toolbars And Extension item, you can change the properties for installed add-ons in the right pane. By selecting an item, you toggle it from enable to disable or vice versa by clicking the button in the lower right corner. In Figure 5.39, you can see that the Shockwave Flash Object add-on is selected and enabled; the button in the lower left corner would be used to disable this add-on.

FIGURE 5.39 The Manage Add-Ons dialog box

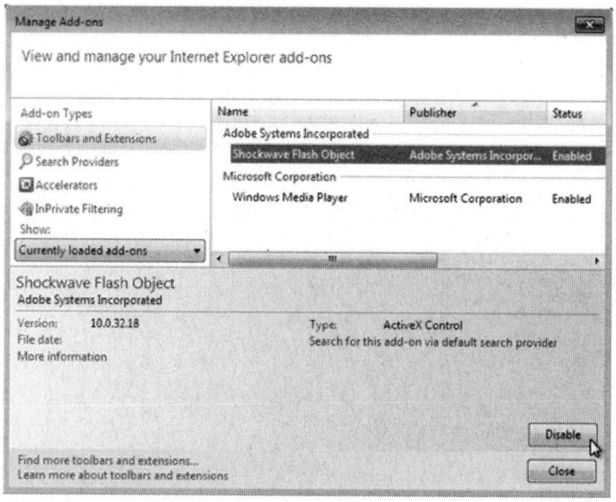

If you were looking for more add-ons for IE8, you could choose the Find More Toolbars And Extensions item in the lower left corner of the Manage Add-Ons dialog box. You can install and manage toolbars as well as search providers as extensions from here. Another feature of many websites are the pop-up windows the website developers include. IE8 includes functionality to block pop-ups dynamically.

Using Protected Mode for IE8

Protected Mode is a feature of Windows 7 for Windows Internet Explorer 8 that forces IE8 to run in a protected, isolated memory space preventing malicious code from writing data outside the Temporary Internet Files directly unless the program trying to write the information is specifically granted access by the user. Protected Mode is enabled by default and displayed in the lower right section of Windows Internet Explorer 8.

You can install software through IE8, but you will need to explicitly allow the modification of the file structure of Windows 7 if the software is going to install outside the protected directory. You can change out of protected mode from the security tab of IE8's internet options. You can get to the Security Tab by selecting the Tools menu and choosing the Internet Options menu choice. You can also open Internet Options by typing "internet options" into the integrated search box in Windows 7. You also have the option of double-clicking the "Protected Mode: On" text within Windows Internet Explorer 8 to open just the Security tab of Internet Options.

To change the Protected Mode settings, click to select or deselect the Enable Protected Mode (requires restarting Internet Explorer) check box. It is recommended that Protected Mode remains active as it provides a greater level of security and safety for the user and does not prohibit an action (installing a program from IE8), it just requires interaction from the user to allow the modification, providing at least a little thought into what's happening within Windows 7.

Configuring Windows Internet Explorer 8 Options

In addition to security and usability options that you can configure in IE8, you can configure other options for managing the browser. Many of the configurations we have discussed in this chapter and have used, the Safety or Tools menu options, to quickly change individual parameters are also available for modification within the Internet Options tabbed dialog box. There are general parameters, security parameters, privacy configurations, content control, connection settings, program options, and advanced settings available for internet options.

General Parameters within Internet Options

You can open the Internet Properties tabbed dialog box by selecting the Tools menu and choosing the Internet Properties menu item or simply typing **"internet options"** into the integrated search box of Windows 7. The General tab (Figure 5.40) allows you to change the default Home Page that displays when Windows Internet Explorer 8 is launched. An interesting feature here is that you can have more than one default Home Page. By entering more than one page in the Home Page text box, each time IE8 is launched all pages will open in their own tab.

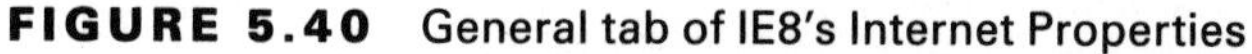

FIGURE 5.40 General tab of IE8's Internet Properties

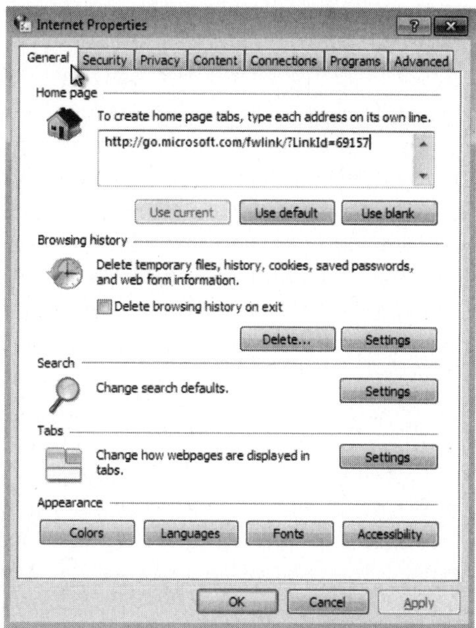

The General tab also allows you to control your Browsing History, Search, Tabs, and Appearance (including accessibility options) settings for the IE8 interface.

Security Parameters within Internet Options

The Security tab of IE8's Internet Options not only gives you access to control Protected Mode as seen earlier in this section, but gives you the ability to set security settings on the specific zones you may browse to as understood by Windows Internet Explorer 8. The zones are the Internet, Local Intranet, Trusted Sites, and Restricted Sites. You can set the behavior of IE8 individually for each zone and even individual sites within each zone.

Privacy Configurations within Internet Options

The privacy tab of IE8's Internet Options allows the management of privacy settings for the Internet Zone; this is the cookie management for specific sites. You can also control the settings for Pop-up Blocker and your InPrivate Filtering and InPrivate Browsing here.

The Pop-up blocker allows you to prevent unwanted internet pop-ups from appearing while you are online. We have all been on websites where pop-up windows start appearing. With the IE8 pop-up blocker, you can prevent this from happening. To access the Pop-up Blocker Settings dialog box, you can click Start, open Internet Explorer, click Tools, click Pop-Up Blocker, and click Pop-up Blocker Settings.

To block cookies from any websites that do not have a compact privacy policy, you should set the privacy setting to High. The High setting prevents IE8 from saving cookies for websites that do not contain a compact privacy policy and cookies that have the potential of saving information that can be used to contact you without your explicit consent.

Content Control within Internet Properties

Figure 5.41 shows the Content tab of Windows Internet Explorer 8's Internet Properties. There are parental controls to manage which sites are available through web filtering and to monitor website access through an Activity Monitor. There has to be a privileged account with a password set to enforce parental controls. InPrivate Browsing is also not allowed when parental controls are in place.

FIGURE 5.41 Content tab of the Internet Properties dialog box

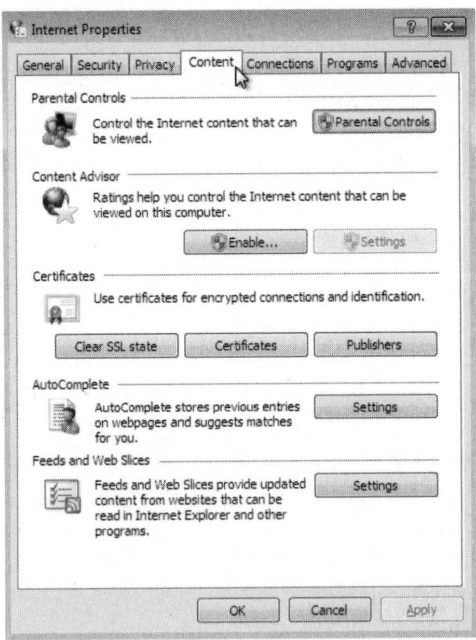

Content Advisor settings can be enabled from the Content tab, allowing a display of rated sites as users browse to different locations. Certificate management for secure

browsing is managed through the Content tab as well. You have the ability to manage AutoComplete functionality as well as RSS feeds and Web Slice data from within the Content tab.

Connection Settings within Internet Options

The Connections tab of Windows Internet Explorer 8's Internet Options dialog box allow you to manage the way IE8 gains access to the network. You can initiate the Connect To The Internet wizard from this tab as well as set up a Virtual Private Network (VPN). If you are using dial-up networking, this connection is also configured from the Connections tab. Local Area Network (LAN) general settings are configured through the Connections tab, which also includes specifying a proxy server if you need to use one (this is typical across many corporate sites, to provide a better level of anonymity for internet surfing).

Program Options within Internet Options

The Programs tab of the IE8 Internet Options dialog box allows you to control which browser you are using as your default web browser. You can manage add-ons specific to IE8 in the Programs tab as well. You can set up an application to allow for HTML editing and set up default programs to be used for internet services such as email.

Advanced Options within Internet Options

The Advanced tab of the IE8 Internet Options dialog box allows you to configure advanced configuration settings for Windows Internet Explorer 8. Some of the advanced configuration items include accessibility settings, browsing settings, international browsing settings, encoding settings, multimedia parameters, printing parameters, and general security settings. You can control whether links are underlined, whether pictures should be displayed, which versions of the secure communication protocols or SSL are used, background colors, and many other parameters.

In addition to being able to change the advanced settings, you also have the option to Restore Advanced Settings To Their Original Configurations or to even Reset Internet Explorer Settings, which resets all IE8 settings (not just the advanced settings) to the default configuration.

Windows Internet Explorer 8, with all of its new and exciting features for user browsing, safety, and security, provides a solid foundation for today's users to enjoy internet surfing. It also provides administrators with the comfort that the users will be on the network safely. Many of the enhancements provide the administrators with more peace of mind about the integrity of the network as well as being able to suppress the intentions of cybercriminals in regard to users without dramatically affecting the surfers.

Summary

Devices and hardware are two very important components that must be properly configured in Windows 7 to guarantee the best possible machine performance. Using Device Manager is a way to help manage these devices and drivers.

Another important task in managing Windows 7 is the proper configuration of applications. Many older applications may not function properly in Windows 7, so Microsoft has given you some tools to help these applications work correctly. You can run applications in XP Mode or Compatibility Mode or using shims.

Applications are an important part of any computer. One application that is very important to most of us is Internet Explorer. Internet Explorer 8 is included with Windows 7 and has many new features and security enhancements so that the user can get the most out of their browsing experience.

In the next chapter, we will discuss how to configure users, groups, and security within the Windows 7 environment.

Exam Essentials

Know how to verify if drivers are signed. Be sure to understand that Microsoft provides a utility for users to verify whether their drivers are signed on their machine called `Sigverif.exe`. `Sigverif.exe` is an application that is included with Windows 7: it will scan your machine and verify that all drivers are properly signed. If they are not signed, `Sigverif.exe` will show you which drivers are not signed.

Be able to associate file extensions. Understand how to associate a file to a particular application. For example, you may want all files with the `.asx` filename extension to be played through Windows Media Player. Know that you can set these file extension associations in Default Programs in Control Panel.

Know how to configure devices and drivers. Understand how to configure devices and drivers in Device Manager. Know how to roll back drivers and how to update drivers when newer versions are released. Know Device Staging and how to add devices in Device Manager.

Know how older applications can work in Windows 7. Understand how to allow older applications to work with Windows 7. You can run applications in XP Mode or compatibility mode or use shims that are created by Microsoft.

Be able to configure privacy settings in IE8. Know how to enable and disable cookies. Know when it is useful to use cookies and when cookies should be blocked. Cookies are files that are placed on your system. Not having files placed on your system increases security. Know how to set an InPrivate session to verify that nothing is saved during an internet session.

Know how to configure and manage IE8. Know how to enable and disable add-ons and how to boot IE8 without add-ons. Know how to grant a site the ability to display pop-ups and how to enable and disable Pop-up Blocker. Know how to enable and disable Phishing Filter and how to configure the web Content Filter. Be able to edit the Allow and Block lists.

Review Questions

1. You are the network administrator for your organization. You have been asked by the owner of the company to verify that all drivers installed on the Windows 7 machines are signed drivers. How do you accomplish this task?

   A. Run `Verify.exe` at the command prompt.

   B. Run a scan in Device manager.

   C. Run `Sigverif.exe` at the command prompt.

   D. Run `Drivers.exe` at the command prompt.

2. You are the network administrator for your organization. You are asked by your manager to modify a few file extensions that are associated with Internet Explorer. How can you accomplish this task?

   A. In Control Panel, open Default Programs and then click Set Associations. Set the proper file extensions.

   B. In Internet Explorer, set extensions on the extension tab.

   C. In Control Panel, open System and then click Set Associations. Set the proper file extensions.

   D. In Internet Explorer, set extensions on the advanced tab.

3. You are the network administrator for a large organization. You are in charge of implementing company policies. One company policy states that you have to prevent Internet Explorer from saving any data during a user's browsing session. How do you accomplish this?

   A. Set the Internet Security settings to disabled.

   B. Run the browsers in the InPrivate session.

   C. InPrivate sessions should be disabled.

   D. Private sessions should be enabled.

4. You are the network administrator for a large organization. A user calls you and says that when they try to connect to the internal website, they are prompted for authentication. The user has the rights to access the internal site due to the fact that all users and computers are part of a domain and the internal website uses Integrated Windows Authentication. How do you make sure that the user is automatically authenticated when they connect?

   A. Change the user's local permissions to administrator.

   B. The Local site's URL should be added to the Local internet zone.

   C. The Local site's security credentials should be added to the trusted sites zone.

   D. The internet security level should be lowered to lowest.

5. You are the network administrator for your organization. Your organization has been using Windows XP, and you are now switching all users to Windows 7 Professional. Some of the XP applications do not run properly in Windows 7. How can you allow these applications to run on Windows 7?

   A. Run the applications in XP mode.

   B. Get newer versions of the applications.

   C. Disable the Windows 7 Compatibility Mode.

   D. Write your own shim to solve the issues.

6. You are using Windows 7 Home edition and you have an XP application that worked well with XP but is having issues running on Windows 7. What steps can you take to help solve this issue?

   A. Change the Applications security settings.

   B. Change the Applications Compatibility Mode to Windows XP.

   C. Enable the Windows 7 operating system to XP Compatible.

   D. Upgrade the application.

7. Which versions of Windows 7 has XP mode automatically built into the operating system? Choose all that apply.

   A. Install and use Windows Virtual PC

   B. Enterprise Edition

   C. Ultimate Edition

   D. Professional Edition

8. You are the network administrator for a large organization. One of your users calls you and states that they think they are having issues with their network card. What tool can you use to see if the hardware is working properly?

   A. Device Hardware Utility

   B. Manage Hardware Utility

   C. Device Manager

   D. Device Configuration

9. You are the network administrator for a large organization. You have a Windows 7 machine that is working fine but you downloaded a newer version of the network adapter driver. You install the new network adapter driver on the Windows 7 machine. After you load the driver, the network device stops working properly. Which tool should you use to help you fix the problem?

   A. Driver Rollback

   B. Driver Repair Utility

   C. Reverse Driver Application

   D. Windows 7 Driver Compatibility tool

10. You have installed Windows 7 with Internet Explorer 8 and now some of the websites that you used to visit no longer display their content correctly. How can you solve this issue?

    A. Download the IE8 Compatibility utility.

    B. Enable the IE8 Compatibility view.

    C. Run the Application Compatibility Mode.

    D. Install the IE7 viewer.

11. You are a help desk technician for your company. You are configuring Internet Explorer, and you want to ensure that cookies that are stored on the computer are not accessible to any websites. Which privacy setting should you configure to accomplish your goal?

    A. Block All Cookies

    B. High

    C. Medium High

    D. Medium

12. You are the network administrator for a large organization that is thinking of switching from Windows XP to Windows 7. Your manager is worried about applications not being compatible with Windows 7. What options do you have to make sure applications work with Windows 7? (Choose all that apply.)

    A. XP Mode

    B. Shims

    C. Application Compatibility Mode

    D. Windows 7 Compatibility Utility

13. You have recently installed Windows 7 on your computer. You are configuring Internet Explorer, and you want to ensure that cookies are not saved from any website that does not have a compact privacy policy. Which privacy setting should you configure to accomplish your goal?

    A. Block All Cookies

    B. High

    C. Medium High

    D. Medium

14. Your network administrator has provided you with a new laptop with Windows 7 installed on it. You are using Internet Explorer. When typing search phrases into the Instant Search box, you discover that search results are being displayed only for `Amazon.com`. You want search phrases to search the Web, not `Amazon.com`. What should you do?

    A. Disable all add-ons.

    B. Configure Internet Explorer as your default browser.

    C. Add additional web-based search providers in the Manage IE add-ons section.

    D. Configure a web-based search provider as your default home page.

15. You have downloaded and installed several Internet Explorer add-ons. You want to view the add-ons that have been used during your current browsing session. Which option of the Manage Add-Ons dialog box should you select to view this information?
    - A. Add-Ons That Have Been Used By Internet Explorer
    - B. Currently Loaded Add-Ons button in Internet Explorer
    - C. Add-Ons That Run Without Requiring Permission
    - D. Downloaded ActiveX Controls (32-bit)

16. You are the network manager for a large organization. Your company is switching from Windows XP to Windows 7 and needs to have XP Mode automatically built into the operating system. Which Windows 7 editions can you use? (Choose all that apply.)
    - A. Basic Edition
    - B. Enterprise Edition
    - C. Home Edition
    - D. Ultimate Edition

17. You have a manager who wants to be able to watch their stock quotes continually throughout the day. How can you set this up?
    - A. Set up Stock Web Slice.
    - B. Have them keep IE on the stock page.
    - C. Use Microsoft Instant Messenger to watch the stocks.
    - D. Download a stock ticker.

18. You want to set up IE8 so that you prevent your 8-year-old daughter from viewing any website with nudity. How do you accomplish this?
    - A. Enable the IE8 Nudity filter in the Security tab.
    - B. Use Content Advisor and block all sites with nudity.
    - C. Enable the IE8 Nudity filter in the Privacy tab.
    - D. Enable the IE8 Nudity filter in the Advanced tab.

19. You are running a Windows 7 machine. You want to load a copy of Windows Vista on the machine for testing and training. How can you accomplish this?
    - A. Format the machine, load Windows Vista, and then load Windows 7.
    - B. Download Windows Virtual PC and create a Windows Vista virtual hard disk.
    - C. Download Hyper-V and create a Windows Vista virtual hard disk.
    - D. Download Virtual Server and create a Windows Vista virtual hard disk.

20. You recently visited a website that automatically downloaded and installed spyware onto your computer. You want to prevent spyware from being installed in the future. You have enabled Pop-up Blocker. What else can you do to minimize your risk of downloading spyware?
    - A. Enable Phishing Filter.
    - B. Disable all add-ons.
    - C. Delete your browsing history.
    - D. Enable Protected Mode.

Answers to Review Questions

1. C. Running the `Sigverif.exe` program will run a check against all the drivers installed on your machine and then notify you of any drivers that are unsigned.

2. A. The Default Programs icon in Control Panel allows you to set file extension associations to the various programs in Windows 7.

3. B. The InPrivate session prevents the browsing history from being recorded and does not allow temporary internet files to be retained. Cookies, usernames, passwords, and form data will not remain in IE8 following the closing of the InPrivate session, nor will there be any footprints or data pertaining to the InPrivate browsing session.

4. B. Because all users and computers are part of the domain and the internal website uses Integrated Windows Authentication, once you add the URL to the Local internet zone properties, the Windows Authentication will take over.

5. A. Windows XP mode is available on Windows 7 Professional, Ultimate, and Enterprise editions and allows you to run XP applications on Windows 7 properly.

6. B. If a Windows XP application worked before but it is not working correctly in Windows 7, you can set that application to run in Compatibility Mode for a previous operating system.

7. B, C, D. Windows Virtual PC allows you to install previous versions of 32-bit operating system like XP so that you can continue to run applications.

8. C. Device Manager is the utility included with Windows 7 that allows you to configure and manage your devices and hardware. You can also configure your drivers within Device Manager.

9. A. Driver Rollback allows you to replace a newly installed driver with the previous driver. You can do the driver rollback using the Device Manager utility.

10. B. Windows Internet Explorer 8 is a new release of Microsoft's web browser included in Windows 7, and some websites may not be updated to use the new features of IE8 or display their content correctly. Problems may exist, such as misaligned images or text. When you use Compatibility View, IE8 will display a web page the way it would have been displayed in Internet Explorer 7 (which should correct any display issues).

11. A. To block any website from accessing cookies stored on the local computer, you should set the privacy setting to Block All Cookies. The Block All Cookies setting prevents cookies from being saved on the computer and prevents any existing cookies from being read by websites.

12. A, B, C. Windows 7 has some built-in options to make sure your Windows XP applications work with Windows 7. They include XP Mode, shims (created by Microsoft), and Application Compatibility Mode. You can also download and run Windows Virtual PC with a Windows XP virtual hard disk.

13. B. To block cookies from any websites that do not have a compact privacy policy, you should set the privacy setting to High. The High setting prevents any cookies from being saved for websites that do not contain a compact privacy policy, and prevents any cookies from being saved that have the potential of saving information that can be used to contact you without your explicit consent.

14. C. You should configure additional web-based search providers in the IE8 add-ons section. To configure this, click on Tools, Internet Options, and then hit the Settings button in the Search section of the General tab.

15. B. A list of add-ons that have been used by Internet Explorer during the current browsing session can be viewed by selecting the Currently Loaded Add-Ons button in the Internet Explorer option of the Manage Add-Ons dialog box. You can use the Manage Add-Ons dialog box to view, enable, and disable add-ons that have been installed on your computer.

16. B, D. Windows XP Mode is available for Windows 7 Enterprise, Ultimate, and Professional. If you need to run XP in any other version of Windows 7, you must download and use Microsoft Windows Virtual PC.

17. A. Web Slices in Windows Internet Explorer 8 allows IE8 to check for updates of web page content you may frequently want to have. This is an excellent way to check your local weather or stock quotes or even watch an auction item in EBay.

    With Web Slices, you can add the piece of the web page with the content you're looking for to the new favorites bar and IE8 will check it for you and give you a visual clue when the content changes. You can control how often IE8 checks for changes as well as have IE8 play a sound when Web Slice content is found on a page and even when an update to content is discovered.

18. B. The Content Advisor allows you to rate sites for their content. Some of that content may contain use of tobacco, alcohol, nudity, drugs, gambling, etc.

19. B. Windows Virtual PC gives you the ability to set up virtualization on a client operating system. This is beneficial for anyone in the industry who has to do testing or configuration.

20. D. You should enable Protected Mode. Protected Mode isolates Internet Explorer and prevents information from being written outside of the Temporary Internet Files unless you allow it. By enabling Protected Mode, you will be notified before any application is able to write to other areas of the operating system. To enable Protected Mode, open Internet Explorer, click Tools, click Internet Options, click the Security tab, and select the Enable Protected Mode option.

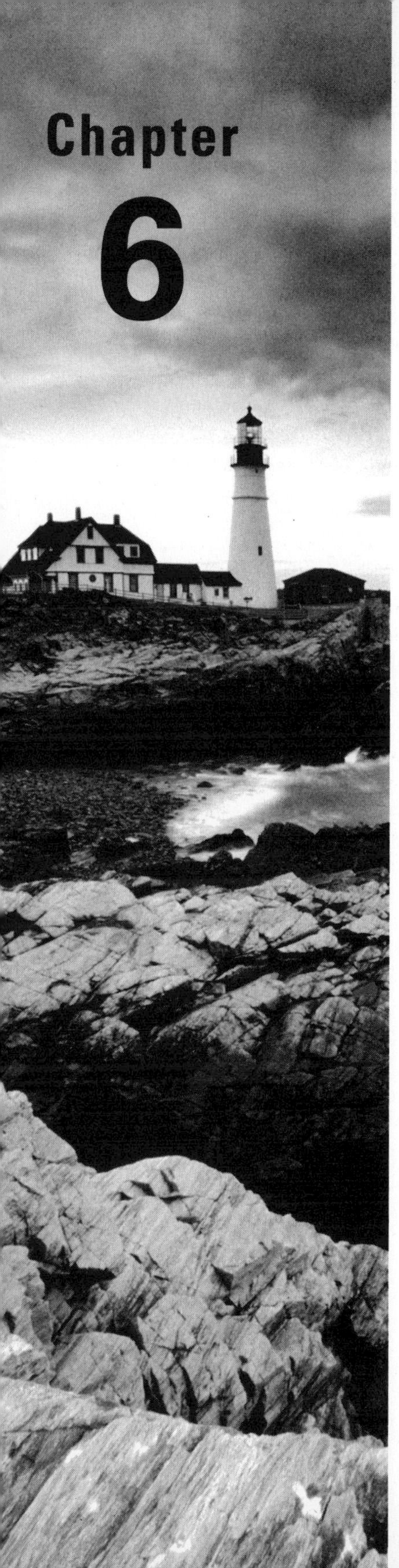

Managing Users, Groups, and Security

MICROSOFT EXAM OBJECTIVES COVERED IN THIS CHAPTER:

✓ **Configure shared resources.**

- This objective may include but is not limited to: folder virtualization; shared folder permissions

✓ **Configure file and folder access.**

- This objective may include but is not limited to: encrypting files and folders by using EFS; configuring NTFS permissions; resolving effective permissions issues; copying files vs. moving files

✓ **Configure user account control (UAC).**

- This objective may include but is not limited to: configuring local security policy; configuring admin vs. standard UAC prompt behaviors; configuring Secure Desktop

✓ **Configure authentication and authorization.**

- This objective may include but is not limited to: resolving authentication issues; configuring rights; managing credentials; managing certificates; smart cards with PIV; elevating user privileges; multifactor authentication

✓ **Configure BitLocker and BitLocker To Go.**

- This objective may include but is not limited to: configuring BitLocker and BitLocker To Go policies; managing Trusted Platform Module (TPM) PINs; configuring startup key storage; data recovery agent support

✓ **Configure application restrictions.**

- This objective may include but is not limited to: setting software restriction policies; setting application control policies; setting through group policy or local security policy

This may be one of the most important chapters in this study guide. Setting up users, groups, and security includes some of the most critical tasks that any IT manager is going to perform.

One of the most fundamental tasks in network management is creating user and group accounts. Without a user account, a user cannot log on to a computer, server, or network.

When users log on, they supply a username and password. Then their user accounts are validated by a security mechanism. In Windows 7, users can log on to a computer locally, or they can log on through Active Directory.

Group accounts are used to ease network administration by grouping users who have similar permission requirements. Groups are an important part of network management. Many administrators are able to accomplish the majority of their management tasks through the use of groups; they rarely assign permissions to individual users. Windows 7 includes built-in local groups, such as Administrators and Backup Operators.

You create and manage local groups through the Local Users And Groups utility. With this utility, you can add groups, change group membership, rename groups, and delete groups.

Windows 7 also offers a wide variety of security options. If the Windows 7 computer is a part of a domain, you can apply security through a group policy object using the Group Policy Management Console. If the Windows 7 computer is not a part of a domain, then you use Local Group Policy Objects to manage local security.

You will learn about the environments in which Windows 7 can be installed and the utilities that are used to manage security. You can use policies to help manage user accounts. Account policies control the logon environment for the computer, such as password and logon restrictions. Local policies specify what users can do once they log on and include auditing, user rights, and security options. You can also manage critical security features through the Windows Security Center.

We will end the chapter with a discussion of NTFS security and shared permissions and how they work independently and together.

Overview of Windows 7 User Accounts

When you install Windows 7, several user accounts are created automatically. You can then create new user accounts. As you already know, user accounts allow a user to access resources.

On Windows 7 computers, you can create local user accounts. If your network has a Windows Server 2008, Windows Server 2003, or Windows Server 2000 domain controller, your network can have domain user accounts as well.

One of the features included with Windows 7 is User Account Control (UAC). User Account Control provides an additional level of security by limiting the level of access that users have when performing normal, everyday tasks. When needed, users can gain elevated access for specific administrative tasks.

In the following sections, you will learn about the default user accounts that are created by Windows 7 and the difference between local and domain user accounts.

Account Types

Windows 7 supports two basic types of user accounts: Administrator and Standard user (see Figure 6.1). Each one of these account is used for specific reasons.

FIGURE 6.1 User Types screen

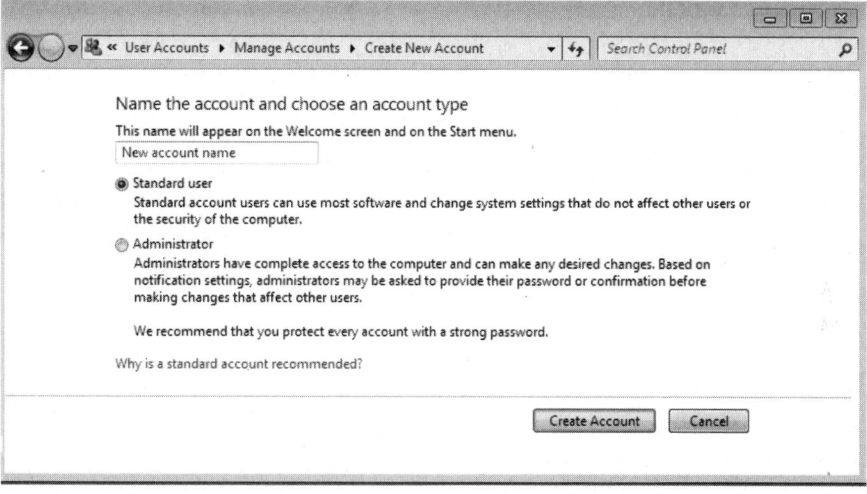

Administrator The administrator account type provides unrestricted access for performing administrative tasks. As a result, administrator accounts should be used only for performing administrative tasks and should not be used for normal computing tasks.

Only administrator accounts can change the Registry. This is important to know because when most software is installed onto a Windows 7 machine, the Registry gets changed. This is why you need administrator rights to install most software.

Standard User The standard user account type should be assigned to every user of the computer. Standard user accounts can perform most day-to-day tasks, such as running

Microsoft Word, accessing email, using Internet Explorer, and so on. Running as a standard user increases security by limiting the possibility of a virus or other malicious code from infecting the computer. Standard user accounts are unable to make systemwide changes, which also helps to increase security.

When you install Windows 7, by default, there are premade accounts called built-in accounts. Let's take a look at them.

Built-in Accounts

Built-in accounts are accounts that are created at the time you install the Windows 7 operating system. Windows 7, when installed into a workgroup environment, has four user accounts (see Figure 6.2).

FIGURE 6.2 Four default accounts

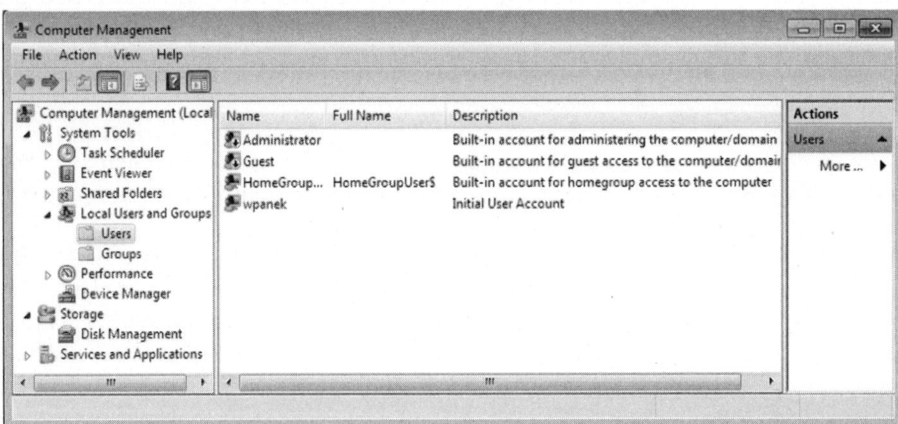

Administrator The Administrator account is a special account that has full control over the computer. The Administrator account can perform all tasks, such as creating users and groups, managing the file system, and setting up printing. Note that the Administrator account is disabled by default.

Guest The Guest account allows users to access the computer even if they do not have a unique username and password. Because of the inherent security risks associated with this type of user, the Guest account is disabled by default. When this account is enabled, it is usually given very limited privileges.

Initial user The initial user account uses the name of the registered user. By default, the initial user is a member of the Administrators group.

HomeGroup user The HomeGroup user is created by default to allow this machine to connect to other machines within the same HomeGroup network. This account is created by default as soon as you set up a HomeGroup.

By default, the name Administrator is given to a user account that is a member of the Administrators group. However, in Windows 7, this user account is disabled by default. You can increase the computer's security by leaving this account disabled and assigning other members to the Administrators group. This way, a malicious user will be unable to log on to the computer using the Administrator user account.

These users are considered local users and their permissions are contained to the Windows 7 machine. A local user's account is an account that must reside on the Windows 7 machine. This account would not let the user access any resources on a networked environment. If you need the user's account to access resources on machines other than their own, you can have users log into the Windows 7 computer as remote users and this would be considered a domain user's account. Let's take a look at the difference between these account types.

Local and Domain User Accounts

Windows 7 supports two kinds of users: local users and domain users. A computer that is running Windows 7 has the ability to store its own user accounts database. The users stored at the local computer are known as local user accounts.

Active Directory is a directory service that is available with the Windows Server 2008, Windows Server 2003, and Windows 2000 Server platforms. It stores information in a central database, called Active Directory, which allows users to have a single user account for the network. The users stored in Active Directory's central database are called domain user accounts.

If you use local user accounts, they must be configured on each computer that the user needs to access within the network. For this reason, domain user accounts are commonly used to manage users on any network larger than 10 users.

On Windows 7, Windows Server 2008, Windows Server 2003, Windows Vista, Windows XP, and Windows 7 computers, you can create local users through the Local Users And Groups utility, as described in the section "Working with User Accounts" later in this chapter. On Windows Server 2008, Windows Server 2003, and Windows 2000 Server domain controllers, you manage users with the Microsoft Active Directory Users and Computers utility.

Active Directory is covered in detail in the *MCTS: Windows Server 2008 Active Directory Configuration Study Guide*, by William Panek and James Chellis (Sybex, 2008).

Now that we have looked at the different types of users and accounts, it's important to understand how to use accounts to log on and log off the local machine or domain.

Logging On and Logging Off

Users must log on to a Windows 7 computer before they can use it. When you create user accounts, you set up the computer to accept the logon information provided by the user. You can log on locally to a Windows 7 computer using a local computer account, or you can log on to a domain using an Active Directory account.

When you install the computer, you specify that it will be a part of a workgroup, which implies a local logon, or that it will be a part of a domain, which implies a domain logon.

When users are ready to stop working on a Windows 7 computer, they should log off. Users can log off through the Windows Security dialog box.

In the following sections, you will learn about local user authentication and how a user logs out of a Windows 7 computer.

Using Local User Logon Authentication

Depending on whether you are logging on to a computer locally or are logging into a domain, Windows 7 uses two different logon procedures. When you log on to a Windows 7 computer locally, you must present a valid username and password (ones that exist within the local accounts database). As part of a successful authentication, the following steps take place:

1. At system startup, the user is prompted to click their username from a list of users who have been created locally. This is significantly different from the Ctrl+Alt+Del logon sequence that was used by earlier versions of Windows. The Ctrl+Alt+Del sequence is still used when you log on to a domain environment. You can also configure the Ctrl+Alt+Del logon sequence as an option in a local environment.
2. The local computer compares the user's logon credentials with the information in the local security database.
3. If the information presented matches the account database, an access token is created. Access tokens are used to identify the user and the groups of which that user is a member.

Access tokens are created only when you log on. If you change group memberships, you need to log off and log on again to update the access token.

The following actions also take place as part of the logon process:

- The system reads the part of the Registry that contains user configuration information.
- The user's profile is loaded. (User profiles are discussed in the section "Setting Up User Profiles, Logon Scripts, and Home Folders" later in this chapter.)

- Any policies that have been assigned to the user through a user or group policy are enforced. (Policies for users are discussed later in this chapter in the section "Managing Security.")
- Any logon scripts that have been assigned are executed. (I'll discuss assigning logon scripts to users in the section "Setting Up User Profiles, Logon Scripts, and Home Folders.")
- Persistent network and printer connections are restored.

Now that you have seen how a local logon process works, let's take a look at logging off a Windows 7 machine.

Logging Off Windows 7

To log off Windows 7, you click Start, point to the arrow next to the Shutdown button, and then click Logoff. Pressing Ctrl+Alt+Del will present you with a screen that will allow you to select whether to lock the computer, switch users, log off, change the password, or start Task Manager.

Real World Scenario

Logging Off Computers

As a network administrator, I used to make it a practice to teach my users to log off their computers every night. What happens in many companies is that users come in on Monday, turn on their computers, and then leave them on and logged in until Friday night.

Having users logged on to a local machine or to a network all week long is a very dangerous practice. This makes it very easy for any other user in the company to sit down at their machine and cause trouble. Have your users get into a practice of logging off at night and locking their keyboard when stepping away for break or lunch.

Now that we understand the different types of accounts on a Windows 7 computer, let's take a look at how to manage these accounts.

Working with User Accounts

To set up and manage your local user accounts, you use the Local Users And Groups utility or the User Accounts option in Control Panel. With either option, you can create, disable, delete, and rename user accounts as well as change user passwords.

Using the Local Users And Groups Utility

There are two common methods for accessing the Local Users And Groups utility:

- You can load Local Users And Groups as a Microsoft Management Console (MMC) snap-in. (See Chapter 3, "Managing Disks," for details on the MMC and the purpose of snap-ins.)
- You can access the Local Users And Groups utility through the Computer Management utility.

In Exercise 6.1, you will add the Local Users And Groups snap-in MMC to the Desktop. This exercise needs to be completed in order to complete other exercises in this chapter.

EXERCISE 6.1

Adding the Local Users And Groups Snap-In

1. Select Start and in the Search box, type **MMC** and press Enter.
2. If a warning box appears, click Yes.
3. Select File ➢ Add/Remove Snap-In.
4. Scroll down the list and highlight Local Users And Groups, and then click the Add button.

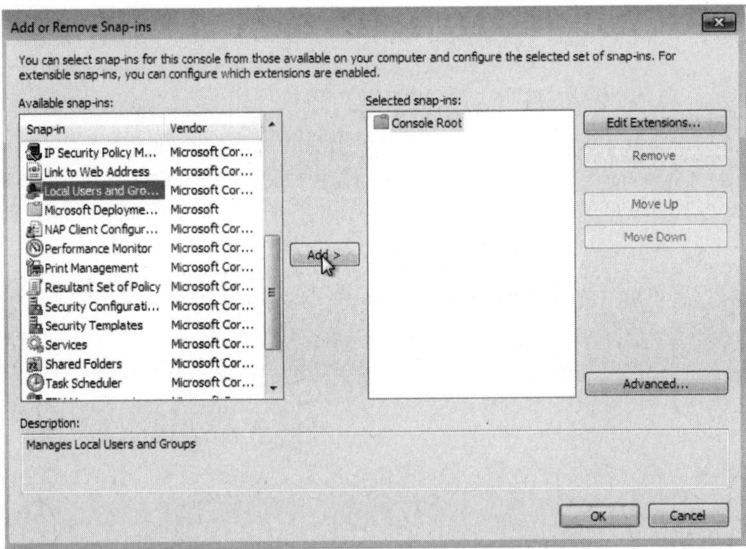

5. In the Choose Target Machine dialog box, click the Finish button to accept the default selection of Local Computer.

6. Click OK in the Add Or Remove Snap-in dialog box.
7. In the MMC window, right-click the Local Users And Groups folder and choose New Window From Here. You will see that Local Users And Groups is now the main window.
8. Click File ➢ Save As. Name the console Local Users And Groups and choose Desktop under the Save In pulldown box. Click the Save button.

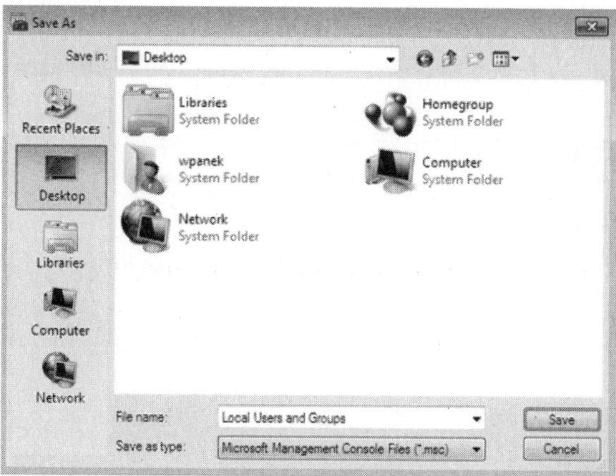

9. Close the MMC snap-in.

You should now see the Local Users And Groups snap-in on the Desktop. You can also open the Local Users And Groups MMC from the Computer Management utility, which you'll do in Exercise 6.2. Complete the following exercise for opening the Local Users And Groups utility from the Computer Management utility.

EXERCISE 6.2

Using the Local Users And Groups Snap-In

1. Select Start, and then right-click Computer and select Manage.
2. In the Computer Management window, expand the System Tools folder and then the Local Users And Groups folder.

If your computer doesn't have the MMC configured, the quickest way to access the Local Users And Groups utility is through the Computer Management utility.

Now let's look at another way to configure users and groups. You can also use the User Accounts option in Control Panel to configure users.

Using the User Accounts Option in Control Panel

The *User Accounts Control (UAC)* Control Panel option provides the ability to manage user accounts in addition to configuring parental controls. To access the User Accounts Control Panel option, click Start ➢ Control Panel ➢ User Accounts. Table 6.1 shows the configurable options in the User Accounts option in Control Panel.

TABLE 6.1 Configurable user account options in Control Panel

Option	Explanation
Change Your Password	This link allows you to change a user's password.
Remove Your Password	This link allows you to remove a password from a user's account.
Change Your Picture	This link allows you to change the account picture.
Change Your Account Name	This link allows you to rename the account.
Change Your Account Type	This link allows you to change your account type between the standard user and administrator account type.
Manage Another Account	This link allows you to configure other accounts on the Windows 7 machine.
Change User Account Control Settings	This link allows you to set the level of notification of when changes are made to your computer. These notifications can prevent potentially hazardous programs from being loaded onto the operating system.
Manage Your Credentials	With this link, you can set up credentials that allow you to easily connect to websites that require usernames and passwords or computers that require certificates.
Create A Password Reset Disk	This link allows you to create a disk that users can use when they forget their password.
Link Online IDs	This link allows you to link an online ID with your Windows account. This makes it easier to share files with other computers.
Manage Your File Encryption Certificates	This link allows you to manage your file encryption certificates.
Configure Advanced User Profile Properties	This link brings you directly to the User's Profile dialog box in Control Panel ➢ System ➢ Advanced ➢ System Settings.
Change My Environment Variables	This link allows you to access the Environment Variables dialog box directly.

Once Windows 7 is installed, you must create user accounts for users who will be accessing the machine. Let's now take a look at how to create new user accounts.

Creating New Users

To create users on a Windows 7 computer, you must be logged on as a user with permission to create a new user, or you must be a member of the Administrators group. In the following sections, you will learn about username rules and conventions, usernames, and security identifiers in more detail.

Username Rules and Conventions

The only real requirement for creating a new user is that you must provide a valid username. To be valid, the name must follow the Windows 7 rules for usernames. However, it's also a good idea to have your own rules for usernames, which form your naming convention.

The following are the Windows 7 rules for usernames:

- A username must be from 1 to 20 characters.
- The username must be unique among all the other user and group names stored on the computer.
- The username cannot contain any of the following characters:

  * / \ [ ] : ; | = , + ? < > “ @

- A username cannot consist exclusively of periods or spaces.

Keeping these rules in mind, you should choose a naming convention (a consistent naming format). For example, consider a user named William Panek. One naming convention might be to use the last name and first initial, for the username WillP or WilliamP. Another naming convention might use the first initial and last name, for the username WPanek. This is the naming convention followed by many mid-size to larger organizations.

You could base usernames on the naming convention defined for email names so that the logon name and the name in the email address match. You should also provide a mechanism that would accommodate duplicate names. For example, if you had a user named Jane Smith and a user named John Smith, you might use a middle initial for usernames, such as JDSmith and JRSmith.

It is also a good practice to come up with a naming convention for groups, printers, and computers.

Real World Scenario

Naming Conventions

As an IT manager, I don't recommend using first name, first initial of last name (WilliamP) as a naming convention. In a mid-size to large company, there is the possibility of having two *WilliamPs*, but the odds that you will have two *WPaneks* are rare.

If you choose to use the first name, first initial of last name option, it can be a lot of work to go back and change this format later if the company grows larger. Choose a naming convention that can grow with the company.

Now let's take a look at how usernames get a special ID number associated with the account and how that number affects your accounts.

Usernames and Security Identifiers

When you create a new user, a *security identifier (SID)* is automatically created on the computer for the user account. The username is a property of the SID. For example, a user SID might look like this:

```
S-1-5-21-823518204-746137067-120266-629-500
```

It's apparent that using SIDs for user identification would make administration a nightmare. Fortunately, for your administrative tasks, you see and use the username instead of the SID.

SIDs have several advantages. Because Windows 7 uses the SID as the user object, you can easily rename a user while still retaining all the user's properties. The reason for this is that all security settings get associated with the SID and not the user account.

SIDs also ensure that if you delete and re-create a user account with the same username, the new user account will not have any of the properties of the old account because it is based on a new, unique SID. Every time you create a new user, a unique SID gets associated. Even if the username is the same as a previously deleted account, the system still sees the username as a new user.

Because every user account gets a unique SID number, it is a good practice to disable instead of delete accounts for users that leave the company or have an extended absence. If you ever need to access the disabled account again, you have the ability.

When you create a new user, there are many options that you have to configure. Table 6.2 describes all the options available in the New User dialog box.

Table 6.2 User account options available in the New User dialog box

Option	Description
User Name	Defines the username for the new account. Choose a name that is consistent with your naming convention (e.g., WPanek). This is the only required field. Usernames are not case sensitive.
Full Name	Allows you to provide more detailed name information. This is typically the user's first and last names (e.g., Will Panek). By default, this field contains the same name as the User Name field.
Description	Typically used to specify a title and/or location (e.g., Sales-Nashville) for the account, but it can be used to provide any additional information about the user.
Password	Assigns the initial password for the user. For security purposes, avoid using readily available information about the user. Passwords are case sensitive.
Confirm Password	Confirms that you typed the password the same way two times to verify that you entered the password correctly.

Option	Description
User Must Change Password At Next Logon	If enabled, forces the user to change the password the first time they log on. This is done to increase security. By default, this option is selected.
User Cannot Change Password	If enabled, prevents a user from changing their password. It is useful for accounts such as Guest and accounts that are shared by more than one user. By default, this option is not selected.
Password Never Expires	If enabled, specifies that the password will never expire, even if a password policy has been specified. For example, you might enable this option if this is a service account and you do not want the administrative overhead of managing password changes. By default, this option is not selected.
Account Is Disabled	If enabled, specifies that this account cannot be used for logon purposes. For example, you might select this option for template accounts or if an account is not currently being used. It helps keep inactive accounts from posing security threats. By default, this option is not selected.

Complete Exercise 6.3 to create a new local user account. Before you complete the following steps, make sure you are logged on as a user with permissions to create new users and have already added the Local Users And Groups snap-in to the MMC.

EXERCISE 6.3

Creating New Users

1. Open the Admin Console MMC Desktop shortcut that was created in a previous exercise and expand the Local Users And Groups snap-in. If a dialog box appears, click Yes.
2. Highlight the Users folder and select Action ➤ New User. The New User dialog box appears.

EXERCISE 6.3 *(continued)*

3. In the User Name text box, type **CPanek**.
4. In the Full Name text box, type **Crystal Panek**.
5. In the Description text box, type **Operations Manager**.
6. Leave the Password and Confirm Password text boxes empty and accept the defaults for the check boxes. Make sure you uncheck the User Must Change Password At Next Logon option. Click the Create button to add the user.
7. Use the New User dialog box to create six more users, filling out the fields as follows:

   Name: **WPanek**; Full Name: **Will Panek**; Description: **IT Admin**; Password: (blank)

   Name: **JDoe**; Full Name: **John Doe**; Description: **Cisco Admin**; Password: (blank)

   Name: **GWashington**; Full Name: **George Washington**; Description: **President**; Password: **P@ssw0rD**

   Name: **JAdams**; Full Name: **John Adams**; Description: **Vice President**; Password: **v!$t@**

   Name: **BFranklin**; Full Name: **Ben Franklin**; Description: **NH Sales Manager**; Password: **P3@ch** (with an uppercase *P*)

   Name: **ALincoln**; Full Name: **Abe Lincoln**; Description: **Tech Support**; Password: **Bearded1** (uppercase *B*)
8. After you've finished creating all of the users, click the Close button to exit the New User dialog box.

You can also create users through the command-line utility NET USER. For more information about this command, type **NET USER /?** at a command prompt.

As I stated earlier, it's good practice to disable accounts for users who leave the company. Let's take a look at the process of disabling accounts.

Disabling User Accounts

When a user account is no longer needed, the account should be disabled or deleted. After you've disabled an account, you can later enable it again to restore it with all of its associated user properties. An account that is deleted, however, can never be recovered.

You might disable an account because a user will not be using it for a period of time, perhaps because that employee is going on vacation or taking a leave of absence. Another reason to disable an account is that you're planning to put another user in that same function.

For example, suppose that Gary, the engineering manager, quits. If you disable his account, when your company hires a new engineering manager, you can simply rename Gary's user account (to the username for the new manager) and enable it. This ensures that the user who takes over Gary's position will have all the same user properties and own all the same resources.

Disabling accounts also provides a security mechanism for special situations. For example, if your company were laying off a group of people, as a security measure, you could disable their accounts at the same time the layoff notices were given out. This prevents those users from inflicting any damage to the company's files after they receive their layoff notice.

In Exercise 6.4, you will disable a user account. Before you complete the follow steps, you should have already created new users in exercise 6.3.

EXERCISE 6.4

Disable Accounts

1. Open the Admin Console MMC Desktop shortcut and expand the Local Users And Groups snap-in.
2. Open the Users folder. Double-click user WPanek to open his Properties dialog box.
3. In the General tab, check the Account Is Disabled box. Click OK.
4. Close the Local Users And Groups MMC.
5. Log off and attempt to log on as WPanek. This should fail because the account is now disabled.
6. Log back on using your user account.

You can also access a user's properties by highlighting the user, right-clicking, and selecting Properties.

Now when users have left a company for a long period of time and you know you no longer need the user account, you can delete it. Let's take a look at how to delete user accounts.

Deleting User Accounts

As noted in the preceding section, you should disable a user account if you are not sure whether the account will ever be needed again. But if the account has been disabled and you know that the user account will never need access to it again, you should delete the account.

To delete a user, open the Local Users And Groups utility, highlight the user account you wish to delete, and click Action to bring up the menu shown in Figure 6.3. Then select Delete. You can also delete an account by clicking on the account and pressing the Delete key on the keyboard.

FIGURE 6.3 Deleting a user account

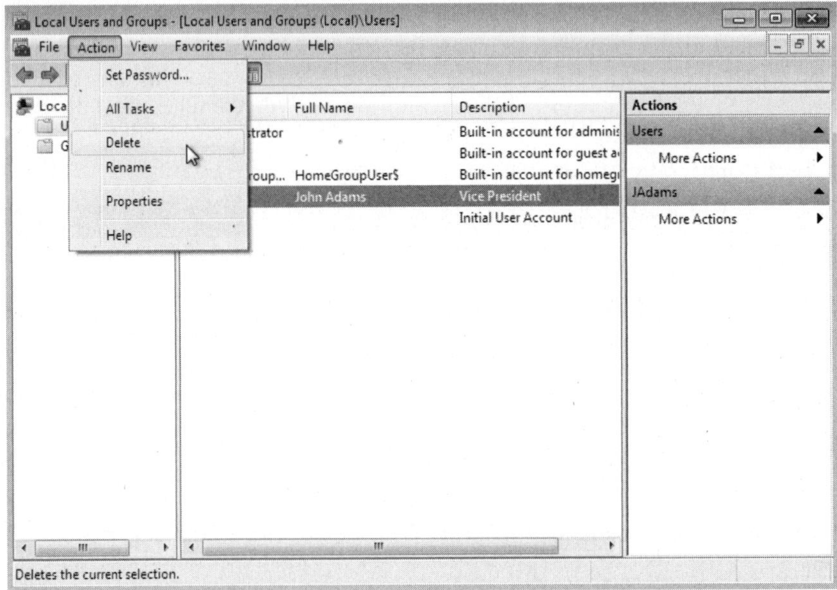

Because deleting an account is a permanent action, you will see the dialog box shown in Figure 6.4, asking you to confirm that you really wish to delete the account. After you click the Yes button here, you will not be able to re-create or re-access the account (unless you restore your local user accounts database from a backup).

FIGURE 6.4 Confirming account deletion

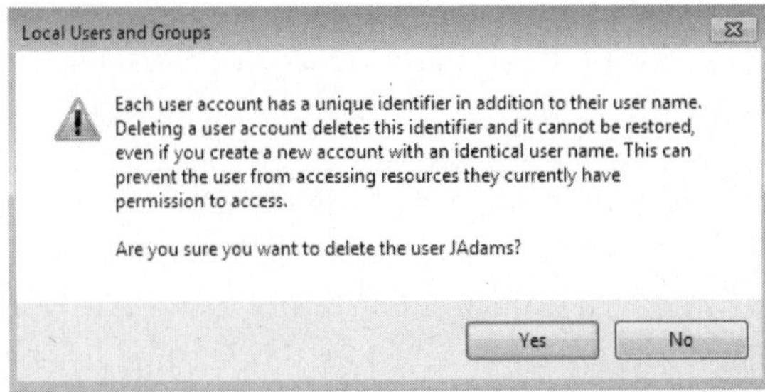

Complete Exercise 6.5 to delete a user account. These steps assume you have completed the previous exercises in this chapter.

EXERCISE 6.5

Deleting a User Account

1. Open the Admin Console MMC Desktop shortcut and expand the Local Users And Groups snap-in.
2. Expand the Users folder and single-click on user JAdams to select his user account.
3. Select Action ➢ Delete. The dialog box for confirming user deletion appears.
4. Click the Yes button to confirm that you wish to delete this user.
5. Close the Local Users And Groups MMC.

Now that you have disabled and deleted accounts, let's take a look at how to rename a user's account.

Renaming User Accounts

Once an account has been created, you can rename it at any time. Renaming a user account allows the user to retain all the associated user properties of the previous username. As noted earlier in the chapter, the name is a property of the SID.

You might want to rename a user account because the user's name has changed (for example, the user got married) or because the name was spelled incorrectly. Also, as explained in the section "Disabling User Accounts," you can rename an existing user's account for a new user, such as someone hired to take an ex-employee's position, when you want the new user to have the same properties.

Complete Exercise 6.6 to rename a user account. These steps assume you have completed all of the previous exercises in this chapter.

EXERCISE 6.6

Renaming a User Account

1. Open the Admin Console MMC Desktop shortcut and expand the Local Users And Groups snap-in.
2. Open the Users folder and highlight user ALincoln.
3. Select Action ➢ Rename.
4. Type the username **RReagan** and press Enter. Notice that the Full Name field retained the original property of Abe Lincoln in the Local Users And Groups utility.
5. Double-click RReagan to open the properties and change the user's full name to Ronald Reagan.

EXERCISE 6.6 *(continued)*

6. Click the User Must Change Password At Next Logon check box.
7. Click OK.
8. Close the Local Users And Groups MMC.

Renaming a user does not change any "hard-coded" names, such as the name of the user's home folder. If you want to change these names as well, you need to modify them manually—for example, through Windows Explorer.

Another very common task that we must deal with is resetting the user's password. Let's take a look at how to do that.

Changing a User's Password

What should you do if a user forgets their password and can't log on? You can't just open a dialog box and see the old password. However, as the administrator, you can change the user's password, and then they can use the new one.

It is very important as IT managers and IT administrators that we teach our users proper security measures that go along with password protection. As you have all probably seen before, the users that tape their password to their monitors or under the keyboards are not using correct security.

It's our job as IT professionals to teach our users proper security, and it always amazes me when I do consulting on how many IT departments don't teach their users properly.

Complete exercise 6.7 to change a user's password. This exercise assumes you have completed all the previous exercises in this chapter.

EXERCISE 6.7

Change a User's Password

1. Open the Admin Console MMC Desktop shortcut and expand the Local Users And Groups snap-in.
2. Open the Users folder and highlight user CPanek.
3. Select Action ➢ Set Password. The Set Password dialog box appears.
4. A warning appears indicating the risks involved in changing the password. Select Proceed.
5. Type the new password and then confirm the password. Click OK.
6. Close the Local Users And Groups MMC.

Now that you have seen how to create users in Windows 7, let's take a look at how to configure and manage your users' properties.

Managing User Properties

For more control over user accounts, you can configure user properties. Through the user's Properties dialog box, you can change the original password options, add the user to existing groups, and specify user profile information.

To open a user's Properties dialog box, access the Local Users And Groups utility, open the Users folder, and double-click the user account. The user's Properties dialog box has tabs for the three main categories of properties: General, Member Of, and Profile.

The General tab contains the information you supplied when you set up the new user account, including the full name and a description, the password options you selected, and whether the account is disabled. If you want to modify any of these properties after you've created the user, simply open the user's Properties dialog box and make the changes on the General tab.

You can use the Member Of tab to manage the user's membership in groups. The Profile tab lets you set properties to customize the user's environment. The following sections discuss the Member Of and Profile tabs in detail.

Managing User Group Membership

The Member Of tab of the user's Properties dialog box displays all the groups that the user belongs to, as shown in Figure 6.5. From this tab, you can add the user to an existing group or remove them from a group. To add a user to a group, click the Add button and select the group that the user should belong to. If you want to remove the user from a group, highlight the group and click the Remove button.

FIGURE 6.5 The Member Of tab of the user's Properties dialog box

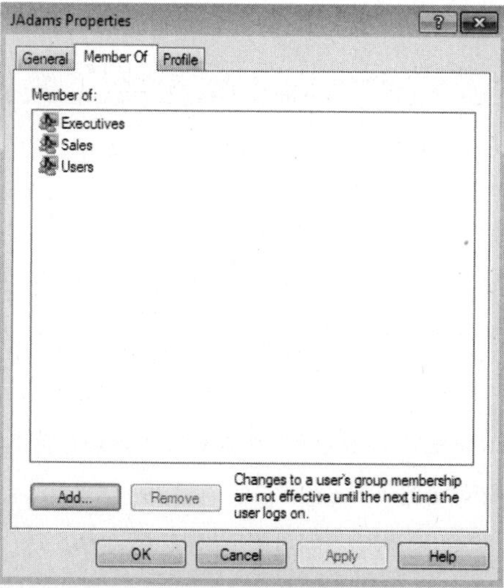

Complete Exercise 6.8 to add a user to an existing group. These steps assume you have completed all the previous exercises in this chapter.

EXERCISE 6.8

Changing a User's Properties

1. Open the Local Users And Groups MMC Desktop snap-in that you created previously.
2. Open the Users folder and double-click user WPanek. The WPanek Properties dialog box appears.
3. Select the Member Of tab and click the Add button. The Select Groups dialog box appears.
4. Under Enter The Object Names To Select, type **Backup Operators**, and click the Check Names button. After the name is confirmed, click OK.
5. Click OK to close the WPanek Properties dialog box.

The final tab in the user's properties is called the Profile tab. Now let's take a look at that Profile tab and what options can be configured within that tab.

Setting Up User Profiles, Logon Scripts, and Home Folders

The Profile tab of the user's Properties dialog box, shown in Figure 6.6, allows you to customize the user's environment. Here, you can specify the following items for the user:

- User profile path
- Logon script
- Home folder

FIGURE 6.6 The Profile tab of the user's Properties dialog box

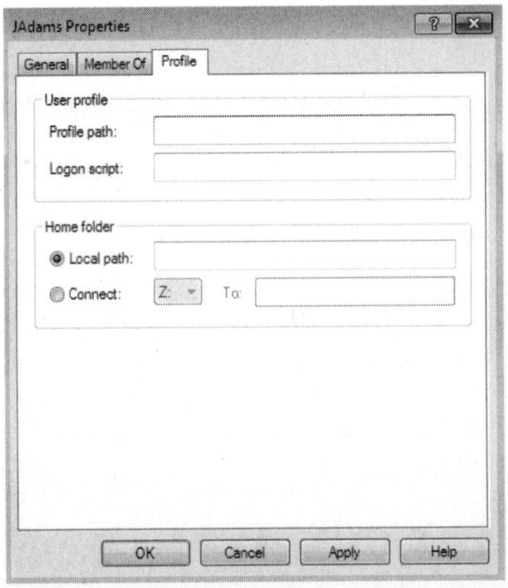

The following sections describe how these properties work and when you might want to use them.

Setting a Profile Path

User profiles contain information about the Windows 7 environment for a specific user. For example, profile settings include the Desktop arrangement, program groups, and screen colors that users see when they log on.

Each time you log on to a Windows 7 computer, the system checks to see if you have a local user profile in the Users folder, which was created on the boot partition when you installed Windows 7.

The first time users log on, they receive a default user profile. A folder that matches the user's logon name is created for the user in the Users folder. The user profile folder that is created holds a file called `NTUSER.DAT` as well as subfolders that contain directory links to the user's Desktop items.

In Exercise 6.9, you'll create two new users and set up local user profiles.

EXERCISE 6.9

Setting up User Profiles

1. Using the Local Users And Groups utility, create two new users: APanek and PPanek. Deselect the User Must Change Password At Next Logon option for each user.
2. Select Start ➢ All Programs ➢ Accessories ➢ Windows Explorer. Expand Computer, then Local Disk (C:), and then Users. Notice that the Users folder does not contain user profile folders for the new users.
3. Log off and log on as APanek.
4. Right-click an open area on the Desktop and select Personalize. In the Personalization dialog box, select a color scheme and click Apply, and then click OK.
5. Right-click an open area on the Desktop and select New ➢ Shortcut. In the Create Shortcut dialog box, type **CALC**. Accept CALC as the name for the shortcut and click Finish.
6. Log off as APanek and log on as PPanek. Notice that user PPanek sees the Desktop configuration stored in the default user profile.
7. Log off as PPanek and log on as APanek. Notice that APanek sees the Desktop configuration you set up in steps 3, 4, and 5.
8. Log off as APanek and log on as your user account. Select Start ➢ All Programs ➢ Accessories ➢ Windows Explorer. Expand Computer, then Local Disk (C:), and then Users. Notice that this folder now contains user profile folders for APanek and PPanek.

The drawback of local user profiles is that they are available only on the computer where they were created. For example, suppose all of your Windows 7 computers are a part of a domain and you use only local user profiles.

User Rick logs on at Computer A and creates a customized user profile. When he logs on to Computer B for the first time, he will receive the default user profile rather than the customized user profile he created on Computer A. For users to access their user profile from any computer they log on to, you need to use roaming profiles; however, these require the use of a network server because they can't be stored on a local Windows 7 computer.

In the next sections, you will learn about how roaming profiles and mandatory profiles can be used. To have a roaming profile or a mandatory profile, your computer must be a part of a network with server access.

Using Roaming Profiles

A roaming profile is stored on a network server and allows users to access their user profile regardless of the client computer to which they're logged on. Roaming profiles provide a consistent Desktop for users who move around, no matter which computer they access. Even if the server that stores the roaming profile is unavailable, the user can still log on using a local profile.

If you are using roaming profiles, the contents of the user's `systemdrive:\Users\UserName` folder will be copied to the local computer each time the roaming profile is accessed. If you have stored large files in any subfolders of your user profile folder, you may notice a significant delay when accessing your profile remotely as opposed to locally.

If this problem occurs, you can reduce the amount of time the roaming profile takes to load by moving the subfolder to another location, such as the user's home directory, or you can use group policy objects within Active Directory to specify that specific folders should be excluded when the roaming profile is loaded.

Using Mandatory Profiles

A *mandatory profile* is a profile that can't be modified by the user. Only members of the Administrators group can manage mandatory profiles. You might consider creating mandatory profiles for users who should maintain consistent Desktops.

For example, suppose you have a group of 20 salespeople who know enough about system configuration to make changes but not enough to fix any problems they create. For ease of support, you could use mandatory profiles. This way, all of the salespeople will always have the same profile, which they will not be able to change.

You can create mandatory profiles for a single user or a group of users. The mandatory profile is stored in a file named `NTUSER.MAN`. A user with a mandatory profile can set different Desktop preferences while logged on, but those settings will not be saved when the user logs off.

You can use only roaming profiles as mandatory profiles. Mandatory profiles do not work for local user profiles.

There is a second type of mandatory profile called super mandatory profile. Let's take a look at this other type of profile.

Using Super Mandatory Profiles

A super mandatory profile is a mandatory user profile with an additional layer of security. With mandatory profiles, a temporary profile is created if the mandatory profile is not available when a user logs on. However, when super mandatory profiles are configured, temporary profiles are not created if the mandatory profile is not available over the network, and the user is unable to log on to the computer.

The process for creating super mandatory profiles is similar to creating mandatory profiles, except that instead of renaming the user folder `Username.v2`, you name the folder `Username.man.v2`.

Real World Scenario

Copying User Profiles

Within your company you have a user, Paige, who logs in with two different user accounts. One account is a regular user account, and the other is an Administrator account used for administration tasks only.

When Paige established all her Desktop preferences and installed the computer's applications, they were installed with the Administrator account. Now when she logs in with the regular user account, she can't access the Desktop and profile settings that were created for her as an administrative user.

To solve this problem, you can copy a local user profile from one user to another (for example, from Paige's administrative account to her regular user account) by choosing Control Panel ➢ System, clicking Advanced System Settings, and clicking the User Profiles Settings button. When you copy a user profile, the following items are copied: Favorites, cookies, documents, Start Menu items, and other unique user Registry settings.

Another configurable item within the Profile tab of the user's properties is using logon scripts. Let's take a look at logon scripts.

Using Logon Scripts

Logon scripts are files that run every time a user logs on to the network. They are usually batch files, but they can be any type of executable file.

You might use logon scripts to set up drive mappings or to run a specific executable file each time a user logs on to the computer. For example, you could run an inventory management file that collects information about the computer's configuration and sends that data to a central management database. Logon scripts are also useful for compatibility with non–Windows 7 clients who want to log on but still maintain consistent settings with their native operating system.

To run a logon script for a user, enter the script name in the Logon Script text box in the Profile tab of the user's Properties dialog box. Another item that can be configured in the Profile tab is the user's home folder. Let's take a look at home folders.

Setting Up Home Folders

Users usually store their personal files and information in a private folder called a home folder. In the Profile tab of the user's Properties dialog box, you can specify the location of a home folder as a local folder or a network folder.

To specify a local path folder, choose the Local Path option and type the path in the text box next to that option. To specify a network path for a folder, choose the Connect option and specify a network path using a Universal Naming Convention (UNC) path.

A UNC consists of the computer name and the share that has been created on the computer. In this case, a network folder should already be created and shared. For example, if you wanted to connect to a folder called `\Users\Will` on a server called SALES, you'd choose the Connect option, select a drive letter that would be mapped to the home directory, and then type **`\\SALES\Users\Will`** in the To box.

If the home folder you are specifying does not exist, Windows 7 will attempt to create the folder for you. You can also use the variable **`%username%`** in place of a specific user's name.

Complete Exercise 6.10 to assign a home folder to a user. These steps assume you have completed all the previous exercises in this chapter.

EXERCISE 6.10

Assigning Home Folders

1. Open the Admin Console MMC Desktop shortcut and expand the Local Users And Groups snap-in.
2. Open the Users folder and double-click user WPanek. The WPanek Properties dialog box appears.
3. Select the Profile tab and click the Local Path radio button to select it.
4. Specify the home folder path by typing **`C:\HomeFolders\WPanek`** in the text box for the Local Path option. Then click OK.
5. Use Windows Explorer to verify that this folder was created.
6. Close the Local Users And Groups MMC.

Real World Scenario

Using Home Folders

As an administrator for a large network, one of my primary responsibilities is to make sure that all data is backed up daily. This has become difficult because daily backup of each user's local hard drive is impractical. You can also have problems with employees deleting important corporate information as they are leaving the company.

After examining the contents of a typical user's local drive, you will realize that most of the local disk space is taken by the operating system and the user's stored applications. This information does not change and does not need to be backed up. What we are primarily concerned with is backing up the user's data.

To more effectively manage this data and accommodate the necessary backup, you should create home folders for each user and store them on a network share. This allows the data to be backed up daily, to be readily accessible should a local computer fail, and to be easily retrieved if the user leaves the company.

Here are the steps to create a home folder that resides on the network. Decide which server will store the users' home folders, create a directory structure that will store the home folders efficiently (for example, `C:\HOME`), and create a single share to the home folder. Then use NTFS and share permissions to ensure that only the specified user has permissions to their home folder. (Setting permissions is covered later in this chapter in the section "Managing Files and Folder Security.") After you create the share and assign permissions, you can specify the location of the home folder through the Profile tab of the user's Properties dialog box.

After creating your user accounts, there is a possibility that you can run into errors or issues with the accounts. In the next section, we will look at how to troubleshoot user account issues.

Troubleshooting User Account Authentication

When a user attempts to log on through Windows 7 and is unable to be authenticated, you will need to track down the reason for the problem.

The following sections offer some suggestions that can help you troubleshoot logon authentication errors for local and domain user accounts.

Troubleshooting Local User Account Authentication

If a local user is having trouble logging on, the problem may be with the username, the password, or the user account itself. The following are some common causes of local logon errors:

Incorrect Username You can verify that the username is correct by checking the Local Users And Groups utility. Verify that the name was spelled correctly.

Incorrect Password Remember that passwords are case sensitive. Is the Caps Lock key on? If you see any messages relating to an expired password or locked-out account, the reason for the problem is obvious. If necessary, you can assign a new password through the Local Users And Groups utility.

Prohibitive User Rights Does the user have permission to log on locally at the computer? By default, the Log On Locally user right is granted to the Users group, so all users can log on to Windows 7 computers.

However, if this user right was modified, you will see an error message stating that the local policy of this computer does not allow interactive logon. The terms *interactive logon* and *local logon* are synonymous and mean that the user is logging on at the computer where the user account is stored on the computer's local database.

A Disabled or Deleted Account You can verify whether an account has been disabled or deleted by checking the account properties through the Local Users And Groups utility.

A Domain Account Logon at the Local Computer If a computer is a part of a domain, the logon dialog box has options for logging on to the domain or to the local computer. Make sure the user has chosen the correct option.

After creating user accounts, normally we place these user accounts into groups. In the next section, I will discuss groups.

Creating and Managing Groups

Groups are an important part of network management. Many administrators are able to accomplish the majority of their management tasks through the use of groups; they rarely assign permissions to individual users.

Windows 7 includes built-in local groups, such as Administrators and Backup Operators. These groups already have all the permissions needed to accomplish specific tasks. Windows 7 also uses default special groups, which are managed by the system. Users become members of special groups based on their requirements for computer and network access.

You can create and manage local groups through the Local Users And Groups utility. With this utility, you can add groups, change group membership, rename groups, and delete groups.

One misconception about groups is that groups have to work with Group Policy Objects (GPOs). This is not correct. Group Policy Objects are a set of rules that allow you to set computer configuration and user configuration options that apply to users or computers. Group policies are typically used with Active Directory and are applied as Group Policy Objects. Group Policy Objects will be discussed in full detail later in this chapter.

In the next sections, you will learn about groups and all the built-in groups. Then you will learn how to create and manage these groups.

Using Built-in Groups

On a Windows 7 computer, default local groups have already been created and assigned all necessary permissions to accomplish basic tasks. In addition, there are built-in special groups that the Windows 7 system handles automatically. These groups are described in the following sections.

Using Default Local Groups

A local group is a group that is stored on the local computer's accounts database. These are the groups to which you can add users and can manage directly on a Windows 7 computer. By default, the following local groups are created on Windows 7 computers:

- Administrators
- Backup Operators
- Cryptographic Operators
- Distributed COM Users
- Event Log Readers
- Guests
- IIS_IUSRS
- Network Configuration Operators
- Performance Log Users
- Performance Monitor Users
- Power Users
- Remote Desktop Users
- Replicator
- Users

We will briefly describe each group, its default permissions, and the users assigned to the group by default.

If possible, you should add users to the built-in local groups rather than creating new groups from scratch. This simplifies administration because the built-in groups already have the appropriate permissions. All you need to do is add the users you want to be members of the group.

The Administrators Group The Administrators group has full permissions and privileges. Its members can grant themselves any permissions they do not have by default to manage all the objects on the computer. (Objects include the file system, printers, and account management.) By default, the Administrator account, which is disabled by default, and the initial user account are members of the Administrators local group.

Assign users to the Administrators group with caution since they will have full permissions to manage the computer.

Members of the Administrators group can perform the following tasks:

- Install the operating system.
- Install and configure hardware device drivers.
- Install system services.
- Install service packs, hot fixes, and Windows updates.
- Upgrade the operating system.
- Repair the operating system.
- Install applications that modify the Windows system files.
- Configure password policies.
- Configure audit policies.
- Manage security logs.
- Create administrative shares.
- Create administrative accounts.
- Modify groups and accounts that have been created by other users.
- Remotely access the Registry.
- Stop or start any service.
- Configure services.
- Increase and manage disk quotas.
- Increase and manage execution priorities.
- Remotely shut down the system.
- Assign and manage user rights.
- Re-enable locked-out and disabled accounts.
- Manage disk properties, including formatting hard drives.
- Modify systemwide environment variables.
- Access any data on the computer.
- Back up and restore all data.

The Backup Operators Group Members of the Backup Operators group have permissions to back up and restore the file system, even if the file system is NTFS and they have not been assigned permissions to access the file system. However, the members of Backup Operators can access the file system only through the Backup utility. To access the file system directly, Backup Operators must have explicit permissions assigned. There are no default members of the Backup Operators local group.

The Cryptographic Operators Group The Cryptographic Operators group has access to perform cryptographic operations on the computer. There are no default members of the Cryptographic Operators local group.

The Distributed COM Users Group The Distributed COM Users group has the ability to launch and run Distributed COM objects on the computer. There are no default members of the Distributed COM Users local group.

The Event Log Readers Group The Event Log Readers group has access to read the event log on the local computer. There are no default members of the Event Log Readers local group.

The Guests Group The Guests group has limited access to the computer. This group is provided so that you can allow people who are not regular users to access specific network resources. As a general rule, most administrators do not allow Guest access because it poses a potential security risk. By default, the Guest user account is a member of the Guests local group.

The IIS_IUSRS Group The IIS_IUSRS group is used by Internet Information Services (IIS). The NT AUTHORITY\IUSR user account is a member of the IIS_IUSRS group by default.

The Network Configuration Operators Group Members of the Network Configuration Operators group have some administrative rights to manage the computer's network configuration—for example, editing the computer's TCP/IP settings.

The Performance Log Users Group The Performance Log Users group has the ability to access and schedule logging of performance counters and can create and manage trace counters on the computer.

The Performance Monitor Users Group The Performance Monitor Users group has the ability to access and view performance counter information on the computer. Users who are members of this group can access performance counters both locally and remotely.

The Power Users Group The Power Users group is included in Windows 7 for backward compatibility. The Power Users group is included to ensure that computers upgraded from Windows XP function as before with regard to folders that allow access to members of the group. Otherwise, the Power Users group has limited administrative rights.

The Remote Desktop Users Group Member of the Remote Desktop Users group allows members of the group to log on remotely for the purpose of using the Remote Desktop service.

The Replicator Group The Replicator group is intended to support directory replication, which is a feature used by domain servers. Only domain users who will start the replication service should be assigned to this group. The Replicator local group has no default members.

The Users Group The Users group is intended for end users who should have very limited system access. If you have installed a fresh copy of Windows 7, the default settings for the Users group prohibit its members from compromising the operating system or program files. By default, all users who have been created on the computer, except Guest, are members of the Users local group.

Windows 7 also uses special groups. In the next section, we will look at special groups and how they work.

Using Special Groups

Special groups can be used by the system or by administrators. Membership in these groups is automatic if certain criteria are met. You cannot manage special groups through the Local Users And Groups utility, but an administrator can add these special groups to resources. Table 6.3 describes several of the special groups that are built into Windows 7.

TABLE 6.3 Special Groups in Windows 7

Group	Description
Creator Owner	This is the account that created or took ownership of an object. This is typically a user account. Each object (files, folders, printers, and print jobs) has an owner. Members of the Creator Owner group have special permissions to resources. For example, if you are a regular user who has submitted 12 print jobs to a printer, you can manipulate your print jobs as Creator Owner, but you can't manage any print jobs submitted by other users.
Everyone	This group includes anyone who could possibly access the computer. The Everyone group includes all users who have been defined on the computer (including Guest), plus (if your computer is a part of a domain) all users within the domain. If the domain has trust relationships with other domains, all users in the trusted domains are part of the Everyone group as well.The exception to automatic group membership with the Everyone group is that members of the Anonymous Logon group are not included as a part of the Everyone group.
Interactive	This group includes all users who use the computer's resources locally. Local users belong to the Interactive group.
Network	This group includes users who access the computer's resources over a network connection. Network users belong to the Network group.

Group	Description
Authenticated Users	This group includes users who access the Windows 7 operating system through a valid username and password. Users who can log on belong to the Authenticated Users group.
Anonymous Logon	This group includes users who access the computer through anonymous logons. When users gain access through special accounts created for anonymous access to Windows 7 services, they become members of the Anonymous Logon group.
Batch	This group includes users who log on as a user account that is used only to run a batch job. Batch job accounts are members of the Batch group.
Dial-up	This group includes users who log on to the network from a dial-up connection. Dial-up users are members of the Dialup group.
Service	This group includes users who log on as a user account that is used only to run a service. You can configure the use of user accounts for logon through the Services program, and these accounts become members of the Service group.
System	When the system accesses specific functions as a user, that process becomes a member of the System group.
Terminal Server User	This group includes users who log on through Terminal Services. These users become members of the Terminal Server User group.

Now that we have looked at the different types of groups, let's take a look at how to manage and work with these groups. In the next section we will discuss how to work with groups.

To work with groups, you can use the Local Users And Groups utility. Let's take a look at how to create new groups.

Creating Groups

To create a group, you must be logged on as a member of the Administrators group. The Administrators group has full permissions to manage users and groups.

As you do in your choices for usernames, keep your naming conventions in mind when assigning names to groups. When you create a local group, consider the following guidelines:

- The group name should be descriptive (for example, Accounting Data Users).
- The group name must be unique to the computer, different from all other group names and usernames that exist on that computer.
- Group names can be up to 256 characters. It is best to use alphanumeric characters for ease of administration. The backslash (\) character is not allowed.

Creating groups is similar to creating users, and it is a fairly easy process. After you've added the Local Users And Groups MMC or use Local Users And Groups through Computer Management, expand it to see the Users and Groups folders. Right-click the Groups folder and select New Group from the context menu. This brings up the New Group dialog box, shown in Figure 6.7.

FIGURE 6.7 The New Group dialog box

The only required entry in the New Group dialog box is the group name. If appropriate, you can enter a description for the group, and you can add (or remove) group members. When you're ready to create the new group, click the Create button.

Complete exercise 6.11 to create two new local groups.

EXERCISE 6.11

Creating Groups

1. Open the Admin Console MMC Desktop shortcut you created and expand the Local Users And Groups snap-in.
2. Right-click the Groups folder and select New Group.
3. In the New Group dialog box, type **Data Users** in the Group Name text box. Click the Create button.
4. In the New Group dialog box, type **Application Users** in the Group Name text box. Click the Create button.

After the groups are created, you will have to manage the groups and their membership. In the next section, we will look at managing groups.

Managing Group Membership

After you've created a group, you can add members to it. As mentioned earlier, you can put the same user in multiple groups. You can easily add and remove users through a group's Properties dialog box, shown in Figure 6.8. To access this dialog box from the Groups folder in the Local Users And Groups utility, double-click the group you want to manage.

FIGURE 6.8 A group Properties dialog box

From the group's Properties dialog box, you can change the group's description and add or remove group members. When you click the Add button to add members, the Select Users dialog box appears (Figure 6.9).

FIGURE 6.9 The Select Users dialog box

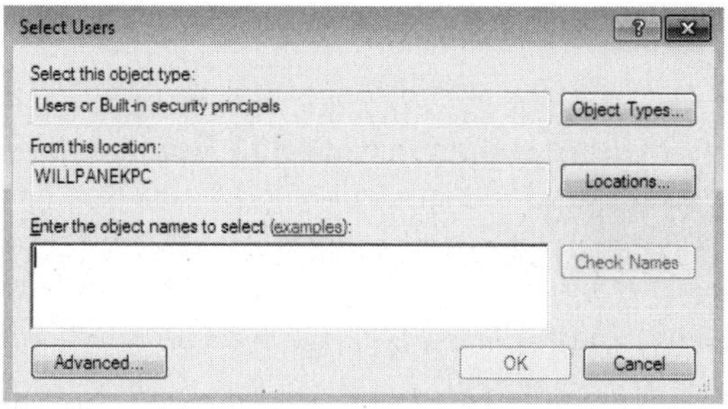

In the Select Users dialog box, you enter the object names of the users you want to add. You can use the Check Names button to validate the users against the database. Select the user accounts you wish to add and click Add. Click the OK button to add the selected users to the group.

Although the special groups that were covered earlier in the chapter are listed in this dialog box, you cannot manage the membership of these special groups.

To remove a member from the group, select the member in the Members list of the Properties dialog box and click the Remove button.

In Exercise 6.12, you'll create new user accounts and then add these users to one of the groups you created in the previous steps.

EXERCISE 6.12

Adding Accounts to Groups

1. Open the Admin Console MMC shortcut you created and expand the Local Users And Groups snap-in.
2. Create two new users: JDoe and DDoe. Deselect the User Must Change Password At Next Logon option for each user.
3. Expand the Groups folder.
4. Double-click the Data Users group.
5. In the Data Users Properties dialog box, click the Add button.
6. In the Select Users dialog box, type the username **JDoe**; then click OK. Click Add and type the username **DDoe**; then click OK.
7. In the Data Users Properties dialog box, you will see that the users have both been added to the group. Click OK to close the group's Properties dialog box.

There may come a point when a specific group is no longer needed. In the next section, we will look at how to delete a group from the Local Users And Groups utility.

Deleting Groups

If you are sure that you will never again want to use a particular group, you can delete it. Once a group is deleted, you lose all permissions assignments that have been specified for the group.

To delete a group, right-click the group and choose Delete from the context menu. You will see a warning that once a group is deleted, it is gone for good. Click the Yes button if you're sure you want to delete the group.

If you delete a group and give another group the same name, the new group won't be created with the same properties as the deleted group because, as with users, groups get unique SIDs assigned at the time of creation.

Creating users and groups is one of the most important tasks that we as IT members can do. On a Windows 7 machine, creating users and groups is an easy and straightforward process.

Now that you understand how to create users and groups, you need to know how to manage security. In the next sections, we will look at how to secure Windows 7.

Managing Security

Windows 7 offers a wide variety of security options. If the Windows 7 computer is a part of a domain, then you can apply security through a Group Policy Object using the Group Policy Management Console. If the Windows 7 computer is not a part of a domain, then you use Local Group Policy Objects to manage local security.

In the following sections, you will learn about the different environments that Windows 7 can be installed in and the utilities that are used to manage security.

You can use policies to help manage user accounts. Account policies control the logon environment for the computer, such as password and logon restrictions. Local policies specify what users can do once they log on and include auditing, user rights, and security options. You can also manage critical security features through the Windows Security Center.

We will continue with NTFS security and shared permissions and how they work independently and together.

Managing Security Configurations

The tools you use to manage Windows 7 computer security configurations depend on whether the Windows 7 computer is a part of a Windows 2000, Windows 2003, or Windows 2008 domain environment.

If the Windows 7 client is not a part of a domain, then you apply security settings through *Local Group Policy Objects (LGPOs)*. LGPOs are sets of security configuration settings that are applied to users and computers. LGPOs are created and stored on the Windows 7 computer.

If your Windows 7 computer is a part of a domain, which uses the services of Active Directory, then you typically manage and configure security through Group Policy objects (GPOs). Active Directory is the database that contains all of your domain user and group accounts along with all other domain objects.

Group Policy objects are policies that can be placed on either users or computers in the domain. The Group Policy Management Console (GPMC) is a Microsoft Management Console (MMC) snap-in that is used to configure and manage GPOs for users and computers via Active Directory.

Windows 7 computers that are part of a domain still have LGPOs, and you can use LGPOs in conjunction with the Active Directory group policies (GPOs).

Usage of Group Policy Objects for domains is covered in greater detail in *MCTS: Windows Server 2008 Active Directory Configuration*, by William Panek and James Chellis (Sybex, 2008).

The settings you can apply through the Group Policy utility within Active Directory are more comprehensive than the settings you can apply through LGPOs.

Table 6.4 lists some of the options that can be set for GPOs within Active Directory and which of those options can be applied through LGPOs.

TABLE 6.4 Group Policy and LGPO setting options

Group Policy Setting	Available for LGPO?
Software installation	No
Remote Installation Services	Yes
Scripts	Yes
Printers	Yes
Security settings	Yes
Policy-based QOS	Yes
Administrative templates	Yes
Folder redirection	No
Internet Explorer configuration	Yes

Now that we have looked at LGPOs, let's take a look at some of the tools available for creating and managing them.

Using the Group Policy Result Tool

When a user logs on to a computer or domain, a resulting set of policies to be applied is generated based on the LGPOs, site GPOs, domain GPOs, and OU GPOs. The overlapping nature of group policies can make it difficult to determine what group policies will actually be applied to a computer or user.

To help determine what policies will actually be applied, Windows 7 includes a tool called the Group Policy Result Tool, also known as the Resultant Set of Policy (RSoP). You can access this tool through the GPResult command-line utility. The `gpresult` command displays the resulting set of policies that were enforced on the computer and the specified user during the logon process.

The `gpresult` command will display the *Resultant Set of Policy (RSoP)* for the computer and user who is currently logged in. Several options can be used with this command. Table 6.5 shows the different switches that can be used for the `gpresult` command.

TABLE 6.5 `Gpresult` switches

Switch	Explanation
`/F`	Forces `gpresult` to override the file name specified in the `/X` or `/H` command.
`/H`	Saves the report in an HTML format.
`/P`	Specifies the password for a given user context.
`/R`	Displays RSoP summary data.
`/S`	Specifies the remote system to connect to.
`/U`	Specifies the user context under which the command should be executed.
`/V`	Specifies that verbose information should be displayed.
`/X`	Saves the report in XML format.
`/Z`	Specifies that the super verbose information should be displayed.
`/?`	Shows all the `gpresult` command switches.
`/scope`	Specifies whether the user or the computer settings need to be displayed.
`/User`	Specifies the username for which the RSoP data is to be displayed.

In the next section, we will look at how to create and apply Local Group Policy Objects to the Windows 7 machine.

Managing and Applying LGPOs

As we discussed previously, policies that have been linked through Active Directory will, by default, take precedence over any established local group policies. Local group policies are typically applied to computers that are not part of a network or are in a network that does not have a domain controller and thus does not use Active Directory.

Previous versions of Windows (before Vista) contained only one Local Group Policy Object that applied to all of the computer's users unless NTFS permissions were applied to the LGPO. However, Windows 7 and Windows Vista changed that with the addition of Multiple Local Group Policy Objects (MLGPOs). Like Active Directory GPOs, MLGPOs are applied in a certain hierarchical order:

1. Local Computer Policy
2. Administrators and Non-Administrators Local Group Policy
3. User-Specific Group Policy

The Local Computer Policy is the only LGPO that includes computer and user settings; the other LGPOs contain only user settings. Settings applied here will apply to all users of the computer.

The Administrators and Non-Administrators LGPOs were new to Windows Vista and are still included with Windows 7. The Administrators LGPO is applied to users who are members of the built-in local Administrators group. As you might guess, the Non-Administrators LGPO is applied to users who are not members of the local Administrators group. Because each user of a computer can be classified as an administrator or a non-administrator, either one policy or the other will apply.

User-Specific LGPOs are also included with Windows 7. These LGPOs make it possible for specific policy settings to apply to a single user.

As with Active Directory GPOs, any GPO settings applied lower in the hierarchy will override GPO settings applied higher in the hierarchy by default. For example, any user-specific GPO settings will override any conflicting administrator/non-administrator GPO settings or Local Computer Policy settings. And, of course, any AD GPO settings will still override any conflicting LGPO settings.

Domain administrators can disable LGPOs on Windows 7 computers by enabling the Turn Off Local Group Policy Objects Processing domain GPO setting, which you can find under Computer Configuration\Administrative Templates\System\Group Policy.

You apply an LGPO to a Windows 7 computer through the Group Policy Object Editor snap-in within the MMC. Figure 6.10 shows the Local Computer Policy for a Windows 7 computer.

FIGURE 6.10 Local Computer Policy

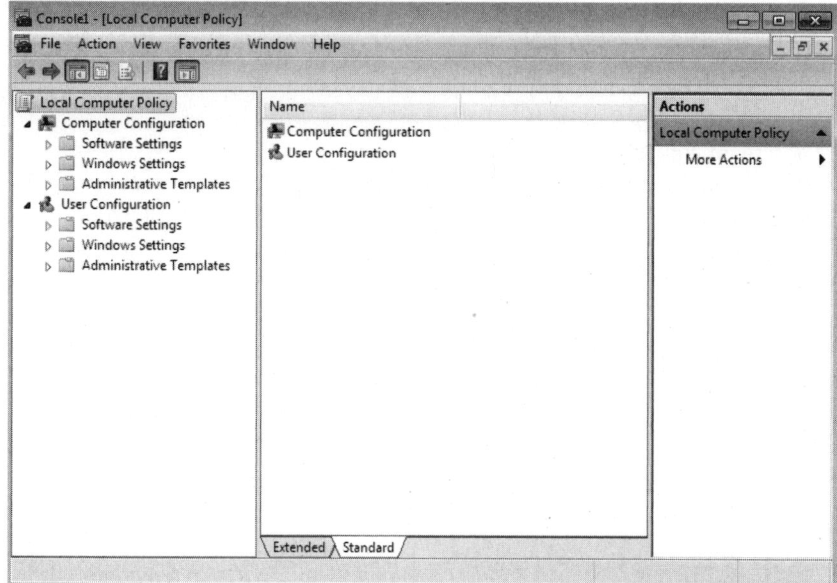

Complete the following exercise to add the Local Computer Policy snap-in to the MMC.

EXERCISE 6.13

Adding the Local Computer Policy Snap-In

1. Open the Admin Console MMC shortcut by typing **MMC** in the Search programs and files box.
2. A User Account Control dialog box appears. Click Yes.
3. Select File ➢ Add/Remove Snap-In.
4. Highlight the Group Policy Object Editor Snap-in and click the Add button.
5. The Group Policy Object specifies Local Computer by default. Click the Finish button.
6. In the Add or Remove Snap-Ins dialog box, click OK.
7. In the left pane, right-click the Local Computer Policy and choose New Windows From Here.
8. Choose File ➢ Save As and name the console **LGPO**. Make sure you save it to the Desktop. Click Save.
9. Close the MMC Admin console.

Now we will look at how to open an LGPO for a specific user account on a Windows 7 machine. Complete Exercise 6.14 to access the Administrators, Non-Administrators, and User-Specific LGPOs.

EXERCISE 6.14

Accessing the LGPO

1. Open the Admin Console MMC shortcut by typing **MMC** in the Windows 7 Search box.
2. Select File ➤ Add/Remove Snap-In.
3. Highlight the Group Policy Object Editor snap-in and click the Add button.
4. Click Browse so that you can browse for a different GPO.
5. Click the Users tab.
6. Select the user you want to access and click OK.
7. In the Select Group Policy Object dialog box, click Finish.
8. In the Add Or Remove Snap-Ins dialog box, click OK. You may close the console when you are done looking at the LGPO settings for the user you chose.

Notice that the Administrators, Non-Administrators, and User-Specific LGPOs contain only User Configuration settings, not Computer Configuration settings.

Now let's take a look at the different security settings that can be configured in the LGPO.

Configuring Local Security Policies

Through the use of the Local Computer Policy, you can set a wide range of security options under Computer Configuration\Windows Settings\Security Settings.

This portion of the Local Computer Policy is also known as the Local Security Policy. The following sections describe in detail how to apply security settings through LGPOs (see Figure 6.11).

FIGURE 6.11 Security Settings of the LGPO

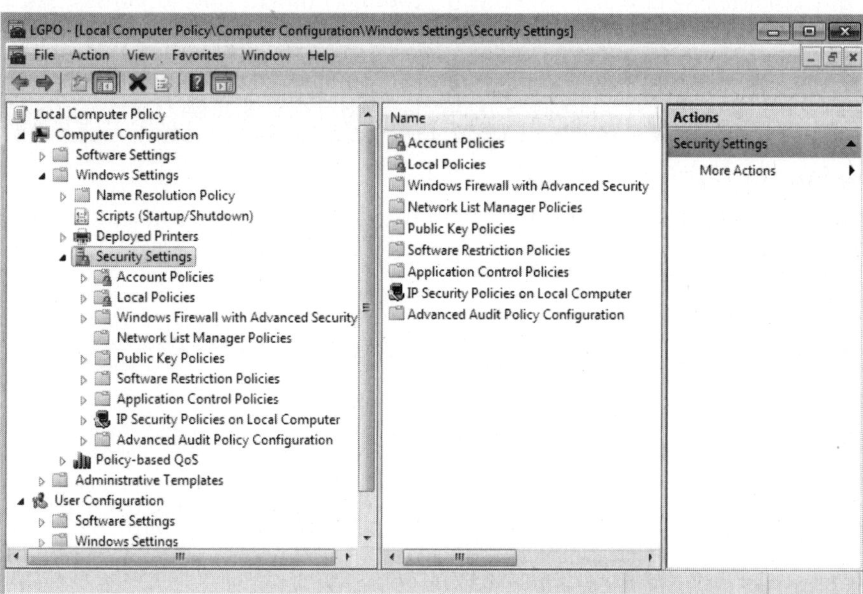

The main areas of security configuration of the LGPO are as follows:

Account Policies Account policies are used to configure password and account lockout features. Some of these settings include password history, maximum password age, minimum password age, minimum password length, password complexity, account lockout duration, account lockout threshold, and whether to reset the account lockout counter afterwards.

Local Policies Local policies are used to configure auditing, user rights, and security options.

Windows Firewall with Advanced Security Windows Firewall with Advanced Security provides network security for Windows computers. Through this LGPO you can set domain, private, and public profiles. You can also set this LGPO to authenticate communications between computers and inbound/outbound rules.

Network List Manager Policies This section allows you to set the network name, icon, and location group policies. Administrators can set Unidentified Networks, Identifying Networks, and All Networks.

Public Key Policies Use the Public Key Policies settings to specify how to manage certificates and certificate life cycles.

Software Restriction Policies The settings under Software Restriction Policies allow you to identify malicious software and control that software's ability to run on the Windows 7 machine. These policies allow an administrator to protect the Microsoft Windows 7 operating system against security threats such as viruses and Trojan horse programs.

Application Control Policies This section allows you to set up AppLocker. You can use AppLocker to configure a Denied list and an Accepted list for applications. Applications that are configured on the Denied list will not run on the system and applications on the Accepted list will operate properly.

IP Security Policies on Local Computer This section allows you to configure the IPsec policies. IPsec is a way to secure data packets at the IP level of the message.

Advanced Audit Policy Configuration Advanced Audit Policy Configuration settings can be used to provide detailed control over audit policies. This section also allows you to configure auditing to help show administrators either successful or unsuccessful attacks on their network.

You can also access the Local Security Policy by running `secpol.msc` or by opening Control Panel and selecting Administrative Tools ➢ Local Security Policy.

Now that you have seen all the options in the security section of the LGPO, let's take a look at account policies and local policies in more detail.

Using Account Policies

Account policies are used to specify the user account properties that relate to the logon process. They allow you to configure computer security settings for passwords and account lockout specifications.

If security is not an issue—perhaps because you are using your Windows 7 computer at home—then you don't need to bother with account policies. If, on the other hand, security is important—for example, because your computer provides access to payroll information—then you should set very restrictive account policies.

Account policies at the LGPO level apply only to local user accounts, not domain accounts. To ensure that user account security is configured for domain user accounts, you need to configure these policies at the domain GPO level.

To access the Account Policies folder from the MMC, follow this path: Local Computer Policy\Computer Configuration\Windows Settings\Security Settings\Account Policies. You will look at all these folders and how to use them throughout the rest of this chapter.

In the following sections you will learn about the password policies and account lockout policies that define how security is applied to account policies.

Setting Password Policies

Password policies ensure that security requirements are enforced on the computer. It is important to understand that password policies are set on a per-computer basis; they cannot be configured for specific users. Figure 6.12 shows the password policies, which are described in Table 6.6.

FIGURE 6.12 The password policies

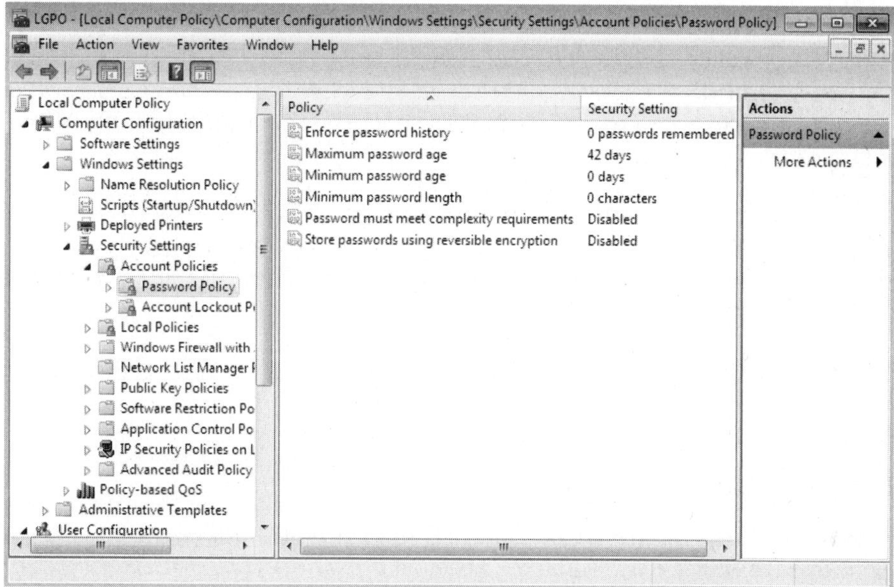

TABLE 6.6 Password policy options

Policy	Description	Default	Minimum	Maximum
Enforce Password History	Keeps track of user's password history	Remember 0 Passwords	Same as default	Remember 24 Passwords
Maximum Password Age	Determines maximum number of days user can keep valid password	Keep Password For 42 Days	Keep Password For 1 Day	Keep Password For Up To 999 Days
Minimum Password Age	Specifies how long password must be kept before it can be changed	0 Days (Password can be changed immediately.)	Same as default	998 Days

TABLE 6.6 Password policy options *(continued)*

Policy	Description	Default	Minimum	Maximum
Minimum Password Length	Specifies minimum number of characters password must contain	0 Characters (No password required.)	Same as default	127 Characters
Password Must Meet Complexity Requirements	Requires that passwords meet minimum levels of complexity	Disabled		
Store Passwords Using Reversible Encryption	Specifies higher level of encryption for stored user passwords	Disabled		

You can use the password policies in Table 6.6 as follows:

Enforce Password History Prevents users from repeatedly using the same passwords. Users must create a new password when their password expires or is changed.

Maximum Password Age Forces users to change their password after the maximum password age is exceeded. Setting this value to 0 will specify that the password will never expire.

Minimum Password Age Prevents users from changing their password several times in rapid succession in order to defeat the purpose of the Enforce Password History policy.

Minimum Password Length Ensures that users create a password and specifies the length requirement for that password. If this option isn't set, users are not required to create a password at all.

Password Must Meet Complexity Requirements Passwords must be six characters or longer and cannot contain the user's account name or any part of the user's full name. In addition, passwords must contain three of the following character types:

- English uppercase characters (A through Z)
- English lowercase characters (a through z)
- Decimal digits (0 through 9)
- Symbols (such as !, @, #, $, and %)

Store Passwords Using Reversible Encryption Provides a higher level of security for user passwords. This is required for Challenge Handshake Authentication Protocol (CHAP) authentication through remote access or Internet Authentication Services (IAS) and for Digest Authentication with Internet Information Services (IIS).

Complete Exercise 6.15 to configure password policies for your computer. These steps assume that you have added the Local Computer Policy snap-in to the MMC completed in earlier exercises.

EXERCISE 6.15

Configuring Password Policy

1. Open the LGPO MMC shortcut that you created earlier.
2. Expand the Local Computer Policy snap-in.
3. Expand the folders as follows: Computer Configuration\Windows Settings\Security Settings\Account Policies\Password Policy.
4. Open the Enforce Password History policy. On the Local Security Setting tab, specify that five passwords will be remembered. Click OK.
5. Open the Maximum Password Age policy. On the Local Security Setting tab, specify that the password expires in 60 days. Click OK.

Let's now take a look at how to set and manage the policies in the Account Lockout Policies section.

Setting Account Lockout Policies

The account lockout policies specify how many invalid logon attempts should be tolerated. You configure the account lockout policies so that after *x* number of unsuccessful logon attempts within *y* number of minutes, the account will be locked for a specified amount of time or until the administrator unlocks it.

Account lockout policies are similar to a bank's arrangements for ATM access code security. You have a certain number of chances to enter the correct PIN. That way, anyone who steals your card can't just keep guessing your access code until they get it right. Typically, after three unsuccessful attempts, the ATM takes the card. Then you need to request a new card from the bank. Figure 6.13 shows the account lockout policies, which are described in Table 6.7.

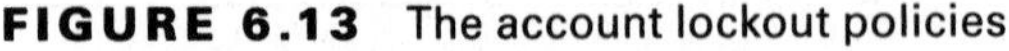

FIGURE 6.13 The account lockout policies

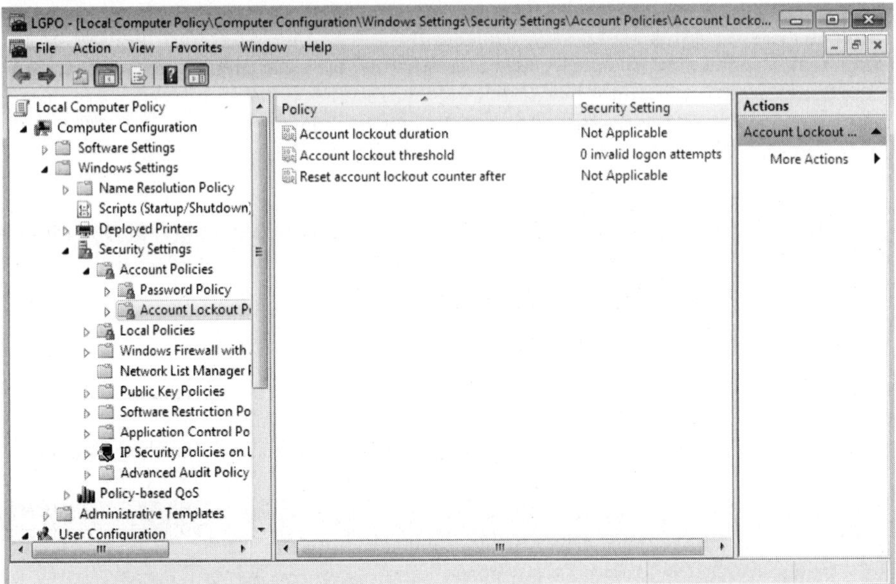

The Account Lockout Duration and Reset Account Lockout Counter After policies will be disabled until a value is specified for the Account Lockout Threshold policy. After the Account Lockout Threshold policy is set, the Account Lockout Duration and Reset Account Lockout Counter After policies will be set to 30 minutes. If you set Account Lockout Duration to 0, the account will remain locked out until an administrator unlocks it.

The Reset Account Lockout Counter After value must be equal to or less than the Account Lockout Duration value.

TABLE 6.7 Account Lockout Policy options

Policy	Description	Default	Minimum	Maximum
Account Lockout Duration	Specifies how long account will remain locked if account lockout threshold is reached	Disabled (If Account Lockout Threshold is enabled, 30 minutes.)	Same as default	99,999 Minutes

Policy	Description	Default	Minimum	Maximum
Account Lockout Threshold	Specifies number of invalid attempts allowed before account is locked out	0 (Disabled; account will not be locked out.)	Same as default	999 Attempts
Reset Account Lockout Counter After	Specifies how long counter will remember unsuccessful logon attempts	Disabled (If Account Lockout Threshold is enabled, 30 minutes.)	Same as default	99,999 Minutes

Complete Exercise 6.16 to configure account lockout policies and test their effects.

EXERCISE 6.16

Configuring Account Lockout Policies

1. Open the LGPO MMC shortcut.
2. Expand the Local Computer Policy snap-in.
3. Expand the folders as follows: Computer Configuration\Windows Settings\Security Settings\Account Policies\Account Lockout Policy.
4. Open the Account Lockout Threshold policy. On the Local Security Setting tab, specify that the account will lock after three invalid logon attempts. Click OK.
5. Accept the suggested value changes for the Account Lockout Duration and Reset Account Lockout Counter After policies by clicking OK.
6. Open the Account Lockout Duration policy. On the Local Security Setting tab, specify that the account will remain locked for 5 minutes. Click OK.
7. Accept the suggested value changes for the Reset Account Lockout Counter After policy by clicking OK.
8. Log off your Administrator account. Try to log on as one of the accounts that have been created on this Windows 7 machine and enter an incorrect password four times.
9. After you see the error message stating that the referenced account has been locked out, log on as an administrator.
10. To unlock the account, open the Local Users And Groups snap-in in the MMC, expand the Users folder, and double-click the user.
11. On the General tab of the user's Properties dialog box, click to remove the check mark from the Account Is Locked Out check box. Then click OK.

In the next section, we will discuss how to control a user or computer after they have logged into the Windows 7 machine.

Using Local Policies

As you learned in the preceding section, account policies are used to control logon procedures. When you want to control what a user can do after logging on, you use local policies. With local policies, you can implement auditing, specify user rights, and set security options.

To use local policies, first add the Local Computer Policy snap-in to the MMC. Then, from the MMC, follow this path to access the Local Policies folders: Local Computer Policy\Computer Configuration\Windows Settings\Security Settings\Local Policies. Figure 6.14 shows the three Local Policies folders: Audit Policy, User Rights Assignment, and Security Options. You will look at each of those in the following sections.

FIGURE 6.14 Accessing the Local Policies folders

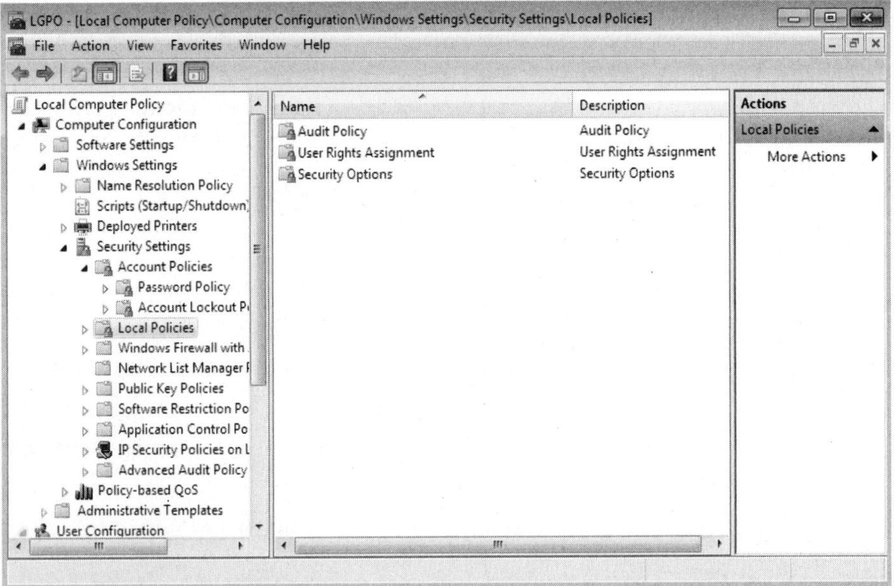

Setting Audit Policies

Audit policies can be implemented to track the success or failure of specified user actions. You audit events that pertain to user management through the audit policies. By tracking certain events, you can create a history of specific tasks, such as user creation and successful or unsuccessful logon attempts. You can also identify security violations that arise when users attempt to access system management tasks for which they do not have permission.

Auditing Failed Attempts

As an IT manager, you have to make sure that you monitor failed attempts to access resources. A failed attempt to access a resource usually means that someone tried to access the resource and they were denied due to insufficient privileges.

Users who try to go to areas for which they do not have permission usually fall into two categories: hackers and people who are just curious to see what they can get away with. Both are very dangerous.

If a user is trying to access an area in which they do not belong, make sure to warn the user about the attacks. This is very common on a network and needs to be nipped in the bud immediately.

When you define an audit policy, you can choose to audit success or failure of specific events. The success of an event means that the task was successfully accomplished. The failure of an event means that the task was not successfully accomplished.

By default, auditing is not enabled, and it must be manually configured. Once auditing has been configured, you can see the results of the audit in the security log using the Event Viewer utility.

Figure 6.15 shows the audit policies, which are described in Table 6.8.

FIGURE 6.15 The audit policies

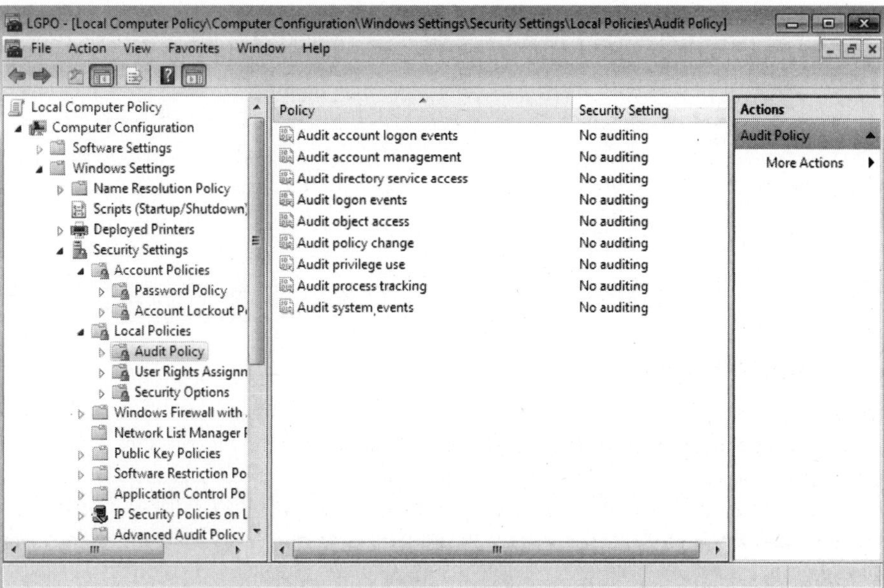

TABLE 6.8 Audit policy options

Policy	Description
Audit Account Logon Events	Tracks when a user logs on or logs off either their local machine or the domain (if domain auditing is enabled)
Audit Account Management	Tracks user and group account creation, deletion, and management actions, such as password changes
Audit Directory Service Access	Tracks directory service accesses
Audit Logon Events	Audits events related to logon, such as running a logon script, accessing a roaming profile. and accessing a server
Audit Object Access	Enables auditing of access to files, folders, and printers
Audit Policy Change	Tracks any changes to the audit policies, trust policies, or user rights assignment policies
Audit Privilege Use	Tracks users exercising a user right
Audit Process Tracking	Tracks events such as activating a program, accessing an object, and exiting a process
Audit System Events	Tracks system events such as shutting down or restarting the computer as well as events that relate to the security log in Event Viewer

After you set the Audit Object Access policy to enable auditing of object access, you must enable file auditing through NTFS security or print auditing through printer security.

Complete Exercise 6.17 to configure audit policies and view their results.

EXERCISE 6.17

Configuring Audit Policies

1. Open the LGOP MMC shortcut.
2. Expand the Local Computer Policy snap-in.
3. Expand the folders as follows: Computer Configuration\Windows Settings\Security Settings\Local Policies\Audit Policy.
4. Open the Audit Account Logon Events policy. Check the Success and Failure boxes. Click OK.

5. Open the Audit Account Management policy. Check the Success and Failure boxes. Click OK.
6. Log off of your Administrator account. Attempt to log back on as your Administrator account with an incorrect password. The logon should fail (because the password is incorrect).
7. Log on as an administrator.
8. Select Start, right-click Computer, and choose Manage to open Event Viewer.
9. From Event Viewer, open the Security log by selecting Windows Logs ➤ Security. You should see the audited events listed with a Task Category of Credential Validation.

In the next section, we will look at how to configure user rights on a Windows 7 machine.

Assigning User Rights

The user rights policies determine what rights a user or group has on the computer. User rights apply to the system. They are not the same as permissions, which apply to a specific object (permissions are discussed later in this chapter, in “Managing File and Folder Security”).

An example of a user right is the Back Up Files And Directories right. This right allows a user to back up files and folders even if the user does not have permissions that have been defined through NTFS file system permissions. The other user rights are similar because they deal with system access as opposed to resource access.

Figure 6.16 shows the user rights policies, which are described in Table 6.9.

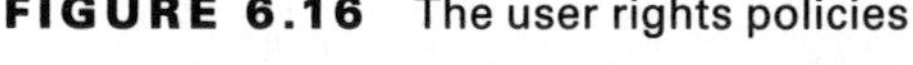

FIGURE 6.16 The user rights policies

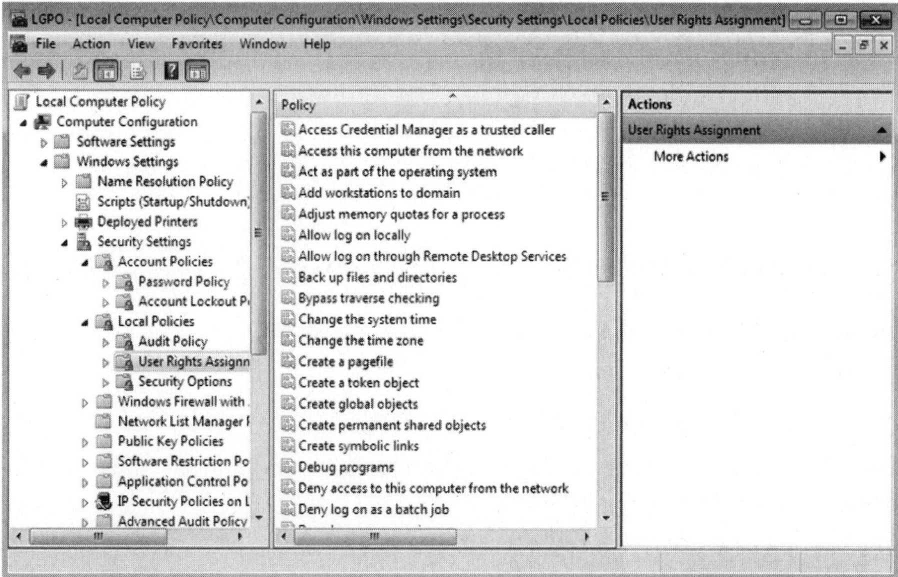

TABLE 6.9 User Rights Assignment Policy Options

Right	Description
Access Credential Manager As A Trusted Caller	Used to back up and restore Credential Manager.
Access This Computer From The Network	Allows a user to access the computer from the network.
Act As Part Of The Operating System	Allows low-level authentication services to authenticate as any user.
Add Workstations To Domain	Allows a user to create a computer account on the domain.
Adjust Memory Quotas For A Process	Allows you to configure how much memory can be used by a specific process.
Allow Log On Locally	Allows a user to log on at the physical computer.
Allow Log On Through Terminal Services	Gives a user permission to log on through Terminal Services. Does not affect Windows 2000 computers prior to SP2.
Back Up Files And Directories	Allows a user to back up all files and directories regardless of how the file and directory permissions have been set.
Bypass Traverse Checking	Allows a user to pass through and traverse the directory structure, even if that user does not have permissions to list the contents of the directory.
Change The System Time	Allows a user to change the internal time and date on the computer.
Change The Time Zone	Allows a user to change the time zone.
Create A Pagefile	Allows a user to create or change the size of a page file.
Create A Token Object	Allows a process to create a token if the process uses an internal API to create the token.
Create Global Objects	Allows a user to create global objects when connected using Terminal Server.
Create Permanent Shared Objects	Allows a process to create directory objects through Object Manager.

Right	Description
Create Symbolic Links	Allows a user to create a symbolic link.
Debug Programs	Allows a user to attach a debugging program to any process.
Deny Access To This Computer From The Network	Allows you to deny specific users or groups access to this computer from the network. Overrides the Access This Computer From The Network policy for accounts present in both policies.
Deny Log On As A Batch Job	Allows you to prevent specific users or groups from logging on as a batch file. Overrides the Log On As A Batch Job policy for accounts present in both policies.
Deny Log On As A Service	Allows you to prevent specific users or groups from logging on as a service. Overrides the Log On As A Service policy for accounts present in both policies.
Deny Log On Locally	Allows you to deny specific users or groups access to the computer locally. Overrides the Log On Locally policy for accounts present in both policies.
Deny Log On Through Terminal Services	Specifies that a user is not able to log on through Terminal Services. Does not affect Windows 2000 computers prior to SP2.
Enable Computer And User Accounts To Be Trusted For Delegation	Allows a user or group to set the Trusted For Delegation setting for a user or computer object.
Force Shutdown From A Remote System	Allows the system to be shut down by a user at a remote location on the network.
Generate Security Audits	Allows a user, group, or process to make entries in the security log.
Impersonate A Client After Authentication	Enables programs running on behalf of a user to impersonate a client.
Increase A Process Working Set	Allows the size of a process working set to be increased.
Increase Scheduling Priority	Specifies that a process can increase or decrease the priority that is assigned to another process.
Load And Unload Device Drivers	Allows a user to dynamically unload and load device drivers. This right does not apply to Plug And Play drivers.

TABLE 6.9 User Rights Assignment Policy Options *(continued)*

Right	Description
Lock Pages In Memory	Allows an account to create a process that runs only in physical RAM, preventing it from being paged.
Log On As A Batch Job	Allows a process to log on to the system and run a file that contains one or more operating system commands.
Log On As A Service	Allows a service to log on in order to run.
Manage Auditing And Security Log	Allows a user to enable object access auditing for files and other Active Directory objects. This right does not allow a user to enable general object access auditing in the Local Security Policy.
Modify An Object Label	Allows a user to change the integrity level of files, folders, or other objects.
Modify Firmware Environment Variables	Allows a user to install or upgrade Windows. It also allows a user or process to modify the firmware environment variables stored in NVRAM of non-x86-based computers. This right does *not* affect the modification of system environment variables or user environment variables.
Perform Volume Maintenance Tasks	Allows a user to perform volume maintenance tasks such as defragmentation and error checking.
Profile Single Process	Allows a user to monitor nonsystem processes through performance-monitoring tools.
Profile System Performance	Allows a user to monitor system processes through performance-monitoring tools.
Remove Computer From Docking Station	Allows a user to undock a laptop through the Windows 7 user interface.
Replace a Process Level Token	Allows a process, such as Task Scheduler, to call an API to start another service.
Restore Files And Directories	Allows a user to restore files and directories regardless of file and directory permissions.
Shut Down The System	Allows a user to shut down the Windows 7 computer locally.

Right	Description
Synchronize Directory Service Data	Allows a user to synchronize Active Directory data.
Take Ownership Of Files or Other Objects	Allows a user to take ownership of system objects, such as files, folders, printers, and processes.

In Exercise 6.08, you'll apply a user rights policy.

EXERCISE 6.18

Applying User Rights

1. Open the LGOP MMC shortcut.
2. Expand the Local Computer Policy snap-in.
3. Expand the folders as follows: Computer Configuration\Windows Settings\Security Settings\Local Policies\User Rights Assignment.
4. Open the Log On As A Service user right.
5. Click the Add User Or Group button. The Select Users Or Groups dialog box appears.
6. Click the Advanced button, and then select Find Now.
7. Select a user. Click OK.
8. Click OK in the Select Users Or Groups dialog box.
9. In the Log On As A Service Properties dialog box, click OK.

In the next section, we will look at how users can install resources on Windows 7 without being an administrator by using User Account Control.

Configuring User Account Control

Most administrators have had to wrestle with the balance between security and enabling applications to run correctly. In the past, some applications simply would not run correctly under Windows unless the user running the application was a local administrator.

Unfortunately, granting local administrator permissions to a user also allows the user to install software and hardware, change configuration settings, modify local user accounts, and delete critical files. Even more troubling is the fact that malware that infects a computer while an administrator is logged in is also able to perform those same functions.

Limited user accounts in Windows XP were supposed to allow applications to run correctly and allow users to perform necessary tasks. However, in practical application, it did not work as advertised. Many applications require that users have permissions to write to protected folders and to the Registry, and limited user accounts did not allow users to do so.

Windows 7's answer to the problem is User Account Control (UAC). UAC enables non-administrator users to perform standard tasks, such as install a printer, configure a VPN or wireless connection, and install updates, while preventing them from performing tasks that require administrative privileges, such as installing applications.

Managing Privilege Elevation

UAC protects computers by requiring privilege elevation for all users, even users who are members of the local Administrators group. As you have no doubt seen by now, UAC will prompt you for permission when performing a task that requires privilege elevation. This prevents malware from silently launching processes without your knowledge.

Privilege elevation is required for any feature that contains the four-color security shield. For example, the small shield shown on the Change Date And Time button in the Date And Time dialog box in Figure 6.17 indicates an action that requires privilege elevation.

FIGURE 6.17 Date And Time dialog box

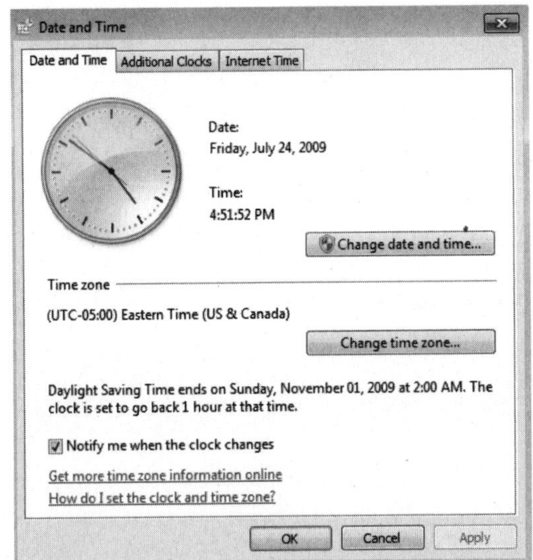

Now let's take a look at how to elevate privileges for users.

Elevated Privileges for Users

By default, local administrators are logged on as standard users. When administrators attempt to perform a task that requires privilege escalation, they are prompted for confirmation by default. This can require administrators to authenticate when performing a task that requires privilege escalation by changing the User Account Control: Behavior Of The Elevation Prompt For Administrators In Admin Approval Mode policy setting to Prompt For Credentials. On the other hand, if you don't want UAC to prompt administrators for confirmation when elevating privileges, you can change the policy setting to Elevate Without Prompting.

Non-administrator accounts are called standard users. When standard users attempt to perform a task that requires privilege elevation, they are prompted for a password of a user account that has administrative privileges. You cannot configure UAC to automatically allow standard users to perform administrative tasks, nor can you configure UAC to prompt a standard user for confirmation before performing administrative tasks. If you do not want standard users to be prompted for credentials when attempting to perform administrative tasks, you can automatically deny elevation requests by changing the User Account Control: Behavior Of The Elevation Prompt For Standard Users policy setting to Automatically Deny Elevation Requests.

The built-in Administrator account, though disabled by default, is not affected by UAC. UAC will not prompt the Administrator account for elevation of privileges. Thus, it is important to use a normal user account whenever possible and use the built-in Administrator account only when absolutely necessary.

Complete the following exercise to see how UAC affects administrator and non-administrator accounts differently.

EXERCISE 6.19

Seeing How UAC Affects Accounts

1. Log on to Windows 7 as a non-administrator account.
2. Select Start ➤ Control Panel ➤ Large Icons View ➤ Windows Firewall.
3. Click the Turn Windows Firewall On Or Off link on the left side. The UAC box should prompt you for permission to continue. Click Yes. You should not be allowed access to the Windows Firewall Settings dialog box.

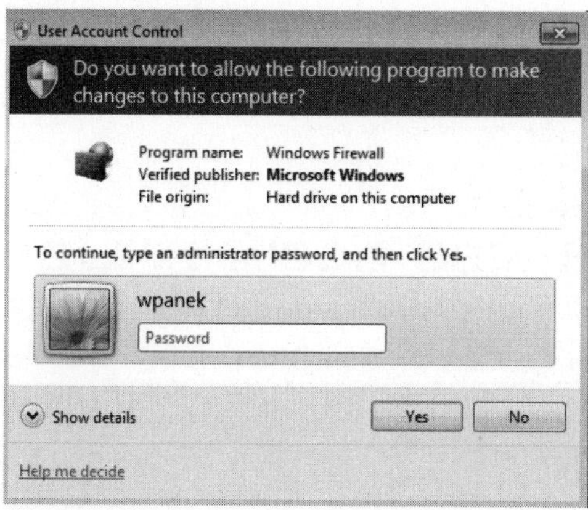

EXERCISE 6.19 *(continued)*

4. Log off and log on as the Administrator account.
5. Select Start ➢ Control Panel ➢ Large Icons View ➢ Windows Firewall.
6. Click the Turn Windows Firewall On Or Off link.
7. You should automatically go to the Windows Firewall screen. Close the Windows Firewall screen.

Let's now take a look at elevating privileges for executable applications.

Elevated Privileges for Executables

You can also enable an executable file to run with elevated privileges. To do so, on a one-time basis, you can right-click a shortcut or executable and select Run As Administrator.

But what if you need to configure an application to always run with elevated privileges for a user? To do so, log in as an administrator, right-click a shortcut or executable, and select Properties. On the Compatibility tab, check the Run This Program As An Administrator check box. If the Run This Program As An Administrator check box is unavailable, the program is blocked from permanently running as an administrator, the program doesn't need administrative privileges, or you are not logged on as an administrator.

Many applications that are installed on a Windows 7 machine need to have access to the Registry. Windows 7 protects the Registry from non-administrator accounts. Let's take a look at how this works.

Registry and File Virtualization

Windows 7 uses a feature called Registry and File Virtualization to enable non-administrator users to run applications that previously required administrative privileges to run correctly. As discussed earlier, some applications write to the Registry and to protected folders, such as `C:\Windows` and `C:\Program Files`. For non-administrator users, Windows 7 redirects any attempts to write to protected locations to a per-user location. By doing so, Windows 7 enables users to use the application successfully while it protects critical areas of the system.

Next we will look at other areas of security.

Using Advanced Security Options

In the following sections, we will look at some of the advanced security options that you can configure to protect a Windows 7 machine. We will take a look at the Action Center, shown in Figure 6.18.

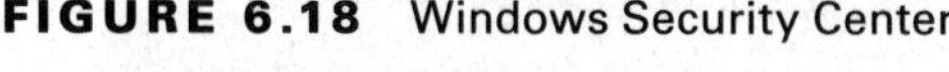

FIGURE 6.18 Windows Security Center

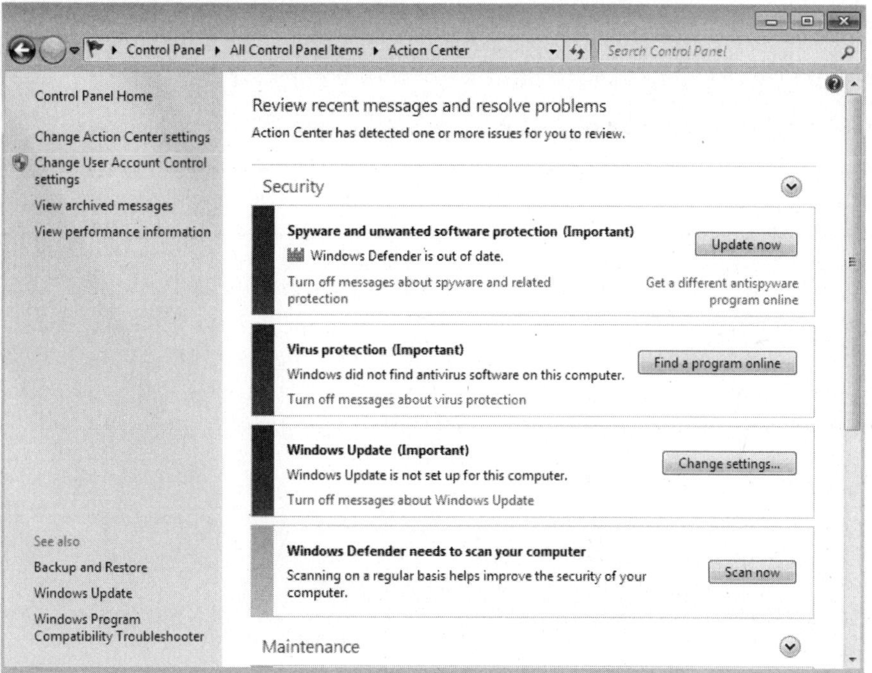

The Action Center is designed to allow you to monitor and configure critical settings through a centralized dialog box. Critical settings include those for automatic updating, malware protection, and other security settings. Malware protection includes virus protection and spyware protection (included through Windows Defender).

Let's start by taking a look at how to configure the Action Center.

Configuring the Action Center

These days, having a firewall just isn't enough. Spyware and viruses are becoming more widespread, more sophisticated, and more dangerous. Users can unintentionally pick up spyware and viruses by visiting websites or by installing an application in which spyware and viruses are bundled.

Even worse, malicious software cannot typically be uninstalled. Thus, antispyware and virus protection applications are also required to ensure that your computer remains protected. Let's take a look at some of the different ways that you can protect your Windows 7 computers using the Action Center.

Using Windows Defender

Windows 7 comes with an antispyware application called *Windows Defender*, formerly known as Microsoft AntiSpyware. Windows Defender offers real-time protection from spyware and other unwanted software. You can also configure Windows Defender to scan for spyware on a regular basis.

Like antivirus programs, Windows Defender relies on definitions, which are used to determine whether a file contains spyware. Out-of-date definitions can cause Windows Defender to not detect some spyware. Windows Update is used to regularly update the definitions used by Windows Defender so that the latest spyware can be detected. You can also configure Windows Defender to manually check for updates using Windows Update.

To access Windows Defender (see Figure 6.19), click Start ➤ Control Panel ➤ Large Icons View ➤ Windows Defender. The status appears at the bottom of the screen and includes time of the last scan, the scan schedule, the real-time protection status, and the definition version.

FIGURE 6.19 Windows Defender

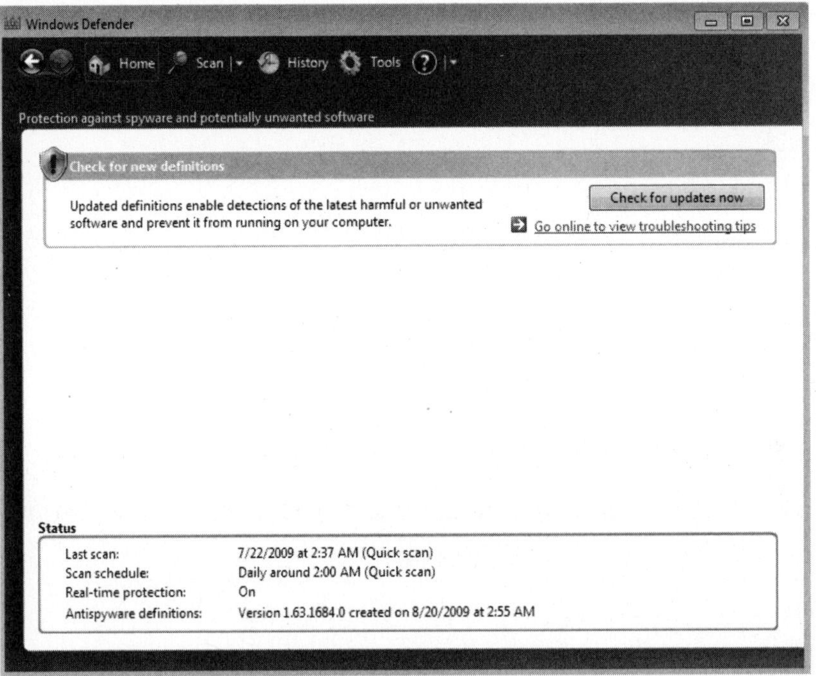

Let's take a look at how you can scan the system for spyware using Windows Defender.

Performing a Manual Scan

You can configure Windows Defender to perform a manual scan of your computer at any time. There are three different types of scans that can be performed:

- Quick Scan checks only where spyware is most likely to be found.
- Full Scan checks all memory, running processes, and folders.
- Custom Scan checks only the drives and folders that you select.

By default, Windows Defender performs a Quick Scan every morning at 2:00 a.m. You can change this setting by using the Tools menu option as shown in Figure 6.20.

FIGURE 6.20 The Options page in Windows Defender

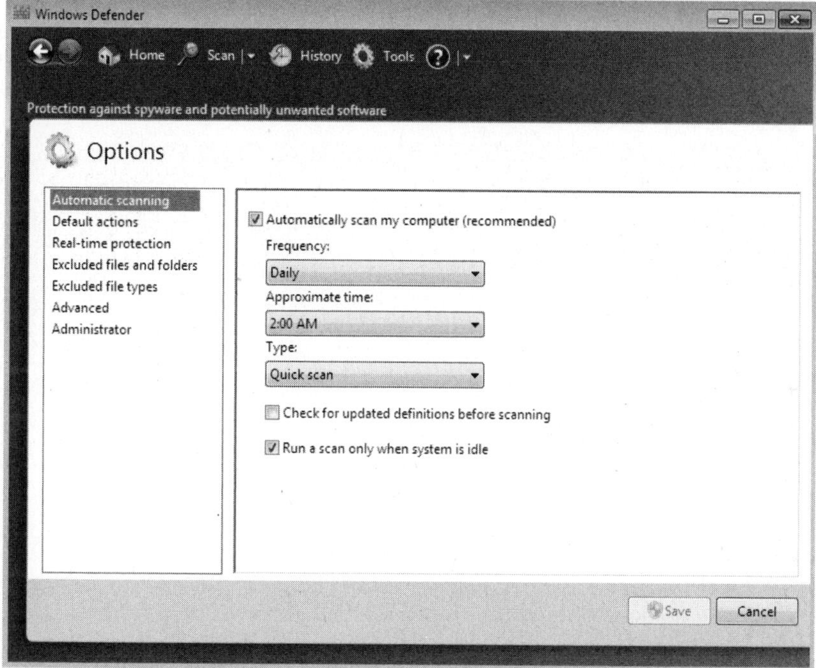

Programs are classified into four spyware alert levels (see Figure 6.21):

- Severe
- High
- Medium
- Low

FIGURE 6.21 Spyware alert levels

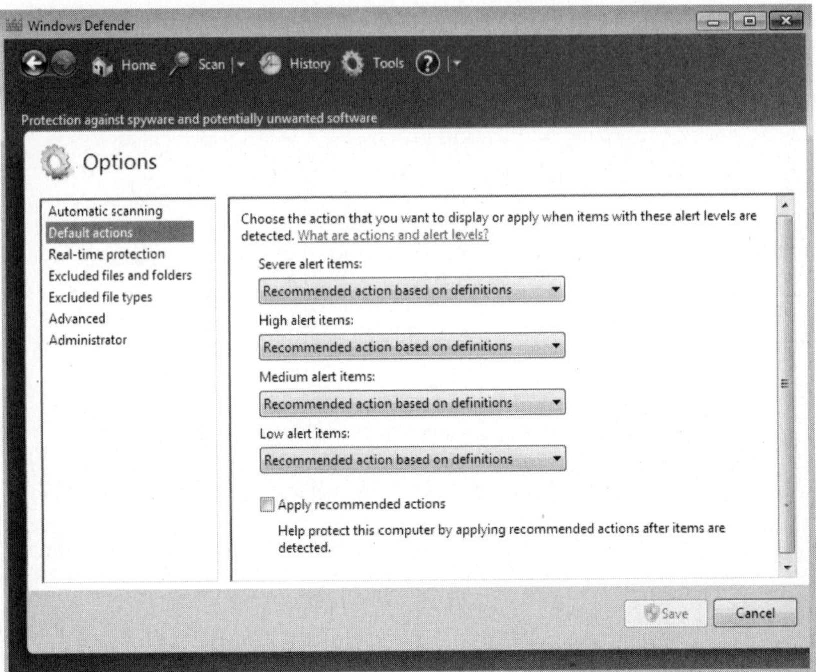

Depending on the alert level, you can choose to have Windows Defender ignore, quarantine, remove, or always allow software.

In the next section we will look at how to configure the many different options of Windows Defender.

Configuring Windows Defender

The Tools menu is used to configure Windows Defender. As shown in Figure 6.22, the following items can be accessed through the Tools menu:

- Options
- Microsoft SpyNet
- Quarantined Items
- Allowed Items
- Windows Defender Website
- Microsoft Malware Protection Center

FIGURE 6.22 Windows Defender Tools And Settings page

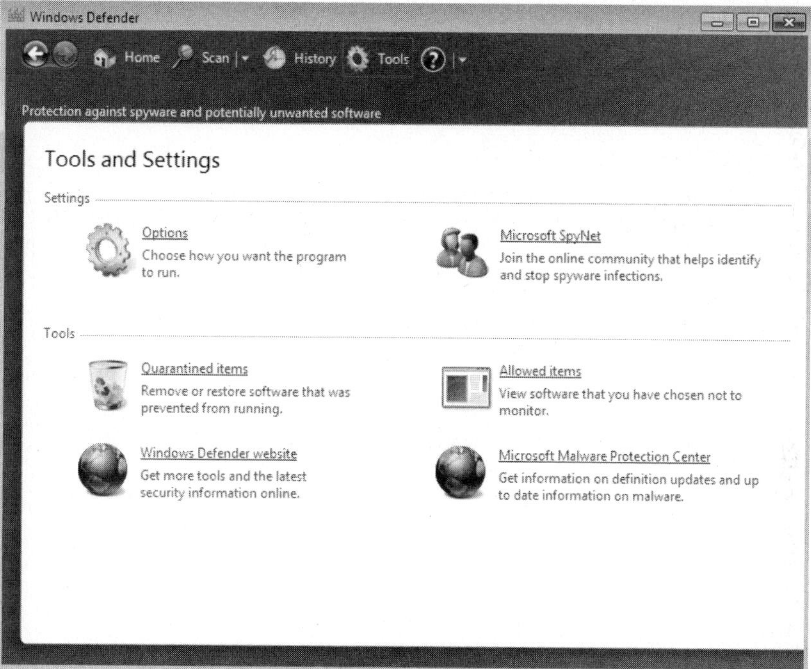

Let's take a look at each one of these Windows Defender Tools options in greater detail.

Options

Clicking Options on the Tools menu will enable you to configure the default behavior of Windows Defender. You can configure the following options:

- Automatic Scanning configures Windows Defender to automatically scan your computer. You can also configure how often automatic scans should occur, the time that scans will occur, the type of scan to perform, whether definitions should be updated before scanning, and whether the default actions should be taken on any spyware that is found.
- Default Actions configures the actions Windows Defender should take on high, medium, and low alert items. You can configure each level so that Windows Defender can take the default action for that level, always remove the item, or always ignore the item.
- Real-Time Protection configures whether real-time protection is enabled, which security agents you want to run, how you should be notified about threats, and whether a Windows Defender icon is displayed in the notification area.
- Excluded Files And Folders allows you to set up files and folders that are to be excluded during a scan.

- Excluded File Types lets you configure certain file types that will be excluded from a scan, as shown in Figure 6.23. For example, you can exclude all files with the `.doc` filenname extension if needed.

FIGURE 6.23 Excluded File Types

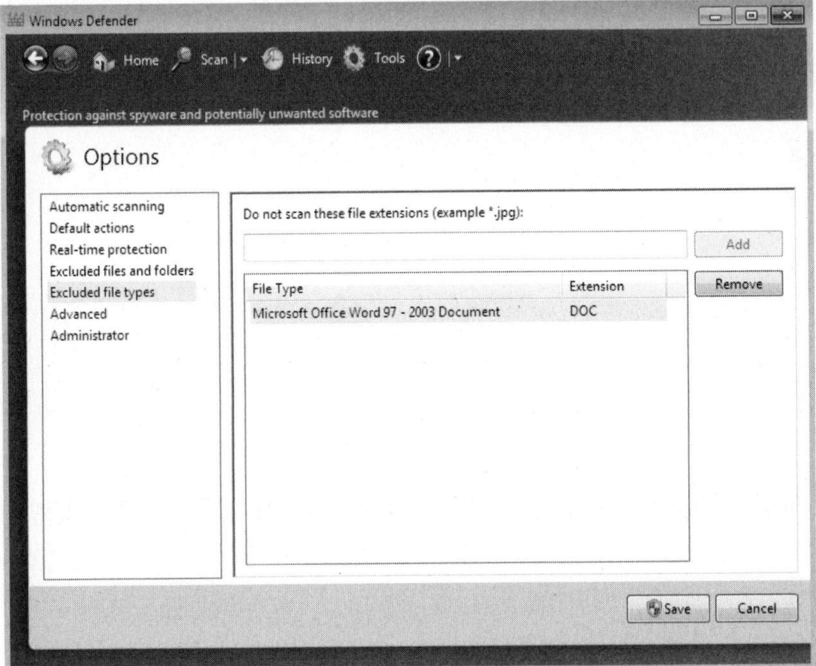

- The options on the Advanced page configure whether archived files and folders are scanned, whether email is scanned, whether removable drives are scanned, whether heuristics are used to detect unanalyzed software, whether a restore point is created before removing spyware, and which file locations are exempt from scanning.
- The options on the Administrator page configure whether Windows Defender is enabled and whether you display items from all users on this computer.

The next option that we will look at from the Windows Defenders Tools is Microsoft SpyNet.

Microsoft SpyNet

Microsoft SpyNet is an online community that can help you find out how others respond to software that has not yet been classified by Microsoft. Participation in SpyNet is voluntary (see Figure 6.24), and a subscription is free. If you choose to participate, your observations will be added to the community so that others can learn from your experiences.

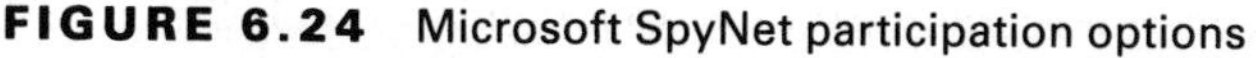

FIGURE 6.24 Microsoft SpyNet participation options

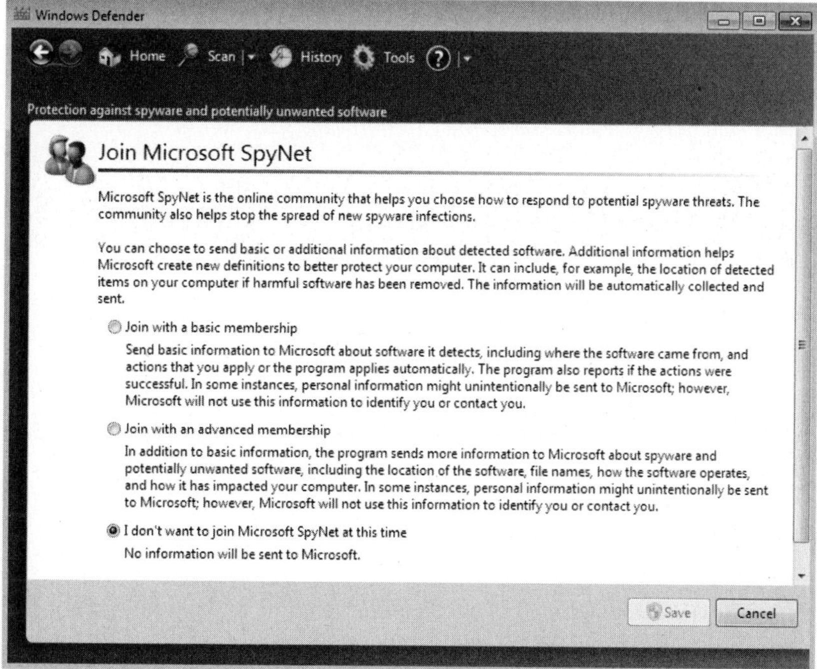

To join the SpyNet community, click Microsoft SpyNet on the Tools menu, then choose either a basic or advanced membership. The level of membership will specify how much information is sent to Microsoft when potentially unwanted software is found on your computer.

By default, I Do Not Want To Join Microsoft SpyNet at this time is selected, but you can choose to participate in SpyNet by selecting the appropriate radio button. If you choose not to participate, no information will be sent to Microsoft and Windows Defender will not alert you regarding unanalyzed software.

Quarantined Items

Software that has been quarantined by Windows Defender is placed in Quarantined Items. Quarantined software will remain here until you remove it. If you find that a legitimate application is accidentally removed by Windows Defender, you can restore the application from Quarantined Items.

Allowed Items

Software that has been marked as allowed will be added to the Allowed Items list. Only trusted software should be added to this list. Windows Defender will not alert you regarding any software found on the Allowed Items list. If you find that a potentially dangerous application has been added to theAllowed Items list, you can remove it from the list so that Windows Defender can detect it.

Windows Defender Website

Clicking Windows Defender Website will open up Internet Explorer and take you to the Windows Defender website. Here, you can find information on Windows Defender, spyware, and security.

Microsoft Malware Protection Center

Clicking Microsoft Malware Protection Center will open up Internet Explorer and take you to the Malware Protection Center website. Here, you can find information on anti-malware research and responses.

History Menu Option

There is also a History menu option next to the tools option. The History menu option is used to see what actions have been taken by Windows Defender. Information is included about each application, the alert level, the action taken, the date, and the status. Information will be retained until you click the Clear History button.

Windows firewalls will be covered in detail in Chapter 7, "Configuring Network Connectivity."

In the next section, we will look at using Windows BitLocker Drive Encryption and how it can help you protect your hard drive.

Using BitLocker Drive Encryption

To prevent individuals from stealing your computer and viewing personal and sensitive data found on your hard disk, some editions of Windows 7 come with a new feature called *BitLocker Drive Encryption*. BitLocker encrypts the entire system drive. New files added to this drive are encrypted automatically, and files moved from this drive to another drive or computer are decrypted automatically.

Only Windows 7 Enterprise and Ultimate include BitLocker Drive Encryption and only the operating system drive (usually C:) or internal hard drives can be encrypted with BitLocker. Files on other types of drives must be encrypted using BitLocker To Go.

BitLocker uses a Trusted Platform Module (TPM) version 1.2 or higher to store the security key. A TPM is a chip that is found in newer computers. If you do not have a computer with a TPM, you can store the key on a removable USB drive. The USB drive will be required each time you start the computer so that the system drive can be decrypted.

If the TPM discovers a potential security risk, such as a disk error or changes made to BIOS, hardware, system files, or startup components, the system drive will not be unlocked until you enter the 48-digit BitLocker recovery password or use a USB drive with a recovery key as a recovery agent.

The BitLocker recovery password is very important. Do not lose it, or you may not be able to unlock the drive. Even if you do not have a TPM, be sure to keep your recovery password in case your USB drive becomes lost or corrupted.

BitLocker must be set up within either the Local Group Policy editor or through the BitLocker icon in Control Panel. One advantage of using BitLocker is that you can prevent any unencrypted data from being copied onto a removable disk, thus protecting a Windows 7 machine.

BitLocker requires that you have a hard disk with at least two partitions, both formatted with NTFS. One partition will be the system partition that will be encrypted. The other partition will be the active partition that is used to start the computer; this partition will remain unencrypted.

In the next section, we will look at two of the most important security features available: proper permissions and file- and folder-level security.

Managing File and Folder Security

Setting up proper file and folder security is one of the most important tasks that an IT professional can perform. If permissions and security are not properly configured, users will be able to access resources that they shouldn't.

File and folder security defines what access a user has to local resources. You can limit access by applying security for files and folders. You should know what NTFS security permissions are and how they are applied.

A powerful feature of networking is the ability to allow network access to local folders. In Windows 7, it is very easy to share folders. You can also apply security to shared folders in a manner that is similar to applying NTFS permissions. Once you share a folder, users with appropriate access rights can access the folders through a variety of methods.

Before diving into the security section of folders, let's first take a look at some folder options.

Folder Options

The Windows 7 Folder Options dialog box allows you to configure many properties associated with files and folders, such as what you see when you access folders and how Windows searches through files and folders. To open the Folder Options dialog box, click Start ➤ Computer, then select Folder And Search Options under the Organize drop-down list. You can also access Folder Options through its icon by choosing Control Panel ➤ Large Icons View ➤ Folder Options. The Folder Options dialog box has three tabs: General, View, and Search. The options on each of these tabs are described in the following sections.

Folder General Options

The General tab of the Folder Options dialog box, shown in Figure 6.25, includes the following options:

- Whether folders are opened all in the same window when a user is browsing folders or each folder is opened in a separate window
- Whether a user opens items with a single mouse click or a double-click
- Whether to have the navigation pane show all folders and automatically expand to the current folder

FIGURE 6.25 The General tab of the Folder Options dialog box

Folder View Options

The options on the View tab of the Folder Options dialog box, shown in Figure 6.26, are used to configure what users see when they open files and folders. For example, you can change the default setting so that hidden files and folders are displayed. Table 6.10 describes the View tab options.

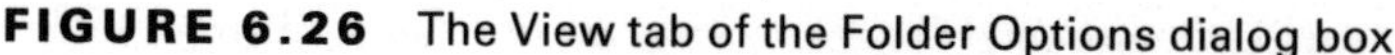

FIGURE 6.26 The View tab of the Folder Options dialog box

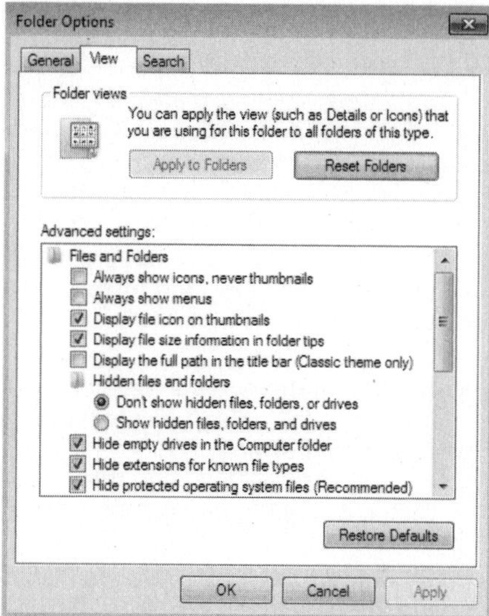

TABLE 6.10 Folder view options

Option	Description	Default Value
Always Show Icons, Never Thumbnails	Shows icons for files instead of thumbnail previews.	Not selected
Always Show Menus	Shows the File, Edit, View, Tools, and Help menus when you're browsing for files.	Not selected
Display File Icon On Thumbnails	Displays the file icon on thumbnails.	Enabled
Display File Size Information In Folder Tips	Specifies whether the file size is automatically displayed when you hover your mouse over a folder.	Enabled
Display the Full Path In The Title Bar (Classic Theme Only)	Specifies whether the title bar shows an abbreviated path of your location. Enabling this option displays the full path, such as `C:\Word Documents\Sybex\Windows 7 Book\Chapter 9`, as opposed to showing an abbreviated path such as `Chapter 6`.	Not selected

TABLE 6.10 Folder view options *(continued)*

Option	Description	Default Value
Hidden Files And Folders	Specifies whether files and folders with the Hidden attribute are listed. Choosing Show Hidden Files, Folders, Or Drives displays these items.	Don't Show Hidden Files, Folders, And Drives
Hide Empty Drives In The Computer Folder	This option will prevent drives that are empty in the Computer folder from being displayed.	Enabled
Hide Extensions For Known File Types	By default, filename extensions, which identify known file types (such as `.doc` for Word files and `.xls` for Excel files) are not shown. Disabling this option displays all filename extensions.	Enabled
Hide Protected Operating System Files (Recommended)	By default, operating system files are not shown, which protects operating system files from being modified or deleted by a user. Disabling this option displays the operating system files.	Enabled
Launch Folder Windows In A Separate Process	By default, when you open a folder, it shares memory with the previous folders that were opened. Enabling this option opens folders in separate parts of memory, which increases the stability of Windows 7 but can slightly decrease the performance of the computer.	Not selected
Show Drive Letters	Specifies whether drive letters are shown in the Computer folder. When disabled, only the name of the disk or device will be shown.	Enabled
Show Encrypted Or Compressed NTFS Files In Color	Displays encrypted or compressed files in an alternate color when they are displayed in a folder window.	Enabled
Show Pop-Up Description For Folder And Desktop Items	Displays whether a pop-up tooltip is displayed when you hover your mouse over files and folders.	Enabled
Show Preview Handlers In Preview Pane	Shows the contents of files in the preview pane.	Enabled

Option	Description	Default Value
Use Check Boxes To Select Items	Adds a check box next to each file and folder so that one or more of them may be selected. Actions can then be performed on selected items.	Not selected
Use Sharing Wizard (Recommended)	This option allows you to share a folder using a simplified sharing method.	Enabled
When Typing Into List View	Selects whether text is automatically typed into the search box or whether the typed item is selected in the view.	Select The Typed Item In The View

Search Options

The Search tab of the Folder Options dialog box, shown in Figure 6.27, is used to configure how Windows 7 searches for files. You can choose for Windows 7 to search by filename only, by filenames and contents, or by a combination of the two, depending on whether indexing is enabled. You can also select from the following options:

- Include subfolders
- Find partial matches
- Use natural language searches
- Don't use the index when searching the file system
- Include system directories in non-indexed locations
- Include compressed files in non-indexed locations

FIGURE 6.27 The Search tab of the Folder Options dialog box

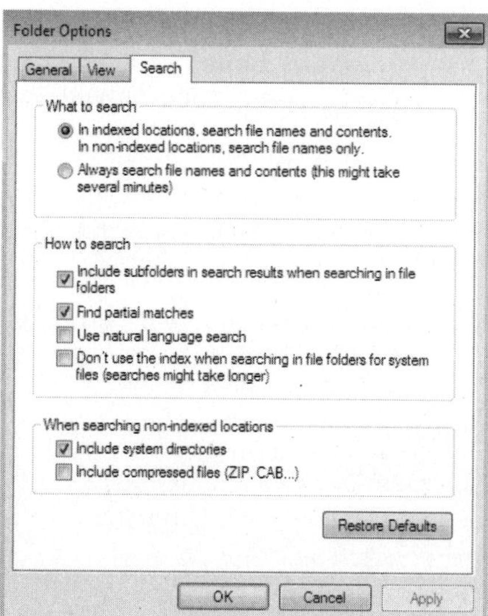

To search for files and folders, click Start ➢ Search and type your query in the search box. In the next section, we will look at how to secure these folders and files.

Securing Access to Files and Folders

On NTFS partitions, you can specify the access each user has to specific folders or files on the partition based on the user's logon name and group associations. Access control consists of rights and permissions. A right (also referred to as a privilege) is an authorization to perform a specific action.

Permissions are authorizations to perform specific operations on specific objects. The owner of an object or any user who has the necessary rights to modify permissions can apply permissions to NTFS objects. If permissions are not explicitly granted within NTFS, then they are implicitly denied. Permissions can also be explicitly denied, which then overrides explicitly granted permissions.

The following sections describe design goals for access control as well as how to apply NTFS permissions and some techniques for optimizing local access. Let's take a look at design goals for setting up security.

Design Goals for Access Control

Before you start applying NTFS permissions to resources, you should develop design goals for access control as a part of your overall security strategy. Basic security strategy suggests that you provide each user and group with the minimum level of permissions needed for job functionality. Some of the considerations when planning access control include the following:

- Defining the resources that are included within your network—in this case, the files and folders residing on the file system
- Defining which resources will put your organization at risk, including defining the resources and defining the risk of damage if the resource was compromised
- Developing security strategies that address possible threats and minimize security risks
- Defining groups that security can be applied to based on users within the group membership who have common access requirements, and applying permissions to groups as opposed to users
- Applying additional security settings through Group Policy if your Windows 7 clients are part of an Active Directory network
- Using additional security features, such as Encrypted File System (EFS), to provide additional levels of security or file auditing to track access to critical files and folders

After you have decided what your design goals are, you can start applying your NTFS permissions.

Applying NTFS Permissions

NTFS permissions control access to NTFS files and folders. This is based on the technology that was originally developed for Windows NT. Ultimately, the person who owns an object has complete control over the object. You configure access by allowing or denying NTFS permissions to users and groups.

Normally, NTFS permissions are cumulative, based on group memberships if the user has been allowed access. This means that the user gets the highest level of security from all the different groups they belong to. However, if the user had been denied access through user or group membership, those permissions override the allowed permissions. Windows 7 offers seven levels of NTFS permissions plus special permissions:

Full Control This permission allows the following rights:

- Traverse folders and execute files (programs) in the folders. The ability to traverse folders allows you to access files and folders in lower subdirectories, even if you do not have permissions to access specific portions of the directory path.
- List the contents of a folder and read the data in a folder's files.
- See a folder's or file's attributes.
- Change a folder's or file's attributes.
- Create new files and write data to the files.
- Create new folders and append data to the files.
- Delete subfolders and files.
- Delete files.
- Compress files.
- Change permissions for files and folders.
- Take ownership of files and folders.

If you select the Full Control permission, all permissions will be checked by default and can't be unchecked.

Modify This permission allows the following rights:

- Traverse folders and execute files in the folders.
- List the contents of a folder and read the data in a folder's files.
- See a file's or folder's attributes.
- Change a file's or folder's attributes.
- Create new files and write data to the files.
- Create new folders and append data to the files.
- Delete files.

If you select the Modify permission, the Read & Execute, List Folder Contents, Read, and Write permissions will be checked by default and can't be unchecked.

Read & Execute This permission allows the following rights:

- Traverse folders and execute files in the folders.
- List the contents of a folder and read the data in a folder's files.
- See a file's or folder's attributes.

If you select the Read & Execute permission, the List Folder Contents and Read permissions will be checked by default and can't be unchecked.

List Folder Contents This permission allows the following rights:

- Traverse folders.
- List the contents of a folder.
- See a file's or folder's attributes.

Read This permission allows the following rights:

- List the contents of a folder and read the data in a folder's files.
- See a file's or folder's attributes.
- View ownership.

Write This permission allows the following rights:

- Overwrite a file.
- View file ownership and permissions.
- Change a file's or folder's attributes.
- Create new files and write data to the files.
- Create new folders and append data to the files.

Special Permissions This allows you to configure any permissions beyond the normal permissions, like auditing, and take ownership.

Any user with Full Control access can manage the security of a folder. However, to access folders, a user must have physical access to the computer as well as a valid logon name and password. By default, regular users can't access folders over the network unless the folders have been shared. Sharing folders is covered in the section "Creating Shared Folders" later in this chapter.

To apply NTFS permissions, right-click the file or folder to which you want to control access, select Properties from the context menu, then select the Security tab. The Security tab lists the users and groups that have been assigned permissions to the file or folder. When you click a user or group in the top half of the dialog box, you see the permissions that have been allowed or denied for that user or group in the bottom half.

Complete Exercise 6.20 to manage NTFS security.

EXERCISE 6.20

Managing NTFS Security

1. Right-click the file or folder to which you want to control access, select Properties from the context menu, and click the Security tab.
2. Click the Edit button to modify permissions.

3. Click the Add button to open the Select Users Or Groups dialog box. You can select users from the computer's local database or from the domain you are in (or trusted domains) by typing in the user or group name in the Enter The Object Names To Select portion of the dialog box and clicking OK.

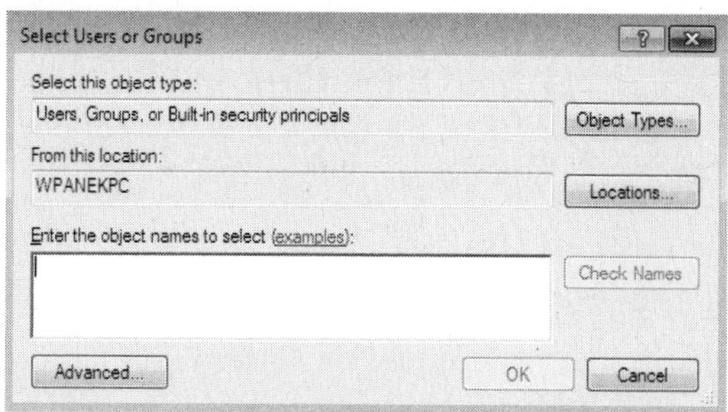

4. You return to the Security tab of the folder Properties dialog box. Highlight a user or group in the top list box, and in the Permissions list, specify the NTFS permissions to be allowed or denied. When you have finished, click OK.

Through the Advanced button of the Security tab, you can configure more granular NTFS permissions, such as Traverse Folder and Read Attributes permissions.

To remove the NTFS permissions for a user, computer, or group, highlight that entity in the Security tab and click the Remove button. Be careful when you remove NTFS permissions. You won't be asked to confirm their removal as you are when deleting most other types of items in Windows 7.

Controlling Permission Inheritance

Normally, the directory structure is organized in a hierarchical manner. This means you are likely to have subfolders in the folders to which you apply permissions. In Windows 7, by default, the parent folder's permissions are applied to any files or subfolders in that folder as well as any subsequently created objects. These are called inherited permissions.

You can specify how permissions are inherited by subfolders and files by clicking the Advanced button on the Security tab of a folder's Properties dialog box. This calls up the Permissions tab of the Advanced Security Settings dialog box. To edit these options, click the Change Permissions button. You can edit the following options:

- Include inheritable permissions from this object's parent
- Replace all existing inheritable permissions on all descendants with inheritable permissions from this object

If an Allow or a Deny check box in the Permissions list on the Security tab has a shaded check mark, this indicates that the permission was inherited from an upper-level folder.

If the check mark is not shaded, it means the permission was applied at the selected folder. This is known as an explicitly assigned permission. Knowing which permissions are inherited and which are explicitly assigned is useful when you need to troubleshoot permissions.

Understanding Ownership and Security Descriptors

When an object is initially created on an NTFS partition, an associated security descriptor is created. A security descriptor contains the following information:

- The user or group that owns the object
- The users and groups that are allowed or denied access to the object
- The users and groups whose access to the object will be audited

After an object is created, the Creator Owner of the object has full permissions to change the information in the security descriptor, even for members of the Administrators group. You can view the owner of an object from the Security tab of the specified folder's Properties by clicking the Advanced button. Then click the Owner tab to see who the owner of the object is. From this dialog box you can change the owner of the object.

Although the owner of an object can set the permissions of an object so that the administrator can't access the object, the administrator or any member of the Administrators group can take ownership of an object and thus manage the object's permissions. When you take ownership of an object, you can specify whether you want to replace the owner on subdirectories and objects of the object. If you would like to see who owns a directory from the command prompt, type **`dir /q`**.

In the next section, we will discuss how to determine the effective permissions of a file or folder.

Determining Effective Permissions

To determine a user's effective rights (the rights the user actually has to a file or folder), add all of the permissions that have been allowed through the user's assignments based on that user's username and group associations. After you determine what the user is allowed, you subtract any permissions that have been denied the user through the username or group associations.

As an example, suppose that user Marilyn is a member of both the Accounting and Execs groups. The following assignments have been made to the Accounting group permissions:

Permission	Allow	Deny
Full Control		
Modify	X	
Read & Execute	X	

Permission	Allow	Deny
List Folder Contents		
Read		
Write		

The following assignments have been made to the Execs group permissions:

Permission	Allow	Deny
Full Control		
Modify		
Read & Execute		
List Folder Contents		
Read	X	
Write		

To determine Marilyn's effective rights, you combine the permissions that have been assigned. The result is that Marilyn's effective rights are Modify, Read & Execute, and Read, so she basically has Modify (the highest right).

As another example, suppose that user Dan is a member of both the Sales and Temps groups. The following assignments have been made to the Sales group permissions:

Permission	Allow	Deny
Full Control		
Modify	X	
Read & Execute	X	
List Folder Contents	X	
Read	X	
Write	X	

The following assignments have been made to the Temps group permissions:

Permission	Allow	Deny
Full Control		
Modify		X
Read & Execute		
List Folder Contents		
Read		
Write		X

To determine Dan's effective rights, you start by seeing what Dan has been allowed: Modify, Read & Execute, List Folder Contents, Read, and Write permissions. You then remove anything that he is denied: Modify and Write permissions. In this case, Dan's effective rights are Read & Execute, List Folder Contents, and Read. Now let's take a look at how to see what rights users have.

Viewing Effective Permissions

If permissions have been applied at the user and group levels and inheritance is involved, it can sometimes be confusing to determine what the effective permissions are. To help identify which effective permissions will actually be applied, you can view them from the Effective Permissions tab of Advanced Security Settings, or you can use the ICACLS command-line utility.

To see what the effective permissions are for a user or group, you click the Select button and then type in the user or group name. Then click OK. If a box is checked and not shaded, then explicit permissions have been applied at that level. If the box is shaded, then the permissions to that object were inherited.

The ICACLS command-line utility can also be used to display or modify user access rights. The options associated with the ICACLS command are as follows:

- `/grant` grants permissions.
- `/remove` revokes permissions.
- `/deny` denies permissions.
- `/setintegritylevel` sets an integrity level of Low, Medium, or High.

One issue that IT people run into is what happens to the security when you move or copy a file or folder. Let's take a look at NTFS permissions when moved or copied.

Determining NTFS Permissions for Copied or Moved Files

When you copy or move NTFS files, the permissions that have been set for those files might change. The following guidelines can be used to predict what will happen:

- If you move a file from one folder to another folder on the same volume, the file will retain the original NTFS permissions.
- If you move a file from one folder to another folder between different NTFS volumes, the file is treated as a copy and will have the same permissions as the destination folder.
- If you copy a file from one folder to another folder on the same volume or on a different volume, the file will have the same permissions as the destination folder.
- If you copy or move a file or folder to a FAT partition, it will not retain any NTFS permissions.

Now that you have seen how to deal with the NTFS security, you need to understand shared permissions. In the next section, we will look at sharing resources.

Managing Network Access

In every network, there are resources to which the users need to gain access. As IT professionals, we share these resources so that our users can do their jobs.

Sharing is the process of allowing network users access to a resource located on a computer. A network share provides a single location to manage shared data used by many users. Sharing also allows an administrator to install an application once, as opposed to installing it locally at each computer, and to manage the application from a single location.

The following sections describe how to create and manage shared folders, configure share permissions, and provide access to shared resources.

Creating Shared Folders

You can share a folder in two ways. To use the Sharing Wizard, right-click a folder and select Share. If the Sharing Wizard feature is enabled, you will see the File Sharing screen. Here, you can add local users.

However, you cannot use the Sharing Wizard to share resources with domain users. To share a folder with domain users, you should right-click the folder and select Properties, then select the Sharing tab, shown in Figure 6.28.

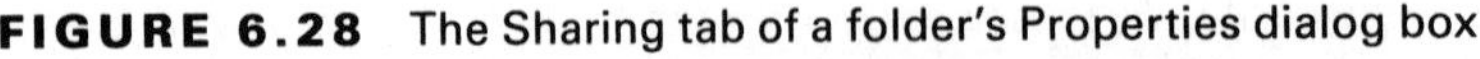

FIGURE 6.28 The Sharing tab of a folder's Properties dialog box

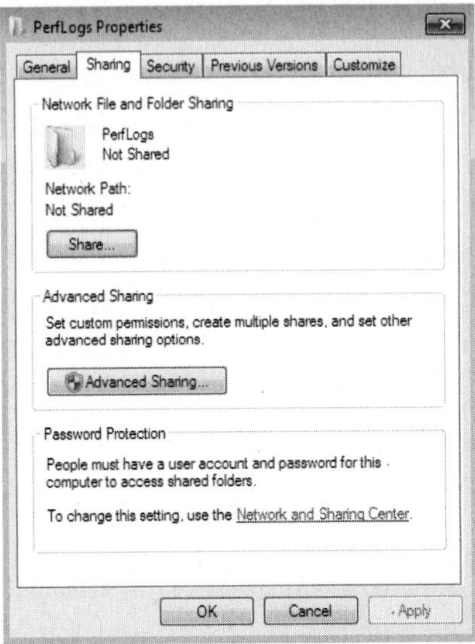

The Share button will take you to the Sharing Wizard. To configure Advanced Sharing, click the Advanced Sharing button, which will open up the Advanced Sharing dialog box. When you share a folder, you can configure the options listed in Table 6.11.

TABLE 6.11 Share folder options

Option	Description
Share This Folder	Makes the folder available through local access and network access
Share Name	A descriptive name by which users will access the folder
Comments	Additional descriptive information about the share (optional)
Limit The Number Of Simultaneous Users To	The maximum number of connections to the share at any one time (no more than 10 users can simultaneously access a share on a Windows 7 computer)
Permissions	How users will access the folder over the network
Caching	How folders are cached when the folder is offline

If you share a folder and then decide that you do not want to share it, just deselect the Share This Folder check box. You can easily tell that a folder has been shared by the group icon located at the bottom left of the folder icon. The following also holds true:

- Only folders, not files, can be shared.
- Share permissions can be applied only to folders and not to files.
- If a folder is shared over the network and a user is accessing it locally, then share permissions will not apply to the local user; only NTFS permissions will apply.
- If a shared folder is copied, the original folder will still be shared but not the copy.
- If a shared folder is moved, the folder will no longer be shared.
- If the shared folder will be accessed by a mixed environment of clients, including some that do not support long filenames, you should use the 8.3 naming format for files.
- Folders can be shared through the Net Share command-line utility.

Now let's take a look at configuring share permissions for your users.

Configuring Share Permissions

You can control users' access to shared folders by assigning share permissions. Share permissions are less complex than NTFS permissions and can be applied only to folders (unlike NTFS permissions, which can be applied to files and folders).

To assign share permissions, click the Permissions button in the Advanced Sharing dialog box. This brings up the Permissions dialog box, shown in Figure 6.29.

FIGURE 6.29 The Permissions dialog box

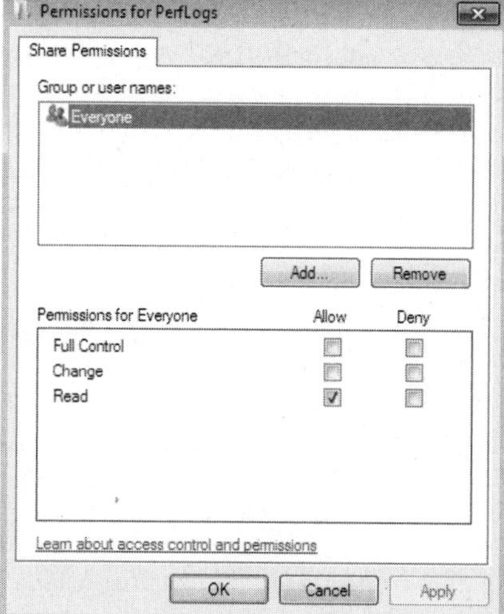

You can assign three types of share permissions:

Full Control Allows full access to the shared folder.

Change Allows users to change data within a file or to delete files.

Read Allows a user to view and execute files in the shared folder. Read is the default permission on shared folders for the Everyone group.

Shared folders do not use the same concept of inheritance as NTFS folders. If you share a folder, there is no way to block access to lower-level resources through share permissions.

When applying conflicting share and NTFS permissions, the most restrictive permissions apply. Remember that share and NTFS permissions are both applied only when a user is accessing a shared resource over a network. Only NTFS permissions apply to a user accessing a resource locally.

So, for example, if a user's NTFS security settings on a resource were Read and the share permission on the same resource was Full Control, the user would have Read permission only when they connect to that resource. The most restrictive set of permissions wins.

Summary

In this chapter, we started with how to create and manage user and group accounts. We looked at the different tools that can be used to create users in Windows 7.

We also looked at Windows 7 security. I showed you the difference between LGPOs, which are applied at the local level, and GPOs, which are applied through a Windows 2000, 2003, or Windows 2008 domain, and how they are applied.

We looked at account policies, which control the logon process. The two types of account policies are password and account lockout policies. We also looked at local policies, which control what a user can do at the computer. The three types of local policies are audit, user rights, and security options policies.

We looked at some of the advanced security items like how to use the Group Policy Result Tool to analyze current configuration settings, how to use User Account Control, and how to use BitLocker Drive Encryption.

Finally, we looked at how to configure NTFS permissions and Share permissions.

Exam Essentials

Be able to create and manage user accounts. When creating user accounts, be aware of the requirements for doing so. Understand User Account Control. Know how to rename and delete user accounts. Be able to manage all user properties.

Know how to configure and manage local user authentication. Understand the options that can be configured to manage local user authentication and when these options would be used to create a more secure environment. Be able to specify where local user authentication options are configured.

Know how to manage local groups. Understand the local groups that are created on Windows 7 computers by default, and be familiar with the rights each group has. Know how to create and manage new groups.

Know how to set local group policies. Understand the purpose of account policies and local policies. Know the purpose and implementation of account policies for managing password policies and account lockout policies. Understand the purpose and implementation of local policies and how they can be applied to users and groups for audit policies, user rights assignments, and security options.

Understand User Account Control. Understand the purpose and features of User Account Control. Be familiar with Registry and file virtualization. Understand privilege escalation. Know the basics of the new UAC Group Policy settings.

Know how to use Windows Security Center. Be able to use Windows Security Center to monitor and configure the settings for Windows Firewall, Automatic Updating, Malware Protection, and Other Security Settings.

Know how to use Windows Defender. Be able to configure and use Windows Defender. Understand how Quarantine works. Know the purpose of Microsoft SpyNet.

Know how to use BitLocker Drive Encryption. Understand the purpose and requirements of BitLocker Drive Encryption. Know which editions of Windows 7 (Enterprise and Ultimate) include BitLocker.

Understand NTFS and share permissions. Be able to configure security permissions and know the difference between NTFS and share permissions.

Review Questions

1. You have a user that has access to the applications folder on your network server. This user belongs to the following groups:

NTFS	
Sales	Read only
Marketing	Full Control
Shared Permissions	
Sales	Read only
Marketing	Change

When this user logs into the applications folder from their Windows 7 machine, what are their effective permissions?

   A. Full Control
   B. Read only
   C. Change
   D. Read and Write

2. You are setting up a machine for a home user who does not know much about computers. You do not want to make the user a local administrator but you do want to give this user the right to change Windows Updates manually. How can you configure this?

   A. Modify the LGPO for Windows Update to allow the user to make changes manually.
   B. Explain to the user how to log on as the Administrator account.
   C. Set Windows Update modifications to anyone.
   D. This can't be done. Only administrators can change Windows Update.

3. You are the administrator for a large organization with multiple Windows Server 2008 domain controllers and multiple domains. You have a Windows 7 machine that is set up for all users to access. You have an application called `StellApp.exe` that everyone on this Windows 7 computer can use except for the sales group. How do you stop the sales group from accessing this one application?

   A. Deny the Everyone group the rights to the application.
   B. Create an executable rule from the Application Control Policy.
   C. Create a security role from the Application Control Policy.
   D. Give the Everyone group full control of the application.

4. You have a Windows 7 machine that multiple users access. All users have the rights to use USB removable devices but you need to deny one user from using USB removable devices. How do you accomplish this?

   A. Deny the one user from using the machine.

   B. Set a USB rule on Hardware Manager.

   C. Deny all users from using USB devices.

   D. Create a removable storage access policy through an LGPO.

5. You are the system administrator for a large organization. You have a Windows 7 machine that all users can access. There is a folder on the Windows 7 machine called Apps. You need to set up auditing on this folder. How do you accomplish this task?

   A. From the Local Group Policy, enable Directory Service Access.

   B. From the Local Group Policy, enable Audit Object Access.

   C. From the Local Group Policy, enable Account Access.

   D. From the Local Group Policy, enable File And Folder Access.

6. You have a user named Will who has access to the Finance folder on your network server. Will belongs to the following groups:

NTFS	
Admin	Full Control
Finance	Modify
Shared Permissions	
Admin	Full Control
Finance	Change

   When Will logs into the Finance folder from his Windows 7 machine, what are his effective permissions?

   A. Full Control

   B. Read only

   C. Change

   D. Read and Write

7. You are the network administrator for a large organization. You have a Windows 7 machine that needs to prevent any user from copying unencrypted files from the Windows 7 machine to any removable disk. How do you accomplish this task?

   A. Within the System icon in Control Panel, set the BitLocker Drive Encryption.

   B. Within the Hardware icon in Control Panel, set the BitLocker Drive Encryption.

   C. Within the Device Manager icon in Control Panel, set the BitLocker Drive Encryption.

   D. Within a Local Group Policy, set the BitLocker Drive Encryption.

8. In which editions of Windows 7 can you enable BitLocker? (Choose all that apply.)

   A. Windows 7 Home Edition

   B. Windows 7 Basic Edition

   C. Windows 7 Ultimate Edition

   D. Windows 7 Enterprise Edition

9. You organization has decided to install a Windows Server Update Service (WSUS). You have a Windows 7 machine that needs to have the updates done from the WSUS server instead of directly from Microsoft's website. How do you accomplish this?

   A. Modify the Local Group Policy for the Windows Update to receive updates from the WSUS server.

   B. Modify the Windows Update icon in Control Panel to receive updates from the WSUS server.

   C. Modify the System icon in Control Panel for the Windows Update to receive updates from the WSUS server.

   D. Modify the WSUS server to force this Windows 7 machine to receive updates from the WSUS server.

10. Your network's security has been breached. You are trying to redefine security so that a user cannot repeatedly attempt user logon with different passwords. To accomplish this, which of the following items (in the Local Security Settings dialog box shown here) should you define?

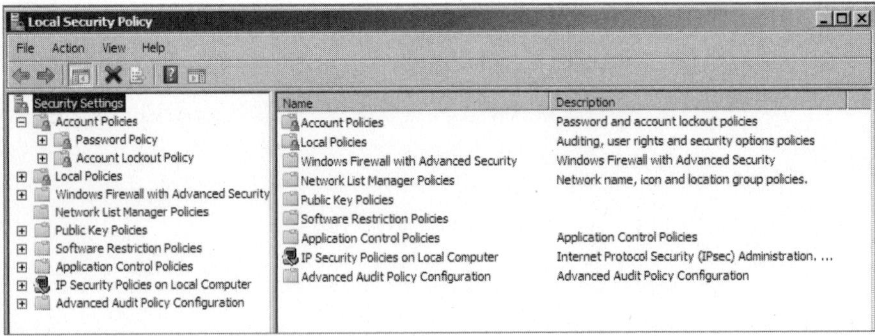

   A. Password Policy

   B. Account Lockout Policy

   C. Audit Policy

   D. Security Options

11. You are the network administrator for a Fortune 500 company. The accounting department has recently purchased a custom application for running financial models. To run properly, the application requires that you make some changes to the computer policy. You decide to deploy the changes through a Local Group Policy setting. You suspect that the policy is not being applied properly because of a conflict somewhere with another Local Group Policy setting. What command should you run to see a listing of how the group policies have been applied to the computer and the user?

    A. GPResult

    B. GPOResult

    C. GPAudit

    D. GPInfo

12. You have a Windows 7 computer that is located in an unsecured area. You want to track usage of the computer by recording user logon and logoff events. To do this, which of the following auditing policies must be enabled?

    A. Audit Account Logon Events

    B. Audit Account Management

    C. Audit Process Tracking

    D. Audit System Events

13. You are the administrator for a printing company. After you configure the Password Must Meet Complexity Requirements policy, several users have problems when changing their passwords. Which of the following passwords meet the minimum complexity requirements? (Choose all that apply.)

    A. aBc-1

    B. Abcde!

    C. 1247445Np

    D. !@#$%^&*(-[]

14. You are the system administrator for Stellacon Corp. You have a computer that is shared by many users. You want to ensure that when users press Ctrl+Alt+Del to log on, they do not see the name of the last user. What do you configure?

    A. Set the security option Clear User Settings When Users Log Off.

    B. Set the security option Interactive Logon: Do Not Display Last User Name In Logon Screen.

    C. Set the security option Prevent Users From Seeing Last User Name.

    D. Configure nothing; this is the default setting.

15. Mary has access to the R&D folder on your network server. Mary's user belongs to the following groups:

NTFS	
Sales	Read only
Marketing	Read only
Shared Permissions	
Sales	Read only
Marketing	Change

When Mary logs into the R&D folder from her Windows 7 machine, what are her effective permissions?

A. Full Control

B. Read only

C. Change

D. Read and Write

16. You have recently hired Will as an assistant for network administration. You have not decided how much responsibility you want Will to have. In the meantime, you want Will to be able to restore files on Windows 7 computers in your network, but you do not want Will to be able to run the backups. What is the minimum assignment that will allow Will to complete this task?

A. Add Will to the Administrators group.

B. Grant Will the Read right to the root of each volume he will back up.

C. Add Will to the Backup Operators group.

D. Grant Will the user right Restore Files And Directories.

17. You are the network administrator of a medium-sized company. Your company requires a fair degree of security and you have been tasked with defining and implementing a security policy. You have configured password policies so that users must change their passwords every 30 days. Which password policy would you implement if you want to prevent users from reusing passwords they have used recently?

A. Passwords Must Be Advanced

B. Enforce Password History

C. Passwords Must Be Unique

D. Passwords Must Meet Complexity Requirements

18. You have a network folder that resides on an NTFS partition on a Windows 7 computer. NTFS permissions and Share permissions have been applied. Which of the following statements best describes how Share permissions and NTFS permissions work together if they have been applied to the same folder?

A. The NTFS permissions will always take precedence.

B. The Share permissions will always take precedence.

C. The system will look at the cumulative Share permissions and the cumulative NTFS permissions. Whichever set is less restrictive will be applied.

D. The system will look at the cumulative Share permissions and the cumulative NTFS permissions. Whichever set is more restrictive will be applied.

19. You are the network administrator for a bookstore. You install Windows 7 on a new computer. Before you connect the computer to the Internet, you want to ensure that the appropriate features are enabled. You open Windows Security Center and notice that there are features that require addressing. Which of the following features are not included with Windows 7?

A. Firewall protection

B. Spyware protection

C. Virus protection

D. Automatic update protection

20. You are the Active Directory administrator for your company. A Windows 7 computer has been purchased for the finance department, and you want to monitor it for unauthorized access. You configure the Audit Object Access policy to audit both success and failure events. However, when you look at the security event log a few days later, you do not see any entries related to file access. What is the most likely reason for this behavior?

A. Auditing has not been enabled for the appropriate files and folders.

B. A conflicting Group Policy setting is overriding your configuration.

C. Another administrator has disabled your Group Policy setting.

D. Object access events are found in the system event log.

Answers to Review Questions

1. C. To figure out a user's rights, you must first add up what their effective NTFS rights are and their effective Shared permissions. Then the most restrictive set takes precedence. So in this example, the user's NTFS rights were Full Control and the Shared permissions were Change, so Change would be the effective permission.

2. A. You do not want this user to have any administrator rights. To allow this user to change Windows Update manually, you must set this in a LGPO.

3. B. Application Control Policy (AppLocker) allows you to configure a Denied list and an Accepted list for applications or users. Applications that are configured on the Denied list will not run on the system or by specific groups and applications on the Accepted list will operate properly.

4. D. LGPOs are policies that you can set on a local Windows 7 machine to limit hardware and user usage. You also have the ability to control individual users within the Local Group Policy.

5. B. Audit Object Access enables auditing of access to files, folders, and printers.

6. A. Will's NTFS rights were Full Control and the Shared permissions were Full Control, so Full Control would be the effective permission.

7. D. Windows 7 comes with a new feature called BitLocker Drive Encryption. BitLocker encrypts the entire system drive. New files added to this drive are encrypted automatically. To configure BitLocker, you must either use a Local Group Policy or use the BitLocker icon in Control Panel.

8. C, D. BitLocker Drive Encryption is a data protection feature available in Windows Enterprise and Ultimate editions of Windows 7.

9. A. Within Windows Update, you cannot specify a WSUS server. You need to specify the WSUS server through the use of a Local Group Policy.

10. B. Account Lockout Policy, a subset of Account Policy, is used to specify options that prevent a user from attempting multiple failed logon attempts. If the Account Lockout Threshold value is exceeded, the account will be locked. The account can be reset based on a specified amount of time or through administrator intervention.

11. A. The Group Policy Result Tool is accessed through the GPResult command-line utility. The `gpresult` command displays the resulting set of policies that were enforced on the computer and the specified user during the logon process.

12. A. Audit Account Logon Events is used to track when a user logs on, logs off, or makes a network connection. You can configure auditing for success or failure, and audited events can be tracked through Event Viewer.

13. B, C. The password Abcde! meets complexity requirements because it is at least six characters long and contains uppercase letters, lowercase letters, and symbols. The password 1247445Np meets complexity requirements because it is at least six characters long and contains uppercase letters, lowercase letters, and numbers. Complex passwords must be at least six characters long and contain three of the four types of characters—uppercase letters, lowercase letters, numbers, and symbols.

14. B. The security option Interactive Logon: Do Not Display Last User Name is used to prevent the last username in the logon screen from being displayed in the logon dialog box. This option is commonly used in environments where computers are used publicly.

15. B. Mary's NTFS rights were Read only and the Shared permissions were Change, so Read only would be the effective permission.

16. D. The Restore Files And Directories user right allows a user to restore files and directories regardless of file and directory permissions. Assigning this user right is an alternative to making a user a member of the Backup Operators group.

17. B. The Enforce Password History policy allows the system to keep track of a user's password history for up to 24 passwords. This prevents a user from using the same password over and over again.

18. D. When both NTFS and Share permissions have been applied, the system looks at the effective rights for NTFS and Share permissions and then applies the most restrictive of the cumulative permissions. If a resource has been shared, and you access it from the local computer where the resource resides, then you will be governed only by the NTFS permissions.

19. C. Virus protection is not included with Windows 7 and should be purchased separately. Windows Firewall, Windows Defender, and Windows Update are included with Windows 7.

20. A. The most likely reason there are no file access entries in the security event log is that you did not enable auditing for the appropriate files and folders. This behavior is true of print auditing as well.

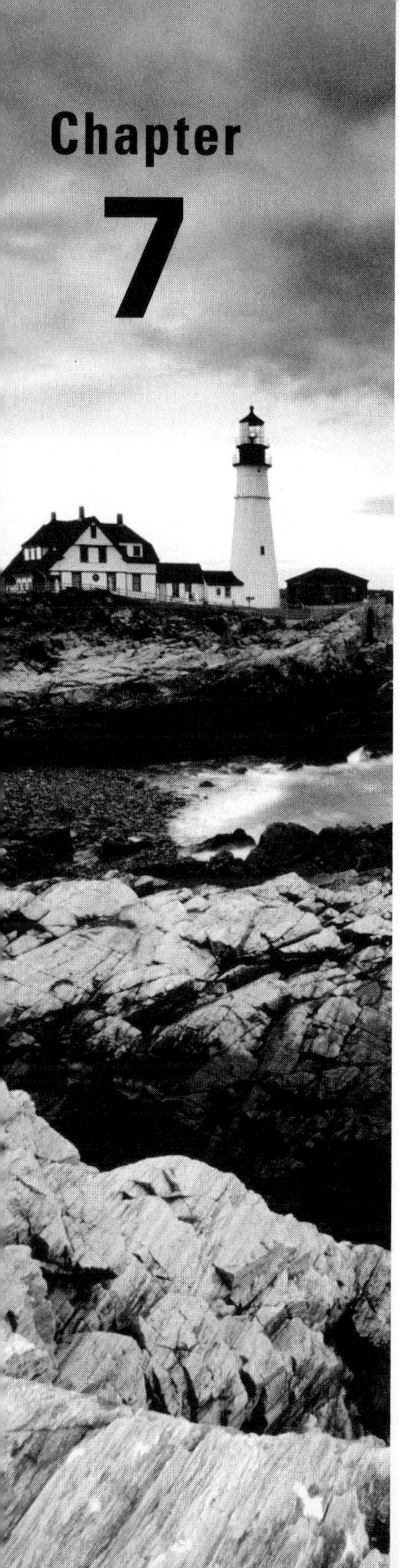

Configuring Network Connectivity

MICROSOFT EXAM OBJECTIVES COVERED IN THIS CHAPTER:

✓ **Configure IPv4 network settings.**

- This objective may include but is not limited to: connecting to a network; configuring name resolution; setting up a connection for a network; network locations; resolving connectivity issues; APIPA

✓ **Configure IPv6.**

- This objective may include but is not limited to: configuring name resolution; connecting to a network; setting up a network connection; network locations; resolving connectivity issues; link local multicast name resolution

✓ **Configure networking settings.**

- This objective may include but is not limited to: adding a physical connected (wired) or wireless device; connecting to a wireless network; configuring security settings on the client; setting preferred wireless networks; configuring network adapters; configuring location-aware printing

✓ **Configure Windows Firewall.**

- This objective may include but is not limited to: configuring rules for multiple profiles; allowing or denying an application; network-profile-specific rules; configuring notifications; configuring authentication exceptions

✓ **Configure remote management.**

- This objective may include but is not limited to: remote management methods; configuring remote management tools; executing PowerShell commands

- ✓ **Configure BranchCache.**
  - This objective may include but is not limited to: distributed cache mode vs. hosted mode; network infrastructure requirements; configuring settings; certificate management
- ✓ **Configure shared resources.**
  - This objective may include but is not limited to: configuring HomeGroup
- ✓ **Configure DirectAccess.**
  - This objective may include but is not limited to: configuring client side; configuring authentication; network infrastructure requirements
- ✓ **Configure a VHD.**
  - This objective may include but is not limited to: creating, deploying, booting, mounting, and updating VHDs; offline updates; offline servicing

In most organizations, Windows 7 will be a member of a domain. Therefore, it's very important to know how to properly configure Windows 7 in a domain environment.

In this chapter, we discuss Active Directory and how to configure Windows 7 to work within the Windows Server 2008 R2 domain environment. You will look at how to connect to a Windows Server 2008 domain by using both IPv4 and IPv6. You will also look at connecting Windows 7 to a network by using either a wireless or wired connection and working with the Windows 7 HomeGroup.

You will look at how to protect your network by using firewalls and also using the Windows 7 firewall. We discuss the different ways that you can manage your network and Windows 7 machines remotely.

Another technology that we present in this chapter is virtualization. This is one of the fastest growing and hottest technologies to hit the market in the past few years. Server virtualization gives an organization the ability to run multiple operating systems, called *virtual machines*, on a single machine. You will look at how to make Windows 7 run as a virtual machine.

Understanding Networking

The first thing we have to discuss is Microsoft's network model types. The way you design your network is going to determine how you set up the rest of the computers and servers on that network.

The choice you make here will be determined by many factors. The number of users on your network or the amount of money you can spend will help determine your network design.

Microsoft uses two networking models: domain-based networks and peer-to-peer networks. We will start our discussion with the peer-to-peer model.

Windows Peer-to-Peer Network

When setting up a Microsoft Windows *peer-to-peer network* (also referred to as a *workgroup network*), it is important to understand that all computers on the network are equal. All of the peer-to-peer computers, also referred to as *nodes*, simultaneously act as both clients and servers.

Peer-to-peer networks are no more than Microsoft Windows XP, Windows Vista, and Windows 7 machines connected by a centralized connection such as a router or hub (see Figure 7.1).

FIGURE 7.1 Peer-to-peer model

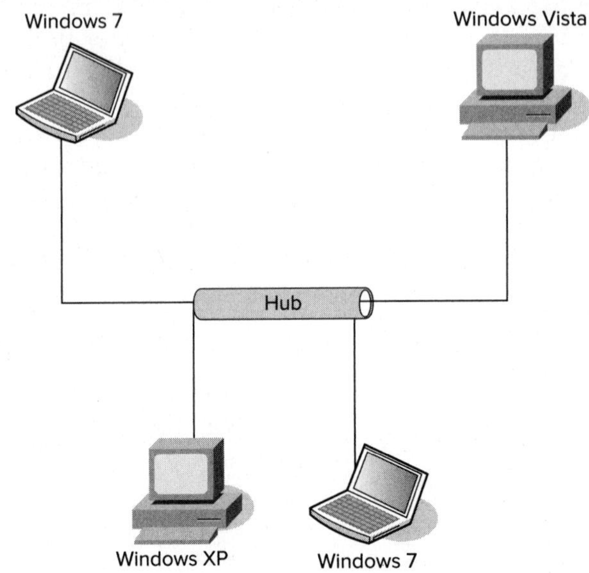

To learn more about Microsoft Windows 7 peer-to-peer networks, see *MCTS: Windows Server 2008 Network Infrastructure Configuration Study Guide* (Exam 70-642) by William Panek, Tylor Wentworth, and James Chellis (Sybex, 2008).

One of the biggest debates among IT professionals is when to use a peer-to-peer network. These types of networks have their place in the networking world. Most of you at home use this type of network. All computers connect by a small Internet router.

Well, it's the same for companies. You would use this network in a small environment with 10 users or fewer. This enables small organizations to still share resources without needing expensive equipment, server software, or an internal IT department.

But just like everything that is good, there is a downside to peer-to-peer networks. The biggest downside is manageability. Many new IT people like working on a small peer-to-peer network because of its size, but in fact a network with 10 users and 10 computers can be very difficult to manage. Because there is no server to centralize user accounts, each Microsoft Windows XP, Windows Vista, or Windows 7 computer must have a user account and password. So if you have 10 users with 10 computers, and all 10 users must be able to access all 10 computers, you end up creating 100 accounts (10 accounts on each machine times 10 machines).

Another disadvantage of peer-to-peer networks is backups. Most IT departments do not back up individual user machines, and because there is no centralized server for data storage, data recoverability can be an issue.

So now that you have seen the advantages and disadvantages of a peer-to-peer network, let's discuss the advantages and disadvantages of a domain-based network.

Windows Server 2008 Active Directory Network

A *domain-based network* is a network that uses Microsoft's Active Directory. *Active Directory* is a single distributed database that contains all the objects contained within your network. Some of these objects are user accounts, group accounts, and published objects (folders and printers).

The first of many advantages to Active Directory is centralized management. As we just stated, the Active Directory database contains all the network information within a single, distributed, data repository. Due to the fact that these objects are all located in the same database, an administrator can easily manage the domain from one location.

Another major advantage to using Active Directory is domain security. An administrator has the advantage of creating a single username and password for all users within the domain. This password can be used to access all resources that an individual has the proper rights to access. An administrator can determine, based on job function or position, which files or folders a user can obtain. In our earlier peer-to-peer example, you needed to create 100 accounts. Now with a domain, you would need to create only the 10 accounts.

An Active Directory structure is made up of one or more domains. A *domain* is a logical grouping of objects within your organization. For example, if we had the Stellacon.com domain, all users in that domain should be members of the Stellacon.com organization. The objects that are contained within a domain do not need to be in the same physical location. Domains can span the entire globe even though they are part of the same organization.

One of the advantages to using domains is the ability to have child domains. A *child domain* is a subdomain of another domain. You can build child domains based on physical locations, departments, and so forth. Figure 7.2 shows the hierarchy structure of Stellacon.com with its child domains (based on geographic location).

Microsoft domains are represented as triangles. It is important to remember that when taking any Microsoft exam.

FIGURE 7.2 Domain structure

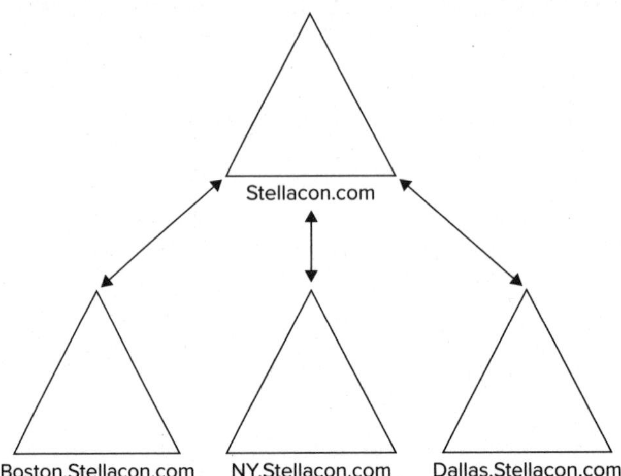

One of the benefits of creating child domains is scalability. Active Directory has the ability to store millions of objects within a single domain, but child domains give an administrator the flexibility to design a structure layout that meets their organizational needs.

When setting up child domains, the parent and child domains already establish a trust relationship. *Trusts* allow users to be granted access to resources in a domain even when their accounts reside in a different domain. To make administration of trust relationships easier, Microsoft has made transitive two-way trusts the default relationship between domains. This means that by default, all domains within the same forest automatically trust one another. As shown in Figure 7.2, Stellacon.com automatically trusts Boston.Stellacon.com, NY.Stellacon.com, and Dallas.Stellacon.com. This means that all child domains implicitly trust one another.

The last Active Directory advantage that we will discuss is an extensible schema. The Active Directory schema contains all the objects and attributes of the database. For example, when you create a new user by using the Active Directory Users and Computers snap-in, the system asks you to fill in the user's first name, last name, username, password, and so forth. These fields are the attributes of Active Directory, and these fields make up the schema. An administrator has the ability to change or expand these fields based on organizational needs.

Real World Scenario

Changing the Schema

You may be asking yourself why an organization would need to change the schema. Many years ago, when I got out of the military and before I got into the computer industry, I used to cast toilets for American Standard. I made 50 toilets a day. When working for American Standard, I had an employee number of 343. All my toilets were stamped 343 (so the company knew who made the product) on the bottom base of the toilet. My time card did not even have my name, just my number.

This number is an example of a field that would need to be added to a schema. I would have an account in Active Directory with my name, but there would need to be a field that showed my employee number. You may have to adjust your Active Directory schema based on your organization's requirements.

The major disadvantage to an Active Directory model is cost. When setting up an Active Directory domain, an organization needs a powerful enough machine to handle the Windows Server 2008 R2 operating system. Also most companies that decide to use a domain-based organization will require the IT personnel to manage and maintain the network infrastructure.

In the next section, you will look at some of the server terminology that is used in the remainder of this chapter.

Microsoft Networking Terms and Roles

Now that you have seen the two networking models that Microsoft offers, let's talk about some Microsoft networking terms and roles. You will be familiar with some of these terms, but it's always good to get a refresher.

Server A *server* is a machine that users connect to so they can access resources located on that machine. These resources can be files, printers, applications, and so forth. Usually the type of server is dependent on the resource that the user needs. For example, a print server is a server that controls printers. A file server contains files. Application servers can run applications for the users. Sometimes you will hear a server referred to by the specific application that it may be running. For example, someone may say, "That's our SQL server or Exchange server."

Domain Controller This is a server that contains a replica of Active Directory. As we mentioned earlier in this chapter, Active Directory is your database that contains all the objects in your network. A *domain controller* is a server that contains this database. Years ago (NT 3.51 and NT 4.0), we used to have a Primary Domain Controller (PDC) and Backup Domain Controllers (BDCs), but that's not true today. All domain controllers are equal in a Windows Server 2008 R2 network. Some domain controllers may contain extra roles, but they all have the same copy of Active Directory.

Member Server A *member server* is a server that is a member of a domain-based network but does not contain a copy of Active Directory. For example, it is recommended that Microsoft Exchange be loaded on a member server instead of a domain controller. Both domain controllers and member servers can act as file, print, or application servers. It just depends on whether you need that server to have a replica of Active Directory.

Standalone Server A *standalone server* is not a member of a domain. Many organizations may use this type of server for virtualization. For example, say you load Windows Server 2008 with Hyper-V (Microsoft's virtualization server) on a standalone server. You can then create virtual machines that act as domain controllers to run the network.

Client Machine A *client machine* is a computer that normally is used by a company's end users. The most common operating systems for a client machine are Windows XP, Windows Vista, and Windows 7.

DNS Server A *Domain Name Service (DNS)* server has the DNS service running on it. DNS is a name resolution service that turns a host name into a TCP/IP address (forward lookup). DNS also has the ability to turn a TCP/IP address into a name (reverse lookup). When you install an operating system onto a computer, you assign that computer a host name. The problem is that computers talk to each other by using the TCP/IP protocol (example: 192.168.1.100). It would be very difficult for most users to remember all the different TCP/IP addresses on a network. So normally you connect to a machine by using its host name. DNS does the conversion of host name to TCP/IP address for you.

The easiest way to understand how this works is to think of your phone number. If someone wants to call you but doesn't have your telephone number, they call information. They give information your name and they get your phone number. Well, this is how a network works. DNS is information on your network. You give DNS a host name, and it returns a network telephone number (TCP/IP address). DNS is a requirement if you want to install Active Directory. You can install DNS before or during the Active Directory installation. DNS can help resolve either IPv4 or IPv6 TCP/IP addresses (explained later in this chapter, in the "Understanding TCP/IP" section).

The reason that DNS can resolve both IPv4 and IPv6 is because of the Link Local Multicast Name Resolution, or LLMNR, protocol. The Link Local Multicast Name Resolution protocol is based on DNS packet formats that allow both IPv4 and IPv6 hosts to perform name resolution for hosts on the same local network.

DHCP Server *A Dynamic Host Configuration Protocol (DHCP)* server is the server that runs the DHCP service. DHCP is the server on the network that assigns TCP/IP information to your computers dynamically. Every computer needs three settings to operate properly (with the Internet and intranet): a TCP/IP number, a subnet mask, and a default gateway (router number). Your computers can get this minimum information two ways: manually (someone assigns the TCP/IP information) or dynamically (automatically installed). DHCP can assign more than just these three settings. DHCP can assign any TCP/IP configuration information (DNS server, WINS server, time servers, and so forth).

In the preceding DNS section, we stated that DNS was information on your network. Well, following this example, DHCP would be the phone company. DHCP is the component that assigns the telephone number (TCP/IP number).

If you are using DHCP and your Windows 7 machine receives a 169.254.*x*.*x* TCP/IP address, your client was not able to connect to the DHCP server. Windows 7 machines will automatically assign themselves a 169.254.*x*.*x* TCP/IP number when DHCP is unavailable. This is called Automatic Private IP Addressing (APIPA). DHCP can issue either IPv4 or IPv6 TCP/IP addresses.

Global Catalog The *Global Catalog* is a database of all Active Directory objects without all of the attributes. In other words, the Global Catalog is a partial representation of the Active Directory objects. Think of the Global Catalog as an index. If you needed to look something up in this Windows 7 book, you would go to the index and find what page you need to turn to. You would not just randomly look through the book for the information. This is what the Global Catalog does on your Active Directory domain. When you need to find a resource in the domain (user, published printer, and so forth), you can search the Global Catalog to find its location.

Domain controllers need to use a Global Catalog to help with user authentication. Global Catalogs are a requirement on an Active Directory domain. All domain controllers can be Global Catalogs, but this is not always a good practice. Your network should have at least two Global Catalogs for redundancy, but too many can cause too much Global Catalog replication traffic.

To learn more about Microsoft Active Directory networks, See *MCTS: Windows Server 2008 Active Directory Configuration Study Guide* (Exam 70-640) by William Panek and James Chellis (Wiley, 2008).

Before we can connect a Windows 7 machine to the domain, we must first set up the Network Interface Card (NIC) that will allow the machines to communicate with each other.

Configuring Windows 7 NIC Devices

A *network interface card (NIC)* is a hardware component used to connect computers or other devices to the network. NICs are responsible for providing the physical connection that recognizes the physical address of the device where they are installed.

The Open System Interconnect (OSI) model defines the encapsulation technique that builds the basic data structure for data transport across an internetwork. The OSI model provides interoperability between hardware vendors, network protocols, and applications. The physical address is the OSI model layer 2 address, or for Ethernet technologies, the MAC address (Media Access Control address). This is not the IP address, which is the OSI layer 3 or Network layer address, also generically defined as the logical address.

The most common place you see network adapters installed are computers, but you also see NICs installed in network printers and specialized devices such as Intrusion Detection Systems (IDSs) and firewalls. We generically call the interface between our network devices and the software components of the machines *network adapters*. Network adapters do not need to be separate cards; they can be built in, as in the case of most PCs today or other network-ready devices such as network cameras or network media players. These adapters (and all other hardware devices) need a driver to communicate with the Windows 7 operating system.

Before you physically install a NIC or network adapter, it's important to read the vendor's instructions that come with the hardware. Most network adapters you get today should be self-configuring, using Plug And Play capabilities. After you install a network adapter that supports Plug And Play, it should work following the installation procedure (which should be automated if the vendor says it is). You might have to restart, but our operating systems are getting much better with this, and you might just get lucky and be all right immediately.

If you happen to have a network adapter that is not Plug And Play, the operating system should detect the new piece of hardware and start a wizard that leads you through the process of loading the adapter's driver and setting initial configuration parameters. You can see your network connection and manage the network connection properties through the Network and Sharing Center.

Configuring a Network Adapter

After you have installed the network adapter, you configure it through its Properties dialog box. There are several ways to get to the network adapter property pages, one being the Network and Sharing Center, another through Computer Management, and yet a third directly through Device Manager. You will look at the Network and Sharing Center in detail later in this chapter.

Let's use the Device Manager applet for the network adapter configuration here. To access the Properties dialog box, choose Start and type **Device Manager** in the Windows 7 search box. This launches Device Manager. You can also right-click Computer from the Start menu and choose Manage from the context menu to get to the Computer Management Microsoft Management Console (MMC) or applet that lets you access Device Manager, as shown in Figure 7.3.

FIGURE 7.3 Device Manager from the Computer Management MMC

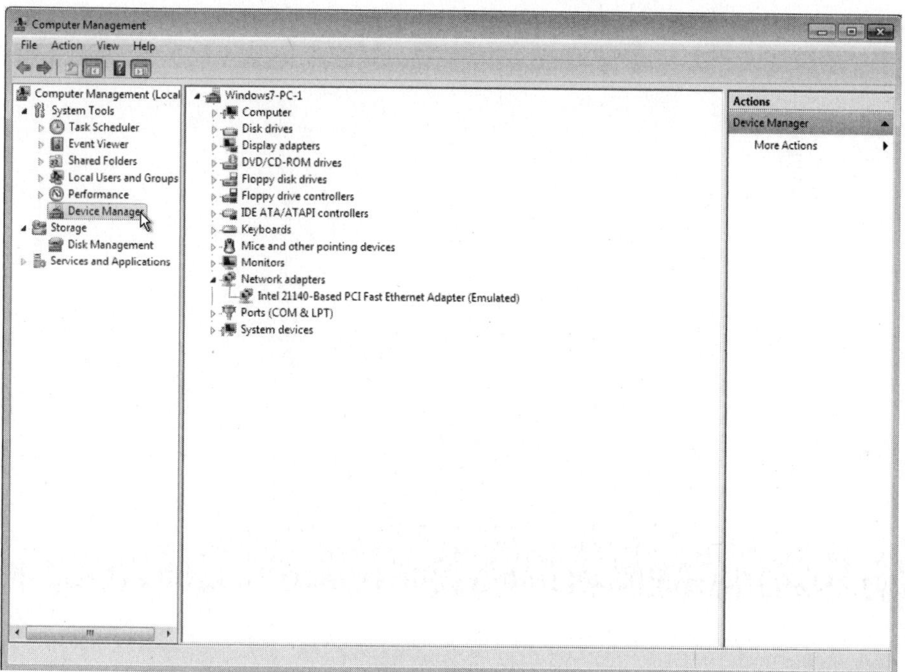

Figure 7.3 shows the Network Adapters item expanded, and the adapter is installed in my machine. Having Computer Management open is a great way to open Device Manager, as this particular MMC has numerous other installed plug-ins available to administrators that might be helpful as we work with our machines.

Accessing the network adapter properties allows us to view and change configuration parameters of the adapter (yes, its properties). You do this by right-clicking the adapter in Device Manager and selecting Properties from the context menu. Figure 7.4 shows the Properties page and the tabs available for my network adapter. Depending on the hardware manufacturer, you will see various tabbed pages available.

FIGURE 7.4 Network Adapter Properties page

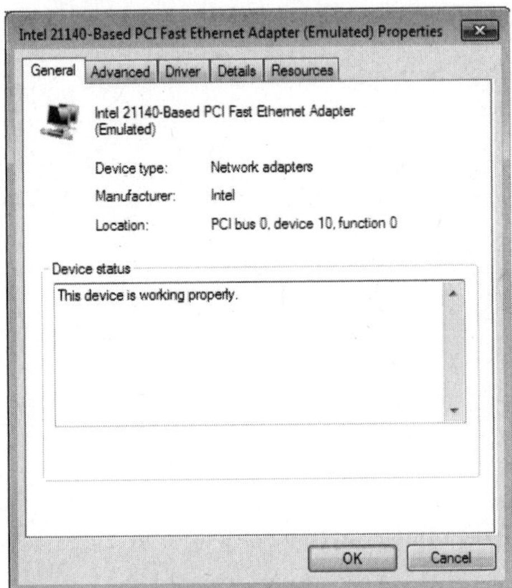

Network Adapter Properties: General Tab

The General tab of the network adapter Properties dialog box shows the name of the adapter, the device type, the manufacturer, and the location. The Device Status box reports whether the device is working properly or not. In the case of the latter ("not"), the Device Status box gives you an error code and a brief description of what Windows 7 identifies as the issue. You can perform an Internet search for the error code(s) if the text is not sufficient. The other tabs provide the following information:

Advanced Tab The contents of the Advanced tab of a network adapter's Properties dialog box vary depending on the network adapter and driver that you are using. Figure 7.5 shows an example of the Advanced tab for my Fast Ethernet adapter. There are several properties available in the Property list box, with the value configured in the Value box. To configure options in this dialog box, choose the property you want to modify in the Property list box and specify the desired value for the property in the Value box on the right. I have selected the Connection Type property and opened the drop-down list box to show you the options for my network adapter.

FIGURE 7.5 Advanced tab of the Network Adapters Properties page

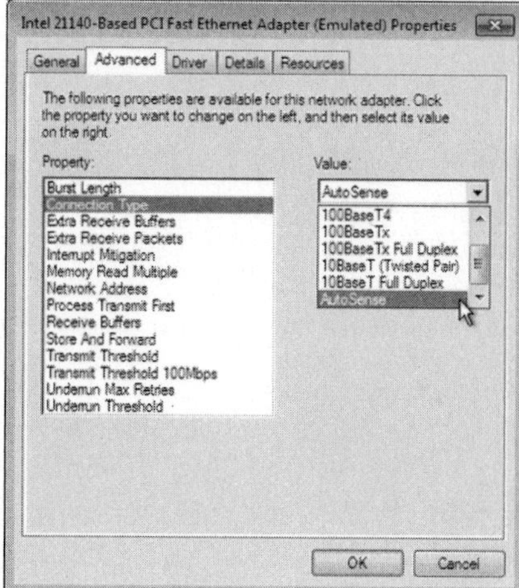

Driver Tab The Driver tab of the network adapter Properties dialog box provides the following information about your driver:

- The driver provider
- The date the driver was released
- The driver version (useful in determining whether you have the latest driver installed)
- The digital signer (the company that provides the digital signature for driver signing)

The Driver tab for my adapter is shown in Figure 7.6. The information here varies from driver to driver and even from vendor to vendor.

FIGURE 7.6 Driver tab of the Network Adapters Properties page

Clicking the Driver Details button on the Driver tab brings up the Driver File Details dialog box that provides the following details about the driver:

- The location of the driver file (useful for troubleshooting)
- The original provider of the driver
- The file version (useful for troubleshooting)
- Copyright information about the driver
- The digital signer for the driver

The Update Driver button starts a wizard to step you through upgrading the driver for an existing device.

The Roll Back Driver button allows you to roll back to the previously installed driver if you update your network driver and encounter problems. In Figure 7.6, the Roll Back Driver button is gray (not available) because we have not updated the driver or a previous driver is not available.

The Disable button is used to disable the device. After you disable the device, the Disable button changes into an Enable button, which you can use to enable the device.

The Uninstall button removes the driver from your computer's configuration. You would uninstall the driver if you were going to remove the device from your system or if you want to completely remove the driver configuration from your system so you can reinstall it from scratch either automatically or manually.

Details Tab The Details tab of the network adapter's Properties dialog box lists the resource settings for your network adapter. Information found on the Details tab varies by hardware device. I have included the Details tab information from my adapter in Figure 7.7, with the Property drop-down list box expanded to show the options for my hardware.

FIGURE 7.7 Details tab of the Network Adapter Properties page

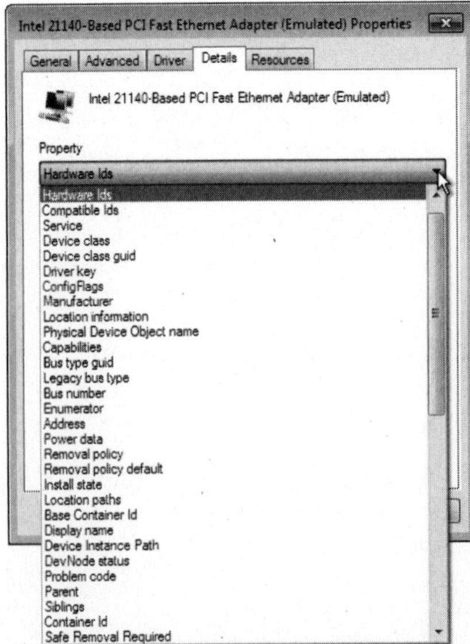

Resources Tab The Resources tab of the network adapter's Properties dialog box lists the resource settings for your network adapter. Resources include interrupt request (IRQ), memory, and input/output (I/O) resources. This information can be important for troubleshooting if other devices are trying to use the same resource settings. This is not normally the case as Windows 7 and the Plug And Play specification should set up nonconflicting parameters. If there are issues, the Conflicting Device list box at the bottom of the Resources tab shows the conflicts.

When installing the NIC device, you may encounter some problems or errors. Let's take a look at some NIC troubleshooting.

Troubleshooting a Network Adapter

If your network adapter is not working, the problem might be with the hardware, the driver software, or the network protocols. We discuss the layer 3 (network protocol) issues later in this chapter. The following list gives some common layer 1 and layer 2 causes for network adapter problems:

Network Adapter Not on the HCL If the device is not on the Hardware Compatibility List (HCL), use your Internet resources to see if others have discovered a solution, or contact the hardware vendor for advice.

Outdated Driver Make sure that you have the most current driver for your adapter. You can have Windows 7 check for an updated driver from the Driver tab of the Properties page for the adapter by clicking the Update Driver button and having Windows search for a better driver, or check for the latest driver on the hardware vendor's website.

Network Adapter Not Recognized by Windows 7 Check Device Manager to see whether Windows 7 recognizes the adapter. If you don't see your adapter, you can try to manually install it.

Improperly Configured Network Card Verify that the settings for the network card are correct for the parameters known within your network and for the hardware device the machine is connected to.

Cabling Problem Make sure that all network cables are functioning and are the correct type. This includes making sure that the connector is properly seated, the cable is straight or crossed depending on where it's plugged into, and the cable is not broken. This is usually done by looking at the Little Green Light (LGL) for link and activity on the NIC. This does not guarantee a good connection even if the LGLs are illuminated. A single conductor failure in a cable can still have a link light on, but data is not passing.

Bad Network Connection Device Verify that all network connectivity hardware is properly working. For example, on a Fast Ethernet network, make sure the switch and port being used are functioning properly.

Another NIC device that has become increasingly popular is the wireless NIC device. In the next section, you will look at how to configure your wireless adapters.

Configuring Wireless NIC Devices

Wireless technology has matured to the point of becoming cost-effective and secure. The use of wireless network adapters is increasingly popular, scaling well out of the home and into the workplace. Windows 7 supports wireless autoconfiguration, which makes wireless network connections easy to use. Windows 7 will automatically discover the wireless networks available and connect your machine to the preferred network. Although conveniently connected, there are still considerations to take into account—namely, security.

Configuring Wireless Network Settings

If you have a wireless network adapter compatible with Windows 7, it will be automatically recognized by the operating system. This can be a built-in adapter such as most modern laptops come with, a wireless card you install in the machine, or even a wireless USB adapter. After it is installed, it is recognized and shown in Device Manager as well as the Network and Sharing Center within the View Your Active Networks section.

We used Device Manager in the previous section for the network adapter configuration, so let's use the Network and Sharing Center for the wireless network configuration. Figure 7.8 shows the Network and Sharing Center with two active networks, the Wireless Network Connection and the wired Local Area Connection.

FIGURE 7.8 Network and Sharing Center

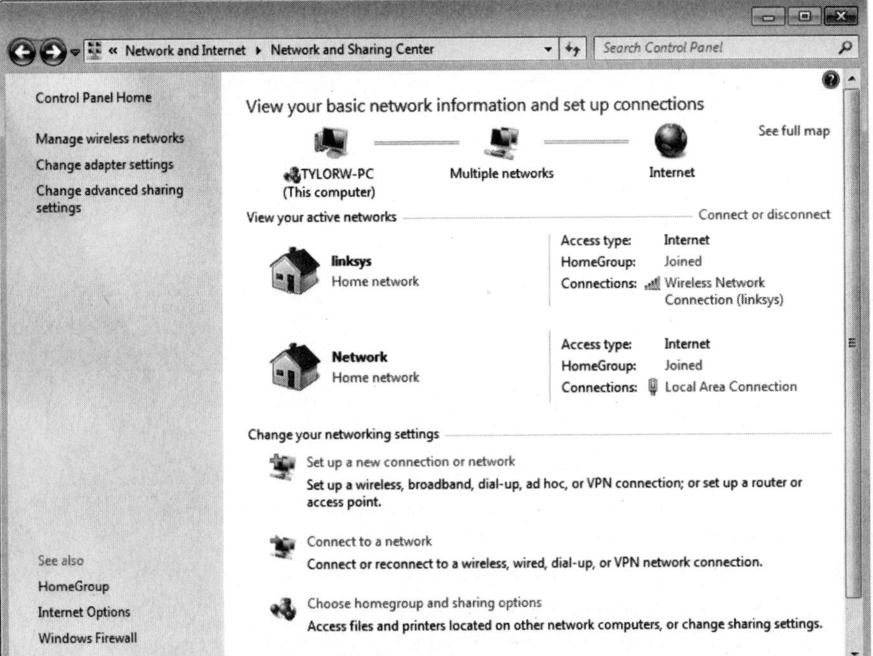

You can view the Network and Sharing Center a few different ways. You can perform any of the following steps to access the Network and Sharing Center:

- Choose Start and type **Network and Sharing Center** in the integrated search box of Windows 7.
- Choose Start ➤ Control Panel ➤ Network and Internet ➤ Network And Sharing Center.
- Choose Start, and then right-click Network and select Properties from the context menu.

Viewing the Wireless Network Connection Status

From the Network and Sharing center, you have easy access to the Wireless Network Connection Status. The Wireless Network Connection Status window gives you an initial look at the status by providing the layer 3 connectivity status (IPv4 and IPv6), media state, service set identifier (SSID) being used, how long the connection has been active (Duration), the negotiated speed of the connection, and the signal quality. The Wireless Network Connection menu choice of the Network and Sharing Center and the Wireless Network Connection Status window are shown in Figure 7.9.

FIGURE 7.9 Wireless Network Connection Status

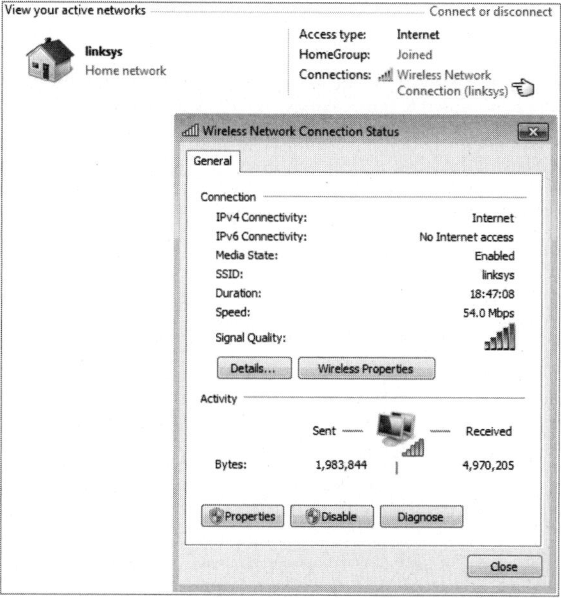

The Details button of the Wireless Network Connection Status window provides, as you probably guessed, detailed information including the actual physical address (layer 2), logical address (layer 3), dynamic addressing parameters (DHCP), name resolution items, and more. After verifying physical layer parameters, this area of properties and status is a great place to verify or troubleshoot logical (driver/software) issues.

Viewing Wireless Network Connection Details

If you have a wireless adapter in your machine, perform Exercise 7.1 to view the Network Connection Details for your Wireless Network Connection.

EXERCISE 7.1

Viewing the Network Connection Details

1. Choose Start and type **Network and Sharing Center** in the Windows 7 integrated search window; press Enter.
2. Select the Wireless Network Connection menu item from the View Your Active Networks section.
3. Click the Details button.
4. Review the Network Connection Details for this connection.

The Wireless Network Connection Status window has an Activity section showing real-time traffic (in bytes) being sent from and received by the wireless network. From the Wireless Network Connection Status window, you also have access to the Wireless Network Connection Properties, which includes access to the wireless adapter configuration pages.

You access the properties page by clicking the Properties button in the Activity section (not the Wireless Properties button in the Connection section; you can identify these buttons as shown previously in Figure 7.9). The Wireless Network Connection Properties window is shown in Figure 7.10.

FIGURE 7.10 Wireless Network Connection Properties window

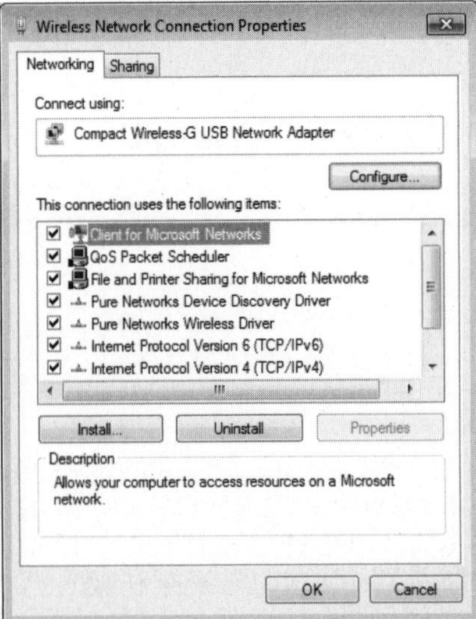

The Wireless Network Connection Properties page has a Networking tab that shows which network adapter is being used for this connection (which you can change if you have more than one available). There is also a tab for configuring Internet Connection Sharing (ICS), which allows other users on your network to access resources through this machine's connection. The This Connection Uses The Following Items section displays the various clients, services, and protocols that are currently available for this connection.

You can install or uninstall network clients, network services, and network protocols by choosing the appropriate button. You can also view the client, service, or protocol properties if they are available by choosing the Properties button for the selected item (if the Properties button is gray, a properties page is not available for the item). From the Wireless Network Connection Properties window, you even have access to the network adapters' hardware configuration property pages. These are the same pages you have access to from Device Manager.

Perform Exercise 7.2 to access the network adapter properties from the Wireless Network Connection Properties page.

EXERCISE 7.2

Viewing Wireless Network Connection Properties

1. Choose Start and type **Network and Sharing Center** in the Windows 7 integrated search window; press Enter.
2. Select the Wireless Network Connection menu item from the View Your Active Networks section.
3. Click the Properties button from the Activity section.
4. Click the Configure button.
5. View the various tabs regarding the network adapter properties.
6. Choose Cancel to return to the Wireless Network Connection Status window.

Configuring Wireless Network Security

Wireless network security is a very large piece of setting up our wireless networks. The focal point for this is the wireless access point or wireless router to which we connect.

Wireless Connection: Infrastructure or Ad Hoc?

We should point out here that you might not always be connecting to an access point or router; these connections are considered infrastructure mode connections. An infrastructure mode connection is similar to our wired connection of a PC to an outlet. Instead, you might connect in an ad hoc fashion, which could be a computer-to-computer connection to share information with other wireless network devices without another wireless device acting as an intermediary.

> Ad hoc connections exist in our wired environment as well, as we would connect two PCs' NICs together by using an Ethernet crossover cable. Securing data transfer in an ad hoc setup is equally important as it is in infrastructure mode, as the data is still traversing between devices using radio frequency (RF), and network sniffers today running the wireless adapter promiscuously (in monitor mode) have no problem viewing the data stream. If the data stream is not encrypted, the sniffers will have access to it.

Whether you are using a small wireless network or a large wireless infrastructure, you should have a plan for secure communication and should configure wireless network security. There are several basic parameters you can configure on your network access devices to increase the security of a wireless network:

- Disable broadcast of the SSID, which is the name of the wireless network. When SSID broadcast is disabled, the wireless network cannot be detected automatically until you manually configure your wireless network card to connect to that SSID.
- Create a Media Access Control (MAC) address filter list so only specifically allowed wireless devices can connect to the wireless network, or require users attempting to connect to supply connection credentials.
- Enable encryption such as Wi-Fi Protected Access (WPA) or WPA2.

For large implementations, there are several vendors supplying wireless access points under the control of a wireless director, software-based controllers that are responsible for allowing access points on the network, providing user access control, and enforcing encryption policies. For smaller implementations, this control functionality is done manually as the wireless routers or access points are set up.

The security policies put in place are configured on the wireless access device and the wireless client. The Windows 7 client components in our case must be set up to match the security settings of the wireless network access devices.

During the setup of most wireless access devices provided by the hardware vendor, the administrator will configure the security parameters. Configuring can be done during the setup program and/or through a web browser that can access the wireless access device configuration pages.

Most of our current devices have a built-in web server to allow the HTTP connection from a web browser. Windows 7 also has the ability to configure the wireless access device if the hardware vendor makes it available. If there is no specific component written, you can launch the web-browser–based configuration from a convenient location—the Network and Sharing Center.

In Exercise 7.3, you will perform the following steps to see how to initiate a Windows 7 wireless access point configuration.

EXERCISE 7.3

Configuring a Wireless Access Point

1. Choose Start and type **Network and Sharing Center** in the Windows 7 integrated search window; press Enter.
2. Choose the Set Up A New Connection Or Network option.
3. Choose Set Up A New Network to configure a new router or access point and then click Next.

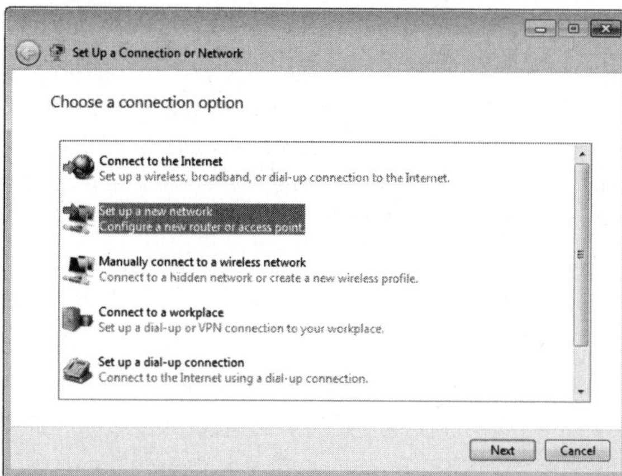

4. Select the wireless access device you want to configure from the Set Up A Network window and click Next.

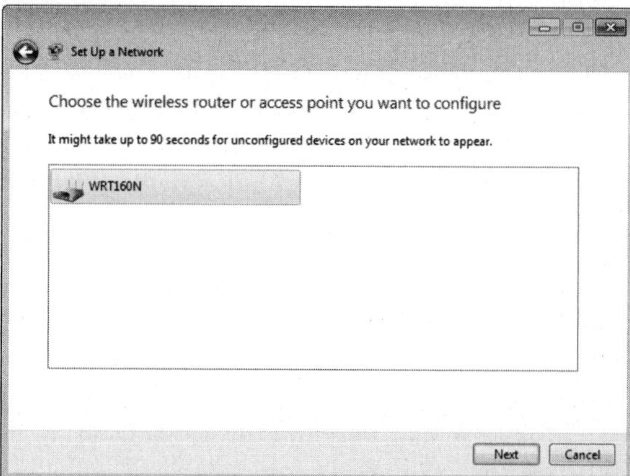

5. Depending on your device, you might be asked to enter a PIN or other identifying parameter to access the device. Enter the PIN and click Next.

6. On the next screen, you will be able to configure the security settings dictated by the wireless security policy to be implemented. The settings defined here need to be configured for each client machine connecting to the wireless network. After making the setting choices, click Next.

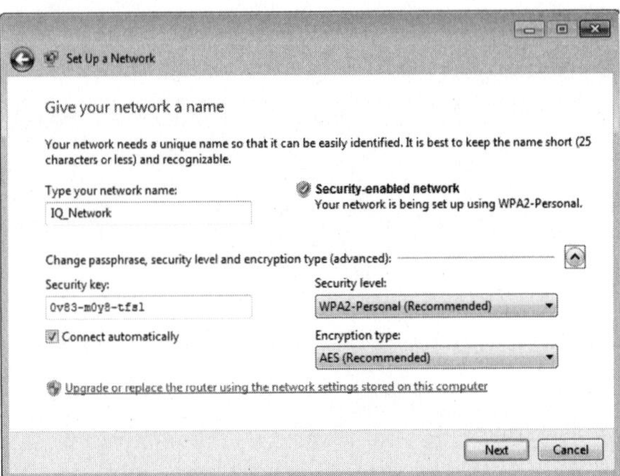

7. The configuration of the wireless network device completes, and you are given a confirmation window. Click Finish to close the window.

Whether you have Windows 7 configure the wireless network connection or you have performed the setup through the manufacturer's process, you still need to configure your Windows 7 client access.

If you have performed the simplest configuration, and there are no security parameters configured (bad idea, by the way), Windows 7 will connect automatically with a quick window showing the wireless network it's connecting to and providing access without much user intervention. Even cancelling the screens will produce a successful (nonsecure) connection. This simple configuration process makes connecting a home or small network easy and straightforward for nontechnical users. However, this is not a good solution.

If you have configured wireless network security (a good idea, by the way), then you need to configure the Windows 7 client with the correct settings. Once again, the configuration screens are available from a convenient location known as the Network and Sharing Center.

In Exercise 7.4, you will perform the following steps to access the Windows 7 client wireless network properties.

EXERCISE 7.4

Accessing the Windows 7 Wireless Properties

1. Choose Start and type **Network and Sharing Center** in the Windows 7 integrated search window; press Enter.

2. Choose the Wireless Network Connection item within the View Your Active Networks section of the Network and Sharing Center.

3. Click the Wireless Properties button within the Connection area of the Wireless Network Connection Status window.

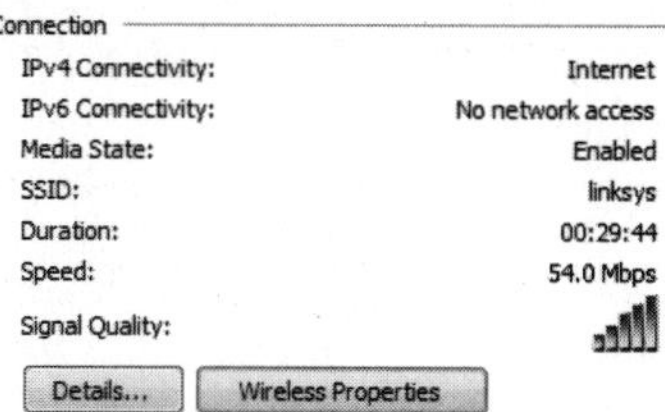

4. The Wireless Network Properties tabbed dialog box opens, displaying the current setup for the wireless network.

Figure 7.11 shows the Connection tab of the Wireless Network Properties tabbed dialog box. From this dialog box, you have the ability to set or change the Windows 7 client configuration.

FIGURE 7.11 Wireless Network Properties tabbed dialog box

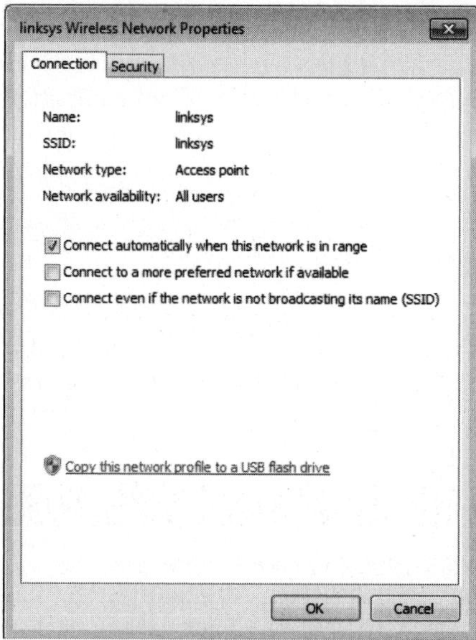

The first tab of the Wireless Network Properties tabbed dialog box is the Connection tab, which displays the following information:

Name The name assigned to the wireless network.

SSID The service set identifier (SSID) of the wireless connection. This defines a friendly name for the wireless network. This is normally an ASCII string and is usually broadcast by default, allowing a machine or users to select a wireless network with which to connect. Some wireless access devices will allow more than one SSID to be available (broadcast) at the same time, creating more than one wireless network within the same device.

Network Type Displays the mode the wireless network is operating in. If the wireless network is in infrastructure mode, this parameter will be Access Point. If the wireless network is ad hoc, this will display Computer-To-Computer.

Network Availability Displays to whom the wireless network is available—All Users or Me Only, for example.

The Connection tab of the Wireless Network Properties tabbed dialog box provides the following types of configuration:

Connect Automatically When This Network Is In Range This option, when selected, allows automatic connection for this wireless network. Deselecting (clearing the check mark) requires the user to select this wireless network for connection.

Connect To A More Preferred Network If Available Windows 7 will attempt to connect to a preferred network (if the Connect Automatically choice is selected). If there is more than one preferred network, Windows 7 might switch back and forth if they are both available at the same time. Clearing this check mark allows the currently connected network to stay connected until it is no longer available, possibly preventing the dropping of data or even dropped connections.

Connect Even If The Network Is Not Broadcasting Its Name (SSID) If the wireless network you are attempting to connect to is not broadcasting its SSID, you must select this option to allow Windows 7 to automatically connect.

There is one more option on the Connection tab of the Wireless Network Properties tab; it is the link to Copy This Network Profile To A USB Flash Drive. Selecting this link launches the Copy Network Settings Wizard, as shown in Figure 7.12.

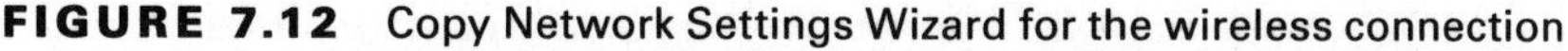

FIGURE 7.12 Copy Network Settings Wizard for the wireless connection

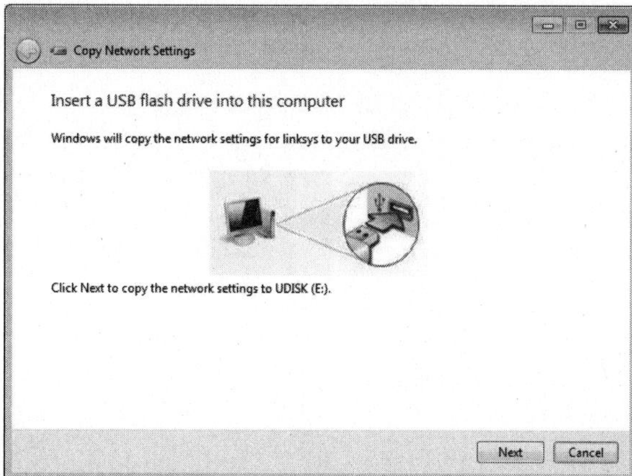

After inserting a USB flash drive, the currently configured wireless network configuration is saved in the form of a `setupSNK.exe` program and a folder named SMRTNTKY with the configuration parameters. Caution should be exercised to protect this information because all the configuration parameters (including security keys) are stored in clear text.

After the files and folder are created and saved, you are presented with a confirmation screen with simple instructions and a link for the detailed information about wireless network configuration. The confirmation page is shown in Figure 7.13.

FIGURE 7.13 Wireless connection copy confirmation window

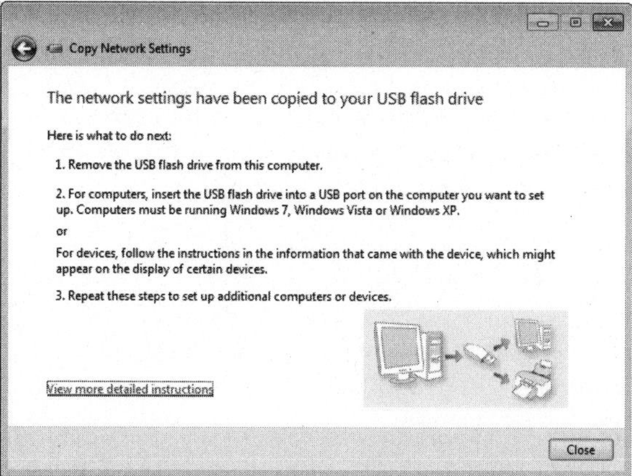

The second tab on the Wireless Network Properties tabbed dialog box is the Security tab. This tab allows the configuration of the security parameters as defined in your security policy and configured on your wireless network access devices.

Figure 7.14 shows the Security tab, the Security Type drop-down box selecting the WPA2-Personal Security choice, and the Encryption Type selecting AES (Advanced Encryption Scheme). You can also see the Network security key as clear text because the Show Characters check box is selected.

FIGURE 7.14 Wireless Network Properties Security tab

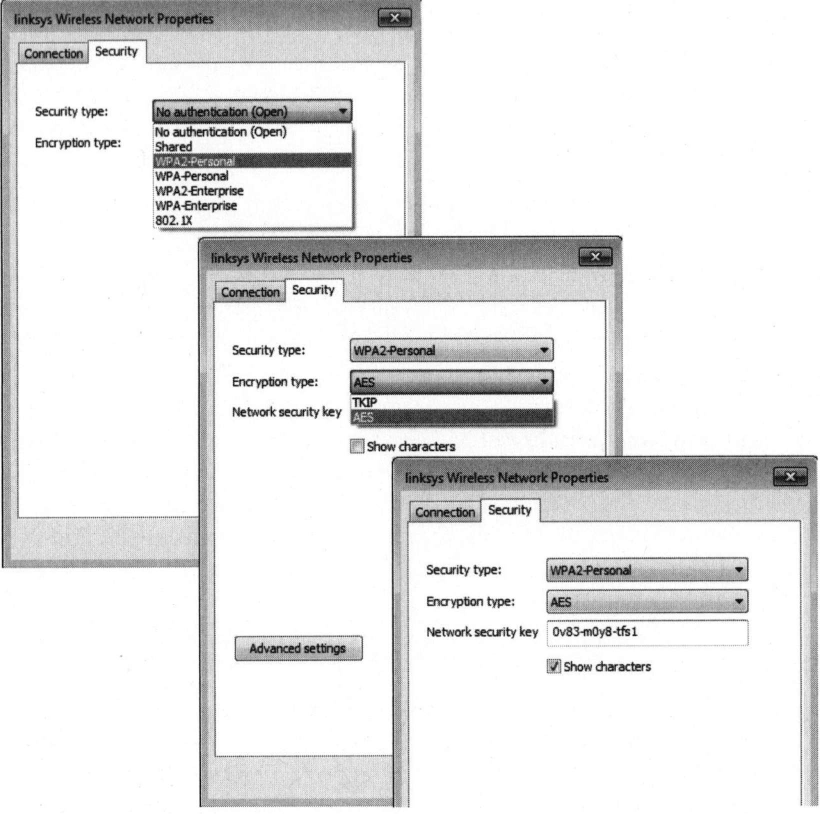

When it comes to WPA, there are two versions: WPA2-Personal and WPA2-Enterprise. WPA2-Personal allows you to set up WPA2 by using a shared password key. WPA2-Enterprise allows you to set up WPA2 by using a server for verification.

Troubleshooting Wireless Connectivity

There are a few common issues with wireless networking you can look at if you're having problems connecting to your wireless network. Following are a few problems and solutions:

Ensure that your wireless card and the access devices are compatible. Cards that are compatible with the 802.11b standard can connect to only 802.11b or 802.11b/g access devices configured to accept b. Cards using 802.11a can connect to only 802.11a or 802.11a/b/g access devices configured to accept a. An 802.11n card needs to connect to an 802.11n access device for efficiency (although most will auto-negotiate to the best spec available). The specification you're using on the card has to be available and turned on in the wireless access device.

Ensure that your wireless network card is enabled. Here's a good one I see regularly: Many newer laptops and tablets have either a switch or a hot-key setting that enables and disables the wireless device. Often a laptop switch will somehow be turned off, or some user will somehow arbitrarily press the key sequence to shut off the PC's wireless radio. The physical layer always seems to be a good place to start looking.

Ensure that the access point signal is available. I find radio frequency (RF) to be a funny thing. You can't see it and you assume that it is everywhere. Not a good assumption. The output power of the signal might be fine, but the RF power is absorbed (okay, we say *attenuated*) as it goes through walls, insulation, or water (which is the main component of leaves). You need to make sure there is nothing that might be causing interference of the wireless signal.

Ensure that the security parameters are configured alike. The SSID, encryption type, encryption algorithm, and passphrase/security key have to be set the same on both the wireless access device and the wireless client. Here's another one I see quite often: In the desire to make the initial setup and the secure setup easier for end users, some hardware vendors have a nice little button that allows the network access device to negotiate a secure set of parameters with the client. In one instance, after the wireless network had been working correctly for a while, a failure showed the parameters to now be incompatible, thanks in large part to someone pressing the easy button just before the failure.

Ensure automatic connections if the SSID is not being broadcast. If you are having trouble connecting to a network that does not broadcast its SSID, select the Connect Even If The Network Is Not Broadcasting check box in the Wireless Network Properties dialog box. I have solved several wireless network connection issues with this fix.

One final thought on troubleshooting in the wireless world: Many times when I go into a small or midsized network, I find that the company (or home user) is connected to a multifunction type of device. These little pieces of plastic we purchase (and call *wireless routers*) are really quite technologically sophisticated. Think of one of these wireless routers; they have switch ports for connecting hard-wired devices on the private network as well as an Internet port to connect to the outside world. The wireless portion of the device is more like another switch port on the private side than anything else, allowing the wireless devices to interact with the hard-wires.

When I troubleshoot and eliminate issues, I start with the hard-wired devices, and see whether they can communicate to each other and the outside (the other side of your wireless router). Try to communicate between the hard-wired and wireless as well, to eliminate the router components. Oh yeah, it's also not the best idea to use the wireless network to configure the wireless devices. Configuring through the wireless interface will ultimately cause you to lose connectivity in the middle of a configuration and may force you to connect with the cable, leaving the access point unusable until you complete the task you started wirelessly.

Another item that we need to configure before we can connect a Windows 7 machine to the domain is the protocol that will allow the Windows 7 machine to communicate with other machines.

Understanding TCP/IP

Transmission Control Protocol/Internet Protocol (TCP/IP) is the most commonly used network protocol. It is actually a suite of protocols that have evolved into the industry standard for network, internetwork, and Internet connectivity. The main protocols providing basic TCP/IP services include Internet Protocol (IP), Transmission Control Protocol (TCP), User Datagram Protocol (UDP), Address Resolution Protocol (ARP), Internet Control Message Protocol (ICMP), and Internet Group Management Protocol (IGMP).

Benefits of Using TCP/IP

TCP/IP as a protocol suite was accepted as an industry standard in the 1980s and continues to be the primary internetworking protocol today! For a default installation of Windows 7, IPv4 and IPv6 are both installed by default. TCP/IP has the following benefits:

- TCP/IP is the most common protocol and is supported by almost all network operating systems. It is the required protocol for Internet access.
- TCP/IP is dependable and scalable for use in small and large networks.
- Support is provided for connectivity across interconnected networks, independent of the operating systems being used at the upper end of the OSI model or the physical components at the lower end of the OSI model.
- TCP/IP provides standard routing services for moving packets over interconnected network segments. Dividing networks into multiple subnetworks (or subnets) optimizes network traffic and facilitates network management.
- TCP/IP is designed to provide data reliability by providing a connection at the transport layer and verifying that each data segment is received and passed to the application requiring the data by retransmitting lost information.
- TCP/IP allows for the classification of data in regard to its importance (Quality of Service). This allows important time-sensitive streams of data (such as Voice over IP) to get preferential treatment.
- TCP/IP is designed to be fault tolerant. It is able to dynamically reroute packets if network links become unavailable (assuming alternate paths exist).
- Protocol applications can provide services such as Dynamic Host Configuration Protocol (DHCP) for TCP/IP configuration and Domain Name Service (DNS) for host name–to–IP address resolution.

- Windows 7 continues to support Automatic Private IP Addressing (APIPA) used by small, local-connection-only networks without a DHCP server, to allow Windows 7 to automatically assign an IP address to itself.
- Support for NetBIOS over TCP/IP (NetBT) is included in Windows 7. NetBIOS is a software specification used for identifying computer resources by name as opposed to IP address. We still use TCP/IP as the network protocol, so we map the NetBIOS name to an IP address.
- The inclusion of Alternate IP Configuration allows users to have a static and a DHCP-assigned IP address mapped to a single network adapter. This feature supports mobile users who roam between different network segments.
- IPv6 incorporates a much larger address space, and more importantly, incorporates many of the additional features of TCP/IP into a standardized protocol. This is important because a vendor who claims to support TCP/IP only has to support the 1980s version, and may not support additional features such as the Internet protocol security features of IPSec. IPv6 as a standard includes these features, allowing a more robust network protocol.

Features of TCP/IP

One of the main features of TCP/IP is that it allows a common structure for network communications across a wide variety of hardware and operating systems and a lot of applications that are specifically written to configure and control it. Several of the features of TCP/IP included with Windows 7 are as follows:

- TCP/IP connectivity tools allowing access to a variety of hosts across a TCP/IP network. TCP/IP tools in Windows 7 include clients for HTTP, FTP, TFTP, Telnet, Finger, and so forth. Server components for the tools are available to install as well.
- Inclusion of a Simple Network Management Protocol (SNMP) agent that can be used to monitor performance and resource use of a TCP/IP host, server, or network hardware devices.
- TCP/IP management and diagnostic tools are provided for maintenance and diagnostic support. TCP/IP management and diagnostic commands include `ipconfig`, `arp`, `ping`, `nbtstat`, `netsh`, `route`, `nslookup`, `tracert`, and `pathping`.
- Support for TCP/IP network printing, enabling you to print to networked print devices.
- Logical and physical multihoming, enabling multiple IP addresses on a single computer for single or multiple network adapters. Multiple network adapters installed on a single computer are normally associated with routing for internetwork connectivity.
- Support for internal IP routing, which enables a Windows 7 computer to route packets between multiple network adapters installed in one machine.
- Support for virtual private networks, which enable you to transmit data securely across a public network via encapsulated and encrypted packets.

Basics of IP Addressing and Configuration

Before you can configure TCP/IP, you should have a basic understanding of TCP/IP configuration and addressing. Let's review TCP/IP addressing. To configure a TCP/IP client, you must specify an IP address, subnet mask, and default gateway (if you're going to communicate outside your local network). Depending on your network, you might want to configure a DNS server, domain name, or maybe even a WINS server.

You can see the Windows 7 TCP/IP version 4 properties window in Figure 7.15. I have included it here as I am going to discuss the different configuration items in the following sections. Although normally set up for automatic configuration, these parameters have been manually assigned in this figure for clarity. We will go through the configuration steps and show how to access this window later in this section.

FIGURE 7.15 Windows 7 TCP/IP version 4 properties

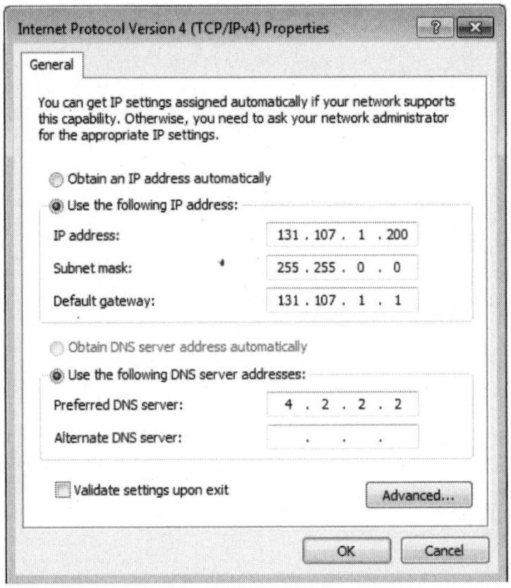

IPv4 Address Types

There are three types of IPv4 addresses: broadcast, multicast, and unicast.

A *broadcast address* is read by all hosts that hear it (the broadcast will not go across a router, so only local devices hear the broadcast). The IPv4 broadcast address is 255.255.255.255; every single bit is a 1.

A *multicast address* is a special address that one or more devices will listen for by joining a multicast group. Not all the local devices respond and process the data in the multicast packet, only the devices configured to listen for it. A multicast address will have a value between 224 and 239 in the first octet (the leftmost number in the dotted decimal representation). A multicast example is 224.0.0.5.

A *unicast IP address* uniquely identifies a computer or device on the network. An IPv4 unicast address is a four-octet, 32-bit address represented as dotted decimal (an example is 131.107.1.200). Each number in the dotted decimal notation is a decimal representation of 8 bits, and the value of each is going to be between 0 and 255 (255 is the numerically largest value that 8 bits can represent). A portion of the IPv4 unicast address is used to identify the network the device is on (or the network of a destination device), and part is used to identify the individual host on the local network or the unique host on a remote network. The IPv4 address scheme is the only address space used by the Internet today, and TCP/IP is the only network protocol used by the Internet today.

IPv4 Address Classes

When the TCP/IP suite was accepted as a standard in the 1980s, there were three classes of unicast IP addresses defined. Depending on the class you use, different parts of the address show the default network portion of the address and the host address. We still refer to these addresses by class, but we no longer really utilize this class structure; we'll explain shortly.

Table 7.1 shows the three classes of network addresses and the number of networks and hosts available for each network class as defined by the original TCP/IP version 4 standard.

TABLE 7.1 IPv4 Class Assignments

Network Class	Address Range of First Octet	Number of Unique Networks Available	Number of Unique Hosts per Network
A	1–126	126	16,777,214
B	128–191	16,384	65,534
C	192–223	2,097,152	254

As you probably noticed, 127 is missing from the address ranges. 127.0.0.1 is the diagnostic loopback address and because of that, no commercial TCP/IP range can start with 127.

The number of octets you can use for either the network ID or the host ID depends on which class you use for your network. For example, if I own a Class B address of 131.107.0.0, the first two octets (131.107) would be the network ID and the last two octets would be the host ID. Table 7.2 shows you the different classes and which octets are the network ID (represented by X) and which octets are the host ID (represented by Y). You are allowed to manipulate only the host IDs (Y) for your organization.

TABLE 7.2 IPv4 Network and Host Octets

Class	Example	Network ID	Host ID
A	17.1.10.10 (X.Y.Y.Y)	17 (X)	1.10.10 (Y.Y.Y)
B	131.107.14.240 (X.X.Y.Y)	131.107 (X.X)	14.240 (Y.Y)
C	192.168.1.10 (X.X.X.Y)	192.168.1 (X.X.X)	10 (Y)

IPv4 Subnet Mask

The *subnet mask* is used to specify which portion of the unicast IPv4 address defines the network value and which portion defines the unique host value. The subnet mask can be shown as either a dotted decimal, as with 255.255.255.0, or as a slash notation (called Classless Inter-Domain Routing, or CIDR), as in /24. The CIDR representation is the number of bits turned on in the subnet mask. For example, 255.255.224.0 is actually 11111 111.11111111.11100000.00000000, which equals 19 bits turned on, or /19.

The 1980s standard for classful network addressing defined the following subnet masks for each class, as shown in Table 7.3.

TABLE 7.3 IPv4 Default Class Subnet Masks

Class	Default Mask	Slash Notation (CIDR)
Class A	255.0.0.0	/8
Class B	255.255.0.0	/16
Class C	255.255.255.0	/24

Another task of the subnet mask is to break down the ranges of your network. For example, 255.255.255.224 allows for six subnets. There should be six TCP/IP ranges that go with the six subnets. In Table 7.4, we show the different ranges for the different subnet masks.

TABLE 7.4 Subnet Mask Ranges

Subnet Mask Number	Ranges
255	1
254	2
252	4

Subnet Mask Number	Ranges
248	8
240	16
224	32
192	64
128	128

Now what does this chart mean to you? Well, let's say that you have a subnet mask of 255.255.255.224. Because 224 allows for six subnets, the six ranges would go by 32. Table 7.5 shows a Class C subnet range for 224. Remember, in any range, you can't use the first number of the range (network ID) or the last number of any range (broadcast).

TABLE 7.5 Class C 224 Subnet Mask Ranges

Subnets	Range	Usable
Range 1	32–63	**33–62**
Range 2	64–95	65–94
Range 3	96–127	97–126
Range 4	128–159	129–158
Range 5	160–191	161–190
Range 6	192–223	193–222

Now if this was a Class B subnet mask, the ranges would include a second octet that you would work with. Table 7.6 shows a Class B 224 subnet mask.

TABLE 7.6 Class B 224 Subnet Mask Range

Subnets	Range	Usable
Range 1	32.0–63.255	32.1–63.254
Range 2	64.0–95.255	64.1–95.254
Range 3	96.0–127.255	96.1–127.254
Range 4	128.0 a-159.255	128.1–159.254
Range 5	160.0–191.255	160.1–191.254
Range 6	192.0–223.255	192.1–223.254

Now if this was a Class A subnet mask, the ranges would include three octets that you would work with. Table 7.7 shows a Class A 224 subnet mask.

TABLE 7.7 Class A 224 Subnet Mask Range

Subnets	Range	Usable
Range 1	32.0.0–63.255.255	32.0.1–63.255.254
Range 2	64.0.0–95.255.255	64.0.1–95.255.254
Range 3	96.0.0–127.255.255	96.0.1–127.255.254
Range 4	128.0.0–159.255.255	128.0.1–159.255.254
Range 5	160.0.0–191.255.255	160.0.1–191.255.254
Range 6	192.0.0–223.255.255	192.0.1–223.255.254

Another way to configure TCP/IP is by using IPv6. In the next section, you will look at using IPv6.

Using IPv6 Addresses

Through most of this section, we have been referencing TCP/IP as the network protocol. However, you should remember that it is really a suite of protocols running in layer 3 and layer 4 of the OSI model. Internet Protocol (IP) is the layer 3 protocol responsible for assigning end devices globally unique addresses (and I mean the whole company for private addresses to the whole Internet for public addresses).

Back in the 1980s, it was unimaginable that we would ever need more than 4 billion addresses, but we do. They (the keepers of the Internet) realized in the 1990s that we were going to have a problem and decided that a new layer 3 was going to be needed. This was not an easy task, and integration into the existing infrastructure was going to take a long time as well.

They (the keepers of the Internet) came up with an interim solution while the new layer 3 protocol became standardized. The interim solution is known as NAT and PAT. NAT/PAT allowed more than one device to use the same IP address on a private network as long as there was one Internet address available. Cool enough, but this is not the real solution.

IPv6 is the solution to the IPv4 address depletion. As time has progressed from the IPv4 standard acceptance in the 1980s, we have needed new and better functionality. However, the way the standards process works around the world is that you can add functionality, but it may or may not be supported in any vendor's TCP/IPv4 network stack. What happened in IPv6 is not only did the address space increase in size, but the additional functionality that may or may not have been included before has become part of the IPv6 standard.

For example, IPv4 is defined as having a variable-length header, which is cumbersome because we need to read an additional piece of data to see how big the header is. Most of the time, the header stays the same, so why not just fix its length and add an extension to the header if we need to carry more information? IPv6 uses a fixed-length IP header with the capability of carrying more information in an extension to the header (known as an *extension header*).

What about the layer 4 piece, TCP and UDP? Those don't need to change; we're changing only layer 3. What about the MAC address and the Ethernet specification? Those don't need to change; we're changing only layer 3. (Okay, we'll have to add a new identifier for the layer 2 header so we know to hand the data to IPv6, but that's for another chapter.)

Microsoft has been including IPv6 in its operating systems since NT4.0; it just has not been enabled by default. Windows 7 (as did Vista) natively supports both IPv4 and IPv6. The main differences you will notice between IPv4 and IPv6 are the format and size of the IP address. IPv6 addresses are 128 bits, typically written as eight groups of four hexadecimal characters. IPv4 addresses, as you saw earlier, are 32 bits—four decimal representations of eight bits. Each of the eight groups of characters is separated by a colon. An example of a valid IPv6 address is 2001:4860:0000:0000:0012:10FF:FECD:00EF.

Leading zeros can be omitted, so we can write our example address as 2001:4860:0:0:12:10FF:FECD:EF. Additionally, a double colon can be used to compress a set of consecutive zeros, so we can write our example address as 2001:4860::12:10FF:FECD:EF. The IPv6 address is 128 bits; when you see a double colon, it's a variable that says to fill enough zeros within the colons to make the address 128 bits. You can have only one set of double colons; two variables in one address is not going to work.

Will we see IPv6 take over the global address space soon? Even with IPv4's lack of address space, we are going to continue to use it for many years. The integration of IPv6 into the infrastructure is going to happen as a joint venture with IPv4 and IPv6 running at the same time in the devices and on some networks.

There are many mechanisms for enabling IPv6 communications over an IPv4 network, including the following:

- Dual stack—a computer or device running both the IPv4 and IPv6 protocol stacks at the same time
- ISATAP—Intra-Site Automatic Tunnel Addressing Protocol
- 6to4—an encapsulation technique for putting IPv6 addresses inside IPv4 addresses
- Teredo tunneling—another encapsulation technique for putting IPv6 traffic inside an IPv4 packet

Some IPv6-to-IPv4 dynamic translation techniques require that a computer's IPv4 address is used as the last 32 bits of the IPv6 address. When these translation techniques are used, it is common to write the last 32 bits as you would typically write an IPv4 address, such as 2001:4850::F8:192.168.122.26.

There are two ways to receive a TCP/IP address (for either IPv4 or IPv6): You can manually assign a TCP/IP address to the Windows 7 machine, or the Windows 7 machine can use DHCP.

Configuring TCP/IP on Windows 7

Windows 7 can use either IPv4 or IPv6 to communicate with other machines on a network, but the Windows 7 machine must receive the TCP/IP address. There are two ways that a Windows 7 machine can get a TCP/IP address: statically or dynamically.

Assigning Static TCP/IP Numbers

As an administrator, it may be necessary to configure a Windows 7 machine manually (static configuration). To configure a Windows 7 machine manually, you must know the following:

- Which TCP/IP address the machine will receive
- What the subnet mask is
- What the default gateway (router's TCP/IP address) is
- What the DNS TCP/IP addresses are

Complete Exercise 7.5 to configure a Windows 7 machine to use a static TCP/IP address. This example uses TCP/IP addresses for a local network, but you can use your own TCP/IP addresses if you know what they should be.

EXERCISE 7.5

Configuring a Static TCP/IP Address

1. Click Start and type **Network and Sharing Center** in the Windows 7 integrated search box.
2. In the Network and Sharing Center window, click the Local Area Connection item in the View Your Active Networks section.

3. Click the Properties button from the Activity section of the Local Area Connection Status box.
4. In the Local Area Connection Properties dialog box, click to select (do not deselect the check box) Internet Protocol Version 4 (TCP/IPv4) and click the Properties button. Manual configuration will work with both IPv4 and IPv6.
5. Under the General tab, click the Use The Following IP Address radio button. Type in the following (unless you want to use your own settings):

   IP Address: **192.168.1.50**

   Subnet Mask: **255.255.255.0**

   Default Gateway: **192.168.1.1**
6. Click the Use The Following DNS Server Addresses radio button and type in **4.2.2.2** (unless you want to use your own settings) in the TCP/IP Address field.
7. Click OK.

Now let's take a look at how to configure a Windows 7 machine to use DHCP.

Configuring a Windows 7 Machine to use DHCP

Dynamic IP configuration assumes that you have a DHCP server on your network that is reachable by the DHCP clients. DHCP servers are configured to automatically provide DHCP clients with all their IP configuration information, including IP address, subnet mask, and DNS server.

For large networks, DHCP is the easiest and most reliable way of managing IP configurations. By default, a Windows 7 machine is configured as a DHCP client for dynamic IP configuration.

Complete Exercise 7.6 to configure a Windows 7 machine to use dynamic IP configuration.

EXERCISE 7.6

Using DHCP

1. Click Start and type **Network and Sharing Center** in the Windows 7 integrated search box.
2. In the Network and Sharing Center window, click the Local Area Connection item in the View Your Active Networks section.
3. Click the Properties button from the Activity section of the Local Area Connection Status box.
4. In the Local Area Connection Properties dialog box, click to select (do not deselect the check box) Internet Protocol Version 4 (TCP/IPv4) and click the Properties button. DHCP will work with both IPv4 and IPv6.

5. Choose the Obtain An IP Address Automatically radio button from the General tab of the Internet Protocol Version 4 (TCP/IPv4) Properties dialog box.
6. Choose the Obtain DNS Server Address Automatically radio button from the General tab of the Internet Protocol Version 4 (TCP/IPv4) Properties dialog box.
7. To use this configuration, click OK to accept the selection and close the dialog box. To exit without saving (if you had a valid static configuration), choose Cancel.

If you are using DHCP and you are not connecting to other machines properly, you can do an `ipconfig /all` to see what your TCP/IP address is. If your TCP/IP address starts with 169.254.*x*.*x*, you are not connecting to the DHCP server and your Windows 7 machine is using APIPA.

Understanding APIPA

Automatic Private IP Addressing (APIPA) is used to automatically assign private IP addresses for home or small business networks that contain a single subnet, have no DHCP server, and are not using static IP addressing. If APIPA is being used, clients will be able to communicate only with other clients on the same subnet that are also using APIPA. The benefit of using APIPA in small networks is that it is less tedious and has less chance of configuration errors than statically assigning IP addresses and configuration.

APIPA is used with Windows 7 under the following conditions:

- When the client is configured as a DHCP client, but no DHCP server is available to service the DHCP request.
- When the client originally obtained a DHCP lease from a DHCP server, but when the client tried to renew the DHCP lease, the DHCP server was unavailable and the lease period expired.

APIPA uses a Class B network address space that has been reserved for its use. The address space is the 169.254.0.0 network, where the range of 169.254.0.1–169.254.255.254 is available for the host to assign to themselves. The steps that APIPA uses are as follows:

1. The Windows 7 client attempts to use a DHCP server for its configuration, but no DHCP servers respond.
2. The Windows 7 client selects a random address from the 169.254.0.1–169.254.255.254 range of addresses and will use a subnet mask of 255.255.0.0.
3. The client uses a duplicate-address detection method to verify that the address it selected is not already in use on the network.
4. If the address is already in use, the client repeats steps 1 and 2. If the address is not already in use, the client configures its network interface with the address it randomly selected. If you note the number of the address the APIPA client can select from (65536 addresses), the odds of selecting a duplicate is very slim.
5. The Windows 7 network client continues to search for a DHCP server every five minutes. If a DHCP server replies to the request, the APIPA configuration is dropped and the client receives new IP configuration settings from the DHCP server.

You can determine whether your network interface has been configured using APIPA by looking at your IP address. You can do this easily from the command interpreter by using the `ipconfig /all` command. Let's take a look at how to test your TCP/IP configuration.

Testing IP Configuration

After you have installed and configured the TCP/IP settings, you can test the IP configuration by using the `ipconfig`, `ping`, and `nbtstat` commands. These commands are also useful in troubleshooting IP configuration errors. You can also graphically view connection details through the Local Area Connection Status of the Network and Sharing Center.

Using the ipconfig command

The `ipconfig` command displays your IP configuration. Table 7.8 lists the command switches that you can use with the `ipconfig` command.

TABLE 7.8 Ipconfig Switches

Switch	Description
/?	Shows all of the help options for `ipconfig`
/all	Shows verbose information about your IP configuration, including your computer's physical address, the DNS server you are using, and whether you are using DHCP
/allcompartments	Shows IP information for all compartments
/release	Releases an IPv4 address that has been assigned through DHCP
/release6	Releases an IPv6 address that has been assigned through DHCP
/renew	Renews an IPv4 address through DHCP
/renew6	Renews an IPv6 address through DHCP
/flushdns	Purges the DNS Resolver cache
/registerdns	Refreshes DHCP leases and re-registers DNS names
/displaydns	Displays the contents of the DNS Resolver Cache
/showclassid	Lists the DHCP class IDs allowed by the computer
/setclassID	Allows you to modify the DHCP class ID

If TCP/IP is still not working properly on the Windows 7 machine, you may need to do some troubleshooting.

TCP/IP Troubleshooting

If you are having trouble connecting to network resources, you might want to check the following:

- If you can access resources on your local subnet but not on a remote subnet, you should check the default gateway settings on your computer. Pinging a remote host and receiving a Destination Unreachable message is also related to default gateway misconfiguration.
- If you can access some but not all resources on your local subnet or remote subnet, you should check your subnet mask settings, the wiring to those resources, or the devices between your computer and those resources.
- Use the `ipconfig` utility to ensure that you are not configured with an APIPA address. If so, determine why you are not receiving IP settings from your DHCP server.
- If you can access a resource (for example, by pinging a computer) by IP address, but not by name, you should check the DNS settings on your computer.

After we have TCP/IP set up on our Windows 7 machine, we can then connect the Windows 7 machine to the network. In the next section, you will look at how to connect Windows 7 to a network.

Configuring Windows 7 on a Network

In a corporate environment, the client machines (Windows XP, Windows Vista, and Windows 7) will be connected to the domain environment. There are two ways to connect the Windows 7 machine to the domain. You can connect the Windows 7 machine to the domain from the Windows 7 operating system or from Active Directory.

Adding Windows 7 to the Domain

It does not matter which way you choose to connect the machine to the domain. I usually connect the Windows 7 machine through the Windows operating system, but either way does the same task.

Having the Windows 7 machine on the domain offers many benefits to administration:

- You can deploy GPOs from one location instead of LGPOs on each machine.
- Users can back up their data to a server. This way, the nightly backups cover user information. Most Windows 7 machines will *not* be backed up separately.

- You can manage users and groups from one central location (Active Directory) instead of on each Windows 7 machine.
- You can manage security to resources on servers instead of resources on each Windows 7 machine.

Complete Exercise 7.7 to connect a Windows 7 machine to a Windows Server 2008 R2 domain.

EXERCISE 7.7

Connecting a Windows 7 Machine to the Domain

1. On the Windows 7 machine, click Start and then right-click Computer. Choose Properties.
2. Under the Computer Name, Domain, And Workgroup section, click the Change Settings link.
3. Click the Change button next to the To Rename This Computer Or Change Its Domain Or Workgroup section.
4. In the Member Of section, click the Domain radio button and type in the name of the Windows Server 2008 domain previously created.

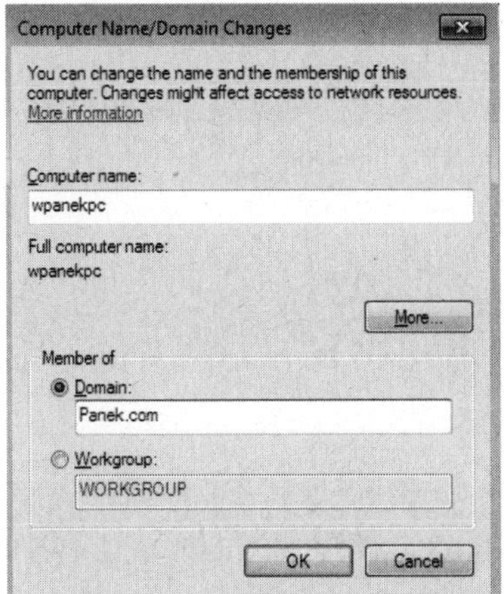

5. A Credentials box appears, asking for the administrator's username and password. Click OK.
6. A dialog box stating that you are part of the domain appears. Click OK and reboot the machine.
7. From the Windows 7 machine, log on to the domain with your username and password.

You also have the ability to create the computer account in the Active Directory Users and Computers MMC snap-in. Complete Exercise 7.8 to add the Windows 7 machine to the domain from the Active Directory snap-in.

EXERCISE 7.8

Adding Windows 7 from Active Directory

1. From the Windows Server 2008 machine, click Start ➤ Administrative Tools ➤ Active Directory Users And Computers.
2. Expand the domain and right-click the Computers OU. Choose New ➤ Computer.
3. In the Computer Name field, type in the name of the Windows 7 computer. Click OK.
4. Double-click the new Windows 7 computer in the right-hand window to open the properties.
5. Take a look at the different tabs and then click the Cancel button.

Another type of network on which you may have to set up Windows 7 is a HomeGroup environment.

Joining and Sharing HomeGroups in Windows 7

Have you ever wanted to share your music, pictures, and documents within your small office or home computers and found the task to be difficult? *HomeGroup* is a new functionality of Windows 7 that simplifies the sharing of music, pictures, and documents within your small office or home network of Windows 7 PCs. HomeGroup allows you to share USB-connected printers too. If you have a printer installed on a Windows 7 computer and it's shared by HomeGroup, it is automatically installed onto the other HomeGroup-enabled Windows 7 PCs. This even extends to domain-joined computers; they can be part of a HomeGroup too. All versions of Windows 7 can use HomeGroups, but only Home Premium, Enterprise, Professional, or Ultimate can create a HomeGroup.

The first step in the process of using HomeGroup for sharing is to create a new HomeGroup or join an existing one. If the Windows 7 network discovery feature is not enabled, you will be asked to create a HomeGroup. In the Network and Sharing Center, select Choose HomeGroup And Sharing Options and then click the Create A HomeGroup button (both items can be seen in Figure 7.16).

FIGURE 7.16 Create a HomeGroup screen

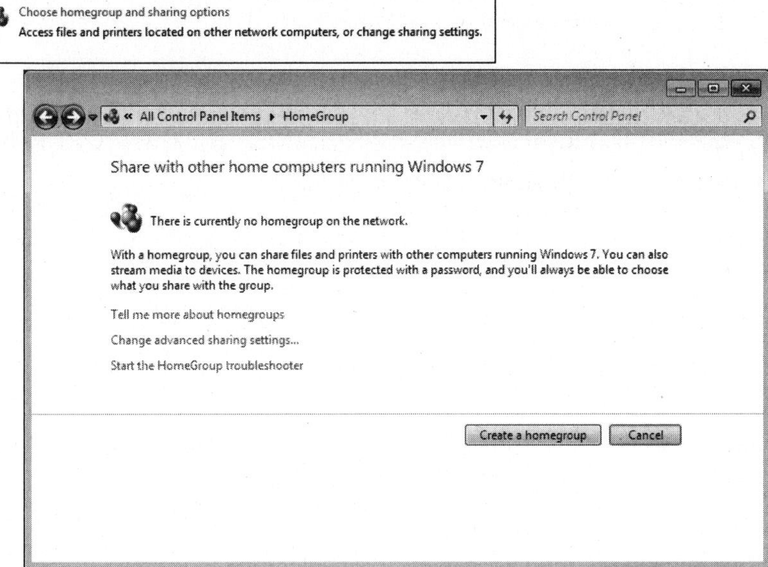

With Windows 7 network discovery turned on (the default), HomeGroup is created automatically. You still need to join the HomeGroup to use the other shared resources and to share yours. From the Network and Sharing Center, you can join an existing HomeGroup by clicking the Join Now button, as shown in Figure 7.17.

FIGURE 7.17 Join an existing HomeGroup

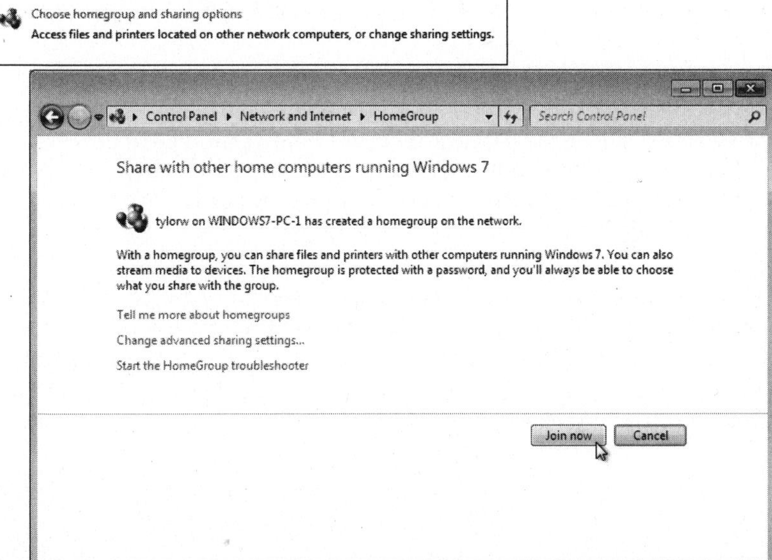

Part of joining a HomeGroup setup is to define the resources that you want to make available to the other members of the HomeGroup. The next screen in the setup (Figure 7.18) lets you choose which resources you want to share.

FIGURE 7.18 HomeGroup sharing selections

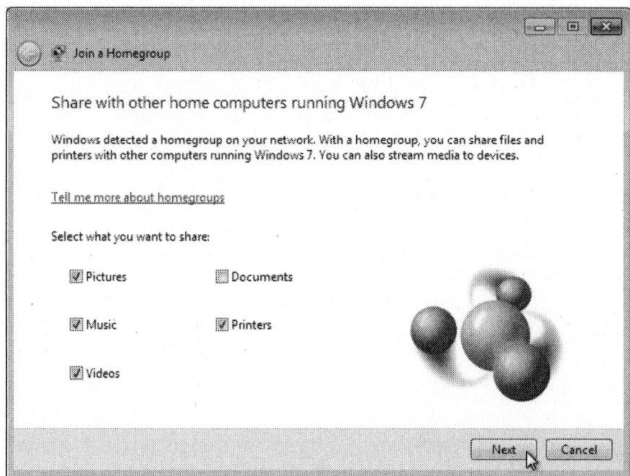

The next step is to enter the HomeGroup password. Windows 7, by default, will recognize a HomeGroup on the network. However, the other Windows 7 machines will not have access to the resources. Allowing any Windows 7 machine connecting to the network to automatically have shared resource access would be a huge security hole. To protect the Windows 7 user resources, a password must be entered to join HomeGroup.

The password for the HomeGroup can be found or changed on the machine that established the HomeGroup. After other machines have joined, each machine has the ability to view or change the password, but they must join the HomeGroup first. The initial machine in the HomeGroup will create a random secure password. To view and/or print the HomeGroup password, use the Choose HomeGroup And Sharing Options selection from the Network and Sharing Center and then choose View Or Print The HomeGroup Password item, as shown in Figure 7.19. Again, this can be done from any Windows 7 machine that is already a member of the HomeGroup, but not from one that wants to join!

Figure 7.20 shows the View And Print Your HomeGroup password screen. For simplicity here, I have changed the password to *password* (not recommended for your network).

FIGURE 7.19 Change HomeGroup settings screen

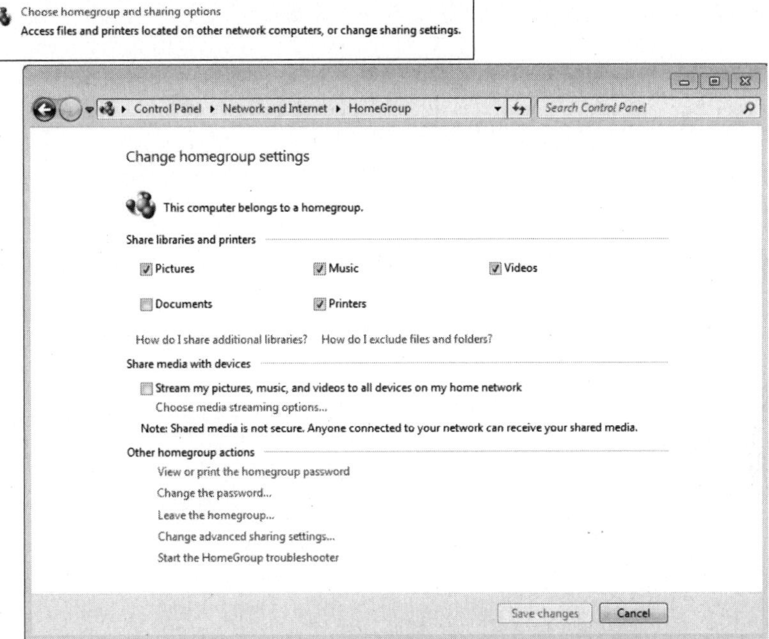

FIGURE 7.20 View And Print Your HomeGroup Password screen

Remember that Windows 7 will initially create a random secure password for the HomeGroup, and you need to visit the View And Print Your HomeGroup Password screen to find out what it is. You will probably want to change it.

To change the password, choose the Change The Password option from the Change HomeGroup Settings page and then select Change The Password from the Change Your HomeGroup Password screen, as shown in Figure 7.21. When you change the HomeGroup password, you need to go to each of the other Windows 7 machines that are members of the HomeGroup and change the password there if you still want the others to share resources.

FIGURE 7.21 Change the HomeGroup password

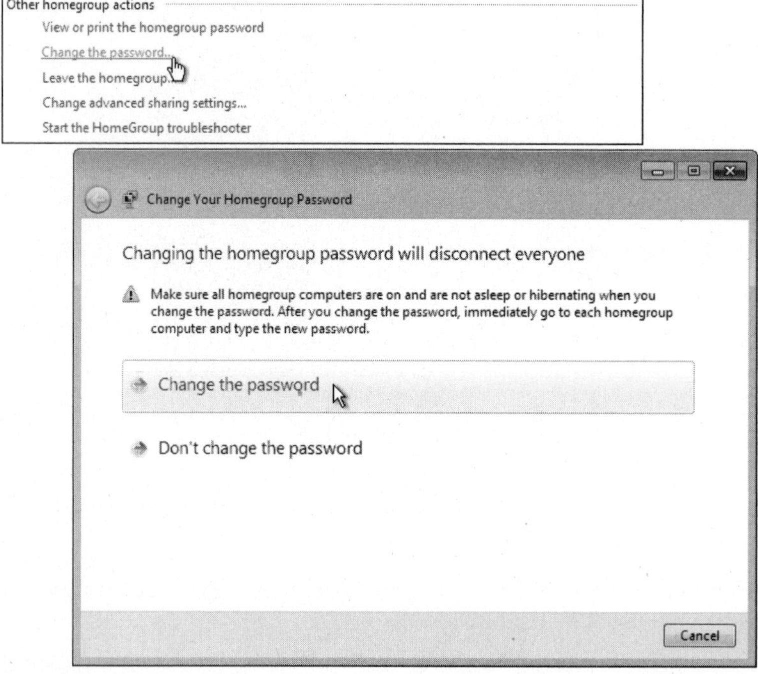

After the HomeGroup is set up, you can see the other members' resources from the HomeGroup option of Windows Explorer or even the Start menu if you customize the Start menu and have added HomeGroup to the displayed options. I have added the HomeGroup option to my Start menu, as shown in Figure 7.22.

FIGURE 7.22 HomeGroup in the Start menu

Choosing the HomeGroup option from the Start menu or choosing Computer and selecting HomeGroup in the Explorer window enables you to see and have access to the other members of your HomeGroup. Figure 7.23 shows the HomeGroup item expanded and one other Windows 7 machine's resources that have joined into the HomeGroup.

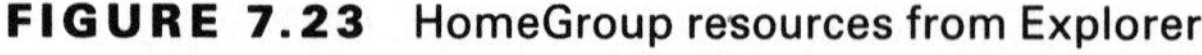

FIGURE 7.23 HomeGroup resources from Explorer

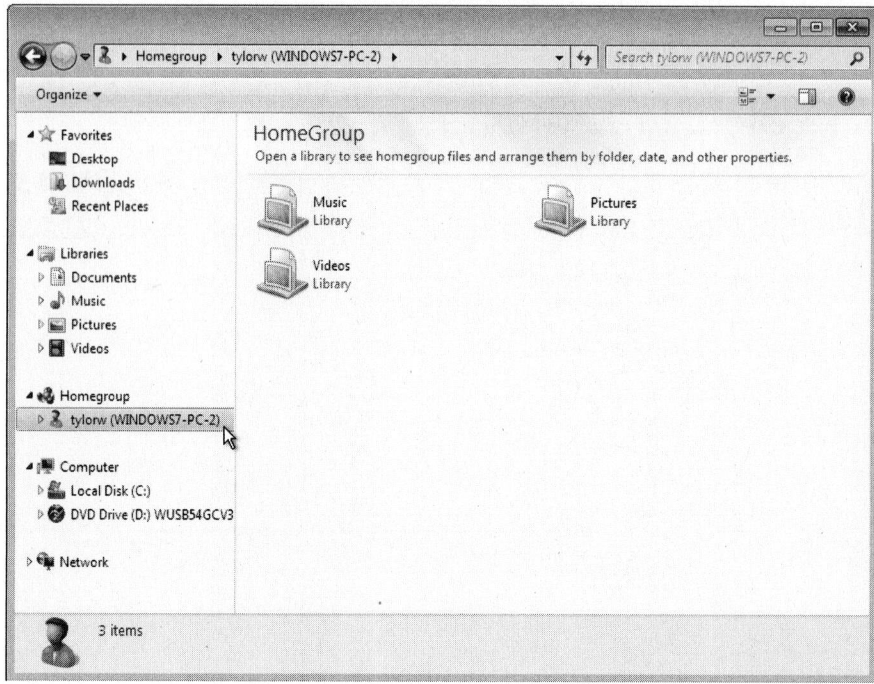

HomeGroups are a great option for users who want to share resources in the Windows 7 environment. But what if you still have non-Windows 7 machines? The legacy function of simply sharing resources and setting permissions still works for Windows 7 and will allow older operating systems to have access to resources shared on Windows 7 machines, as well as allowing users running Windows 7 to have access to the shared resources on Vista and XP.

After you have connected the Windows 7 machine to a network, the next configuration option that has to be set is the Windows 7 firewall. In the next section, you will look at configuring Windows Firewall.

Configuring Windows Firewall

Windows Firewall, which is included with Windows 7, helps prevent unauthorized users or malicious software from accessing your computer. Windows Firewall does not allow unsolicited traffic (traffic that was not sent in response to a request) to pass through the firewall.

You configure Windows Firewall by choosing Start ➢ Control Panel ➢ Large Icons View ➢ Windows Firewall, and then clicking Turn Windows Firewall On Or Off. The Windows Firewall settings dialog box appears, as shown in Figure 7.24.

FIGURE 7.24 Windows Firewall settings dialog box

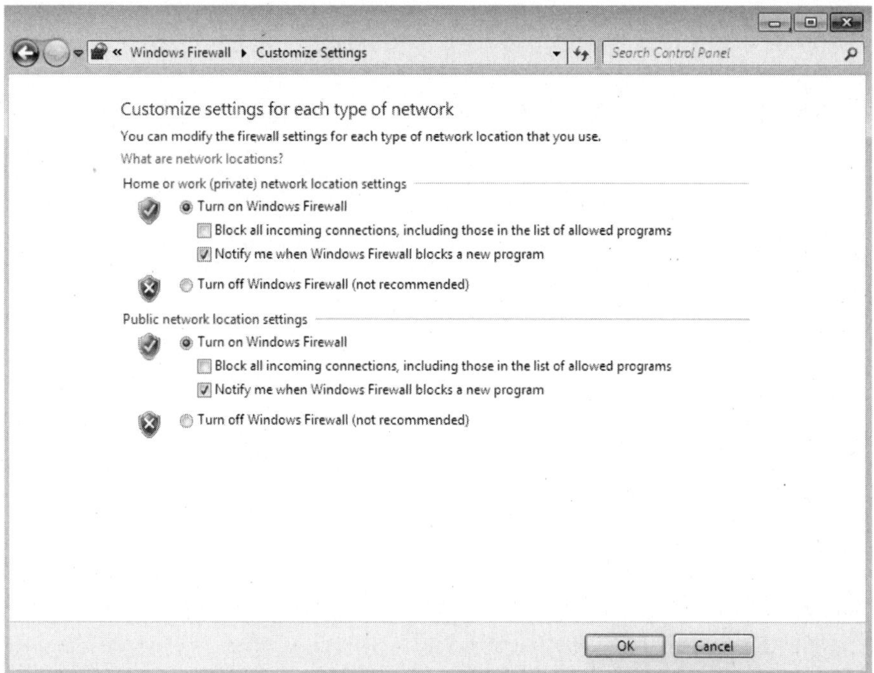

The Windows Firewall settings dialog box allows you to turn Windows Firewall on or off for both private and public networks. The On setting will block external sources except those that are specified on the Exceptions tab. The Off setting will allow external sources to connect.

There is also a check box for Block All Incoming Connections. This feature allows you to connect to networks that are not secure. When Block All Incoming Connections is enabled, exceptions are ignored and no notification will be given when an application is blocked by Windows Firewall.

The exceptions section of the Windows Firewall settings dialog box, shown in Figure 7.25, allows you to define which programs and services should be allowed to pass through Windows Firewall. You can select from a defined list of programs and services or you can use the Allow Another Program button to customize your exceptions.

FIGURE 7.25 Windows Firewall Allowed Programs dialog box

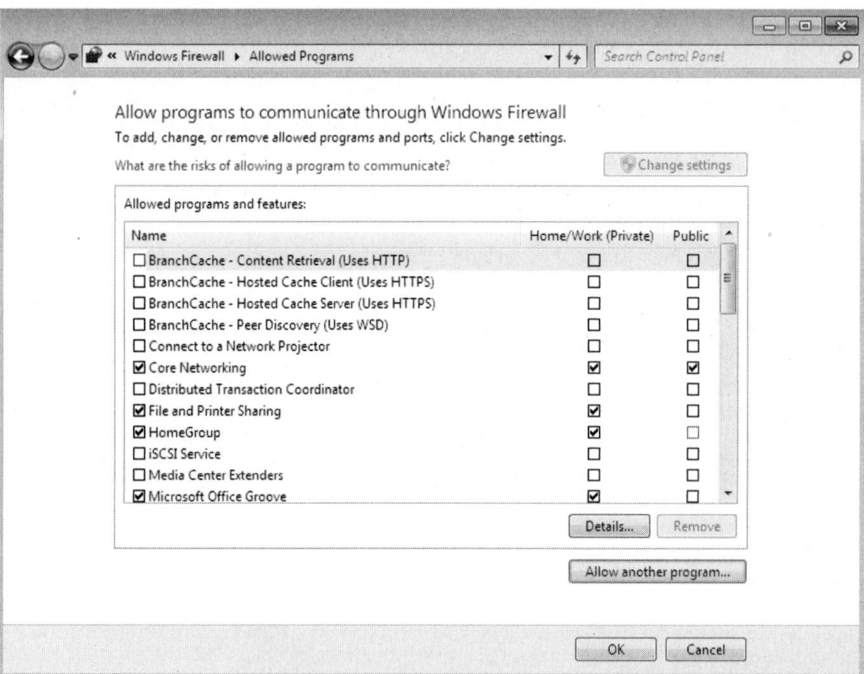

Take great care in enabling exceptions. Exceptions allow traffic to pass through the firewall, which could expose your computer to risk. Remember that the Block All Incoming Connections setting will ignore all exceptions.

Now that you have looked at the basic Windows Firewall settings, let's discuss Windows Firewall with Advanced Security.

Windows Firewall with Advanced Security

You can configure more-advanced settings by configuring Windows Firewall with Advanced Security (WFAS). To access Windows Firewall with Advanced Security, click Start ➢ Control Panel ➢ Large Icons View ➢Windows Firewall and then click the

Advanced Settings link. The Windows Firewall with Advanced Security dialog box appears, as shown in Figure 7.26.

FIGURE 7.26 Windows Firewall with Advanced Security

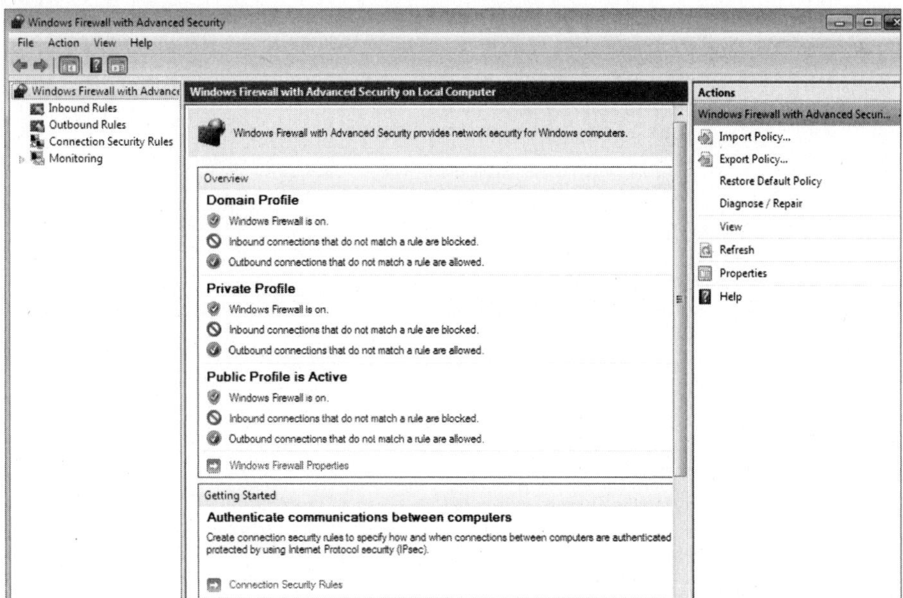

The scope pane to the left shows that you can set up specific inbound and outbound rules, connection security rules, and monitoring rules. The central area shows an overview of the firewall's status, as well as the current profile settings. Let's take a look at these in more detail.

Inbound and Outbound Rules

Inbound and outbound rules consist of many preconfigured rules that can be enabled or disabled. Obviously, inbound rules (see Figure 7.27) monitor inbound traffic, and outbound rules monitor outbound traffic. By default, many are disabled. Double-clicking a rule will bring up its Properties dialog box, as shown in Figure 7.28.

FIGURE 7.27 Inbound rules

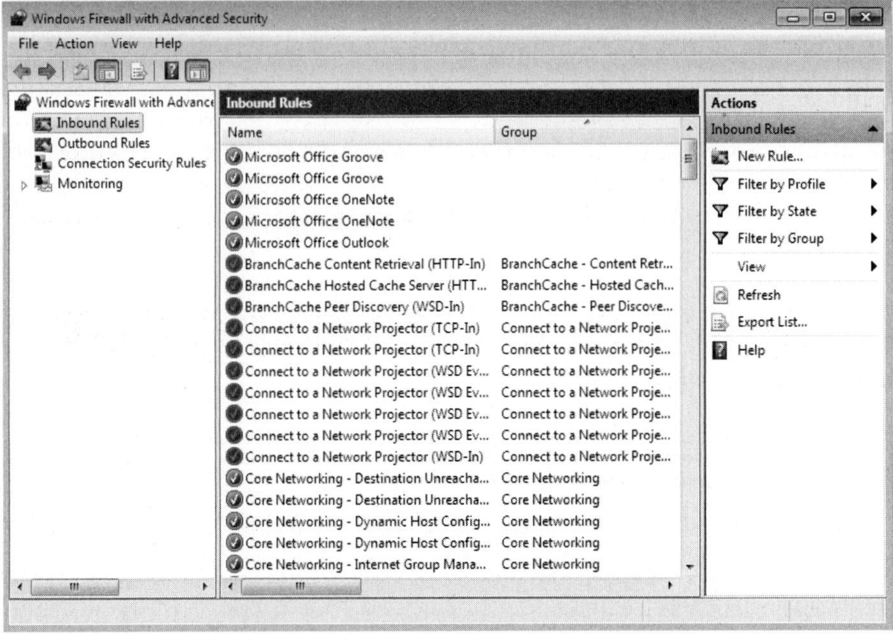

FIGURE 7.28 An inbound rule's Properties dialog box

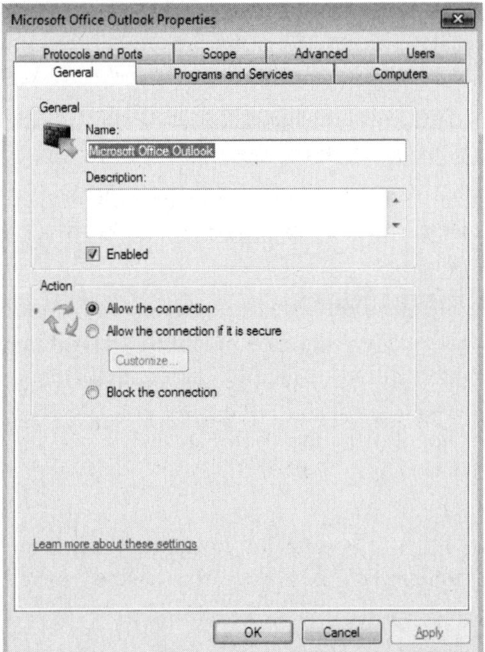

You can filter the rules to make them easier to view. Filtering can be performed based on the profile the rule affects, whether the rule is enabled or disabled, or based on the rule group.

If you can't find a rule that is appropriate for your needs, you can create a new rule by right-clicking Inbound Rules or Outbound Rules in the scope pane, and then selecting New Rule. The New Inbound (or Outbound) Rule Wizard will launch, and you will be asked whether you want to create a rule based on a particular program, protocol or port, predefined category, or custom settings.

Complete Exercise 7.9 to create a new inbound rule that will allow only encrypted TCP traffic.

EXERCISE 7.9

Creating a New Inbound Rule

1. Choose Start ➤Control Panel ➤Large Icon View ➤Windows Firewall.
2. Click Advanced Settings on the left side.
3. Right-click Inbound Rules and select New Rule.
4. Choose a Rule Type. For this exercise, let's choose Custom so we can see all the options available to us. Then click Next.
5. Choose the programs or services that are affected by this rule. For this exercise, let's choose All Programs. Then click Next.
6. Choose the protocol type, as well as the local and remote port numbers that are affected by this rule. For this exercise, let's choose TCP, and ensure that All Ports is selected for both Local Port and Remote Port. Click Next to continue.
7. Choose the local and remote IP addresses that are affected by this rule. Let's choose Any IP Address for both local and remote. Then click Next.
8. Specify whether this rule will allow the connection, allow the connection only if it is secure, or block the connection. Let's select the options Allow The Connection If It Is Secure. Then click Next.
9. Specify whether connections should be allowed only from certain users. You can experiment with these options if you want. Then click Next to continue.
10. Specify whether connections should be allowed only from certain computers. Again you can experiment with these options if you want. Then click Next to continue.
11. Choose which profiles will be affected by this rule. Select one or more profiles and click Next to continue.
12. Give your profile a name and description, and then click Finish. Your custom rule will appear in the list of Inbound Rules, and the rule will be enabled.

13. Double-click on your newly created rule. Notice that you can change the options that you previously configured.
14. Disable the rule by deselecting the Enabled check box. Click OK.

Now let's take a look at setting up connection security rules through Windows Firewall with Advanced Security.

Connection Security Rules

Connection security rules are used to configure how and when authentication occurs. These rules do not specifically allow connections; that's the job of inbound and outbound rules. You can configure the following connection security rules:

- Isolation: To restrict a connection based on authentication criteria
- Authentication Exemption: To specify computers that are exempt from authentication requirements
- Server-to-Server: To authenticate connections between computers
- Tunnel: To authenticate connections between gateway computers
- Custom

The final section you will look at for Windows Firewall with Advanced Security is the Monitoring section.

Monitoring

The Monitoring section shows detailed information about the firewall configurations for the Domain Profile, Private Profile, and Public Profile settings. These network location profiles determine what settings are enforced for private networks, public networks, and networks connected to a domain.

Real World Scenario

Firewalls

When doing consulting, it always make me laugh when I see small to mid-size companies using Microsoft Windows firewalls and no other protection. Microsoft Windows firewalls should be your *last* line of defense. You need to make sure that you have good hardware firewalls that separate your network from the world.

Also watch Windows firewalls when it comes to printing. I have run into many situations where a printer that needs to talk to the operating system has issues when Windows Firewall is enabled. If this happens, make sure that the printer is allowed in the Allowed Programs section.

In the next section, you will look at how to configure your Windows 7 machine remotely.

Configuring Remote Management

There are a few ways that you can help Windows 7 users remotely. A couple of ways, Remote Assistance and Remote Desktop, we covered in Chapter 4, "Managing the Windows 7 Environment." But there are some other tools that you can use to help manage Windows 7—such as Windows Remote Management and Windows PowerShell.

Windows Remote Management

The *Windows Remote Management (WinRM)* utility is Microsoft's version of the WS-Management Protocol. The WS-Management Protocol is an industry standard protocol that allows different vendor operating systems and hardware to work together. There are three main ways to access the WinRM utility:

- WinRM command-line tool
- WinRM scripting objects
- Windows Remote Shell command-line tool

The WinRM utility allows you to remotely execute commands and obtain management data from local and remote computers. You can use the WinRM utility on both Windows-based operating systems and non-Windows-based operating systems.

Table 7.9 shows the different command-line WinRM commands and descriptions of what each command will accomplish.

TABLE 7.9 WinRM Commands and Descriptions

Command	Description
`WinRM g` or `WinRM get`	Retrieves management information
`WinRM s` or `WinRM set`	Modifies management information
`WinRM c` or `WinRM create`	Creates a new instance on the managed resources
`WinRM d` or `WinRM delete`	Removes an instance from a managed resource
`WinRM e` or `WinRM enumerate`	Lists all instances of a managed resource
`WinRM i` or `WinRM invoke`	Executes a method on a managed resource
`WinRM id` or `WinRM identity`	Determines whether a WS-Management implementation is running on a remote machine

TABLE 7.9 WinRM Commands and Descriptions *(continued)*

Command	Description
`WinRM quickconfig`	Configures a machine to accept WS-Management commands from a remote machine
`WinRM configSDDL`	Modifies an existing security descriptor for a Uniform Resource Identifier (URI)
`WinRM helpmsg`	Displays error messages for an error code

Now that you have looked at WinRM, let's take a look at how to remotely manage a Windows 7 machine by using the Windows PowerShell utility.

Windows PowerShell

Windows PowerShell is a command-line scripting utility that allows you to remotely execute commands on a Windows 7 machine. Windows PowerShell is a command line utility that was specifically designed for system administrators to allow for remote administration.

One of the advantages of Windows PowerShell is that Windows PowerShell introduced the concept of a cmdlet. A *cmdlet* is a command that is built into Windows PowerShell. There are over 100 built-in cmdlets, and you can build your own cmdlets and allow others to use these homemade cmdlets.

Another advantage of Windows PowerShell is that Windows PowerShell allows you to gain access to a file system on a computer. Windows PowerShell also allows you to access the Registry, digital certificate stores, and other data stores.

Table 7.10 defines a few of the cmdlets in Windows PowerShell.

TABLE 7.10 Windows PowerShell cmdlets

cmdlet	Definition
`Clear-History`	Deletes entries from the command history
`Invoke-command`	Runs commands on local or remote computers
`Start-job`	Starts a Windows PowerShell background job
`Stop-job`	Stops a Windows PowerShell background job
`Remove-job`	Deletes a Windows PowerShell background job

cmdlet	Definition
`Import-Module`	Adds modules to the current session
`Receive-job`	Gets the results of a Windows PowerShell background job
`Format-table`	Shows the results in a table format
`Out-file`	Sends the job results to a file
`Get-Date`	Gets the date and time
`Set-Date`	Sets the system time and date on a computer
`Get-event`	Gets an event in the event queue
`New-event`	Creates a new event
`Trace-command`	Configures and starts a trace of a command on a machine

Complete Exercise 7.10 to start the Windows PowerShell utility.

EXERCISE 7.10

Starting the Windows PowerShell

1. Start the Windows PowerShell utility by clicking Start ➢ All Programs ➢ Accessories ➢ Windows PowerShell ➢ Windows PowerShell. The utility is just called Windows PowerShell and it is under the Windows PowerShell folder.

```
Windows PowerShell
Windows PowerShell
Copyright (C) 2009 Microsoft Corporation. All rights reserved.

PS C:\Users>
```

2. When the Windows PowerShell utility starts, type **Help** and press Enter. This will show you the Windows PowerShell syntax and some of the commands included with Windows PowerShell.

3. At the Windows PowerShell command prompt, type **Get-Date**. This will show you the system's date and time.
4. At the Windows command prompt, type **Help ***. This will show you all the cmdlet commands that you can use.
5. Close the Windows PowerShell utility.

Using the WinRM and Windows PowerShell utilities gives you the ability to remotely configure and administer a Windows 7 machine. Now let's take a look at BranchCache.

Understanding BranchCache

BranchCache is a new technology that has been introduced in Windows Server 2008 R2 and Windows 7. BranchCache allows an organization with slower links between offices to cache data so downloads between offices do not have to occur each time a file is accessed.

For example, say John comes into work and logs in to the network. John accesses the corporate website and downloads a media file that takes four minutes to download. With BranchCache enabled, when Judy comes into work and connects to the corporate website and tries to download the same media file, the file will be cached from the previous download, and Judy will have immediate access to the file.

There are two types of BranchCache configurations that you can set up—distributed cache mode and hosted mode:

Distributed Cache Mode In the distributed cache mode configuration, all Windows 7 client machines cache the files locally on the client machines. So in the preceding example, after John downloaded the media file, Judy would receive the cached media file from John's Windows 7 machine.

Hosted Mode In the hosted mode configuration, the cache files are cached on a local (within the site) Windows Server 2008 R2 machine. So in the preceding example, after John downloaded the media file, the cached file would be placed on a Windows Server 2008 machine by default and all other users (Judy) would download the media file from the Windows Server 2008 R2 machine.

Distributed Cache Mode Requirements

If you decide to install BranchCache in the distributed cache mode configuration, a hosted cache server running Windows Server 2008 R2 is not required at the branch office. To set up distributed cache mode, the client machines must be running either Windows 7 Enterprise Edition or Windows 7 Ultimate Edition.

The Windows 7 machines would download the data files from the content servers at the main branch office, and then these Windows 7 machines become the local cache servers. To set up distributed cache mode, you must install a Windows Server 2008 R2 content server at the main office first. After the content server is installed, physical connections (WAN or VPN connections) between the sites and branch offices must be established.

Client computers running Windows 7 have BranchCache installed by default, but you must, however, enable and configure BranchCache and configure firewall exceptions. Complete Exercise 7.11 to configure BranchCache firewall rule exceptions.

EXERCISE 7.11

Configuring BranchCache Firewall Exceptions

1. On a domain controller, click Start ➤Administrative Tools ➤ Group Policy Management. This opens the Group Policy Management console.
2. In the Group Policy Management console, expand the following path: Forest ➤Domains ➤Group Policy Objects. Make sure that the domain you choose contains the BranchCache Windows 7 client computer accounts that you want to configure.
3. In the Group Policy Management console, right-click Group Policy Objects and select Create And Link Group Policy Here. Name the policy **BranchCache Client** and press Enter. Right-click BranchCache Client and click Edit. The Group Policy Management Editor console opens.
4. In the Group Policy Management Editor console, expand the following path: Computer Configuration ➤Policies ➤Windows Settings ➤Security Settings ➤Windows Firewall with Advanced Security ➤Windows Firewall with Advanced Security ➤LDAP ➤Inbound Rules.
5. Right-click Inbound Rules and then click New Rule. The New Inbound Rule Wizard opens.
6. In Rule Type, click Predefined, expand the list of choices, and then click BranchCache—Content Retrieval (Uses HTTP). Click Next.
7. In Predefined Rules, click Next.
8. In Action, ensure that Allow The Connection is selected, and then click Finish. You must select Allow The Connection for the BranchCache client to be able to receive traffic on this port.
9. Now to create the WS-Discovery firewall exception, right-click Inbound Rules, and click New Rule. The New Inbound Rule Wizard opens.
10. In Rule Type, click Predefined, expand the list of choices, and then click BranchCache—Peer Discovery (Uses WSD). Click Next.
11. In Predefined Rules, click Next.
12. In Action, ensure that Allow The Connection is selected, and then click Finish.
13. In the Group Policy Management Editor console, right-click Outbound Rules, and then click New Rule. The New Outbound Rule Wizard opens.

14. In Rule Type, click Predefined, expand the list of choices, and then click BranchCache—Content Retrieval (Uses HTTP). Click Next.
15. In Predefined Rules, click Next.
16. In Action, ensure that Allow The Connection is selected, and then click Finish.
17. Create the WS-Discovery firewall exception by right-clicking Outbound Rules, and then click New Rule. The New Outbound Rule Wizard opens.
18. In Rule Type, click Predefined, expand the list of choices, and then click BranchCache—Peer Discovery (Uses WSD). Click Next.
19. In Predefined Rules, click Next.
20. In Action, ensure that Allow The Connection is selected, and then click Finish.

Now that you have looked at the distributed cache mode configuration, let's take a look at the hosted mode configuration.

Hosted Mode Requirements

To set up a hosted mode BranchCache configuration, you must first set up a Windows Server 2008 R2 hosted cache server at the main and branch offices. You also need Windows 7 Enterprise or Windows 7 Ultimate computers at the branch offices.

The Windows 7 machines download the data from the main cache server, and then the hosted cache servers at the branch offices obtain a copy of the downloaded data for other users to access.

Your network infrastructure must also allow for physical connections between the main office and the branch offices. These connections can be VPNs or some type of WAN links. After these requirements are met, your cache server must obtain a server certificate so the client computers in the branch offices can positively identify the cache servers.

To learn how to configure a certificate server, see *MCTS: Windows Server 2008 Network Infrastructure Configuration Study Guide* (Exam 70-642) by William Panek, Tyler Wentworth, and James Chellis (Sybex, 2008).

Exercise 7.12 walks you through the process of installing the BranchCache feature on a Windows Server 2008 R2 machine. To accomplish this exercise, you must be logged in to the Windows Server 2008 machine as an administrator.

EXERCISE 7.12

Installing BranchCache on a Windows Server 2008 R2 machine

1. Open the Server Manager by clicking Start ➤ Administrative Tools ➤ Server Manager.
2. In Server Manager, right-click Features and then choose the Add Feature link.

3. The Add Features Wizard starts. Select the BranchCache check box and click Next.
4. At the Confirm Installation Selections screen, click Install.
5. After the BranchCache feature installs, click Close.
6. In the Server Manager left window pane, double-click Configuration and then click Services.
7. In the Services detail pane, double-click BranchCache.
8. The BranchCache Properties dialog box appears. Click the General tab and then click Start. Click OK.
9. Close Server Manager.

Make sure to repeat this exercise on all branch office cache servers. Now one of the requirements for BranchCache was a physical connection between the main office and the branch offices. In the next section, you will look at configuring DirectAccess.

Configuring DirectAccess

DirectAccess is new to the Windows Server 2008 R2 and Windows 7 operating systems. *DirectAccess* enables a remote user to work on their corporate network when they are away from the office without the need of a VPN. As long as the remote user is connected to the Internet, DirectAccess will automatically connect the remote user to the corporate network without the need of any user intervention.

When a user's DirectAccess-enabled laptop is connected to the Internet, a bidirectional connection is automatically established with the user's corporate network. Because the connection is bidirectional, the IT administrator can also remotely manage the Windows 7 machine while the machine is away from the network.

DirectAccess vs. VPNs

There are a few problems with using VPNs to connect to a network. One issue is that when a user gets disconnected from their VPN connection, they must reestablish the VPN connection.

Another issue with VPNs is that many organizations filter VPN connection traffic. It may not be possible for an organization to open a firewall to allow VPN traffic. Also if your intranet and your Internet connections are the same as your VPN connections, this can cause your Internet connections to be slower.

DirectAccess does not face the same limitations of a VPN. DirectAccess allows a laptop or desktop that is configured properly to automatically connect by using a bidirectional connection between the client and the server.

To establish this connection, DirectAccess uses Internet Protocol Security (IPsec) and IPv6. IPsec provides a high level of security between the client and the server, and IPv6 is the protocol that the machines use.

Understanding How DirectAccess Works

To better understand DirectAccess, it helps to understand how DirectAccess operates. The following steps, taken from the Microsoft white papers, show how DirectAccess operates.

1. The Windows 7 DirectAccess client determines whether the machine is connected to a network or to the Internet.
2. The Windows 7 DirectAccess computer tries to connect to the web server specified during the DirectAccess setup configuration.
3. The Windows 7 DirectAccess client computer connects to the Windows Server 2008 R2 DirectAccess server using IPv6 and IPsec. Because most users connect to the Internet by using IPv4, the client establishes an IPv6-over-IPv4 tunnel using 6to4 or Teredo.
4. If an organization has a firewall that prevents the DirectAccess client computer using 6to4 or Teredo from connecting to the DirectAccess server, the Windows 7 client automatically attempts to connect by using the IP-HTTPS protocol.
5. As part of establishing the IPsec session, the Windows 7 DirectAccess client and server authenticate each other by using computer certificates for authentication.
6. The DirectAccess server uses Active Directory membership, and the DirectAccess server verifies that the computer and user are authorized to connect by using DirectAccess.
7. The DirectAccess server begins forwarding traffic from the DirectAccess client to the intranet resources to which the user has been granted access.

Now that you understand how DirectAccess works, let's take a look at the requirements for setting up DirectAccess on your network.

Knowing the DirectAccess Infrastructure Requirements

To set up DirectAccess, your network infrastructure must meet some minimum requirements. The following show the requirements for setting up DirectAccess:

- Windows Server 2008 R2 configured to use DirectAccess. The Windows Server 2008 machine will be set up as a multihomed system. This means that your server will need two network adapters so one adapter is connected directly to the Internet and a second adapter is connected to the intranet. Each network adapter will be configured with its own TCP/IP address.

- Windows 7 client machines configured to use DirectAccess.
- Minimum of one domain controller and one DNS server running Windows Server 2008 SP2 or Windows Server 2008 R2.
- Certificate authority (CA) server that will issue computer certificates, smart card certificates, or health certificates.
- IPsec policies to specify protection for traffic.
- IPv6 on the DirectAccess server that uses ISATAP, Teredo, or 6to4.

Complete Exercise 7.13 to install the DirectAccess feature onto a Windows Server 2008 R2 machine. Remember that the DirectAccess feature needs to be installed on Windows Server 2008 R2.

EXERCISE 7.13

Installing the DirectAccess Feature

1. Start Server Manager by clicking Start ➢ Administrative Tools ➢ Server Manager.
2. In the left window pane, click Features.
3. In the right window, click the Add Feature link.
4. Click the DirectAccess Management Console check box.
5. A dialog box may appear, asking you to install any other features required by DirectAccess. Click the Add Required Features button.
6. Click Next and then click the Install button.
7. Verify that the installation was complete and then close Server Manager.

After the DirectAccess feature is installed, in the Administrative Tools section, the DirectAccess Manager will appear. When you start the DirectAccess Manager, click Setup and the DirectAccess Setup Wizard will start.

The setup wizard (see Figure 7.29) walks you through a four-stage process (Setting up the Remote Clients, DirectAccess Server, Infrastructure Servers, and Application Servers) and it will allow you to choose which Windows 7 computers can use DirectAccess. Follow the wizard to complete the installation. To complete the setup and allow this to function properly, you also need to set up a certificate server, domain controller, and DNS.

FIGURE 7.29 DirectAccess Setup Wizard stages

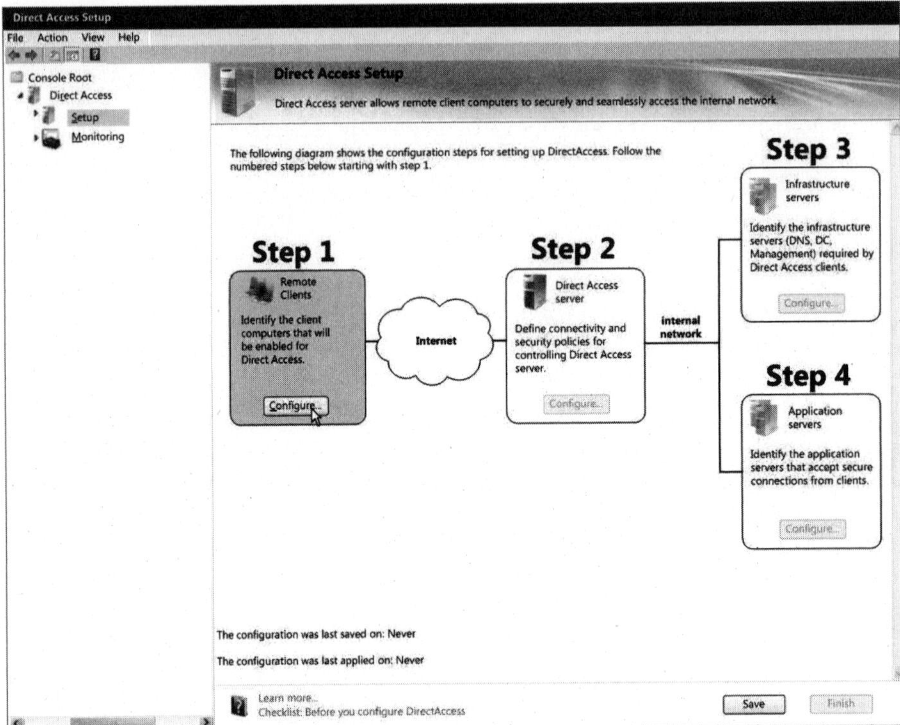

Finally, in this chapter you will look at how to run Windows 7 in a virtualized environment by using either Microsoft Hyper-V or Microsoft Virtual PC.

Understanding Virtualization

Server *virtualization* gives an organization the ability to run multiple operating systems, called *virtual machines*, on a single machine. The ability to run multiple operating systems on a single machine will help an organization reduce their hardware costs and allow an organization to reduce their IT department overhead.

Many organizations have started to move their servers over to virtualized servers. But you do not need to just use virtualization for your servers. You can also use virtualization for client operating systems such as Windows 7. In the next sections, you will look at the two most common ways to use Microsoft products to virtually set up Windows 7: Windows Virtual PC and Hyper-V. Microsoft has just released a new version of virtualization with the Windows Server 2008 R2 operating system called Hyper-V, and that's where we will start.

Understanding Microsoft Hyper-V

Hyper-V is not Microsoft's first attempt at virtualization. Microsoft has been doing virtualization for years. There were two versions of virtualization that IT teams have used in the past. The two Microsoft virtualization products that you may have used before are Microsoft Virtual PC and Microsoft Virtual Server 2005.

Microsoft *Hyper-V* is the next generation hypervisor-based virtualization technology. With the release of Microsoft Windows Server 2008, Microsoft has now incorporated server virtualization into the operating system with the release of Hyper-V. This gives an organization the ability to take full advantage of the next generation of 64-bit server hardware.

Let's imagine an IT department for any size organization. You come in one morning before everyone else (common in our field) and see that one of your servers has crashed. The first thing that's going to happen is your heart is going to drop into your stomach. After that, you will start trying to fix the error and you may even need to rebuild the machine. Now your heart is racing, and your blood pressure is going through the roof because you need to get this server up and running before anyone else comes into work. We have all been there before.

Now let's imagine the same situation, but all of your servers are running Hyper-V. When you come in and see your crash, you know you can relax. All you need to do is move the Hyper-V virtual machine to another machine, and you are back up and running. This is what Hyper-V can do for you. Hyper-V is a role-based feature that allows an organization to have multiple virtual machines (multiple operating systems including Windows 7) on a single Windows Server 2008 machine.

A virtual machine (VM) is an implementation of an operating system that runs in its own virtualization window. The advantage of using virtual machines is that you can have multiple VMs on the same Windows Server 2008 machine. Each VM can have its own unique resources running on its operating system. An administrator can now run multiple operating systems (including non-Windows–based systems) or run multiple server roles in their own virtual machines, thus allowing an organization more flexibility without the need for more servers. One of the greatest advantages of Hyper-V technology is that you have the ability to run both 32-bit and 64-bit applications within the virtual environment.

To learn more about Microsoft Hyper-V, see *MCTS: Windows Server Virtualization Configuration Study Guide* (Exam 70-652) by William Panek (Wiley, 2009).

In the next section, you will install the Windows 7 operating system in Hyper-V as a virtual machine.

Creating a Hyper-V Windows 7 Virtual Machine

As we explained in the preceding section, a virtual machine is an operating system that is running within the Microsoft Hyper-V or Microsoft Virtual PC environments. You can run multiple virtual machines on the same physical machine. By placing multiple virtual machines on the same physical machine, Hyper-V and Virtual PC allow you to maximize performance by utilizing hardware resources.

The *hypervisor*, in Hyper-V, is a 64-bit mechanism that allows Hyper-V to run multiple virtual machines on the same physical machine. The hypervisor's job is to create and manage the partitions between virtual machines. The hypervisor is a thin software layer that sits between the virtual machines and the hardware.

Virtual machines are full operating systems that run in a virtualized environment. The end users that connect to the virtual machines do not know the difference between a normal machine or a virtualized machine. Because of this, you can set up your virtual machine environment the same way you would set up a normal machine.

Complete Exercise 7.14 to install Windows 7 as a virtual machine. To complete this exercise, you must be running Windows Server 2008 R2 with Hyper-V along with virtualization enabled on the BIOS.

EXERCISE 7.14

Making Windows 7 a .VHD

1. Start the Hyper-V Manager by clicking Start ➢ Administrative Tools ➢ Hyper-V Manager.
2. When the Hyper-V Manager starts, click the New, Virtual Machine link under the Actions section.
3. Click Next at the Before You Begin screen.
4. At the Specify Name And Location screen, type **Win7VM** in the Name field. Leave the default location. Click Next.
5. At the Assign Memory screen, type **1024MB** and click Next.
6. At the Configure Networking screen, pull down the Connection type and choose your network adapter. Click Next.
7. We are going to create a virtual hard disk at the Connect Virtual Hard Disk screen. Click Create A New Virtual Hard Disk.
8. Type **`Win7.vhd`** and make the hard drive size 20 GB. Click Next.
9. At the Summary screen, select the Start The Virtual Machine After It Is Created check box and click Finish.

10. When the Win7VM starts, you will receive a boot failure. Click the Media menu option. Click the DVD Drive option and then Capture Your DVD Drive. Then click Enter.
11. The Windows 7 installation should start. Install the Windows 7 Enterprise Edition as normal.

One item that you may have to configure when booting into a Windows 7 virtual machine is the boot configuration file, or `bcdedit`. The `bcdedit` file was discussed in detail in Chapter 1, "Windows 7 Installation."

Make sure you understand what and how the `bcdedit` configuration file works. You will see multiple exam questions on this topic on the Microsoft Windows 7 exam (70-680).

Now, it may not be feasible to set up a Windows Server 2008 machine with Hyper-V to run Windows 7. So there is a better way for client operating systems—Microsoft Virtual PC.

Understanding Windows Virtual PC

Microsoft also has a virtualization environment that can operate on its client software called Windows Virtual PC. *Windows Virtual PC* enables you to create and manage virtual machines without the need of a server operating system. The advantage here is that you can run server operating systems in a client environment such as Windows XP, Windows Vista, or Windows 7.

Windows Virtual PC was covered in detail in Chapter 5, "Configuring Hardware and Applications." I mention it here again in this chapter because we are discussing virtualization.

In Chapter 5, you downloaded and installed Windows Virtual PC. You also created a Windows 7 virtual hard disk. Now that you have created a Windows 7 virtual machine for Virtual PC, let's go ahead and start the Windows 7 operating system on the virtual PC. Complete the following steps to run the Windows 7 Virtual PC virtual machine:

1. Open Windows Virtual PC.
2. Click the Windows 7 machine (VirtualWin7) and click the Start button.
3. When Windows 7 starts, log in as usual.

To do a Ctrl+Alt+Delete in Virtual PC, you can use right-Alt/Delete. You can go into a full screen mode by clicking right-Alt/Enter. Do the same command to get out of full screen mode. When you use the mouse within Virtual PC, to release the mouse and go back to the host machine, press the right Alt key.

Implementing Windows 7 in a Virtual PC environment enables you to start testing and learning about the new operating system before implementing it into your organization.

Virtualization is a fast-growing technology that many IT departments have embraced. If you have not started using virtualization yet, start doing your homework now before you fall behind the curve. Virtualization can save your organization money and downtime and make you look great as the IT person who implemented it.

Summary

In this chapter, we discussed the different types of Windows networks: domain based and peer-to-peer (workgroup) based. We also discussed a newer, easier way to set up a workgroup-based network by using HomeGroups.

Computers need to use some type of communication device, and that is called a NIC device. You can set up Windows 7 to use both wired and wireless NIC devices. Windows 7 also has new features included to help with setting up your wireless networks.

To allow computers to communicate on a network, you must use a protocol. A *protocol* is a set of communication standards that all computers will use. The main protocol that Windows 7 uses is TCP/IP. There are two versions of TCP/IP that Windows 7 can use, IPv4 and IPv6. IPv4 is the most commonly used protocol, but IPv6 is the newest version of TCP/IP and gives organizations flexibility and growth potential.

In this chapter, we also discussed using Windows Firewall with Advanced Security. Windows Firewall helps prevent unauthorized users from connecting to the Windows 7 operating system. Windows Firewall is an extra line of defense, but it *should not* replace a perimeter firewall for your network.

We showed how to use remote management tools such as WinRM to help configure your operating systems remotely. We also presented BranchCache and DirectAccess and how to configure these utilities.

Finally, in this chapter we discussed virtualization. We looked at how to turn Windows 7 into a virtualized operating system and how to use Windows Hyper-V and Virtual PC to run these virtual Windows 7 operating systems.

Exam Essentials

Understand IPv4 and IPv6. Know and understand IPv4 and IPv6. Understand how to configure and maintain both IPv4 and IPv6 networks. Know how to subnet an IPv4 network. Understand that APIPA will automatically assign an IP address to a Windows 7 machine if DHCP is not available.

Understand how to configure network settings. Know how to install and configure both wired and wireless networks. Understand how Windows 7 has built-in wireless network support. Know how to set up your preferred wireless network.

Know how to configure Windows Firewall. Know how to set up and maintain Windows Firewall with Advanced Security. Know that you can set up inbound and outbound rules by using Windows Firewall. Know how to allow or deny applications by using Windows Firewall.

Understand the different remote management tools. Know the different remote management tools such as the Windows Remote Management (WinRM) utility and Windows PowerShell. Know how to configure these tools for remote management.

Understand BranchCache. Understand that BranchCache helps remote locations access resources without using excessive bandwidth. Know the difference between distributed cache mode and hosted mode. Know what the network requirements are to use BranchCache and how to configure BranchCache.

Understand DirectAccess. Understand that DirectAccess allows remote users to connect to an organization's network without the need of using a VPN. Know that DirectAccess needs to run on Windows Server 2008 R2 and understand the different infrastructure requirements to run DirectAccess.

Know Windows 7 virtualization. Know how to turn a Windows 7 operating system into a virtual machine. Understand that you must configure the `bcdedit` file to boot a machine into a Windows 7 virtual machine. Know that you can use both Microsoft Hyper-V and Windows Virtual PC to run a Windows 7 virtual machine.

Review Questions

1. You are the network administrator for a large organization that has decided to implement DirectAccess. What are some of the requirements needed to install DirectAccess? Choose all that apply.
   - **A.** Windows Server 2008 R2 running the DirectAccess feature
   - **B.** Windows certificate authority server
   - **C.** DNS
   - **D.** WINS
2. You are the network administrator for a midsize company that uses Windows Server 2008 R2 and Windows 7. All Windows 7 machines receive their IP address from DHCP. You have a Windows 7 machine and need to identify its IPv6 address. How can you accomplish this task? Choose all that apply.
   - **A.** Click Details from the network connection status.
   - **B.** Type **ipconfig /all** at the command prompt.
   - **C.** Type **ipconfig /view** at the command prompt.
   - **D.** Choose properties of My Computer.
3. You are hired by friends to set up a network in their home. They have four machines in their home that are all connected by a router. There is currently no network in place. They want to be able to share audio and video files among their family members. How can you set up the network? Choose two.
   - **A.** Install a Windows Server 2008 R2 domain controller.
   - **B.** Create a HomeGroup.
   - **C.** All audio and video files should be moved to the media library.
   - **D.** Move all audio and video files to a shared folder on the Windows Server 2008 R2 machine.

4. You are the network administrator for an organization with two sites (as shown in the diagram). You need to install a new Windows 7 machine into site 1. Which TCP/IP address can you assign to the new Windows 7 machine?

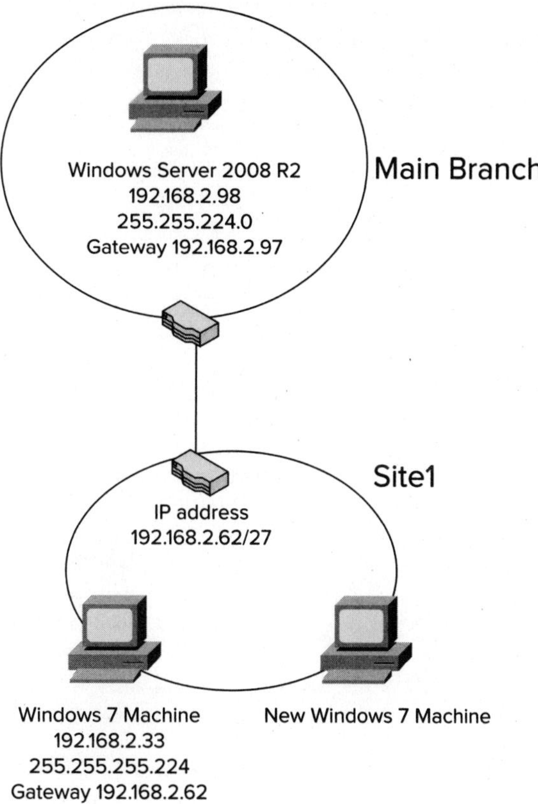

A. 192.168.2.32

B. 192.168.2.31

C. 192.168.2.41

D. 192.168.2.63

5. You are the network administrator for a large organization that has decided to use DirectAccess. You have configured all requirements for DirectAccess. You have a Windows 7 machine that is not connecting through DirectAccess. You run an `ipconfig` and get the following information:

   Ethernet adapter local area connection

   Connection-specific DNS suffix: Stellacon.com

   IPv4 address: 192.168.20.40

   Subnet mask: 255.255.255.0

   Default gateway: 192.168.20.1

   There are no other configuration settings for this Windows 7 machine. What needs to be done first to configure this machine to use DirectAccess?

   A. Enable IPv6 on the network adapter

   B. Remove the connection-specific DNS suffix

   C. Remove the default gateway

   D. Change the subnet mask

6. You are the network administrator for a midsize company that uses both desktops and laptops. All laptops use Windows 7 and have been connected to a wireless access point. You disable the service set identifier (SSID), and now your laptops can no longer connect to the access point. What do you need to do to allow the laptops to connect?

   A. Reboot the laptops.

   B. Modify the wireless network connection settings on the laptops.

   C. Reboot the access point.

   D. Disconnect and reconnect the laptops to the domain.

7. You have made a Windows 7 virtual hard disk (`.vhd`) and installed that `.vhd` onto a machine. You want to be sure that the machine boots up using the Windows 7 `.vhd`. What do you need to modify?

   A. Disk Management

   B. Fdisk

   C. `bcdedit`

   D. `boot.ini`

8. You are the network administrator for a midsize company that uses both desktops and laptops. All laptops use Windows 7 and have been connected to a wireless access point that is configured to use Advanced Encryption Standard (AES) security. There is no preshared password key being used. You need to connect a new Windows 7 laptop to the access point. How would you set up the security setting on the laptop?

   A. WPA2-Personal

   B. WPA2-Enterprise

   C. WPA-Personal

   D. WAP security

9. You are the network administrator for a large organization that uses Windows Server 2008 R2 and Windows 7. You have two Windows 7 machines named Client1 and Client2. You want to be able to remotely execute commands on Client2 from Client1's machine. How can you accomplish this task?

   A. Run WinRM `quickconfig` on Client1

   B. Run WinRM `quickconfig` on Client2

   C. Run WinRM `execute` on Client1

   D. Run WinRM `execute` on Client2

10. You are the network administrator for a small organization that has decided to switch the company's TCP/IP subnet mask. They have chosen to use 255.255.255.240. What do the subnet ranges go by in a 240 subnet mask?

    A. 4

    B. 8

    C. 16

    D. 32

11. You have two DHCP servers on your network. Your computer accidentally received the wrong IP and DNS server configuration from a DHCP server that was misconfigured. The DHCP server with the incorrect configuration has been disabled. What commands could you use to release and renew your computer's DHCP configuration? Choose two.

    A. `ipconfig /release`

    B. `ipconfig /registerdhcp`

    C. `ipconfig /renew`

    D. `ipconfig /flushdhcp`

12. You are the network administrator for your company. Your service provider has assigned you the network address 192.168.154.0. You have been granted the entire range to use. What class of address have you been assigned?

    A. Class A

    B. Class B

    C. Class C

    D. Class D

13. You are the network administrator for your company. After configuring a new computer and connecting it to the network, you discover that you cannot access any of the computers on the remote subnet by IP address. You can access some of the computers on the local subnet by IP address. What is the most likely problem?

    A. Incorrectly defined IP address

    B. Incorrectly defined subnet mask

    C. Incorrectly defined default gateway

    D. Incorrectly defined DNS server

14. A user cannot access a server in the domain. After troubleshooting, you determine that the user cannot access the server by name but can access the server by IP address. What is the most likely problem?

    A. Incorrectly defined IP address

    B. Incorrectly defined subnet mask

    C. Incorrectly defined DHCP server

    D. Incorrectly defined DNS server

15. You have a Windows 7 machine that needs to have a static TCP/IP address. You assign the IP address to the machine and you now want to register the computer with DNS. How can you do this from the Windows 7 machine?

    A. `ipconfig /renewDNS`

    B. `ipconfig /flushDNS`

    C. `ipconfig /DNS`

    D. `ipconfig /registerDNS`

16. You are the network administrator for a large organization that has just opened a new site location. The new site location has a slow link between the site and the main office. What can you implement to help with the slower link between the main site and the remote site?

    A. BranchCache

    B. SiteCache

    C. LinkCache

    D. BranchLink

17. You need to set up a Windows 7 machine for testing and training. You want to set this Windows 7 machine up on an XP machine and you want to keep the XP machine as the primary operating system. What utility can you use to create a Windows 7 testing and training environment?

    A. Microsoft Hyper-V

    B. Windows Virtual PC

    C. Microsoft Virtual Server

    D. Microsoft Virtualization Server

18. You are the network administrator for a large organization that has implemented a new site. All machines in the remote site are Windows 7. The new site link is slow, and you want to implement BranchCache. You do not want to implement a BranchCache server in the remote location. How would you configure BranchCache?

    A. Hosted mode

    B. Distributed cache mode

    C. Shared mode

    D. Server mode

19. You are the network administrator for a small organization. Your organization has implemented Windows 7 on all client machines. You want to implement another line of security on the Windows 7 machine so unauthorized users can't access the machines. What can you implement on the Windows 7 machines?

A. Windows Data Protection

B. Windows Encryption Protection

C. Windows Firewall

D. Windows Secure Data Protocol

20. You are the network administrator for a large organization with many laptop users who go on the road. You want these users to be able to connect to the network without using a VPN or taking over the server console. What can you implement?

A. DirectAccess

B. Remote Access

C. Remote Desktop

D. Remote Server

Answers to Review Questions

1. A, B, C. To implement DirectAccess, your network must have a Windows Server 2008 R2 machine with the DirectAccess feature installed. You must also have a certificate authority (CA) server to issue a certificate to the DirectAccess clients. You must also have a domain controller and DNS server.

2. A, B. You can see what the IPv6 address is by clicking the Details button from the network connection status or by typing **ipconfig /all**. There is no such command as `ipconfig /view`, and the My Computer properties will not show IP address configuration information.

3. B, C. Create a new HomeGroup and set the password. Use that password and join all computers to the same HomeGroup. By default, all files in the media library are available to all members of the HomeGroup.

4. C. The company's subnet mask is 255.255.224.0. This subnet mask uses subnet ranges of 32. So the subnet's layout is 32–63, 64–95, 96–127, 128–159, 160–191 and 192–223. Now when you subnet, you can't use the first or last number of any range. The first number represents the network ID, and the last number represents the broadcast. So because the router and the one Windows 7 computer fall within the 32–63 range, your new Windows 7 machine must fall within this range. 32 is the network ID and can't be used, and 63 is the broadcast and can't be used. So the only available addresses are from 33–62, and the only available unused IP address in that range is 192.168.2.41.

5. A. IPv6 is a requirement of DirectAccess, and you need to have IPv6 enabled on this Windows 7 machine.

6. B. You need to change the wireless network connection settings on the laptops to allow these laptop users to connect to the reconfigured access point.

7. C. To allow the Windows 7 `.vhd` file to be the default operating system, you must configure the `bcdedit` command. The `bcdedit` command replaced the `boot.ini` file when Microsoft Vista was released.

8. B. When it comes to WPA, there are two versions: WPA2-Personal and WPA2-Enterprise. WPA2-Personal allows you to set up WPA2 by using a shared password key. WPA2-Enterprise allows you to set up WPA2 by using a server for verification. Because all users are using AES with no shared password key, WPA2-Enterprise is the setting that you would choose.

9. B. The WinRM `quickconfig` command configures a machine to accept WS-Management commands from a remote machine.

10. C. On a 240 subnet mask, the ranges go by 16. Because this is a Class C, the ranges would be 16–31, 32–47, 48–63, 64–79, 80–95, 96–111, 112–127, 128–143, 144–159, 160–175, 176–191, 192–207, 208–223, and 224–239. Now remember, in a Class C address, these are not all usable. You have to subtract the first number (network ID) and the last number (broadcast).

11. A, C. The `ipconfig /release` and the `ipconfig /renew` commands will allow your machine to receive a new IP address from the DHCP server.

12. C. Because the first octet starts with 192, it's a Class C. If the first octet starts with 1–126, it's a Class A. 128–191 is a Class B, and 192–223 is a Class C.

13. C. The default gateway is the router's IP address. The default gateway allows you to get from your subnet to another subnet.

14. D. The DNS server turns a host name into an IP address so you can connect to a machine by the machine name. If you can connect to a machine by using the TCP/IP address but not the name, DNS is the issue.

15. D. `Ipconfig /registerDNS` will automatically register the Windows 7 machine with the DNS server. The registration will include the Windows 7 machine name and the IP address.

16. A. BranchCache enables an organization with slower links between offices to cache data so that downloads between offices do not have to occur each time a file is accessed.

17. B. Windows Virtual PC is a client version of virtualization software. Microsoft Hyper-V and Microsoft Virtual Server are both virtualization software that require the Windows Server operating system. Because you are running Windows XP, you would use Windows Virtual PC.

18. B. There are only two types of BranchCache modes: hosted and distributed cache. Hosted mode requires a BranchCache server in the remote location, and distributed cache mode uses the Windows 7 machines in the remote locations as distribution points.

19. C. Windows Firewall, which is included with Windows 7, helps to prevent unauthorized users or malicious software from accessing your computer. Windows Firewall does not allow unsolicited traffic (traffic that was not sent in response to a request) to pass through the firewall.

20. A. DirectAccess enables remote users to work on their corporate network when they are away from the office without the need of a VPN. As long as the remote user is connected to the Internet, DirectAccess will automatically connect the remote user to the corporate network without the need of any user intervention.

Monitoring and Maintaining Windows 7

MICROSOFT EXAM OBJECTIVES COVERED IN THIS CHAPTER:

✓ **Monitor systems.**

- This objective may include but is not limited to: configuring event logging; filtering event logs; event subscriptions; data collection sets; generating a system diagnostics report

✓ **Configure performance settings.**

- This objective may include but is not limited to: configuring the hard drive cache; configuring network performance

If you want an optimized Windows 7 installation, you must monitor its reliability and performance. Windows 7 comes with many tools to track memory, processor activity, the disk subsystem, and the network subsystem, as well as other computer subsystems.

There are tools available to provide baseline statistics for each of the subsystems so you can track changes over time, better evaluate issues that pertain to your Windows 7 machine, and make changes to proactively affect declining performance.

In this chapter, you will learn how to monitor, maintain, troubleshoot, and optimize Windows 7 by using the following utilities: Performance Monitor, Reliability Monitor, System Information, Task Manager, Configuration, Task Scheduler, and Event Viewer. Each of these tools provides information about the operating system and hardware status.

Understanding Windows 7 Performance Optimization

Before you can optimize the performance of Windows 7, you must monitor the operating system's critical subsystems to determine how each is currently performing and what (if anything) is causing system bottlenecks that negatively affect performance. Windows 7 ships with many tools that you can use to monitor system performance. The monitoring tools enable you to assess your server's current health and determine what requirements are available to improve its present condition.

Performance Monitor is a tool that you can use to perform the following tasks:

- Create baselines
- Identify system bottlenecks
- Determine trends
- Test configuration changes or tuning efforts
- Create alert thresholds

Creating Baselines

A *baseline* is a snapshot of how your system is currently performing. Suppose that your computer's hardware has not changed over the last six months, but the computer seems to be performing more slowly now than it did six months ago. If you have been using the Performance Monitor utility and taking baseline logs, as well as noting the changes in your workload, you can more easily determine what resources are causing the system to slow down. If you simply note that Windows 7 seems to be running more slowly, without any supporting statistics, you will not have any idea what is causing your problems.

You should create baselines at the following times:

- When the system is first configured, without any load
- At regular intervals of typical usage
- Whenever any changes are made to the system's hardware or software configuration

Baselines are particularly useful for determining the effect of changes that you make to your computer. For example, if you are adding more memory to your computer, you should take baselines before and after you install the memory to determine the effect of the change. Along with hardware changes, system configuration modifications also can affect your computer's performance, so you should create baselines before and after you make any changes to your Windows 7 configuration.

For the most part, Windows 7 is a self-tuning operating system. If you decide to tweak the operating system, you should take baselines before and after each change. If you do not notice a performance gain after the tweak, you should consider returning the computer to its original configuration; some tweaks might cause more problems than they solve.

Identifying System Bottlenecks

A *bottleneck* is a system resource that is inefficient compared with the rest of the computer system as a whole. The bottleneck can cause the rest of the system to run slowly.

You need to pinpoint the cause of a bottleneck to correct it. Consider a system that has a Pentium 4 3.0 GHz processor with 1,024 MB of RAM. You might consider changing to a more advanced processor. However, if your applications are memory-intensive and lack of memory is your bottleneck, then upgrading your processor will not eliminate the problem.

By using Performance Monitor, you can measure the performance of the various parts of your system, which allows you to identify system bottlenecks in a scientific manner. You will learn how to set counters to monitor your network and spot bottlenecks in the "Optimizing Windows 7 with Performance Monitor" section later in this chapter.

Determining Trends

Many of us tend to manage situations reactively instead of proactively. With reactive management, you focus on a problem when it occurs; with proactive management, you take steps to avoid the problem before it happens. In a perfect world, all management would be proactive. Performance Monitor is a great tool for proactive network management. If you are creating baselines on a regular basis, you can identify system trends. For example, if you notice average CPU utilization increasing 5 percent every month, you can assume that within the next six months, you're going to have a problem. Before performance becomes so slow that your system is not responding, you can upgrade the hardware.

Testing Configuration Changes or Tuning Efforts

When you make configuration changes or tune your computer, you might want to measure the effects of those changes. When you make configuration changes, the following recommendations apply:

Make only one change at a time. If you are making configuration changes for tuning, and you make multiple changes at one time, it is difficult to quantify the effect of each individual change. In addition, some changes might have a negative impact that, if you have made multiple changes, may be difficult to identify.

Repeat monitoring with each individual change you make. This will help you determine whether additional tuning is required.

As you make changes, check the Event Viewer event log files. Some performance changes will generate events within Event Viewer that should be reviewed. Event Viewer is covered in more detail in the "Using Event Viewer" section later in this chapter.

Using Alerts for Problem Notification

Performance Monitor provides another tool for proactive management in the form of alerts. Through data collector sets, you can specify alert thresholds (when a counter reaches a specified value) and have the utility notify you when these thresholds are reached. For example, you could specify that if one of your hard drive's logical disks has less than 10 percent of free space, you want to be notified. Once alerted, you can add more disk space or delete unneeded files before you run out of disk space. Setting up Performance Monitor and using its capabilities is a boon to you as an administrator to keep Windows 7 optimized.

Optimizing Windows 7 with Performance Monitor

The *Performance Monitor* utility is used to measure the performance of a local or a remote computer on the network. Performance Monitor enables you to do the following:

- Collect data from your local computer or remote computers on the network. You can collect data from a single computer or multiple computers concurrently.
- View data as it is being collected in real time, or historically from collected data.
- Have full control over the selection of what data will be collected, by selecting which specific objects and counters will be collected.
- Choose the sampling parameters that will be used, meaning the time interval that you want to use for collecting data points and the time period that will be used for data collection.
- Determine the format in which data will be viewed—in line, histogram bar, or report views.
- Create HTML pages for viewing data.
- Create specific configurations for monitoring data that can then be exported to other computers for performance monitoring.

In order to view data on remote computers, you need to have administrative rights to the remote computer, and the Remote Registry Service must be enabled and running on the remote computer. Also, make sure your firewall allows the ability to remote in.

Windows 7 Performance Monitor includes the new *data collector set*. This tool works with performance logs, telling Performance Monitor where the logs are stored and when the log needs to run. The data collector sets also define the credentials used to run the set.

Data collector sets are used to collect data into a log so that the data can be reviewed. You can view the log files with Performance Monitor, as described in the previous section.

Data collector sets can collect the following data:

- Performance counters
- Event trace data
- System configuration information

Windows 7 includes the following four data collector sets that are stored within the System subfolder:

- LAN Diagnostics
- System Diagnostics
- System Performance
- Wireless Diagnostics

Through Performance Monitor, you can view current data or data from a log file. When you view current data, you are monitoring real-time activity. When you view data from a log file, you are importing a log file from a previous session.

To access Performance Monitor, choose Start ➢ Control Panel ➢ System and Security ➢ Administrative Tools ➢ Performance Monitor (double-click), or type **perfmon** from the Windows 7 search box. Figure 8.1 shows the main Performance Monitor window when it is initially opened without configuration.

FIGURE 8.1 Windows 7 Performance Monitor

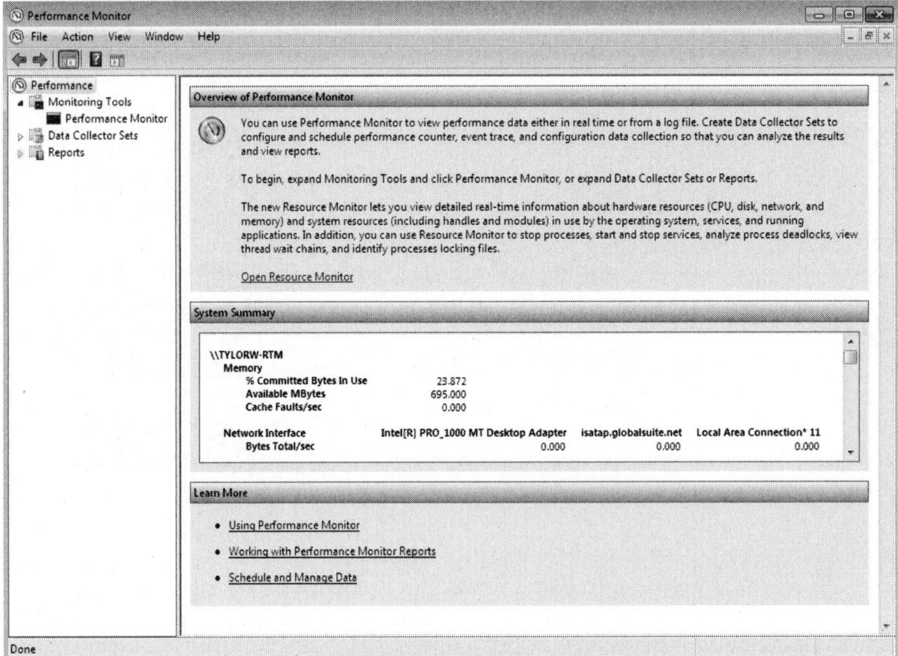

When you first start Performance Monitor, the Overview Of Performance Monitor page is displayed. The System Summary pane of this page gives a quick snapshot of which resources are being used in your computer. Notice the four initial resources tracked: Memory, Network Interface, Physical Disk, and Processor Information. You can view detailed information about each resource by choosing the Open Resource Monitor link or by typing **Resmon** from the Windows 7 search box.

Using Resource Monitor

The Resource Monitor window was integrated into the Reliability and Performance utility of Windows Vista, but has been given its own dialog box in Windows 7. Figure 8.2 shows the Resource Monitor tabbed dialog box.

FIGURE 8.2 Windows 7 Resource Monitor

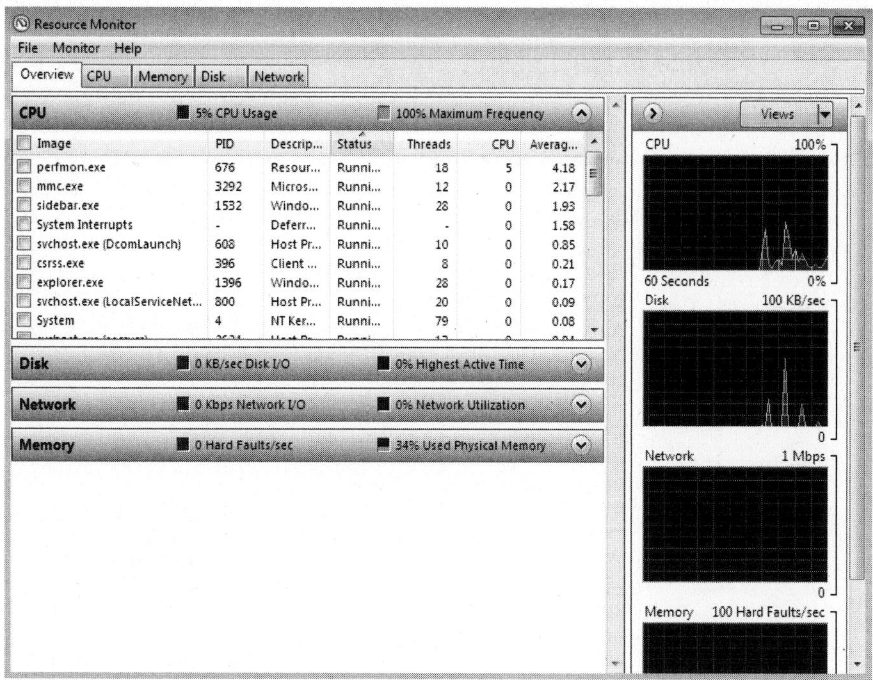

The Overview tab of the Resource Monitor dialog box is open by default and gives you a fair amount of detail in terms of a graphical representation on the right side. The main window of the Resource Monitor dialog box gives you an overview of the four major subsystems monitored by default (CPU, Disk, Network, and Memory). You expand or compress each of the four items by clicking the arrow in the right of the item title bar, as shown in Figure 8.3. For example, if you want to view details about the memory being used by the processes of Windows 7, click the arrow to expand Memory, and you can view each process, process ID, and memory allocation by physical, shared, and private allotment.

FIGURE 8.3 Expand or collapse the Resource Monitor item arrow

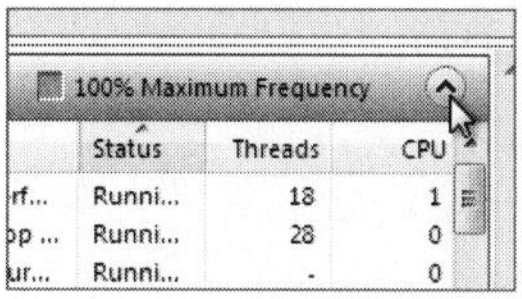

The other tabs of Resource Monitor give detailed information with regard to each of the major subsystems of Windows 7. The CPU tab of Resource Monitor displays the individual process currently running on the machine as well as the process ID (PID), a brief description, the running status of the process, the number of threads the process is running, current CPU utilization, and average CPU utilization. You also have services details, application handle details, and module details available by expanding each item. The CPU tab of Resource Monitor is shown in Figure 8.4. The right side of the CPU tab also offers a graphical representation of real-time statistics indicating percentages for CPU total usage and service CPU usage.

FIGURE 8.4 The CPU tab of Resource Monitor

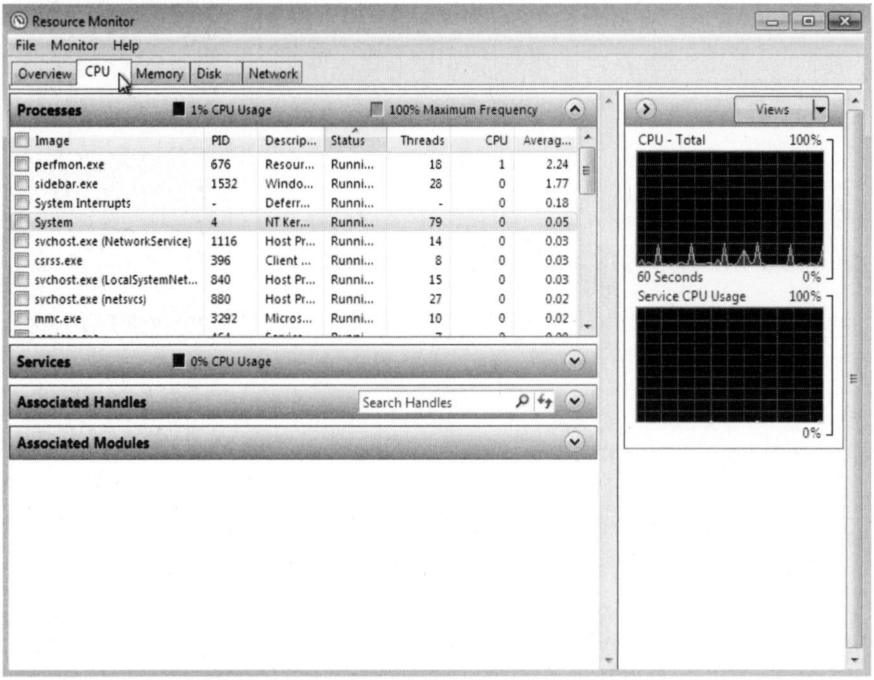

The Memory tab of Resource Monitor shows the process information as displayed in the CPU tab, with an overview of memory allocation in the form of a graphical representation. The right side of the display also shows you real-time information about the physical memory, currently allocated memory called the Commit Charge, and Hard Faults/Sec (the number of memory accesses that are not actually in RAM, but in a page file waiting to be used). The Memory tab of Resource Monitor is shown in Figure 8.5.

FIGURE 8.5 The Memory tab of Resource Monitor

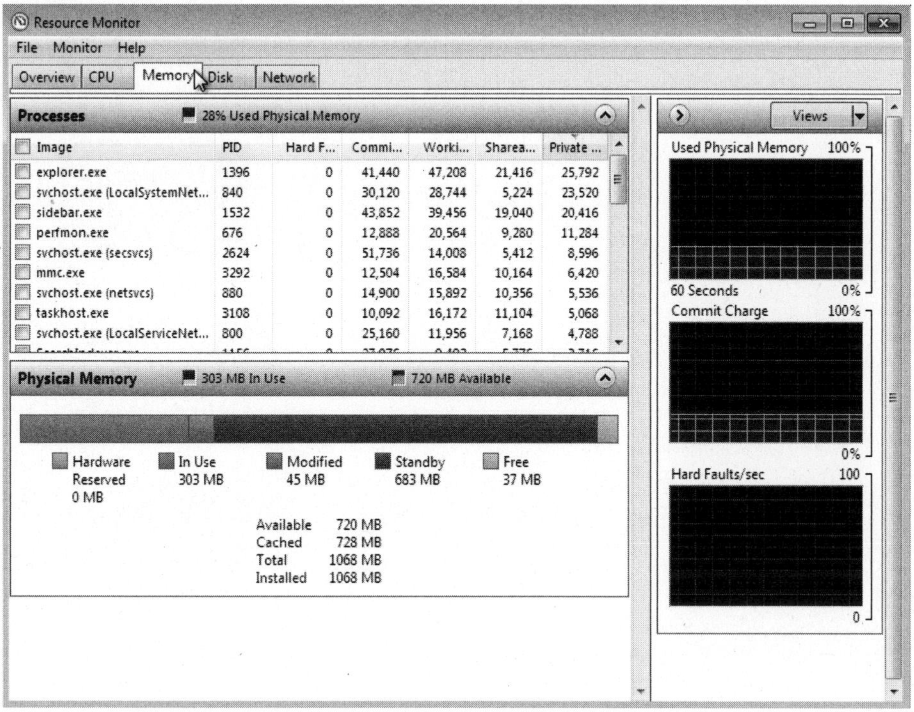

The Disk tab of Resource Monitor is used to display the disk activity of your machine. The items available to view are the Processes With Disk Activity, Disk Activity, and Storage statistics. You can see the Disk tab in Figure 8.6, including the real-time graphical representation of Disk transfer in KB/sec and Disk Queue Length (the amount of transfer currently waiting for transfer to RAM for processing).

FIGURE 8.6 The Disk tab of Resource Monitor

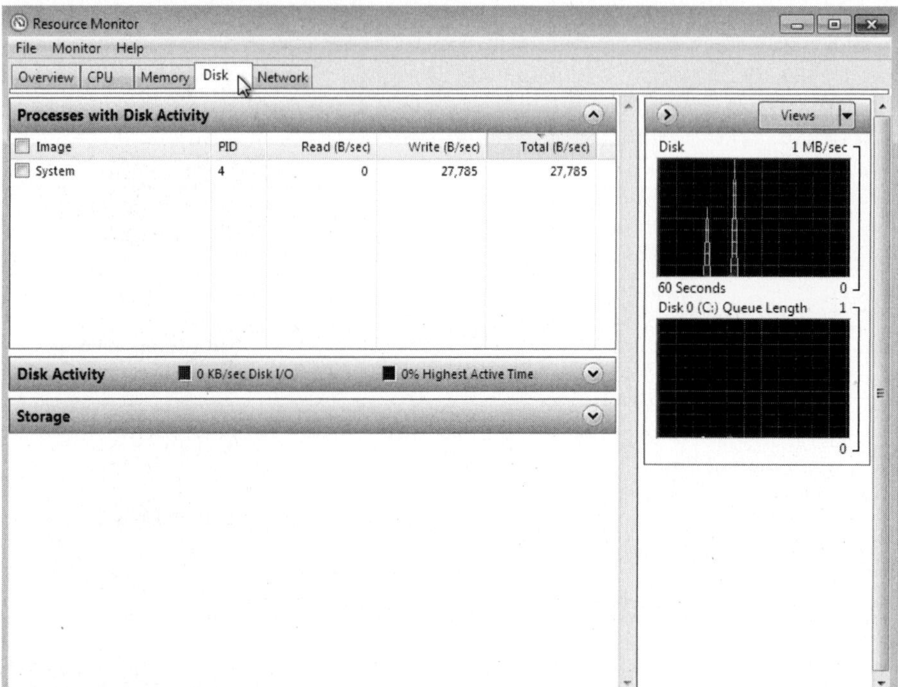

The Network tab of Resource Monitor shows network utilization as well as network protocol information. The items available for detailed information include Processes With Network Activity, Network Activity, TCP Connections, and Listening Ports. We've had this information available to us in previous versions of Windows, but this is one convenient location for a slew of useful network information. As shown in Figure 8.7, the Network tab offers a huge amount of useful network information (I have opened the Listening Ports item in the figure) as well as the real-time graphical information for Network data transfer, open TCP Connections, and Local Area Connection usage as a percentage.

FIGURE 8.7 The Network tab of Resource Monitor

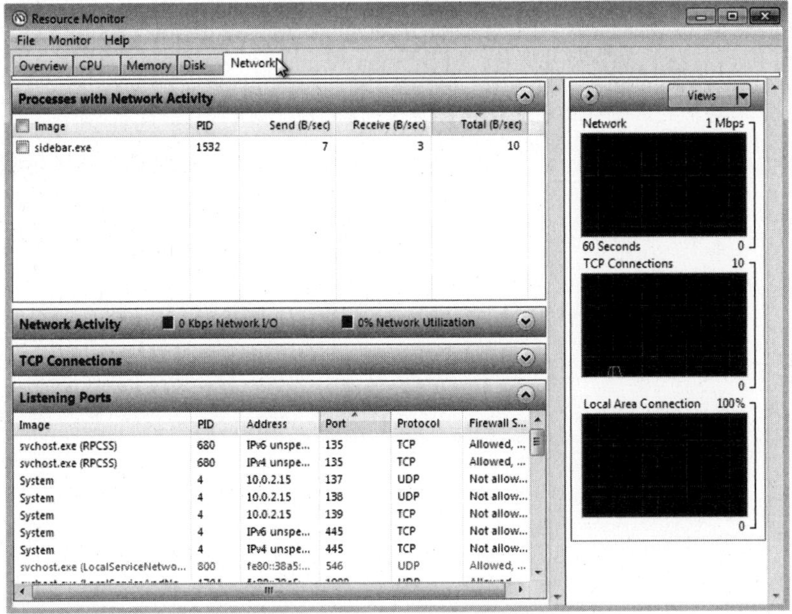

Real World Scenario

The Great Network Tab in Resource Monitor

I am a packet sniffer and network utilization geek and have been for some time. I constantly talk with other administrators about resources being used in their servers and client machines that are associated with many network attributes. It's always important for me to see just which applications are using the network in terms of the ports they have open on my machine. I use TCPView (downloadable from Microsoft's website) on a regular basis to see what's happening.

Making the association to the ports open, the processes using resources, the applications associated with the ports and processes, and just how much bandwidth is being used has always had me looking between applications and utility outputs. I have a regimen that I use and recommend to administrators to monitor this information—but now the Resource Monitor Network tab has consolidated these details into one convenient spot. Nice! The tab provides a regular data display as well as real-time graphical views, making me drool.

I have found myself returning to Resource Monitor time and time again to see what my Windows 7 machine is doing and have caught many of my colleagues doing the same thing. Take a look; if you've ever considered looking at the connections being made into or out of your computer, you will love the Network tab of Resource Monitor (okay, the other tabs are pretty good, too).

It is important to monitor resources such as hard drive cache and network performance. Monitoring these resources enables you to configure them for peak performance in Windows 7.

For monitoring system activity other than what is provided by the Resource Overview tab and Resource Monitor, you must use more of the Performance Monitor features.

Utilizing Customized Counters in Performance Monitor

You can add numerous counters from any of the subsystems within Windows 7. To access the configurable Performance Monitor window, select the Performance Monitor item in the left pane, as shown in Figure 8.8.

FIGURE 8.8 Customizable Performance Monitor window

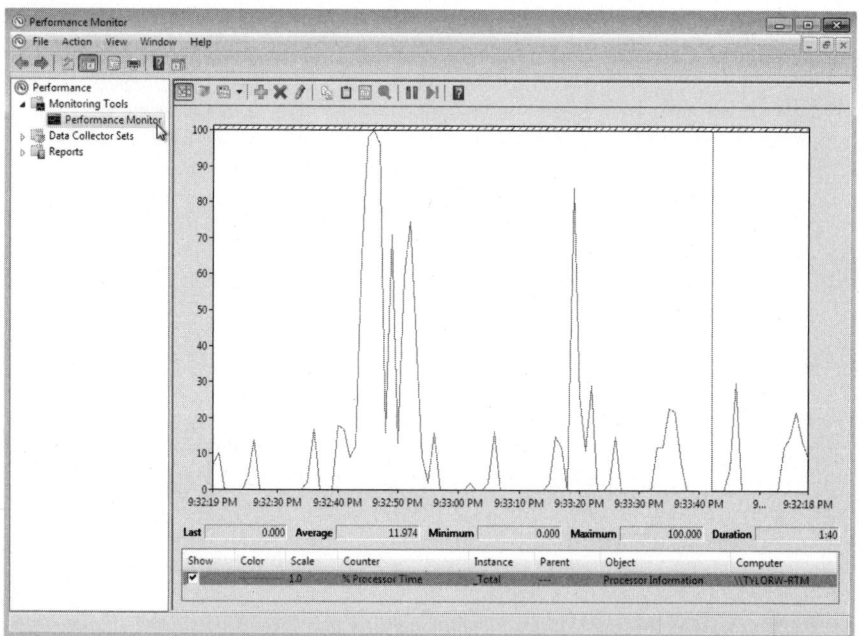

Customizable counters are listed at the bottom of the Performance Monitor window. By default, only the % Processor Time counter is tracked for the local computer. The fields just above the counter list will contain data based on the counter that is highlighted in the list, as follows:

Last Displays the most current data

Average Shows the average of the counter

Minimum Shows the lowest value that has been recorded for the counter

Maximum Shows the highest value that has been recorded for the counter

Duration Shows how long the counter has been tracking data

Before we add counters to Performance Monitor, we need to discuss the three Performance Monitor views.

Selecting the Appropriate View

Click the Change Graph Type button on the Performance Monitor toolbar to see your data in one of three views, as shown in Figure 8.9.

FIGURE 8.9 Change Graph Type button

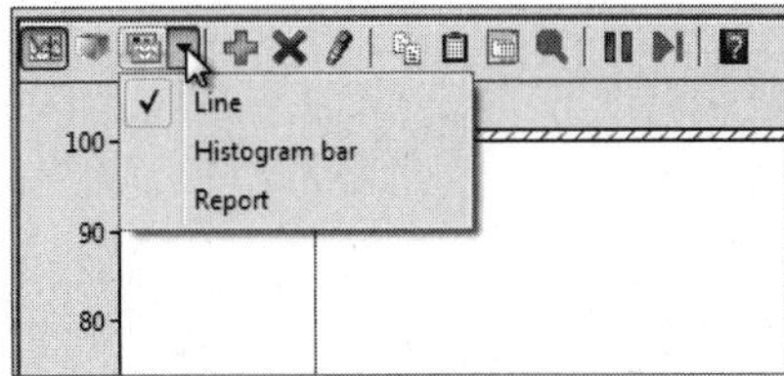

Line View The line view is Performance Monitor's default view. It's useful for viewing a small number of counters in a graphical format. The main advantage of line view is that you can see how the data has been tracked during the defined time period.

Histogram Bar View The histogram view, shown in Figure 8.10, shows the Performance Monitor data in a bar graph. This view is useful for examining large amounts of data. However, it shows performance only for the current period. You do not see a record of performance over time, as you do with the line view.

FIGURE 8.10 Performance Monitor histogram bar view

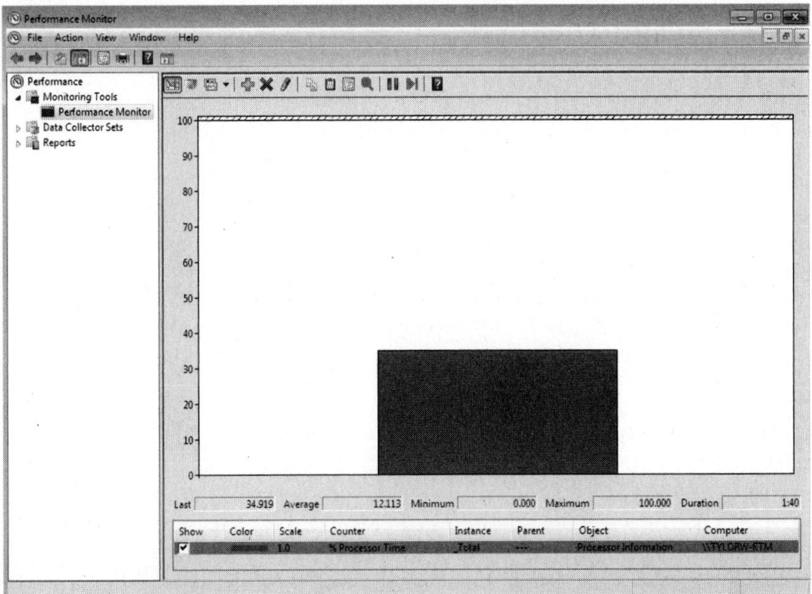

Report View The report view, shown in Figure 8.11, offers a logical text-based report of all the counters that are being tracked through Performance Monitor. Only the current session's data is displayed. The advantage of the report view is that it allows you to easily track large numbers of counters in real time. It is important to note that when you view data in real-time format, the data can appear skewed as applications and processes are started. It is typically more useful to view data as an average over a specified interval.

FIGURE 8.11 Performance Monitor report view

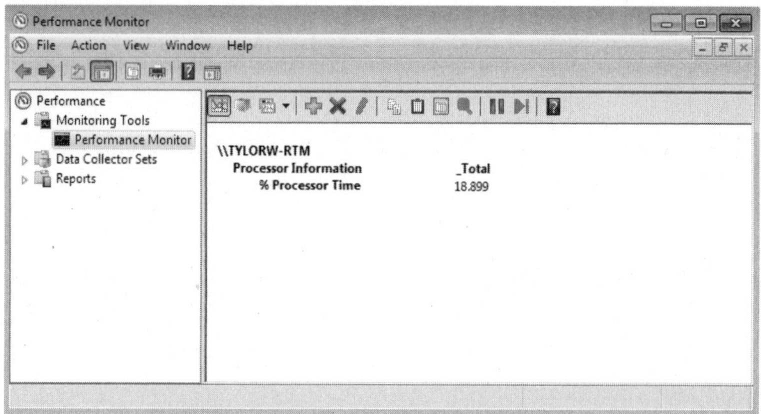

Complete Exercise 8.1 to add counters.

EXERCISE 8.1

Adding Counters

1. In Performance Monitor, click the Add button on the toolbar, which looks like a green plus sign (+). This brings up the Add Counters dialog box.
2. In the Add Counters dialog box, ensure that the Select Counters From The Computer drop-down list displays <Local Computer> so you can monitor the local computer. Alternatively, to select counters from a specific computer, pick a computer from the drop-down list.
3. Select a performance object from the drop-down list. All Windows 7 system resources are tracked as performance objects, such as Cache, Memory, Paging File, Process, and Processor.
4. Select the counter or counters within the performance object that you want to track. Each performance object has an associated set of counters. Counters are used to track specific information regarding a performance object. For example, the PhysicalDisk performance object has a % Disk Time counter, which will tell you how busy a disk has been in servicing read and write requests. PhysicalDisk also has %

Disk Read Time and % Disk Write Time counters, which show you what percentage of disk requests are read requests and what percentage are write requests, respectively.

5. Select <All Instances> to track all the associated instances or pick specific instances from the list box.
6. Click the Add button to add the counters for the performance object.
7. Repeat steps 2 through 6 to specify any additional counters you want to track. When you finish, click OK.

After you've added counters, you can select a specific counter by highlighting it in Performance Monitor. To highlight a counter, click it and then click the Highlight button (which looks like a highlighter) on the Performance Monitor toolbar, or select the counter and press Ctrl+H.

To stop showing data for a counter, deselect the check box under Show for that counter. To remove a counter, highlight it in Performance Monitor and click the Delete button on the toolbar. The Delete button looks like a red X.

Managing Performance Monitor Properties

To configure the Performance Monitor properties, click the Properties button on the Performance Monitor toolbar, and the Performance Monitor Properties dialog box opens, as shown in Figure 8.12.

FIGURE 8.12 Performance Monitor Properties

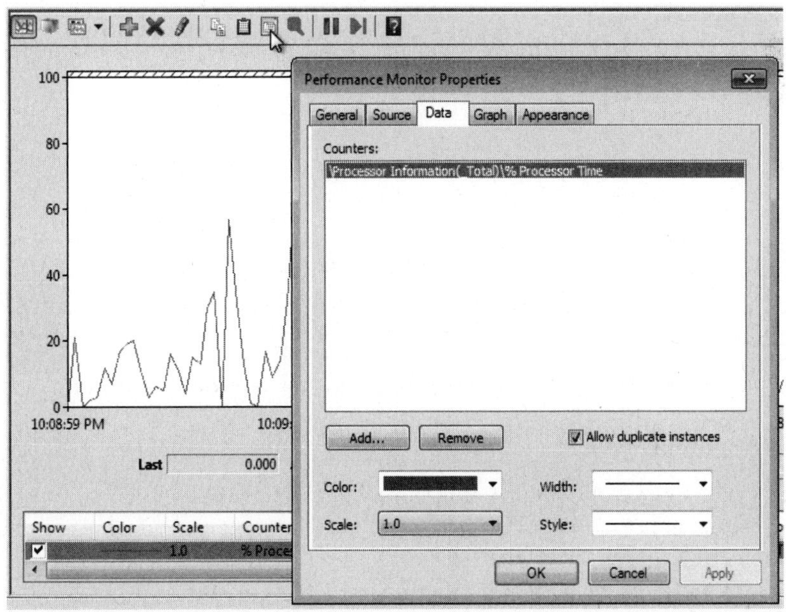

The Performance Monitor Properties dialog box has the following five tabs—General, Source, Data, Graph, and Appearance. You can configure the following properties on each of these tabs:

General Tab The General tab of the Performance Monitor Properties dialog box, as shown in Figure 8.13, contains the following options:

- The display elements that will be used: legend, value bar, and/or toolbar
- The data that will be displayed: default (for reports or histograms, this is current data; for logs, this is average data), current, minimum, maximum, or average
- How often the data is updated, in seconds

FIGURE 8.13 Performance counter properties General tab

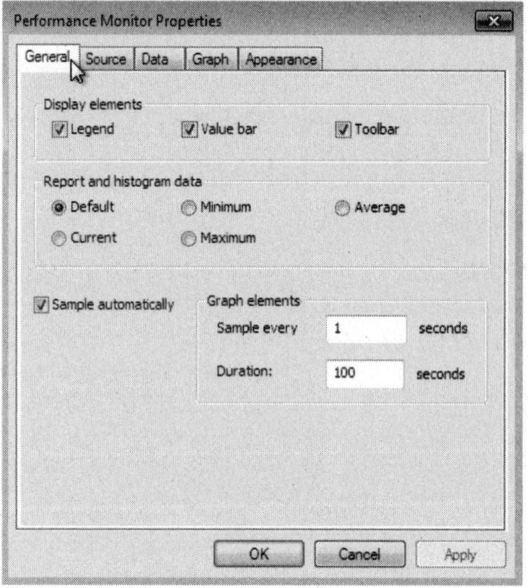

Source Tab The Source tab, shown in Figure 8.14, enables you to specify the data source. This can be current activity, or it can be data that has been collected in a log file or database. If you import data, you can specify the time range that you want to view.

FIGURE 8.14 Performance counter properties Source tab

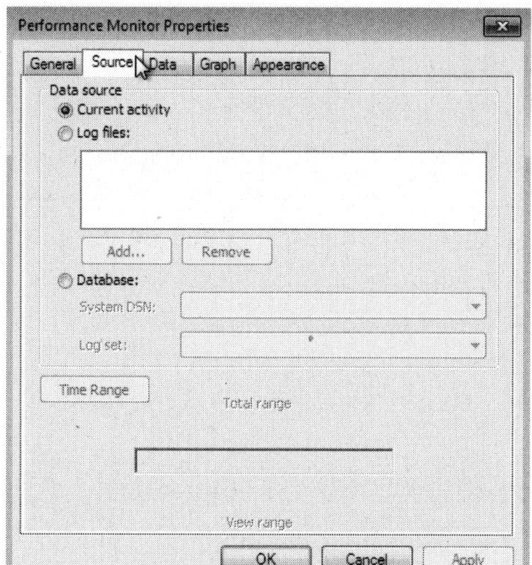

Data Tab The Data tab (the default tab, which is active when the Properties dialog box opens) lets you specify the counters that you want to track. You can add and remove counters by clicking the Add and Remove buttons. You can also select a specific counter and define the color, scale, width, and style that are used to represent the counter in the graph.

Graph Tab The Graph tab, shown in Figure 8.15, contains the following options, which you can apply to the line or histogram bar view:

- Whether the data will scroll or wrap (line view only)
- A title
- A vertical axis label
- Whether you will show a vertical grid, a horizontal grid, vertical scale numbers, and/or time axis labels
- The minimum and maximum numbers for the vertical scale

FIGURE 8.15 Performance counter properties Graph tab

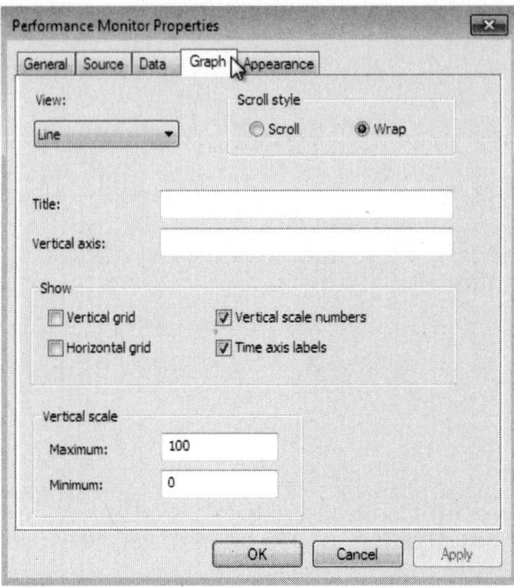

Appearance Tab The Appearance tab of the Performance Monitor Properties dialog box, shown in Figure 8.16, has options for customizing the colors and fonts used in the Performance Monitor display.

FIGURE 8.16 Performance counter properties Appearance tab

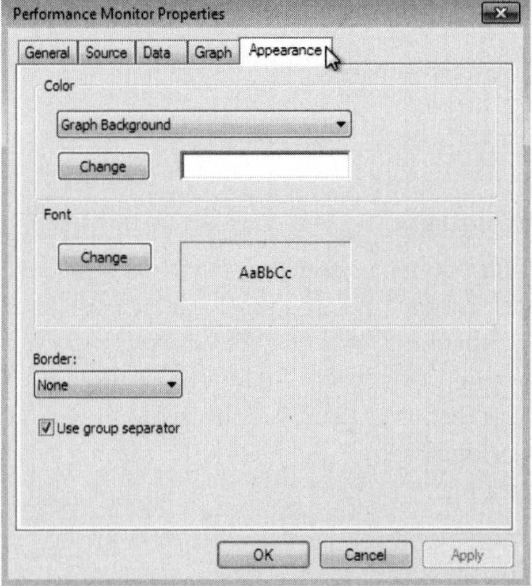

After you have set counters and viewed them in real time, you might be interested in collecting the data over time and saving it to a file so you can maintain a baseline of data for comparison. You do this in Performance Monitor by using data collector sets.

Managing Performance Monitor Data with Collector Sets

The data collector set portion of Performance Monitor is shown in Figure 8.17. *Data collector sets* are used to collect data into a log so that the data can be reviewed and saved for comparison at a later date (baselining). You can view the log files with Performance Monitor, as described in the previous section, "Managing Performance Monitor Properies" (in the "Source Tab" subsection).

FIGURE 8.17 Performance Monitor data collector set configuration

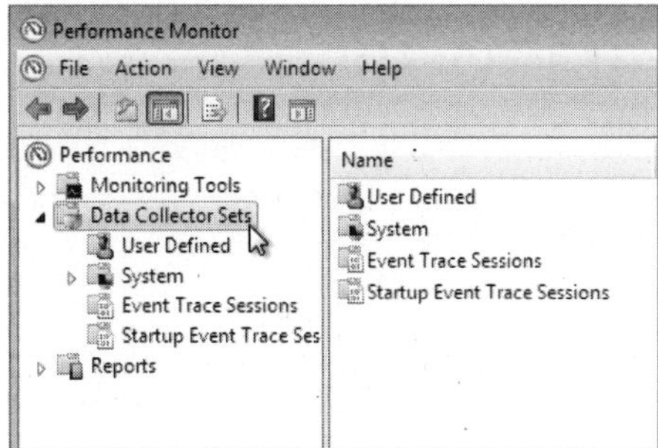

Data collector sets can collect the following data:

- Performance counters
- Event trace data
- System configuration information

There are two built-in data collector sets that track multiple counters for system diagnostics and system performance. You can also create your own user-defined data collector sets and save them for later use. You can view the reports from these data collector sets within the Reports folder in Performance Monitor.

Performance counter logs record data about hardware usage and the activity of system services. You can configure logging to occur manually or on a predefined schedule. Perform Exercise 8.2 to create a data log.

EXERCISE 8.2

Creating a Data Log

1. Expand Data Collector Sets and right-click User Defined. Select New and then select Data Collector Set from the pop-up menu.
2. In the Create New Data Collector Set dialog box that appears, type a name for the collector set and choose whether to create the set from a template or to create it manually; then click the Next button.
3. If you chose to create the set from a template, follow the prompts to create the set. After the set is created, you can modify it. If you chose to create the set manually, you are asked whether you want to create data logs or a performance counter alert. Data logs can consist of the following types of data:
   - Performance counters
   - Event trace data
   - System configuration information
   - After you select the data you want to collect, click Next.
4. Add the performance counters you want to collect and click Next after each data type.
5. You are asked where to save the data. Browse to the location, click OK, and then click Next.
6. You are asked under which user account the data collector set should run, and whether the data collector set should be edited, started, or saved. After you make your selections, click Finish.

Creating an Alert

Alerts can be generated when a specific counter rises above or falls below a specified value. You can configure alerts to log an entry in the application event log and/or start a data collector set. Creating an alert is similar to creating a performance counter data log except you are required to specify the alert conditions. You create an alert by creating a user-defined collector set, manually specifying counters. In the Create New Data Collector Wizard, you have the option of selecting a Performance Counter Alert radio button. For example, you might configure a performance counter alert that will log an entry whenever the % Free Space counter for C: falls below 5 percent. After you create the alert, you can modify the alert parameters by right-clicking the data collector and selecting Properties.

After you create the data collector sets and set the alerts, you will want to run the sets and save the logs periodically. Reviewing the logs gives you a proactive approach to managing your Windows 7 performance.

Now let's take a look at how to manage Windows 7 performance.

Managing System Performance

By analyzing data, you can determine whether any resources are placing an excessive load on your computer, resulting in a system slowdown. The following list gives some of the causes of poor system performance:

- A resource is insufficient to handle the load that is being placed upon it, and the component might need to be upgraded, or additional components might be required.
- If a resource has multiple instances, the resources might not be evenly balancing the workload, and the workload might need to be balanced over the multiple instances more effectively.
- A resource might be malfunctioning. In this case, the resource should be repaired or replaced.
- A specific program might be allocating resources improperly or inefficiently, in which case the program needs to be rewritten or another application should be used.
- A resource might be configured improperly and causing excessive resource usage, and need to be reconfigured.

There are four main subsystems that you should monitor. You should configure counters in your data collector set for each of the following:

- The memory subsystem
- The processor subsystem
- The disk subsystem
- The network subsystem

Each subsystem should be examined over time to evaluate Windows 7 performance.

Monitoring and Optimizing Memory

When the operating system needs a program or process, the first place it looks is in physical memory. If the required program or process is not in physical memory, the system looks in logical memory (the page file). If the program or process is not in logical memory, the system then must retrieve the program or process from the hard disk. It can take thousands of times longer to access information from the hard disk than to get it from physical RAM. If your computer is using excessive paging, that is an indication that your computer does not have enough physical memory.

Insufficient memory is the most likely cause of system bottlenecks. If you have no idea what is causing a system bottleneck, memory is usually a good place to start checking. To determine how memory is being used, you need to examine the following two areas:

Physical Memory The physical RAM you have installed on your computer. You should have as much memory as either your machine or budget can handle. It's actually a good idea to have more memory than you think you will need just to be on the safe side. As you've probably noticed, each time you add or upgrade applications, you require more system memory.

Page File Logical memory exists on your hard drive. If you are using excessive paging (swapping between the page file and physical RAM) or hard page faults, it's a clear sign that you need to add more memory.

The first step in memory management is determining how much memory your computer has installed and what the appropriate memory requirements are based on the operating system requirements and the applications and services you are running on your computer.

Key Counters to Track for Memory Management

The following three counters are the three most important counters for monitoring memory:

Memory ➢ Available MBytes Memory ➢ Available MBytes measures the amount of physical memory that is available to run processes on the computer. If this number is less than 20 percent of your installed memory, it indicates that you might have an overall shortage of physical memory for your computer, or you possibly have an application that is not releasing memory properly. You should consider adding more memory or evaluating application memory usage.

Memory ➢ Pages/Sec Memory ➢ Pages/Sec shows the number of times the requested information was not in memory and had to be retrieved from disk. This counter's value should be below 20; for optimal performance, it should be 4 or 5. If the number is above 20, you should add memory or research paging file use more thoroughly. Sometimes a high Pages/Sec counter is indicative of a program that is using a memory-mapped file.

Paging File ➢ % Usage Paging File ➢ % Usage indicates the percentage of the allocated page file that is currently in use. If this number is consistently over 70 percent, you might need to add more memory or increase the size of the page file. You should track this counter in conjunction with Available MBytes and Pages/Sec.

The counters listed previously work together to show what is happening on your system. Use the Paging File ➢ % Usage counter value in conjunction with the Memory ➢ Available MBytes and Memory ➢ Pages/Sec counters to determine how much paging is occurring on your computer.

Along with memory counters, processor (or CPU) counters are valuable in evaluating Windows 7 performance.

Managing Processor Performance

Processor bottlenecks can develop when the threads of a process require more processing cycles than are currently available. In this case, the process will wait in a processor queue, and system responsiveness will be slower than if process requests could be immediately served. The most common causes of processor bottlenecks are processor-intensive applications and other subsystem components that generate excessive processor interrupts (for example, disk or network subsystems).

In a workstation environment, processors are usually not the source of bottlenecks. However, you should still monitor this subsystem to make sure that processor utilization is at an efficient level.

Let's now take a look at some of the key counters that you need to track when watching the processor.

Key Counters to Track for the Processor

You can track processor utilization through the Processor and System objects to determine whether a processor bottleneck exists. The following three counters are the most important counters for monitoring the system processor:

Processor ➤ % Processor Time Processor ➤ % Processor Time measures the time that the processor spends responding to system requests. If this value is consistently above an average of 85 percent, you might have a processor bottleneck. The Processor ➤ % User Time and Processor ➤ % Privileged Time counters combine to show the total % Processor Time counter. You can monitor these counters individually for more detail.

Processor ➤ Interrupts/Sec Processor ➤ Interrupts/Sec shows the average number of hardware interrupts received by the processor each second. If this value is more than 3,000, you might have a problem with a program or hardware that is generating spurious interrupts. (This value will vary in optimization based on the processor type; you'll need to do a little research for your specific processor to see the appropriate value.)

System ➤ Processor Queue Length System ➤ Processor Queue Length is used to determine whether a processor bottleneck is due to high levels of demand for processor time. If a queue of two or more items exists for an extended period of time, a processor bottleneck might be indicated. If you suspect that a processor bottleneck is due to excessive hardware I/O requests, then you should also monitor the System ➤ File Control Bytes/Sec counter.

Tuning and Upgrading the Processor

If you suspect that you have a processor bottleneck, you can try the following solutions:

- Use applications that are less processor-intensive.
- Upgrade your processor.
- If your computer supports multiple processors, add one.

The Memory and Processor subsystem objects are important counters to evaluate in determining your Windows 7 performance. You should also look at the hard drive or disk subsystem to check for issues as well.

Managing the Disk Subsystem

Disk access is the amount of time your disk subsystem takes to retrieve data that is requested by the operating system. The two factors that determine how quickly your disk subsystem will respond to system requests are the average disk access time on your hard drive and the speed of your disk controller.

Key Counters to Track for the Disk Subsystem

You can monitor the PhysicalDisk object, which is the sum of all logical drives on a single physical drive, or you can monitor the LogicalDisk object, which represents a specific logical disk. The more important counters for monitoring the disk subsystem are as follows:

PhysicalDisk ➢ % Disk Time and LogicalDisk ➢ % Disk Time PhysicalDisk ➢ % Disk Time and LogicalDisk ➢ % Disk Time show the amount of time the disk is busy because it is servicing read or write requests. If your disk is busy more than 90 percent of the time, you will improve performance by adding another disk channel and splitting the disk I/O requests between the channels.

PhysicalDisk ➢ Current Disk Queue Length and LogicalDisk ➢ Current Disk Queue Length PhysicalDisk ➢ Current Disk Queue Length and LogicalDisk ➢ Current Disk Queue Length indicate the number of outstanding disk requests that are waiting to be processed. On average, this value should be less than 2.

LogicalDisk ➢ % Free Space LogicalDisk ➢ % Free Space specifies how much free disk space is available. This counter should indicate at least 15 percent.

Tuning and Upgrading the Disk Subsystem

When you suspect that you have a disk subsystem bottleneck, the first thing you should check is your memory subsystem. Insufficient physical memory can cause excessive paging, which in turn affects the disk subsystem.

If you do not have a memory problem, try the following solutions to improve disk performance:

- Use faster disks and controllers.
- Confirm that you have the latest drivers for your disk adapters.
- Use disk striping to take advantage of multiple I/O channels.
- Balance heavily used files on multiple I/O channels.
- Add another disk controller for load balancing.
- Use Disk Defragmenter to consolidate files so that disk space and data access are optimized.

After you evaluate the first three subsystems—memory, processor, and disk—you also need to look at the network subsystem to optimize your Windows 7 performance.

Optimizing the Network Subsystem

Windows 7 does not have a built-in mechanism for monitoring the entire network. However, you can monitor and optimize the traffic that is generated on your Windows 7 machine. You can monitor the network interface (your network card) and the network protocols that have been installed on your computer.

Network bottlenecks are indicated when network traffic exceeds the capacity that can be supported by the local area network (LAN). Typically, you would monitor this activity on a network-wide basis—for example, with the Network Monitor utility that ships with Windows Server 2003.

Key Counters to Track for the Network Subsystem

If you are using the Performance Monitor utility to monitor local network traffic, the following two counters are useful for monitoring the network subsystem:

Network Interface ➤ Bytes Total/Sec Network Interface ➤ Bytes Total/Sec measures the total number of bytes sent or received from the network interface and includes all network protocols.

TCPv4 > Segments/Sec TCPv4 ➤ Segments/Sec measures the number of bytes sent or received from the network interface and includes only the TCPv4 protocol.

Tuning and Upgrading the Network Subsystem

You can use the following guidelines to help optimize and minimize network traffic:

- Install and configure only the network protocols you need.
- Use network cards that take advantage of your bus speed.
- Use faster network cards—for example, 100 Mbps Ethernet or 1 Gbps Ethernet instead of 10 Mbps Ethernet.

A feature was added to Windows Vista as part of Performance Monitor known as Reliability Monitor (hence the Windows Vista tool named *Reliability and Performance Monitor*). In Windows 7, Microsoft removed the tool from Performance Monitor and added Reliability Monitor as its own tool.

Using Reliability Monitor

Reliability Monitor is a new stand-alone feature in Windows 7 that provides an overview of the stability of your computer. In Windows Vista, Reliability Monitor was included in Performance Monitor. Figure 8.18 shows the Windows 7 Reliability Monitor window. You can access Reliability Monitor by typing **Reliability Monitor** into the Windows 7 search box.

FIGURE 8.18 Windows 7 Reliability Monitor

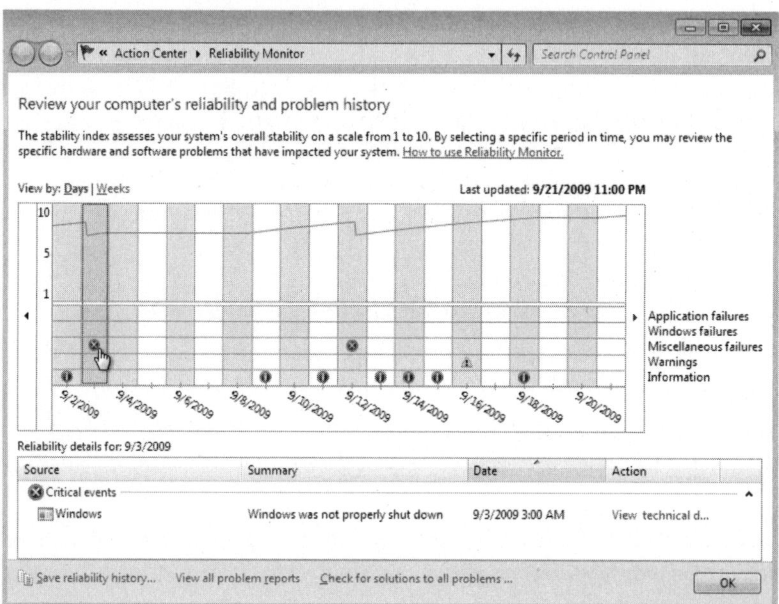

If something is causing system instability, Reliability Monitor can provide details about the problem. This data is collected and stored in the following five categories in the lower half of the display window:

- Application failures: Programs that hang or crash
- Windows failures: Includes operating system and boot failures
- Miscellaneous failures: Includes unexpected shutdowns
- Warnings: Items that are detrimental, but not failures
- Information: Informational messages that Windows 7 issues

The upper half of the graphical display indicates the relative reliability of your Windows 7 machine on a scale of 1 to 10 (1 being horrible and 10 being completely reliable). The tracked reliability items are displayed in a time view that can be changed to view by days or weeks by clicking the View By: Days | Weeks item in the upper left of the Reliability Monitor window. Details about failures, warnings, and informational messages can be accessed by clicking the icon in the graphical window in the time period displayed.

If you notice a recurring problem, you can choose Check For Solutions To All Problems at the bottom of the window. Windows 7 will then check the issues and report to you potential solutions. You can view all the problems that Reliability Monitor has detected by choosing View All Problem Reports, also located at the bottom of the Reliability Monitor window. By selecting Save Reliability History at the bottom of the window, you can save the current report in XML format.

Performance Monitor and Resource Monitor are great utilities for evaluating your Windows 7 computer. Several other tools are also available for you to learn about your system information.

Using Windows 7 Tools to Discover System Information

Windows 7 contains many other tools to discover system information about your computer. Some of the tools you should be familiar with include the following:

- System Information
- Task Manager
- Performance Information and Tools

System Information

You can use the System Information utility, shown in Figure 8.19, to show details about your hardware, software, and resources. Type **msinfo32** in the Windows 7 search box to launch this utility.

FIGURE 8.19 System Information dialog box

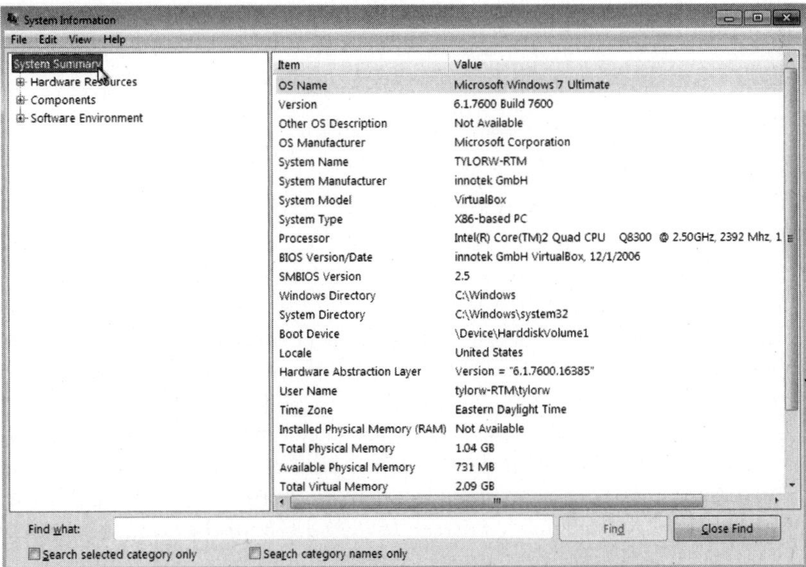

A great deal of information is available about how to use this application. Click the fields in the left pane, and details will be displayed in the right pane. You can also search for a term by typing it in the Find What field at the bottom of the page. This utility has been available in many releases of the Windows product.

Task Manager

The Task Manager utility shows the applications and processes that are currently running on your computer, as well as CPU and memory usage information. To access Task Manager, press Ctrl+Alt+Delete and click Start Task Manager. Alternatively, right-click an empty area in the Taskbar and select Task Manager from the context menu, or type **task manager** into the Windows 7 search box. The Task Manager dialog box has the following six main tabs that I discuss in the sections that follow:

- Applications
- Processes
- Services
- Performance
- Networking
- Users

Managing Application Tasks in Task Manager

The Applications tab of the Task Manager dialog box, shown in Figure 8.20, lists all of the applications that are currently running on the computer. For each task, you will see the name of the task and the current status (running, not responding, or stopped).

FIGURE 8.20 Applications tab in Task Manager

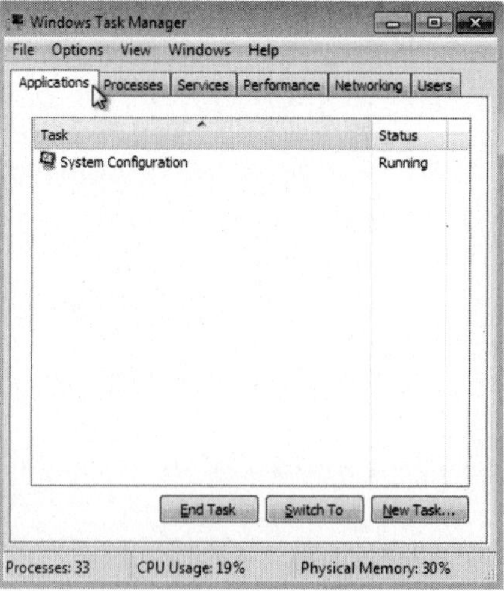

To close an application, select it in the Task Manager window and click the End Task button at the bottom of the dialog box. To make the application window active, select it and click the Switch To button. If you want to start an application that isn't running, click the New Task button and specify the location and name of the program you wish to start.

Managing Process Tasks in Task Manager

The Processes tab of the Task Manager dialog box, shown in Figure 8.21, lists all the processes that are currently running on the computer. This is a convenient way to get a quick look at how your system is performing. For each process, you will see the Image Name (the name of the process), the User Name (the user account that is running the process), CPU (the amount of CPU utilization for the process), Memory—Private Working Set (the amount of memory that is being used by the process), and Description (a description of the process).

FIGURE 8.21 Processes tab in Task Manager

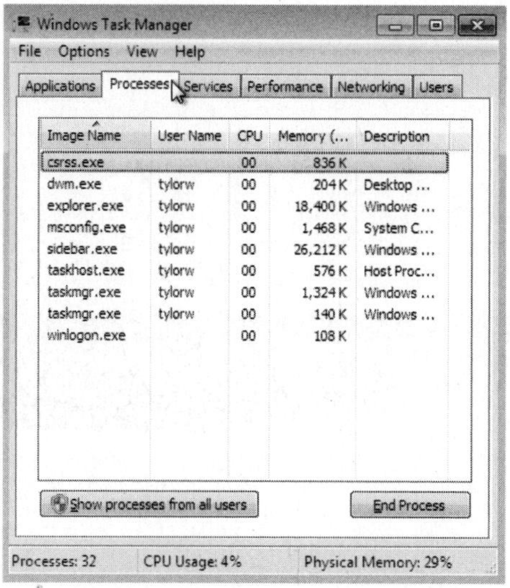

From the Processes tab, you can organize the listing and control processes as follows:

- To organize the processes, click the column headings. For example, if you click the CPU column, the listing will start with the processes that use the most CPU resources. If you click the CPU column a second time, the listing will be reversed so the processes that use the least CPU resources are listed first.
- To manage a process, right-click it and choose an option from the context menu. You can choose to end the process, end the process tree, debug the process, specify virtualization, create a dump file, or set the priority of the process (to Realtime, High,

Above Normal, Normal, Below Normal, or Low). If your computer has multiple processors installed, you can also set processor affinity (the process of associating a specific process with a specific processor) for a process.

- To customize the counters that are listed, choose View ➢ Select Columns. This brings up the Select Columns dialog box, where you can select various information you want to see listed on the Processes tab.

Within the Processes tab in Task Manager, you can also stop a process and manage process priority.

Stopping Processes You might need to stop a process that isn't executing properly. To stop a specific process, select the process you want to stop in the Task Manager's Processes tab and click the End Process button. Task Manager displays a Warning dialog box. Click the End Process button to terminate the process. If you right-click a process, you can end the specific process or you can use the option End Process Tree. The End Process Tree option ends all processes that have been created either directly or indirectly by the process.

Managing Process Priority You can manage process priority through Task Manager. To change the priority of a process that is already running, use the Processes tab of Task Manager. Right-click the process you want to manage and select Set Priority from the context menu. You can select from Realtime, High, Above Normal, Normal, Below Normal, and Low priorities. As you might expect, applications launch at Normal priority by default.

Perform Exercise 8.3 to set a process priority and end a process from within Task Manager.

EXERCISE 8.3

Setting Processes

1. Right-click an empty space on your Taskbar and select Task Manager from the context menu.
2. On the Applications tab, click the New Task button.
3. In the Create A New Task dialog box, type **calc** and click OK.
4. Click the Processes tab. Right-click `calc.exe` and select Set Priority, then Low. In the Task Manager Warning dialog box, click the Change Priority button to continue.
5. Right-click `calc.exe` and select End Process. In the Task Manager Warning dialog box, click the End Process button.

Restarting Your Windows 7 Desktop

Windows 7 is much better at closing all graphical displays when programs close or crash than other Windows legacy operating systems. But I have still had issues when something stays on my desktop that shouldn't. A piece of a window, some graphic component, or just some distracting piece of junk that is not supposed to be there just hangs around.

Most of the time you'll see users reboot their machine to clean up the desktop. I know I used to. Using the Processes tab of Task Manager can provide a solution to this problem. If you select the `explorer.exe` process and end it, you will see your desktop programs, icons, and random stuck graphics go away (and not come back). You can then just restart the `explorer.exe` process (the desktop) by choosing File ➢ New Task and typing **`explorer.exe`** to bring back your desktop (Task Manager stays with the ending of the Explorer process). This is a much faster and more efficient way of restoring your desktop without rebooting.

Managing Services in Task Manager

The Services tab of the Task Manager dialog box, shown in Figure 8.22, lists all the services that can run on the computer. For each service, you will see the Name (the name of the service), PID (the associated process identifier), Description (a description of the service), Status (whether a process is Running or Stopped), and Group (the service group).

FIGURE 8.22 Services tab of Task Manager

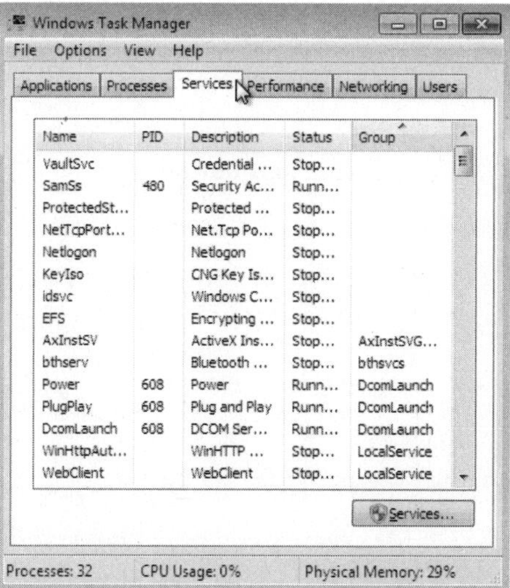

To start a stopped service, click the service and select Start Service. To stop a running service, click the service and select Stop Service. You can also open the Services tool by clicking the Services button. The Services tool enables you to specify whether a process starts automatically, automatically with a delayed start, manually, or is disabled.

Managing Performance Tasks in Task Manager

The Performance tab of the Task Manager dialog box, shown in Figure 8.23, provides an overview of your computer's CPU and memory usage. The Performance tab is similar to the information tracked by Performance Monitor.

FIGURE 8.23 Performance tab of Task Manager

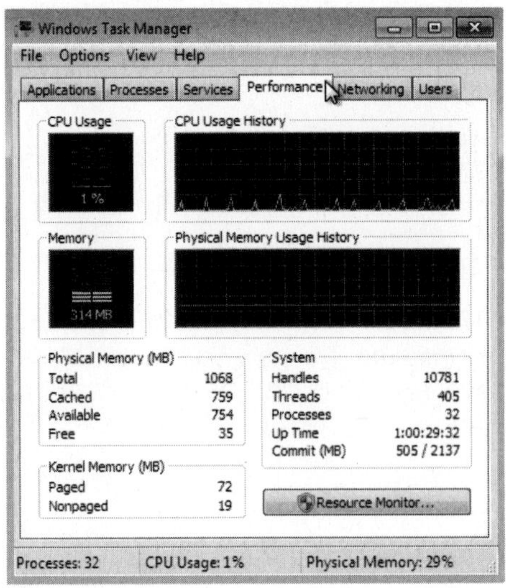

The Performance tab shows the following information:

- CPU usage, in real time and in a history graph
- Memory usage, in real time and in a history graph
- Physical memory statistics
- Kernel memory statistics
- System totals for handles, threads, processes, uptime, and the page file

Click the Resource Monitor button to launch Resource Monitor, which you can also find in Performance Monitor.

Managing Networking Tasks in Task Manager

The Networking tab of the Task Manager dialog box, shown in Figure 8.24, provides an overview of your networking usage. Statistics for each adapter are displayed at the bottom of the dialog box.

FIGURE 8.24 Networking tab of Task Manager

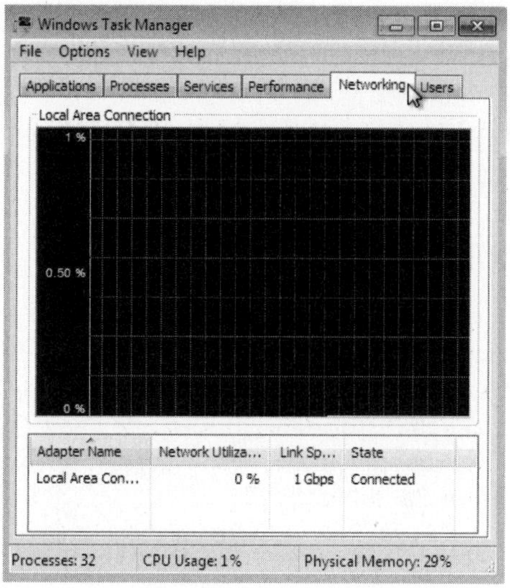

Managing Users in Task Manager

The Users tab of the Task Manager dialog box, shown in Figure 8.25, shows the active and disconnected users on your computer. For each user, you will see the User (the name of the user), ID (the current user ID), Status (whether Active or Disconnected), Client Name, and Session (whether the user is connected via the console session or by another method, such as Remote Desktop).

FIGURE 8.25 Users tab of Task Manager

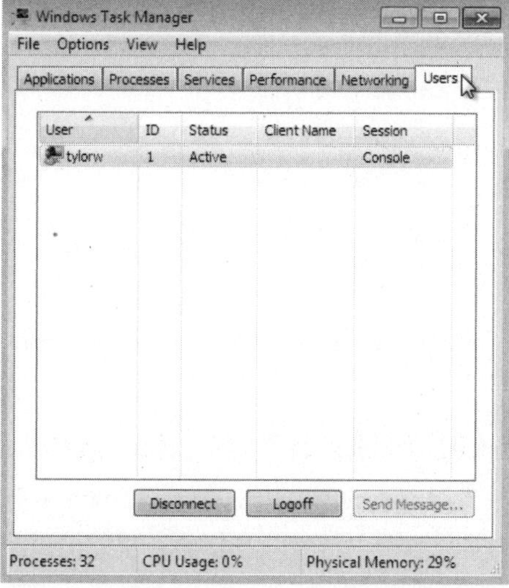

To send a message to a user, select the user and click the Send Message button. To connect to a user session, right-click the user and select Connect. To disconnect a user session, select the user and click the Disconnect button. To log off a user, select the user and click the Logoff button.

In addition to `msinfo32` and Task Manager (`taskman.exe`), Windows 7 has another tool to show you how well your machine is currently working: Performance Information and Tools.

Performance Information and Tools

If you enjoy seeing how well your computer performs by running benchmarking applications that provide a score rating, then you will love Performance Information and Tools, shown in Figure 8.26. This utility provides a numerical score that lets you know how well your system performs. To launch Performance Information and Tools, click Start ➢ Control Panel ➢ System And Maintenance ➢ Performance Information And Tools, or simply type **Performance Information** in the Windows 7 search box.

FIGURE 8.26 Performance Information And Tools window

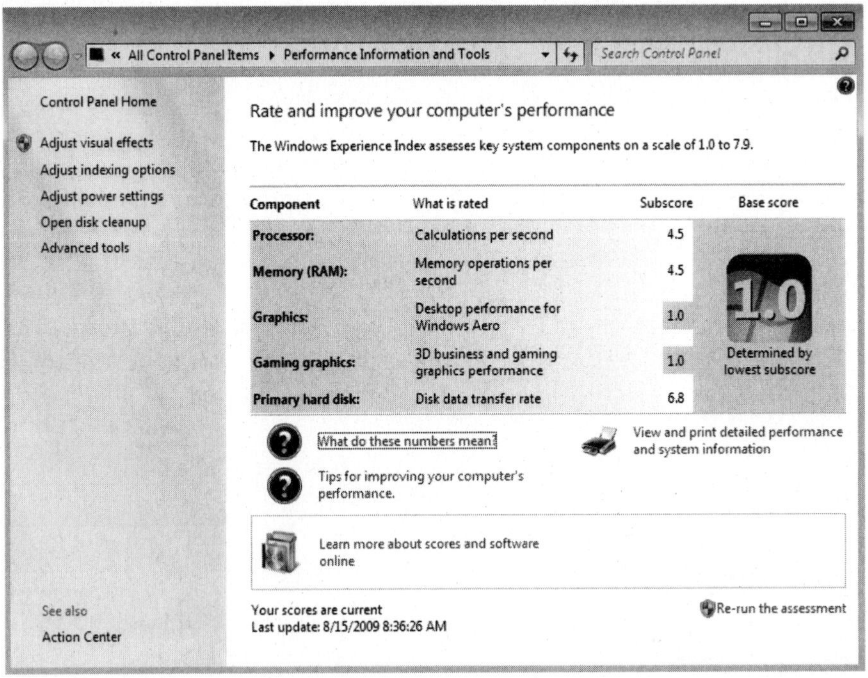

The main pane reveals a calculated score, called the Windows Experience Index. The Windows Experience Index base score is calculated by taking the lowest subscore among five rated components:

- Processor, based on calculations per second
- Memory (RAM), based on memory operations per second
- Graphics, based on Windows Aero performance
- Gaming Graphics, based on 3D graphics performance
- Primary Hard Disk, based on disk transfer rate

A computer with a base score of 1 or 2 will be able to perform only the most basic tasks. A base score of 3 indicates that a computer can run Windows Aero and all but the most advanced Windows 7 features. A base score of 4 or 5 should be able to run all Windows 7 features, as well as play graphically intensive 3D games.

Each component subscore determines how well each individual component performs. Because the base score is equal to the lowest component subscore, the Windows Experience Index base score should give you an overview of how well your computer should run applications. This enables application developers to give their applications a numerical rating so consumers can easily figure out whether the application will run well on their computer.

If an application requires a higher base score than your computer has, it might be time to upgrade your hardware. After you install new hardware, you can select Update My Score to have Windows 7 recalculate your Windows Experience Index base score.

The left pane of Performance Information and Tools contains useful links to help you improve the performance of your computer. Click Adjust Visual Effects to bring up the Visual Effects tab of the Performance Options dialog box, which you can use for configuring how Windows will graphically display windows, menu items, and icons. Click Adjust Indexing Options to launch Indexing Options, which can improve the speed of searching files on your computer. Click Adjust Indexing Options to launch the Indexing Options dialog box, where you can choose which resources on your Windows 7 machine are included in indexing.

Click Adjust Power Settings to launch Power Options, which you can use to adjust your power plan. Click Open Disk Cleanup to launch Disk Cleanup Options so you can clean up unnecessary files on your hard disk. Finally, click Advanced Tools to launch a list of tools that you can use to further improve your computer's performance, including the following tools:

- Clear all Windows Experience Index Scores and re-rate the system
- View Performance Details in Event Log
- Open Performance Monitor
- Open Resource Monitor
- Open Task Manager
- View Advanced System Details in System Information

- Adjust the Appearance and Performance of Windows
- Open Disk Defragmenter
- Generate a System Health Report

The Performance Information And Tools menu is a great display of your system and a launching point for many tools within Windows 7. Another useful tool that has been around in many versions of Windows and is still available in Windows 7 is the System Configuration utility, or `msconfig`.

Using System Configuration

You can use the System Configuration utility to help you view and troubleshoot how Windows 7 starts and what programs and services launch at startup. You might recognize this utility as `msconfig.exe`. To launch this utility, run `msconfig.exe` from the Windows 7 search box. The General tab, shown in Figure 8.27, is used to specify startup options. You can choose from the following three startup options:

- Normal Startup, which loads all device drivers and services
- Diagnostic Startup, which loads basic services and drivers
- Selective Startup, from which you can choose whether to load system services, load startup items, and use the original boot configuration

FIGURE 8.27 System Configuration General tab

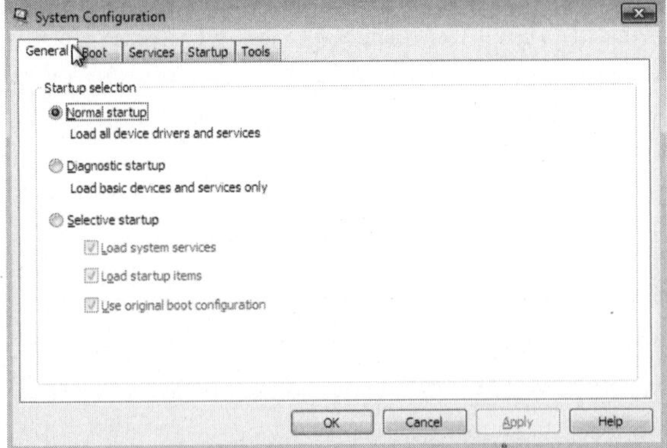

The Boot tab, shown in Figure 8.28, is used to configure whether Windows boots in Safe mode, runs an Active Directory repair, boots to a graphical user interface (GUI), logs boot information, boots in VGA mode, and displays driver names while booting. Select any of the options on this screen to change the settings on the General tab; conversely, select Normal Startup on the General tab to clear the settings on the Boot tab.

FIGURE 8.28 System Configuration Boot tab

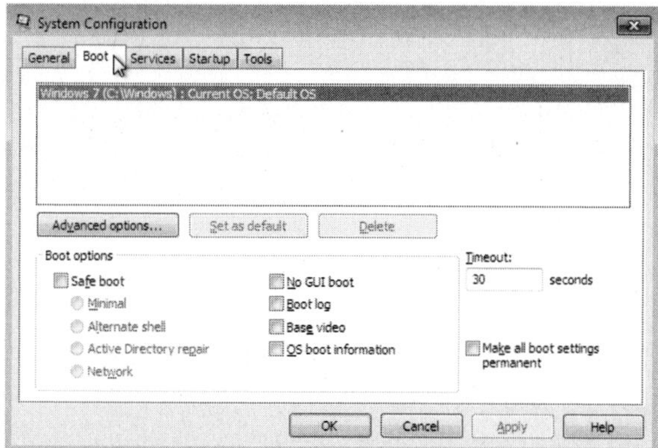

The Services tab is used to list Windows 7 services and indicate which services are running. You can deselect services on this tab so they do not launch at startup. Select any of the services on this screen to change the settings on the General tab; conversely, select Normal Startup on the General tab to clear the settings on the Services tab. The Services tab of the System Configuration tool is shown in Figure 8.29.

FIGURE 8.29 System Configuration Services tab

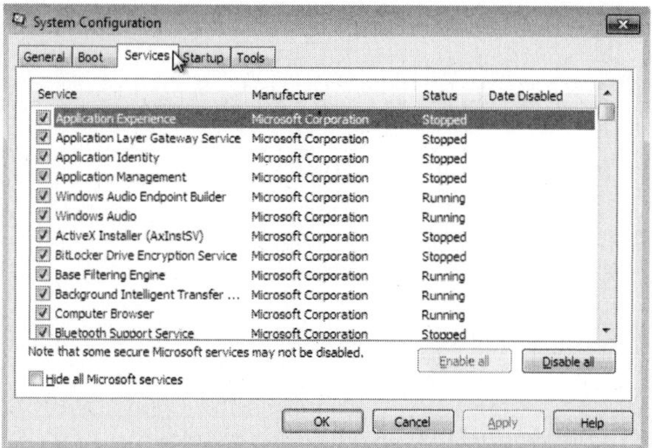

The Startup tab, as shown in Figure 8.30, shows applications that start when Windows 7 starts. You can deselect applications on this tab so they do not launch at startup. If you've read through the previous two paragraphs, you can probably guess that selecting any of the services on this screen changes the settings on the General tab, and selecting Normal Startup on the General tab clears the settings on the Startup tab.

FIGURE 8.30 System Configuration Startup tab

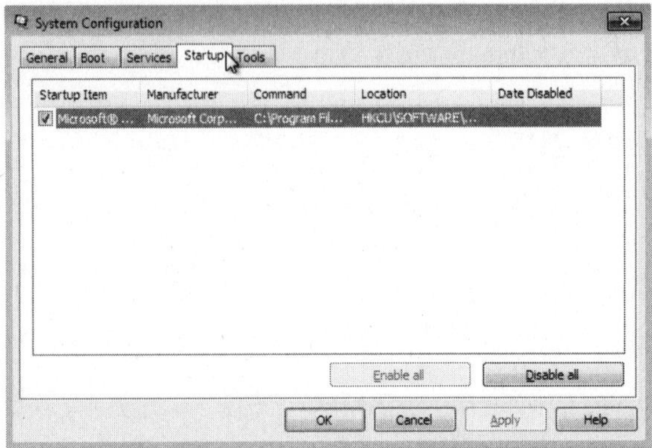

The Tools tab, as shown in Figure 8.31, shows tools that you can launch from System Configuration. Simply click the tool name and click Launch to launch the tool. You can launch the following tools from this tab:

- About Windows
- Change UAC Settings
- Action Center
- Windows Troubleshooting
- Computer Management
- System Information
- Event Viewer
- Programs
- System Properties
- Internet Options
- Internet Protocol Configuration
- Performance Monitor
- Resource Monitor
- Task Manager
- Command Prompt
- Registry Editor
- Remote Assistance
- System Restore

FIGURE 8.31 System Configuration Tools tab

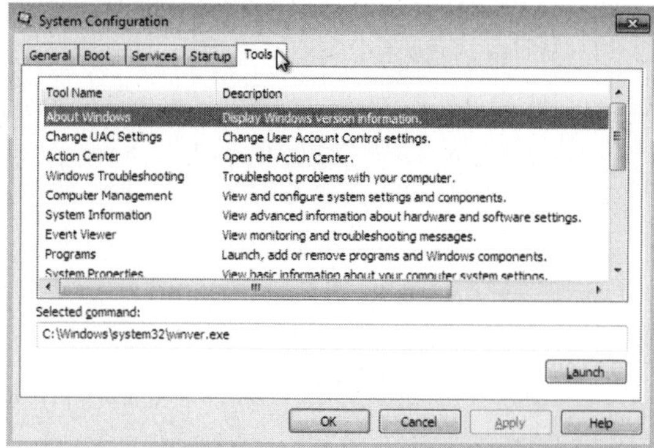

From the Tools tab, you can manually launch many of the utilities offered by Windows 7. You also have the ability to automatically launch utilities by using the Task Scheduler.

Setting Up Task Scheduler

Task Scheduler is a utility in Windows 7 that allows you to schedule actions to occur at specified intervals. Windows 7 Task Scheduler can be accessed by typing **Task Scheduler** into the Windows 7 search box. This launches the application, as shown in Figure 8.32.

FIGURE 8.32 Windows 7 Task Scheduler

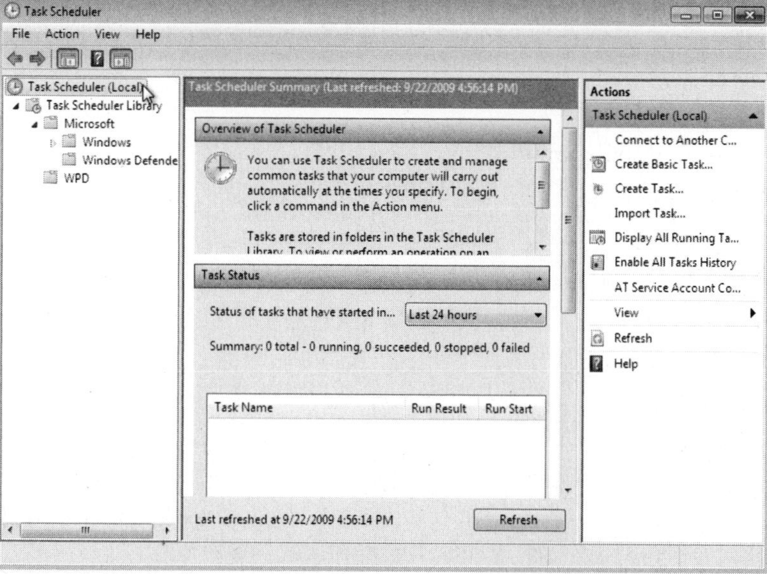

After Task Scheduler starts, you can create a scheduled task.

Creating a Scheduled Task

You can create a basic task by selecting the Create Basic Task menu item in the Actions pane on the right side of Task Scheduler, as shown in Figure 8.33.

FIGURE 8.33 Creating a basic task in Task Scheduler

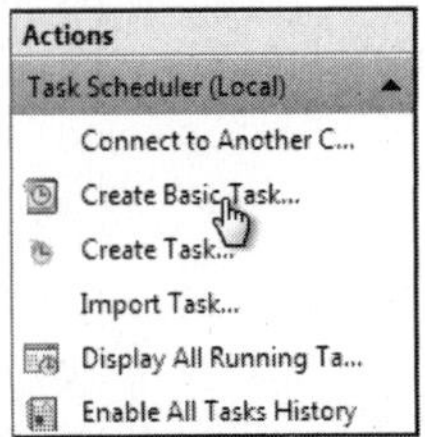

By creating a basic task, a Task Manager Wizard lets you set any of your Windows programs to run automatically at a specific time and at a set interval, such as daily, weekly, or monthly. For example, you might schedule an application to run daily at 2 a.m. Actions can be performed at the following events (called *triggers*) available in the Task Manager Wizard:

- Daily, or once every number of days (such as once every three days)
- Weekly, or on certain days of the week, or every number of weeks (such as every four weeks on Monday)
- Monthly, or on selected days of the month, or only on selected months
- One time only
- When the computer starts
- When you log on
- When a specific event is logged

If you've chosen a time trigger, you configure the time/date when the action will occur. When a trigger is activated, Task Scheduler can perform the following actions:

- Start a program
- Send an email
- Display a message

Perform the following steps in Exercise 8.4 to set up a scheduled task to launch Windows 7 Calculator at a predetermined weekly time.

EXERCISE 8.4

Scheduling a Task to Launch

1. Click Start and type **Task Scheduler** into the Windows 7 search box, or choose Start ➢ Control Panel ➢ System and Security ➢ Administrative Tools and then double-click Task Scheduler.
2. In the Actions pane of the Task Scheduler window, select Create Basic Task.
3. The Create Basic Task Wizard appears; type **Monday's calculator** as a name for your task and a description, and then click Next.
4. Select how often you want the action to occur. For this example, select Weekly and click Next to continue.
5. Specify that the action should occur every Monday at 9 a.m. and click Next.
6. Select the Start A Program radio button and click Next.
7. Browse for the Calculator application at `C:\Windows\system32\calc.exe`. Click Next.
8. The final dialog box shows your selections for the scheduled task; click Finish.

Select the Windows folder in the left pane and then select the arrow to expand the folder's contents and reveal a complete set of preconfigured tasks. Figure 8.34 shows the Windows folder expanded and the Defrag task selected. You can view the Defrag task settings, edit the task, and even run the Defrag task manually if you desire.

FIGURE 8.34 Task Scheduler preconfigured Defrag task

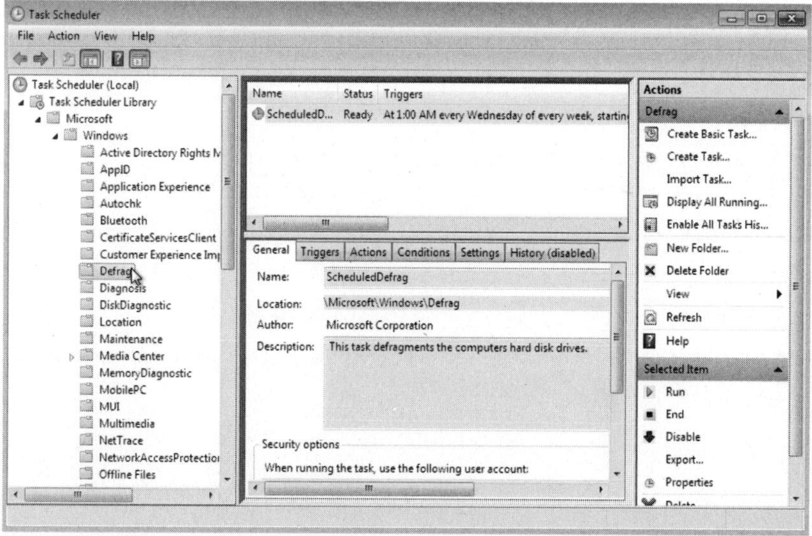

Task Scheduler also enables you to run tasks manually by selecting the task and clicking Run in the right pane. Select a task and click Disable to disable a task.

Managing Scheduled Task Properties

You can manage a scheduled task through its Properties dialog box. To access this dialog box, right-click the task you want to manage and choose Properties from the context menu, as shown in Figure 8.35.

FIGURE 8.35 Scheduled task properties access

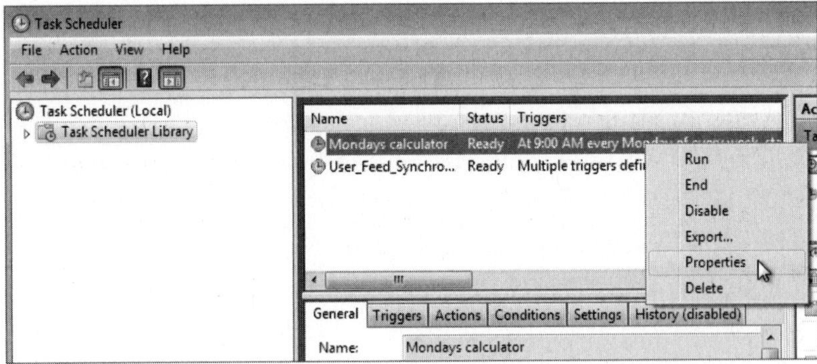

The scheduled task's Properties dialog box has six tabs for configuration, as follows:

- General
- Triggers
- Actions
- Conditions
- Settings
- History

Each options tab is described here:

General Tab On the General tab, you can configure the following options:

- The description of the task
- The username or group to be used to run the specified task
- Whether the task is run when the user is logged off
- Whether the task is hidden

Triggers Tab The Triggers tab shows the schedule configured for the task. You can click Edit to edit the trigger, which brings up the Edit Trigger dialog box. You can also click New to create a new trigger or click Delete to delete an existing trigger.

Actions Tab The Actions tab shows the action that is configured for the task. You can click Edit to edit the action, which brings up the Edit Action dialog box. You can also click New to create a new action or click Delete to delete an existing action.

Conditions Tab The Conditions tab shows the conditions associated with the task. The options in the Idle section are useful if the computer must be idle when the task is run. You can specify how long the computer must be idle before the task begins and whether the task should be stopped if the computer ceases to be idle. The options in the Power section are applicable when the computer on which the task runs is battery powered. You can specify that the task should not start if the computer is running from batteries and choose to stop the task if battery mode begins. You can also select whether to wake the computer in order to run the task. The option in the Network section defines whether the task starts when a particular network connection is available.

Settings Tab The Settings tab provides settings that affect the task's behavior as follows:

- Whether the task can be run on demand
- Whether the task should be restarted if it is missed
- How often the task should be restarted if it fails
- When to stop the task if it runs a long time
- Whether you can force the task to stop
- When the task should be deleted
- What actions should occur if the task is already running

History Tab The History tab shows historical information regarding the task, including the task's start time, stop time, and whether the task completed successfully. Once set up, the scheduled task should commence at the appropriate time. If not, you might need to troubleshoot it.

Troubleshooting Scheduled Tasks

If you are trying to use Task Scheduler and the tasks are not properly being executed, one of the following troubleshooting options might resolve the problem:

- If a scheduled task does not run as expected, right-click the task and select Properties. In the Task Scheduler Library, ensure that the task status is Ready. In the task's Properties page, verify that the schedule has been defined on the Triggers tab.
- If the scheduled task is a command-line utility, make sure that you have properly defined the command-line utility, including any options that are required for the utility to run properly.

- Verify that the user who is configured to run the scheduled task has the necessary permissions for the task to be run.
- Within the Task Status section, check the task status to see when the task last ran successfully, if ever.
- Verify that the Task Scheduler service has been enabled on the computer if no tasks can be run on the computer.

Task Scheduler is a great utility that you can use to run scheduled maintenance applications and proactively maintain a Windows 7 system. If issues occur within Windows 7, you will use a different utility, called Event Viewer, to view these events.

Using Event Viewer

Event Viewer, shown in Figure 8.36, enables you to view event logs that are created by the operating system. This utility is useful when troubleshooting problems that occur on your computer.

FIGURE 8.36 Windows 7 Event Viewer

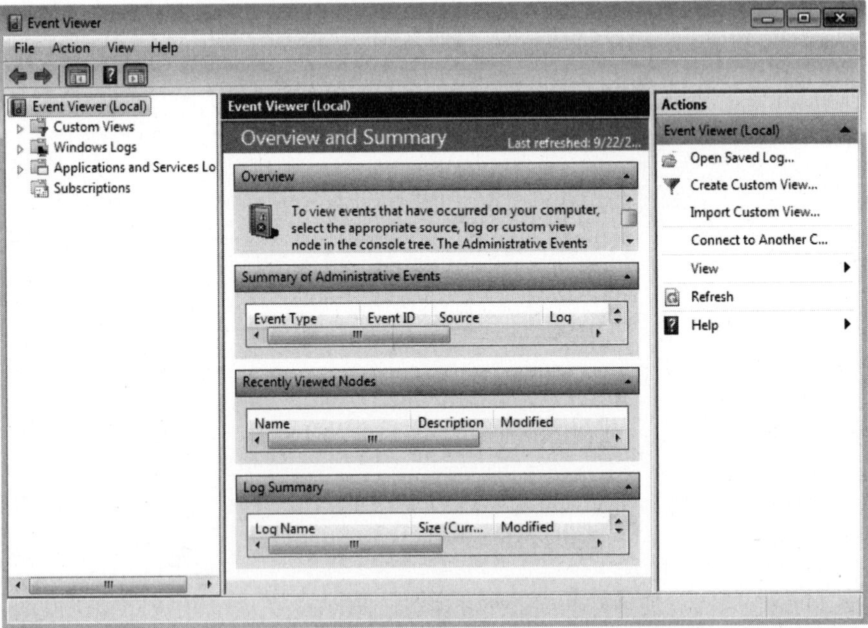

Whenever an error occurs, an event is usually placed in one or more event logs. To open Event Viewer, click Start ➤ Control Panel ➤ System and Security ➤ Administrative Tools ➤ View Event Logs.

Whereas old versions of Event Viewer contained only the Application, Security, and System logs, the Windows 7 version of Event Viewer contains the following Windows logs:

- Application
- Security
- Setup
- System
- Forwarded Events

The *Application log* is used to log events relating to applications, such as whether an application, driver, or service fails. The *Security log* is used to log security events, such as successful or failed logon events. The *Setup log* is used only by domain controllers, so it doesn't have much practical use in Windows 7. The *System log* is used to log events related to the operating system and related services. The *Forwarded Events log* is used to collect events that have been forwarded from other computers.

To configure log settings, right-click the log that you want to configure and select Properties. The Log Properties dialog box appears. The Application log properties are shown in Figure 8.37.

FIGURE 8.37 Event Viewer Application log properties

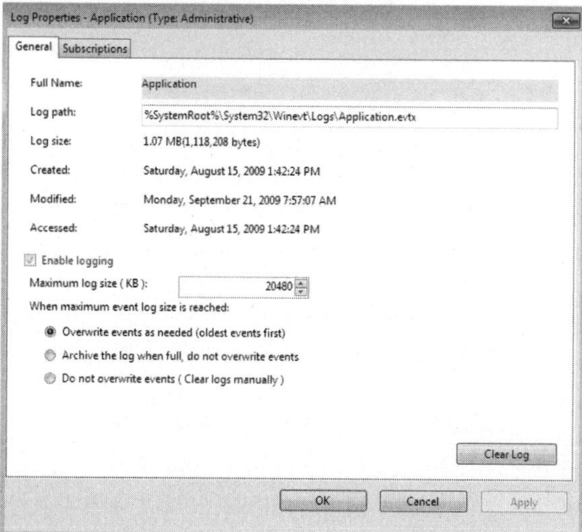

The Log Properties dialog box shows the following information:

- The full name of the log
- Where the log is stored
- The size of the log
- When the log was created, modified, and accessed
- Whether logging is enabled for the log
- The maximum log size in KB
- The action that occurs when the log reaches the maximum size

The left pane of Event Viewer is where you find the Windows logs noted previously, but it also contains other logs and views that can be helpful when troubleshooting a specific application. The Custom Views section can be used to create a view that contains only the information you want to see, such as only events in a particular log or only Critical events. One custom view, Administrative Events, is created for you by default, as shown in Figure 8.38.

FIGURE 8.38 Event Viewer Custom Views: Administrative Events

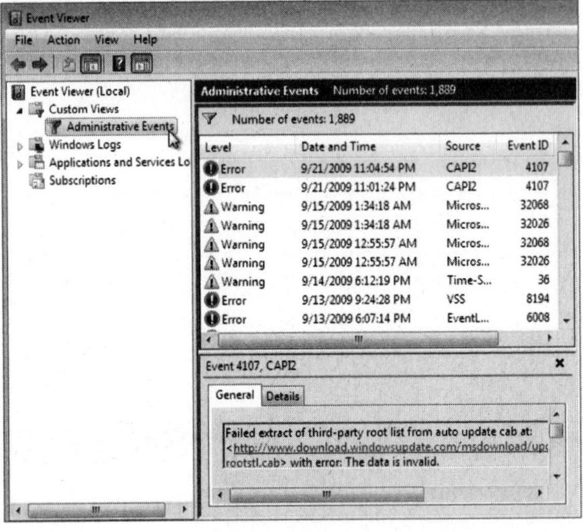

The Administrative Events view contains Critical, Error, and Warning events from all logs, enabling you to easily view only the most important events. Another section in the left pane contains logs that relate to Applications and Services, as shown in Figure 8.39.

FIGURE 8.39 Event Viewer Application and Services log

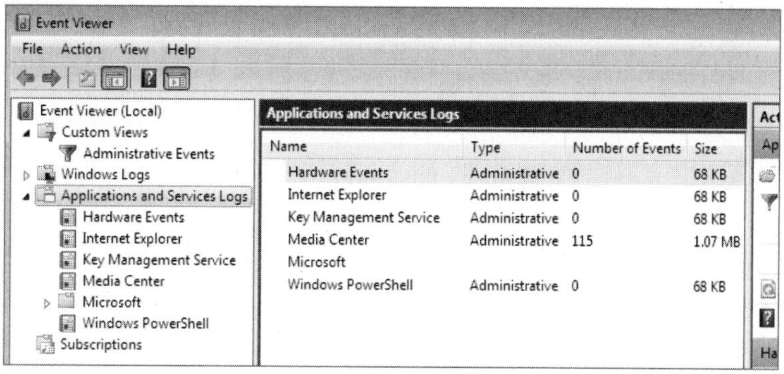

The Microsoft folder within the Application and Services log contains many other logs related to specific Microsoft components and applications.

The Subscription folder enables you to receive event logs from other computers. Having other machines send events to one machine is useful to us as it gives us one central repository to view events from multiple locations. To use subscriptions, you must start the Windows Event Collector Service.

The center pane of Event Viewer displays the events and information that relates to those events. You can also view a summary of your administrative events, which contains a count of Critical, Error, Warning, Information, Audit Success, and Audit Failure events. A count of these events is displayed for the last hour, day, and week, and the total number of events is also provided. Each event is assigned an event level of Critical, Error, Warning, Information, or Verbose.

The right pane of Event Viewer enables you to perform actions related to items you have selected in the left and center panes. You can save logs, open saved logs, create or import views, clear logs, filter logs, and find logs with certain keywords. You can also attach a task to an event. Clicking Attach Task To This Event opens the Create Basic Task Wizard in Task Scheduler so you can easily create a task related to the selected event.

Perform Exercise 8.5 to view events in Event Viewer and set log properties.

EXERCISE 8.5

Viewing Events in Event Viewer

1. Choose Start ➤ Control Panel ➤ System And Security ➤ Administrative Tools ➤ View Event Logs, or type **`Event Viewer`** into the Windows 7 search box.
2. Open Windows Logs and click System in the left pane of the Event Viewer window to display the System log events.

EXERCISE 8.5 *(continued)*

3. Double-click the first event in the center pane of the Event Viewer window to see its Event Properties dialog box.
4. After you view the Event Properties, click the Close button to close the dialog box.
5. Right-click System in the left pane of the Event Viewer window and select Properties.
6. Configure the System log to archive the log file when it is full by clicking Archive The Log File When Full; Do Not Overwrite Events; click OK to close the dialog box.
7. Right-click System in the left pane of the Event Viewer window and select Filter Current Log.
8. Select the check boxes next to Critical and Error boxes; then click OK (you will see only Critical and Error events listed in the System log).
9. Right-click System and select Clear Log.
10. A dialog box appears that asks whether you want to save the System log before you clear it; click the Save And Clear button.
11. Specify the path and filename for the log file, and then click the Save button (the events will be saved in an `.evtx` file, and the events will be cleared from the System log).

When you are investigating a Windows 7 problem, Event Viewer is one of the first places that you should look.

Summary

In this chapter, you learned how to monitor, maintain, troubleshoot, and optimize Windows 7. To monitor Windows 7 properly, Microsoft includes many utilities including Performance Monitor, Reliability Monitor, System Information, Task Manager, System Configuration, Task Scheduler, and Event Viewer. Each of these tools provides information about the operating system and hardware status.

It is important to monitor Windows 7 so you can see where the system is performing badly (if it is performing badly). Windows 7 allows you to track memory, processor activity, the disk subsystem, the network subsystem, and many other computer subsystems.

The tools included with Windows 7 allow you to provide baseline statistics for each of the subsystems so you can track changes over time, better evaluate issues that pertain to the Windows 7 machine, and make changes to proactively affect declining performance.

Exam Essentials

Be able to monitor and troubleshoot Windows 7 performance. Know which utilities can be used to track Windows 7 performance events and issues. Know how to track and identify performance problems related to memory, the processor, the disk subsystem, and the network subsystem. Be able to correct system bottlenecks when they are identified.

Know how to use Task Scheduler to automate system tasks. Understand the purpose of Task Scheduler. Be able to configure Task Scheduler and identify problems that would keep it from running properly.

Understand how to configure monitoring tools. Know how to troubleshoot by using Task Manager, Event Viewer, System Information, Performance Information and Tools, and Problem Reports and Solutions.

Review Questions

1. You are the network manager for a small company. You have a junior IT administrator who did some installations last week on a Windows 7 machine. How can you see what applications were installed last week on the Windows 7 machine?
   A. View the informational events of Reliability Monitor.
   B. Open Control Panel, Add/Remove programs.
   C. Check Event Viewer system logs.
   D. View the data collector sets.
2. You are the network administrator for Stellacon Corporation. Users in the sales department have been complaining that the Sales application is slow to load. Using Performance Monitor, you create a baseline report for one of the computers, monitoring memory, the processor, the disk subsystem, and the network subsystem. You notice that the disk subsystem has a high load of activity. What other subsystem should you monitor before you can know for sure whether you have a disk subsystem bottleneck?
   A. Memory
   B. Processor
   C. Network
   D. Application
3. Your accounting department runs a processor-intensive application and you are trying to determine whether their current computers need to have the processors upgraded. You load a test computer with a configuration identical to the production computers' and run a program that simulates a typical user's workload. You monitor the Processor ➢ % Processor Time counter. What average value for this counter would indicate a processor bottleneck?
   A. Over 5 percent
   B. Over 50 percent
   C. Over 60 percent
   D. Over 85 percent
4. You are the network administrator for a large corporation. The accounting department requires that a specific application, `STELLAPP.EXE`, be run every day to create daily reports on accounting activity. The application needs to be run at 6 p.m. on Monday through Friday. The accounting manager has asked you to automate the process so reports are generated on the specified schedule without any user interaction. Which Windows 7 utility should you use?
   A. Task Scheduler
   B. Automated Scheduler
   C. Task Manager
   D. Task Automater

5. You are the network administrator for a large company. The payroll manager has Windows 7 installed on her desktop computer. The computer has the following configuration:

   - Dual Pentium 4 processors
   - 1 GB of RAM
   - Two physical SCSI disks
   - Disk 0 has volume C:
   - Disk 1 has volume D:
   - 1.5 GB page file on partition C:
   - 100 Mbps Fast Ethernet NIC

   The payroll manager requires the use of a database application. She has come to you to report that when the database application is running, the computer slows down very significantly, and she is unable to run any other applications. You run Reliability and Performance Monitor on her computer and record the following information when the database application is running:

   - Sustained processor utilization is at 100 percent for both processors.
   - There are a significant number of hard page faults.

   When you record the data for the computer when the database application is not running, you record the following information:

   - Average processor utilization is at 30 percent.
   - There are a significant number of hard page faults.

   The database application is critical to the finance manager's job. In order to be able to better manage her productivity, which two of the following actions will have the greatest impact on optimizing her computer's performance? Choose two.

   A. Upgrade the processors in her computer.

   B. Add memory to the computer.

   C. Split the page file over D: and E:.

   D. Increase the page file to 3 GB.

6. You are the network administrator for an organization that has decided to migrate to Windows 7. Part of your job requires that you are able to complete the following:

   - Collect data from the local or remote Windows 7 computers on the network. You can collect data from a single computer or multiple computers concurrently.
   - View data as it is being collected in real time, or historically from collected data.

   Which Windows 7 application can you use to achieve your task?

   A. Event Viewer

   B. Computer Monitor

   C. Windows 7 Monitor

   D. Performance Monitor

7. You are the network administrator for a large organization. You are running Windows 7 machines throughout your network along with Windows Server 2008 R2. You need to use Event Viewer to review event logs for Critical and Error events only. You need to see *all* of these events from the logs. What do you do to achieve this?

   A. Use the Administrative Events view.

   B. Create a custom view and choose Administrative Events.

   C. Do a search on the system log for all of these events.

   D. Create a custom view and select Critical, Error, and Verbose for all logs.

8. You are the network administrator for an organization that runs Windows Server 2008 R2 and Windows 7. You are asked by your IT manager to collect performance data on a Windows 7 machine, for a period of three weeks. The IT manager wants CPU utilization, disk utilization, and memory utilization all included in the data collected. How should you accomplish this?

   A. Create a user-defined data collector set.

   B. Create a custom performance set.

   C. Create a trace event.

   D. Create a session data collector set.

9. While using Performance Monitor, you use the following output mode.

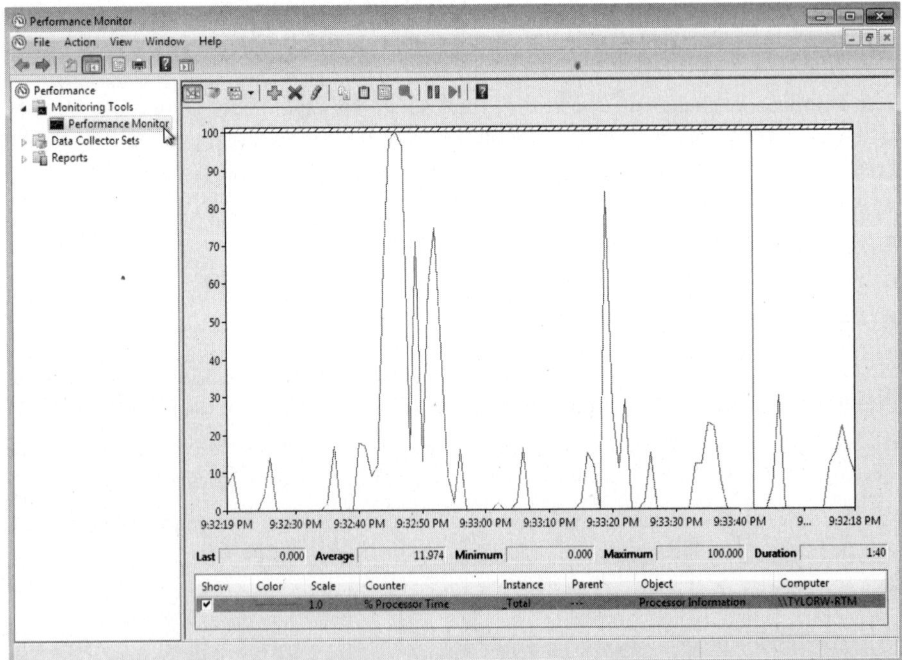

Which output mode are you using?

A. Histogram bar view

B. Graph view

C. Report view

D. Line view

10. While using Performance Monitor, you use the following output mode.

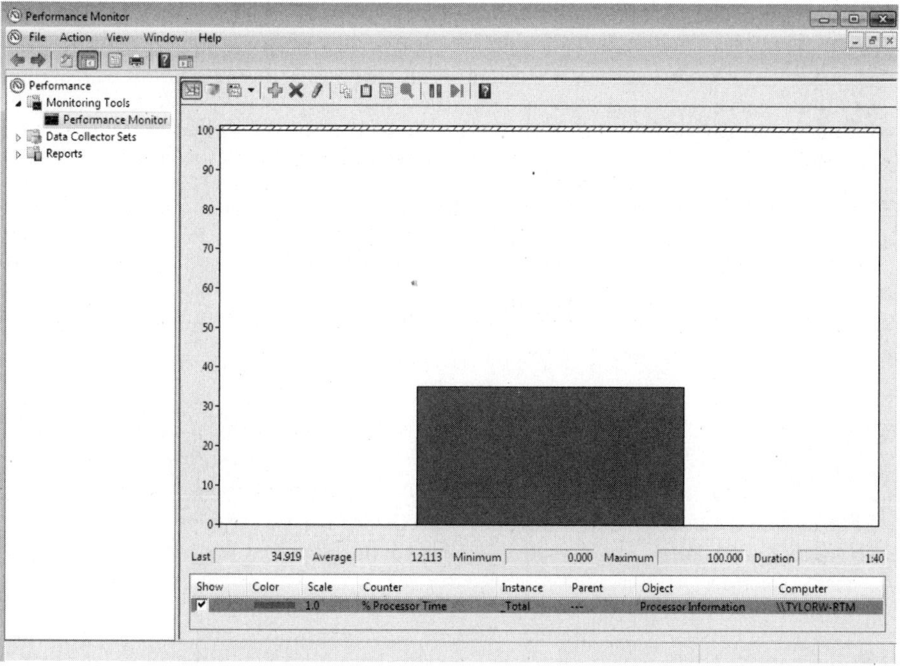

Which output mode are you using?

A. Histogram bar view

B. Graph view

C. Report view

D. Line view

Answers to Review Questions

1. A. By viewing the informational events of Reliability Monitor, you will be able to see which application got installed by the installation date.

2. A. You should check the memory counters. If your computer does not have enough memory, it can cause excessive paging, which may be perceived as a disk subsystem bottleneck.

3. D. If the average Processor ➢ % Processor Time counter is consistently above 85 percent, a processor bottleneck may be indicated. Normally this number will spike up and down over time. A spike over 85 percent is not necessarily alarming. If the average is over 85 percent, then a bottleneck is indicated and a second processor or a faster one should be installed.

4. A. To automate scheduled tasks, you use Task Scheduler. You can schedule tasks to be run based on the schedule you specify and the user account that should be used to run the task.

5. A, B. The greatest improvement in performance for this computer can be obtained by upgrading the processors and adding more physical RAM. Because the database application is using 100 percent processor utilization over a sustained period, you need to upgrade the processors. The hard page faults indicate that you also have a memory bottleneck. Although moving or increasing the page file might have an impact on performance, neither would have as large an impact as adding more physical memory.

6. D. Performance Monitor enables you to collect data from your local computer or remote Windows 7 machine, from a single computer or multiple computers concurrently; view data as it is being collected in real time, or historically from collected data; have full control over the selection of what data will be collected, by selecting which specific objects and counters will be collected; choose the sampling parameters that will be used, meaning the time interval that you want to use for collecting data points and the time period that will be used for data collection.

7. D. You would have to create a custom view to achieve this task. You could not use the Administrative Events view (default custom view) because it also includes all warnings.

8. A. Data collector sets are used to collect data into a log so the data can be reviewed. You can view the log files with Performance Monitor.

9. D. The graphic is an example of a line view output. The three options are line view, histogram bar view, and report view.

10. A. The graphic is an example of a histogram bar view output. The three options are line view, histogram bar view, and report view.

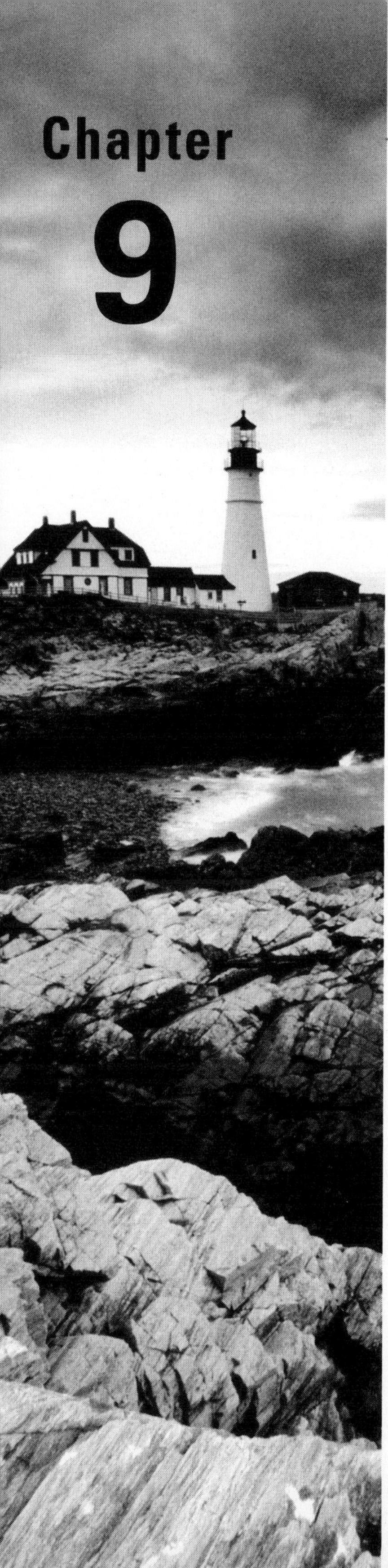

Configuring Backups and Recovery

MICROSOFT EXAM OBJECTIVES COVERED IN THIS CHAPTER:

✓ **Configure backup.**

- This objective may include but is not limited to: creating a system recovery disk; backing up files, folders, or full system; scheduling backups

✓ **Configure system recovery options.**

- This objective may include but is not limited to: configuring system restore points; restoring system settings; Last Known Good Configuration; complete restore; Driver Rollback

✓ **Configure file recovery options.**

- This objective may include but is not limited to: configuring file restore points; restoring previous versions of files and folders; restoring damaged or deleted files by using shadow copies; restoring user profiles

Windows 7 has a full backup and restore application to enable you to maintain a backup copy of any of the Windows 7 component files and data files that are considered critical to the operation of your day-to-day business. You can use the backup of the files to restore them if they become unusable (corrupt, deleted, or even modified and you want to go back to the original).

In this chapter, we also explain the following recovery tools:

- Advanced Boot Options menu, including Safe mode
- Startup Repair tool
- Backup and Restore Center
- System Protection

Safeguarding Your Computer and Recovering from Disaster

One of the worst events you will experience is a computer that won't boot. An even worse experience is discovering that there is no recent backup for that computer.

The first step in preparing for disaster recovery is to expect that a disaster will happen at some point and take proactive measures to plan your recovery before the failure occurs. Here are some of the preparations you can make:

- Keep your computer up-to-date with Windows Update (covered in Chapter 1, "Windows 7 Installation").
- Perform regular system backups.
- Use current software to scan for malware (such as viruses, spyware, and adware) and make sure you have the most recent updates.
- Perform regular administrative functions, such as monitoring the logs in the Event Viewer utility.

If you can't start Windows 7, there are several options and utilities that can be used to identify and resolve Windows errors. The following is a broad list of troubleshooting options:

- If you have recently made a change to your computer's configuration by installing a new device driver or application and Windows 7 will not load properly, you can use the Last Known Good Configuration, roll back the driver, or use System Restore to restore a previous system configuration.

- If you can boot your computer to Safe mode, and you suspect that you have a system conflict, you can temporarily disable an application or processes, troubleshoot services, or uninstall software.
- If your computer will not boot to Safe mode, you can use the Startup Repair tool to replace corrupted system files.
- If necessary, you can use the Backup and Restore Center utility to restore personal files from backup media and to restore a complete image of your computer.
- You can also use Driver Rollback. If you install a driver that causes issues on your system, you can use the Driver Rollback utility to return the driver to its previous version.

Table 9.1 summarizes all of the Windows 7 utilities and options that can be used to assist in performing system recovery. All these Windows 7 recovery techniques are covered in detail in this chapter.

TABLE 9.1 Windows 7 Recovery Techniques

Recovery Technique	When to Use
Event Viewer	If the Windows 7 operating system can be loaded through Normal or Safe mode, one of the first places to look for hints about the problem is Event Viewer. Event Viewer displays System, Security, and Application logs.
Safe mode	This is generally your starting point for system recovery. Safe mode loads the absolute minimum of services and drivers that are needed to boot Windows 7. If you can load Safe mode, you may be able to troubleshoot devices or services that keep Windows 7 from loading normally.
Last Known Good Configuration	This option can help if you made changes to your computer and are now having problems. Last Known Good Configuration is an Advanced Boot Options menu item that you can select during startup. It loads the configuration that was used the last time the computer booted successfully. This option will not help if you have hardware errors.
Startup Repair tool	This tool can restore system files from the Windows 7 media. This option will not help if you have hardware errors.
Backup and Restore Center	You should use this utility to safeguard your computer. Through the Backup utility, you can back up and restore personal files on your computer. You can also create and restore images of your entire computer.
System Restore	System Restore is used to create known checkpoints of your system's configuration. In the event that your system becomes misconfigured, you can restore the system configuration to an earlier checkpoint.

Using Advanced Boot Options

The Windows 7 advanced startup options can be used to troubleshoot errors that keep Windows 7 from successfully booting. Figure 9.1 shows the Advanced Boot Options screen.

FIGURE 9.1 Advanced Boot Options screen

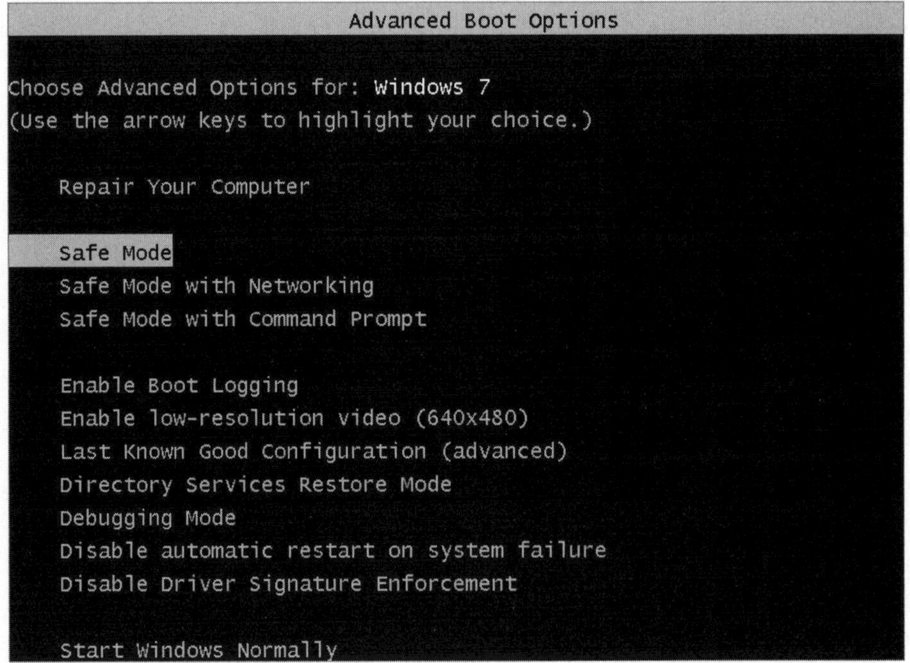

To access the Windows 7 advanced startup options, start or reboot the computer and press the F8 key after the firmware POST process, but before Windows 7 is loaded. This will bring up the Advanced Boot Options menu, which offers numerous options for booting Windows 7.

These advanced startup options are covered in the following three sections.

Starting in Safe Mode

When your computer will not start, one of the fundamental troubleshooting techniques is to simplify the configuration as much as possible. This is especially important when you do not know the cause of your problem and you have a complex configuration. After you have simplified the configuration, you can determine whether the problem is in the basic configuration or is a result of your complex configuration.

If the problem is in the basic configuration, you have a starting point for troubleshooting. If the problem is not in the basic configuration, you should proceed to restore each configuration option you removed, one at a time. This helps you to identify what is causing the error.

If Windows 7 will not load, you can attempt to load the operating system through *Safe mode*. When you run Windows 7 in Safe mode, you are simplifying your Windows configuration as much as possible. Safe mode loads only the drivers needed to get the computer up and running.

The drivers that are loaded with Safe mode include basic files and drivers for the mouse, monitor, keyboard, hard drive, standard video driver, and default system services. Safe mode is considered a diagnostic mode, so you do not have access to all of the features and devices in Windows 7 that you have access to when you boot normally, including networking capabilities.

A computer booted to Safe mode will show *Safe Mode* in the four corners of your desktop, as shown in Figure 9.2.

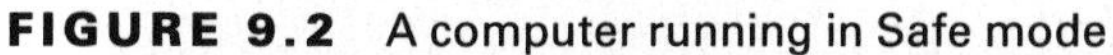
FIGURE 9.2 A computer running in Safe mode

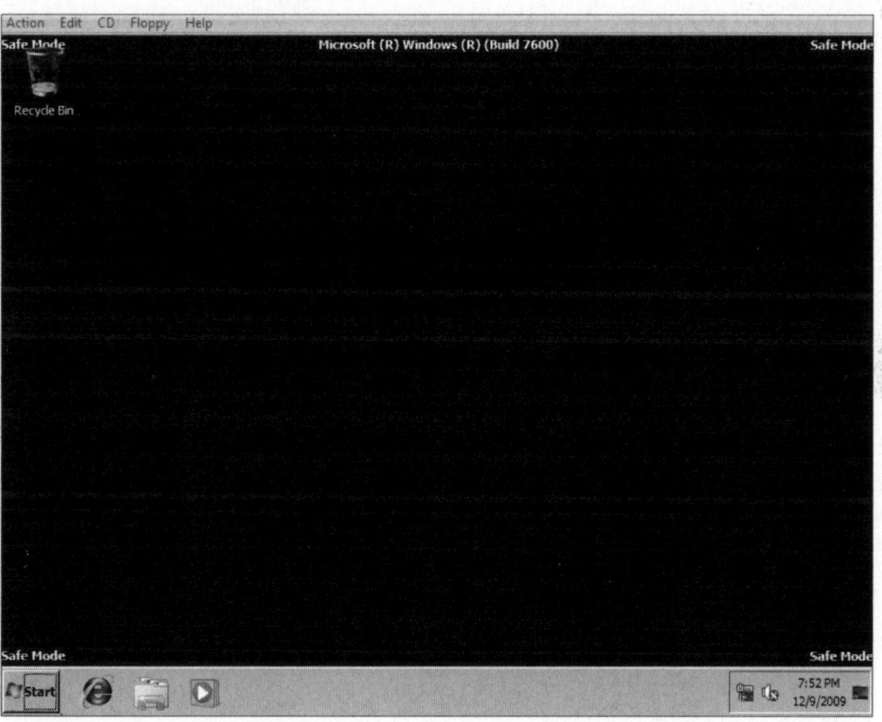

If you boot to Safe mode, check all of your computer's hardware and software settings in Device Manager and try to determine why Windows 7 will not boot properly. After you take steps to fix the problem, try to boot to Windows 7 as you normally would.

In Exercise 9.1, you will boot your computer to Safe mode.

EXERCISE 9.1

Booting Your Computer to Safe Mode

1. If your computer is currently running, choose Start ➢ Shutdown ➢ Restart.
2. During the boot process, press the F8 key to access the Advanced Boot Options menu.
3. Highlight Safe Mode and press Enter.
4. When Windows 7 starts, log in.
5. You will see a Help And Support dialog box letting you know what Safe mode is. Exit Help And Support.
6. You should see in the lower-right corner that a network connection is not available.
7. Choose Start ➢ Control Panel. Notice that most of the Control Panel icons are not available. If you are having a problem with a driver, you can open Device Manager and uninstall or roll back the driver.
8. Don't restart your computer yet; you will do this as a part of the next exercise.

Enabling Boot Logging

Boot logging creates a log file that tracks the loading of drivers and services. When you choose the Enable Boot Logging option from the Advanced Boot Options menu, Windows 7 loads normally, not in Safe mode. This allows you to log all of the processes that take place during a normal boot sequence.

This log file can be used to troubleshoot the boot process. When logging is enabled, the log file is written to `\WINDOWS\Ntbtlog.txt`. A sample of the `Ntbtlog.txt` file is shown in Figure 9.3.

FIGURE 9.3 The Windows 7 boot log file

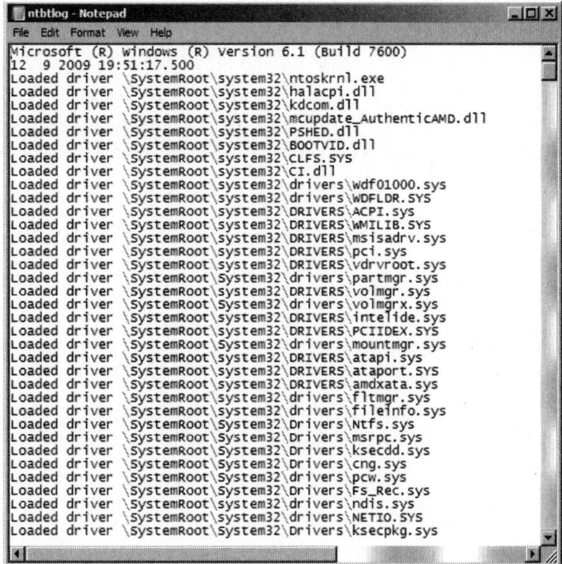


```
Microsoft (R) Windows (R) Version 6.1 (Build 7600)
12  9 2009 19:51:17.500
Loaded driver \SystemRoot\system32\ntoskrnl.exe
Loaded driver \SystemRoot\system32\halacpi.dll
Loaded driver \SystemRoot\system32\kdcom.dll
Loaded driver \SystemRoot\system32\mcupdate_AuthenticAMD.dll
Loaded driver \SystemRoot\system32\PSHED.dll
Loaded driver \SystemRoot\system32\BOOTVID.dll
Loaded driver \SystemRoot\system32\CLFS.SYS
Loaded driver \SystemRoot\system32\CI.dll
Loaded driver \SystemRoot\system32\drivers\wdf01000.sys
Loaded driver \SystemRoot\system32\drivers\WDFLDR.SYS
Loaded driver \SystemRoot\system32\DRIVERS\ACPI.sys
Loaded driver \SystemRoot\system32\DRIVERS\WMILIB.SYS
Loaded driver \SystemRoot\system32\DRIVERS\msisadrv.sys
Loaded driver \SystemRoot\system32\DRIVERS\pci.sys
Loaded driver \SystemRoot\system32\DRIVERS\vdrvroot.sys
Loaded driver \SystemRoot\System32\drivers\partmgr.sys
Loaded driver \SystemRoot\system32\DRIVERS\volmgr.sys
Loaded driver \SystemRoot\System32\drivers\volmgrx.sys
Loaded driver \SystemRoot\system32\DRIVERS\intelide.sys
Loaded driver \SystemRoot\system32\DRIVERS\PCIIDEX.SYS
Loaded driver \SystemRoot\System32\drivers\mountmgr.sys
Loaded driver \SystemRoot\system32\DRIVERS\atapi.sys
Loaded driver \SystemRoot\system32\DRIVERS\ataport.SYS
Loaded driver \SystemRoot\system32\DRIVERS\amdxata.sys
Loaded driver \SystemRoot\system32\drivers\fltmgr.sys
Loaded driver \SystemRoot\system32\drivers\fileinfo.sys
Loaded driver \SystemRoot\System32\Drivers\Ntfs.sys
Loaded driver \SystemRoot\System32\Drivers\msrpc.sys
Loaded driver \SystemRoot\System32\Drivers\ksecdd.sys
Loaded driver \SystemRoot\System32\Drivers\cng.sys
Loaded driver \SystemRoot\System32\drivers\pcw.sys
Loaded driver \SystemRoot\System32\Drivers\Fs_Rec.sys
Loaded driver \SystemRoot\system32\drivers\ndis.sys
Loaded driver \SystemRoot\system32\drivers\NETIO.SYS
Loaded driver \SystemRoot\System32\Drivers\ksecpkg.sys
```

In Exercise 9.2, you will create and access a boot log file.

EXERCISE 9.2

Using Boot Logging

1. Start your computer. If it is already running, choose Start ➢ Restart.
2. During the boot process, press the F8 key to access the Advanced Boot Options menu.
3. Highlight Enable Boot Logging and press Enter.
4. When Windows 7 starts, log in.
5. Choose Start ➢ Computer and browse to `C:\WINDOWS\Ntbtlog.txt`. Double-click this file.
6. Examine the contents of your boot log file.
7. Shut down your computer and restart it without using Advanced Boot Options.

The boot log file is cumulative. Each time you boot to Safe mode, you are writing to this file. This enables you to make changes, reboot, and see whether you have fixed any problems. If you want to start from scratch, you should manually delete this file and reboot to an Advanced Boot Options menu selection that supports logging.

Using Other Advanced Boot Options Menu Modes

In this section, you will learn about additional Advanced Boot Options menu modes. These include the following:

Safe Mode With Networking This is the same as the Safe mode option but adds networking features. You might use this mode if you need networking capabilities to download drivers or service packs from a network location.

Safe Mode With Command Prompt This starts the computer in Safe mode, but after you log in to Windows 7, only a command prompt is displayed. This mode does not provide access to the desktop. Experienced troubleshooters use this mode.

Enable Low-Resolution Video (640×480) This loads a standard VGA driver without starting the computer in Safe mode. You might use this mode if you changed your video driver, did not test it, and tried to boot to Windows 7 with a bad driver that would not allow you to access video. The Enable VGA mode bails you out by loading a default driver, providing access to video so that you can properly install (and test!) the correct driver for your computer.

Safe mode starts Windows 7 at a resolution of 800×600.

Last Known Good Configuration (Advanced) This boots Windows 7 by using the Registry information that was saved the last time the computer was successfully booted. You would use this option to restore configuration information if you improperly configured the computer and did not successfully reboot it. When you use the Last Known Good Configuration option, you lose any system configuration changes that were made since the computer last successfully booted.

Directory Services Restore Mode This option is used for domain controllers only and is not relevant to Windows 7.

Debugging Mode This runs the Kernel Debugger, if it is installed. The Kernel Debugger is an advanced troubleshooting utility.

Disable Automatic Restart On System Failure This prevents Windows from restarting when a critical error causes Windows to fail. This option should be used only when Windows fails every time you restart so that you are not able to access the desktop or any configuration options.

Disable Driver Signature Enforcement This allows drivers to be installed even if they do not contain valid signatures.

Start Windows Normally This boots to Windows 7 in the default manner. This option is on the Advanced Boot Options menu in case you accidentally hit F8 during the boot process but really wanted to boot Windows 7 normally.

In the next section, you will look at using the Startup Repair tool.

Using the Startup Repair Tool

If your Windows 7 computer will not boot because of missing or corrupted system files, you can use the *Startup Repair tool* to correct these problems. Startup Repair cannot repair hardware failures. Additionally, Startup Repair cannot recover personal files that have been corrupted, damaged by viruses, or deleted. To ensure that you can recover your personal files, you should use the Backup and Restore utility discussed in the next section.

To use the Startup Repair tool, follow these steps:

1. Boot your computer using the Windows 7 media.
2. When the Install Windows dialog box appears, select the language, time and currency format, and the keyboard or input method. Click Next to continue.
3. The Install Now button appears in the center of the screen. Click Repair Your Computer in the lower-left corner.
4. Select the operating system to recover and click Next. If you do not see your operating system, you might need to load your hard disk drivers by clicking the Load Drivers button.
5. The System Recovery Options dialog box appears. You can choose one of the following options:
   - Startup Repair
   - System Restore
   - Windows Complete PC Restore
   - Windows Memory Diagnostic Tool
   - Command Prompt

   Choose Startup Repair to continue.
6. Startup Repair checks your computer for problems and attempts to repair them. After Startup Repair has finished, click Shut Down or Restart.

If you were not provided the Windows 7 media when you purchased your computer, the computer manufacturer might have placed the files on a recovery partition, or they might have replaced the Startup Repair tool with one of their own. Check with the manufacturer for more information.

If Startup Repair is unable to correct the problem, you might have to reinstall Windows 7. This should be done as a last resort. This is a reason why you should always back up your Windows 7 machine. In the next section, you will look at the Backup and Recovery tools.

Maintaining Windows 7 with Backup and Restore

The Windows 7 *Backup and Restore utility* enables you to create and restore backups. Backups protect your data in the event of system failure by storing the data on another medium, such a hard disk, CD, DVD, or network location. If your original data is lost because of corruption, deletion, or media failure, you can restore the data by using your saved backup.

To access Backup and Restore, type **Backup and Restore** in the Windows 7 search box. Alternatively, you can choose Start ➢ Control Panel, choose either small or large icon view, and then click Backup And Restore. The Backup and Restore center is shown in Figure 9.4.

FIGURE 9.4 Windows 7 Backup and Restore

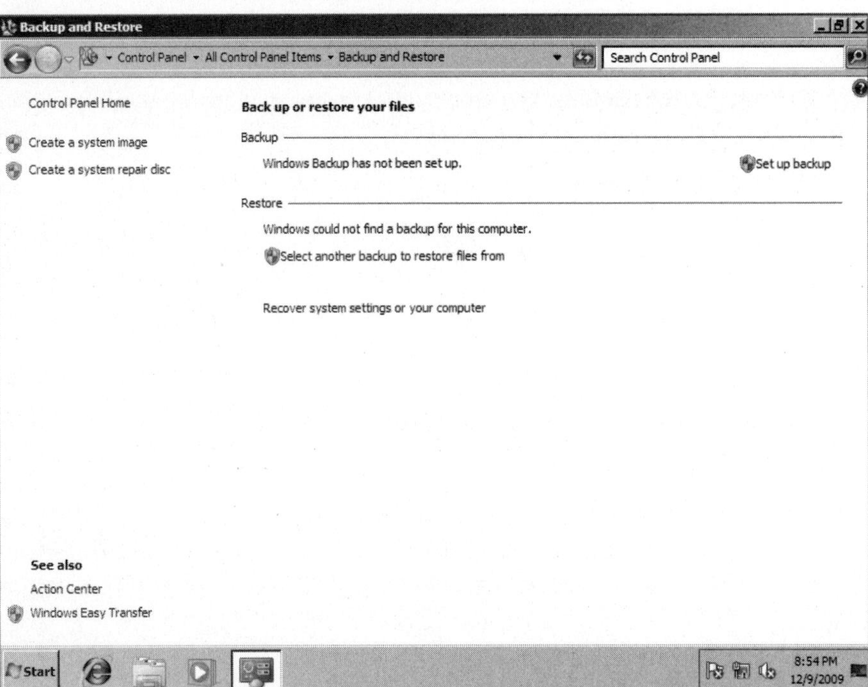

Creating a Backup

You can see in the previous figure that no backups of this Windows 7 machine have been taken. To set up a backup, choose the Set Up Backup link in the right side of the Backup And Restore window. Choosing Set Up Backup launches a wizard that takes you through the process of creating a backup. The Backup Wizard first asks you for a location to save your backup. This location can be a hard disk (removable or fixed), a CD, a DVD, or even a network location (if you have Windows 7 Premium or Ultimate).

Next you are asked to either let Windows 7 choose the files and folders to back up or let you manually select the resources you want to back up. In your manual selection, you can choose just the data libraries of Windows 7 for you as a user, or other users. You can also choose to create a backup of the Windows 7 system files. If you want to choose other files and folders, you have the option of selecting any resources individually on your hard disk(s).

The final page of the wizard enables you to view the items you have selected as well as set up a schedule for your backups to occur. If you're happy with the setup, click the Save Settings And Run Backup button. The backup commences, and you are able to restore the resources if necessary in the future. Figure 9.5 shows my Windows 7 machine right after I chose to save settings and run a backup. You can see the backup in progress and the history of my backups.

FIGURE 9.5 Windows 7 initial backup in progress

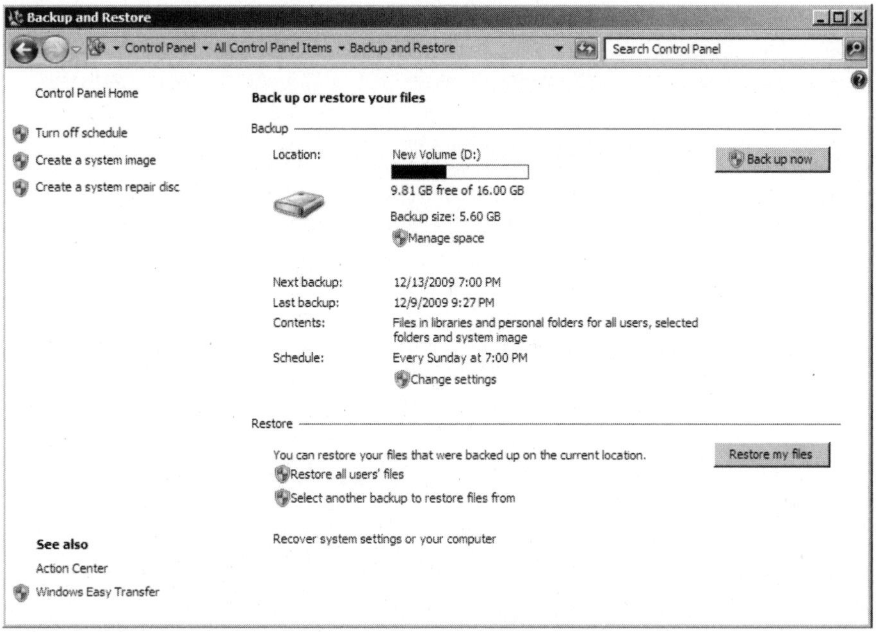

In Exercise 9.3, you will make a backup of your files. This exercise assumes that you haven't yet configured an automatic backup.

EXERCISE 9.3

Backing Up Files

1. Choose Start ➢ Control Panel ➢ Backup And Restore Center.
2. Click the Set Up Backup link.
3. Select the location where you want to save your backup, and then click Next. In our example, we will use our D: drive.

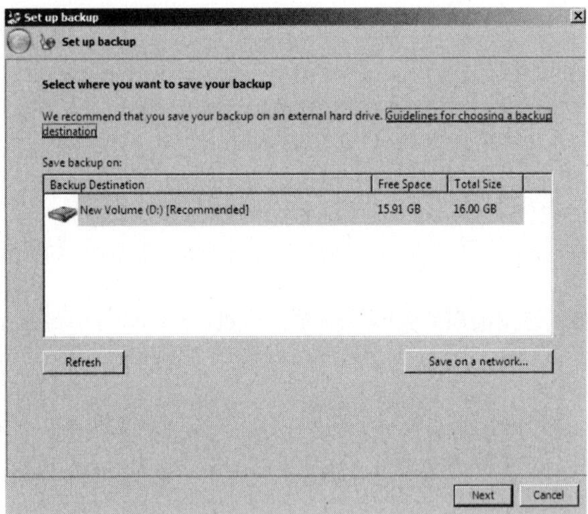

4. The Set Up Backup screen appears. Click the Let Me Choose radio button and click Next.

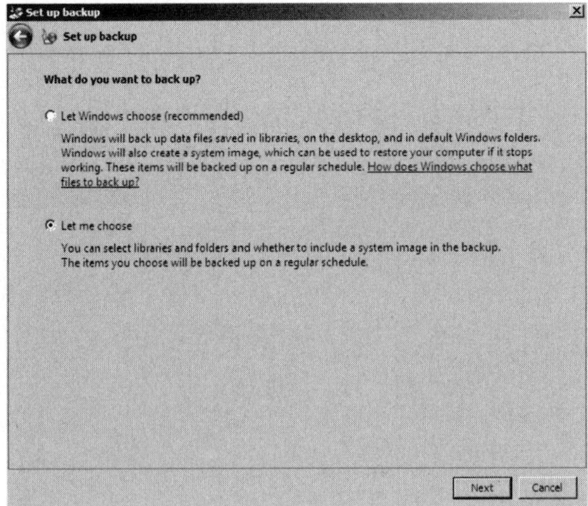

5. Select the files that you would like to back up. Click Next.

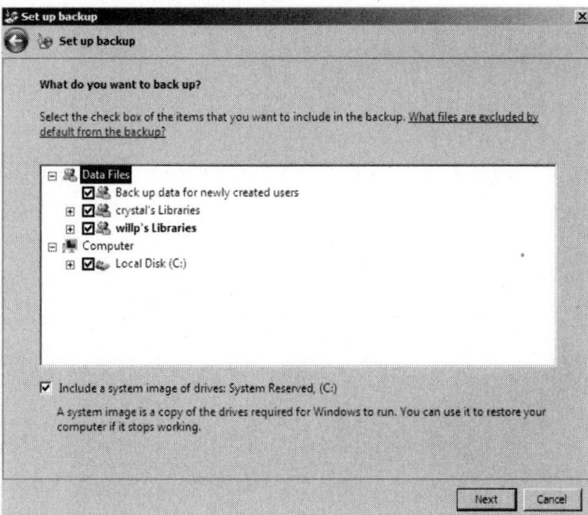

6. At the Backup Summary screen, you can also select how often you want a backup to be automatically performed. To start the backup, click the Save Settings And Start Backup button.

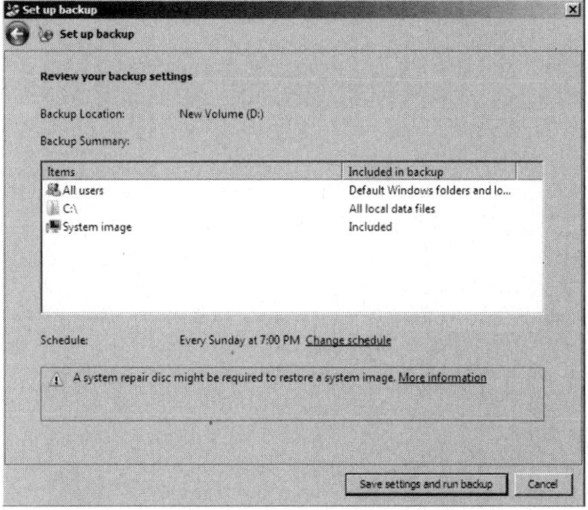

Windows begins backing up files, and a progress indicator indicates how the backup is progressing.

EXERCISE 9.3 *(continued)*

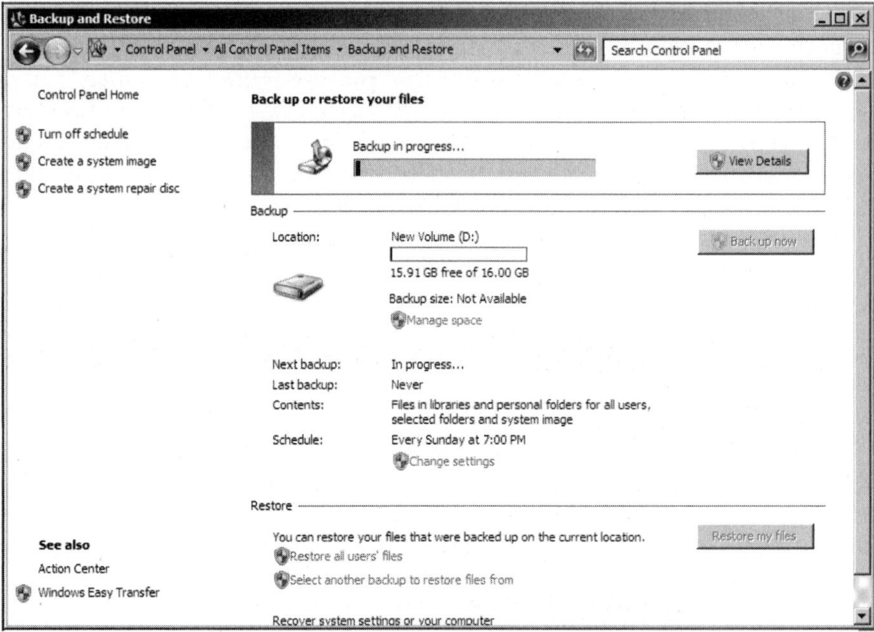

7. When the backup is complete, click Close.

After you have created your backup, you can restore system files and user data files with the restore utility.

Restoring Files from a Backup

If you have lost or destroyed files that you still want on your Windows 7 system, you can restore them from your backup. To restore files to your computer, launch the Backup and Restore program by typing **Backup and Restore** in the Windows 7 search box. Assuming the media where your backup was saved is available, you can click the Restore My Files button.

Click the Restore My Files button to launch a restore wizard that prompts you to search for the files you want to restore. You can select multiple files and folders. When you have selected all the files and folders you want to restore, click Next and you will have one final option—to restore to the original location or pick an alternate location for restoration. After you make the restore location decision, choose Restore. The restore operation commences, and your original files and folders are available for you from the backup media.

You also have options in the Backup And Restore window to restore all users' files or to select another backup to restore files from. You would use this second option if you saved your backup to multiple locations, and the last one (the one listed in the backup section) is not the set of backup files you want to use in your current session. Other than just restoring files and folders, you have the choice to use other advanced backup options.

In Exercise 9.4, you will restore some files. This exercise assumes that you created a backup in Exercise 9.3.

EXERCISE 9.4

Restoring Files

1. Choose Start ➢ Control Panel ➢ Backup And Restore Center.
2. Click the Restore Files button.
3. At the Restore Files screen, click the Browse For Folders button.

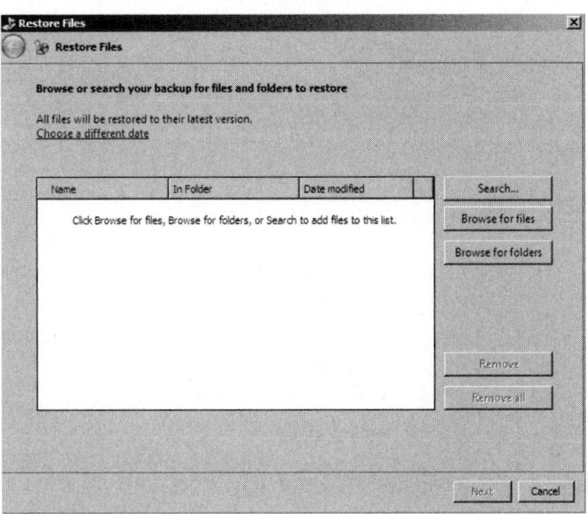

4. Click the Microsoft Windows Backup link in the left window. Then double-click the backup that you created in the previous exercise. Choose the folder that you want to restore (we chose the Program Files folder) and click Add. Click Next to continue.
5. Select whether you want files saved in the original location or a different location. To begin the restore, select Restore.

EXERCISE 9.4 *(continued)*

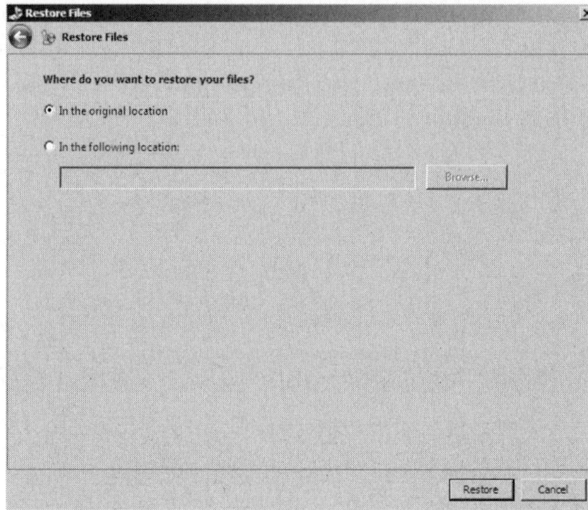

6. When the restore is complete, click Finish.

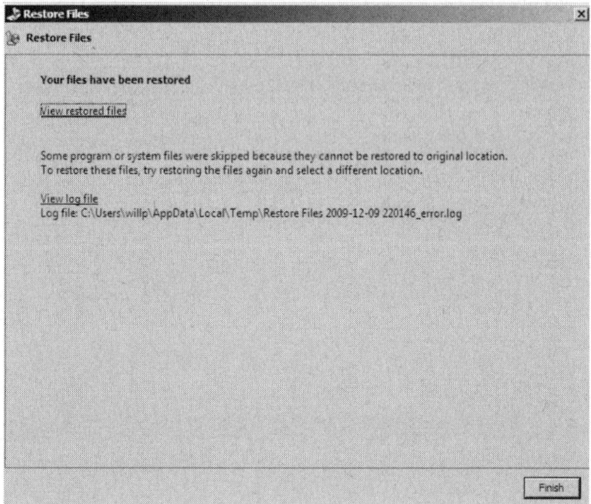

Using Advanced Backup Options

In the main Backup And Restore window, you have options in the left pane to turn off the schedule, create a system image, and create a system repair disk.

Choosing the Turn Off Schedule option lets you take your backup out of the current backup scheduling as seen in Task Scheduler. Creating a system image lets you back up critical operating system files for restoration later if your operating system has become corrupt. Creating a system repair disc allows you to create a bootable disc with which you will have a limited set of repair utilities and the ability to restore your backup files if necessary.

Creating a System Image

A *system image* enables you to take a snapshot of the entire hard disk and capture that image to a specific location so you can restore that image at a later date.

To create a system image of your entire computer, select the Create A System Image link on the left side of the Backup And Restore utility. When creating a system image, you can save that image to a hard disk, DVD, or a network location (see Figure 9.6).

FIGURE 9.6 Create A System Image screen

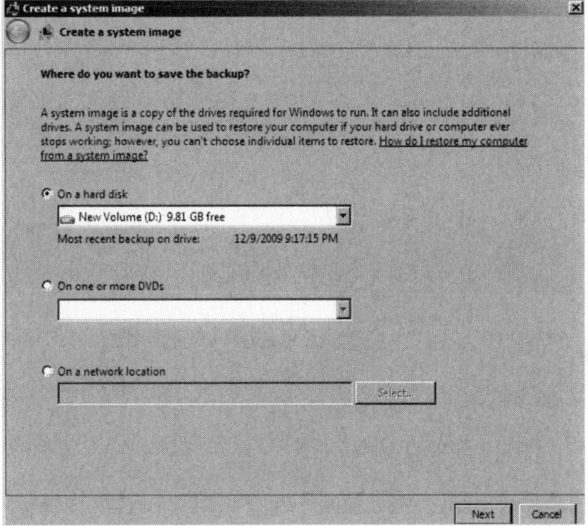

You cannot save the backup to multiple CDs or to a USB flash drive.

In Exercise 9.5, you will create a system image and save it to a local hard disk.

EXERCISE 9.5

Creating a System Image

1. Choose Start ➢ Control Panel ➢ Backup And Restore Center.
2. Click the Create A System Image link.
3. Choose the location where you want to save the image. We are choosing the local D: drive. Click Next.
4. At the Summary screen, click Start Backup.
5. A dialog box appears, asking whether you want to create a system repair disk. Click the No button. If you want to create a system repair disk, you will need a DVD burner and DVD.

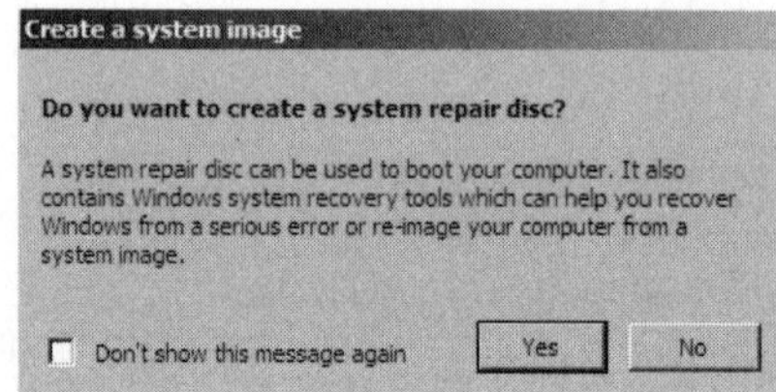

6. When the image is complete, click the Close button.

After you create a system image disk, you may need to restore it. Let's take a look at the steps needed to complete a restore.

Restoring an Image

To restore an image, you must perform the following steps:

1. Boot your computer by using the Windows 7 media, or use the recovery partition instructions provided by your computer manufacturer.
2. When the Install Windows dialog box appears, select the language, time and currency format, and the keyboard or input method. Click Next to continue.
3. The Install Now button appears in the center of the screen. Click Repair Your Computer in the lower-left corner.
4. Select the operating system to recover and click Next. If you do not see your operating system, you might need to load your hard disk drivers by clicking the Load Drivers button.
5. The System Recovery Options dialog box appears. You can choose one of the following options:

- Startup Repair
- System Restore
- Windows Complete PC Restore
- Windows Memory Diagnostic Tool
- Command Prompt

Choose Windows Complete PC Restore to continue.

6. Select the recommended image, or select Restore A Different Backup. Click Next to continue.
7. If you selected Restore A Different Backup, follow the prompts to select the location of the image and the image you want to restore.
8. You will be asked to review your selections. Press Finish to continue.
9. You will be asked to confirm your decision. Click the check box and click OK to restore the image.

If you were not provided the Windows 7 media when you purchased your computer, the computer manufacturer might have placed the files on a recovery partition. Check with the manufacturer for more information.

There's one more option for restoring your Windows 7 configuration, known as System Protection.

Using System Protection

System Protection is a feature of Windows 7 that creates a backup and saves the configuration information of your computer's system files and settings on a regular basis. System Protection saves previous versions of saved configurations rather than just overwriting them. This makes it possible to return to multiple configurations in your Windows 7 history, known as *restore points*. These restore points are created before most significant events, such as installing a new driver. Restore points are also created automatically every seven days. System Protection is turned on by default in Windows 7 for any drive formatted with NTFS.

You manage System Protection and the restore points from the System Protection tab of the System Properties dialog box, as shown in Figure 9.7. You can also access this tab directly by typing **Restore Point** into the Windows 7 search box or by clicking the Recovery icon in Control Panel.

FIGURE 9.7 System Protection in System Properties

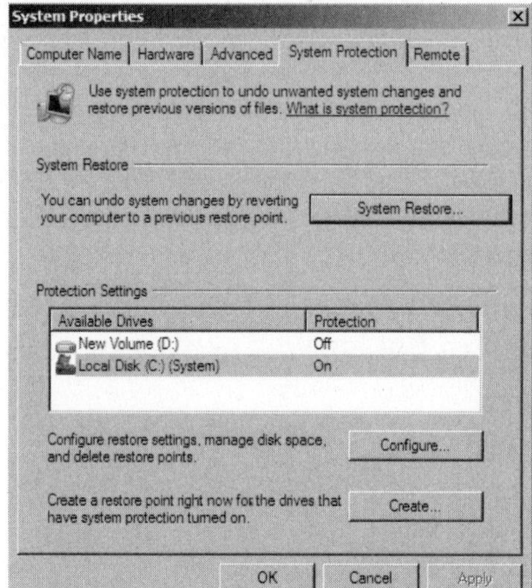

Clicking the System Restore button launches the System Restore Wizard, which walks you through the process of returning Windows 7 to a previous point in time. Also within the System Protection tab of the System Properties dialog box is the Protection Settings section, where you can configure any of your available drives.

Select the drive that you would like to modify the configuration of and click the Configure button. The System Protection configuration dialog box for the drive appears, as shown in Figure 9.8.

FIGURE 9.8 System restore points in System Protection

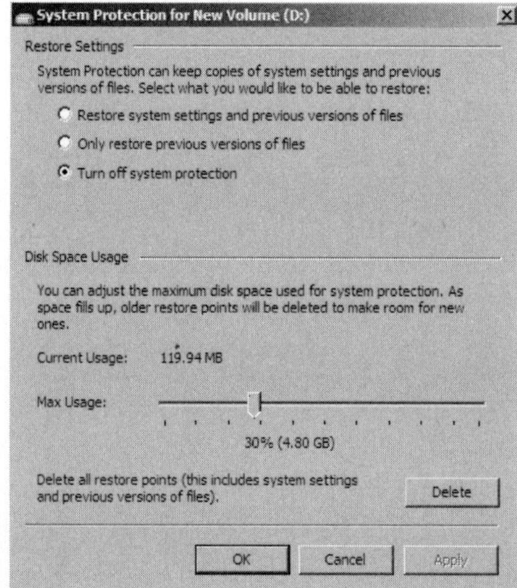

The System Protection for the selected disk properties box allows you to enable or disable system protection for the drive. When you enable protection, you can opt for previous versions of files or previous versions of files and system settings. You also have the ability to set the maximum usage that your restore points will use for storage.

One final function of the System Protection dialog box for the selected disk is to delete all restore points (including system settings and previous versions of files) by clicking the Delete button.

Creating Restore Points

Restore points contain Registry and system information as they were at a certain point in time. These restore points are created at the following times:

- Weekly
- Before installing applications or drivers
- Before significant system events
- Before System Restore is used to restore files (so you can undo the changes if necessary)
- Manually upon request

In Exercise 9.6, you will manually create a restore point.

EXERCISE 9.6

Creating a Restore Point

1. Click Start and then right-click Computer.
2. When the System Properties appears, click the System Protection tab.
3. Click the Create button on the bottom of the screen next to the Create A Restore Point Right Now section.

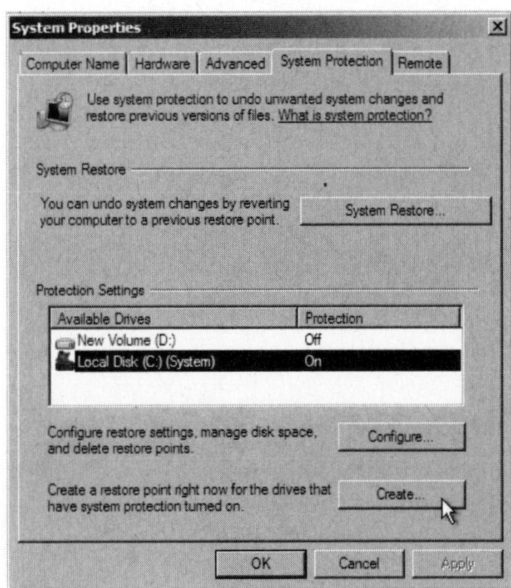

EXERCISE 9.6 *(continued)*

4. At the System Protection dialog box, enter a description (we entered *test09*) for the restore point. Click Create.
5. A dialog box states that the restore point was created. Click Close.

Now after a restore point is created, you may need to restore the restore point. Let's take a look at how to restore a restore point.

Restoring Restore Points

You can restore previously created restore points with System Restore. The restore operation will restore system files and settings, but will not affect your personal files.

System Restore will also remove any programs that have been installed since the restore point was created.

In Exercise 9.7, you will restore a restore point.

EXERCISE 9.7

Restoring a Restore Point

1. Click Start and then right-click Computer.
2. When the System Properties screen appears, click the System Protection tab.
3. Click the System Restore box. Click Next at the Welcome screen to continue.
4. Choose a restore point (test09), and click Next to continue.

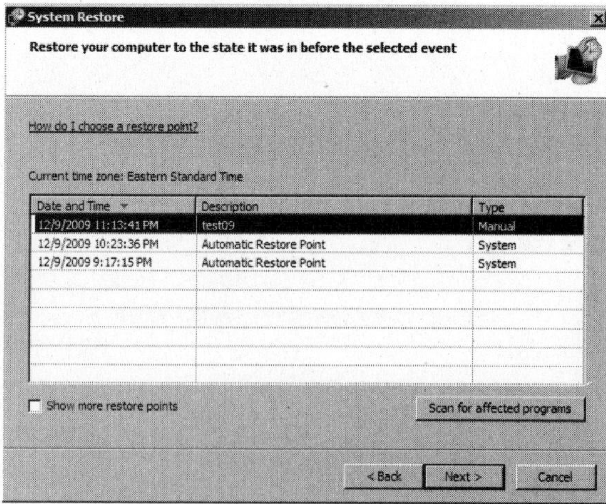

5. Review your restore point selection, and click Finish to continue.
6. Confirm that you want System Restore to continue, and click Yes to continue.

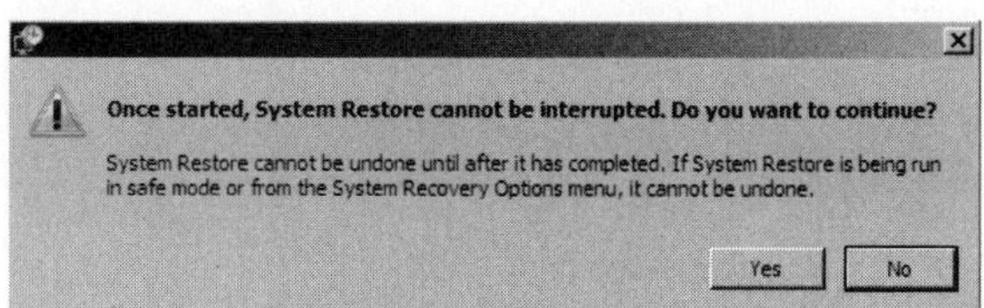

7. System Restore will restore your system and reboot your computer to apply the changes. You should see a message stating that System Restore has restored your computer. Click OK to close the dialog box.

If your computer will not boot, you can also perform the following steps to use System Restore:

1. Boot your computer by using the Windows 7 media, or use the recovery partition instructions provided by your computer manufacturer.
2. When the Install Windows dialog box appears, select the language, time and currency format, and the keyboard or input method. Click Next to continue.
3. The Install Now button appears in the center of the screen. Click Repair Your Computer in the lower-left corner.
4. Select the operating system to recover and click Next. If you do not see your operating system, you might need to load your hard disk drivers by clicking the Load Drivers button.
5. The System Recovery Options dialog box appears. It provides the following options:
   - Startup Repair
   - System Restore
   - Windows Complete PC Restore
   - Windows Memory Diagnostic Tool
   - Command Prompt

   Choose System Restore to continue.
6. Follow the prompts to restore the restore point. The prompts will be similar to those in Exercise 9.7.

Troubleshooting System Restore

If System Restore does not fix your problems, you can either undo the restore or attempt to restore an earlier restore point. If neither of these options works, you could try to use the Startup Repair tool if the problem is related to missing or corrupted system files.

Summary

In this chapter, you looked at the different ways to recover and protect your Windows 7 machine from hardware and software issues. We discussed using the Advanced Boot Options such as Last Known Good, Safe mode, Debugging mode, and VGA mode. We also discussed the advantage of using the Driver Rollback utility.

Another important item that needs to be completed on a Windows 7 machine is backups and restores. Backing up a Windows 7 machine protects it in the event of a hardware or software failure.

We also discussed how to back up a complete copy of Windows 7 by using images. An image allows you to copy the entire Windows 7 machine and then re-image the machine in the event of a major failure. Another way to protect data is by the use of shadow copies. Shadow copies (System Protection) allow you to keep previous versions of data and revert back to that previous version in the event of a problem.

Exam Essentials

Understand the different options for managing system recovery. Know how to use the Startup Repair tool, System Restore, and the Backup and Restore Center, and when it is appropriate to use each option.

Be able to perform file recovery with the Backup and Restore Center and shadow copies. Understand the options that are supported through the Backup and Restore Center and the files that are backed up using this tool. Know how to manually create a shadow copy and how to keep only the last shadow copy versions.

Know how to troubleshoot using Advanced Boot Options. Be able to list the options that can be accessed through Advanced Boot Options, and know when it is appropriate to use each option. Know the difference between Last Known Good Configuration, Safe mode, Debugging mode, and VGA mode.

Review Questions

1. You are the network administrator for a large organization that uses both Windows Server 2008 R2 and Windows 7. One of the Windows 7 machines needs to be backed up daily. You perform an image backup on the Windows 7 machine. The Windows 7 machine then gets struck by a virus and will not start up properly. What can you do to get the Windows 7 machine up and running the fastest possible way?

    A. Because of the virus, the best thing is to rebuild the machine from scratch.

    B. Start the computer from the Windows 7 DVD and then use the System Image Recovery tool.

    C. Start the computer from the Windows 7 DVD and then use the Image Restore utility.

    D. Use a Windows 7 boot disk and run the Image Restore utility.

2. You need to back up Windows 7, but the backup must be backed up to a local disk drive. When you start the backup, you see the following screen:

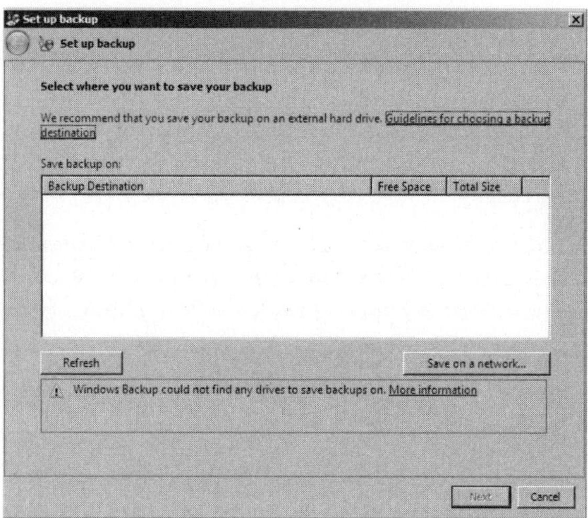

    What action do you need to perform?

    A. Log on as the backup administrator.

    B. Log on as the system administrator.

    C. Add a local hard disk to the machine by using Computer Management and then run the backup again.

    D. Run the backup utility in protected mode.

3. You are the system administrator for a large organization that uses Windows Server R2 and Windows 7. You have a Windows 7 machine and have enabled System Protection. You want the machine to retain only the last System Protection snapshot that was taken. What should you do?

   A. Run Disk Cleanup for System Restore and then run Shadow Copies.

   B. Disable Shadow Copies and run System Protection.

   C. Set the Keep Only Last Shadow Copy option in System Protection.

   D. Enable Shadow Copies and then set the Keep Only Last Shadow Copy option.

4. You are the network administrator for a small company. You manage the computers for the marketing department, all of which are running the Windows 7 operating system. You are making several configuration changes to the manager's computer to enhance performance. Before you make any changes, you want to create a restore point that can be used if any problems arise. How do you manually create a restore point?

   A. By using the System Restore utility

   B. By using the System Protection tab of the System Properties dialog box

   C. By using the System Configuration utility

   D. By using the Startup Repair tool

5. Your computer uses a SCSI adapter that supports a SCSI drive, which contains your Windows 7 system and boot partitions. After updating the SCSI driver, you restart your computer, but Windows 7 will not load. You need to get this computer up and running as quickly as possible. Which of the following repair strategies should you try first to correct your problem?

   A. Restore your computer's configuration with your last backup.

   B. Boot your computer with the Last Known Good Configuration.

   C. Boot your computer with the Safe Mode option.

   D. Boot your computer to the Recovery Console and manually copy the old driver back to the computer.

6. You are about to install a new driver for your CD-ROM drive, but you are not 100 percent sure that you are using the correct driver. Which of the following options will allow you to most easily return your computer to the previous state if the new driver is not correct?

   A. Safe Mode

   B. Roll Back Driver

   C. System Restore utility

   D. Startup Repair Tool

7. After you updated Will's computer, his system files became corrupted due to a virus and now need to be restored. Which of the following processes should you use to fix the problem?

   A. Restore a backup.

   B. Restore an image.

   C. Use the Startup Repair tool.

   D. Boot to Safe mode.

8. You are unable to boot your Windows 7 computer, so you decide to boot the computer to Safe mode. Which of the following statements regarding Safe mode is false?
   - **A.** When the computer is booted to Safe mode, there is no network access.
   - **B.** Safe mode loads all the drivers for the hardware that is installed on the computer.
   - **C.** When you run Safe mode, boot logging is automatically enabled.
   - **D.** When you run Safe mode, the screen resolution is set to 8030×600.

9. You have been having problems with your Windows 7 computer. You decide to start the computer by using the Enable Boot Logging option on the Advanced Boot Options menu. Where can you find the log file that is created?
   - **A.** `\Windows\ntbtlog.txt`
   - **B.** `\Windows\System32\ntbtlog.txt`
   - **C.** `\Windows\ntboot.log`
   - **D.** `\Windows\System32\ntboot.log`

10. You have purchased a new computer with Windows 7 installed. After modifying the system so that it is configured just how you want it, you want to back up the system so that if anything happens, you can restore the files and settings. Which of the following should you do?
    - **A.** Back up your files by using the Back Up Files button in the Backup And Restore Center.
    - **B.** Create an image of your computer by using the Create An Image link in the Backup And Restore Center.
    - **C.** Use the System Repair tool to take an image of your computer.
    - **D.** Use Shadow Copies to create a previous version of the files.

11. You have a computer that runs Windows 7. You upgrade the network adapter driver on the computer. After the upgrade, you can no longer access network resources. You open Device Manager and see a warning symbol next to the network adapter. You need to restore access to network resources. What should you do?
    - **A.** Roll back the network adapter driver.
    - **B.** Assign a static IP address to the network adapter.
    - **C.** Disable the network adapter and scan for hardware changes.
    - **D.** Uninstall the network adapter and scan for hardware changes.

12. You need to back up the existing data on a computer before you install a new application. You also need to ensure that you are able to recover individual user files that are replaced or deleted during the installation. What should you do?
    - **A.** Create a System Restore point.
    - **B.** Perform an Automated System Recovery (ASR) backup and restore.
    - **C.** In the Backup And Restore Center window, click the Back Up Now button.
    - **D.** In the Backup And Restore Center window, click the Back Up Computer button.

13. Your data recovery strategy must meet the following requirements:
    - Back up all data files and folders in `C:\Data`.
    - Restore individual files and folders in `C:\Data`.
    - Ensure that data is backed up to and restored from external media.

    What should you do?

    A. Use the Previous Versions feature to restore the files and folders.

    B. Use the System Restore feature to perform backup and restore operations.

    C. Use the NTBackup utility to back up and restore individual files and folders.

    D. Use the Backup And Restore Center to back up and restore files.

14. You need to ensure that you can recover system configuration and data if your computer hard disk fails. What should you do?

    A. Create a system restore point.

    B. Create a backup of all file categories.

    C. Create a Complete PC Backup and Restore image.

    D. Perform an Automated System Recovery (ASR) backup.

15. You have a computer that runs Windows 7. Your computer has two volumes, C: and D:. Both volumes are formatted by using the NTFS file system. You need to disable previous versions on the D: volume. What should you do?

    A. From System Properties, modify the System Protection settings.

    B. From the properties of the D: volume, modify the Quota settings.

    C. From the properties of the D: volume, modify the Sharing settings.

    D. From the Disk Management snap-in, convert the hard disk drive that contains the D: volume to Dynamic.

16. You have a computer that runs Windows 7. You configure a backup job to back up all files and folders on an external NTFS file system hard disk drive. The backup job fails to back up all files that have the encryption attribute set. You need to back up all encrypted files. The backed up files must remain encrypted. What should you do?

    A. Manually copy the encrypted files to the external hard disk drive.

    B. Schedule a backup job to occur when you are not logged on to the computer.

    C. Enable Volume Shadow Copy on the external drive and schedule a backup job.

    D. Add the certificate of the local administrator account to the list of users who can transparently access the files, and schedule a backup job.

17. You have a computer that runs Windows 7. You use Windows Complete PC Backup and Restore to create a backup image. You need to perform a complete restore of the computer. What are two possible ways to begin the restore? (Each correct answer presents a complete solution. Choose two.)

A. Open the Windows Backup And Restore Center and click Advanced Restore.

B. Open the Windows Backup And Restore Center and click Restore Computer.

C. Start your computer. From the Advanced Boot Options menu, select Repair Your Computer.

D. Start the computer by using the Windows 7 installation media. Select Repair Your Computer.

18. You are the network administrator for your organization. You are asked by a junior administrator when he should create restore points. Which of the following are times when restore points should be created? Choose all that apply.

A. Weekly

B. Before installing applications or drivers

C. Before significant system events

D. Before System Restore is used to restore files (so you can undo the changes if necessary)

19. You install Windows 7 on a new computer. You update the video card driver and restart the computer. When you start the computer, the screen flickers and then goes blank. You restart the computer and receive the same result. You need to configure the video card driver. What should you do first?

A. Restart the computer in Safe mode.

B. Restart the computer in Debugging mode.

C. Restart the computer in low-resolution video mode.

D. Insert the Windows 7 installation media into the computer, restart, and use System Recovery to perform a startup repair.

20. You are asked by your managers to start a Windows 7 machine to allow for Kernel Debugging. How would you start the machine?

A. Advanced options, Kernel Mode

B. Advanced options, Debugging Mode

C. Advanced options, Kernel Debugging Mode

D. Advanced options, Safe Mode

Answers to Review Questions

1. B. After starting the machine with the Windows 7 DVD, you can use the System Image Recovery tool to reload the backup image that you created.

2. C. When you are using the backup utility and no local disks are present, you must either configure an installed disk or physically install a hard disk before running the backup utility. You can also save your backups to a network location.

3. A. You have to run the Disk Cleanup utility to delete the previous versions and then run Shadow Copies in System Protection. There is no Keep Only Last Shadow Copy option.

4. B. To manually create a restore point or to restore your computer to a previous restore point, you use the System Protection tab of the System Properties dialog box. Although System Restore uses restore points, you do not use the System Restore utility to create a restore point.

5. B. If you need to get a stalled computer up and running as quickly as possible, you should start with the Last Known Good Configuration option. This option is used when you've made changes to your computer's hardware configuration and are having problems restarting. The Last Known Good Configuration will revert to the configuration used the last time the computer was successfully booted. Although this option helps overcome configuration errors, it will not help for hardware errors.

6. B. The Roll Back Driver option is the easiest way to roll back to a known good driver. You could also use the System Restore utility to roll back your computer to a known restore point if you make harmful changes to your computer, but Driver Rollback is easier and faster.

7. C. To quickly repair the system files, you can use the Startup Repair tool. You can restore an image by using the Backup And Repair Center, but it is faster to use the Startup Repair tool. Additionally, you will not lose any personal files by using the Startup Repair tool. Alternatively, you could try to use System Restore to go back to a previous checkpoint.

8. B. When you run your computer in Safe mode, you simplify your Windows 7 configuration. Only the drivers that are needed to get the computer up and running are loaded.

9. A. When you enable boot logging, the file created is `\Windows\ntbtlog.txt`. This log file is used to troubleshoot the boot process.

10. B. You should create an image of your computer by using the Create An Image link in the Backup And Restore Center. Images back up everything on your computer. File backups cannot be used to back up system files and settings.

11. A. The Roll Back Driver option is the fastest way to return the driver to the previous version. You could also use System Restore, but Driver Rollback is easier and faster.

12. C. The Backup Now button allows you to start a backup and configure a Windows 7 backup.

13. D. If you need to back up and restore your Windows 7 machine, you need to use the Windows 7 Backup And Restore Center.

14. C. Using images allows you to back up and restore your entire Windows 7 machine instead of just certain parts of data.

15. A. If you need to disable previous versions on the D: volume, this needs to be done from the System Protection settings from the computer system properties.

16. A. You have to manually copy all the encrypted files because the backup software will not work with the encrypted files in Windows 7.

17. C, D. There are two ways to repair system files on Windows 7. You can do it by using the installation CD and choosing Repair during the installation or you can boot to the advanced options and select Repair.

18. A, B, C, D. Restore points allow you to bring your system back to a previous point in time, and they should be created at all of the times listed.

19. A. Starting the computer in Safe mode loads the basic VGA drivers and allows you to fix any video issues including using the Driver Rollback utility.

20. B. Debugging mode runs the Kernel Debugger. The Kernel Debugger is an advanced troubleshooting utility.

About the Companion CD

IN THIS APPENDIX:

- ✓ What you'll find on the CD
- ✓ System requirements
- ✓ Using the CD
- ✓ Troubleshooting

What You'll Find on the CD

The following sections are arranged by category and summarize the software and other goodies you'll find on the CD. If you need help with installing the items provided on the CD, refer to the installation instructions in the section "Using the CD" later in this appendix.

Sybex Test Engine

For Windows

The CD contains the Sybex test engine, which includes two bonus exams located only on the CD.

PDF of Glossary of Terms

For Windows

We have included an electronic version of the glossary in PDF format. You can view the electronic version of the glossary with Adobe Reader.

Adobe Reader

For Windows

We've also included a copy of Adobe Reader so you can view PDF files that accompany the book's content. For more information on Adobe Reader or to check for a newer version, visit Adobe's website at `www.adobe.com/products/reader/`.

Electronic Flashcards

For PC and Pocket PC

These handy electronic flashcards are just what they sound like. One side contains a question or fill-in-the-blank sentence, and the other side shows the answer.

System Requirements

Make sure your computer meets the minimum system requirements shown in the following list. If your computer doesn't match up to most of these requirements, you may have problems using the software and files on the companion CD. For the latest and greatest information, please refer to the Readme file located at the root of the CD-ROM.

- A PC running Microsoft Windows 98, Windows 2000, Windows NT4 (with SP4 or later), Windows Me, Windows XP, Windows Vista, or Windows 7
- An Internet connection
- A CD-ROM drive

Using the CD

To install the items from the CD to your hard drive, follow these steps:

1. Insert the CD into your computer's CD-ROM drive. The license agreement appears.

Windows users: The interface won't launch if you have Autorun disabled. In that case, click Start ➢ Run (for Windows Vista or Windows 7, Start ➢ All Programs ➢ Accessories ➢ Run). In the dialog box that appears, type `D:\Start.exe`. (Replace *D* with the proper letter if your CD drive uses a different letter. If you don't know the letter, see how your CD drive is listed under My Computer.) Click OK.

2. Read the license agreement, and then click the Accept button if you want to use the CD.

The CD interface appears. The interface allows you to access the content with just one or two clicks.

Troubleshooting

Wiley has attempted to provide programs that work on most computers with the minimum system requirements. Alas, your computer may differ, and some programs may not work properly for some reason.

The two likeliest problems are that you don't have enough memory (RAM) for the programs you want to use or you have other programs running that are affecting the installation or running of a program. If you get an error message such as "Not enough memory" or "Setup cannot continue," try one or more of the following suggestions and then try using the software again:

Turn off any antivirus software running on your computer. Installation programs sometimes mimic virus activity and may make your computer incorrectly believe that it's being infected by a virus.

Close all running programs. The more programs you have running, the less memory is available to other programs. Installation programs typically update files and programs, so if you keep other programs running, installation may not work properly.

Have your local computer store add more RAM to your computer. This is, admittedly, a drastic and somewhat expensive step. However, adding more memory can really help the speed of your computer and allow more programs to run at the same time.

Customer Care

If you have trouble with the book's companion CD-ROM, please call the Wiley Product Technical Support phone number at (800) 762-2974. Outside the United States, call +1(317) 572-3994. You can also contact Wiley Product Technical Support at `http://sybex.custhelp.com`. John Wiley & Sons will provide technical support only for installation and other general quality-control items. For technical support on the applications themselves, consult the program's vendor or author.

To place additional orders or to request information about other Wiley products, please call (877) 762-2974.

Glossary

A

Active Directory Server database that contains all the objects of the domain.

B

Backup And Restore utility Windows 7 tool that allows you to back up and restore data on the machine.

baseline Snapshot of how your system is currently performing.

BitLocker Drive Encryption Encrypts an entire system drive. New files added to this drive are encrypted automatically.

boot logging The process of creating a log file that tracks the loading of drivers and services during system startup.

BranchCache A feature of Windows 7 that allows two locations to share resources over a slow connection using minimum bandwidth. BranchCache caches data either on a BranchCache server or on Windows 7 machines.

D

data collector sets Used to collect data into a log so that the data can be reviewed.

Device Manager Utility used to view and manage devices on a machine.

DirectAccess New feature that allows remote users to connect to their network without the need of a VPN.

Domain Name Service (DNS) Hostname resolution service. DNS turns a hostname into a TCP/IP address or a TCP/IP address into a hostname.

driver Software that allows hardware to work with an operating system.

dual-booting Booting multiple operating systems on the same physical machine.

E

Encrypting File System (EFS) Windows 7 technology that is used to store encrypted files on NTFS partitions.

Event Viewer Windows feature that enables you to view event logs that are created by the operating system.

F

FAT32 Updated version of File Allocation Table (FAT) that supports smaller cluster sizes.

H

Hardware Compatibility List (HCL) An extensive list of computers and peripheral hardware that has been tested with the Windows 7 operating system.

HomeGroup HomeGroups are small local networks that you can easily configure at home and work. Also a Windows 7 peer-to-peer network that allows home users to easily connect machines together and share data.

Hyper-V Windows Server 2008 R2 version of virtualization software.

L

Last Known Good Configuration Restores the Registry to the last previous version.

Layer 2 Tunneling Protocol (L2TP) Tunneling protocol that has no built-in encryption. L2TP uses IPSec for security.

Local Group Policy Objects (LGPOs) Set of security configuration settings that are applied to users and computers. LGPOs are created and stored on the Windows 7 computer.

M

mandatory profile Roaming profile that is mandatory for a user to use.

Microsoft Assessment And Planning Utility that will locate computers on a network and then perform a thorough inventory of these computers.

Microsoft Deployment Toolkit (MDT) Utility for automating desktop and server deployment.

Microsoft Management Console (MMC) Console framework for application management that provides a common environment for snap-ins.

Microsoft SpyNet An online community that can help you know how others respond to software that has not yet been classified by Microsoft.

network interface card (NIC) Hardware that allows a Windows 7 machine to connect to a network or device.

N

NTFS Allows partitions to be up to 16 TB with 4 KB clusters or 256 TB with 6 4KB clusters and offers comprehensive folder- and file-level security.

P

Performance Monitor Utility that allows you to measure the performance of the various parts of your system.

Point-to-Point Tunneling Protocol (PPTP) Point-to-point protocol that has built-in encryption for tunneling. Used with Windows Server 2003.

R

Redundant Array of Independent Disks (RAID) Allows an administrator to recover data from a single hard disk failure.

Reliability Monitor Stand-alone feature in Windows 7 that provides an overview of the stability of the computer.

Remote Assistance A tool that allows an individual to connect to a machine and assist the user in the same session.

Remote Desktop A tool that allows a user to take over a machines session remotely. The local user will not be able to see what is happening during the Remote Desktop connection.

Resultant Set of Policy (RSOP) Tool that allows you to see how GPOs are configured.

S

safe mode A mode that allows the Windows 7 machine to load using just the basic default drivers.

Secure Socket Tunneling Protocol (SSTP) Newest tunneling protocol with Windows Server 2008 server. SSPT allows encapsulated Point-to-Point Protocol (PPP) packets to be transmitted over an HTTP connection.

security identification (SID) number Unique number that identifies an object.

security identifier (SID) Unique identification given to Active Directory security objects.

shim Code written by Microsoft that allows older applications to work with Windows 7.

simple volume A volume that contains hard disk space from a single dynamic drive.

spanned volume A volume that contains hard disk space from multiple dynamic disks.

Startup Repair Tool Tool that allows you to repair missing Windows 7 system files.

striped volume Volumes that store data in equal stripes between two or more (up to 32) dynamic drives.

System Image Allows you to take an image of the entire Windows 7 machine in the event of a major failure.

System Preparation Tool Utility that creates an image that can be deployed by a third-party application for installing multiple systems.

System Protection Utility that allows you to create and revert restore points.

T

Task Scheduler Utility that allows you to schedule tasks or applications to be run at specific times.

Transmission Control Protocol/Internet Protocol (TCP/IP) Suite of protocols that allows machines to talk on the network or Internet.

Trusts A connection between domains that allows users to connect from one domain to another.

U

Upgrade Advisor Windows 7 Setup program that can check the compatibility of your system, devices, and installed applications and then provide a compatibility report.

User Account Control (UAC) Provides the ability to manage user accounts, in addition to configuring parental controls.

User State Migration Tool (USMT) A tool used to migrate large numbers of users over automated deployments.

V

virtual machines Virtualization operating system inserts.

Virtual PC Virtualization client that allows you to run multiple operating systems on a machine.

W

Web Slice Allows IE8 to check for updates to web page content you may frequently want to have.

Windows Automated Installation Kit Set of utilities and documentation that allows an administrator to configure and deploy Windows operating systems.

Windows Defender Utility that offers real-time protection from spyware and other unwanted software.

Windows Deployment Services This utility is a suite of components that allows you to remotely install Windows 7 on client computers.

Windows Easy Transfer Tool used to transfer files and settings from one computer to another.

Windows Firewall Security software that helps prevent unauthorized users from gaining access to a Windows 7 machine.

Windows PowerShell Command-line scripting utility that allows you to remotely execute commands on a Windows 7 machine.

Windows Remote Management (WinRM) Microsoft's version of the WS-Management Protocol. The WS-Management Protocol is an industry-standard protocol that allows different vendor operating systems and hardware to work together.

Windows Update Utility that allows you to connect to Microsoft's website and download patches and security updates.

X

XP Mode Mode that allows Windows XP applications to run on a Windows 7 operating system. XP Mode is available on Windows 7 Enterprise, Professional, and Ultimate editions.

Index

Note to the Reader: Throughout this index **boldfaced** page numbers indicate primary discussions of a topic. *Italicized* page numbers indicate illustrations.

Symbols

A

B

C

E

F

G

J

K

L

M

N

O

P

S

T

U

V

W

X

Z

Wiley Publishing, Inc.
End-User License Agreement

READ THIS. You should carefully read these terms and conditions before opening the software packet(s) included with this book "Book". This is a license agreement "Agreement" between you and Wiley Publishing, Inc. "WPI". By opening the accompanying software packet(s), you acknowledge that you have read and accept the following terms and conditions. If you do not agree and do not want to be bound by such terms and conditions, promptly return the Book and the unopened software packet(s) to the place you obtained them for a full refund.

1. License Grant. WPI grants to you (either an individual or entity) a nonexclusive license to use one copy of the enclosed software program(s) (collectively, the "Software," solely for your own personal or business purposes on a single computer (whether a standard computer or a workstation component of a multi-user network). The Software is in use on a computer when it is loaded into temporary memory (RAM) or installed into permanent memory (hard disk, CD-ROM, or other storage device). WPI reserves all rights not expressly granted herein.

2. Ownership. WPI is the owner of all right, title, and interest, including copyright, in and to the compilation of the Software recorded on the physical packet included with this Book "Software Media". Copyright to the individual programs recorded on the Software Media is owned by the author or other authorized copyright owner of each program. Ownership of the Software and all proprietary rights relating thereto remain with WPI and its licensers.

3. Restrictions On Use and Transfer.

(a) You may only (i) make one copy of the Software for backup or archival purposes, or (ii) transfer the Software to a single hard disk, provided that you keep the original for backup or archival purposes. You may not (i) rent or lease the Software, (ii) copy or reproduce the Software through a LAN or other network system or through any computer subscriber system or bulletin-board system, or (iii) modify, adapt, or create derivative works based on the Software.

(b) You may not reverse engineer, decompile, or disassemble the Software. You may transfer the Software and user documentation on a permanent basis, provided that the transferee agrees to accept the terms and conditions of this Agreement and you retain no copies. If the Software is an update or has been updated, any transfer must include the most recent update and all prior versions.

4. Restrictions on Use of Individual Programs. You must follow the individual requirements and restrictions detailed for each individual program in the About the CD-ROM appendix of this Book or on the Software Media. These limitations are also contained in the individual license agreements recorded on the Software Media. These limitations may include a requirement that after using the program for a specified period of time, the user must pay a registration fee or discontinue use. By opening the Software packet(s), you will be agreeing to abide by the licenses and restrictions for these individual programs that are detailed in the About the CD-ROM appendix and/or on the Software Media. None of the material on this Software Media or listed in this Book may ever be redistributed, in original or modified form, for commercial purposes.

5. Limited Warranty.

(a) WPI warrants that the Software and Software Media are free from defects in materials and workmanship under normal use for a period of sixty (60) days from the date of purchase of this Book. If WPI receives notification within the warranty period of defects in materials or workmanship, WPI will replace the defective Software Media.

(b) WPI AND THE AUTHOR(S) OF THE BOOK DISCLAIM ALL OTHER WARRANTIES, EXPRESS OR IMPLIED, INCLUDING WITHOUT LIMITATION IMPLIED WARRANTIES OF MERCHANTABILITY AND FITNESS FOR A PARTICULAR PURPOSE, WITH RESPECT TO THE SOFTWARE, THE PROGRAMS, THE SOURCE CODE CONTAINED THEREIN, AND/OR THE TECHNIQUES DESCRIBED IN THIS BOOK. WPI DOES NOT WARRANT THAT THE FUNCTIONS CONTAINED IN THE SOFTWARE WILL MEET YOUR REQUIREMENTS OR THAT THE OPERATION OF THE SOFTWARE WILL BE ERROR FREE.

(c) This limited warranty gives you specific legal rights, and you may have other rights that vary from jurisdiction to jurisdiction.

6. Remedies.

(a) WPI's entire liability and your exclusive remedy for defects in materials and workmanship shall be limited to replacement of the Software Media, which may be returned to WPI with a copy of your receipt at the following address: Software Media Fulfillment Department, Attn.: *MCTS: Microsoft Windows 7 Configuration Study Guide*, Wiley Publishing, Inc., 10475 Crosspoint Blvd., Indianapolis, IN 46256, or call 1-800-762-2974. Please allow four to six weeks for delivery. This Limited Warranty is void if failure of the Software Media has resulted from accident, abuse, or misapplication. Any replacement Software Media will be warranted for the remainder of the original warranty period or thirty (30) days, whichever is longer.

(b) In no event shall WPI or the author be liable for any damages whatsoever (including without limitation damages for loss of business profits, business interruption, loss of business information, or any other pecuniary loss) arising from the use of or inability to use the Book or the Software, even if WPI has been advised of the possibility of such damages.

(c) Because some jurisdictions do not allow the exclusion or limitation of liability for consequential or incidental damages, the above limitation or exclusion may not apply to you.

7. U.S. Government Restricted Rights. Use, duplication, or disclosure of the Software for or on behalf of the United States of America, its agencies and/or instrumentalities "U.S. Government" is subject to restrictions as stated in paragraph (c)(1)(ii) of the Rights in Technical Data and Computer Software clause of DFARS 252.227-7013, or subparagraphs (c) (1) and (2) of the Commercial Computer Software - Restricted Rights clause at FAR 52.227-19, and in similar clauses in the NASA FAR supplement, as applicable.

8. General. This Agreement constitutes the entire understanding of the parties and revokes and supersedes all prior agreements, oral or written, between them and may not be modified or amended except in a writing signed by both parties hereto that specifically refers to this Agreement. This Agreement shall take precedence over any other documents that may be in conflict herewith. If any one or more provisions contained in this Agreement are held by any court or tribunal to be invalid, illegal, or otherwise unenforceable, each and every other provision shall remain in full force and effect.